ASIAN COURTS IN CONTEXT

The rise of Asia in global political and economic developments has been facilitated in part by a profound transformation of Asian courts. This book provides the most up-to-date and comprehensive analysis of these courts, explaining how their structures differ from courts in the West and how they have been shaped by the current challenges facing Asia. Contributors from across the continent analyze fourteen selected Asian jurisdictions representing varying degrees of development: Japan, Korea, Taiwan, India, Indonesia, Mongolia, the Philippines, Hong Kong, Singapore, Bangladesh, Malaysia, Thailand, China and Vietnam. Setting the courts of each region in the context of their country's economic, political and social dynamics, this book shows how and why Asian courts have undergone such profound transformations in recent years and predicts the future trajectories of tradition, transition and globalization to suggest the challenges and developments that lie ahead.

JIUNN-RONG YEH is University Chair Professor in the College of Law at the National Taiwan University.

WEN-CHEN CHANG is Professor in the College of Law at the National Taiwan University.

ASIAN COURTS IN CONTEXT

Edited by

JIUNN-RONG YEH

and

WEN-CHEN CHANG

CAMBRIDGE
UNIVERSITY PRESS

CAMBRIDGE
UNIVERSITY PRESS

University Printing House, Cambridge CB2 8BS, United Kingdom

Cambridge University Press is part of the University of Cambridge.

It furthers the University's mission by disseminating knowledge in the pursuit of education, learning and research at the highest international levels of excellence.

www.cambridge.org
Information on this title: www.cambridge.org/9781107066083

First published 2015

A catalogue record for this publication is available from the British Library

Library of Congress Cataloguing in Publication data
Asian courts in context / edited by Jiunn-rong Yeh and Wen-Chen Chang.
pages. cm
Includes bibliographical references and index.
ISBN 978-1-107-06608-3
1. Courts–East Asia. 2. Courts–South Asia. 3. Courts–Southeast Asia.
I. Yeh, Jiunn-rong, editor. II. Chang, Wen-Chen, editor.
KNC459.A975 2014
347.5′01–dc23
2014022409

ISBN 978-1-107-06608-3 Hardback

CONTENTS

FIGURES

TABLES

CONTRIBUTORS

BATBOLD AMARSANAA is Vice Director of the National Legal Institute of Mongolia and a member of the Judicial Qualifications Committee of Mongolia. His primary areas of research include company and business law, comparative law, private international law and insurance law.

WEN-CHEN CHANG is Professor at National Taiwan University College of Law. She focuses her teaching and research on comparative constitutions, international human rights, international environmental law, administrative law, and law and society.

YEOW CHOY CHOONG is Professor and former Dean at the Faculty of Law, University of Malaya, Malaysia. His primary areas of research include transnational civil litigation, international commercial arbitration and the administration of the civil justice system.

WEIXIA GU is Assistant Professor at the Faculty of Law, University of Hong Kong. She specializes in commercial arbitration, business dispute resolution, conflict of laws, and civil justice, particularly with respect to China and Greater China.

RIDWANUL HOQUE is Associate Professor of Law, University of Dhaka, Bangladesh. His research interests include comparative constitutional theory, judicial politics, law and society, migration law, and Islamic family law.

HIKMAHANTO JUWANA is Professor of Law and former Dean at the Faculty of Law, University of Indonesia, Jakarta, Indonesia. He specializes in international law, Indonesian business law, competition law, and contract law.

NORIKAZU KAWAGISHI is Professor of Constitutional Law at the Faculty of Political Science and Economics Law School, Waseda University, Japan. He is a constitutional law expert whose research interests are mainly in freedom of expression and constitutionalism.

JONGCHEOL KIM is Professor of Law at Yonsei University School of Law in Seoul, South Korea. He is a leading scholar of Korean constitutional law who writes extensively in both Korean and English.

JAYANTH KRISHNAN is the Charles L. Whistler Faculty Fellow and Professor of Law at the Indiana University Maurer School of Law, United States. His academic research focuses are mainly on the legal profession, law and globalization, and legal education, with a special emphasis on how these areas intersect in India.

PUI YIN LO is a barrister who has been in private practice in Hong Kong for twenty years. He has appeared before courts of various levels, including the Privy Council and the Hong Kong Court of Final Appeal. His specializations include constitutional and administrative law, and protection of human rights. He is the author of two books on the Hong Kong Basic Law.

NATTAPORN NAKORNIN is former Lecturer in Law at Faculty of Law, Chulalongkorn University, with specialization in criminal law and criminal procedure. She is admitted to the Thai Bar and is presently a Judge at the Judicial Training Institute.

PIP NICHOLSON is Professor of Law and Director of the Asian Law Centre, Melbourne Law School, Australia. Her current research and teaching focuses are primarily on law and legal change in transitional countries and cross-cultural legal research.

RAUL C. PANGALANGAN is Professor of Law and former Dean at the University of the Philippines. He is a leading authority on constitutional law in the Philippines and specializes in public international law and constitutional law.

PAWAT SATAYANURUG is Lecturer in Law at Faculty of Law, Chulalongkorn University, with specialization in public international law, international criminal law, and international human rights law. He is presently pursuing a doctoral degree at University of Zurich, Switzerland.

KEVIN Y. L. TAN is concurrently Adjunct Professor of Law at the National University of Singapore and Adjunct Professor of International Law at the S. Rajaratnam School of International Studies, Nanyang Technological University. He is a leading scholar of Singapore constitutional law, human rights, legal history and comparative law in Southeast Asia.

JIUNN-RONG YEH is University Chair Professor at National Taiwan University College of Law. He previously has served as a Minister in the Taiwanese Government and Vice-Dean of his College, and also taught in many overseas universities. His teaching and research focuses are primarily on comparative constitutional law, environmental law and administrative law. He has published widely in both Chinese and English and is the author and editor of nineteen books.

ACKNOWLEDGMENTS

In the process of putting this book together, we have accumulated many intellectual and other debts. We would like to first acknowledge the Institute for Advanced Studies in Humanities and Social Sciences of National Taiwan University, whose Top University Research Project enabled us to invite all contributors of this book to hold a conference in March 2012 for the discussion of draft chapters, to acquire research materials, and to employ research and editing assistants. We are especially grateful to the generous support of the Dean of the Institute, Distinguished Professor Chun-Chieh Huang.

Together with three other colleagues at the College of Law, National Taiwan University – Professor Andrew Jen-Guang Lin, Professor Kuan-Ling Shen and Professor Chung-Jau Wu – we have, since August 2011, formed a collaborative research team on "Courts in East Asia and Legal Transplant" under the auspices of the Institute for Advanced Studies in Humanities and Social Sciences of National Taiwan University. The publication of this book has been one of the many items on the research agenda set in this collaboration. We especially acknowledge the intellectual contributions of these three colleagues to this book as well as to the chapter on Taiwan. We hope our other intellectual collaborations will also soon come to fruition.

We are enormously indebted to all of the contributors to this book. Without their most generous intellectual contributions, the publication of this book would not be possible. Special gratitude must be extended to Sabrina Su, our English language editor, for her meticulous editing efforts and willingness to work with us on a very pressing schedule. We are also greatly indebted to Dr Chun-Yuan Lin, Szu-Chen Kuo and Shao-Man Lee for their relentless efforts in assisting in the preparation of the manuscript. Thanks too to our students and research assistants, Ju-Ching Huang, Jo-Tzu Ma, Yi-Li Lee, Chia-ching Chen, Yan-Lin Li, Pei-Jung Li, Wei Chen, Wen-Wei Chen and Po-Cheng Lin, for their assistance in editing and checking the styles throughout this book.

In this endeavor, we must also thank Cambridge University Press for agreeing to publish this book, and for all of their efforts in guiding us through getting the manuscript to press.

January 2014

Jiunn-rong Yeh
and Wen-Chen Chang

1

Introduction

Asian courts in context: tradition, transition and globalization

JIUNN-RONG YEH AND WEN-CHEN CHANG

The recent rise of Asia in both economic and political power has attracted wide attention.[1] Since World War II, economic development in Asia has surpassed that of many countries in other regions. First was the rapid economic recovery of Japan in the 1960s, followed by the miraculous economic growth of the four Asian tigers or dragons – South Korea, Taiwan, Hong Kong and Singapore – in the 1980s.[2] This economic miracle has continued into the first decade of the twenty-first century despite the global economic recession. China, India, Indonesia and Thailand, as well as many other Asian states, have become some of the fastest growing economies of the world.[3] With the economic decline of the West, the rise of the Asian market has shifted the world's economic center of gravity towards Asia.

Politically, Asia has also undergone profound transformations. An unprecedented number of Asian states have transitioned into constitutional democracies. Japan adopted a postwar democratic constitution in 1946, followed by India in 1949. Following a similar trajectory to that of the West centuries earlier, a strong wave of democratization swept

[1] For scholarly discussions on the rise of Asia, see e.g. F. B. Tipton, *The Rise of Asia: Economics, Society, and Politics in the Contemporary Asia* (University of Hawaii Press, 1998).

[2] See e.g. P. Krugman, "The myth of Asia's miracle," *Foreign Affairs*, 73(6) (1994), 62–78; R. Wade, *Governing the Market: Economic Theory and the Role of Government in East Asian Industrialization* (Princeton University Press, 1990); H. L. Root, *Small Countries, Big Lessons: Governance and the Rise of East Asia* (Oxford University Press, 1996).

[3] See e.g. S. Radelet, J. Sachs and J.-W. Lee, "The determinants and prospects of economic growth in Asia," *International Economic Journal*, 15(3) (2001), 1; M. Younis, X. X. Lin, Y. Sharahili and S. Selvarathinam, "Political stability and economic growth in Asia," *American Journal of Applied Sciences*, 5 (2008), 203, 205.

over Asia in the late 1980s and early 1990s.[4] In 1987, both South Korea and the Philippines adopted new constitutions. Mongolia adopted a new constitution in 1992. Taiwan undertook seven rounds of constitutional revisions in the 1990s and 2000s, while Indonesia proceeded with four stages of constitutional reform between 1999 and 2002. Thailand created a new constitution in 1997 and again in 2007.[5] Among these, some, such as India, Japan, Taiwan and South Korea, have successfully embraced vibrant democracies, while others have continued to face varying degrees of difficulties and challenges.[6]

Political and constitutional reforms also took place in socialist systems. Vietnam adopted a new constitution in 1992. The 1982 Constitution of the People's Republic of China (PRC) was amended in 1988, 1993, 1999 and 2004. As the renowned political scientist Larry Diamond declared in 2008, "More than any other region, Asia will determine the global fate of democracy in the next two to three decades."[7]

The rapid economic development and profound political transitions that have taken place in Asia have inevitably brought about the transformation of the region's legal institutions, and of its courts in particular. In many jurisdictions, courts have been created or reformed in order to cope with fast-growing economies as well as to facilitate the rule of law and protection of individual rights. Over the past few decades, for example, constitutional courts have been created in Taiwan, South Korea, Mongolia, Cambodia, Thailand, Indonesia and Myanmar.[8] Specialized courts – particularly those with jurisdiction over economic matters concerning tax, bankruptcy, and intellectual property law, among others – have been mushrooming in

4 For general discussions on the waves of democratization around the globe, see e.g. S. P. Huntington, *The Third Wave: Democratization in the Late 20th Century* (University of Oklahoma Press, 1993). For democratization in Asia, see e.g. A. Croissant, "From transition to defective democracy: mapping Asian democratization," *Democratization*, 11(5) (2004), 156, 157; J.-r. Yeh and W.-C. Chang, "The emergence of East Asian constitutionalism: features in comparison," *American Journal of Comparative Law*, 56 (2011), 805, 807.

5 D. C. Shin, "The third wave in East Asia: comparative and dynamic perspective," *Taiwan Journal of Democracy*, 4(2) (2008), 91, 99–101.

6 For discussion of the causes and difficulties of democratization in Asia, please see J. Lee, "Primary causes of Asian democratization: dispelling conventional myths," *Asian Survey*, 42 (2002), 821–37.

7 L. Diamond, *The Spirit of Democracy* (New York: Times Books, 2008), p. 212.

8 See the subsequent chapters of South Korea, Taiwan, Mongolia and Thailand. For general discussions of constitutional courts in Asia, see also T. Ginsburg, *Judicial Review in New Democracies: Constitutional Courts in Asian Cases* (Cambridge University Press, 2003); W.-C. Chang, K. Y. L. Tan, L.-a. Thio and J.-r. Yeh, *Constitutionalism in Asia: Cases and Materials* (Oxford: Hart Publishing, 2014), pp. 328–42.

Asia.[9] More importantly, the emphasis on courts and their functions in economic and political developments have led to the undertaking of large-scale judicial reforms aimed at facilitating judicial independence or even democratization of the judiciary. It is not a coincidence that varying degrees of lay participation in courts have been introduced in some Asian jurisdictions, even those with civil law traditions such as Japan, South Korea and Taiwan.[10]

Despite this ongoing transformation of courts in Asia, few academic works have provided systematic and contextual analyses of Asian courts and their changing functions.[11] How have courts been structured or restructured in response to recent economic and political changes in Asia? Are there distinctive features in the ways that Asian courts are organized and operate? What are the economic, political, social and cultural functions that Asian courts are expected to deliver? In what ways and to what extent are Asian courts different from courts in the West? The main purpose of this book is to provide answers to these key questions that are not yet fully researched and systematically studied in the existing scholarship on Asian courts and their functional dynamics. Fourteen jurisdictions – those of Bangladesh, China, Hong Kong, India, Indonesia, Japan, Malaysia, Mongolia, the Philippines, Singapore, South Korea, Taiwan, Thailand, and Vietnam – are included in this book.

This introduction is divided into five parts. First, we elaborate on the methodology of this book and explain why we adopt an institutional approach to the study of courts and their functional dynamics. Second, we articulate three conceptual dimensions of analysis – tradition and transplantation, transition and construction, and globalization and competition – in order to place the discussion of courts and their functional dynamics into their corresponding contexts. Third, we provide the rationale for the outline and structure of this book. The fourth and fifth parts of this introduction represent key comparative results of the

[9] See the following discussion of 4.1.5.

[10] See the subsequent chapters: N. Kawagishi, "Towards a more responsive judiciary: courts and judicial power in Japan," this volume, section 2.2; J. Kim, "Courts in the Republic of Korea: featuring a built-in authoritarian legacy of centralization and bureaucratization," this volume, section 1.4; W.-C. Chang, "Courts and judicial reform in Taiwan: gradual transformations towards the guardian of constitutionalism and rule of law," this volume, section 1.2.

[11] Recent exceptional efforts include: A. Harding and P. Nicholson (eds.), *New Courts in Asia* (New York: Routledge, 2010); B. Dressel (ed.), *The Judicialization of Politics in Asia* (New York: Routledge, 2012).

fourteen selected jurisdictions in this book. The fourth part addresses comparisons of the structures of courts, judges and their qualifications and appointments, citizens' relationships with the judiciary and their access to justice, and the styles of judicial decisions. The fifth part includes comparisons of the functional dynamics in the fourteen selected jurisdictions along the three analytical dimensions described in the second part: tradition and transplantation, transition and construction, and globalization and competition.

1 Methodology: starting with Martin Shapiro and an institutional approach to courts

While most legal studies focus on legal doctrines and judicial interpretations, a few approaches emphasize courts as an institution and observe their functional dynamics. A pioneer in this approach was Martin Shapiro, whose analysis of courts was published in 1981.[12] Shapiro focused on courts as an institution for legal research, attempting to explore the meaning and function of courts in response to legal systems and social contexts. He initially depicted a prototype of courts prevailing in American society, which consisted of four elements: independence, adversarialism, decision making according to pre-existing rules, and winner-take-all results.[13] However, through a comparative study of courts in Britain, Imperial China, Western Europe and traditional Islamic societies, Shapiro believed that such an American prototype is just a myth. Most courts have not always reflected such a prototype, and courts in most societies were often used as mechanisms of social control.

Shapiro's study of courts and their functional dynamics has made at least two important contributions to contemporary legal scholarship on courts. First, Shapiro opened up a new institutional approach to courts. Courts and judicial processes have since been viewed as important subjects in legal scholarship. Second, Shapiro departed from a relatively narrow and Western-centered view on courts, pointing out that what matters is the function of courts in different social contexts and political systems.

As a result of Shapiro's work, an increasing number of legal scholars – especially socio-legal scholars – have begun to adopt just such an

[12] M. Shapiro, *Courts: A Comparative and Political Analysis* (University of Chicago Press, 1981), pp. 1–4.

[13] *Ibid.*

institutional approach and to understand courts as institutions operating in particular political systems and social contexts. Some scholars have focused their attention on the policy-making functions of courts and have even viewed courts as strategic players central to policy-making processes.[14] Others have relied on the principal-agent or related theories and have attempted to delineate the relationship between the courts and the political branches.[15] Still others have elaborated on the attitudes of judges, examining if the personal preferences of judges or other similar factors may affect judicial decisions.[16] Within this body of scholarship, courts are generally understood both as legal institutions and as political institutions interacting with other legal or political institutions and responding to political, economic, social and cultural dynamics. This dynamic understanding of courts has recently become quite popular in the legal discourse of the United Sates as well as elsewhere.

Context also matters. Inspired by Shapiro's study of courts in various contexts, a number of scholars have begun extending their research beyond the United States, attempting to observe the structures and operations of courts in different social contexts and political systems. For example, John Ferejohn and Pasquale Pasquino have studied the origins and practices of European constitutional adjudication, arguing that judicial review can function well even in civil law systems.[17] Alec Stone has suggested that the Constitutional Council of France has gradually gained public trust as a result of the complex interactions between the Constitutional Council and the political branches.[18] Gretchen

[14] L. Epstein and T. Walker, "The role of the Supreme Court in American society: playing the reconstruction game" in L. Epstein (ed.), *Contemplating Court* (Washington, DC: Congressional Quarterly Press, 1995), pp. 315–46; S. Brenner and H. J. Spaeth, *Stare Indecisis: The Alteration of Precedents on the Supreme Court, 1946–1992* (Cambridge University Press, 1995).

[15] J. Brent, "An agent and two principals: U.S. Court of Appeals responses to Employment Division, Department of Human Resources v. Smith and the Religious Freedom Restoration Act," *American Politics Quarterly*, 27 (1999), 236–66; D. Songer, J. A. Segal and C. Cameron, "The hierarchy of justice: testing a principal–agent model of Supreme Court–circuit court interactions," *American Journal of Political Science*, 38 (1994), 673–96.

[16] See J. A. Segal and H. J. Spaeth, *The Supreme Court and the Attitudinal Model Revisited* (Cambridge University Press, 2002).

[17] Ginsburg, *Judicial Review in New Democracies*; S. Issacharoff, "Constitutional courts and democratic hedging," *Georgetown Law Journal*, 99 (2011), 961–1012; J. Ferejohn and P. Pasquino, "Constitutional adjudication: lessons from Europe," *Texas Law Review*, 82 (2004), 1671–704.

[18] A. Stone, *The Birth of Judicial Politics in France: The Constitutional Council in Comparative Perspective* (Oxford University Press, 1992).

Helmke and Julio Rios-Figueroa have studied the courts in Latin America, inquiring how institutions, partisan politics and public support may shape the relations of the courts with the political branches.[19] Theunis Roux has studied the Constitutional Court of South Africa and found it to be a pragmatic actor.[20] Tom Ginsburg has studied the constitutional courts in new democracies in Asia and developed an insurance theory to explain how constitutional review may be created in the course of turbulent political transition. In a global context, David Caron has studied international courts and tribunals, finding that these courts may shoulder a wide range of political functions.[21] Neal Tate and Torbjörn Vallinder provide contextualized explanations for the global expansion of judicial power in politics.[22] All of these scholars have attempted to uncover the multiple facets of courts in different contexts, which may correspondingly change the functions of courts. For example, recently, Ginsburg and Moustafa have extended the study of courts to the context of authoritarian regimes and found that courts may still exert some influence over politics there.[23]

Thirty years have passed since the publication of Shapiro's seminal work. The study of Asian courts and their functional dynamics in response to fast-changing political, economic, social and cultural contexts has been far from abundant. Only recently have there been scholarly publications addressing the creation of constitutional courts or special courts in various Asian jurisdictions.[24] It is evident that more contextualized, dynamic and comprehensive studies of Asian courts and their functional dynamics are needed. We hope that this book contributes substantially to the achievement of this important goal.

[19] G. Helmke and J. Rios-Figueroa, *Courts in Latin America* (Cambridge University Press, 2011).

[20] T. Roux, "Principle and pragmatism on the Constitutional Court of South Africa," *International Journal of Constitutional Law*, 7 (2009), 106–38.

[21] D. D. Caron, "Toward a political theory of international courts and tribunals," *Berkeley Journal of International Law*, 24 (2007), 401–23.

[22] C. N. Tate and T. Vallinder, "The global expansion of judicial power: the judicialization of politics" in Tate and Vallinder (eds.), *The Global Expansion of Judicial Power* (New York University Press, 1995), pp. 1–10.

[23] See T. Moustafa and T. Ginsburg, "Introduction: the function of courts in authoritarian politics" in T. Moustafa and T. Ginsburg (eds.), *Rule by Law: The Politics of Courts in Authoritarian Regimes* (Cambridge University Press, 2008), pp. 1–22.

[24] Harding and Nicholson, *New Courts in Asia*; Dressel, *The Judicialization of Politics in Asia*.

2 Asian courts in context: three dimensions

Studying courts in Asia is not an easy task. We must understand the courts as well as "Asia". In the past, Western scholars often viewed Asia as "exceptional" or "exotic" and therefore either misrepresented Asian societies and their institutions or ignored them entirely. Another common perception of Asia was related to the "Asian values" discourse perpetuated by some Asian political leaders, in which Asian traditions were thought unfit for liberal constitutionalism.[25] Asian cultures were understood as valuing the family more highly than the individual, preferring authority over personal freedoms, and emphasizing obligations more than rights.[26] The discourse of "Asian values" was even manipulated by some into rhetoric justifying the existence of authoritarian regimes.[27] Both views, however, have mistakenly treated "Asia" as a monolithic society, ignoring the diversity and dynamics of such a vast region.

What is the best approach to capturing the diversity and dynamics of Asia and studying Asian courts and their functions without running the risk of over-essentializing "Asia" or the West? We suggest three analytical concepts that are crucial for the study of Asian courts and their functional dynamics: (1) tradition and transplantation, (2) transition and construction, and (3) globalization and competition. We elaborate on these concepts below, and, in the last part of this introduction, we will rely on them to conduct comparative analyses of the functional dynamics of the courts in the fourteen selected jurisdictions.

2.1 Tradition and transplantation

Courts in Asia are neither indigenous nor entirely transplanted from the West. In most cases, Asian courts have developed as a result of rather complex interactions between tradition and foreign transplantations.

One of the traditional functions of courts – dispute resolution – had long existed in various cultures throughout Asia[28] but was not always

[25] For discussion of how modern constitutionalism developed in East Asia has gradually departed from the Asian values discourse, see Yeh and Chang, "Emergence of East Asian constitutionalism."

[26] Transcript of an interview with Lee Kuan Yew: see F. Zakaria, "Culture is destiny: a conversation with Lee Kuan Yew," *Foreign Affairs*, 73 (1994), 109, 111. See also K. Engle, "Culture and human rights: the Asian values debate in context," *New York University Journal of International Law and Politics*, 32 (2000), 291–333.

[27] Yeh and Chang, "Emergence of East Asian constitutionalism."

[28] E.g. Shapiro, *Courts*, pp. 160–1.

shouldered by courts in a modern or Western sense of the word. For example, in imperial China, a mayor was expected to exercise all executive, legislative and judicial powers.[29] Most Asian jurisdictions established modern legal and judicial systems within the last two or three centuries, and the extent to which their various traditions and cultures may still affect the workings of their modern courts and their functional dynamics is especially intriguing.

The adoption or transplantation of legal institutions is a complex and dynamic process. The direction of transplantation is not always from the West to the East. Nor is it the case that tradition or other contextual factors have no impact on such processes. The present judicial systems in Asia have been asymmetrically influenced by the West through externally imposed colonization, internally triggered modernization, or the consequences of wars, among other forces.[30] The sources and directions of these influences are complex. For example, in the late nineteenth century, Japan created a modern judicial system mostly by following Germany's example. Yet the organization and operation of Japan's courts today are dictated by the Constitution it adopted after World War II under pressure from the United States. How these two different sources – in addition to tradition and other contextual factors – may have impacted the Japanese courts has long motivated scholarly inquiry.[31] Likewise, in Taiwan, the transplantation of legal and judicial systems was quite dynamic and complex, having been shaped by the Chinese imperial system, Japanese colonialism, and modernization, both internally triggered and influenced by the West.[32] It is evident that the complexity and dynamics of courts in Asia cannot be fully understood without analysis from the perspectives of both tradition and transplantation.

2.2 *Transition and construction*

Transition is another key concept in understanding the functional dynamics of Asian courts. In the course of a democratic transition, courts may serve as catalysts for democratization, as facilitator for departing

[29] *Ibid.* p. 172.

[30] W.-C. Chang, "East Asian foundations for constitutionalism: three models reconstructed," *National Taiwan University Law Review*, 3(2) (2008), 111–41.

[31] N. Kadomatsu, "Judicial governance through resolution of legal disputes? A Japanese perspective," *National Taiwan University Law Review*, 4(2) (2009), 141–62.

[32] Chang, "East Asian foundations for constitutionalism."

authoritarian rulers or as adjudicators of political conflicts.[33] In a process of economic transition, courts may be keys to economic stability and growth.[34]

As discussed in the beginning of this introduction, the majority of Asian states have experienced rapid and significant transitions in their political, economic and social systems. These transitions will inevitably continue to affect courts, to varying degrees. Some effects may lead to court reform. Others may – in unexpected and more profound ways – challenge the institutional capacities of courts in these changing contexts. Faced with such unprecedented challenges, Asian courts and judges may need to be innovative in formulating possible solutions.

For example, both South Korea and Taiwan underwent democratization in the late 1980s and 1990s. Both countries' democratization resulted in the empowerment of constitutional courts, particularly for resolving highly contested political disputes.[35] In an unexpected turn of events, both constitutional courts had to decide the fates of their countries' top political leadership: the impeachment of President Roh Moo-Hyun of South Korea in 2004 and the criminal investigation of President Chen Shui-Bian of Taiwan in 2007.[36] Perhaps not coincidentally, both constitutional courts developed similar strategies to resolve disputes while leaving ample space for political engagement.[37] Yet, successful resolutions notwithstanding, both constitutional courts have faced political

[33] A. Trochev, *Judging Russia: Constitutional Court in Russian Politics 1990–2006* (Cambridge University Press, 2008); L. Hilbink, *Judges Beyond Politics in Democracy and Dictatorship: Lessons from Chile* (Cambridge University Press, 2007); S. Issacharoff, "Constitutionalizing democracy in fractured societies," *Journal of International Affairs*, 58 (2004), 73–93; A. Barak, "The role of a supreme court in a democracy," *Hastings Law Journal*, 53 (2002), 1205–16.

[34] E.g. L. P. Feld and S. Voigtd, "Economic growth and judicial independence: cross-country evidence using a new set of indicators," *European Journal of Political Economy*, 19 (2003), 497–527 (arguing that real GDP growth per capita is positively related to de facto judicial independence); S. Gloppen, R. Gargarella and E. Skaar, "Introduction: the accountability function of the courts in new democracies" in S. Gloppen, R. Gargarella and El. Skaar (eds.), *Democratization and the Judiciary: The Accountability Functions of Courts in New Democracies* (London: Frank Cass, 2004), pp. 1–4.

[35] J.-r. Yeh, "Presidential politics and judicial facilitation of political dialogue between political actors in new Asian democracies: comparing the South Korean and Taiwanese experiences," *International Journal of Constitutional Law*, 8(4) (2011), 911–49; W.-C. Chang, "Strategic judicial responses in politically charged cases: East Asian experiences," *International Journal of Constitutional Law*, 8(4) (2010), 885–910.

[36] Chang, "Strategic judicial responses."

[37] Yeh, "Presidential politics"; Chang, "Strategic judicial responses."

setbacks and challenges to their institutional integrity, such as politicization of the judicial appointment process.[38]

In China and Vietnam, profound transitions from socialist systems to market economies have occurred. Increasing demands for judicial decisions related to entitlements and rights in the market have triggered large-scale reforms of the legal education and judicial systems.[39] Similar reforms have also occurred in other emerging markets, such as Indonesia, Mongolia and Thailand, among others. Courts in Asia are greatly influenced by these transitions and at the same time are expected to take on the resulting challenges. This is the second indispensable dimension for studying the functional dynamics of Asian courts.

2.3 *Globalization and competition*

The third of the dimensions guiding our analysis is that of globalization and the competition it accelerates. Aided by advanced technology and the development of the internet, globalization is mobilizing goods, capital, and even human beings on a global scale at ever increasing speeds.

Global trade, first and foremost, demands conflict resolution mechanisms for international legal disputes. It is no surprise that entry into the World Trade Organization (WTO) often brings about judicial reforms. China's membership in 2001 was the catalyst for both constitutional and judicial reforms in the following decade.[40] Alternatively, global economic crises may also impact the restructuring of courts and the roles of judges. The 1997 Asian financial crisis, for example, had significant impacts on legal and judicial reforms in South Korea, Thailand and Indonesia.[41] Large-scale financial reforms resulting from

[38] Yeh, "Presidential politics"; Chang, "Courts and judicial reform in Taiwan," this volume, section 5.1; Chang, "Strategic judicial responses."

[39] W. Gu, "Courts in China: judiciary in the economic and societal transitions," this volume, section 6.1; P. Nicholson, "Renovating courts: the role of courts in contemporary Vietnam," this volume, sections 1, 2.

[40] C. X. Lin, "A quiet revolution: an overview of China's judicial reform," *Asian-Pacific Law & Policy Journal*, 4 (2003), 255–319; P. Potter, "Legal reform in China: institutions, culture and selective adaptation," *Law & Social Inquiry*, 29 (2004), 465, 473; Gu, "Courts in China," this volume, section 6.1.

[41] M. Kawai and H. Schmiegelow, *Financial Crisis as a Catalyst of Legal Reforms: The Case of Asia* (Tokyo: Asian Development Bank Institute, 2013).

the global economic crisis of 2009 gave rise to the restructuring of courts, particularly in the area of commercial disputes.[42]

In addition, globalization may also bring about the emergence of a global community of courts, in which judges around the world view each other as colleagues in a common enterprise and begin dialogue with each other.[43] In a globally connected judicial network, the ways in which Asian courts and judges might position and identify themselves becomes an intriguing issue. Would Asian courts and judges be more willing to depart from their traditions and make changes in their strategies or attitudes? Would they be more likely to engage in global judicial dialogues, to refer to foreign precedents or to adopt more cosmopolitan perspectives?

Courts in Asia are multifaceted, complex, dynamic, and continually evolving. They struggle between tradition and foreign influences, adapt themselves to profound transitions that often demand constructive innovation, and engage in global dialogues in an increasingly competitive world economy. These three dimensions interconnect and intertwine, contributing to the design, operation, and functioning of courts in Asia.

3 Structure of this book

In order to provide systematic and contextual analyses of Asian courts and their functional dynamics, we include fourteen jurisdictions into this book. They are Bangladesh, China, Hong Kong, India, Indonesia, Japan, Malaysia, Mongolia, the Philippines, Singapore, South Korea, Taiwan, Thailand, and Vietnam. We further divide them into two groups in Part I and Part II.

Part I includes the five most advanced economies, Japan and the four Asian tigers or dragons. Among them, Japan, South Korea and Taiwan have experienced successful democratic transitions, while Hong Kong and Singapore are still gradually opening up to electoral competition. Part II includes developing economies in Asia. Among these jurisdictions, some, such as India, Indonesia, Mongolia and the Philippines, have

42 See *ibid.* See also F. Lee and S. Ali, "Resolving financial disputes in the context of global civil justice reforms," *International Journal of Business and Social Science*, 2(7) (2011), 37–51.

43 A.-M. Slaughter, "Judicial globalization," *Virginia Journal of International Law*, 40 (2000), 1103–24; A.-M. Slaughter, "A global community of courts," *Harvard International Law Journal*, 44 (2003), 191–220.

transitioned into democracies, while others, such as Bangladesh, Malaysia and Thailand, are still struggling with the ongoing process of democratization. Also noteworthy are China and Vietnam. Both remain socialist systems despite having developed more open market economies with high rates of economic growth in recent years.

All of the country chapters attempt to provide an updated and systematic discussion of the courts and their functional dynamics in their jurisdictions. Each chapter may include but is not limited to the following topics: (1) a general description of the judicial system and recent reforms, (2) the judicial appointment process and judicial independence, (3) sources of law and styles of judicial decisions, (4) alternative dispute resolution processes, (5) influences on the judicial system, and (6) the functions of courts and evaluations of their performance. In discussing the functions of courts, some of the chapters pay special attention to the functions that courts may deliver even in the context of authoritarian regimes. As suggested by Ginsburg and Moustafa, courts in such contexts may (1) provide for social control and sideline political opposition, (2) legitimize regimes, (3) strengthen bureaucratic control, (4) facilitate trade and investment, and (5) reinforce controversial policies.[44]

This common framework enables us to conduct systematic and comparative analyses across these jurisdictions. We provide the results of these comparisons below, first through the lens of institutional structures –including courts, judges, citizens' relationships with courts and the styles of judicial decisions – and, second, along the three dimensions of tradition, transition and globalization. By conducting these comparisons of various Asian court systems and their functional dynamics, we hope to illustrate what may be common amongst them and what may be unique in responding to their particular contexts, as well as to shed light on further comparisons between Asia and other regions.

4 Asian courts in comparative profile

The country chapters that follow illuminate basic features of the courts in each jurisdiction. We take the liberty of summarizing them here and conducting comparisons along four aspects: (1) structures of courts, (2) quality of judges, (3) citizens' relationships with the courts, and (4) styles and interpretive approaches of judicial decisions.

[44] Moustafa and Ginsburg, "Introduction."

4.1 Structures of courts

All of the country chapters provide general information on court structure, and most provide information on the number of courts. Based on the information available, we find that the number of courts varies significantly across jurisdictions. Such disparity in number of courts is often – but not always – related to the size of the country's territory or population. Including all tiers of courts, there are up to 3,500 courts in China, while there are only 14 courts in Hong Kong.[45] In between, there are 35 courts in Taiwan, 79 courts in Mongolia, around 550 courts in Japan, 700 courts in Bangladesh, 785 courts in Indonesia, and 720 courts in Vietnam.[46]

The varying numbers of courts notwithstanding, the structures of courts across the jurisdictions covered in this book share some basic features. First, the judicial systems of these jurisdictions are unitary in nature. The adoption of judicial federalism is rare in Asia. Second, the majority of jurisdictions follow a typical judicial structure consisting of three tiers of courts and three instances of trials. Third, the creation of a constitutional court with a centralized system of judicial review is a common trend. Fourth, most jurisdictions have a single supreme court. The adoption of a single or multiple supreme courts in Asia does not always correspond with the existence of a civil or common law tradition. Last but not least is the recent emergence of special courts or tribunals in response to specific economic and social challenges. We discuss each of these features in the following.

4.1.1 Judicial federalism

In Asia, most states have adopted unitary – rather than federal – systems of government.[47] The majority of judicial systems are thus unitary in nature. Intriguingly, however, even in a few federal states such as India and Malaysia, a unitary judicial system prevails. In India, "a case based

[45] Gu, "Courts in China," this volume, section 1.3; P. Y. Lo, "Hong Kong: common law courts in China," this volume, section 1.3.

[46] Chang, "Courts and judicial reform in Taiwan," this volume, section 1.3; B. Amarsanaa, "The fledgling courts and adjudication system in Mongolia," this volume, section 2.1; Kawagishi, "Judicial power in Japan," this volume, section 2; R. Hoque, "Courts and the adjudication system in Bangladesh: in quest of viable reforms," this volume, section 1; H. Juwana, "Courts in Indonesia: a mix of western and local character," this volume, section 1.4; Nicholson, "Renovating courts," this volume, section 2.2.

[47] G. Hassall and C. Saunders, *Asia-Pacific Constitutional Systems* (Cambridge University Press, 2002).

on either a state or central governmental law may originate in the lower courts and work its way up this unified chain, ultimately to the Supreme Court."[48] This practice is certainly quite different from those of federal states in the West, for example the United States or Germany, which also usually have federal judicial systems.[49]

4.1.2 Tiers of courts and instances of trials

The majority of country chapters describe a typical structure of courts with three tiers and three instances. At the same time, in order to accommodate small claims and to enhance litigation efficiency, only two tiers or two instances exist in many jurisdictions for designated types of litigation. Perhaps the most interesting contrast is between Singapore and China: the former generally provides two instances for trials while the latter provides up to four instances.[50]

4.1.3 The establishment of constitutional courts and models of judicial review

A recent trend noted by scholars of comparative constitutionalism has been the establishment, particularly in European countries, of constitutional courts with centralized systems of judicial review.[51] Such a trend seems also to have extended to Asia.[52] Thus far, seven constitutional courts or tribunals with centralized powers of judicial review have been established in Asian jurisdictions, including Taiwan (created in 1948), South Korea (1987), Mongolia (1992), Cambodia (1993), Thailand (1997), Indonesia (2001) and Myanmar (2008).[53] These constitutional courts are usually vested with exclusive power in reviewing the constitutionality of laws and regulations at the request of the executive branch, parliament, lower courts or citizens. Some of these courts are also vested with the power to decide on the impeachment of the president and

48 Y. C. Choong, "Courts in Malaysia and judiciary initiated reforms," this volume, section 1.1; J. Krishnan, "Legitimacy of courts and the dilemma of their proliferation: the significance of judicial power in India," this volume, section 1.1.

49 N. Dorsen, M. Rosenfeld, A. Sajo and S. Baer, *Comparative Constitutionalism: Cases and Materials*, 2nd edn. (Eagan, MN: West, 2010).

50 K. Y. L. Tan, "As efficient as the best businesses: Singapore's judicial system," this volume, section 3; Gu, "Courts in China," this volume, section 1.2.

51 See e.g. A. Stone Sweet, *Governing with Judges: Constitutional Politics in Europe* (Oxford University Press, 2000).

52 Ginsburg, *Judicial Review in New Democracies*.

53 For further discussions on these Asian constitutional courts, see Chang et al., *Constitutionalism in Asia*.

high-level government officials or on the dissolution of unconstitutional political parties, which may lead the courts to be involved with highly charged political issues.[54]

A centralized system in which judicial review is vested in a constitutional court, however, is not the only model in Asia. The other model, a decentralized system with diffused exercise of judicial review at all levels of courts, prevails in jurisdictions that have experienced British colonial rule or American occupation. In this book, Bangladesh, Hong Kong, India, Japan, Malaysia, the Philippines and Singapore represent this type of system.[55] As has been the case in countries with centralized systems, the courts – especially the supreme courts – in countries with decentralized systems have in recent years exhibited varying degrees of judicial activism in invalidating unconstitutional statutes or expanding standing to sue to permit greater protection of individual rights or the public interest.[56]

It should be noted that hybrid systems of judicial review also exist in many jurisdictions. For example, in Singapore, notwithstanding its decentralized system, the Constitutional Tribunal was created in 1994 and invoked once in 1995, when President Ong Teng Cheong referred to the Tribunal a question concerning the constitutional scope of his power.[57] In South Korea and Taiwan, although the power to review the constitutionality of laws is centralized in each country's Constitutional Court, the courts of general jurisdiction may still have the power to review the constitutionality of administrative regulations.[58]

4.1.4 Single or multiple supreme courts

Another interesting feature in the structure of courts is the existence of a single or multiple supreme courts. In a civil law system, multiple supreme courts may exist, each with jurisdiction over a different area of law. Most

[54] *Ibid.* See also Chang, "Strategic judicial responses."

[55] Krishnan, "Legitimacy of courts," this volume, section 1.1; Hoque, "Courts in Bangladesh," this volume, section 1.1.2; Kawagishi, "Judicial power in Japan," this volume, sections 1,5; Lo, "Hong Kong," this volume, sections 1.1,6; Choong, "Courts in Malaysia," this volume, section 1.1; R. C. Pangalangan, "The Philippines' post-Marcos judiciary: the institutional turn and the populist backlash," this volume, section 1.1; Tan, "Singapore's judicial system," this volume, section 3.

[56] Hoque, "Courts in Bangladesh," this volume, section 5.1; Krishnan, "Legitimacy of courts," this volume, section 5; Lo, "Hong Kong," this volume, section 6; Kawagishi, "Judicial power in Japan," this volume, section 5; Pangalangan, "The Philippines' post-Marcos judiciary," this volume, section 2.

[57] *Constitutional Reference No. 1 of 1995* [1995] 2 SLR 201.

[58] Chang et al., *Constitutionalism in Asia.*

illustrative in comparative constitutional law is the federal judicial structure of Germany, in which five federal supreme courts have been created and respectively vested with final jurisdiction over ordinary, administrative, financial, labor, and social matters.[59] In France, the Court of Cassation is the supreme court for civil and criminal cases while the Council of State acts as the final court of appeal over administrative litigation. In common law systems, however, the primary model is that of a single court at the apex of the judiciary acting as the final court of appeal for all jurisdictions.

Intriguingly, in Asia, the adoption of a single or multiple supreme courts does not always correspond with the civil or common law division. The model of a single supreme court exists in most Asian common law systems as well as in some civil law and socialist systems. Among civil law systems, Japan, Korea, Indonesia and Mongolia have a single supreme court. The socialist systems of China and Vietnam also have only one top court.[60] The model of multiple supreme courts has been adopted in Taiwan and Thailand. Each has one supreme court for civil and criminal matters and another for administrative matters; however, Thailand also has a supreme military court, for a total of three supreme courts.[61]

4.1.5 The emergence of special courts or tribunals

The last – and perhaps most important – feature in the structure of courts in Asia is the recent emergence of special courts or tribunals aside from constitutional or administrative courts. These special courts or tribunals have been created both within and outside the courts of general – civil or criminal – jurisdiction. The majority of the country chapters report such a trend.[62]

59 German Basic Law, Art. 95.

60 Gu, "Courts in China," this volume, section 1.1; Juwana, "Courts in Indonesia," this volume, section 1.1; Kawagishi, "Judicial power in Japan," this volume, section 2.3; Kim, "Courts in the Republic of Korea," this volume, section 1.1; Nicholson, "Renovating courts," this volume, section 2.1; Choong, "Courts in Malaysia," this volume, section 1.1; Pangalangan, "The Philippines' post-Marcos Judiciary," this volume, section 1.1; Amarsanaa, "Courts in Mongolia," this volume, section 1.1; Lo, "Hong Kong," this volume, section 1.2; Hoque, "Courts in Bangladesh," this volume, section 1.1; Tan, "Singapore's judicial system," this volume, section 3.1.

61 P. Satayanurug and N. Nakornin, "Courts in Thailand: progressive development as the country's pillar of justice," this volume, section 1.1.4.

62 E.g. Chang, "Courts and judicial reform in Taiwan," this volume, section 1.1; Krishnan, "Legitimacy of courts," this volume, sections 1.1, 6. For discussion of the recent trend in the increasing number of special courts, see also Harding and Nicholson (eds.), *New Courts in Asia*, pp. 315–68.

These special courts cover a wide range of jurisdictions: from traditional jurisdictions (such as military law), to special civic or criminal jurisdictions (such as matters related to small claims, traffic accidents, family, children or religion), to market-oriented jurisdictions (such as commerce, intellectual property, consumer protection or labor matters). Not all special courts or tribunals are recent creations. For example, Japan created its family court after World War II.[63] The military court or court-martial existed in China, Malaysia, South Korea, Taiwan and Vietnam, among others.[64] Religious courts have been in place in Malaysia and Singapore for decades.[65] Some jurisdictions, Hong Kong for example, have gradually set up special tribunals since the 1970s. However, as illustrated below, the mushrooming of special courts or tribunals is indeed a recent phenomenon in most of the jurisdictions included in this book.

From a comparative perspective, Bangladesh has the highest number of special courts or tribunals. In addition, India, Indonesia, Malaysia, the Philippines and Thailand also have quite a number of special courts or tribunals. In contrast, Japan, Korea, Taiwan and Singapore have fewer special courts or tribunals. In what follows, we find that in Asia these special courts or tribunals are created primarily in response to economic and related challenges, and they may also be created as accommodations for specific needs in matters concerning family, religion or indigenous minorities. However, the structural design of these special courts or tribunals remains a serious challenge to their effective functioning and independence.

4.1.5.1 Responses to economic and related challenges The recent mushrooming of special courts or tribunals in Asia has occurred primarily in response to escalating economic and related challenges. Even in those jurisdictions with fewer special courts or tribunals overall, commercial or intellectual property courts or tribunals have been established. For example, Singapore alone has three special commercial courts, and Taiwan recently created an intellectual property court.[66]

[63] Kawagishi, "Judicial power in Japan," this volume, section 2.1.

[64] E.g. Kim, "Courts in the Republic of Korea," this volume, section 1.3; Chang, "Courts and judicial reform in Taiwan," this volume, section 1.1.

[65] Choong, "Courts in Malaysia," this volume, section 1.3; Tan, "Singapore's judicial system," this volume, sections 1.3, 3.2.2.

[66] Tan, "Singapore's judicial system," this volume, section 3.2.1; Chang, "Courts and judicial reform in Taiwan," this volume, section 1.1.

Bangladesh serves as a prime example of the creation of special courts or tribunals to tackle a wide array of economic and related issues. These special courts or tribunals include: the money loan courts, the environment courts, the labor courts and labor appellate tribunals, the suppression of acid crimes tribunal, the speedy trial tribunal, the law and order disruptive crimes tribunal, and the court of the special judge (an anti-corruption court). According to Ridwanul Hoque, these special tribunals were created in response to the phenomenal growth in offenses that occurred after Bangladesh gained independence.[67]

Similarly, India also has a vast array of "quasi-judicial" courts, as well as a raft of alternative specialized forums including labor courts, consumer courts, and motor accident vehicle courts.[68] In Indonesia, special courts, the majority of which were created in recent decades, include the tax court, the commercial courts, the labor court, and the human rights court.[69] Special courts or tribunals in Malaysia include the industrial courts, the tribunal for consumer claims, the tribunal for homebuyer claims, and the public service tribunal. The most special of these special courts is "the special court" established in 1993 to hear "any proceedings by or against the *Yang di-Pertuan Agong* (the Ruler of a State) in his personal capacity."[70]

In Hong Kong, special courts or tribunals include the labor tribunal, the lands tribunal, the small claims tribunal, the obscene articles tribunal and the coroner's court, which investigates questionable death. The most recent creation is the competition tribunal, which was established in 2013.[71] In Thailand, special courts established by law include the labor court, the tax court, the intellectual property and international trade court, and the bankruptcy court.[72] In the Philippines, the court of tax appeal and the anti-corruption court were created.[73]

Even in socialist legal systems, special courts for resolving particular economic disputes have been created. In China, the intellectual property tribunals and environmental tribunals are two such examples.[74] In Vietnam, special courts include the economic court and the labor court.[75]

[67] Hoque, "Courts in Bangladesh," this volume, sections 1.5, 1.6.
[68] Krishnan, "Legitimacy of courts," this volume, section 1.1.
[69] Juwana, "Courts in Indonesia," this volume, sections 1.1, 1.2.
[70] See Malaysia Federal Constitution, Part XV.
[71] Lo, "Hong Kong," this volume, section 1.2.
[72] Satayanurug and Nakornin, "Courts in Thailand," this volume, section 1.2.
[73] Pangalangan, "The Philippines' post-Marcos judiciary," this volume, section 1.2.
[74] Gu, "Courts in China," this volume, section 1.1.
[75] Nicholson, "Renovating courts," this volume, section 2.2.

4.1.5.2 Accommodations for matters related to family, religion and indigenous minorities Special courts or tribunals may also be created to accommodate special needs in matters concerning family, women and/or children, religion, and indigenous or ethnic minorities. In nearly all the jurisdictions covered in this book (the exceptions being Hong Kong and Mongolia), special courts or tribunals for matters related to family, children or women have been created. Most jurisdictions have one special court for family matters, while some jurisdictions have more than one. For example, Bangladesh has family courts, children's courts and the *Nari O Shishu Nirjatan Daman* tribunal (for offenses against women and children).[76] India has both family courts and women's courts.[77]

Special religious courts have been created in Indonesia, Malaysia, Singapore and the Philippines. In Indonesia, both religious courts and Syari'ah tribunals exist, each with different jurisdictions. The religious courts have jurisdiction over family and civil matters, while the Syari'ah tribunals have jurisdiction over cases involving Muslims who violate Syari'ah law.[78] In Singapore, Malaysia and the Philippines, the Syari'ah (Shari'a) courts are the only religious courts that apply personal or relevant Syari'ah laws to the cases under their jurisdiction. It is intriguing to note that not all jurisdictions in Asia with Muslim populations or religious minorities have created special Muslim or religious courts. For example, in Bangladesh and India, while Muslim, Hindu or other religious personal laws are formally recognized, disputes related to those laws are adjudicated in the ordinary civil courts.[79]

Also noteworthy is the structure of religious courts, which may be designed differently from the courts of general jurisdiction. For example, in Malaysia, some extent of judicial federalism is accorded to the religious courts although not to the courts of general jurisdiction. According to Yeow Choy Choong, "*Syariah* Courts come within the purview of each of the States and the Federal Territories in the Federation. *Syariah* Courts are state courts established under various state laws, which also provide for their constitution, jurisdiction and procedure. Besides the *Syariah* Courts, a hierarchy of state Native Courts exists in Sabah and Sarawak to hear disputes among natives."[80]

[76] Hoque, "Courts in Bangladesh," this volume, sections 1.4, 1.5.
[77] Krishnan, "Legitimacy of courts," this volume, section 1.1.
[78] Juwana, "Courts in Indonesia," this volume, section 1.2.1.
[79] Hoque, "Courts in Bangladesh," this volume, section 1.5.1; Krishnan, "Legitimacy of courts," this volume, section 4.2.
[80] Choong, "Courts in Malaysia," this volume, section 1.1.

The need for special courts or tribunals to accommodate differences in culture, custom or language is also strong among indigenous communities or ethnic minorities. However, only a few jurisdictions have created special indigenous courts. India created *Lok Adalats* (the people's courts).[81] Bangladesh established a special division in the administration of justice in the Chittagong Hill-Tracts for indigenous people.[82] In Taiwan, notwithstanding the legal basis for indigenous courts provided in the Basic Law on Indigenous Peoples of 2005, no such court has yet been created.[83]

4.1.5.3 The challenge of structural design The key structural design issue in creating special courts or tribunals is determining where in the general structure of the courts to place these special courts. Typically there are three models. The first model is to place these special courts or tribunals entirely outside the general structure of the courts. The problems with this model, however, are that the decisions of the special courts or tribunals may not be appealable to the general courts, and that the top court may lack supervisory power over these special courts or tribunals. As a result, judicial independence or integrity may be undermined if political institutions are able to interfere with these special courts or tribunals.

The second model stands as the opposite of the first model. In this model, special courts or tribunals are typically created as special district or high courts or as special tribunals in district or high courts. The advantages of this model are that the top court continues to enjoy final supervisory power over all special jurisdictions, and that judicial integrity and independence may be better preserved. The problem with this model, however, is that these special courts or tribunals may not be "special" at all, as the judges of these special courts or tribunals may still be drawn from those serving in the general jurisdictions and therefore lack the kind of special expertise needed.

The third model, which places a greater emphasis on the special expertise of the decision-makers, is a model of "quasi-judicial" tribunals. Under this model, special courts or tribunals are created by transforming administrative agencies into quasi-judicial tribunals and bureaucrats into judges, reflecting what the recent scholarship of comparative

81 Krishnan, "Legitimacy of courts," this volume, section 5.
82 Hoque, "Courts in Bangladesh," this volume, section 1.6.
83 Chang, "Courts and judicial reform in Taiwan," this volume, section 1.1.

administrative law terms as "judicialization of administrative powers."[84] The advantage of this model is the enhanced capacity of these adjudicators when compared to general judges. Yet the particular challenge of this model is one of ensuring the independence and integrity of these "quasi-judicial" tribunals.

In Asia and among the jurisdictions covered in this book, the second model is most popular, the first is less so, and the third model is mostly found in India. The first model, in which special courts or tribunals are placed outside the general structure of the courts, is typically used in the creation of military or martial courts. The maritime courts in China, the military courts in China and Vietnam, the human rights court and religious court in Indonesia, the martial courts in Malaysia, and some special courts in Bangladesh are established this way.[85] The second model prevails in most jurisdictions. All special courts in India, Japan, the Philippines, Singapore, South Korea, Taiwan and Thailand, as well as most special courts in Bangladesh, China, Indonesia, Malaysia and Vietnam, have been established under this model.[86] The third, quasi-judicial, model, in which quasi-judicial administrative tribunals hear appeals, with a state or central apex agency being the administrative court of last resort, is mostly observed in India.[87]

4.2 Quality of judges

As the number of courts varies significantly across the jurisdictions covered in this book, so does the number of judges. China has the highest

[84] See e.g. T. Ginsburg, "The judicialization of administrative governance: causes, consequences and limits" in T. Ginsburg and A. H. Y. Chen (eds.), *Administrative Law and Governance in Asia: Comparative Perspectives* (New York: Routledge, 2009), pp. 1–19; C. Scott, "Agencification, regulation and judicialization: American exceptionalism and other ways of life" in Ginsburg and Chen (eds.), *Administrative Law and Governance in Asia: Comparative Perspectives*, pp. 38–58.

[85] Gu, "Courts in China," this volume, section 1.1; Nicholson, "Renovating courts," this volume, section 1; Juwana, "Courts in Indonesia," this volume, sections 1.2.1, 1.2.6; Choong, "Courts in Malaysia," this volume, section 1.4; Hoque, "Courts in Bangladesh," this volume, section 1.3.1.

[86] Krishnan, "Legitimacy of courts," this volume, section 1.1; Kawagishi, "Judicial power in Japan," this volume, section 2.1; Pangalangan, "The Philippines' post-Marcos judiciary," this volume, section 1.2; Tan, "Singapore's judicial system," this volume, section 3.2; Kim, "Courts in the Republic of Korea," this volume, section 1.1; Chang, "Courts and judicial reform in Taiwan," this volume, section 1.1; Satayanurug and Nakornin, "Courts in Thailand," this volume, section 1.1.2.

[87] Krishnan, "Legitimacy of courts," this volume, section 1.1.

number of judges – around 193,000 – at all levels of courts. Among these, 500 serve as judges of the Supreme People's Court.[88] In contrast, Hong Kong and Singapore each have fewer than 200 judges.[89] Between these extremes, there is wide variation: 463 judges in Mongolia, 813 judges in Malaysia, 1,700 judges and magistrates in Bangladesh, 2,070 judges in Taiwan, 2,218 judges in the Philippines, 4,000 judges in Thailand, around 4,500 judges in Vietnam, and 7,780 judges in Indonesia.[90]

Consequently, the number of judges per 100,000 inhabitants also varies greatly from jurisdiction to jurisdiction, from 0.0512 in Vietnam, to 1.3 in India, 2.66 in Hong Kong, 4.9 in Korea, 9 in Taiwan, 14.37 in China, and 16 in Mongolia.[91] However, the ratio of judges to population does not necessarily indicate the quality of the judiciary or correlate with the country's degree of political and economic development. What actually affects the quality of the judiciary across jurisdictions thus remains intriguing. The following sections discuss and compare across the jurisdictions covered in this book the following four aspects of the judiciary that may – in varying degrees – affect judicial quality: the qualifications of judges, the judicial appointment process, the terms and tenure of judges, and judicial training and legal education.

4.2.1 Qualifications of judges

As is typically the case for all other civil servants, a common requirement for judges of all levels is that they hold citizenship of the country in which they serve. For example, the Constitution of the Philippines provides that no person shall be appointed to be a member of the Supreme Court or any lower collegiate court unless he or she is a natural-born citizen of the

88 Gu, "Courts in China," this volume, section 1.3.

89 Lo, "Hong Kong," this volume, section 1.3; Tan, "Singapore's judicial system," this volume, section 3.1.

90 Amarsanaa, "Courts in Mongolia," this volume, section 2.1; Choong, "Courts in Malaysia," this volume, section 1.1; Hoque, "Courts in Bangladesh," this volume, section 1; Chang, "Courts and judicial reform in Taiwan," this volume, section 1.3; Pangalangan, "The Philippines' post-Marcos judiciary," this volume, Table 10.1; Satayanurug and Nakornin, "Courts in Thailand," this volume, section 1.4; Nicholson, "Renovating courts," this volume, section 2.2; Juwana, "Courts in Indonesia," this volume, section 1.4.

91 Nicholson, "Renovating courts," this volume, section 2.2; Krishnan, "Legitimacy of courts," this volume, section 1.2; Lo, "Hong Kong," this volume, section 1.3; Kim, "Courts in the Republic of Korea," this volume, section 1.5; Chang, "Courts and judicial reform in Taiwan," this volume, section 1.3; Gu, "Courts in China," this volume, section 1.2; Amarsanaa, "Courts in Mongolia," this volume, section 2.1.

Philippines.[92] The Constitution of Mongolia stipulates Mongolian nationality as one of the prerequisites for qualifying as a judge.[93] The Federal Constitution of Malaysia also includes a similar requirement.[94]

Noticeably, however, in Hong Kong, the Basic Law authorizes the Court of Final Appeal to invite judges from other common law jurisdictions to sit on the bench.[95] In addition, the Basic Law also permits the recruitment of lower-court judges from other common law jurisdictions.[96] At present, the Court of Final Appeal consists of the Chief Justice, three permanent judges and five non-permanent judges from Hong Kong, and twelve non-permanent judges from other common law jurisdictions.[97] Non-permanent foreign judges have typically been retired judges from the United Kingdom and Australia. As one non-permanent foreign judge commented, "a function of a judge from another common law jurisdiction was to give particular consideration to whether a proposed decision of the Court of Final Appeal was in accord with general principles of the common law."[98] Notwithstanding the deliberation function, having foreign judges serve on the top court has become a unique feature of the judiciary in Hong Kong, striking a delicate balance between its two identities as an autonomous common law jurisdiction and an integral part of China.

Aside from nationality, other qualifications of judges may vary with different tiers of courts or with courts of different specialties. We discuss them separately in the following.

4.2.1.1 Judges of lower courts Exam-based qualification is typical for entry-level judges across jurisdictions in Asia. In civil law jurisdictions such as China, Indonesia, Japan, Mongolia, South Korea, Taiwan and Thailand, any law graduate or qualified individual who intends to become a judge must take an exam.[99] Even among common law

92 Constitution of the Philippines, Art. 8 (7) (1).

93 Article 51(3) of the Constitution of Mongolia stipulates that a Mongolian national of thirty-five years of age with higher legal education and experience in judicial practice of not less than ten years may be appointed as a judge of the Supreme Court.

94 Federal Constitution of Malaysia, Art. 123.

95 Basic Law of the HKSAR, Art. 82.

96 Basic Law of the HKSAR, Art. 92.

97 Lo, "Hong Kong," this volume, section 1.3.

98 *Chen Li Hung & Anor* v. *Ting Lei Miao & Ors* (2000) 3 HKCFAR 9 (CFA). See also P. Y. Lo, *The Hong Kong Basic Law* (Butterworths: LexisNexis, 2011), p. 479.

99 Gu, "Courts in China," this volume, section 2.1; Juwana, "Courts in Indonesia," this volume, section 3.1; Kawagishi, "Judicial power in Japan," this volume, section 3.1; Amarsanaa, "Courts in Mongolia," this volume, section 2.2; Kim, "Courts in the Republic of Korea," this volume, section 4.2.2; Chang, "Courts and judicial reform in Taiwan," this

jurisdictions, where judges are usually recruited from among experienced lawyers, a number of jurisdictions in Asia, such as Bangladesh and India, may still require exam passage for entry-level judges. In Bangladesh, for example, judges and magistrates of the junior judiciary have since 2007 been selected through exams covering both legal and non-legal subjects. In India, while judges may be recruited from among experienced lawyers, most judges come to the lower courts by taking a series of civil servants' exams following their law school graduation.[100]

These exams are typically administered by the judiciary, the Ministry of Justice or an independent government organ. For example, the exams are administered by the Supreme Court in Indonesia and the Philippines, by the Ministry of Justice in Japan and South Korea, by the Judicial Service Commission in Bangladesh, and by an independent constitutional organ, the Examination Yuan, in Taiwan.[101]

Most noteworthy is the competitiveness of these exams, as reported in many jurisdictions. In Bangladesh, for example, the pass rate is around 10 percent, but it was only 6 percent in 2012.[102] In China, according to the Ministry of Justice, the pass rate in 2004 was 11.22 percent.[103] In Thailand, the exams are open to all eligible lawyers who intend to become judges and are extremely competitive. According to Satayanurug and Nakornin, "the recent open examination for judge recruitment saw only 15 out of more than 8,000 candidates successfully pass the examination, joining the already scarce number of judges on duty."[104]

East Asian jurisdictions including Japan, South Korea and Taiwan perhaps saw the most competitive exams for judges. In Taiwan, the pass rate is on average 1 percent,[105] compared to the average pass rate of 8 percent for the qualifying exams taken by those intending to become

volume, section 2.1; Satayanurug and Nakornin, "Courts in Thailand," this volume, section 3.1.1.

[100] Krishnan, "Legitimacy of courts," this volume, section 1.2.

[101] Juwana, "Courts in Indonesia," this volume, section 3.1; Pangalangan, "The Philippines' post-Marcos judiciary," this volume, section 3.1; Hoque, "Courts in Bangladesh," this volume, section 2.1; Kim, "Courts in the Republic of Korea," this volume, section 4.2.2; Chang, "Courts and judicial reform in Taiwan," this volume, section 2.1.

[102] Hoque, "Courts in Bangladesh," this volume, section 2.1.

[103] Ministry of Justice, China, www.moj.gov.cn/sfks/content/2009-05/31/content_1098045.htm?node=8010.

[104] Satayanurug and Nakornin, "Courts in Thailand," this volume, section 6.3.2.

[105] Statistics compiled by Ministry of Examination, Taiwan, wwwc.moex.gov.tw/main/ExamReport/wFrmExamStatistics.aspx?menu_id=158.

lawyers.[106] Prior to the recent reforms of the legal education system in both Japan and South Korea, the pass rate for the judges' exam in Japan was on average 2–3 percent,[107] similar to the pass rate for the lawyers' exam,[108] while the pass rate for the lawyers' exam in South Korea was on average less than 5 percent,[109] and the pass rate for the judges' exams was well below that.[110] Both Japan and South Korea undertook legal education reforms respectively in 2004 and in 2007, one of which was to create American-style law schools and permit only graduates of those schools to take the exams required to become lawyers or judges. After the reforms, in Japan, the pass rate for the judges' exam was set at about 40 percent,[111] but it was reportedly only 25 percent in 2011.[112] In South Korea, according to Kim, for the first two post-reform bar exams, in 2011 and 2012, the pass rate was fixed at around 75 percent, and entry-level judges were to be appointed from among law clerks or practicing lawyers with more than five years of legal experience.[113]

Having passed the exams, prospective judges are usually required to undergo further training at a judicial training institute and/or through apprenticeships at the courts for one or two years. As indicated above, in a few jurisdictions such as South Korea, Taiwan and Thailand, the recruitment of judges has become diversified, extending beyond a traditional exam process to the recruitment of experienced lawyers or legal scholars.[114] Interestingly, however, in some of those jurisdictions, for example Thailand, competitive exams may still be required for experienced lawyers or law professors who intend to become judges.[115]

[106] Statistics compiled by Ministry of Examination, Taiwan, wwwc.moex.gov.tw/main/ExamReport/wFrmExamStatistics.aspx?menu_id=158. See also Chang, "Courts and judicial reform in Taiwan," this volume, section 2.3.

[107] Statistics compiled by Ministry of Justice, Japan, www.moj.go.jp/content/000006745.pdf.

[108] Statistics compiled by Ministry of Justice, Japan, www.moj.go.jp/content/000006745.pdf.

[109] J. Kim, "Socrates v. Confucius: an analysis of South Korea's implementation of the American law school model," *Asian-Pacific Law & Policy Journal*, 10 (2009) 322, 326.

[110] Kim, "Courts in the Republic of Korea," this volume, section 4.2.2.

[111] M. J. Wilson, "U.S. legal education methods and ideals: application to the Japanese and Korean systems," *Cardozo Journal of International & Comparative Law*, 18 (2010), 295, 339–40.

[112] M. Tanikawa, "A Japanese legal exam that sets the bar high," *New York Times*, 10 July 2011, www.nytimes.com/2011/07/11/world/asia/11iht-educLede11.html?pagewanted=all&_r=0.

[113] Kim, "Courts in the Republic of Korea," this volume, section 4.2.2.

[114] For example, Chang, "Courts and judicial reform in Taiwan," this volume, section 2.1.

[115] That is the special appointment exam in addition to the open exam for all lawyers with bachelor of law degrees and the knowledge exam for lawyers with master of law degrees or higher qualifications: Satayanurug and Nakornin, "Courts in Thailand," this volume, section 3.1.1.

As discussed earlier, judges in common law jurisdictions are generally recruited from among experienced lawyers. Hence, in order to be qualified as a judge, one must first be qualified as a lawyer. For example, in Hong Kong, in order to be eligible for appointment as a judge, one must be qualified to practice as a lawyer in a court in Hong Kong or any other common law jurisdiction and have, since becoming so qualified, practiced as a lawyer in such a court, or served as an officer of the government for at least a specified period of time.[116] In some jurisdictions, additional requirements may be stipulated. In the Philippines, for example, eligible lawyers who intend to apply for judicial posts must attend an additional pre-judicature program offered by the Philippine Judicial Academy.[117]

In nearly all jurisdictions, a law degree is a prerequisite for qualifying to be a judge. In China, however, a law degree is not a prerequisite. With or without a law degree, one can become a judge by passing the unified national judicial exam and having one to three years of working experience in the courts.[118] According to Gu, "in the early 1980s, approximately two-thirds of Chinese judges did not have a law degree, and one-third of them were retired from the military."[119] In order to solve this problem, the Judge Law as amended in 2001 requires that judges without law degrees obtain further training at the national or local judicial training institutes.[120]

4.2.1.2 Judges of supreme courts Usually there are no additional qualification requirements for judges of supreme courts except experience as a judge or some other qualified legal professional for a certain period of time. In most common law jurisdictions, for example Bangladesh, Malaysia and Singapore, the typical required length of experience is ten years.[121] In civil law jurisdictions, the required length of experience generally depends on the period of time necessary for climbing up the judicial ladder from the bottom tier to the top court.

For example, in Japan, the justices of the Supreme Court are appointed from among "learned persons with extensive knowledge of laws, who are

[116] Lo, "Hong Kong," this volume, section 3.1.
[117] Pangalangan, "The Philippines' post-Marcos judiciary," this volume, section 3.1.
[118] Article 9 of the Judges' Law. [119] Gu, "Courts in China," this volume, section 2.1.
[120] *Ibid.*
[121] Hoque, "Courts in Bangladesh," this volume, section 2.1; Choong, "Courts in Malaysia," this volume, section 3.1.2; Tan, "Singapore's judicial system," this volume, section 2.1.

not less than forty years old" as stipulated in the law.[122] The same Act also requires that at least ten out of fifteen justices of the Supreme Court should be persons who have held one or two of the following positions for a total period of twenty years or more: (1) president of the high court, (2) judge, (3) judge of the summary court, (4) public prosecutor, (5) attorney, or (6) professor or associate professor of law at a university.[123] According to Kawagishi, although the law permits the justices to be appointed at the age of forty, no justices have yet been appointed in their forties. Instead, justices are generally appointed in their sixties because of the work experience requirements and the mandatory retirement age of seventy.[124]

Perhaps due to the high prestige of supreme courts and the gatekeeping function of the appointment process discussed below, the lack of specific qualifications for top court judges does not seem to bring about serious concerns. In Singapore, for example, according to Tan, for the past twenty years, most appointees were well-respected and highly experienced legal practitioners, and the general public perception is that those who are eventually appointed to the bench have been appointed primarily on the basis of merit.[125] However, in Bangladesh, concerns were expressed regarding the lack of statutory criteria for the selection of top court judges, especially when the appointment process became non-transparent or even politicized.[126]

4.2.1.3 Judges of constitutional courts Qualifications for constitutional court judges are similar to those for judges at top courts. However, due to the political nature of constitutional adjudication, additional qualifications may be stipulated for constitutional court judges.

For example, in Thailand, the Constitution specifically requires that, aside from being judges and qualified persons in the field of law, two out of the nine justices of the Constitutional Court be selected from "qualified persons in the field of political science, public administration or other social science, who really possess knowledge and expertise in the administration of the State affairs."[127] Similarly, in Cambodia, the members of the Constitutional Council must have considerable work

[122] The Court Act, Art. 41(1) (Japan). [123] The Court Act, Art. 41(2) (Japan).
[124] Kawagishi, "Judicial power in Japan," this volume, section 3.1.
[125] Tan, "Singapore's judicial system," this volume, section 2.1.
[126] Hoque, "Courts in Bangladesh," this volume, section 2.2.
[127] Constitution of Thailand, s. 204 (1) (4).

experience and a higher-education degree in law, administration, diplomacy or economics.[128] In Mongolia, aside from legal qualifications, a justice of the Constitutional Court must also have a high level of political experience.[129]

In Taiwan, in order to be eligible for appointment as a Justice of the Constitutional Court, a candidate must: (1) have served as a Justice of the Supreme Court for more than ten years with a distinguished record; (2) have served as a Member of the Legislative Yuan for more than nine years with distinguished contributions; (3) have been a professor in a major field of law at a university for more than ten years and authored publications in a specialized field; (4) have served as a Justice of the International Court, or have had authoritative works published in the fields of public or comparative law; or (5) be a person of high repute in the field of legal research who has had political experience. In addition, the law requires that the number of Justices qualifying under any single category of qualifications listed above not exceed one-third of the total number of Justices. In practice, however, half of the Justices come from academic backgrounds, and half are career judges.[130]

4.2.1.4 Judges of special courts or tribunals With the emergence of special courts or tribunals, finding qualified judges for such courts or tribunals may become a concern. Intriguingly, however, there are often no additional qualifications required for judges of special courts or tribunals other than being qualified as judges. The lack of special expertise of these judges may generate doubts regarding the functions of these special courts or tribunals and the quality of their decisions. For example, in China, according to Gu, a general shortage of judicial expertise in the area of commercial law has resulted in misapplication of rules or even denial of enforcement of arbitral awards.[131]

In order to address such problems, some jurisdictions place emphasis on judges' experience in specific areas of adjudication or on their specialization in certain areas of law. For example, in Taiwan, family court judges are to be appointed from among those who have experience, expertise and enthusiasm in the adjudication of family matters,[132] and intellectual

[128] Constitution of Cambodia, Art. 138. [129] Constitution of Mongolia, Art. 65(2).

[130] W.-C. Chang, "The role of judicial review in consolidating democracy: the case of Taiwan,"*Asia Law Review*, 2(2) (2005), 73–88.

[131] Gu, "Courts in China," this volume, section 2.1.

[132] Juvenile and Family Court Act, Art. 20 (Taiwan).

property court judges are to be appointed from among those specializing in intellectual property laws.[133] Additional ways to strengthen the expertise of courts or tribunals are to appoint specialists as assistants to judges[134] or to rely to a greater degree on experts during the adjudication process.

Most exceptional perhaps is the recruitment of associate judges who are specialized laypersons in relevant fields for adjudication of special courts and tribunals in Thailand. According to Satayanurug and Nakornin, these specialized associate judges are appointed for temporary terms on special courts, including the juvenile and family court, the labor court, and the intellectual property and international trade court.[135]

4.2.2 Appointment of judges

As with the required qualifications for judges, the method and process of judicial appointment may vary by type of court. In Asia, judges of lower courts are generally appointed by the chief executive on the basis of their qualifications or their performance on competitive exams. The appointment of Supreme Court or constitutional court judges, however, may involve power-sharing mechanisms between the executive and legislature and have greater political accountability.

4.2.2.1 Appointment of lower court judges In Asia, lower court judges serving in general or special jurisdictions are typically appointed by the chief executive based on exam performance or other qualifications. As discussed above, the exams are usually administered by the judiciary, and certifications of qualifications are provided by law schools or bar associations. As a result, despite being made by the chief executive, judicial appointments are generally merit-based, and political interference is rare and insubstantial. Especially noteworthy is the fact that lower court judges in South Korea are appointed by the Chief Justice of the Supreme Court with the consent of the Conference of Supreme Court Justices.[136]

133 Intellectual Property Court Act, Art. 13 (Taiwan).

134 For example, in Taiwan, technical experts are appointed to assist judges of the intellectual property courts to review the cases as stipulated in Article 15 of the Intellectual Property Court Act. In addition, according to the Juvenile and Family Court Act, specialized social workers or psychologists may also be appointed as special investigators by the family courts.

135 Satayanurug and Nakornin, "Courts in Thailand," this volume, section 3.1.3.

136 Constitution of the Republic of Korea, Art. 103. See also Kim, "Courts in the Republic of Korea," this volume, section 4.2.1.

Elite-centered judicial appointments, however, are not without criticism. For example, in South Korea, according to Kim, "the fact that judges have been appointed from a state-controlled group with a highly homogenized and bureaucratic culture" has facilitated the bureaucratization of the judiciary.[137] In Taiwan, similar criticisms were also expressed, which triggered the enactment of the Judge Act in 2011, in which a few reform measures on judicial appointments were undertaken.[138] Most important was the creation of a judicial council – reflecting a recent trend in other countries[139] – composed of representatives of the judiciary, the bar, the legal community, the political branches of government or civil society, to participate in the process of judicial appointment.[140]

Similar judicial councils have also been created in other jurisdictions. For instance, in Malaysia, the Judicial Appointments Commission consists of high-ranking members of the judiciary and four other "eminent persons" who are not members of the executive or public service.[141] A similar commission in Hong Kong consists of local judges, members of the legal profession and eminent persons from other sectors.[142] In the Philippines, the Judicial and Bar Council, composed of former government officials and judges, is empowered to supply a shortlist of judicial appointees to the president.[143]

4.2.2.2 Appointment of Supreme Court judges Due to the institutional prominence of the Supreme Court having the final power of adjudication in any given jurisdiction, appointments to the Supreme Court may involve greater political checks and balances. Unlike the power to appoint lower court judges, which is usually held by the chief executive, the power to appoint Supreme Court judges is more likely to be shared among the executive, legislative and judicial branches. Ranging from lesser to greater power-sharing mechanisms, the appointment of Supreme Court justices in Asia may follow one of four models.[144]

137 Kim, "Courts in the Republic of Korea," this volume, section 4.2.2.

138 Chang, "Courts and judicial reform in Taiwan," this volume, section 2.1.

139 See e.g. N. Garopa and T. Ginsburg, "Guarding the guardians: judicial councils and judicial independence," *American Journal of Comparative Law*, 57 (2009), 103, 119–121.

140 Chang, "Courts and judicial reform in Taiwan," this volume, section 2.1.

141 Choong, "Courts in Malaysia," this volume, section 3.1.2.

142 Lo, "Hong Kong," this volume, section 3.1.

143 Pangalangan, "The Philippines' post-Marcos judiciary," this volume, section 2.2.

144 See also Chang et al., *Constitutionalism in Asia*.

The first is the executive model, in which justices are appointed solely by the president or the cabinet. Japan and Bangladesh stand out as typical examples. In Japan, the justices of the Supreme Court are appointed by the cabinet, and the Chief Justice is appointed by the Emperor upon the designation of the cabinet. In Bangladesh, the Chief Justice and other Justices of the Supreme Court are appointed by the President.[145]

The second model is executive appointment in consultation with the judiciary, usually with the Chief Justice of the Supreme Court. China, India and Singapore follow this model. In China, the judges of the Supreme People's Court are appointed by the Standing Committee of the National People's Congress upon the recommendation of the president of the Supreme People's Court.[146] The Constitution of India prescribes that justices of the Supreme Court, with the exception of the Chief Justice, shall be appointed by the President with the consultation of the Chief Justice.[147] In addition, the Supreme Court recently issued decisions requiring that the four most senior justices below the Chief Justice also be consulted in such appointments.[148] In Singapore, the judges of the Supreme Court are appointed by the President on the advice of the Prime Minister, following the Prime Minister's consultation of the Chief Justice.[149]

The third model is executive appointment with consultation of judicial councils or commissions. Hong Kong and the Philippines follow this model.[150] As stated above, judicial councils are composed of representatives of the judiciary, the political branches, the legal community or civil society. The last and fourth model involves power-sharing elements in the appointment process, which are much more common in constitutional court appointments than in supreme court appointments. Under this model, the justices of the Supreme Court are appointed by the executive with parliamentary consent. For example, in South Korea, justices of the Supreme Court are appointed by the President on the recommendation of the Chief Justice and with the consent of the National Assembly.[151]

145 Kawagishi, "Judicial power in Japan," this volume, pp. 000–00; Hoque, 'Courts in Bangladesh," this volume, section 3.
146 Constitution of the People's Republic of China, Art. 67(11).
147 Constitution of India, Art. 124.
148 Krishnan, "Legitimacy of courts," this volume, section 2.
149 Constitution of Singapore, Art. 95.
150 Basic Law of HKSAR, Art. 88; Pangalangan, "The Philippines' post-Marcos judiciary," this volume, section 2.2.
151 Constitution of the Republic of Korea, Art. 104.

4.2.2.3 Appointment of constitutional court judges Due to the political nature of constitutional adjudication, the appointment of constitutional court justices typically involves power-sharing mechanisms between the political branches. There are basically two models: the cooperation model and the representation model.[152]

The cooperation model requires the two political branches – the executive and legislative – to complete the appointment of all constitutional court justices. For example, in Taiwan, all justices of the Constitutional Court are appointed by the president with the consent of the legislature. In contrast, the representation model emphasizes the different interests of the government branches in appointing constitutional court justices. Under this model, the executive, legislative and judicial branches share the power to appoint constitutional court justices, usually with each appointing one-third. The Constitutional Courts of Indonesia, Mongolia and South Korea have adopted this model.[153]

Most complex is the appointment of constitutional court justices in Thailand, which involves elements of both the cooperation and representation models. The King nominally appoints the nine justices of the Constitutional Court, five of whom are selected by the judiciary, with the other four selected by the Senate from a list submitted by a selection committee whose membership is prescribed by the Constitution and includes representatives of the judiciary and legislature.[154]

4.2.3 Terms and tenure of judges

The guarantee of life tenure is essential to securing the independence of judges. The majority of jurisdictions in Asia provide such a guarantee for judges, who shall hold office during good behavior until he or she attains the age of retirement. Particularly noteworthy is the ten-year renewable terms of lower court judges in Japan and South Korea. Both countries' constitutions stipulate that lower court judges serve for a ten-year term with the privilege of reappointment.[155] In observance of the principle of judicial independence, however, in both jurisdictions this clause has been interpreted in such a way as to provide judges in good standing with guaranteed tenure until the age of retirement.[156]

[152] Chang et al., *Constitutionalism in Asia.* [153] Chang et al., *Constitutionalism in Asia.*
[154] Constitution of Thailand, s. 206.
[155] Kawagishi, "Judicial power in Japan," this volume, section 4; Kim, "Courts in the Republic of Korea," this volume, section 4.2.3.
[156] Kawagishi, "Judicial power in Japan," this volume, section 4; Kim, "Courts in the Republic of Korea," this volume, section 4.2.3.

Intriguingly, the two socialist legal systems – China and Vietnam – included in this book have not provided judges with life tenure. In Vietnam, judges are appointed for a term of five years and may be reappointed, giving the party-state strong controls over the judiciary.[157] In China, judges of all levels are appointed and removed by the standing committees of the people's congresses at the corresponding level, and the presidents of courts at all levels are elected and removed by the people's congress at that level. According to Gu, the lack of a tenure system has exacerbated judicial corruption and the shortage of talent in the judiciary, as skilled lawyers prefer to work elsewhere.[158]

While life tenure fosters judicial independence, it may compromise judicial accountability, which is of particular importance to the court of last resort. This also explains why some jurisdictions, for example South Korea, have adopted a more political and power-sharing model for the appointment of Supreme Court justices. Similar considerations may underlie restrictions on tenure for top court justices. In South Korea, the Chief Justice of the Supreme Court serves only for a term of six years while other justices hold six-year terms with one-time renewability.[159] In Japan, the justices of the Supreme Court must retire at the age of seventy but are usually appointed around the age of sixty, rendering a de facto term limit of about ten years.[160] In Korea, the relatively short terms of top court justices – while they ensure some degree of accountability – have raised concerns about political bias and judicial corruption, according to Kim.[161]

Due to the political nature of constitutional adjudication, constitutional court justices are usually subject to fixed terms. As stated above, there are seven constitutional courts or councils in Asia: Taiwan (created in 1948), South Korea (1987), Mongolia (1992), Cambodia (1993), Thailand (1997), Indonesia (2001) and Myanmar (2008). Other than Taiwan, which has fifteen constitutional court justices, all other Asian constitutional courts have nine justices each. The terms of constitutional court justices range from five years in Indonesia and Myanmar, to six years in Mongolia and South Korea, eight years in Taiwan and nine years in Thailand. In all of the jurisdictions except South Korea, the terms of

157 Nicholson, "Renovating courts," this volume, section 3.3.
158 Gu, "Courts in China," this volume, section 2.1.
159 Kim, "Courts in the Republic of Korea," this volume, section 1.4.
160 Kawagishi, "Judicial power in Japan," this volume, section 3.1.
161 Kim, "Courts in the Republic of Korea," this volume, section 4.2.3.

constitutional justices are non-renewable.[162] In Taiwan, prior to 2003, the justices of the Constitutional Court enjoyed renewable terms of nine years, but after 2003, as a result of a constitutional revision, they now only serve non-renewable terms of eight years.[163]

Another category of judges who may not be guaranteed life tenure is that of "additional judges", "supernumerary judges" or "contract judges" appointed due to a shortage of judges. Only a very small number of jurisdictions – for example, India and Singapore – report the existence of such judges. The Constitution of India permits the appointment of an "additional" judge due to the increase of workload or a shortage of judges for a period not exceeding two years.[164] In Singapore, a shortage of High Court judges led to an amendment to Article 94 of the Constitution to permit the appointment of "supernumerary" or "contract" judges in 1971. This allowed judges of the Supreme Court who were compelled to retire at the age of sixty-five to stay on as judges on a contractual basis, usually for terms of one to three years. In addition, difficulties in persuading senior legal practitioners to accept appointments to the bench led to an amendment to the Constitution in 1979 to create the post of Judicial Commissioner, which can be filled on a temporary basis. The term of a Judicial Commissioner is between six months and three years, and, after serving his or her term, the Judicial Commissioner is allowed to return to private business. According to Tan, constitutional permission for such temporary judicial appointments is problematic and may compromise judicial independence, although thus far there has never been any suggestion that any judge or judicial commissioner was appointed for political reasons.[165]

Life tenure guarantees the continuation of one's judgeship during good behavior until the age of retirement is reached. In the case of misbehavior or an inability to discharge his or her duties, a judge may be impeached and dismissed. Impeachment is thus the primary method for the dismissal of judges across all jurisdictions.[166] However, the country chapters of this

162 Constitution of Mongolia, Art. 65; Constitution of Cambodia, Art. 137; Constitution of Thailand, s. 208; Constitution of Indonesia, Art. 24C; Constitution of the Republic of the Union of Myanmar, Art. 335.

163 Chang, "Role of judicial review."

164 Constitution of India, Art. 224. For relevant discussions, see Chang et al., *Constitutionalism in Asia*, ch. 5.

165 Tan, "Singapore's judicial system," this volume, section 2.2.

166 Chang, "Courts and judicial reform in Taiwan," this volume, section 2; Satayanurug and Nakornin, "Courts in Thailand," this volume, section 3.2.2.

book have not reported many cases of impeachment, with the exception of the Philippines. According to Pangalangan, the impeachment of judges, especially the impeachment of the Chief Justice of the Supreme Court most recently in 2012, has become a form of political backlash against the already politicized court.[167] Also noteworthy is the system of popular review of judges in Japan. Article 79 of the Constitution stipulates that the appointment of Supreme Court judges shall be reviewed by the people at the first general election of members of the House of Representatives following their appointment and shall be reviewed again at the first general election of members of the House of Representatives after a lapse of ten years, and that if the majority of the voters favors the dismissal of a judge, he or she shall then be dismissed.[168] Thus far, no judge has been dismissed through this process.

4.2.4 Judicial training and legal education

Legal education and judicial training serve as the foundation for the quality of the judiciary. Legal education in Asia is primarily offered at the undergraduate level across all jurisdictions in both civil and common law systems. As in Europe and Latin America, it is typical in a civil law system for legal education to be offered at the undergraduate level. Among common law systems in Asia, undergraduate legal education primarily reflects British colonial influence, as is the case in Bangladesh, Hong Kong, India, Malaysia and Singapore. The exception is the Philippines, whose legal education system reflects American colonial influence dating back to the early twentieth century. According to Pangalangan, the American style of law teaching was introduced in 1911 with the establishment of the University of the Philippines' College of Law, which offered a three-year professional course in law. Later, a two-year pre-law undergraduate course was required, which was expanded into a four-year course in 1960.[169]

Also noteworthy is a recent American influence on the reform of legal education in Asia. As indicated above, Japan and South Korea undertook legal education reforms respectively in 2004 and 2007, in which American-style law schools were created and case-law methods emphasized. In both places, the reform plan was to permit only graduates from the limited number of high-quality law schools to become legal

[167] Pangalangan, "The Philippines' post-Marcos judiciary," this volume, section 2.4.

[168] See the Constitution of Japan, Art. 79, para. 3; the Act on Popular Review of the Supreme Court Justices (Act no. 136, 20 November 1947), Art. 32 and Art. 35, para. 1.

[169] Pangalangan, "The Philippines' post-Marcos judiciary," this volume, section 3.1.

professionals.[170] In Taiwan, a similar reform was also undertaken, proceeding with dual tracks: (1) an undergraduate law degree track, and (2) a graduate law degree track for those with undergraduate degrees in a subject other than law.[171] Mongolia also adopted a similar two-track legal education system.[172]

As expressed in the country chapters, the challenges of legal education in Asia are twofold. The first challenge is the homogeneous and bureaucratic nature of legal professionals resulting from elite-centered legal education systems and competitive examination processes. This challenge has been most apparent in Japan, Korea and Taiwan.[173] For example, in Korea, according to Kim, the judiciary consists mostly of graduates from the top five universities.[174] The second challenge is the poor quality of legal education due to a lack of resources, as exacerbated in India, Mongolia and China, particularly in rural areas.[175] In China, the quality of legal education has recently substantially improved as a result of both government reforms and overseas funding. Yet, the fact that a law degree is not a prerequisite for becoming a lawyer or a judge, continues to undermine the importance of legal education.

Perhaps due to concerns with the quality of legal education, many jurisdictions included in this book provide further training for judges, prior to appointment and/or during their terms of service. Nearly all of the jurisdictions provide in-service training as part of continuing legal education. However, pre-appointment training is mostly only offered in civil law jurisdictions. For example, Japan, Taiwan, Korea, Indonesia, Thailand, Vietnam and China provide pre-appointment training ranging from eight months to two years.[176] In contrast, in most common law

170 Kawagishi, "Judicial power in Japan," this volume, section 4; Kim, "Courts in the Republic of Korea," this volume, section 4.2.2.

171 Chang, "Courts and judicial reform in Taiwan," this volume, section 2.3.2.

172 Amarsanaa, "Courts in Mongolia," section 3.1.

173 Kawagishi, "Judicial power in Japan," this volume, section 4; Kim, "Courts in the Republic of Korea," this volume, section 4.2.2; Chang, "Courts and judicial reform in Taiwan," this volume, section 2.3.2.

174 Kim, "Courts in the Republic of Korea," this volume, section 4.2.2.

175 Amarsanaa, "Courts in Mongolia," this volume, section 3.1; Gu, "Courts in China," this volume, section 7; Krishnan, "Legitimacy of courts," this volume, section 3.1.

176 Kawagishi, "Judicial power in Japan," this volume, section 3.1; Kim, "Courts in the Republic of Korea," this volume, section 4.2.2; Chang, "Courts and judicial reform in Taiwan," this volume, section 2.3.2; Juwana, "Courts in Indonesia," this volume, section 3.3; Satayanurug and Nakornin, "Courts in Thailand," this volume, section 3.3; Nicholson, "Renovating courts," this volume, section 3.5; Gu, "Courts in China," this volume, section 2.3.

jurisdictions, for example Singapore and Hong Kong, there is no formal training for judges prior to their appointment to the bench.[177] The exception is the Philippines, in which the Pre-Judicature Program is provided for prospective judges.[178] The difference in the provision of pre-appointment training between civil and common law systems lies in the fact that prospective judges in common law systems are generally experienced lawyers whereas in civil law systems they are often young graduates who have just passed their exams. Also noteworthy is that in some jurisdictions these judicial training programs are offered by the judiciary, while in others they are provided by the Ministry of Justice.[179]

Problems with the quality of judicial training in some jurisdictions have been reported. For example, in Vietnam, the lack of resources for judicial training, especially in rural areas, has become a serious concern.[180] In China, the lack of professional training, particularly for judges serving at special courts or tribunals, has already affected the quality of judicial decisions.[181]

4.3 *Citizens and courts*

Unlike the executive and legislative branches, which are directly or indirectly elected by and accountable to the people, the judiciary is usually not formed upon such a democratic foundation nor burdened with such political accountability. This does not mean, however, that the judiciary is disconnected to the people or unaccountable to them. To the contrary, the relationships between citizens and courts are manifold.

For one, citizens are users of judicial services. Ensuring that citizens have fair and sufficient access to justice is of the highest importance to any government that upholds the rule of law. Citizens' satisfaction with the judiciary as well as judicial efficiency are thus important benchmarks of the performance of the judiciary. In addition to being users of judicial services, citizens may participate in trials as jury members or even lay judges. Finally, citizens may also have some influence over or even directly participate in judicial administration by monitoring judicial

177 Tan, "Singapore's judicial system," this volume, section 2.3; Lo, "Hong Kong," this volume, section 3.1.

178 Pangalangan, "The Philippines' post-Marcos judiciary," this volume, section 3.2.

179 Nicholson, "Renovating courts," this volume, section 3.5; Chang, "Courts and judicial reform in Taiwan," this volume, section 2.3.2.

180 Nicholson, "Renovating courts," this volume, section 3.5.

181 Gu, "Courts in China," this volume, section 2.1.

operations, criticizing judicial decisions or serving on judicial committees that include citizen participation.[182]

The following sections include comparative discussions of citizen participation in trials, citizens' access to justice and citizens' satisfaction with the judiciary across the Asian jurisdictions covered in this book.

4.3.1 Citizen participation in trials

The jury system was first introduced in Asia primarily in the common law jurisdictions of British colonies during the period of colonization. The use of juries was restricted to a very limited number of cases. Interestingly, upon gaining independence, most former colonies abolished the jury system. For example, Bangladesh, India, Malaysia and Singapore have all abolished the jury system.[183] The reasons for abolition are complex. According to Tan, at least one reason was concern over the quality of jury decisions, as jury members might be unsophisticated, insufficiently educated to appreciate the proceedings in court or susceptible to media and public influence.[184] The former British colony that has not abolished the jury system is Hong Kong, which sets out provisions for the jury system in the Jury Ordinance.[185] Also noteworthy is the Philippines, which, despite being a common law jurisdiction, never adopted the jury system, partly because the American colonial government deliberately did not adopt such a system.[186]

In contrast with the abolition of the jury system in common law jurisdictions, civil law jurisdictions in Asia have in recent years witnessed the trend of enhancing citizen participation in the judiciary or democratizing the judiciary by adopting systems incorporating citizen juries or lay judges. Japan, South Korea and Taiwan have all witnessed such trends. In Japan, the Act creating the system of *Saiban-in* (lay judge) participation in criminal justice cases was established in 2004 and became effective in 2009. The system of lay judges applies to cases involving crimes punishable by the death penalty or life imprisonment or cases involving intentionally committed crimes that caused the deaths of the victims.[187] In

[182] See for example the discussion in Kim, "Courts in the Republic of Korea," this volume, section 1.4.

[183] Tan, "Singapore's judicial system," this volume, section 3.3; Choong, "Courts in Malaysia," this volume, section 1.2; Hoque, "Courts in Bangladesh," this volume, section 1.

[184] Tan, "Singapore's judicial system," this volume, section 3.3.

[185] Lo, "Hong Kong," this volume, section 1.2.

[186] Pangalangan, "The Philippines' post-Marcos judiciary," this volume, section 4.1.

[187] Kawagishi, "Judicial power in Japan," this volume, sections 2.2, 3.2.

2008, a quasi-jury system or "participatory trial system" was introduced in Korea. This new system applies to only a limited category of criminal cases, and the verdicts of jurors do not bind the courts.[188] In 2012, the Judicial Yuan of Taiwan proposed a system of public trial observation, in which the opinions of lay observers are only advisory. This proposal was sent to the legislature for floor discussion.[189]

Also noteworthy is the institution of people's assessors with the judiciary in socialist legal systems, a reflection of democratic supervision of the administration of justice. Both China and Vietnam still maintain this system.[190] However, according to Gu, the use of people's assessors has declined in China over the years, as those who participated in the trials made few contributions to the decision-making process.[191]

4.3.2 Citizen's access to justice

Ensuring fair and sufficient access to justice for all citizens involves a great many institutional and substantive arrangements in the operation of the judicial – especially the litigation – system. The following sections compare a few key aspects across the various jurisdictions: (1) the number of lawyers, (2) litigation fees and legal aid, and (3) the possibility of public interest litigation.

4.3.2.1 The number of lawyers In general, the number of lawyers has been rising across the Asian jurisdictions covered in this book. In the two socialist legal systems whose economies have become increasingly market-oriented, the growth in the number of lawyers is astonishing. In China, the number of full-time lawyers increased by a factor of thirty in two decades, from 6,213 in 1981 to 192,546 in 2011.[192] In Vietnam, there were 369 lawyers in 1991, rising to 2,100 lawyers in 2001 and 5,250 lawyers in 2010, a fourteen-fold increase overall.[193] In Mongolia, there is one lawyer for every 2,700 inhabitants.[194] In India, there is one lawyer

188 Kim, "Courts in the Republic of Korea," this volume, section 1.4.
189 Chang, "Courts and judicial reform in Taiwan," this volume, section 1.2.
190 Gu, "Courts in China," this volume, section 1.2; Nicholson, "Renovating courts," this volume, section 2.1.
191 Gu, "Courts in China," this volume, section 1.2.
192 Gu, "Courts in China," this volume, section 3.1.
193 Nicholson, "Renovating courts," this volume, section 3.6 (fn. 131).
194 Amarsanaa, "Courts in Mongolia," this volume, section 3.2.

for every 1,000 inhabitants.[195] Other jurisdictions such as South Korea and Taiwan also reported an increase in the number of lawyers.[196]

Notwithstanding the increase in the number of lawyers, serious shortages of lawyers may still exist in some developing jurisdictions, especially in rural areas or with respect to certain areas of law, such as civil rights or politically sensitive issues. For example, in Indonesia, public defense lawyers and pro-bono civil rights lawyers are scarce.[197] In China, with a population of over one billion, there are 0.2 million lawyers, most of whom are located in cities.[198]

4.3.2.2 Litigation costs and legal aid Litigation costs may be an impediment to citizens' access to justice. In Hong Kong and Singapore, litigation costs are relatively high.[199] In other jurisdictions, litigation costs seem more affordable. For example, Nicholson reports affordable litigation costs for most individuals and firms in Vietnam, in which if the value of the dispute is below VND 40,000,000 (US $1,921.00), the court fees (*án phí*) are VND 4,000,000 (US $192.12).[200] In Taiwan and Mongolia, the court of first instance assesses the price or value of the claim and charges a litigation fee based on this assessment, and no litigation fee is required for petitions before the constitutional court.[201]

Another concern regarding citizens' access to justice is the high cost of legal expertise. In some developed jurisdictions, for example Singapore, the cost of legal counsel may be so high as to render access to justice merely illusory.[202] In developing jurisdictions, for example Vietnam, the cost of legal expertise may be relatively affordable.[203] However, additional costs such as bribery may exist. For example, according to Krishnan, in India, the non-systematic, non-transparent fee collection structure can be an impediment to access to justice.[204] In Indonesia,

[195] Krishnan, "Legitimacy of courts," this volume, section 3.2.
[196] E.g. Chang, "Courts and judicial reform in Taiwan," this volume, section 2.4.5; Kim, "Courts in the Republic of Korea," this volume, section 2.3.
[197] Juwana, "Courts in Indonesia," this volume, section 3.4.2.
[198] Gu, "Courts in China," this volume, section 3.1.
[199] Lo, "Hong Kong," this volume, section 3.3.2; Tan, "Singapore's judicial system," this volume, section 3.4.2.
[200] Nicholson, "Renovating courts," this volume, section 3.6.
[201] Chang, "Courts and judicial reform in Taiwan," this volume, section 2.4.2; Amarsanaa, "Courts in Mongolia," this volume, section 3.2.
[202] Tan, "Singapore's judicial system," this volume, section 3.4.2.
[203] Nicholson, "Renovating courts," this volume, section 3.6.
[204] Krishnan, "Legitimacy of courts," this volume, section 3.2.

lawyer's fees and bribery are often intertwined, and a recent report indicates that judicial costs are 122.7 percent of the amount of monetary compensation claimed.[205]

In nearly all of the jurisdictions included in this book, legal aid is provided through government programs, sometimes in collaboration with bar associations.[206] These legal aid programs typically provide litigation expenses,[207] legal services,[208] or legal advice.[209]

4.3.2.3 Public interest litigation In order to have standing to sue, a person usually needs to demonstrate that his or her constitutionally or legally protected rights or interests have been infringed by the respondent. This doctrine of standing to sue or *locus standi* is generally recognized in jurisdictions across Asia.[210] However, such a doctrine may be an impediment to citizens' access to justice in cases involving public rights or the public interest – for example, in environmental protection or social policy cases – in which everyone's right or interest is minute or remote.[211]

A few Asian jurisdictions have developed quite liberal doctrines to allow such public interest litigation. Most representative are India and the Philippines. The Supreme Court of India extended standing to sue to "any member of the public" if "a legal wrong or a legal injury is caused to such person or determinate class of persons by reason of poverty, helplessness or disability or socially or economically disadvantaged position, unable to approach the Court for relief."[212] In the

205 Juwana, "Courts in Indonesia," this volume, section 3.4.2.

206 Hoque, "Courts in Bangladesh," this volume, section 1.2; Choong, "Courts in Malaysia," this volume, section 3.3.1; Gu, "Courts in China," this volume, section 3.1; Lo, "Hong Kong," this volume, section 3.3.2; Satayanurug and Nakornin, "Courts in Thailand," this volume, section 3.4.3; Chang, "Courts and judicial reform in Taiwan," this volume, section 2.4.3; Nicholson, "Renovating courts," this volume, section 3.6; Juwana, "Courts in Indonesia," this volume, section 3.4.1.

207 Hoque, "Courts in Bangladesh," this volume, section 4.3.2.3; Lo, "Hong Kong," this volume, section 3.3.2; Juwana, "Courts in Indonesia," this volume, section 3.4.1.

208 Lo, "Hong Kong," this volume, section 3.3.2; Choong, "Courts in Malaysia," this volume, section 3.3.1; Chang, "Courts and judicial reform in Taiwan," this volume, section 2.4.3; Tan, "Singapore's judicial system," this volume, section 3.4.3; Nicholson, "Renovating courts," this volume, section 3.6; Satayanurug and Nakornin, "Courts in Thailand," this volume, section 3.4.3.

209 Lo, "Hong Kong," this volume, section 3.3.2; Nicholson, "Renovating courts," this volume, section 3.6; Satayanurug and Nakornin, "Courts in Thailand," this volume, section 3.4.3.

210 Chang et al., *Constitutionalism in Asia*, ch. 5.

211 *Ibid.*

212 *SP Gupta* v. *Union of India* [1982] AIR SC 149, para. 17.

Philippines, the Supreme Court grants standing to sue so long as the issue at stake is "of transcendental importance to the public" or "if the issues raised are of paramount public interest, and if they immeasurably affect the social, economic, and moral well-being of the people."[213] Aside from India and the Philippines, the courts in Bangladesh, Hong Kong and Taiwan as well as the Supreme Court in Indonesia have in recent years demonstrated similarly liberal attitudes toward public interest litigation.[214]

Not all jurisdictions have, however, recognized public interest litigation so liberally. In Malaysia, for example, according to Choong, the court's attitude towards public interest litigation has been like a pendulum, swinging back and forth between liberal and conservative ends and at present falling in the middle of the spectrum.[215] A similar swing also occurred in China. According to Gu, while the former Chief Justice Xiao Yang of the Supreme People's Court was receptive to public interest suits, since the current Chief Justice took office in 2008, greater restrictions have been in place.[216] In Mongolia, according to Amarsanaa, "there is no legal ground authorizing public interest litigation."[217] In Singapore, according to Tan, due to the way that the legal doctrine was interpreted, it "has meant that there has practically been no public interest litigation in Singapore."[218]

Also noteworthy is an intriguing function of the Chinese courts in which the courts accept visits and letters from people who have grievances or complaints. This is known as the 'letters and visits' system (*Xingfang*), applying not only to the courts but – most importantly – also to the people's congresses and government organs at all levels.[219] In a way, the judiciary's acceptance and management of these informal letters or visits may be deemed an alternative to public interest litigation.

[213] *Chavez* v. *Presidential Commission on Good Government*, GR No. 130716, 9 Dec. 1998 (Supreme Court, Philippines).

[214] Hoque, "Courts in Bangladesh," this volume, section 2.4; Chang, "Courts and judicial reform in Taiwan," this volume, section 2.4.1; Lo, "Hong Kong," this volume, section 3.3.2; Krishnan, "Legitimacy of courts," this volume, section 5; Juwana, "Courts in Indonesia," this volume, section 3.4.1.

[215] Choong, "Courts in Malaysia," this volume, section 3.3.2.

[216] Gu, "Courts in China," this volume, section 6.2.1.

[217] Amarsanaa, "Courts in Mongolia," this volume, section 3.2.

[218] Tan, "Singapore's judicial system," this volume, section 3.4.1.

[219] Gu, "Courts in China," this volume, section 3.2.

4.3.3 Citizens' satisfaction with the judiciary

The country chapters report varying levels of judicial performance. Some jurisdictions report high efficiency. For example, the courts in Hong Kong, Japan, Mongolia, Singapore and South Korea have displayed very high clearance rates and short clearance periods.[220] Most noteworthy is Singapore. According to Tan, "Singapore operates one of the most efficient court systems in the world."[221] In contrast, the courts in China, India and Vietnam have exhibited very poor records in efficiency, leading to calls for immediate reforms.[222] The performance of the courts in Taiwan seems to lie in the middle,[223] lagging behind frontrunners Hong Kong, Japan, Singapore and Korea but faring better than China, India and Vietnam.

Notwithstanding these varying degrees of performance, nearly all country chapters report a general public attitude in which judges and the judiciary are respected and held in high esteem.[224] The courts in Hong Kong are considered independent and impartial.[225] In contrast, corruption is reported in Bangladesh, China and Indonesia, among others,[226] and the professionalism of the judiciary is still a serious concern, especially among the business community.[227] In Korea, with the bureaucratization and centralization of the judiciary, public confidence in the courts has declined.[228] In Taiwan, the legal and political communities generally hold critical views of judicial integrity.[229] It seems that despite the public's respect for the judiciary in these jurisdictions, public confidence in the courts still has room for improvement.

220 Kim, "Courts in the Republic of Korea," this volume, section 1.5; Lo, "Hong Kong," this volume, section 1; Kawagishi, "Judicial power in Japan," this volume, section 2.4; Amarsanaa, "Courts in Mongolia," this volume, section 2.1; Tan, "Singapore's judicial system," this volume, section 3.1.

221 Tan, "Singapore's judicial system," this volume, section 3.1.

222 Nicholson, "Renovating courts," this volume, section 3.1; Gu, "Courts in China," this volume, section 7; Krishnan, "Legitimacy of courts," this volume, section 3.1.

223 Chang, "Courts and judicial reform in Taiwan," this volume, section 1.3.

224 Tan, "Singapore's judicial system," this volume, section 6; Hoque, "Courts in Bangladesh," this volume, section 5.4; Krishnan, "Legitimacy of courts," this volume, section 3.1; Satayanurug and Nakornin, "Courts in Thailand," this volume, section 6.2.

225 Lo, "Hong Kong," this volume, section 6.

226 Hoque, "Courts in Bangladesh," this volume, section 5.4.

227 Hoque, "Courts in Bangladesh," this volume, section 5.4; Gu, "Courts in China," this volume, section 2.1.

228 Kim, "Courts in the Republic of Korea," this volume, section 5.

229 Chang, "Courts and judicial reform in Taiwan," this volume, section 6.2.

4.4 *The styles and interpretive approaches of judicial decisions*

The fourth and last aspect in our comparisons of the jurisdictions included in this book encompasses the styles and interpretive approaches of judicial decisions, which are likely to be affected by the differences among the various legal systems. The following sections include comparative discussions of the length and style of judgments; approaches to law, judicial precedent and other authorities; and, lastly, references to foreign law.

4.4.1 The length and style of judicial decisions

Judgments in civil law systems and socialist legal systems tend to be short, as is the case in China, Mongolia, South Korea, Thailand, Taiwan and Vietnam.[230] However, Indonesia, which has a civil law system, is an exception and has relatively longer judicial decisions, as they usually include the entire argument of each litigant party.[231] In common law jurisdictions such as Hong Kong, India and Singapore, the judgments are likely to be lengthy.[232] Hong Kong serves as an interesting case, as the courts operate in two official languages, and the style and length of a judgment tends to be determined by the language in which the hearing is conducted. According to Lo, "If a judgment is given in Chinese after a hearing in Chinese, the text of the judgment might be much terser than if the argument had been conducted in English, with the parties and the court tending to summarize the applicable common law precedents and case reports (which are usually available only in English)."[233]

Also noteworthy is whether courts adopt a fixed format for writing judgments. Courts in most jurisdictions have adopted fixed formats for writing judgments.[234] However, courts in China have not yet done so.[235] Having a fixed format for writing judgments does not necessarily guarantee their length or quality. Nevertheless, a fixed format does ensure that some basic elements are included in each judgment, such

230 Nicholson, "Renovating courts," this volume, section 4.2; Gu, "Courts in China," this volume, section 4.2.

231 Juwana, "Courts in Indonesia," this volume, section 4.2.

232 Lo, "Hong Kong," this volume, section 4.2; Tan, "Singapore's judicial system," this volume, section 4.2.

233 Lo, "Hong Kong," this volume, section 4.2.

234 Chang, "Courts and judicial reform in Taiwan," this volume, section 4.2; Nicholson, "Renovating courts," this volume, section 4.2; Satayanurug and Nakornin, "Courts in Thailand," this volume, section 4.2; Gu, "Courts in China," this volume, section 4.2.

235 Gu, "Courts in China," this volume, section 4.2.

as the legal issues that were deliberated, and it can also facilitate detailed analyses of these issues.[236] In China, in order to improve the quality of judicial decisions, some model judgments have been issued to serve as style guides for judges.[237] In Vietnam, teaching judges how to write judgments has been incorporated into legal education and judicial training.[238]

The tiers or jurisdictions of courts may also affect the length of their judgments. In Singapore, according to Tan, "Court of Appeal decisions tend to be much longer than those of the High Court, especially when the Court of Appeal is trying to settle controversial points of law in which there are conflicting authorities," and "typical Court of Appeal judgments range between 30 and 60 pages on the average," while "High Court decisions are typically half that length except where the facts are highly complex or where there are many witnesses."[239] Similarly, the Constitutional Court of Thailand issues lengthier judgments that contain complicated factual and legal issues and significant political implications.[240] Bangladesh has also witnessed lengthy judgments in constitutional cases, while ordinary judgments are of medium length.[241]

Difficult legal terminology or legal jargon contained in court judgments may also affect the communicative functions or social legitimacy of courts. As reported in South Korea and Thailand, legal terms can be difficult for non-lawyers to comprehend,[242] and the writing style of court judgments often poses a barrier to lay comprehension.[243]

4.4.2 Approaches to law, judicial precedent and other authorities

The text-based interpretive approach has gained the most popularity in most jurisdictions in Asia,[244] while the purposive approach serves as a supplementary method of legal interpretation.[245] Other interpretive methods – for example, the historical approach – are used comparatively

[236] Juwana, "Courts in Indonesia," this volume, section 4.2; Amarsanaa, "Courts in Mongolia," this volume, section 4; Gu, "Courts in China," this volume, section 4.2.
[237] Gu, "Courts in China," this volume, section 4.2.
[238] Nicholson, "Renovating courts," this volume, section 4.2.
[239] Tan, "Singapore's judicial system," this volume, section 4.2.
[240] Satayanurug and Nakornin, "Courts in Thailand," this volume, section 4.2.
[241] Hoque, "Courts in Bangladesh," this volume, section 3.2.
[242] Satayanurug and Nakornin, "Courts in Thailand," this volume, section 4.2.
[243] Kim, "Courts in the Republic of Korea," this volume, section 3.2.
[244] Chang et al., *Constitutionalism in Asia*, ch. 5. [245] *Ibid.*

more often in the courts of Singapore and Hong Kong.[246] The Supreme Court of India is renowned for its expansive understanding of the living law, permitting legal interpretation to respond to changing times and circumstances.[247] In Bangladesh, following independence in 1971, according to Hoque, "the judges gradually began to abandon strict literalism in favor of a legal spirit-based method of interpretation"[248] as a way to break from the retrogressive decisions of former ruler Pakistan. Yet, when dealing with sensitive issues involving extra-constitutional or emergency regimes, the courts still follow rather mechanistic, text-based interpretive methods.[249]

In common law jurisdictions such as Bangladesh, Hong Kong, India, Malaysia and Singapore, courts apply law as well as precedents, and they may even include precedents of other common law jurisdictions.[250] Although civil law systems do not adopt the *stare decisis* doctrine, the courts in Indonesia, South Korea and Taiwan may nevertheless apply precedents, especially those rendered by the top courts or special courts in exceptional cases.[251] In Taiwan, the system of *Pan-li* has been in place, in which selected decisions of the top courts – particularly regarding the ways in which laws are interpreted or applied in given circumstances – are announced and accorded with de jure binding effects upon the entire judiciary.[252] China has also adopted a similar system, and upper court decisions usually hold strong influence or even de facto binding effects on the lower courts.[253]

Indigenous sources of law are applied in some Asian courts. For instance, Singapore and Malaysian courts apply Muslim law and customary laws of the Malay, Chinese and Hindu communities.[254] Bangladesh and Indian courts embrace Muslim law and various personal laws regarding religious issues.[255] Indonesia recognizes *adat* law, which is closely connected to religion, belief and tradition.[256]

[246] Lo, "Hong Kong," this volume, section 4.4; Tan, "Singapore's judicial system," this volume, section 4.4.

[247] Krishnan, "Legitimacy of courts," this volume, p. 270; Chang et al., *Constitutionalism in Asia*, ch. 5.

[248] Hoque, "Courts in Bangladesh," this volume, section 3.3.

[249] *Ibid.*

[250] Choong, "Courts in Malaysia," this volume, section 2.1.

[251] Juwana, "Courts in Indonesia," this volume, section 4.3.

[252] Chang, "Courts and judicial reform in Taiwan," this volume, section 3.1.

[253] Gu, "Courts in China," this volume, section 4.2.

[254] Tan, "Singapore's judicial system," this volume, section 4.1.3; Choong, "Courts in Malaysia," this volume, section 2.1.

[255] Krishnan, "Legitimacy of courts," this volume, section 4.2; Hoque, "Courts in Bangladesh," this volume, section 3.1.

[256] Juwana, "Courts in Indonesia," this volume, section 2.4.

The courts in China and Vietnam have included "socialist thinking" in their judgments. Communist party documents, policies, and direct guidance serve as key tools for judges.[257] The Chinese courts are required to use adjudicative activities to educate citizens to be loyal to the socialist motherland.[258]

4.4.3 Reference to foreign law

In recent years, there has been a global trend in which courts mutually refer to one another in judicial decisions.[259] Such judicial dialogue, as measured by foreign law citations in court judgments, has not been as evident in Asia as in other regions such as Europe or North America.[260] We find two contrasting attitudes in the courts across Asia towards references to foreign law: one embracing and the other resisting.

On the side of embracing comparative and foreign law, the courts of Hong Kong stand out. In Japan, South Korea and Taiwan, while the appearance of comparative or foreign law in court judgments is rare, their influences are actually very strong according to extensive interviews of judges by legal scholars.[261] On the side of resistance are Malaysia, Mongolia and Singapore. Mongolian courts represent an extreme case, in which no foreign authorities have ever been referred to in judicial decisions.[262] Attitudes towards foreign law references may vary across different tiers or jurisdictions of courts. For example, in Bangladesh, lower courts are relatively reluctant to cite foreign law in their decisions, but the Supreme Court has embraced comparative and foreign law.[263]

5 Functional dynamics of Asian courts in context: tradition, transition and globalization

We have examined in comparative perspective the structures of courts, the quality of judges, citizens' relationships with the courts, and the styles

[257] Nicholson, 'Renovating courts," this volume, section 4.3.
[258] Gu, "Courts in China," this volume, section 4.2.
[259] D. S. Law and W.-C. Chang, "The limits of global judicial dialogue," *Washington Law Review*, 86(3) (2011), 523–77.
[260] *Ibid.* [261] *Ibid.* 539–40.
[262] Amarsanaa, "Courts in Mongolia," this volume, section 4; L.-a. Thio, "Beyond the 'four walls' in an age of transnational judicial conversations: civil liberties, rights theories and constitutional adjudication in Malaysia and Singapore," *Columbia Journal of Asian Law*, 19 (2006), 428–518.
[263] Hoque, "Courts in Bangladesh," this volume, section 3.3.

of judicial decisions in the selected fourteen Asian jurisdictions. It is quite intriguing why some jurisdictions share certain features while others do not, as well as what may affect the common or different dynamics represented in these different jurisdictions.

In our comparative study of these jurisdictions, for example, we find that the type of legal system – civil law, common law and socialist – may explain some dynamics to varying degrees but not others. One striking example is the adoption of a jury system. As discussed above, most common law jurisdictions – except Hong Kong – have abandoned the system of trial by jury. However, a few civil law jurisdictions, such as Japan, South Korea and Taiwan, have just begun institutionalizing the jury system as a response to calls for "democratizing the judiciary."[264] In socialist legal systems, the use of people's assessors has been in sharp decline. Another example is the heavy reliance throughout Asian jurisdictions, civil law, common law and socialist alike, on competitive exams for recruiting entry-level judges. There are many other examples that render any attempts at finding simple explanations difficult if not impossible.

As we have suggested in the second part of this introduction, the best approach to understanding the dynamics represented in Asian courts is to interpret them through their corresponding political, economic, social and cultural contexts. We argue that three dimensions of analysis are crucial: (1) tradition and transplantation, (2) transition and construction, and (3) globalization and competition. The following sections elaborate on how the dynamics represented in Asian courts may be understood along these respective dimensions.

5.1 Tradition and transplantation

Asian courts have developed from the interwoven influences of colonization, modernization and tradition as well as the resulting transplantation, adaptation and transformation of those influences. Without a doubt, colonization has substantially influenced the establishment of judicial systems in Asia, for example in the former British colonies (Bangladesh, Hong Kong, India, Malaysia and Singapore) covered in this book. Yet, how and why colonization has exerted influences upon some but not all elements of these judicial systems remains to be further examined. In

[264] See the discussion in section 4.3 above.

addition to colonization, modernization also has left a significant imprint on the development of these judicial systems, especially with respect to jurisdictions without colonial experiences such as Japan and Thailand. For many jurisdictions, modernization and colonization have usually been intertwined, resulting in the reception and transplantation of Western legal and judicial systems.[265] In the course of colonization and modernization, deep-rooted traditions and cultures have persisted, grappling with adaptation and transformation. The following discusses (1) colonization and the transplantation of legal and judicial systems; (2) modernization, nationalism and legal adaptation; and (3) tradition, religion and indigenous cultures with regard to their imprints on Asian courts and their functional dynamics.

5.1.1 Colonization and transplantation

Colonial experiences have significantly shaped the modern courts in Asia. These experiences are in no way unitary but instead fairly complex. For some jurisdictions, such as Bangladesh, Hong Kong, India, Malaysia and Singapore, colonization was imposed by a single Western colonial power, the British. For other jurisdictions, such as South Korea and Taiwan, colonization came from within Asia, such as from imperial Japan. Still other jurisdictions experienced multiple colonial rulers. For example, the Philippines were colonized by the Spanish empire for hundreds of years, followed by American occupation in the early twentieth century. The story of Vietnam is even more complex, first having been colonized by the French for hundreds of years and then divided into the north influenced by the Soviets and the south by the Americans.

These colonial experiences have left different imprints on the establishment of legal and judicial systems in different jurisdictions. First, the jurisdictions with a single colonial experience tend to maintain the judicial system established by the colonial regime. Bangladesh, Hong Kong, India, Malaysia and Singapore, among others, are examples.[266] In Singapore, according to Tan, "the common law was introduced to Singapore with the physical arrival of the Second Charter of Justice of 1826, which, among other things, extended the jurisdiction of the Court

[265] See e.g. Chang, "East Asian foundations for constitutionalism," 111–41.

[266] Hoque, "Courts in Bangladesh," this volume, section 1; Lo, "Hong Kong," this volume, section 1; Krishnan, "Legitimacy of courts," this volume, section 1.1; Choong, "Courts in Malaysia," this volume, section 1; and Tan, "Singapore's judicial system," this volume, sections 1, 2.

of Judicature at Penang to the territories of Malacca and Singapore."[267] "Between 1827 and 1955, the entire judiciary was staffed by judges of the elite Colonial Legal Service, either from the United Kingdom or from different parts of the empire, such as Australia and Ceylon."[268] Singapore finally gained independence in 1963 and departed from the Federation of Malaya in 1965. Noticeably however, Singapore's independence did not include full judicial sovereignty. The Judicial Committee of the Privy Council of the UK continued to serve as Singapore's highest court of appeal until 1994.[269]

The relationship between British colonies and the Privy Council is worthy of a special note. As British colonies were not vested with judicial sovereignty, appeals to the Privy Council were mandatory.[270] In Asia, some jurisdictions, such as Singapore and Malaysia, retained this colonial practice even after achieving independence, while others, for example Hong Kong and India, abolished it and created final courts of appeal of their own immediately after independence. However, irrespective of whether appeals to the Privy Council were retained, the courts in these jurisdictions continue to this day to refer to the decisions of the Privy Council, despite the lack of any explicit legal mandate to do so. In Bangladesh, for example, the court has treated the Privy Council's decisions as persuasive authority.[271]

While a single colonial experience may leave a stronger imprint on the judicial system, exceptions or complications may still exist. In Indonesia, for example, according to Juwana, the colonial Dutch government did not apply Dutch law to indigenous Indonesians but instead created a separate judicial system. With the independence of Indonesia in 1945, Dutch influence also came to an end.[272]

Second, multiple or even divided colonial experiences usually complicate the patterns of legal and judicial transplantation. For example, in the Philippines, despite Spanish colonization for more than three hundred years, the courts and the operation of the judicial system have been more strongly influenced by the American occupation, especially with the enactment of the 1935 Constitution, followed by the 1987 Constitution, both of which were modeled on the American Federal Constitution. Yet, not all aspects of the common law court system were adopted. According to Pangalangan, for example, the American

[267] Tan, "Singapore's judicial system," this volume, section 1. [268] *Ibid.* section 1.1.
[269] *Ibid.* [270] Chang et al., *Constitutionalism in Asia*, ch. 5. [271] *Ibid.*
[272] Juwana, "Courts in Indonesia," this volume, section 2.1.

colonial government did not establish a jury system in the Philippines.[273] Vietnam presents an even more complicated story. After French colonization ended, Vietnam was divided as a result of a devastating war between 1945 and 1975, with the North constructing its legal and judicial system on the Soviet model and the South continuing a complicated system influenced by the French and then by the Americans. Only after the end of the civil war in 1975 was Vietnam united, and it adopted the socialist legal system that persists today.[274] Also complicated was the establishment of the judicial system in Mongolia. Mongolia is a landlocked country neighboring two great powers, China and Russia.[275] Upon independence, Mongolia studied the constitutions of England, Japan and Korea and promulgated its own constitution in 1924.[276] It then borrowed the Soviet system until the late 1990s, followed by the democratization of the country and the adoption of a new constitution in 1992. These foreign influences or quasi-colonial experiences have all contributed to the current mixed judicial system in Mongolia.[277]

Colonization in Asia was not simply from the West. Both South Korea and Taiwan were colonies of imperial Japan, and the establishment of modern judicial systems in both places was heavily influenced by Japan.[278] At the same time, however, in both South Korea and Taiwan, attempts at constructing modernization by borrowing legal and judicial systems from the West had begun earlier than – or at the same time as – Japanese colonization. Thus, in both places, the adoption of legal and judicial systems represented a complex process of Western influences both with and without the colonial imprint of Japan.[279]

273 Pangalangan, "The Philippines' post-Marcos judiciary," this volume, section 4.1.

274 Nicholson, "Renovating courts," this volume, section 1. In Vietnam, Chinese, Russians, Japanese, French, Americans and, more recently, Western countries and organizations in general, have all at some stage sought to influence Vietnamese legal development, sometimes only in particular parts of the country: *ibid.*

275 Amarsanaa, "Courts in Mongolia," this volume, section 1. 276 *Ibid.* section 5.

277 Mongolia studied the constitutions of England, Japan, and Korea when it promulgated the Constitution of 1924, and then borrowed the Soviet system until the late 1990s.

278 For discussion of Japanese colonialism in Asia, see L. Ching, *Becoming "Japanese": Colonial Taiwan and the Politics of Identity Formation* (University of California Press, 2001); R. Myers and M. Peattie (eds.), *The Japanese Colonial Empire* (Princeton University Press, 1984); H. Kang, *Under the Black Umbrella: Voices from Colonial Korea* (Ithaca: Cornell University Press, 2001).

279 See e.g. Kang, *Under the Black Umbrella*, p. I.

5.1.2 Modernization, nationalism and legal adaptation

Modernization in Asia has involved – to varying degrees – the adoption of Western legal and judicial systems, both with and without experiencing colonial rule. For example, despite never having experienced colonial rule, Japan and Thailand began the modernization process by adopting Western laws and courts in the eighteenth and nineteenth centuries.

In Japan, a civil law system largely borrowed from Germany was adopted. With its defeat in World War II and the promulgation of the 1946 Constitution, which was influenced greatly by the American occupation, some elements of common law courts – for example, decentralized judicial review with a single top court – were introduced.[280]

In Thailand, according to Satayanurug and Nakornin, during the Ayutthaya Kingdom in the seventeenth century, "a group of experts and specialists were appointed to assist the King in deciding cases," a system later evolving into the judiciary exercising judicial power in the name of the King.[281] The current judicial system was primarily developed under the Kingdom of Rattanakosin that began in 1782, as the King saw the need for modernization due to social changes and foreign influences.[282] The courts in Thailand have primarily been modeled after a civil law system but modified with common law elements, as many leading legal experts were educated in the common law countries. For example, HRH Prince Rapee Pattanasak, the "Father of Thai Law", received his legal education in the United Kingdom.[283]

In the wake of Western colonization or domination, many Asian jurisdictions saw the development of nationalism, as exemplified by the organization of nationalist political parties, promulgation of nationalist constitutions and domination of nationalist governments.[284] Creating a unitary state under a nationalist government to combat Western colonization or domination was typical rhetoric for establishing modern states and governments in the nineteenth and twentieth centuries in Asia.[285] The lack of federal states and judicial federalism as discussed in the preceding part of this introduction partly reflects such nationalist sentiments.

The emergence of nationalism in many jurisdictions has complicated or undermined Western influence in the adoption of legal and judicial

[280] Kawagishi, "Judicial power in Japan," this volume, section 1.
[281] Satayanurug and Nakornin, "Courts in Thailand," this volume, sections 1, 2.
[282] *Ibid.* [283] *Ibid.*
[284] See e.g. Chang, "East Asian foundations for constitutionalism." [285] *Ibid.*

systems. For example, in Malaysia, Choong stresses that notwithstanding British colonial influence, the structure of courts was significantly changed three times after independence in 1957.[286] Also, in Indonesia, as stated above, the Dutch colonial imprint on the legal and judicial system was moderate, and many features of the courts were established by the 1945 Constitution after independence.[287] Also noteworthy is India. According to Krishnan, following independence in 1947, the ruling Indian National Congress viewed the legal system inherited from the British as unsuitable to a reconstructed India.[288] These developments may explain why many jurisdictions covered by this book present mixed or complex features in their judicial systems that are not always in accordance with any particular legal system.

5.1.3 Tradition, religion and indigenous cultures

Tradition, religion and indigenous cultures may further complicate the dynamics of Asian courts. One aspect of tradition in Asia that may affect the functions of the judicial system is the emphasis on harmony in society and harmonious relationships between individuals.[289] Such an emphasis may stand against the adversarialism embedded in modern litigation and favor informal mechanisms for dispute resolution. For example, in China, according to Gu, "the emphasis on social harmony and the fulfillment of moral obligations have encouraged the use of mediation in dispute resolution in China, both inside and outside the courtroom."[290] Also, in India, against the backdrop of national independence, a proposal to displace modern courts with *panchayats*, a traditional village mechanism to resolve disputes, was made and implemented.[291] However, according to Krishnan, these *panchayats* encountered problems maintaining their independence from personal ties, and thus their use has been in serious decline.[292]

Another feature embedded in various traditions in Asia that may be reflected in the structure of courts is the importance of the maintenance of family relationships, which may be associated with a preference for

[286] Choong, "Courts in Malaysia," this volume, sections 1–3.
[287] Juwana, "Courts in Indonesia," this volume, section 1.
[288] Krishnan, "Legitimacy of courts," this volume, section 5.
[289] L.-a. Thio, "Constitutionalism in illiberal polities" in M. Rosenfeld and A. Sajó (eds.), *The Oxford Handbook of Comparative Constitutional Law* (Oxford University Press, 2012), pp. 142–7.
[290] Gu, "Courts in China," this volume, section 5.
[291] Krishnan, "Legitimacy of courts," this volume, section 5. [292] *Ibid.*

resolving family disputes differently from the ways in which ordinary disputes are resolved. It is quite striking that ten of the fourteen jurisdictions covered in this book have created or assigned special courts or tribunals in which different substantive and procedural rules may apply when dealing with family issues. These jurisdictions include Bangladesh, India, China, Japan, Malaysia, Singapore, Taiwan, Thailand, the Philippines and Vietnam.[293]

The other possible judicial dynamic reflective of tradition is the heavy reliance on competitive exams for recruiting entry-level judges throughout Asian jurisdictions, as illustrated in the previous section. Imperial examinations in Chinese dynasties provided the primary – if not the only – way for ordinary citizens to become part of the state apparatus as civil servants.[294] This tradition also influenced neighboring tribes as imperial China extended its territory over the years.[295] Against this traditional background, examinations are often regarded as a fair and merit-based institution facilitating social and political mobility. Understood this way, it seems unsurprising that, in some Asian jurisdictions, the exams for entering the judiciary – due to the superior status judges enjoy – are deliberately designed to be highly competitive.

Diverse religions including Buddhism, Christianity, Catholicism, Daoism, Hinduism, Shinto and Islam, among others, have contributed to diverse cultural developments in Asia.[296] This distinctive aspect may also be reflected in the judicial systems and functions of the courts. For example, in the view of Hogue, Bangladesh has "been greatly influenced by ancient Hindu, Buddhist, and Muslim periods as well as by the English legal system."[297] As discussed in the previous section, special

[293] Hoque, "Courts in Bangladesh," this volume, section 1.5.1; Krishnan, "Legitimacy of courts," this volume, section 1.1; Gu, "Courts in China," this volume, section 1.1; Kawagishi, "Judicial power in Japan," this volume, section 2.1; Choong, "Courts in Malaysia," this volume, section 1.4; Tan, "Singapore's judicial system," this volume, section 3.2.3; Chang, "Courts and judicial reform in Taiwan," this volume, section 1.1; Satayanurug and Nakornin, "Courts in Thailand," this volume, section 1.3; Pangalangan, "The Philippines' post-Marcos judiciary," this volume, section 1.2; and Nicholson, "Renovating courts," this volume, section 1.

[294] B. A. Elman, *A Cultural History of Civil Examinations in Late Imperial China* (University of California Press, 2000).

[295] H. Liu, "Influence of China's imperial examinations on Japan, Korea and Vietnam," *Frontiers of History in China*, 2 (2007), 493–512.

[296] Discussion on religions in Asia: see e.g. C. F. Keyes, L. Kendall and H. Hardacre, *Asian Visions of Authority: Religion and the Modern States of East and Southeast Asia* (University of Hawaii Press, 1994).

[297] Hoque, "Courts in Bangladesh," this volume, section 1.5.1.

religious courts have been created in Indonesia, Malaysia, Singapore and the Philippines.[298] In Bangladesh and India, religious personal laws in Muslim, Hindu or other religious communities are applied to relevant disputes.[299] The creation of these special religious courts or tribunals, however, has not been without concerns or criticism. For one, jurisdictional conflicts between civil and religious courts may become quite complex, undermining citizens' access to justice.[300] For another, with the emphasis on religious code or traditional rule of conduct, the practice or narrative of religious courts may at times compromise civil rule or functions of state institutions.[301] Yet, there are scholars who view such religious discourse not as entirely subversive, but instead functioning – in perplexing ways – to bolster certain agendas of the civilian government or help sustain overall political stability.[302] In any event, challenges brought by the creation of these special religious courts or tribunals remain critical to the development of Asian judicial systems and must be tackled by a variety of approaches in balance with civil and religious jurisprudence.

Like elsewhere, indigenous peoples and their cultures have gradually gained recognition in Asia. For example, as stated above, Taiwan enacted the Basic Law on Indigenous Peoples in 2005, providing a legal basis for the creation of an indigenous court, which nevertheless is yet to be put in place.[303] In Indonesia and Malaysia, customary laws of indigenous communities are recognized, forming part of the laws.[304] In Bangladesh, according to Hoque, the courts reflect "a pluralist legal system built on a complex of pre-colonial indigenous legal cultures, received Anglo-Indian legal tradition, and post-independence developments. Its pluralistic nature is evident in the existence of customary laws, various personal laws, and semi-official or non-state justice systems alongside the secular state-law and justice systems."[305]

The above statement characterizes not only the Bangladeshi judicial system but also many judicial systems in Asia. In the struggle between

[298] See 4.1.5.2, above (special courts). [299] *Ibid.*

[300] L.-a. Thio, "Jurisdictional imbroglio: civil and religious courts, turf wars and Article 121 (1A) of the Federal Constitution" in A. Harding and H. P. Lee (eds.), *Constitutional Landmarks in Malaysia: The First 50 Years* (LexisNexis, 2007), pp. 197–226.

[301] M. G. Peletz, *Islamic Modern: Religious Courts and Cultural Politics in Malaysia* (Princeton University Press, 2002), pp. 19–20.

[302] *Ibid.* [303] Chang, "Courts and judicial reform in Taiwan," this volume, section 1.1.

[304] Juwana, "Courts in Indonesia," this volume, section 2.4; Choong, "Courts in Malaysia," this volume, section 1.

[305] Hoque, "Courts in Bangladesh," this volume, section 1.

tradition, modernization and colonization, Asian courts present a colorful and complex picture, with various paths and patterns of development through transplantation, adaptation and transformation.

5.2 Transition and construction

Political and economic transitions in the last two or three decades have brought about significant changes in the structure of courts as well as significant reconstruction of judicial functions in and beyond Asia.[306] Almost all jurisdictions covered in this book have experienced profound political and economic transitions. Generally, political transitions demand a neutral and independent judiciary to resolve highly charged political disputes, and economic changes may require capable judges to maintain a properly functioning market. Such transitions inevitably require judicial reforms in which the functions of courts and the roles of judges may be reconstructed against changing political, economic, social and cultural contexts. In the wake of these transitions and reconstructions, judicial independence remains a major concern for the majority of jurisdictions.

5.2.1 Judicial reform and dual transitions

Judicial reforms have been undertaken as responses to dual transitions: economic and political. Unsurprisingly, economic developments in both advanced and developing economies have dominated the discourse of judicial reform and have had profound impacts. For example, advanced economies, particularly Hong Kong and Singapore, have demanded that their judicial systems be efficient and professional in order to attract more foreign investment.[307]

Developing economies have also undertaken judicial reforms in order to ease investor concerns and remove obstacles to the operation of more open and transparent markets. For example, in Malaysia, judicial reforms to resolve the backlog of cases and delays in the litigation process have been seriously undertaken since 2008.[308] In China, judicial reforms have

[306] In Asia, see Ginsburg, *Judicial Review in New Democracies*. Beyond Asia, see, e.g., J. J. Linz and A. Stepan, *Problems of Democratic Transition and Consolidation: Southern Europe, South America, and Post-Communist Europe* (Baltimore: Johns Hopkins University Press, 1996); R. Hirschl, *Towards Juristocracy: The Origins and Consequences of the New Constitutionalism* (Harvard University Press, 2007).

[307] Tan, "Singapore's judicial system," this volume, section 5.1.

[308] Choong, "Courts in Malaysia," this volume, section 5.

since 1999 been placed high on the government's five-year reform agendas.[309] These reforms, including improving the quality of judges, reconstructing the structure of courts and encouraging the use of mediation or alternative dispute resolution mechanisms, have to varying degrees responded to changing dynamics in urban and rural China.[310] Yet, in the view of Gu, as "judicial reform is bound to clash with the political agenda of the party-state," the implementation and effectiveness of any reforms have been constrained.[311]

Indeed, economic and political transitions occur in tandem, and judicial reforms may be undertaken to respond to these transitions. Without a doubt, capable and independent judges, high-quality judicial decisions, and transparent and efficient judicial processes help foster a healthy economy and a well-functioning political system. However, in different jurisdictions, the agendas for judicial reform may be different. For example, Bangladesh and India have focused on the issues of incompetent judges and the delayed delivery of justice.[312] Indonesia and Malaysia have put corruption at the top of their judicial reform agendas.[313] In Vietnam, issues concerning judicial independence and the quality of judges were the main agenda items in the 2002 round of reforms, while more accessible, transparent and democratic judicial procedures were the target of the judicial reforms of 2005.[314]

Judicial reforms in advanced jurisdictions may target issues concerning "democratization of the judiciary," or enhancement of citizens' participation in the judiciary. As stated above, in contrast with the common law jurisdictions that abandoned the jury system after gaining independence, the three civil law jurisdictions – Japan, South Korea and Taiwan – recently began implementing jury systems for deepening public participation in the judiciary. Reforms concerning the recruitment of judges and the legal education system have also been pursued in these three jurisdictions, in which American-style law schools have been introduced

[309] Gu, "Courts in China," this volume, section 6.1. [310] *Ibid.*

[311] Gu, "Courts in China," this volume, section 7; J.-r. Yeh and W.-C. Chang, "Challenges and prospects for Asian courts," this volume, section 2.2.

[312] Krishnan, "Legitimacy of courts," this volume, section 1.2; Hoque, "Courts in Bangladesh," this volume, section 5.3.

[313] Juwana, "Courts in Indonesia," this volume, section 3.2; Choong, "Courts in Malaysia," this volume, section 5.

[314] Nicholson, "Renovating courts," this volume, section 2.1.

in the hope of producing judges who are more capable of resolving conflicts regarding diverse issues.[315]

Also noteworthy are the strengthening of constitutional litigation and the establishment of constitutional courts in the wake of democratic transitions.[316] As stated above, a number of constitutional courts or constitutional tribunals have been recently created in Asia. Even in decentralized systems of judicial review, a few top courts have functioned effectively to implement constitutionalism and rule of law. Nevertheless, whether such profound transformation of constitutional litigation or successful operation of constitutional courts may continue depends considerably upon political contingencies and regime stability. For example, in Thailand, the Constitution of 1997 (BE 2540) was abolished as a result of the military coup in 2006. The operation of the Constitutional Court was obstructed despite the quick restoration along with other institutions in the Constitution of 2007.[317] In China, the beginning years of the 2000s saw a few exercises of constitutional review of government actions.[318] Most exemplary was the *Qi Yuling* case in which the court referred to the constitutional right to education in resolving the dispute on college enrollment.[319] Yet, in 2008, the Supreme People's Court issued an opinion stating that the judicial interpretation on the *Qi Yuling* case ceased to apply.[320] Meanwhile, the judicial reform plan in 2009 also became conservative following a leadership change in the judiciary.[321] It is evident that judicial reforms and the degrees of open economy and free democracy are interdependent. Absent the continuing progress in economic or political transitions,

[315] Kawagishi, "Judicial power in Japan," this volume, section 1; Kim, "Courts in the Republic of Korea," this volume, sections 1.4, 2.3; Chang, "Courts and judicial reform in Taiwan," this volume, section 2.3.2.

[316] For discussion of the global expansion of judicial review, see T. Ginsburg, "The global spread of constitutional review" in K. Whittington and D. Keleman (eds.), *Oxford Handbook of Law and Politics* (Oxford University Press, 2008), pp. 81–98.

[317] T. Ginsburg, "Constitutional afterlife: the continuing impact of Thailand's postpolitical constitution," *International Journal of Constitutional Law*, 7(1) (2009), 83–105.

[318] See e.g. Q. Zhang, "A constitution without constitutionalism? The path of constitutional development in China," *International Journal of Constitutional Law*, 8(4) (2010), 950, 960.

[319] For this case and related discussion, see Chang et al., *Constitutionalism in Asia*, ch. 5.

[320] [2008] Law Interpretation No. 15.

[321] Gu, "Courts in China," this volume, section 6.1. These changes have prompted some to characterize it as "China's turn against law." See e.g. C. F. Minzner, "China's turn against law," *American Journal of Comparative Law*, 59(4) (2011), 935–84.

judicial reforms and consequently the functions of courts may be constrained substantially.

5.2.2 Changing functions of courts

According to Martin Shapiro, the traditional function of courts is to resolve legal disputes and – in so doing – maintain the stability of the legal order.[322] This is the most basic function of courts recognized by nearly all of the jurisdictions in Asia. Tan's comment that "the Singapore courts see themselves as playing an important role in maintaining law and order"[323] can be applied to all of the judicial systems covered in this book.

The maintenance of legal order often facilitates the stability of social order, referring – in substantial part – to the function of the criminal justice system. A few country chapters, for example those describing Bangladesh, Indonesia, Thailand and Singapore, comment on the importance of the criminal justice system and the function of courts in maintaining social order or even social control on the basis of law.[324]

Facing varying extents of economic and political transition, the courts in the fourteen jurisdictions covered in this book have presented a considerable variety of dynamics in their respective functions. As suggested by Ginsburg and Moustafa, one key function of courts – especially for those in an authoritarian context or even in a context of democratic transition – often is to legitimize government policies.[325] Such a function has been noted in a few jurisdictions. For example, in Vietnam, Nicholson sees Vietnamese courts today as still partly a political institution, in that the courts "work for the party-state and must resolve matters in accordance with a complex hierarchy of influences, only one of which is law."[326] In Bangladesh, Hogue notes that "the Supreme Court of Bangladesh has often paid due deference to the government's policies."[327] The chapters on Thailand

322 Shapiro, *Courts*, pp. 1–5.

323 Tan, "Singapore's judicial system," this volume, section 5.1.

324 Hoque, "Courts in Bangladesh," this volume, section 5.1; Juwana, "Courts in Indonesia," this volume, section 5.1; Satayanurug and Nakornin, "Courts in Thailand," this volume, section 6.1; and Tan, "Singapore's judicial system," this volume, section 5.1.

325 Moustafa and Ginsburg, "Introduction," pp. 5–7; and section 1 above.

326 Nicholson, "Renovating courts," this volume, section 6.

327 Hoque, "Courts in Bangladesh," this volume, section 5.1.

and Singapore also comment on the role of the judiciary in legitimizing government policies.[328]

Noticeably, however, these courts do not just merely legitimize government policies. For example, in Singapore, according to Tan, while "the courts do not see themselves as natural adversaries of the executive,"[329] they nevertheless try to impartially "ensure the government stay on the correct side of law."[330] In Thailand, Satayanurug and Nakornin note that while the courts may legitimize government policies, they may also strike down government policies on the grounds of illegitimacy.[331] The central administrative court of Thailand just ruled against a major government policy on the grounds that it illegally bypassed the required public hearings and referendum.[332] Similarly, in Bangladesh, Hogue states that the Supreme Court of Bangladesh may intervene "in policy matters when constitutional ideals or norms are at stake" or "during times of extra-constitutional or overweening governments."[333] Nevertheless, effective judicial checks and balances with the exercise of government powers remain sporadic in these jurisdictions as constrained by limited progress of political reforms.[334]

Another function of courts – especially pivotal to those jurisdictions in economic transition – is their capacity to secure "credible commitments in market functions of the economic sphere" in the words of Ginsburg and Moustafa.[335] A number of chapters note this function, which has also been an important driving force for judicial reforms. For example, "as one of the world's most important trading and financial centers," Singapore's courts "are particularly conscious of the need to provide the most impartial and high-quality decisions."[336] Yet, not all courts have been capable of securing commitments in the market. In Bangladesh, for

[328] Satayanurug and Nakornin, "Courts in Thailand," this volume, section 6.1.2; Tan, "Singapore's judicial system," this volume, section 5.2.

[329] Tan, "Singapore's judicial system," this volume, section 5.2. [330] *Ibid.*

[331] Satayanurug and Nakornin, "Courts in Thailand," this volume, section 6.1.2.

[332] *Ibid.* [333] Hoque, "Courts in Bangladesh," this volume, section 5.2.

[334] See e.g. R. Hoque, *Judicial Activism in Bangladesh: A Golden Mean Approach* (Cambridge Scholars Publishing, 2011), pp. 263–70; C. C. Gan, "Administrative law and judicialized governance in Malaysia: the Indian connection" in Ginsburg and Chen (eds.), *Administrative Law and Governance in Asia: Comparative Perspectives*, pp. 257–86; G. Silverstein, "Singapore: the exception that proves rules matters" in Moustafa and Ginsburg (eds.), *Rule by Law: The Politics of Courts in Authoritarian Regimes*, pp. 73–101.

[335] See Moustafa and Ginsburg, "Introduction," pp. 8–9; and section 1 above.

[336] Tan, "Singapore's judicial system," this volume, section 5.3.

example, Hoque notes that the Supreme Court has shown "limited fulfillment of its commitment in the market sector" as it may sustain certain government measures for "the country's ailing economy."[337] Juwana also discusses the fact that nationalistic sentiments embedded in relevant laws or government policies in Indonesia have undermined market functions to a certain extent. As the government agency charged with enforcing Indonesia's competition law "has tended to go against foreign companies and to protect national interests," the function of courts in the economic sphere has been constrained.[338]

Facilitating the smooth operation of the market is certainly not the only market-related function of courts. Sometimes, courts may be required to address market malfunctions, especially regarding consumers, workers, minorities, the environment, or compensatory and reparatory justice. The courts in India stand out in providing such functions. According to Krishnan, the Supreme Court of India in particular has been "on the forefront of rights-protection and rights-activism over the last thirty-five years."[339] Satayanurug and Nakornin also note that Thai courts have performed this essential function, particularly in the areas of consumer protection and the environment.[340] Tan notes that such judicial functions in Singapore are very limited, due to the virtual absence of public interest litigation, but the recent passage of a consumer protection law may begin to foster the expansion of these functions.[341] Also noteworthy are the constraints placed by the political environment on such judicial functions. In China, for example, according to Gu, as the "Sanlu tainted milk" case in 2009 has indicated, the function of courts is still limited and "is perhaps, undermined, by the political agenda of the Party."[342] Whether the courts can address rights-based litigation will be determined by the Communist Party.[343] Hoque also notes the limited readiness of the courts in Bangladesh to use litigation as a tool for reparatory and compensatory justice.[344]

The functions of courts in times of political transition are also quite dynamic. Courts may facilitate the process of or uphold the results of democratization, and they are expected to protect human rights and

[337] Hoque, "Courts in Bangladesh," this volume, section 5.1.
[338] Juwana, "Courts in Indonesia," this volume, section 5.3.
[339] Krishnan, "Legitimacy of courts," this volume, section 1.
[340] Satayanurug and Nakornin, "Courts in Thailand," this volume, section 6.1.3.
[341] Tan, "Singapore's judicial system," this volume, section 5.4.
[342] Gu, "Courts in China," this volume, section 6.2.1. [343] *Ibid.*
[344] Hoque, "Courts in Bangladesh," this volume, section 5.1.

resolve political conflicts uninhibitedly.[345] In general, courts in many jurisdictions covered in this book, such as India, Japan, South Korea and Taiwan, among others, have exhibited such functions to varying degrees.[346] Many courts – especially constitutional courts – such as those in Bangladesh, Indonesia, Taiwan, Thailand and South Korea have been shouldered with the responsibility of resolving political conflicts between different government branches or even political parties.[347] As reported in Taiwan and South Korea, judicial involvement in political conflicts has begun generating problems of "politicization of the judiciary."[348] In Thailand, the decisions of the Constitutional Court regarding electoral disputes and dissolutions of political parties had placed it into the center of a political storm, partially causing the 2006 coup and impacting on the reform of the 2007 Constitution.[349] Similarly, in Indonesia, the Constitutional Court has not only intervened in electoral disputes but also directed the application of electoral laws and regulations. In a recent case, it even provided a legal guideline commanding how the ballot should be conducted.[350] These judicial interventions in contentious politics often trigger political setbacks for the courts, rendering critical challenges to institutional integrity and judicial independence.

Also noteworthy is a quite distinctive function of courts in Hong Kong. As noted by Lo, the common law system of Hong Kong and the efforts of courts in sustaining it have facilitated the success of the "One Country, Two Systems" model for China's governance of Hong Kong.[351]

[345] Ginsburg, *Judicial Review in New Democracies*; Chang, "Role of judicial review"; J.-r. Yeh and W.-C. Chang, "The changing landscape of modern constitutionalism: Transitional perspective," *National Taiwan University Law Review*, 4(1) (2009), 145–83.

[346] Krishnan, "Legitimacy of courts," this volume, section 1; Kawagishi, "Judicial power in Japan," this volume, section 5; Kim, "Courts in the Republic of Korea," this volume, section 2.3; and Chang, "Courts and judicial reform in Taiwan," this volume, section 5.1.

[347] Hoque, "Courts in Bangladesh," this volume, section 1.1.2; Juwana, "Courts in Indonesia," this volume, section 5.2; Chang, "Courts and judicial reform in Taiwan," this volume, section 5.1; Satayanurug and Nakornin, "Courts in Thailand," this volume, section 6.1.2; and Kim, "Courts in the Republic of Korea," this volume, section 2.3.

[348] Chang, "Courts and judicial reform in Taiwan," this volume, section 5.1; Kim, "Courts in the Republic of Korea," this volume, section 4.3.3.2.

[349] B. Dressel, "Judicialization of politics or politicization of the judiciary? Considerations from recent events in Thailand," *International Journal of Constitutional Law*, 23(5) (2010), 671–91; Ginsburg, "Constitutional afterlife," pp. 83–105.

[350] B. Dressel and M. Mietzner, "A tale of two courts: the judicialization of electoral politics in Asia," *Governance: An International Journal of Policy, Administration, and Institutions*, 25(3) (2012), 391–414, 404.

[351] Lo, "Hong Kong," this volume, section 6.

In the course of economic and political transitions, the capabilities of courts may be tested, enhancing or undermining their reputation or legitimacy. For example, the courts in Taiwan and South Korea have been praised for their successful functioning in times of democratic transition.[352] At the same time, however, having adjudicated many political controversies, both courts have also suffered "politicization," and their impartiality may be questioned from time to time.[353] Mongolia's courts are perceived negatively by the majority of the legal community partly because of their poor performance in times of transition.[354] Similarly, in Indonesia, courts have also been questioned with regard to their capacity to deal with a divided society and with political transitions.[355]

5.2.3 Judicial independence in the context of transition

Judicial independence is crucial to the exercise of judicial power in any constitutional democracy that upholds checks and balances between the branches of government. It is even more so in the context of profound economic and political transitions, as courts must strike a delicate balance among powerful stakeholders in the market or in politics.

It seems that in the majority of Asian jurisdictions covered in this book, judicial independence has been ensured, albeit to quite varying extents. Noticeably, however, judicial independence has still not been guaranteed in China and Vietnam, both of which have socialist legal systems and are politically dominated by the Communist party. According to Gu, in China, judicial independence has suffered from dual threats: political supervision within the court from the Party Committee and outside the court from the Party Political and Legal Affairs Committee.[356] In addition, local governments may also interfere with courts through financial control, since the courts are financed by the local governments of their corresponding levels.[357] In Vietnam, judicial independence is undermined by the fact that the judicial budget

[352] Chang, "Courts and judicial reform in Taiwan," this volume, section 5.1; and Kim, "Courts in the Republic of Korea," this volume, section 2.3; Ginsburg, *Judicial Review in New Democracies*, pp. 106–57, 206–46.

[353] Chang, "Courts and judicial reform in Taiwan," this volume, section 5.1; Kim, "Courts in the Republic of Korea," this volume, section 4.3.2.2.

[354] Ginsburg, *Judicial Review in New Democracies*, pp. 158–205.

[355] Juwana, "Courts in Indonesia," this volume, section 5.2.

[356] Gu, "Courts in China," this volume, section 2.2. [357] *Ibid.*

is substantially controlled by the Standing Committee of the National Assembly.[358]

Judicial administration may also affect judicial independence. In Japan, according to Kawagishi, the performance evaluations of judges that affect promotions, salary increases or transfers have long been criticized as being "carried out in a black box."[359] In Thailand, as Satayanurug and Nakornin report, the operation of judicial administration, including recruitment and budgets, has not been completely independent from the government or immune from political interference.[360] In Malaysia, according to Choong, political appointments and transfer decisions of the Chief Justice have negative impacts on judicial independence.[361]

Last but not least is the issue of judicial corruption. Some country chapters, for example those describing Indonesia, Malaysia, Taiwan and Thailand, discuss or briefly touch upon this issue.[362] However, the extent of judicial corruption in Asia remains to be further researched. One striking observation is that judicial corruption in some jurisdictions does not seem to seriously affect the reputation of the judiciary. For example, in Thailand, poll results indicated that while most of the public viewed judicial corruption as pervasive, the courts remained the most respected government branch.[363]

5.3 *Globalization and competition*

The progress of globalization further brings Asian courts into a global context, connecting them to regional and international economic, political, and, eventually, legal and judicial systems.[364] As scholars have pointed out, the development of globalization has created a global

[358] Nicholson, "Renovating courts," this volume, section 5.
[359] Kawagishi, "Judicial power in Japan," this volume, section 4.
[360] Satayanurug and Nakornin, "Courts in Thailand," this volume, section 3.2.
[361] Choong, "Courts in Malaysia," this volume, section 3.2.
[362] Satayanurug and Nakornin, "Courts in Thailand," this volume, section 6.3; Choong, "Courts in Malaysia," this volume, section 3.2; Juwana, "Courts in Indonesia," this volume, section 7; and Chang, "Courts and judicial reform in Taiwan," this volume, section 6.2.
[363] Satayanurug and Nakornin, "Courts in Thailand," this volume, section 6.2.
[364] J.-r. Yeh and W.-C. Chang, "The emergence of transnational constitutionalism: its features, challenges and solutions," *Penn State International Law Review*, 27 (2008), 89–124; V. C. Jackson, *Constitutional Engagement in a Transnational Era* (Oxford University Press, 2010).

community of judges and facilitated global judicial dialogues,[365] a phenomenon that has – to some extent – also occurred in Asia.[366]

In the context of global competition, the features most relevant to functional dynamics of courts include: (1) the convergence of laws, especially regarding an increased reference to foreign and international laws in the courts; (2) the creation of new special courts for meeting the challenges of global economic competition; and (3) the emergence of alternative dispute resolution methods demanded by fast-growing global trade.

5.3.1 The convergence of laws

The first indication of globalization is an increased reference to foreign or international laws in the courts. As stated in the previous section, quite a number of the jurisdictions covered in this book have embraced comparative and foreign laws in their judicial decisions, while a few have continued to resist such a trend.[367]

The courts of Hong Kong stand out in embracing global norms. According to the Court of Final Appeal in Hong Kong, in interpreting the provisions of the Basic Law and human rights statutes, "the Court may consider it appropriate to take account of the established principles of international jurisprudence as well as decisions of international and national courts and tribunals on like or substantially similar provisions in other international instruments and national constitutions."[368]

Part of the reason for the global convergence of laws is related to the protection of universal human rights. In Indonesia, for example, the Human Rights Court has been expected to wholeheartedly embrace international human rights laws, and both the Constitutional Court and the Administrative Court have begun applying international human rights laws and general international principles.[369] Similar trends have also occurred in other jurisdictions such as Hong Kong, Japan, Taiwan and South Korea.[370]

[365] Jackson, *Constitutional Engagement in a Transnational Era*; Slaughter, "Judicial globalization"; Slaughter, "A global community of courts."

[366] Law and Chang, "The limits of global judicial dialogue." [367] Section 4.4.3 above.

[368] *Shun Kwok Sher* v. *HKSAR*, 5 HKCFAR 381 (2003); Lo, "Hong Kong," this volume, section 4.4.

[369] Juwana, "Courts in Indonesia," this volume, section 4.4.

[370] For Hong Kong, Lo, "Hong Kong," this volume, section 4.1. For Japan, see A. Ejima, "A gap between the apparent and hidden attitudes of the Supreme Court of Japan towards foreign precedents" in T. Groppi and M.-C. Ponthoreau (eds.), *The Use of Foreign*

A noteworthy issue is whether differences in legal systems are associated with attitudes towards referencing comparative and international laws in judicial decisions. While common laws courts generally are receptive to foreign or international laws, studies have not yet confirmed such a link.[371] In the fourteen jurisdictions covered in this book, the jurisdictions that have embraced foreign and international laws in judicial decisions include both common law and civil law jurisdictions. In addition, the jurisdictions that have continued to resist such a trend, such as Malaysia, Mongolia and Singapore, also include both common law and civil law jurisdictions.

5.3.2 Creation of new special courts

As discussed in the previous section, the recent mushrooming of special courts in Asia has occurred particularly in response to economic challenges. Even in those jurisdictions with relatively fewer special courts overall, special courts on trade or intellectual property have still been established.[372]

The creation of these special courts on commerce, trade, and intellectual property, among other areas, seems to be in response to market competition as well as global trade laws. For example, five intellectual property courts or tribunals have recently been created in China, Malaysia, Singapore, Taiwan and Thailand.[373] Such a phenomenon seems reflective of the demand for protection of intellectual property under international trade laws. For example, according to Gu, China established the intellectual property tribunal in tandem with its accession to the World Trade Organization (WTO) in 2001.[374] In Thailand, the central intellectual property and international trade court was established to meet the demands of the WTO and related trade agreements.[375]

Precedents by Constitutional Judges (Oxford: Hart Publishing, 2013), pp. 273–300; for South Korea and Taiwan, see W.-C. Chang, "The convergence of constitutions and international human rights: Taiwan and South Korea in comparison," *North Carolina Journal of International Law and Commercial Regulation*, 36 (2011), 593–624.

371 See e.g. C. Saunders, "Towards a global constitutional gene pool," *National Taiwan University Law Review*, 4(3) (2009), 1–38; Groppi and Ponthoreau (eds.), *The Use of Foreign Precedents by Constitutional Judges*.

372 Section 4.1.5.2 above.

373 Gu, "Courts in China," this volume, section 1.1; Choong, "Courts in Malaysia," this volume, section 1.4; Tan, "Singapore's judicial system," this volume, section 3.2.1; Chang, "Courts and judicial reform in Taiwan," this volume, section 1.1; and Satayanurug and Nakornin, "Courts in Thailand," this volume, section 1.3.

374 Gu, "Courts in China," this volume, section 1.1.

375 Satayanurug and Nakornin, "Courts in Thailand," this volume, section 2.4.

International organizations or multilateral trade agreements may also facilitate the creation of special courts. In the wake of the global economic crisis, the need for support from international financial mechanisms may increase, and these international loan agencies often stipulate conditions for lending, such as the enactment of certain laws or the creation of certain courts or tribunals. For example, in exchange for financing from the International Monetary Fund and World Bank, Indonesia enacted a series of laws regarding fair competition, bankruptcy and intellectual property and created corresponding special courts.[376] Upon its recovery from the economic crisis, South Korea entered into free trade agreements with the European Union and United States. Under these free trade agreements, the exercise of relevant judicial powers became subject to the Investor State Dispute Settlement clause, and the legal services market was opened to foreign competition. According to Kim, these new measures, taken against the backdrop of economic crises in a globalized era, have had an immense impact on the judicial system in South Korea.[377]

5.3.3 The emergence of alternative dispute resolution

The expansion of global markets naturally leads to demand for efficient and cost-conscious dispute resolution mechanisms and flexible and pragmatic rules. As a result, an increasing number of trade disputes and trade agreements prefer alternative dispute resolution (ADR) to traditional litigation, which is often time-consuming and very costly.

In keeping with the region's rise in economic power in the global era, the majority of Asian jurisdictions have established or improved their respective ADR mechanisms in order to attract international investment or facilitate global competitiveness. For example, Singapore, whose strong economy has continued to grow for many years, established an independent international arbitration center in July 1991 to promote international arbitration.[378] Other advanced economies have also created similar mechanisms or enacted special laws. For example, Taiwan revised its Arbitration Law in 1998 to facilitate commercial and trade arbitration.[379]

376 Juwana, "Courts in Indonesia," this volume, section 2.1.
377 Kim, "Courts in the Republic of Korea," this volume, section 2.3.
378 Tan, "Singapore's judicial system," this volume, section 6.1.
379 Chang, "Courts and judicial reform in Taiwan," this volume, section 4.1.

Many developing or fast-growing economies in the region followed suit. For example, China promulgated its Arbitration Law in 1994; Indonesia enacted its Arbitration and Alternative Dispute Resolution Act in 1999; Bangladesh revised its Arbitration Law in 2001 and revised relevant laws again in 2003 and 2006; Malaysia enacted its Arbitration Act in 2005; Vietnam promulgated its Commercial Arbitration Law in 2012.[380]

Most noteworthy is the convergence of these arbitration laws with international standards. For example, in Thailand, the relevant laws have been significantly modeled after the Model Law on International Commercial Arbitration prepared by the United Nations Commission on International Trade Law in order to ensure that arbitration is on par with international standards.[381] Also, in China, the judiciary has been trying to bring the development of arbitration closer to international norms and standards.[382]

With the rise of global markets, judicial efficiency and capacity to deal with international trade disputes may become an important benchmark by which courts are evaluated and compared. The courts of Hong Kong have often been described as "internationalist," while the courts of Singapore are highly praised because they are "as efficient as the best businesses."[383] Evidently, the process of globalization has begun changing our perceptions of laws as well as courts. The tasks of courts in a global era are certainly changing and becoming more challenging.

In this introduction, we have elaborated on the methodology of this book and explained why we adopt an institutional approach to the study of courts and their functional dynamics. Based on the contributions of the fourteen country chapters, we have been able to provide a comparative analysis across these jurisdictions on the structures of courts, the quality of judges, citizens' relationships with the courts, and the styles of judicial decisions. We further elaborate on these comparative dynamics against the contexts of tradition, transition and globalization. As these analyses have demonstrated, the courts in Asia present a wide spectrum of functional dynamics that have worked in tandem with the recent

[380] Gu, "Courts in China," this volume, section 5; Juwana, "Courts in Indonesia," this volume, section 6.1; Hoque, "Courts in Bangladesh," this volume, section 4.1; Choong, "Courts in Malaysia," this volume, section 4.1; Nicholson, "Renovating courts," this volume, section 5.

[381] Satayanurug and Nakornin, "Courts in Thailand," this volume, section 5.

[382] Gu, "Courts in China," this volume, section 5.2.

[383] Tan, "Singapore's judicial system," this volume, section 1; Lo, "Hong Kong," this volume, section 4.1.

profound economic and political transitions that have occurred throughout the region. After the chapters describing the fourteen selected jurisdictions, we will elaborate further in the conclusion on the prospects and challenges that lie ahead.

References

Barak, A. "The role of a supreme court in a democracy," *Hastings Law Journal*, 53 (2002), 1205–16

Brenner, S. and Spaeth, H. J. *Stare Indecisis: The Alteration of Precedents on the Supreme Court, 1946–1992* (Cambridge University Press, 1995)

Brent, J. "An agent and two principals: U.S. Court of Appeals responses to Employment Division, Department of Human Resources v. Smith and the Religious Freedom Restoration Act," *American Politics Quarterly*, 27 (1999), 236–66

Caron, D. D. "Toward a political theory of international courts and tribunals," *Berkeley Journal of International Law*, 24 (2007), 401–23

Chang, W.-C. "East Asian foundations for constitutionalism: three models reconstructed," *National Taiwan University Law Review*, 3(2) (2008), 111–41

Chang, W.-C. "Strategic judicial responses in politically charged cases: East Asian experiences," *International Journal of Constitutional Law*, 8(4) (2010), 885–910

Chang, W.-C. "The convergence of constitutions and international human rights: Taiwan and South Korea in comparison," *North Carolina Journal of International Law and Commercial Regulation*, 36 (2011), 593–624

Chang, W.-C. "The role of judicial review in consolidating democracy: the case of Taiwan," *Asia Law Review*, 2(2) (2005), 73–88

Chang, W.-C., Tan, K. Y. L., Thio, L.-a. and Yeh, J.-r. *Constitutionalism in Asia: Cases and Materials* (Oxford: Hart Publishing, 2014)

Ching, L. *Becoming "Japanese": Colonial Taiwan and the Politics of Identity Formation* (University of California Press, 2001)

Croissant, A. "From transition to defective democracy: mapping Asian democratization," *Democratization*, 11(5) (2004), 156–78

Diamond, L. *The Spirit of Democracy* (New York: Times Books, 2008)

Dorsen, N., Rosenfeld, M., Sajo, A. and Baer, S. *Comparative Constitutionalism: Cases and Materials*, 2nd edn. (Eagan, MN: West, 2010)

Dressel, B. "Judicialization of politics or politicization of the judiciary? Considerations from recent events in Thailand," *International Journal of Constitutional Law*, 23(5) (2010), 671–91

Dressel, B. (ed.) *The Judicialization of Politics in Asia* (New York: Routledge, 2012)

Dressel, B. and Mietzner, M. "A tale of two courts: the judicialization of electoral politics in Asia," *Governance: An International Journal of Policy, Administration, and Institutions*, 25(3) (2012), 391–414

Ejima, A. "A gap between the apparent and hidden attitudes of the Supreme Court of Japan towards foreign precedents" in Groppi and Ponthoreau (eds.), *The Use of Foreign Precedents by Constitutional Judges*, pp. 273–300

Elman, B. A. *A Cultural History of Civil Examinations in Late Imperial China* (University of California Press, 2000)

Engle, K. "Culture and human rights: the Asian values debate in context," *New York University Journal of International Law and Politics*, 32 (2000), 291–333

Epstein, L. and Walker, T. "The role of the Supreme Court in American society: playing the reconstruction game" in L. Epstein (ed.), *Contemplating Court* (Washington, DC: Congressional Quarterly Press, 1995), pp. 315–46

Feld, L. P. and Voigtd, S. "Economic growth and judicial independence: cross-country evidence using a new set of indicators," *European Journal of Political Economy*, 19 (2003), 497–527

Ferejohn, J. and Pasquino, P. "Constitutional adjudication: lessons from Europe," *Texas Law Review*, 82 (2004), 1671–1704

Gan, C. C. "Administrative law and judicialized governance in Malaysia: The Indian connection" in T. Ginsburg and A. H. Y. Chen (eds.), *Administrative Law and Governance in Asia: Comparative Perspectives* (New York: Routledge, 2009), pp. 257–86

Garopa, N. and Ginsburg, T. "Guarding the guardians: judicial councils and judicial independence," *American Journal of Comparative Law*, 57 (2009), 103–34

Ginsburg, T. "Constitutional afterlife: the continuing impact of Thailand's post-political constitution," *International Journal of Constitutional Law*, 7(1) (2009), 83–105

Ginsburg, T. *Judicial Review in New Democracies: Constitutional Courts in Asian Cases* (Cambridge University Press, 2003)

Ginsburg, T. "The global spread of constitutional review" in K. Whittington and D. Keleman (eds.), *Oxford Handbook of Law and Politics* (Oxford University Press, 2008), pp. 81–98

Ginsburg, T. "The judicialization of administrative governance: causes, consequences and limits" in T. Ginsburg and A. H. Y. Chen (eds.), *Administrative Law and Governance in Asia: Comparative Perspectives* (New York: Routledge, 2009), pp. 1–19

Gloppen, S., Gargarella, R. and Skaar, E. "Introduction: the accountability function of the courts in new democracies" in S. Gloppen, R. Gargarella and E. Skaar (eds.), *Democratization and the Judiciary: The Accountability Functions of Courts in New Democracies* (London: Frank Cass, 2004), pp. 1–4

Groppi, T. and Ponthoreau, M.-C. (eds.) *The Use of Foreign Precedents by Constitutional Judges* (Oxford: Hart Publishing, 2013)

Harding, A. and Nicholson, P. (eds.) *New Courts in Asia* (New York: Routledge, 2010)

Hassall, G. and Saunders, C. *Asia-Pacific Constitutional Systems* (Cambridge University Press, 2002)

Helmke, G. and Rios-Figueroa, J. *Courts in Latin America* (Cambridge University Press, 2011)

Hilbink, L. *Judges Beyond Politics in Democracy and Dictatorship: Lessons from Chile* (Cambridge University Press, 2007)

Hirschl, R. *Towards Juristocracy: The Origins and Consequences of the New Constitutionalism* (Harvard University Press, 2007)

Hoque, R. *Judicial Activism in Bangladesh: A Golden Mean Approach* (Newcastle upon Tyne: Cambridge Scholars Publishing, 2011)

Huntington, S. P. *The Third Wave: Democratization in the Late 20th Century* (University of Oklahoma Press, 1993)

Issacharoff, S. "Constitutionalizing democracy in fractured societies," *Journal of International Affairs*, 58 (2004), 73–93

Issacharoff, S. "Constitutional courts and democratic hedging," *Georgetown Law Journal*, 99 (2011), 961–1012

Jackson, V. C. *Constitutional Engagement in a Transnational Era* (Oxford University Press, 2010)

Kadomatsu, N. "Judicial governance through resolution of legal disputes? A Japanese perspective," *National Taiwan University Law Review*, 4(2) (2009), 141–62

Kang, H. *Under the Black Umbrella: Voices from Colonial Korea* (Ithaca, NY: Cornell University Press, 2001)

Kawai, M. and Schmiegelow, H. *Financial Crisis as a Catalyst of Legal Reforms: The Case of Asia* (Tokyo: Asian Development Bank Institute, 2013)

Keyes, C. F., Kendall, L. and Hardacre, H. *Asian Visions of Authority: Religion and the Modern States of East and Southeast Asia* (University of Hawaii Press, 1994)

Kim, J. "Socrates v. Confucius: an analysis of South Korea's implementation of the American law school model," *Asian-Pacific Law & Policy Journal*, 10 (2009), 322–53

Krugman, P. "The myth of Asia's miracle," *Foreign Affairs*, 73(6) (1994), 62–78

Law, D. S. and Chang, W.-C. "The limits of global judicial dialogue," *Washington Law Review*, 86(3) (2011), 523–77

Lee, F. and Ali, S. "Resolving financial disputes in the context of global civil justice reforms" *International Journal of Business and Social Science*, 2(7) (2011), 37–51

Lee, J. "Primary causes of Asian democratization: dispelling conventional myths," *Asian Survey*, 42 (2002), 821–37

Lin, C. X. "A quiet revolution: an overview of China's judicial reform," *Asian-Pacific Law & Policy Journal*, 4 (2003), 255–319

Linz, J. J. and Stepan, A. *Problems of Democratic Transition and Consolidation: Southern Europe, South America, and Post-Communist Europe* (Baltimore: Johns Hopkins University Press, 1996)

Liu, H. "Influence of China's imperial examinations on Japan, Korea and Vietnam," *Frontiers of History in China*, 2 (2007), 493–512

Lo, P. Y. *The Hong Kong Basic Law* (Butterworths: LexisNexis, 2011)

Minzner, C. F. "China's turn against law," *American Journal of Comparative Law*, 59(4) (2011), 935–84

Moustafa, T. and Ginsburg, T. "Introduction: the function of courts in authoritarian politics" in T. Moustafa and T. Ginsburg (eds.), *Rule by Law: The Politics of Courts in Authoritarian Regimes* (Cambridge University Press, 2008), pp. 1–22

Myers, R. and Peattie, M. (eds.) *The Japanese Colonial Empire* (Princeton University Press, 1984)

Peletz, M. G. *Islamic Modern: Religious Courts and Cultural Politics in Malaysia* (Princeton University Press, 2002)

Potter, P. "Legal reform in China: institutions, culture and selective adaptation," *Law & Social Inquiry*, 29 (2004), 465–95

Radelet, S., Sachs, J. and Lee, J.-W. "The determinants and prospects of economic growth in Asia," *International Economic Journal*, 15(3) (2001), 1–29

Root, H. L. *Small Countries, Big Lessons: Governance and the Rise of East Asia* (Oxford University Press, 1996)

Roux, T. "Principle and pragmatism on the Constitutional Court of South Africa," *International Journal of Constitutional Law*, 7 (2009), 106–38

Saunders, C. "Towards a global constitutional gene pool," *National Taiwan University Law Review*, 4(3) (2009), 1–38

Scott, C. "Agencification, regulation and judicialization: American exceptionalism and other ways of life" in Ginsburg and Chen (eds.), *Administrative Law and Governance in Asia: Comparative Perspectives* (Oxen: Routledge, 2009), pp. 38–58

Segal, J. A. and Spaeth, H. J. *The Supreme Court and the Attitudinal Model Revisited* (Cambridge University Press, 2002)

Shapiro, M. *Courts: A Comparative and Political Analysis* (University of Chicago Press, 1981)

Shin, D. C. "The third wave in East Asia: comparative and dynamic perspective," *Taiwan Journal of Democracy*, 4(2) (2008), 91–131

Silverstein, G. "Singapore: the exception that proves rules matters" in Moustafa and Ginsburg (eds.), *Rule by Law: The Politics of Courts in Authoritarian Regimes*, pp. 73–101

Slaughter, A.-M. "Judicial globalization," *Virginia Journal of International Law*, 40 (2000), 1103–24

Slaughter, A.-M. "A global community of courts," *Harvard International Law Journal*, 44 (2003), 191–220

Songer, D., Segal, J. A. and Cameron, C. "The hierarchy of justice: testing a principal–agent model of Supreme Court–circuit court interactions," *American Journal of Political Science*, 38 (1994), 673–96

Stone, A. *The Birth of Judicial Politics in France: The Constitutional Council in Comparative Perspective* (Oxford University Press, 1992)

Stone Sweet, A. *Governing with Judges: Constitutional Politics in Europe* (Oxford University Press, 2000)

Tanikawa, M. "A Japanese legal exam that sets the bar high," *New York Times*, 10 July 2011

Tate, C. N. and Vallinder, T. "The global expansion of judicial power: the judicialization of politics" in Tate and Vallinder (eds.), *The Global Expansion of Judicial Power* (New York University Press, 1995), pp. 1–10

Thio, L.-a. "Beyond the 'four walls' in an age of transnational judicial conversations: civil liberties, rights theories and constitutional adjudication in Malaysia and Singapore," *Columbia Journal of Asian Law*, 19 (2006), 428–518

Thio, L.-a. "Constitutionalism in illiberal polities" in M. Rosenfeld and A. Sajó (eds.), *The Oxford Handbook of Comparative Constitutional Law* (Oxford University Press, 2012), pp. 133–52

Thio, L.-a. "Jurisdictional imbroglio: civil and religious courts, turf wars and Article 121 (1A) of the Federal Constitution" in A. Harding and H. P. Lee (eds.), *Constitutional Landmarks in Malaysia: The First 50 Years* (Kuala Lumpur: LexisNexis, 2007), pp. 197–226

Tipton, F. B. *The Rise of Asia: Economics, Society, and Politics in the Contemporary Asia* (University of Hawaii Press, 1998)

Trochev, A. *Judging Russia: Constitutional Court in Russian Politics 1990–2006* (Cambridge University Press, 2008)

Wade, R. *Governing the Market: Economic Theory and the Role of Government in East Asian Industrialization* (Princeton University Press, 1990)

Wilson, M. J. "U.S. legal education methods and ideals: application to the Japanese and Korean systems," *Cardozo Journal of International & Comparative Law*, 18 (2010), 295–358

Yeh, J.-r. "Presidential politics and judicial facilitation of political dialogue between political actors in new Asian democracies: comparing the South Korean and Taiwanese experiences," *International Journal of Constitutional Law*, 8(4) (2011), 911–49

Yeh, J.-r. and Chang, W.-C. "The changing landscape of modern constitutionalism: transitional perspective," *National Taiwan University Law Review*, 4(1) (2009), 145–83

Yeh, J.-r. and Chang, W.-C. "The emergence of East Asian constitutionalism: features in comparison," *American Journal of Comparative Law*, 59(3) (2011), 805–40

Yeh, J.-r. and Chang, W.-C. "The emergence of transnational constitutionalism: its features, challenges and solutions," *Penn State International Law Review*, 27 (2008), 89–124

Younis, M., Lin, X. X., Sharahili, Y. and Selvarathinam, S. "Political stability and economic growth in Asia," *American Journal of Applied Sciences*, 5 (2008), 203–8

Zakaria, F. "Culture is destiny: A conversation with Lee Kuan Yew," *Foreign Affairs*, 73 (1994), 109–25

Zhang, Q. "A constitution without constitutionalism? The path of constitutional development in China," *International Journal of Constitutional Law*, 8(4) (2010), 950–76

PART I

Courts in advanced economies

2

Towards a more responsive judiciary: courts and judicial power in Japan

NORIKAZU KAWAGISHI

Following the collapse of the regime under the Constitution of the Empire of Japan, the liberal democratization of Japanese society has been the most pressing issue in postwar Japan. The current Japanese Constitution, which was promulgated on 3 November 1946 and took effect half a year later, fortified the judiciary, vesting the highest court in Japan with autonomous institutional authority and the power of judicial review. The expansion of judicial power over administrative cases, strengthening judicial independence, and the conception of constitutional rights with judicial review promised to fulfill expectations for a new era immediately after the establishment of the new constitutional system.

However, the Supreme Court and the judiciary as a whole have played a relatively minor role in the liberal democratization of postwar Japanese society. It can by no means be said that administrative and constitutional litigation, in particular, are or have been as lively as they were expected to be when the current Constitution was promulgated. That is why nobody has earnestly applauded or reproached the Supreme Court.

Around the end of the twentieth century, the Japanese government started an eagerly awaited discussion on judicial reform. In July 1999, the Cabinet established the Justice System Reform Council to "clarify the role to be played by justice in Japanese society in the twenty-first century examining and deliberating fundamental measures necessary for the realization of a justice system that is easy for the people to utilize, participation by the people in the justice system, achievement of a legal profession as it should be and strengthening the functions thereof, and other reforms of the justice system, as well as improvements in the infrastructure of that system."[1] On 12 June 2001, the Council reported to the Cabinet its final opinions, titled "For a Justice System to Support Japan in the Twenty-First

[1] The Law Concerning Establishment of the Justice System Reform Council (Act no. 68, 1999), Art. 2(1).

Century." New institutions have been introduced such as a lay judge system, a new system of law schools and a new bar examination, a Lower Courts Judges Designation Consultation Commission, and amendments of administrative litigation law. In shaking off its traditional state of being practically inactive, the Supreme Court has recently taken on a somewhat greater burden in furthering the liberal democratization of society.

In this chapter, I explore the current status of Japanese courts and the roles the judiciary has played. Topics include: the concept of judicial power; the organization of courts as a whole, including the Supreme Court; judgeship; judicial independence; and judicial review.[2]

1 Judicial power

The Constitution of Japan provides that "The whole judicial power is vested in a Supreme Court and in such inferior courts as are established by law."[3] However, the constitutional provisions do not define what is included in this judicial power. A commonly accepted view – and that of the Supreme Court of Japan – is that judicial power is the state's power to adjudicate concrete controversies by interpreting and applying the law.

A historical rather than theoretical understanding of judicial power has been emphasized in postwar constitutional scholarship in Japan. This is because postwar constitutional change brought an expansion of judicial power. The court system changed from one modeled after the continental European system to one modeled after the Anglo-American system. In the old constitutional regime,[4] the courts of the judicial branch heard only civil and criminal cases,[5] and administrative cases had to be presented to the administrative court, which was situated only in Tokyo

[2] For general discussions on courts and judicial power in Japan, see, e.g., H. Kaneko and M. Takeshita, *Saiban Ho*, 4th edn. (Tokyo: Yuhikaku Publishing, 1999); M. Ichikawa et al., *Gendai no Saiban*, 6th edn. (Tokyo: Yuhikaku Publishing, 2013); S. Kisa et al., *Gendai Shiho*, 5th edn. (Tokyo: Nihon Hyōron Sha, 2009); N. Ashibe, revised by K. Takahashi, *Kenpo*, 5th edn. (Tokyo: Iwanami Shoten, 2011); K. Sato, *Nihonkoku Kenpo Ron* (Tokyo: Seibundo, 2011); T. Nonaka et al., *Kenpo II*, 5th edn. (Tokyo: Yuhikaku, 2012); Y. Hasebe, *Kenpo*, 5th edn. (Tokyo: Hatsubai Saiensusha, 2011).

[3] The Constitution of Japan, Art. 76(1).

[4] The Constitution of the Empire of Japan, Art. 57(1) ("The Judicature shall be exercised by the Courts of Law according to law, in the name of the Emperor."); Art. 61 ("No suit at law, which relates to rights alleged to have been infringed by the illegal measures of the administrative authorities, and which shall come within the competency of the Court of Administrative Litigation specially established by law, shall be taken cognizance of by Court of Law.").

[5] *Saibansho Kosei Ho* (Court Organization Act), Art. 2. This law, Act no. 6, 1890, was repealed on 3 May 1947, when the Constitution of Japan became effective.

as both the court of first instance and last resort. Judgments of the administrative court were not eligible for retrial.[6] Standing to sue against any allegedly illegal measures of the administrative authorities was narrowly defined in the Administrative Justice Act.[7] In sharp contrast, the current constitution prohibits the establishment of any extraordinary tribunal system in general and specifically prohibits the granting of final judicial power to administrative organs.[8] All judicial power is now vested in the courts of the judicial branch,[9] which thus hear not only civil and criminal but also administrative cases.

Constitutional scholars who witnessed this structural change understandably felt there was little room for a rational explanation of this judicial expansion. They tended to underscore the dependence of the conception of the judicature on historical incidents such as constitutional rewriting. As constitutional reform was complete with the promulgation of the new Constitution, the Constitution itself became the focus of debate centered on interpretive methodologies. Some constitutional scholars have challenged the established view of judicial power and tried to theorize a constitutional requirement of a concrete case.

Unlike the US Constitution,[10] the constitutional text of Japan never refers to words such as "case" or "controversy." However, the commonly accepted view argues that the judicature provided for in the Constitution holds the power to decide legal disputes. Article 3, paragraph 1 of the *Saibansho Ho* (Court Act) well represents this viewpoint: "Courts shall, except as specifically provided for in the Constitution of Japan, decide all legal disputes, and have such other powers as are specifically provided for by law."[11] The Supreme Court has interpreted legal disputes as disputes that "relate to the existence of concrete rights and duties or legal relations between the parties" and that "can be finally settled by the application of law".[12]

6 *Gyosei Saiban Ho* (the Administrative Justice Act), Art. 19. This law, Act no. 48, 1890, was also repealed on 3 May 1947.

7 The Administrative Justice Act, Art. 15.

8 Article 76(2) of the Constitution of Japan reads: "No extraordinary tribunal shall be established, nor shall any organ or agency of the Executive be given final judicial power." See also Art. 3(2) of the Court Act. For reform of the administrative adjudication system, see A. C. Oppler, *Legal Reform in Occupied Japan: A Participant Looks Back* (Princeton University Press, 1976), pp. 83–4.

9 The Constitution of Japan, Art. 76(1).

10 See the US Constitution, Art. 3.

11 The Court Act, no. 59 of 16 April 1947, materializes the commands of Article 76(1) of the Constitution of Japan.

12 See, e.g., the *Wooden Mandala* Case, Supreme Court Judgment, 7 April 1981, *Minshu* 35-10-1369.

Judicial courts also exercise "such other powers as are specifically provided for by law."[13] These powers include judicial decisions on non-contentious cases,[14] adjudications of domestic relations,[15] citizen actions, and interagency actions. A citizen action is defined as "an action seeking correction of an act conducted by an agency of the State or of a public entity which does not conform to laws, regulations, and rules, which is filed by a person based on his/her status as a voter or any other status that is irrelevant to his/her legal interest."[16] An interagency action is "an action relating to a dispute between agencies of the State and/or a public entity(ies) over issues concerning which of these agencies has the authority, or the exercise thereof."[17] These two are objective actions that "may be filed only by persons specified by Acts in cases provided for in Acts."[18]

Judicial courts may sometimes fail to exert their powers due to certain limits. Two types of limits are recognized. Internal limits of judicial powers include the following: abstract legal issues; disputes that cannot be definitively resolved by the application of law, such as a conflict over a religious doctrine or the truth of an academic theory; and legislative and administrative discretionary acts.[19] The second type of limits encompasses those that are policy-oriented and in that sense external. First of all, the Constitution itself acknowledges exceptions to judicial power, such as disputes related to the qualifications of members of the House of Representatives and House of Councillors and to the trials of impeached judges.[20] Other external limits are as follows: exceptions deriving from international customs and treaties[21] and from paying due respect to autonomous judgments of co-equal branches of government. In addition, the Supreme Court has defined additional exceptions through interpretation. It held that the *Tenno* (Emperor) should be excluded from any

[13] The Court Act, Art. 3(1). [14] See the Non-Contentious Cases Procedure Act.

[15] See the Family Cases Procedure Act.

[16] The Administrative Case Litigation Act, Art. 5.

[17] The Administrative Case Litigation Act, Art. 6.

[18] The Administrative Case Litigation Act, Art. 42.

[19] However, when legislative and administrative acts are made beyond the bounds of a discretionary power or by an abuse of such power, judicial courts can review these acts. See, e.g., the Administrative Case Litigation Act, Art. 30.

[20] The Constitution of Japan, Arts. 55 and 64.

[21] See Art. 17(3)(a) of the Agreement under Article VI of the Treaty of Mutual Cooperation and Security between Japan and the United States of America, regarding Facilities and Areas and the Status of United States Armed Forces in Japan, Washington, 19 January 1960, 373 UNTS 207.

status as a defendant in a civil action because the Constitution has designated him as "the symbol of the State and of the unity of the people."[22] It has also recognized that judicial courts should refrain from intervening in certain highly important acts of government (the political question doctrine).[23] Some constitutional scholars have criticized these positions because of their dubious foundations on the liberal and fortified judicial system of the postwar Constitution.

2 The organization of courts

As we stated earlier, according to the Constitution, "the whole judicial power is vested in a Supreme Court and in such inferior courts as are established by law."[24] The current Japanese judicial system consists of one Supreme Court and the following four kinds of inferior courts established by the Court Act: high courts, district courts, family courts, and summary courts.

2.1 Summary courts and family courts

As courts of first instance, summary courts hear relatively minor cases, such as those in which the value of the property in dispute does not exceed 1,400,000 yen and those in which the crimes in question are (1) punishable with a fine or lighter penalties, (2) punishable with a fine as an optional penalty, or (3) are related to gambling, embezzlement, or acceptance of stolen property.[25] With some exceptions, summary courts may not impose an imprisonment-without-work or heavier penalty.[26] Because administrative cases are usually complex and influential, however, district courts rather than summary courts hear them, regardless of the value of the disputed property.

In summary courts, special proceedings that are less rigid and speedier than full proceedings are available in civil cases and criminal cases by

[22] Supreme Court Judgment, 20 November 1989, *Minshu* 43-10-1160.

[23] The *Sunakawa* Case (Violation of the Special Criminal Law enacted in consequence of the Administrative Agreement under Article III of the Security Treaty between Japan and the United States of America), Supreme Court Judgment, Grand Bench, 16 December 1959, *Keishu* 13-13-3225; the *Tomabeji* Case (a case concerning the power of the court to review the validity of the dissolution of the House of Representatives), Supreme Court Judgment, Grand Bench, 8 June 1960, *Minshu* 14-7-1206.

[24] The Constitution of Japan, Art. 76(1).

[25] The Court Act, Art. 33(1).

[26] The Court Act, Art. 33(2).

request or with the consent of the interested parties.[27] However, this special treatment may not deny interested parties the right to have a trial with ordinary proceedings. Summary courts also offer institutions of conciliation to settle through negotiation civil disputes that occur in citizens' everyday lives.[28] As of 2013 there are 438 summary courts throughout the country. A single judge handles cases in summary courts.[29] Appeals from a summary court are carried to a district court and final appeals to a high court.

Family courts were established as part of the judicial reforms of the postwar era. Family courts as a judicial institution have for the most part been highly regarded because they provide ordinary citizens with basic access to measures for settling disputes with the people closest to them. Recent judicial reforms have thus vested family courts with jurisdiction over personal status litigation, a matter that was previously under the jurisdiction of district courts.

Family courts have jurisdiction over matters concerning families, as well as cases involving juveniles. Specifically, they deal with "[t]rial and decision, and conciliation for cases relating to families as provided for by the Family Cases Procedure Act"; "[j]udicial decision of the first instance relating to personal status provided for by the Personal Status Litigation Act"; and "[t]rial and decision for matters for protecting juveniles as provided for by the Juvenile Act".[30] Family cases deal with rulings on adult guardianship, curatorship or assistance, adjudication of disappearance, special adoptions, loss of parental authority, minor guardianship, the sharing of living expenses between husband and wife, the division of inherited property, the contributory portion to inherited property, and so on.[31] Conciliation in family courts generally covers not only family affairs but also personal status matters.[32] A party wishing to file a lawsuit on matters that family courts may conciliate must first file for conciliation with a family court.[33]

Family courts also handle cases involving juveniles (persons under 20 years of age). The Juvenile Act was enacted to "subject delinquent Juveniles to protective measures to correct their personality traits and modify their environment, and to implement special measures for juvenile

[27] See the Code of Civil Procedure, Part VI, Special Provisions Concerning Actions on Small Claims, and the Code of Criminal Procedure, Part VI, Summary Proceedings.

[28] The Court Act, Art. 34. [29] The Court Act, Art. 35. [30] The Court Act, Art. 31-3.

[31] See the Family Cases Procedure Act, Art. 39 and appendices 1 and 2.

[32] See the Family Cases Procedure Act, Art. 244.

[33] See the Family Cases Procedure Act, Art. 257.

criminal cases, for the purpose of Juveniles' sound development."[34] Any juvenile charged with committing criminal or delinquent acts is first taken from police custody and the public prosecutor's office to a family court.[35] As a result of an investigation into the nature of the crime and circumstances, however, family courts may refer juvenile crime cases back to the public prosecutor's office to follow official criminal procedure.[36] Hearings in juvenile cases are not open to the public[37] and are "conducted cordially and amicably" to "encourage the delinquent Juvenile to introspect about the own delinquency of the Juvenile."[38]

In family courts, as a general rule, a single judge hears and decides a case.[39] However, certain cases that meet the following conditions will be heard and decided by a panel of judges: (1) cases that a panel has previously ruled must be heard or decided by a panel of judges; and (2) cases that are required by another law to be heard and decided by a panel of judges.[40] In family court cases, family court probation officers and research law clerks play a pivotal role in settling disputes. There are 50 family courts, with 203 branches. Each family court has territorial jurisdiction, which is identical to that of the prefecture in which it is located, with the exception of the family courts in Hokkaido, where there are four family courts because of its geographical size. A family court and its branches' territorial jurisdiction are the same as that of a district court and its branches. Family courts may have departments.[41]

The institution of family courts was once challenged as an unconstitutional extraordinary tribunal. Defending the legitimacy of family courts, the Supreme Court held that extraordinary tribunals were defined as courts that do not belong to the organization of ordinary courts that exercise judicial powers, as opposed to courts that merely have jurisdiction over special matters.[42]

2.2 *District courts and high courts*

District courts are generally first instance courts for civil and criminal cases unless the law provides for the original jurisdiction of other

[34] The Juvenile Act, Art. 1.
[35] See the Juvenile Act, Art. 3.
[36] See the Juvenile Act, Art. 20.
[37] See the Juvenile Act, Art. 22(2).
[38] The Juvenile Act, Art. 22(1).
[39] The Court Act, Art. 31-4(1).
[40] The Court Act, Art. 31-4(2).
[41] See the Supreme Court Rule on the Administrative Affairs of Inferior Courts (Kakyu Saibansho Jimushori Kisoku), Art. 4.
[42] Supreme Court Judgment, Grand Bench, 30 May 1956, *Keishu* 10-5-756.

courts.[43] District courts always hear administrative cases. District courts also exert appellate jurisdiction over appeals against judgments, rulings, and the orders of summary courts.[44] Finally, district courts have jurisdiction over the following:[45] civil execution proceedings provided for by the Civil Execution Act;[46] bankruptcy proceedings provided for by the Bankruptcy Act;[47] civil rehabilitation cases provided for by the Civil Rehabilitation Act;[48] non-contentious company cases provided for by the Company Act;[49] and non-contentious cases over land lease rights provided for by the Act on Land and Building Leases.[50] District courts are the most common and comprehensive lower courts in the Japanese court system.

Generally, a single judge presides over cases in district courts. However, a panel of three judges is required in the following: cases in which "a panel has made a ruling to the effect that it will conduct proceedings and give judgments"; cases "involving crimes punishable with the death penalty, life imprisonment with work, imprisonment with or without work for a minimum period not less than one year"; appeals from summary courts; and cases designated so by laws other than the Court Act.[51] Since 21 May 2009, in particular, the following types of cases have been heard by a panel of three professional judges and six *saiban-in* (lay judges): (1) cases involving crimes punishable with the death penalty or life imprisonment, and (2) cases involving intentionally committed crimes that caused the death of the victim and that are among the types of cases listed in Article 26(2)(ii) of the Court Act as requiring a panel.[52] These cases are related to serious crimes such as homicide, robbery causing death or injury, injury causing death, dangerous driving causing death or injury, arson of inhabited buildings, kidnapping for ransom, and the smuggling of stimulants for the purpose of profit.

There are 50 district courts with 203 branches throughout Japan. District courts have "*bu*" (departments), and their branches may also have departments.[53] The largest and most important district court is the Tokyo District Court, which has one branch in Tachikawa City and a

[43] See the Court Act, Art. 24(1) and (2). [44] See the Court Act, Art. 24(3) and (4).
[45] See the Court Act, Art. 25. [46] See the Civil Execution Act, Art. 3.
[47] See the Bankruptcy Act, Art. 2(3). [48] See the Civil Rehabilitation Act, Art. 5.
[49] See the Company Act, Art. 868. [50] See the Act on Land and Building Leases, Art. 41.
[51] See the Court Act, Art. 26.
[52] See the Act Concerning Participation of Lay Judges in Criminal Trials, Art. 2.
[53] See the Supreme Court Rule on Administrative Affairs of Inferior Courts, Art. 4.

total of fifty-four civil departments and twenty-four criminal departments, including those of the Tachikawa branch.

High courts, which are the highest of the inferior courts, have appellate jurisdiction over appeals from district courts and family courts.[54] More precisely, in civil cases, high courts review (1) appeals filed against judgments rendered by district courts in first instance proceedings and by family courts, and (2) final appeals filed against judgments rendered by district courts on appeals of judgments by summary courts. High courts also review direct civil appeals filed against judgments by summary courts. In criminal cases, high courts review appeals against judgments rendered by either district courts or summary courts. High courts review appeals against rulings and orders rendered by district courts and family courts, as well as appeals against rulings and orders rendered by summary courts in criminal cases, except those over which the Supreme Court has jurisdiction as provided for in the codes of procedure.[55]

High courts also have first instance jurisdiction in special cases as provided for by law when speedy resolutions of disputes are desirable and required. For example, actions alleging the invalidity of elections and elected candidates provided for in the Public Offices Election Act must be filed with high courts.[56] High courts also review the decisions of administrative agencies with quasi-judicial powers such as the Fair Trade Commission or the Patent Office. In fact, the Tokyo High Court has exclusive jurisdiction over these cases.[57] In addition, high courts have first instance jurisdiction to hear criminal cases related to insurrection.[58]

A high court consists of a president and a certain number of judges.[59] As a general rule, a panel of three judges hears cases in high courts. However, a panel of five judges is required by specific laws in cases such as criminal cases involving insurrection[60] and those reviewing decisions of the Fair Trade Commission.[61]

Eight high courts are located in Tokyo, Osaka, Nagoya, Hiroshima, Fukuoka, Sendai, Sapporo, and Takamatsu. The Supreme Court may

[54] See the Court Act, Art. 16. [55] See the Court Act, Art. 7(2).

[56] See, e.g., the Public Offices Election Act, Arts. 204 and 208.

[57] See the Act on Prohibition of Private Monopolization and Maintenance of Fair Trade, Arts. 85–87; the Patent Act, Art. 178; and the Trademark Act, Art. 68.

[58] See the Court Act, Art. 16(4); the Criminal Code, Arts. 77–79.

[59] See the Court Act, Art. 15. [60] See the Court Act, Art. 18(2).

[61] See the Act on Prohibition of Private Monopolization and Maintenance of Fair Trade, Art. 87(2).

establish high court branches.[62] Since 1 April 2005, as a result of recent judicial reforms, the Tokyo High Court has had the special branch of the Intellectual Property High Court, which specializes in handling intellectual property cases.[63] High courts have "*bu*" (departments), and their branches also may have departments.[64]

2.3 The Supreme Court

The Supreme Court is the highest court in Japan and the only court the Constitution of Japan directly prescribes to be established. The Supreme Court is the court of final instance and is vested with judicial review power; thus it reviews the constitutionality of statutes and other government actions as well as final appeals in ordinary cases.[65]

The Supreme Court conducts proceedings and delivers decisions through either the grand bench or a petty bench. The grand bench or full bench is a panel comprised of all fifteen Justices sitting together. The Chief Justice presides over proceedings and decisions of the grand bench. The Supreme Court has three petty benches, each of which is composed of five Justices (though the Chief Justice has recently not participated in petty bench proceedings and decisions).[66] Nine or more Justices on the grand bench and three or more Justices on each petty bench constitute a quorum to hear and determine cases.[67]

All cases on final appeal are first assigned to one of the three petty benches. If a case is found to involve an issue of whether any law, order, rule, or disposition conflicts with the Constitution, a petty bench will adjudicate the case where there is a precedent on the same issue; however, where no such precedent exists, the grand bench must adjudicate the matter. The Court Act enumerates three types of cases that the grand bench must hear: (1) cases in which a determination is to be made on the

[62] See the Court Act, Art. 22(1). Currently, Nagoya High Court has Kanazawa branch, Hiroshima High Court has Okayama and Matsue branches, Fukuoka High Court has Miyazaki and Naha branches, and Sendai High Court has Akita branch.

[63] See the Act for Establishment of the Intellectual Property High Court, Art. 2.

[64] See the Supreme Court Rule on the Administrative Affairs of Inferior Courts (Kakyu Saibansho Jimushori Kisoku), Art. 4.

[65] See the Constitution of Japan, Arts. 76 and 81.

[66] See the Court Act, Art. 9; the Supreme Court Rule on Administrative Affairs of the Supreme Court (Saiko Saibansho Jimushori Kisoku), Arts. 1 and 2.

[67] See the Court Act, Art. 9; the Supreme Court Rule on Administrative Affairs of the Supreme Court, Art. 2(2).

constitutionality of a law, order, rule, or disposition, based on the argument by a party (except cases where the opinion is the same as that of a judicial decision previously rendered through the grand bench in which the constitutionality of an act, order, rule, or disposition is recognized); (2) cases other than those referred to in the preceding item when any law, order, rule, or disposition is to be decided as unconstitutional; and (3) cases where an opinion concerning interpretation and application of the Constitution or of any other laws and regulations is contrary to that of a judicial decision previously rendered by the Supreme Court.[68]

A Supreme Court proceeding begins with the filing of a petition of final appeal on the part of a party to a judgment of a lower court, generally of a high court. Because it mainly determines questions of law, the Supreme Court renders judicial decisions, as a rule, based upon an examination of documents alone (final appeal briefs and the records of the lower courts). If a final appeal is groundless, the Supreme Court may dismiss the final appeal with prejudice on the merits by a judgment, without oral argument. If, however, the Supreme Court finds a final appeal well grounded, a judgment is passed after it hears oral arguments.

The Supreme Court exercises jurisdiction of final appeals.[69] It also deals with appeals against the rulings of a lower court specifically provided for in the codes of civil and criminal procedure. In addition, the Supreme Court has powers specially provided for in laws other than the Court Act.[70] One such law gives the Supreme Court original and final jurisdiction in proceedings involving the impeachment of commissioners of the National Personnel Authority, which is provided for in the National Public Service Act.[71]

A final appeal to the Supreme Court is permissible in the following instances: (1) an appeal lodged against a judgment rendered in the first or second instance by a high court; (2) a direct appeal sought against a judgment rendered by a district court or a family court, or a judgment in criminal cases rendered by a summary court as a court of first instance; (3) an appeal filed with a high court and transferred to the Supreme Court for a special reason; (4) a special appeal to the court of last resort made against a judgment in a civil case rendered by a high court as the final appellate court; and (5) an extraordinary appeal to the court of last

[68] The Court Act, Art. 10. [69] The Court Act, Art. 7(1). [70] The Court Act, Art. 8.
[71] The National Public Service Act, Art. 9.

resort lodged by the Prosecutor-General against a final and binding judgment in a criminal case.[72]

In criminal cases, the Supreme Court may hear a final appeal against a high court judgment of first or second instance on the following grounds: (1) there is a violation of the Constitution or an error in the interpretation of the Constitution; (2) a determination has been rendered that conflicts with a Supreme Court precedent; or (3) in the event that there is no Supreme Court precedent, a determination has been rendered that conflicts with a precedent of the former Supreme Court (*daishin'in*) or a high court that was the court of final instance, or that conflicts with a precedent of a high court that was the court of second instance after the enforcement date of the Code of Criminal Procedure.[73] In addition, the Supreme Court as the court of final instance may accept a case that is deemed to involve important matters relating to the interpretation of laws and regulations pursuant to the Rules of Court.[74]

In civil and administrative cases, the Supreme Court may hear a final appeal only on the grounds that (1) a judgment of the lower courts contains a misconstruction of the Constitution[75] or any other violation of the Constitution, or (2) there are serious violations of provisions regarding the procedure of the lower courts, which are listed in the Code of Civil Procedure as the absolute reasons for the final appeal.[76] Furthermore, the Supreme Court as the final appellate court may consider an appeal when the judgment being appealed either contains a determination that is inconsistent with the Supreme Court's precedents or is found to involve material matters concerning the construction of laws and regulations.[77]

Each year the Supreme Court accepts about 5,000 civil and administrative cases and 4,000 criminal cases.[78] The judicial docket of the Supreme Court is always overflowing with cases. The Justices are so

[72] Supreme Court of Japan, Overview of the Judicial System in Japan, www.courts.go.jp/english/judicial_sys/overview_of/overview/index.html#01.

[73] The Code of Criminal Procedure, Art. 405.

[74] The Code of Criminal Procedure, Art. 406.

[75] The Code of Civil Procedure, Art. 312(1).

[76] The Code of Civil Procedure, Art. 312(2).

[77] The Code of Civil Procedure, Art. 318(1).

[78] In 2010, with respect to civil and administrative cases, the Supreme Court accepted 5,321 new cases and completed 4,989 cases; with respect to criminal cases, it accepted 4,024 new cases and completed 3,987 cases: *Shiho Tokei Nenkan 2010* (The Annual Report of Judicial Statistics 2010).

busily occupied with final appeal cases that it is difficult for them to wrestle with time-consuming and complicated constitutional issues. This is surely one of the reasons that the Japanese Supreme Court is inactive in constitutional litigation.

In addition to the fact that Supreme Court Justices are extremely busy in their regular work as the final appellate court, some of the justices are also unfamiliar with judicial work itself because they were not career judges prior to their appointment to the Supreme Court. Judicial research officials are thus available for assisting the judicial work of the Supreme Court Justices. These officials are typically appointed by the Supreme Court from among career judges with an average of fifteen years of experience. Currently there is one chief, three senior officials (one each for the civil, administrative, and criminal departments), and thirty judicial research officials. The position of chief judicial research official is usually a precursor to a Supreme Court Justiceship. In fact, seven recent chief officials were actually appointed as Justices. It is said that judicial officials are heavily engaged in preparing judgments.

2.4 *Performance of Courts*

Tables 2.1 to 2.3 include selected data on the caseloads of the Supreme Court, high courts, district courts, summary courts and family courts. Since 2000, grounds for as-of-right final appeals have been limited in civil cases to reduce the number of cases the Supreme Court must deal with, and instead a system in which appellants must seek the court's leave to pursue final appeals has been introduced. The caseloads for all levels of courts are, not surprisingly, steadily rising. Notably, at the Supreme Court, civil/administrative cases outnumber criminal cases, but the opposite is true at the high courts. Civil/administrative cases also outnumber criminal cases at the district courts and family courts[79] while their numbers are comparable at the summary courts.[80]

These data show that newly accepted cases have dramatically increased in the past sixty years. People have relied more and more on litigation as a tool for resolving disputes. They have thus expected the judiciary to be

[79] For example, in 2012, while the family courts have newly accepted 857,237 domestic relations cases and finished 853,604 domestic relations cases, they have only accepted 134,185 Juvenile disciplinary cases and finished 139,302 Juvenile disciplinary cases.

[80] For instance, in 2012, the number of civil/administrative cases in summary courts newly accepted is 987,098 and the number of criminal cases is 802,955.

Table 2.1: *Selected data on the caseload of the Supreme Court*

Supreme Court	Civil/ Administrative cases newly accepted	Civil/ Administrative cases terminated	Criminal cases newly accepted	Criminal cases terminated
1949	502	260	5,014	4,204
1960	2,074	2,004	4,717	4,721
1980	3,010	2,923	2,187	2,251
2000	6,476 (5,044)	6,179 (4,915)	2,901	2,908
2010	7,410 (5,321)	6,905 (4,989)	4,924	3,987
2012	8,169 (5,868)	8,336 (5,992)	4,142	4,258

Source: Supreme Court of Japan, *Shiho Tokei Nenkan 2012* (Annual Report of Judicial Statistics 2012).

Table 2.2: *Selected data on the caseload of high courts*

High courts	Civil/ Administrative cases newly accepted	Civil/ Administrative cases terminated	Criminal cases newly accepted	Criminal cases terminated
1949	4,661	3,282	36,194	27,607
1960	18,979	18,259	19,608	19,036
1980	19,981	20,215	11,092	11,210
2000	37,275	38,022	10,199	9,936
2010	41,171	39,329	10,419	10,477
2012	43,564	44,066	10,566	10,600

Source: Supreme Court of Japan, *Shiho Tokei Nenkan 2012* (Annual Report of Judicial Statistics 2012).

a forum where complex interests are considered and handled. The Supreme Court and lower courts must attempt to live up to these high expectations by responding to social demand. The judiciary's will and ability to assume a greater burden are most relevant here.

3 Judgeship

The Constitution of Japan differentiates judges into three categories: a Chief Justice, Justices of the Supreme Court, and judges of lower

Table 2.3: *Selected data on the caseload of district courts*

District courts	Civil/ Administrative cases newly accepted	Civil/ Administrative cases terminated	Criminal cases newly accepted	Criminal cases terminated
1949	112,592	104,513	113,932	108,493
1960	341,588	327,229	357,731	360,950
1980	569,345	549,441	265,268	268,461
2000	1,161,498	1,193,703	316,462	314,010
2010	817,062	841,760	285,691	287,655
2012	668,737	688,366	281,899	283,618

Source: Supreme Court of Japan, *Shiho Tokei Nenkan 2012* (Annual Report of Judicial Statistics 2012).

courts.[81] While Chief Justices are designated by the Cabinet and appointed by the *Tenno* (Emperor), Justices are appointed by the Cabinet.[82] In addition, to facilitate citizen participation in the judiciary, the Diet passed a law in 2004 requiring selected citizens to participate as "*saiban-in*", lay judges, in trials for certain severe crimes. The system of lay judges started in 2009.

3.1 Career judges: Chief Justice, Supreme Court Justices and lower courts judges

The constitutional categories of judges are further broken down into six official titles given to judges, as provided for by the Court Act. These are the Chief Justice and fourteen Justices of the Supreme Court, presidents of high courts, judges, assistant judges, and summary court judges.[83] The presidents of district courts, family courts, and summary courts and chief judges of a panel are important titles in a practical sense but are not official titles.

In Japan, which belongs to the civil law tradition, judges are usually selected, trained, and promoted within the judicial bureaucracy. After passing the bar examination and spending one year as a legal apprentice at the Legal Training and Research Institute attached to the Supreme

[81] See the Constitution of Japan, Arts. 79 and 80; the Court Act, Art. 39(1) and (2).
[82] See the Constitution of Japan, Arts. 6 and 79. [83] See the Court Act, Art. 5.

Court, assistant judges are appointed from among those who have recently finished their legal apprenticeships. However, the career system allows exceptions in order to allow those with more diversified backgrounds to serve as judges at both the entry and high-end levels.

Summary court judges are different from assistant judges in their career path. Summary court judges do not necessarily need to pass the bar examination, which is generally a prerequisite for assistant judges. Because, as described earlier, summary courts handle cases that are relatively uncomplicated but that are most closely related to the everyday life of citizens, the accessibility to a summary court judgeship is considered an important factor in the selection process. Summary court judges may be selected from among the following: (1) former presidents and judges of the high courts; (2) current and former assistant judges, public prosecutors, attorneys, research law clerks, court administrative officials, professors at the Legal Training and Research Institute, professors at the Training and Research Institute for Court Officials, and law officials or law instructors at the Ministry of Justice, who have served in these positions for at least three years; and (3) "persons who have been engaged in judicial affairs for many years, or who possess the knowledge and experience necessary for performing the duties of a judge of summary courts."[84]

Recruiting Justices of the Supreme Court, who are at the apex of the judicial system, is also very different from recruitment of ordinary judges. The Supreme Court comprises one Chief Justice and fourteen Associate Justices. The appointments of the Chief and Associate Justices are popularly reviewed (in a process similar to a judicial retention referendum) at the first general election of members of the House of Representatives following their appointment. They are popularly reviewed "again at the first general election of members of the House of Representatives after a lapse of ten years, and in the same manner thereafter."[85] Because execution of this popular review is linked to a general election of members of the House of Representatives, the nature of the popular review is disputable. If we interpret it as a recall, that interpretation encounters difficulty because it would allow some justices to be dismissed without having achieved enough as a justice if a popular review occurs too soon after his or her appointment. Thus, some constitutional scholars argue that the popular review is both an ex-post approval of appointment by

[84] See the Court Act, Arts. 44 and 45.

[85] The Constitution of Japan, Art. 79(2).

the Cabinet and a recall. In the current review system, an eligible voter may cast either a vote in favor of dismissal or a blank vote for each justice to be reviewed. Because a voter cannot cast a vote affirmatively in favor of retention, blank votes are not regarded as votes that represent non-confidence. The Supreme Court itself held that popular review is a kind of recall and thus that the current review system, which tries to evaluate an affirmative will to dismiss among the people, is not unconstitutional.[86] So far no justices have been dismissed by popular review. As a result, the effectiveness of this institution has been seriously challenged. Many constitutional scholars propose a change of voting system to one in which eligible voters may express their will in three ways: dismiss, retain, or blank.

Justices of the Supreme Court are appointed from among "learned persons with extensive knowledge of law, who are not less than forty years old."[87] Although the Act allows Justices to be appointed at the age of forty, no Justices have yet been appointed in their forties. In fact,

[86] See the Supreme Court Judgment, Grand Bench, 20 February 1952, *Minshu*, 6-2-122.
[87] Article 41 of the Court Act reads:

(1) Justices of the Supreme Court shall be appointed from learned persons with extensive knowledge of law, who are not less than forty years old. At least ten of them shall be persons who have held one or two of the positions set forth in item (i) or (ii) for not less than ten years, or one or more of the positions set forth in the following items for the total period of twenty years or more.
 (i) President of the High Court
 (ii) Judges
 (iii) Judges of the Summary Court
 (iv) Public Prosecutors
 (v) Attorneys
 (vi) Professors or associate professors of law of universities that shall be determined by law.
(2) For the purpose of the application of the provisions of the preceding paragraph, if persons who have held the positions referred to in items (i) and (ii) of the preceding paragraph for at least five years, or one or more of the positions referred to in items (iii) through (vi) of the preceding paragraph for not less than ten years, also have held positions of assistant judge, research law clerk, Secretary General of the Supreme Court, court administrative official, professor of the Legal Training and Research Institute, professor of the Training and Research Institute for Court Officials, Administrative Vice-Minister of the Ministry of Justice, law official of the Ministry of Justice, or law instructor of the Ministry of Justice, then, such position shall be deemed to be those referred to in items (iii) through (vi) of the said paragraph.
(3) For the purpose of the application of the provisions of the preceding two paragraphs, the period of service in the positions set forth in items (iii) to (v) of paragraph 1 and in the preceding paragraph shall be counted only from the completion of training as legal apprentice.

Justices generally tend to be appointed in their sixties. Because the mandatory retirement age for Justices is seventy,[88] they generally serve less than ten years on the Supreme Court. A justice therefore usually undergoes a popular review of his or her appointment only once. The relatively short tenure of Justices allows for strong leadership by the Chief Justice.

As a matter of practice, a system using lenient quotas of recruiting sources has been adopted. As of September 2013, the Justices of the Supreme Court consisted of six career judges, four attorneys-at-law, two prosecutors, two government officials, and one scholar (an ex-judge). The Chief Justice has for many years come from the ranks of career judges.[89]

Although the constitutional provisions indicate that the Cabinet designates and appoints the Chief and Associate Justices, it is reportedly the case that, in practice, the incumbent Chief Justice and Secretary General along with a few other high-ranking officials of the General Secretariat consult with the Cabinet and the ruling party, as well as with high-ranking officials at the public prosecutors' office and the president of the Japan Federation of Bar Associations, in identifying candidates.[90] We can readily assume, on the one hand, that persons whom the Cabinet and ruling party determinedly refuse to appoint or designate will have no chance of becoming a Justice, but that, on the other hand, the Cabinet should not have arbitrary power in judicial politics. Because the Diet has nothing to do with the appointment and designation process, transparency in this process is not necessarily guaranteed.

When the Supreme Court commenced its duties after the promulgation of the Constitution of Japan, a Justice Appointment Consultation

(4) In cases where a person has held a position as a professor of law or associate professor of law of a university referred to in item (vi) of paragraph 1 for three years or more, and also has held a position as a judge of Summary Court, public prosecutor (excluding an assistant prosecutor) or attorney, the provisions of the preceding paragraph shall not apply with respect to the period of service in latter positions.

88 The Court Act, Art. 50.

89 Up to now there have been seventeen Chief Justices, twelve of whom have been career judges. The exceptions are the following: the first Chief Justice, Mibuchi Tadao, a lawyer; the second, Tanaka Kotaro, a university professor; the third, Yokota Kisaburo, a university professor; the seventh, Fujibayashi Ekizo, a lawyer; and the eighth, Okahara Masao, a prosecutor.

90 See T. Fujita, *Saikosai kaikoroku (The Memoirs on the Supreme Court)* (Tokyo: Yuhikaku Publishing, 2012); D. S. Law, "The anatomy of a conservative court: judicial review in Japan," *Texas Law Review*, 87 (2009), 1545.

Commission was established to help the Cabinet appoint or designate Justices. However, the commission was abolished after only two unsuccessful submissions of slates of candidates to two successive Cabinets,[91] on the grounds that an advisory commission to nominate candidates for justiceship might unconstitutionally interfere with the power vested solely in the Cabinet to designate and appoint Justices. Since then, no institution for openly reviewing candidates' qualifications for justiceship has been officially established. Recent judicial reform discussions have pointed out that the selection process of Supreme Court Justices should be more objective and transparent.[92] As of September 2013, however, no action had yet materialized.

The Cabinet appoints judges of lower courts from a list of candidates nominated by the Supreme Court.[93] This mechanism is designed to maintain the Cabinet's appointment power and, at the same time, respect judicial autonomy. There has been constitutional debate over whether the Cabinet can refuse to appoint candidates recommended by the Supreme Court. In practice, reportedly, the Supreme Court proposes a list of a fixed number plus one of candidates ranked by preference, and the Cabinet appoints judges from that list. It is said that the Cabinet has never refused a list of candidates proposed by the Supreme Court.

Transparency in the Supreme Court's process of determining the list of candidates has also been an important issue. Legal apprentices who wish to be assistant judges have sometimes been denied without being told the reason(s) for the decision. The Supreme Court has explained that this is because giving the reason(s) for rejection would serve no useful purpose.

[91] At first, the commission submitted a list of candidates to the Yoshida Shigeru Cabinet on 23 April 1947. For the Constitution of Japan to be effective on 3 May 1947, however, the House of Representatives was resolved on March 31 and a general election was held on April 25. Yoshida's Liberal Party was defeated and the Socialist Party gained a plurality of members of the House of Representatives. Kataya Tetsu was designated as prime minister on May 23 and his coalition cabinet was at last officially formed on June 1. The Kataya Cabinet formed the second Justice Appointment Consultation Commission on July 21 and received a list of 30 recommended candidates on July 28. The Supreme Court was formally inaugurated as an institution but there were no chief and associate justices for three months. During that period, the old *Taishin-in* and its justices were substituted for the Supreme Court and its justices. See S. Nishikawa, "Saikosaibansho no ruutsu wo saguru," *Seikei Ronso*, 78 (2009), 1–82.

[92] See the Justice System Reform Council, "Recommendations of the Justice System Reform Council – For a Justice System to Support Japan in the 21st Century," chapter III, part 5, "5. With Regard to How Supreme Court Justices Should Be Appointed, etc." (12 June 2001), www.kantei.go.jp/foreign/judiciary/2001/0612report.html.

[93] See the Constitution of Japan, Art. 80(1).

Many people have suspected that political or ideological judgments lurk in the background. The recent judicial reform has led the Supreme Court to establish the Lower Courts Judges Designation Consultation Commission.[94] This commission consists of eleven members whom the Supreme Court appoints from among judges, public prosecutors, attorneys-at-law, and persons of learning and experience.[95] The current composition of the members is that of two judges, one prosecutor, two lawyers, three professors of law, one professor of economics, one clinical psychologist, and one novelist. The commission has eight regional sub-commissions in the areas where high courts are located.[96] Sub-commissions gather information on candidates, which, along with their opinions on the candidates, they convey to the commission.[97] The Supreme Court must refer without its opinions to the commission's judgments.[98] Every year the commission reviews about 100 candidates. The commission submits reports on the qualifications of the candidates along with its own opinions. As the commission's role is consultative, the Supreme Court makes the final decisions on nominations. The Supreme Court shows those whom it has not nominated the grounds for its decision. When it rejects the commission's recommendations, the Supreme Court is required to inform the commission and to give its reasons. Since the commission's formation on 1 May 2003, no small number of candidates have failed to be recommended to the Supreme Court.

As of May 2013, the numbers of judges prescribed by law are 8 presidents of high courts, 1,889 judges, 1,000 assistant judges, and 806 summary judges.[99] In addition, as stated above, there is one Chief Justice and

[94] The Justice System Reform Council pointed out that "from the standpoint of strengthening the confidence of the people toward the judges, in order to reflect the views of the people in the process whereby the Supreme Court nominates those to be appointed as lower court judges, a body should be established in the Supreme Court, which, upon receiving consultations from the Supreme Court, selects appropriate candidates for designation, and recommends the results of its consideration to the Supreme Court." Justice System Reform Council, "Recommendations of the Justice System Reform Council", chapter III, part 5, "2. Reexamination of Procedures for Appointment of Judges".

[95] The Supreme Court Rule on the Lower Courts Judges Designation Consultation Commission, Arts. 5 and 6.

[96] The Supreme Court Rule on the Lower Courts Judges Designation Consultation Commission, Art. 12.

[97] The Supreme Court Rule on the Lower Courts Judges Designation Consultation Commission, Art. 13.

[98] The Supreme Court Rule on the Lower Courts Judges Designation Consultation Commission, Art. 3.

[99] See the Act Concerning Prescribed Numbers of Court Officials (Act no. 53, 1951), Art. 1.

14 Associate Justices.[100] When assistant judges have served for more than five years, they may – as a legal exception – serve in an official capacity as judge equivalents in order to remedy a shortage of judges.[101]

3.2 *Lay judges*

As part of recent judicial reforms, the Act Concerning *Saiban-in* (Lay Judge) Participation in Criminal Justice[102] was passed in May 2004 and became effective on 21 May 2009. By introducing a new system in which *saiban-in*, who are selected from among ordinary citizens, are involved with criminal proceedings together with professional judges, the legislation has aimed at making a contribution to promoting the people's understanding of the judiciary and elevating their confidence in it.[103] *Saiban-in* are randomly selected for an individual case from the list of *saiban-in* candidates randomly selected once a year from the list of voters eligible to elect members of the House of Representatives.[104] The trials in which *saiban-in* participate deal with the most serious crimes, such as murder, robbery causing death, and arson involving inhabited buildings.[105] *Saiban-in* trials are applicable only to courts of the first instance, namely district courts. Thus, appeals are heard by a panel consisting only of professional judges in courts of the second instance, high courts.

In a *saiban-in* trial, a panel generally consists of six *saiban-in* and three professional judges. However, when a court, in considering and arranging issues and evidence at a pre-trial arrangement proceeding, determines that a charged fact is not contested and, after considering the contents of the case and circumstances, recognizes it as appropriate to do so, it may decide the panel should instead consist of four *saiban-in* and one professional judge.[106] While a panel of *saiban-in* and professional judges deals with finding facts, application of laws and regulations, and sentencing, a panel consisting only of professional judges decides matters on interpretation of laws and regulations and on criminal procedure.[107] Decisions

[100] See the Court Act, Art. 5(1) and (3).

[101] See the Act Concerning the Exceptions to the Authority of Assistant Judges, etc. (Act no. 146, 1948), Art. 1.

[102] Act no. 63, 2004 (hereinafter the *Saiban-in* Act).

[103] The *Saiban-in* Act, Art. 1.

[104] The *Saiban-in* Act, ch. 2, s. 2.

[105] The *Saiban-in* Act limits *saiban-in* trials to cases involving crimes punishable by the death penalty or imprisonment for life or statutory panel cases in which an intentional criminal act has caused the death of a victim. See the *Saiban-in* Act, Art. 2(1).

[106] The *Saiban-in* Act, Art. 2(2) and (3).

[107] The *Saiban-in* Act, Art. 6.

concerning guilt and sentencing are reached when a majority – which must include one professional judge and one *saiban-in* – of a panel of *saiban-in* and professional judges agrees.[108]

Saiban-in may participate in the whole of the trial proceedings, such as examining witnesses, questioning victims or the bereaved, having defendants state relevant matters, participating in deliberations, voting for decisions, and rendering judgments.[109] *Saiban-in* are obliged to appear at the trial on trial dates, express their opinions in deliberations, and not divulge any confidential information that has come to their knowledge in the course of their duties.[110] The observance of such secrecy is protected by the threat of criminal punishment, the harshness of which has been widely criticized because it deters ex-*saiban-in* from sharing their experiences with those around them and thus seems inconsistent with the purpose of the legislation.[111] *Saiban-in* are paid travel expenses, a daily allowance, and an accommodation fee.[112]

During the period from 21 May 2009 to 31 August 2013, *saiban-in* trials handled 7,189 cases, in which 5,513 persons were found guilty and 29 persons not guilty. Twenty persons were sentenced to the death penalty and 119 persons to life imprisonment with forced labor; 1,917 persons filed an appeal to high courts; 489,840 persons were selected as candidates for *saiban-in*, while 32,013 persons were selected as *saiban-in* and 10,974 persons as substitute *saiban-in*. The average trial duration for all 5,547 cases was 6.4 days; for the 2,337 contested cases it was 8.9 days, while for the 3,210 confessed cases it was 4.6 days. The average number of minutes given to deliberation for all cases was 569.3, while for contested cases it was 715.7 and for confessed cases it was 462.7.[113]

Three years after becoming effective, the *Saiban-in* Act required the government to examine the state of implementation of *saiban-in* trials and, if necessary, take measures to ensure that *saiban-in* were playing a full role as one of the foundations of the judicial system in Japan.[114] Thus, *saiban-in* trials are now under review. Ex-*saiban-in* have generally

[108] The *Saiban-in* Act, Art. 66. [109] The *Saiban-in* Act, Arts. 56, 58, 59, 66, 67 and 63.

[110] The *Saiban-in* Act, Arts. 52, 66, and 9.

[111] Punishment is imprisonment with forced labor for not more than six months or a fine of not more than 100,000 yen. See the *Saiban-in* Act, Art. 108(1).

[112] The *Saiban-in* Act, Art. 11.

[113] See Supreme Court of Japan, "Saiban-in saiban no jisshi jokyo ni tsuite" ("On the State of Implementing Saiban-in Trials") 2013, www.saibanin.courts.go.jp/topics/pdf/09_12_05-10jissi_jyoukyou/h25_8_sokuhou.pdf.

[114] The *Saiban-in* Act, supplementary provisions, Art. 9.

evaluated their experiences positively, though most were highly reluctant to be *saiban-in* before they actually served.

Japanese criminal proceedings previously were documentation-oriented; however, since *saiban-in* trials were introduced, direct and oral approaches have become more and more important. Fundamental principles such as presumption of innocence and proof beyond reasonable doubt have been more sharply emphasized because ordinary citizens are now participating in criminal justice. *Saiban-in* trials have gradually but steadily influenced the conduct of criminal proceedings in Japan. Some of the issues that are being reconsidered are fact finding, the increased severity of sentences, the appeal system, the sharing of *saiban-in* experiences, and the influence of media bias on *saiban-in* trials, among others.

4 Judicial independence

The Supreme Court now enjoys autonomy in the judicial system. In the Meiji constitutional regime, the judiciary had a number of autonomous authorities but they were narrowly limited. In the first place, judicial power was exercised in the name of the Emperor,[115] and the judicature was under the supervision of the Ministry of Justice. In marked contrast, the current Constitution vests the Supreme Court with the powers appropriate for an independent governmental body, such as rulemaking and judicial administration. The Supreme Court's rulemaking power is over "the rules of procedure and of practice, and of matters relating to attorneys, the internal discipline of the courts and the administration of judicial affairs."[116] Judicial administration affairs are carried out through the deliberations of the Judicial Assembly and under the general supervision of the Chief Justice of the Supreme Court.[117] All Justices participate in the Judicial Assembly, over which the Chief Justice presides.[118]

Judicial independence has two principles. The first is independence from outside influences. This principle aims to avoid the intervention of political branches in judicial decision-making. This principle is expressed in the constitutional provision that "No disciplinary action against judges shall be administered by any executive organ or agency,"[119] which is generally the most dangerous threat to the judiciary. In Japanese history,

[115] See the Constitution of the Empire of Japan, Art. 57(1).
[116] The Constitution of Japan, Art. 77(1). [117] The Court Act, Art. 12(1).
[118] The Court Act, Art. 12(2). [119] See the Constitution of Japan, Art. 78.

it is said, judicial independence in this sense has been well maintained. Indeed, political interventions have not been reported since the start of Japan's modernization in the Meiji era.

Second, each judge may exercise his or her authority independently. This is internal independence in the judicial system. The following constitutional text clarifies this second principle: "All judges shall be independent in the exercise of their conscience and shall be bound only by this Constitution and the laws."[120] Judges' positions are secure as long as they maintain good behavior.[121] That is, judges may not be removed, transferred, suspended from performing their jobs, or have their salaries reduced[122] against their will, except in cases constitutionally and legally provided for.[123] Lower court judges serve for a ten-year term of office with the privilege of reappointment.[124] While Supreme Court justices and summary court judges must retire at the age of seventy, other lower court judges reach their age limit at sixty-five.[125]

Constitutional and legal exceptions to the guarantee of status as a judge exist in three types of cases. One is, as we have already discussed, dismissal of Supreme Court justices by popular review in which a majority of voters favor a justice's dismissal.[126] Another case in which dismissal is warranted is when a judge is convicted in an impeachment trial.[127] According to the proceedings of public impeachment, the Judge Impeachment Committee, which consists of ten members and five reserve members of the Houses of Representatives and Councillors, respectively, first impeaches judges who have grossly violated their official duties or flagrantly neglected their duties, or are guilty of such malfeasance as to experience substantial loss of their prestige as a judge, either concerning or regardless of their official duties.[128] The Diet then establishes an impeachment court from among seven members and four

[120] The Constitution of Japan, Art. 76(3).

[121] See the Constitution of Japan, Art. 78.

[122] The Constitution of Japan, Arts. 79(5) and 80(2). These provisions are interpreted to protect individual judges. When all public officials have had their salaries reduced by governmental action, the Judicial Assembly has constitutionally decided on a uniform reduction of all judges' salaries. After the earthquake of 11 March 2011, the Diet, on 29 February 2012, established an Act whereby all judges' salaries were reduced for two years in order to help raise funds for reconstruction.

[123] See the Court Act, Art. 48.

[124] See the Constitution of Japan, Arts. 79(2) and 80(1).

[125] See the Court Act, Art. 50.

[126] See the Constitution of Japan, Art. 79(3); the Act on Popular Review of the Supreme Court Justices (Act no. 136, 1947), Arts. 32 and 35(1).

[127] See the Constitution of Japan, Art. 78.

[128] See the Diet Act, Art. 126(1); the Judge Impeachment Act, Art. 2.

reserve members of both Houses respectively for the purpose of trying those judges against whom removal proceedings have been instituted.[129] Because judicial independence is a pivotal principle of constitutionalism, the contents of judgments made by judges in an official capacity are not considered eligible for review by political departments. Thus, errors in judgments do not constitute a cause for impeachment. Dismissal decisions concerning impeached judges must be rendered with the approval of two-thirds of the members of an impeachment court.[130] Dismissal of judges becomes effective as soon as impeachment courts declare dismissal decisions. Because judgments by impeachment courts are final, no appeals are permitted. Upon request by judges dismissed through impeachment trials, impeachment courts may make judgments on recovery of legal qualifications when there is sufficient reason to restore legal qualifications after five years or to repeal dismissal decisions in light of newly discovered evidence.[131] Ordinary judicial courts, even the Supreme Court, have no jurisdiction over impeachment trials. So far, only nine lower court judges have been impeached, seven of whom were dismissed. There have been six requests for recovery of legal qualifications, with the requests being approved in three of these cases.[132] Integrity of judgeship has been generally maintained in Japan.

The third and final category of exceptions is the removal of judges who are declared mentally or physically incompetent to perform their duties.[133] The Judges Status Act provides that judges are to be removed when a judicial decision holds that they are unable to carry out their official duties because of irreparable mental or physical problems.[134] Such decisions against district, family, and summary courts judges are rendered by a panel of five judges in high courts.[135] Such decisions for Supreme Court justices and high court judges are rendered as in both the first and final instance by the grand bench of the Supreme Court, which also hears final appeals of such decisions by the high courts.[136]

As discussed earlier, the Supreme Court also performs judicial administration. The official entity for carrying out administrative matters is the

[129] See the Diet Act, Art. 125(1); the Judge Impeachment Act, Art. 16.
[130] See the Judge Impeachment Act, Art. 31(2) proviso.
[131] See the Judge Impeachment Act, Art. 38.
[132] See the homepage of the Impeachment Court, www.dangai.go.jp/lib/lib1.html.
[133] See the Constitution of Japan, Art. 78; the Court Act, Art. 48.
[134] See the Judges Status Act, Art. 1.
[135] See the Judges Status Act, Art. 3(1) and Art. 4 sentence 1.
[136] See the Judges Status Act, Art. 3(2) and Art. 4 sentence 2.

Judicial Assembly. Because Supreme Court Justices usually struggle with an extremely heavy workload, however, the Chief Justice and the General Secretariat play a pivotal role in judicial administrative affairs. In fact, the Secretary General, who heads the General Secretariat, is also influential in judicial administration in general and in judicial personnel matters in particular. Furthermore, this position is an important recruiting source of Supreme Court Justices. Indeed, six of seventeen Chief Justices occupied this position before their appointments. It is often pointed out that, owing to the General Secretariat's enormous influence over judicial personnel matters, the internal independence of the judiciary has long been in serious question.[137]

Lower court judges are appointed for a ten-year term with the privilege of reappointment. The nature of this application for reappointment has been a controversial issue. The Supreme Court has argued that it maintains the discretion to release a list of designated reappointment candidate judges who have applied for renewal of their terms. However, many constitutional scholars are critical of the Supreme Court's free hand policy because it makes a judge's status insecure. Standards for evaluating eligibility for reappointment are often obscure, or at least not clear and plain. As a result, the guarantee of lower court judges' status covers only a term of ten years. In the career system, almost all judges seek reappointment, and, if they are denied an opportunity to continue their jobs, they face serious difficulties in finding other employment. As a matter of practice, an overwhelming majority of judges have been reappointed. Gaining reappointment may cost career judges their freedom as ordinary citizens, however. An incident in 1971 in which the Supreme Court refused the application of an assistant judge for reappointment has attracted wide attention. Assistant Judge Miyamoto Yasuaki was denied the opportunity to be reappointed without any reason being given. It is widely suspected that the Supreme Court rejected Miyamoto because he belonged to a liberal-left group of judges, lawyers, and scholars. The Supreme Court has never made clear its reason for rejecting him, as the Supreme Court has traditionally explained nothing regarding personnel matters. Many constitutional scholars have questioned this lack of transparency in the reappointment process. The recent judicial reforms have included a new approach to reviewing reappointment applications. In addition to reviewing new applications for judgeships, the Lower

[137] See, e.g., J. M. Ramseyer and E. B. Rasmusen, *Measuring Judicial Independence: Political Economy of Judging in Japan* (University of Chicago Press, 2003).

Courts Judges Designation Consultation Commission now reviews the merits of judges seeking reappointment and reports to the Supreme Court its opinion on the propriety of renewals. Reappointment has thus become to some degree more transparent and objective than before.

Misconduct that is not serious enough to initiate proceedings of impeachment may nevertheless be subject to disciplinary action. As a corollary of judicial independence, the judiciary itself may impose discipline on judges.[138] When judges have violated their official duties, neglected their jobs or degraded themselves, disciplinary action may be taken through judicial decisions.[139] Procedures for judicial disciplinary action are stipulated in the Judges Status Act, which limits disciplinary measures against judges to two kinds: a reprimand or a non-penal administrative fine of not more than 10,000 yen.[140] One vigorously debated case involved the disciplinary action taken against Assistant Judge Teranishi Kazushi. In identifying himself as an assistant judge, Teranishi, at a public meeting that was held to oppose a bill concerning wiretapping for investigating organized crime, said he would decline to make a speech as a panelist because his chief judge had warned him that he might be subject to disciplinary action for participating in the public meeting. A grand bench of the Supreme Court turned down a final appeal by Teranishi and confirmed that he had actively engaged in a political campaign in breach of his official obligations as a judge[141] and should be reprimanded.[142] Five justices, all of whom had practiced law, filed dissenting opinions, pointing out that a disciplinary action against him was inconsistent with the constitutional protection of free expression and that his words and deeds did not fit the legal requirement of active engagement in a political campaign. Constitutional scholars are generally supportive of these dissenting opinions. This case has come to symbolize Japanese judges' lack of civil liberties.

In the career system, personnel performance evaluations to determine promotions, salary increases, and transfers play an important role. There has long been criticism that evaluations are carried out in a black box. The Personnel Affairs Bureau of the General Secretariat of the Supreme Court, which is in charge of personnel matters concerning all judges, has never articulated standards for evaluation. Many people

[138] See the Constitution of Japan, Art. 78 sentence 2. [139] See the Court Act, Art. 49.
[140] See the Judges Status Act, Art. 2.
[141] See the Court Act, Art. 52 item 1 and Art. 49; the Judges Status Act, Art. 2.
[142] See the Supreme Court Decision, Grand Bench, 1 December 1998, *Minshu* 52-9-1761.

suspect that judges who have made decisions that were not welcomed by top executives of the Supreme Court have been given less favorable evaluations and thus end up being penalized in terms of promotion and salary.

To respond to the criticism, the recent judicial reforms have included a measure to render personnel evaluations more transparent and objective. Since 1 April 2004, the Supreme Court has made effective a rule clarifying evaluation items such as the ability to handle cases, the ability to properly administer a section or panel, and such general abilities as judges need to demonstrate in the discharge of their official duties.[143] In paying due attention to judicial independence, the presidents of the courts that judges belong to evaluate the judges' performance from various angles and are required to present the judges evaluated with documents of evaluation upon request. If a judge is dissatisfied with the result of an evaluation, he or she may file a complaint against the court president who filed the evaluation. The presidents of the courts then conduct an investigation and the presidents of high courts may conduct further investigations. As a result of the investigation process, the presidents of courts, if necessary, may amend the results of an evaluation or, if not, record the facts of the complaints and investigations. The judge who filed the complaint is informed of the results of the investigation process.[144] In this way, transparency and objectivity in the performance evaluation process for judges has been realized to a significant degree, although it is too early to conclude that the evaluation system has become sufficiently clear to maintain the independence of judges in the exercise of their powers.

In Japan there has consistently been an argument that a unified system of the legal profession is preferable to a career system. This argument's critique of the career system is that career judges are apt to obediently follow the will of senior judges and to have socially narrow views, owing to a lack of appropriate real-world experience. The recent judicial reforms rejected the Anglo-American style in which persons who desire to be judges must first be practicing lawyers, instead introducing a new system while continuing to emphasize applications from lawyers for judgeships. The new system is one in which assistant judges and public prosecutors who have served for less than ten years are allowed to obtain

[143] See the Supreme Court Rule Concerning Personnel Evaluation of Judges, Art. 3(1). The Supreme Court has made public detailed items and ways of evaluation.

[144] See the Supreme Court Rule Concerning Personnel Evaluation of Judges, Art. 5.

experience as practicing lawyers for two years.[145] Every year, about ten assistant judges and public prosecutors leave office to become attorneys-at-law. While it would be difficult to conclude with certainty that having two years of experience as practicing lawyers serves to enrich the social vision of assistant judges, we might assume a somewhat positive impact when these judges touch on social matters outside the judiciary.

An institution for appointing attorneys-at-law to judgeships has been another important measure to cultivate a wider social perspective among judges within the career system. The Japan Federation of Bar Associations has been enthusiastic in persuading member lawyers to apply for judgeships. However, the invitation has not necessarily been well received because practicing lawyers tend to dislike the restrictions that judges face. As of 1 February 2011, a total of sixty-three judges were ex-lawyers.[146]

To sum up, several measures have been taken to mitigate tight control over judges on the part of the General Secretariat of the Supreme Court. It is still too early to tell, however, whether these measures will lead to a revitalized judiciary.

5 Judicial review

The current Constitution, which became effective on 3 May 1947, introduced the power of constitutional review in Japan. The Supreme Court is now "the court of last resort with power to determine the constitutionality of any law, order, regulation or official act."[147]

The nature of this constitutional review power was once heatedly discussed. A number of constitutional scholars argued that the Constitution allows an abstract review of law by virtue of Article 81. The main reason they gave was that if, as Chief Justice John Marshall of the United States Supreme Court emphasized in *Marbury* v. *Madison*,[148] constitutional interpretation is a part of legal interpretation, and the task the judiciary carries out is the interpretation of law, a constitutional provision on the constitutional review of laws should be understood as a positive power of review. That is, such a provision might be a constitutional foundation for a constitutional court or an abstract review of law.

[145] See the Act Concerning Experiences as Practicing Attorney of Assistant Judges and Public Prosecutors (Act no. 121, 2004).

[146] See the Japan Federation of Bar Associations, *Bengoshi ninkan (jokin) Q&A* (Japan Federation of Bar Associations, 2011), p. 7.

[147] The Constitution of Japan, Art. 81.

[148] *Marbury* v. *Madison*, 5 US (1 Cranch) 137 (1803).

Following this thesis, a constitutional complaint concerning the National Police Reserve was filed directly to the Supreme Court of Japan in 1952.[149] The plaintiff was Suzuki Mosaburo, the Chairman of the Japan Socialist Party and a member of the Diet. He substantially alleged that all actions by the Japanese government since 1 April 1951 in connection with the establishment and maintenance of the National Police Reserve, including not only administrative acts but also actual acts and acts in private law, together with all laws, ordinances, and regulations concerning the establishment and maintenance of the reserve forces, were inconsistent with the constitutional provision for peace (Article 9). He also argued from a procedural point of view that Article 81 had established the Supreme Court as a constitutional court and thus the Supreme Court had proper jurisdiction over abstract review of law without any specific provisions on constitutional litigation.

In supporting a judicial review system, the Supreme Court unanimously rejected these arguments. The Supreme Court held that "under our present system, the decision of a court may be sought only when there exists a concrete legal dispute between specific parties." It continued, "There is no basis whatsoever in the Constitution, laws, or statutes to support the view that the courts have authority to determine the constitutionality of laws, orders, and the like in the abstract and in the absence of a concrete case."

Several years before this judgment, in fact, the Supreme Court had already declared that the power to review the constitutionality of a law is an element of judicial review power and thus a court may examine a concrete case or controversy. The Supreme Court thus contended that a constitutional provision on judicial review power might not be necessary because the power could well be drawn from clauses such as judicial power, supremacy of the Constitution or the obligation of officials to respect and uphold the Constitution (Articles 76, 98 and 99).[150] As a corollary, even lower courts may resort to judicial review as a part of the ordinary exercise of judicial power.[151]

The Supreme Court judgment in the case of the National Police Reserve has been a controlling precedent. In Japan, therefore, constitutional review means judicial review. There is no such thing as a constitutional suit per se. After civil, administrative or criminal litigation is

[149] Supreme Court Judgment, Grand Bench, 8 October 1952, *Minshu* 6-9-783.
[150] Supreme Court Judgment, Grand Bench, 8 July 1948, *Keishu* 2-8-801.
[151] Supreme Court Judgment, Grand Bench, 1 February 1950, *Keishu* 4-2-73.

properly filed in an ordinary judicial court, a court may exercise the power of judicial review. Even if a constitutional issue is appropriately and convincingly presented in a case, the court is understood to have wide discretion over whether to take up the constitutional question. The court is required to declare a judgment on the constitutionality of governmental actions only as far as it is necessary to solve the case. This is a rule of avoidance of constitutional judgments.[152]

Along with a handful of foreign scholars who are interested in Japanese law,[153] most Japanese constitutional scholars have denounced the Supreme Court as inactive and conservative. In constitutional litigation, for example, the Japanese Supreme Court has set a high threshold. Because the Supreme Court has adopted an extremely limited understanding of standing, this narrow approach has been criticized as reservation of litigation law. The Supreme Court has been substantially reluctant and inactive as well. It has almost always supported judgments by political departments. In fact, the Supreme Court has declared a statute unconstitutional only nine times in the past sixty-six years. They are the Patricide Case,[154] the Pharmacy Location Case,[155] the two Malapportionment Cases,[156] the Forest Division Limitation Case,[157] the Post Office Limited Liability Case,[158] the Overseas Voting Rights Case,[159] the Nationality Law Case,[160] and the Statutory Share in the Inheritance of an Illegitimate Child Case.[161] The Supreme Court has also judged a disposition unconstitutional in a few cases.[162] These judgments of unconstitutionality are classified into five

[152] See Justice Brandeis' concurring opinion in *Ashwander* v. *Tennessee Valley Authority*, 297 US 288 (1936).

[153] See, e.g., Ramseyer and Rasmusen, *Measuring Judicial Independence: Political Economy of Judging in Japan*; Law, "The anatomy of a conservative court," 1545. See also, D. S. Law, "Decision making on the Japanese Supreme Court," *Washington University Law Review*, 88 (2011), 1365.

[154] Supreme Court Judgment, Grand Bench, 4 April 1973, *Keishu* 27-3-265.

[155] Supreme Court Judgment, Grand Bench, 30 April 1975, *Minshu* 29-4-572.

[156] Supreme Court Judgment, Grand Bench, 14 April 1976, *Minshu* 30-3-223; Supreme Court Judgment, Grand Bench, 17 July 1985, *Minshu* 39-5-1100.

[157] Supreme Court Judgment, Grand Bench, 22 April 1987, *Minshu* 41-3-408.

[158] Supreme Court Judgment, Grand Bench, 11 September 2002, *Minshu* 56-7-1439.

[159] Supreme Court Judgment, Grand Bench, 14 September 2005, *Minshu* 59-7-2087.

[160] Supreme Court Judgment, Grand Bench, 4 June 2008, *Minshu* 62-6-1367.

[161] Supreme Court Decision, Grand Bench, 4 September 2013, *Minshu* 67-6-1320.

[162] I will mention some of the cases here. The Supreme Court held that the forfeiture of a third party's property without providing him/her with notice and the opportunity to excuse or defend himself/herself violated Articles 29 and 31 of the Constitution and declared it was unconstitutional as applied. (Supreme Court Judgment, Grand Bench,

categories: voting rights, equality, economic freedom and property rights, procedure rights, and religious freedom. An important area that is missing in judicial review is that of protecting freedom of expression. Although there have been many dubious laws and practices restricting free expression, the Supreme Court has never invalidated such laws and practices. Because freedom of expression is one of the most important rights in a liberal democracy, and its restriction is not easily reversed through the political process, the Supreme Court is supposed to play a pivotal role in protecting it. Unfortunately, this assumption, which is commonly a shared understanding in Japanese constitutional scholarship, has not been applicable to Japanese judicial practices. Thus, a general perception among most constitutional scholars is that it is no exaggeration to say that the Japanese Supreme Court has shown only a minimal presence in the liberal democratic process in postwar Japan.

There are several institutional reasons why the Japanese Supreme Court is so inactive. First of all, as we already saw, the Supreme Court Justices are so busy in dealing with ordinary final appeals that it is natural for them to be reluctant to take up constitutional issues, which are generally complicated, troublesome, and time-consuming, even if they would otherwise be willing to do so.[163] The backgrounds of Supreme Court Justices may be another reason. A majority of Justices have been trained to pay due respect to legality. Public prosecutors and governmental officials rarely cast doubt on the constitutionality of established law and practices. Control over judicial personnel by the General Secretariat may be another reason for inactive judicial review. Career judges may tend to avoid constitutional issues because participating in a decision of unconstitutionality could have a negative impact on their performance evaluations by the Supreme Court. A fourth possible reason is the existence and role of the Judicial Research Officials of the Supreme Court. They are veteran career judges of exceptional talent. Some of them are en route to becoming Supreme Court

28 November 1962, *Keishu* 16-11-1593.) The Supreme Court declared that the prefecture's expenditures from public funds to Yasukuni Shrine and Yehime Gokoku Shrine (religious corporations), which held rituals and ceremonies, violated Article 20, paragraph 3 and Article 89. (Supreme Court Judgment, Grand Bench, 2 April 1997, *Minshu* 51-4-1673.) The Supreme Court held that the decision of Sunagawa City in Hokkaido to offer city-owned lands to a joint neighborhood association for use as the site of a Shinto shrine facility without compensation was in violation of Article 89 and the second sentence of Article 20, paragraph 1 of the Constitution. (Supreme Court Judgment, Grand Bench, 20 January 2010, *Minshu* 64-1-1.)

[163] See Table 2.1.

Justices themselves. They might therefore be apt to evade controversial issues when discharging their duties as Judicial Research Officials. Or the Japanese Supreme Court may tend to preserve a pluralist democracy.[164]

A closer examination, however, shows a gradual change in the attitude of the Japanese Supreme Court toward constitutional litigation in the twenty-first century.[165] During the past thirteen years, the Supreme Court has invalidated a statute four times, whereas it did so only five times in the entire fifty-three-year period before that. As a matter of quality, moreover, the Court's more recent judgments of the unconstitutionality of certain laws have had much greater impact on Japanese society than have those made in the last century (with the exception of the Malapportionment Cases). The Supreme Court has now come to occupy a slightly more significant role in the liberal democratic process in Japanese society. We thus acknowledge some political dissatisfaction with the Court's judgments of unconstitutionality, particularly in the Nationality Law Case and the Statutory Share in the Inheritance of an Illegitimate Child Case. Accordingly, we can anticipate that the counter-majoritarian difficulty of judicial review, which we have previously recognized only as an American theory, will be realized even in Japan.

We may be curious about the causes of the Supreme Court's attitudinal change from practically inactive to somewhat more active. We might enumerate as possible explanations the heated arguments for establishing a constitutional court in place of the inactive Supreme Court, the end of the ideological confrontation of regime choice, and the recent changes in political power. It is too early to make any decisive judgment, however, because we cannot foresee at this moment whether the Supreme Court of Japan will continue to be active even in defying the pressures that majoritarian institutions may produce, which are a common feature of constitutional review in a democracy.

6 Conclusion

On 4 August 1947, the Supreme Court officially started its service as the highest court and constitutional court in postwar Japan. In his address to

[164] See Y. Hasebe, "The Supreme Court of Japan: its adjudication on electoral systems and economic freedoms," *International Journal of Constitutional Law*, 5 (2007), 296–307.

[165] For a more detailed examination of this change, see N. Kawagishi, "Japanese Supreme Court: an introduction," *National Taiwan University Law Review*, 8 (2013), 234–44, 255–8.

the people at the beginning of his term of service, the first Chief Justice, Mibuchi Tadahiko, expressed the newly born Court's dedication to justice for the Japanese people. The courts are places, he argued, to defend the people's rights and to realize justice and fairness. Under the new democratic constitution, he continued, the courts need to become courts for the people to the core. To do so, judges should not crouch in the small world of law but open their eyes wider, make their perspectives broader and pay close attention to what politics should be, including the movements of society, transformations in the world, and the direction of people's feelings and opinions. To cope with these, judges should diligently cultivate the requisite insights and abilities.[166]

Since then Japan has experienced marked economic growth and relatively stable social development. Have judges been able to meet Mibuchi's expectations? It may be said in answer to this that they have contained themselves within a relatively small world. Many judges seem to have been trained to concentrate on their own tasks in light of the established order. During the past sixty-six years, the Supreme Court and lower courts have played a limited role rather than fulfill the constitutional promise they once held. We cannot say with confidence that they have truly lived up to Mibuchi's ideals.

Contemporary Japan is replete with social problems – poverty, the fastest aging society in the world, declines in population, intergenerational inequality, conformism and the imposition of orthodox ideas, the impacts of globalization, and so on. Issues such as freedom, equality, and social justice are still pressing. To try to solve these difficult and complicated problems, due respect must be paid to the dignity of the individual, as the current Constitution has underscored. The judiciary in general and the Supreme Court in particular should have made greater contributions to these projects, because constitutional principles matter in the judicial process.[167] To realize Mibuchi's vision, the Supreme Court and lower courts should show leadership worthy of principled institutions in a liberal democracy. As the Supreme Court seems to have come at long last to a change, albeit slight, in its understanding of its task, discussion has only just begun on the role the Supreme Court and the judiciary should play in the contemporary world.

[166] See J. Nomura, *Saikousai Zensaigankan (All Supreme Court Justices)* (Tokyo: Sanseido, 1986), pp. 2–3.

[167] See R. Dworkin, *Taking Rights Seriously* (Harvard University Press, 1978).

References

Ashibe, N. *Kenpo*, 5th edn. (Tokyo: Iwanami Shoten, 2011)

Dworkin, R. *Taking Rights Seriously* (Harvard University Press, 1978)

Fujita, T. *Saikosai kaikoroku (The Memoirs on the Supreme Court)* (Tokyo: Yuhikaku Publishing, 2012)

Hasebe, Y. "The Supreme Court of Japan: its adjudication on electoral systems and economic freedoms," *International Journal of Constitutional Law*, 5 (2007), 296–307

Hasebe, Y. *Kenpo*, 5th edn. (Tokyo: Hatsubai Saiensusha, 2011)

Ichikawa, M., Sakamaki, T. and Yamamoto, K. *Gendai no Saiban*, 6th edn. (Tokyo: Yuhikaku Publishing, 2013)

Japan Federation of Bar Associations. *Bengoshi ninkan (jokin) Q&A* (Japan Federation of Bar Associations, 2011)

Kaneko, H. and Takeshita, M. *Saiban Ho*, 4th edn. (Tokyo: Yuhikaku Publishing, 1999)

Kawagishi, N. "Japanese Supreme Court: an introduction," *National Taiwan University Law Review*, 8 (2013), 231–60

Kisa, S., Miyazawa, S., Sato T., Kawashima, S., Mizutani, N. and Ageishi, K. *Gendai Shiho*, 5th edn. (Tokyo: Nihon Hyōron Sha, 2009)

Law, D. S. "The anatomy of a conservative court: judicial review in Japan," *Texas Law Review*, 87 (2009), 1545–94

Law, D. S. "Decision making on the Japanese Supreme Court," *Washington University Law Review*, 88 (2011), 1365–73

Nishikawa, S. "Saikosaibansho no ruutsu wo saguru," *Seikei Ronso*, 78 (2009), 1–82

Nomura, J. *Saikousai Zensaigankan (All Supreme Court Justices)* (Tokyo: Sanseido, 1986)

Nonaka, T., Nakamura, M., Takahashi, K. and Takami, K. *Kenpo II*, 5th edn. (Tokyo: Yuhikaku Publishing, 2012)

Oppler, A. C. *Legal Reform in Occupied Japan: A Participant Looks Back* (Princeton University Press, 1976)

Ramseyer, J. M. and Rasmusen, E. B. *Measuring Judicial Independence: Political Economy of Judging in Japan* (University of Chicago Press, 2003)

Sato, K. *Nihonkoku Kenpo Ron* (Tokyo: Seibundo, 2011)

3

Courts in the Republic of Korea: featuring a built-in authoritarian legacy of centralization and bureaucratization

JONGCHEOL KIM

This chapter aims to introduce the Korean judicial system to foreign readers who might be interested in comparative research in this field. Focus is given to its structural layout, with special reference to two built-in features: centralization and bureaucratization. These features lead us to the ongoing agenda of judicial reform, the significance of which can be found in the circumstances of Korean democracy since its formal establishment in the Korean Peninsula in the wake of Korea's liberation from the Japanese colonial rule and the ensuing American military regime in 1948. Although the Republic of Korea ("Korea"), internationally known as South Korea, has been recognized as one of the countries that succeed in achieving constitutional democracy together with economic development, there still remains an old legacy of colonial and authoritarian regimes. One example of such a legacy might be the highly centralized and bureaucratic judicial system, accompanied by its less democratic formation and functioning. Therefore, it is not surprising that since the watershed of Korean democratization in 1987, which resulted in a relatively stable and democratic constitutionalism in Korea compared to its predecessors and other Asian countries, judicial reform has been an ongoing project in the Korean democratization process. However, this does not mean that there has been no progress at all in this area; rather, there have been a few notable achievements, such as the successful establishment of a constitutional adjudication system and the introduction of a quasi-jury system in criminal proceedings.

The following begins with a general description of the Korean judicial system featuring the structural layout of the court system and sources and influences of its establishment. Then, I will attempt to analyze and

This work was supported by the National Research Foundation of Korea Grant funded by the Korean Government (NRF-2012S1A3A2033542).

evaluate them in terms of judicial independence, with a view to identifying the system's main features of centralization and bureaucratization.

1 General description of the Korean judicial system

1.1 The hierarchy of the courts and instances of trials

As Korea is a unitary nation in the sense that there is neither a federal system nor sub-national devolutionary territories, the dualist judicial system that can be easily found in a federal state does not exist.

In Korea's unitary judicial system, there are six types of courts: the Supreme Court as the highest court; high court (appellate trial); district court (first instance trial and exceptional appellate trial); patent court (appellate trial); family court (first instance trial); and administrative court (first instance trial).[1] The Supreme Court is the only court established by the Constitution, while the other five courts are constituted by the Court Organization Act as prescribed by Articles 101(2) and 102(3) of the Constitution. General jurisdictions such as civil and criminal proceedings are based upon the three instance system, which is composed of the district court as the court of first instance trial, the high court as the court of second instance trial and the Supreme Court as the ultimate court of appeal. District courts and high courts, sitting in two divisions (civil and criminal), hear both civil and criminal cases. Patent, family, and administrative courts are specialist courts entrusted with specialized jurisdictions. The patent court, ranked on the same level as the high courts, is assigned matters concerned with patents. Family courts deal with matters related to personal status and marriage and its dissolution. The administrative court is designated to hear administrative law issues.

Generally speaking, district courts are courts of first instance dealing with the facts and law of the cases brought before them. However, as the district court is divided between a single-judge division and a three-judge panel, the three judge panel as the court of second instance hears appeals from judgments by the single-judge division, unless the amount in dispute exceeds 50 million KRW.[2] In principle, the single-judge division deals with cases when the sum in dispute exceeds 100 million KRW or is incalculable. The appellate jurisdiction also deals with the facts as well as law of the cases, while the Supreme Court is envisaged to decide only matters related to the law governing the given cases.

[1] Court Organization Act, Art. 3(1).

[2] This case is heard by the High Court.

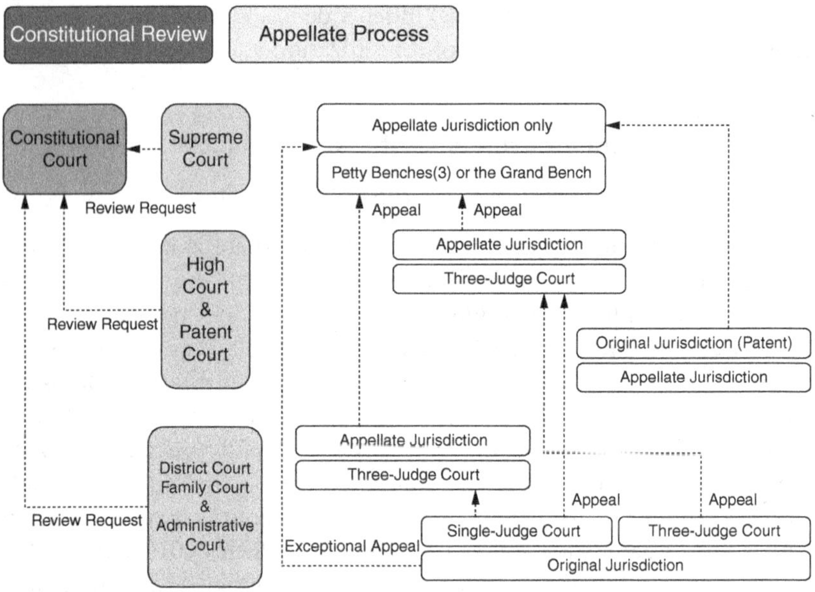

Figure 3.1: The hierarchy and jurisdictions of the courts in Korea

There are eighteen district courts nationwide, while five high courts are located in the major cities of Korea: Seoul, Busan, Daegu, Gwangju and Daejon. There is only one patent court, located in Daejon. Five family courts are located in the same cities where high courts are located.[3] A district court and a family court may establish branch courts and municipal courts (*Si* or *Gun* courts),[4] as prescribed by the Court Organization Act, as well as registration offices as prescribed by the Rule of the Supreme Court.[5] The administrative court is established only in Seoul.

1.2 *Organization of the courts*

The Supreme Court consists of fourteen justices including the Chief Justice.[6] The Chief Justice is appointed by the President with the consent of the National Assembly. Other justices are nominated by the Chief Justice and appointed by the President with the consent of the National Assembly.[7]

[3] There used to be merely two family courts in Seoul and Busan until 1 March 2012 when three family court branches were elevated into the family court.
[4] As of 13 March 2012, there are forty district court branches.
[5] Court Organization Act, Art. 3(2). [6] Court Organization Act, Art. 4(2).
[7] Constitution, Arts. 104(1) and (2).

In principle, the judgment authority of the Supreme Court is exercised by a collegiate panel composed of not less than two-thirds of all the Justices, with the Chief Justice presiding. However, in reality, most cases are dealt with by a panel[8] composed of three or more Justices, unless their opinions are in disagreement, or the cases or controversies fall into the categories that the Court Organization Act designates the principal collegiate panel to consider: (1) where it is deemed that any administrative decree or regulation is in violation of the Constitution or Acts; (2) where it is deemed necessary to modify such opinion on the application of the interpretation of the Constitution, Acts, administrative decrees, and regulations, as was formerly decided by the Supreme Court; and (3) where it is deemed that a trial by a panel is not proper.[9]

Article 102(2) of the Constitution permits the Supreme Court to have judges other than Justices; hence, Article 24 of the Court Organization Act introduces judicial researchers who are mainly appointed from among judges.[10]

The judgment authority of a high court, patent court or administrative court is exercised by a collegiate panel consisting of three judges.[11]

District courts, family courts and their branches consist of single-judge divisions except when a collegiate panel composed of three judges is required by statute.[12]

1.3 Special courts

Since the first Constitution, Korea has had a constitutional adjudication system, though its form varies from that of an independent commission, to that of a judicial review body, to that of a constitutional court. The current form is that of an independent court system. Chapter 6 of the Constitution, which consists of three articles, is designated for the powers and organization of the Constitutional Court, independent from not only the legislative and executive branches but also the judicial branch. The Constitutional Court is entrusted with five exclusive powers: (1) the

[8] Article 102(1) of the Constitution allows the Supreme Court to set up a panel system.

[9] Court Organization Act, Art. 7(1).

[10] As of September 2013, more than one hundred judges are appointed as judicial researchers to support Supreme Court Justices due to their extremely heavy workload.

[11] Court Organization Act, Art. 7(3). However, the collegiate panel of the administrative court may decide, if necessary, whether a single judge alone can exercise judgment authority.

[12] Court Organization Act, Art. 7(4).

constitutional review of Acts upon the request of ordinary courts; (2) impeachment trials; (3) dissolution of political parties; (4) competence disputes between state agencies, between agencies and local governments, and between local governments; and (5) constitutional complaints as prescribed by statute.[13]

The martial court is another special court, in the sense that military officers who are not qualified as judges may hear cases in martial court. However, unlike the Constitutional Court, military trials are subject to the appellate jurisdiction of the Supreme Court, with the exception of military trials under an extraordinary martial law in which no appeal may be allowed in the following types of cases: crimes of soldiers and employees of the military; military espionage; and crimes as defined by statute in regard to sentinels, sentry posts, supply of harmful foods and beverages, and prisoners of war.[14]

1.4 Jury or similar systems of citizen participation in trials

The ways in which citizens can take part in the judicial process are threefold, by and large. First, citizens may participate in judicial administration by, for example, attending a kind of advisory committee on personnel affairs, registration of realties or family relationships, the operation of courts, litigation procedures and other court affairs. Second, citizens may have an influence on the judiciary by proposing judicial policies or monitoring judicial decisions and administration. Third, most importantly, citizens can be involved in judicial judgments as a jury member or lay judge. In the course of Korea's democratization, Korean citizens have acquired all of these means of participating in the judicial process.

First, there is the Judicial Policy Advisory Committee set up by the Chief Justice as the head of judicial administration. Members of this committee are appointed by the Chief Justice from among those highly learned and respected with regard to understanding of judicial policies.[15] As far as judge personnel affairs are concerned, the Judges Personnel

[13] For a general introduction to the Korean constitutional adjudication system, see Jongcheol Kim, "The structure and basic principles of constitutional adjudication in the Republic of Korea" in K. Cho (ed.), *Litigation in Korea* (London: Edward Elgar Publishing, 2010), ch. 6.

[14] Constitution, Arts. 110(1) and (4). However, even in those cases, death sentences may be appealed to the Supreme Court.

[15] Court Organization Act, Art. 25.

Committee is charged with establishing and implementing a basic plan for judicial personnel affairs.[16]

Second, since the 1990s, a civic movement to monitor and reform the judiciary has been active. For example, People's Solidarity for Participatory Democracy ("PSPD"), one of the most powerful social movement associations in Korea, has run a working center for judicial monitoring along with a public interest law center. This civic activist group has had a great impact on judicial reform, such as the reform of the legal education and career development system (i.e. introduction of an American-style law school system)[17] and the Constitutional Court's ruling that a ban on night-time assemblies was an unconstitutional violation of the right to free assembly, among other examples. In 2008, a quasi-jury system called the "juror system" or "participatory trial system" was introduced in the Korean judicial system by the Act on Citizen Participation in Criminal Trials. However, in the new trial system, citizens' participation is recognized only in a very limited category of criminal cases.[18] Furthermore, the jurors' verdicts do not bind the court, so despite jurors' opinions, the presiding judges may decide differently.[19]

Third, lay citizens' participation in trial proceedings is institutionalized, though their power is limited. The limited power of lay jurors even in the new participatory trial system stems from an institutional barrier established by the Constitution. Article 27(1) provides that "All citizens shall have the right to be tried in conformity with the Act by *judges* qualified under the Constitution and the Act" and Article 101(1) of the Constitution stipulates that "Judicial power shall be vested in courts composed of *judges*." Also, other clauses envisaged to guarantee judicial independence explicitly provide strong protection for judges. For example, the minimum terms of all classes of judges are explicitly set by Article 105,[20] and any unfavorable treatment of them is prohibited by

[16] Court Organization Act, Art. 25-2.

[17] In the old system, every judge had to pass an extraordinarily tough state judicial exam and then be trained for two years at the Judicial Research and Training Institute together with those wishing to be prosecutors and private lawyers. This system was part and parcel of a hierarchical judges' career development system and has been criticized as having been a major factor in the creation of the country's highly bureaucratized judiciary. So the repeal of this old system was a first step towards a less bureaucratized judiciary.

[18] Act on Citizen Participation in Criminal Trials, Art. 5.

[19] Act on Citizen Participation in Criminal Trials, Art. 46(5).

[20] The minimum term of office of the Chief Justice and Justices of the Supreme Court is six years, while that of judges other than the Chief Justice and Justices of the Supreme Court is ten years.

Article 106.[21] This strong protection of judges' tenure is strengthened by the constitutional stipulation that judicial power is entrusted not to courts as an institutional entity itself but to courts as composed of special officials, i.e. judges. Such institutionalization of judges in constitutional clauses makes it very difficult for any lay citizen to take part in any stage of a judicial judgment, because such participation itself can be regarded as a violation of the constitutional guarantee of judicial independence, which focuses on judges' personnel protection together with specialization of judicial power.[22]

Since 12 February 2008, when the first participatory trial took place at Daegu District Court, as of 31 December 2011, some 574 cases have been heard through this new juror system, and in 520 of those cases (almost 90.6 percent), the jurors' verdicts were accepted by the judges concerned. In a jurors' survey, 96 percent of the jurors answered that they were satisfied with their exercise of duties as jurors, and the attendance rate of juror candidates was 28.4 percent.[23] The number of cases heard by the new participatory trial system has increased every year, from 64 in 2008 to 95 in 2009 and 165 in 2010.

1.5 Size and performance of the courts

Table 3.1 shows the maximum and actual numbers of judges on various courts. Exclusive of the Chief Justice and Supreme Court Justices, there were 2,552 judges as of 31 December 2011, resulting in a ratio of 4.9 judges per 100,000 inhabitants. Figure 3.2 indicates that the operation of the courts in Korea is very stable. The number of cases remains stable, as do the number of rejections, cases on the merits and non-litigation cases.

As for the distribution of cases, 4,351,411 civil cases represented the majority of the caseload in 2011, occupying about 69.2 per cent of a total

21 Article 106(1) stipulates that "no judge shall be removed from office except by impeachment or a sentence of imprisonment without prison labor or heavier punishment, nor shall he be suspended from office, have his salary reduced, or suffer any other unfavorable treatment except by disciplinary action" and Article 106(2) provides that "in the event a judge is unable to discharge his official duties because of serious mental or physical impairment, he may be retired from office under the conditions as prescribed by Act."

22 In fact, the Constitutional Court ruled that constitutional protection of citizens' rights to judicial access requires the legislature to provide every citizen with at least one chance to be judged both in trial on fact and in trial on law. See Korean Constitutional Court Decision 92Hun-Ga11, 28 September 1995, 7(2) *Korean Constitutional Court Reports* 264.

23 *Annual Report of Courts 2012*, p. 246.

Table 3.1: *Maximum and actual number of judges (as of 31 December 2011)*

	Presidents of HC and PC	Presidents of DC, FC and AC	Senior Judges and Judicial Researchers of HC and PC	Chief of BC	Senior Judges of DC, FC and AC	Judicial Researchers	Judges of HC and PC	Judges of DC and AC	Total
Maximum number	6	21 (+1)	117	42	437 (+34)	94	261	1,886 (−35)	2,844
Actual number	5 (−1)	21 (+1)	104 (+4)	42	366 (+15)	95 (+9)	191 (−24)	1,709 (+53)	2,552 (+76)

*HC: High Court; PC: Patent Court; DC: District Court; BC: Branch Court; FC: Family Court; AC: Administrative Court

Source: Annual Report of Courts 2012, pp. 86, 89

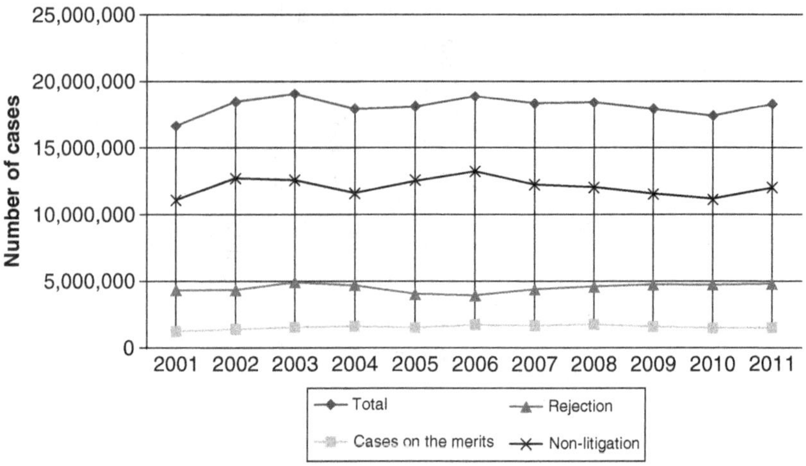

Figure 3.2: Composition of Cases
Source: Annual Report of Courts 2012, p. 534.

of 6,287,823 litigation cases. Criminal cases took second place, with 1,702,897 cases, representing roughly 27.1 per cent of total litigation cases. The number of family cases was 139,789 in the same year. Regarding non-litigation cases, general registration matters and registration matters concerning family relations represented the majority.[24]

Korean courts also seem quite efficient in their disposal of cases. The clearance rate of total cases is generally high and remains stable. According to the *Annual Report of Courts 2012*,[25] the number of cases filed in the courts has been around 18,000,000 each year since 2002, and the courts have disposed of almost the same number of cases. The clearance rate in the past decade has ranged from 98.7 percent (2007) to 100.6 percent (2009). The clearance rate remains high in all kinds of cases. Civil and criminal cases all enjoy a clearance rate of almost 100 percent. The gradually increasing caseload has not seemed to negatively impact the efficiency of the courts. Although the number of civil cases has increased significantly since 2003, the clearance rate has remained the same.[26]

In addition, the average period of clearance indicates efficiency. For civil cases, the average period of a first instance case is 164.9 days if decided by a single judge and 272.2 days if decided by a panel hearing.

[24] *Ibid*. p. 530. [25] *Ibid*. p. 613. [26] *Ibid*. p. 615.

For the Supreme Court, the average period of civil cases is 91.0 days if decided by a single judge and 139.8 days if decided by a panel.[27] As for criminal cases, the average period in the first instance by a panel hearing is 96.3 days if the defendants are held in custody and 139.2 days without detention. For Supreme Court cases decided by a panel hearing, the average period is 59.6 days if the defendants are in custody and 188.7 days without detention. For both administrative and family cases, the majority are generally decided in less than a year.[28]

2 Sources of and influences on the establishment of the judicial system

2.1 The pressure of modernization and Japanese influence in the nineteenth century

The introduction of a Western judicial system to Korea began with the efforts of the enlightened intellectuals in the Chosun Dynasty around the middle of the nineteenth century, but their influence was very limited because the ruling class indulged in a Confucian form of government that refused to adopt any new governmental system. With the growing pressure to open its market to foreign imperialists, however, the Chosun was forced to give up their "closed-door" policy (鎖國政策). This occurred formally with the Japan-Korea Treaty in 1876 (江華島條約), which contained an extraterritoriality clause stating that the Chosun Government did not have law enforcement powers over Japanese citizens in Korea. A group of young reformists equipped with new, Western ideas took advantage of this event, finally winning power in 1894 and pushing ahead with their reform policies, known as the Political Reform (甲午更張). The Reform included the enactment of the Court Composition Act of 1895 ("CCA 1895"), the first modern form of law made by the reformists, in which Western-style courts were established. Article 1 of the CCA 1895 provided five types of courts: the district courts, the courts at open port areas, the circuit court, the high court, the special court. This new system basically consisted of two instances, and both lower and upper courts were divided into dual dimensions. Generally, the high court and the circuit court had appellate jurisdiction, but they were not permanent institutions. Judicial administration was delegated to the Minister of Justice, who had the power to supervise judges, though the

[27] *Ibid.* p. 549. [28] *Ibid.* p. 567.

judges of the circuit court were also allowed to control district courts and the courts at open port areas like Pusan and Wonsan.[29]

However, this reform failed to be completed as planned. First, the reform lasted only two years because the reformists lost power in 1896, when King Gojong of the Chosun took refuge at the Russian legation (俄館播遷). Afterward, most judicial power was generally exercised in the traditional mode until the transfer of judicial power to the Japanese Residency-General (朝鮮統監府) and the so-called Judicial Improvement of Korea (司法改良) from 1907–10.[30] Second, as the reformists' judicial reform efforts were not entirely self-motivated but mostly led by Japanese imperialists, whose underlying intentions were to improve social systems for the purpose of entrenching imperialist interests, the modernization of the judicial system could have been difficult to establish in Korean society.[31]

2.2 *Japanese colonialism*

Without consideration of the impact of Japanese colonialism, any meaningful discussion of Korea's contemporary judicial system is unthinkable. This does not mean that all the developments of the Korean judicial system resulted from Japanese colonialism, but it cannot be denied that the current architecture of the judiciary was first formulated during the Japanese colonial period. Even since Korea's liberation in 1945, the direct and indirect influence of the Japanese judicial system, its judicial practices and its judicial jurisprudence has continued, though the influence of other countries like the USA, Germany and France has replaced it considerably. Considering that before 1945 the Japanese judicial system itself was not formulated according to that of a constitutional democracy, the impact of Japanese colonialism may be found in its negative effects.

[29] See J. Y. Moon, *The Birth of Courts and Prosecutors – The Republic of Korea through the Spectrum of the Judicial History* (Seoul: Yuk Sa Bi Pyeong Sa, 2010), pp. 180–2 (in Korean). For an official description of judicial reform in this period, see also Judicial Development Foundation, *The Judiciary in History* (Seoul: Judicial Development Foundation, 2009), pp. 25–9 (in Korean).

[30] Based on the Japan-Korea Treaty of 1907, the Court Composition Act was promulgated. It established four courts: the Supreme Court, the High Court, the District Court and the Municipal Court. It also introduced a three instance system modeled after the Japanese judicial system. For more information, see Moon, *The Birth of Courts and Prosecutors*, pp. 389–94.

[31] *Ibid.* pp. 194–226.

For example, the legacy of a bureaucratic and centralized colonial judiciary has survived even after liberation.

2.3 Democratization, social movements and the impact of globalization

Democratization goes hand in hand with judicial reform in the direction of enhancing the protection of individual rights, the rule of law and citizens' participation in the decision-making process. For example, the introduction of a constitutional court in the wake of the 1987 People's Uprising resulted in not only the development of democracy and the rule of law but also a significant improvement in public consciousness of the values of constitutional democracy. Since the establishment of the 1987 constitutional arrangements, the agenda of judicial reform has haunted every government. The Kim Young Sam government pursued judicial reform as part of its project of globalization as well as democratization. The dramatic increase in the number of lawyers was made possible in the course of reforms of both legal education and the hierarchical career system of the judiciary. Both the Kim Dae Jung and Roh Moo Hyun governments set up a special commission to pursue judicial reform. Despite this continuous effort over two decades, the achievements of this movement have been relatively unsatisfactory. The introduction of the law school system and citizens' participation trials are a few symbolic reflections of the movement's success. The Lee Myong Bak government was an exception because it was reluctant to reform the judiciary, preferring the old style of a bureaucratic judiciary. Ironically, this retroactive stance backfired, such that the necessity of judicial reform to cope with the resurgence of authoritarian statecraft became more apparent to the general public. The creation of a special committee within the National Assembly in 2010 to discuss judicial reform was the first time in which the legislature took the initiative on this issue. However, this move also faced institutional resistance from the judiciary and the Prosecutors' Office, and the special committee came to an end in 2011 without any significant results. This episode provides reformists and the public with the chance to understand why so many judicial reform initiatives were made in vain. It seems to have been proven that the core of judicial reform lies in how to deconstruct the fortified clan of self-interested lawyers entrenched in a homogenized institutional culture of not only the judiciary and law enforcement forces but also the practicing lawyers association. Judicial reform including reform of the prosecutorial system was one of the top issues in the general election in April and presidential election in December 2012.

With the democratization of society, the growing tensions among different social classes have accelerated social division and conflicts; in response to this, the judicial system also must change. For example, the administrative court was established as a separate specialized court so as to respond to the increasing occurrence of administrative conflicts and the unique character of administrative affairs in comparison to traditional civil cases. Also, with the advent of an aging society together with the increasing nuclearization of the family, family law cases are in transition in terms of their patterns, leading to an increase in mediation or arbitration in family court proceedings. Also, growing concerns about corporate wrongdoing are likely to drive the introduction of new systems in civil proceedings like class action, punitive damages and so on.

Economic crises in a globalized era also have had an immense impact on judicial systems. The need and pressure to accommodate international standards and law in one way or another has fundamentally altered Korea's judicial system. For example, as Korea has entered free trade agreements (FTAs) with the EU and USA, its judicial power is subject to the Investor State Dispute Settlement clause. Also, the opening of Korea's legal services market as part of such FTAs has had an impact on the judicial environment.

3 Sources of law and styles of judicial decisions

3.1 Sources of law

Korea adopted a continental legal system or civil law system as opposed to an Anglo-American legal system or common law system. Therefore, the main sources of law are written laws. Like most democratic countries, Korea has a written constitution as the supreme law of the land. Although it has a fine list of civil, political, cultural, economic and social freedoms and rights, it does not stipulate in detail concrete arrangements for constitutional institutions or their operation, instead delegating a number of matters to the legislature. The election system of the National Assembly, local autonomy, the basic structure of the three basic branches of government, and so on, are all left to be prescribed by Acts. Thus, statute law is the most important source of law, though it is subject to constitutional review by the Constitutional Court.

Presidential and departmental orders as subordinate legislation are other primary sources of law. Article 75 of the Constitution endows the President with the power of enacting presidential orders, while Article 95 of the Constitution gives the Prime Minister and heads of the executive ministries the power of promulgating departmental regulations.

Article 117 of the Constitution entrusts the power to enact legislation regarding local autonomy to local governments. Articles 22 and 23 of the Local Autonomy Act recognize two forms of autonomous legislation: (1) municipal by-laws or ordinances made by local councils; and (2) municipal rules by the heads of local governments. Although the binding force of this type of legislation is limited to the specific area, it is an important source of law because it very much affects people's actual way of life.

Since Article 6(1) of the Constitution stipulates that "Treaties duly concluded and promulgated under the Constitution and the generally recognized rules of international law shall have the same effect as the domestic laws of the Republic of Korea," international treaties and general principles can have binding force in Korea. According to the Korean Constitutional Court, the hierarchical status of international treaties in the domestic legal system may vary depending upon the nature of the treaty-making process and the treaty's contents.[32] Thus, if international treaties are recognized as domestic laws, they can be treated as a kind of statutory law that can invalidate inferior forms of law[33] and even older laws that are at the same level in the hierarchy.[34]

Finally, custom sometimes can be a source of law. Although in 2004 the Korean Constitutional Court recognized a customary constitution with the same force of law as codified constitutional provisions,[35] it has been generally said that in the field of public law, even if custom can be recognized as a source of law, its effect should be limited to supplementing written laws.[36] In the case of private law, customary laws can be recognized as a source of law. Article 1 of the Civil Code recognizes customary laws as a supplementary source of law while Article

[32] Korean Constitutional Court Decision, 29 April 1999, 97Hun-Ka14, 11-1 *Korean Constitutional Court Reports* 273 at 282.

[33] Korean Supreme Court Decision, 22 July 1986, 82Da-Ka1372 cited in Kyun Woo Han, *Korean Administrative Law*, 3rd edn. (2008), p. 11 (in Korean).

[34] Korean Supreme Court Decision, 9 September 2005, 2004Chu10 cited in Kyun Woo Han, *ibid.* p. 11.

[35] Korean Constitutional Court Decision, 21 October 2004, 2004Hun-Ma554 etc., 16-2(Ha) *Korean Constitutional Court Reports* 1.

[36] Han, *Korean Administrative Law*, pp. 12–13.

1 of the Commercial Code gives customary laws higher authority than the Civil Code, such that if commercial customs are in conflict with provisions of the Civil Code, the former prevail over the latter.

3.2 *The style of judicial decisions*

The writing style of judicial judgments is different from that of other types of writing. To make legal elements exact in context, there are a number of formalistic rules, which are one of the main standards against which trainees' writing skills and analytic capabilities are assessed in the main courses of the Judicial Research and Training Institute. For example, requisite facts in civil proceedings or facts charged in criminal proceedings are required to be described according to constitutive elements and principles of the laws applied to such facts, and, if possible, this is to be done in a single sentence.

Another feature of Korean judgments is that there are few citations of sources of the logic and principles that the judges rely on, except for those of laws or cases. Also, the style of judgments is short and concise, and the redundancy or unnecessary metaphor that we often find in American cases is taboo for good judicial writing. It is assumed that there would be concerns that such citations or redundant pedantic expressions could distort the genuine intention of the courts' jurisprudence or make it vulnerable to outside criticisms of the main jurisprudence. However, this does not mean that the judgments are written in very plain and readable language. Lay citizens may have difficulty understanding judgments, because of the usage of legal terms as well as the highly sophisticated writing style.

3.3 *Can judges make law?*

Although Korea is a civil law country and thus case law or judge-made law is not regarded as law, this does not mean that case law does not have any meaningful role in the Korean legal system. Indeed, the differentiation between the two types of legal systems is not an absolute one but a relative one. For one thing, even in the civil law system, the statutory interpretation of higher courts is, in reality, regarded as a highly authoritative standard for lower courts to use to interpret and apply statute laws in cases or controversies, although they have no binding force. As mentioned before, the hierarchical career system in the Korean judiciary has a great impact on judges, such that they must seriously consider the precedents set by the Supreme Court. Otherwise, they would face disadvantages in their career evaluations, which could be used against them in future personnel administration. However, judges' self-censorship in judicial judgments should not be exaggerated. If the precedents do not reflect social development, they can be challenged by lower courts.

Korean judges' self-esteem and sense of duty to keep Korean society moving in a desirable direction are relatively high, so, if they feel there are evident flaws in written laws, they are sometimes quick to take a stance in interpreting those laws. For example, the Supreme Court defied the clear meaning of Article 47(1) of the Constitutional Court Act,[37] in which the retroactive effect of a decision of unconstitutionality was limited to cases involving penal laws, by expanding the retroactive effect to non-penal laws.[38]

3.4 *Interpretive method*

The dominant interpretive method is a formalistic one. The analytic elements of law and the jurisprudence of relevant precedents are the main tools of judicial reasoning. Sometimes foreign legislation of relevance is used to supplement the main line of reasoning, but there are few cases that directly cite foreign case law or academic resources.

4 Judicial independence

Generally speaking, judicial independence can be viewed from three perspectives: functional independence, personal independence, institutional independence.

4.1 *Functional independence*

Functional independence, or independence from the intervention of other branches of government in the function with which the judiciary has been entrusted by the Constitution, is the most vital element. That is, independence in delivering judgments in cases or controversies is an

[37] The provision stipulates that "Any law or provisions thereof decided as unconstitutional shall lose its effect from the day on which the decision is made: Provided, That the law or provisions relating to any penalty shall lose its effect retroactively."

[38] Korean Supreme Court Decision, 16 July 1993, 93Da3783 cited in the Korean Constitutional Court, *A Brief Introduction to Practices of Constitutional Adjudication*, 2nd edn. (2008), pp. 152–3 (in Korean).

essential function of the judiciary. Article 103 of the Constitution declares that "Judges shall rule independently according to their conscience and in conformity with the Constitution and laws."

In past authoritarian regimes, outside threats – in particular, political and administrative threats – to judicial independence were the main concerns for Koreans. However, while governmental intervention seems to have decreased as part of the process of democratization (though problems still remained, especially during the Lee Myong Bak government),[39] internal threats have been drawing more concern than ever before. In the wake of more than one hundred days of candlelight demonstrations against American beef imports[40] across the nation in 2008, which seriously damaged the ability to govern of the newly launched Lee Myong Bak government, some young judges accused President Shin Young Chul of Seoul Central District Court ("SCDC") of recklessly intervening in a number of criminal cases involving those indicted for violation of the night-time assembly and demonstration prohibition, and of doing so by sending emails to and/or calling the judges assigned to those cases to persuade them not to decide in favor of the defendants. It is also alleged that, at first, SCDC President Shin assigned most of these demonstration offense cases to a particular judge whose conservative stance in this area was well known, but, after being challenged on this by other judges, he changed the way such cases were assigned. SCDC President Shin argued that he did not intervene in the cases substantively but instead did so for the purpose of efficient judicial administration, merely asking junior judges to accelerate the speed with

[39] Conservative lawyers and newspapers condemned young judges whose decisions were alleged to be in favor of liberals or progressives in some politically sensitive cases. For example, in criminal cases about the joint declarations on current issues by the National Teachers' Union ("NTU") in 2008, court decisions between the first instance and second instance trials and those between the first instance trials were split, and those judges who released the union teachers by denying any breach of the teachers' statutory duty of non-participation in collective activities were attacked by conservative forces including the Minister of Education, Science and Technology and the Minister of Justice. Another example occurred when a lawmaker of the ruling Hannara Party, National Assemblyman Cho Jun Hyuk, made public the list of teachers who were affiliated with the NTU, defying a court prohibition. He and his party's spokesperson publically condemned the judge who ordered him not to open that list as a left-leaning, biased judge.

[40] They were first initiated to challenge Lee Myong Bak government's policy of opening domestic markets to American beef suspected of being infected with mad cow disease, but, as the demonstrations continued, public discontent with comprehensive political and social issues like the restructuring of labor relations in the public sector and strict regulation of citizens' freedom of expression became their focus.

which they handled the cases. However, considering that one of the judges in charge of the cases referred the question of the constitutionality of the prohibition to the Constitutional Court, and judicial practice in such a case is to hold the original case pending until the Constitutional Court issues its decision, the SCDC President's intervention cannot be justified in the name of efficient judicial administration. Indeed, the Supreme Court Ethics Committee found that there were unsuitable activities on the part of SCDC President Shin, and the Chief Justice of the Supreme Court warned that he must not engage in such misconduct again. What inflamed more public suspicion in this case is the fact that President Shin, who had lost two previous chances to be appointed as a Supreme Court Justice, was on the list of promising candidates for the next Justice. Interestingly, he was appointed as the next Justice despite public concerns about his unsuitable actions, while Judge Park Jae Young, the very young judge who allegedly challenged President Shin's actions, resigned from office.

4.2 *Judges' personal independence: judicial appointments and guarantees*

4.2.1 Judicial appointments

The functional independence of the judiciary cannot really be guaranteed without judges' personal independence. In particular, personnel matters are the most important factor in guaranteeing judges' personal independence. In this regard, the term of office is one concern, and another is the danger of dismissal or disadvantage.

According to Chapter 5 of the Constitution, there are three classes of judges: (1) the Chief Justice of the Supreme Court, (2) Supreme Court Justices, and (3) ordinary judges other than the Chief Justice and Justices of the Supreme Court. The Chief Justice serves a single six-year term and is appointed by the President with the consent of the National Assembly. Justices of the Supreme Court serve six-year, one-time renewable terms and are appointed by the President on the recommendation of the Chief Justice and with the consent of the National Assembly.[41] The total number of Justices including the Chief Justice is fixed at fourteen according to Article 4(2) of the Court Organization Act. Other judges, whose minimum term is ten years with renewability until the statutory

[41] Constitution, Arts. 104(1) and (2).

retirement age, are appointed by the Chief Justice with the consent of the Supreme Court Justices Council. The number of all judges is prescribed separately by statute, but the number of judges assigned to each court is decided by the Rules of the Supreme Court.[42]

In Korea, judges on good behavior are well protected from any threat or danger of dismissal and any disadvantages in relation to their exercise of judicial power. Judges can be dismissed from office only by impeachment or a sentence of imprisonment without prison labor or heavier punishment. Only disciplinary action based upon reasonable evidence and due process can suspend judges from office, reduce their salaries, or make them suffer any other unfavorable treatment.[43] Even in the event that a judge is unable to discharge his official duties because of serious mental or physical impairment, he may be retired from office under the conditions as prescribed by statute.[44]

4.2.2 Qualifications and training system of judges

All justices and judges must meet the qualifications for judges prescribed by statute. At the moment, only those who meet the qualifications to be lawyers can be appointed as judges. The problem with this system lies in the state-controlled and highly homogenized judicial career system. Until recently, only a small number[45] of elites who passed the notorious state judicial exam and were trained for two years in a closed and condensed program at the Judicial Research and Training Institute (JRTI)[46] could qualify to be judges.[47] They were selected mainly on the basis of their exam results, both at the judicial examination and at the JRTI, with not

[42] Court Organization Act, Art. 5(3). [43] Constitution, Art. 106(1).

[44] Constitution, Art. 106(2).

[45] The number of successful candidates was fewer than one hundred per year when those who now occupy the most senior judgeships began their careers in their early twenties. In the early 1980s, the number was increased to around 300 per year, and since the end of the 1990s until 2010, the number reached around 1,000.

[46] Besides the JRTI, there is another training institute affiliated with the Supreme Court: the Training Institute for Court Officials. This institute provides a training and development program for court clerks, marshals and other staff members of the judiciary.

[47] An exception to this is the Military Judiciary Examination designed to select judge advocates, which has been the other route to becoming a lawyer. Successful candidates are required to complete the lawyer training program at JRTI and serve as a military judicial officer in the army, navy or air force for at least ten years to be fully qualified to practice as lawyers or judges. However, this institute's quotas are very limited, and the possibility of judge advocates from this track being chosen as judges has been very low, so the National Judicial Examination can be said to be in practical terms the only route to becoming a lawyer and ultimately a judge. Incidentally, successful candidates of the

much consideration of their educational background. Moreover, since they were trained together with future prosecutors and practicing lawyers in a closed atmosphere, they were often under suspicion of "JRTI cronyism". As far as the patronage problem in judicial appointments is concerned, the more serious problems stem from college or high school cliques or regionalism. The "Big 5" universities, namely Seoul National, Korea, Yonsei, Hanyang and Sungkyungwan Universities, dominate the judicial personnel map, which can definitely increase the homogeneity of the judiciary.

In 2010, graduates affiliated with the "Big 5" universities together represented 89 percent of new judges.[48] The top judiciary is even more homogeneous with respect to graduates of prestigious universities. For example, statistics published in 2003 show that 83.6 percent of senior judges are affiliated with Seoul National University. The same report also shows a similar pattern in qualified lawyers: only 7.6 percent of lawyers qualified in 2003 were not affiliated with the "Big 5".[49]

To address the homogeneity of career judges (though this was surely not the only purpose), the introduction of an American-style law school system with a bar exam replacing the old judicial exam took place in 2007. The JRTI is scheduled to be abolished, at least for the purpose of training newly qualified lawyers,[50] until 2019. New judges will be appointed from law clerks or practicing lawyers with more than five years of legal experience.

Despite this legal education reform, the total number of law school students is still tightly controlled by the Minister of Education.[51] Furthermore, the newly introduced bar exam is also controlled by the Minister of Justice.[52] In other words, the number of successful candidates and the methods of selecting them are all controlled by the

National Judicial Examination are entitled to serve as judge advocates as part of their military obligation after training at JRTI.

48 *Hangyeoreh 21*, 799, 26 February 2010 (in Korean).

49 The statistics are relatively old, but it is safe to assume that the pattern has continued until the present.

50 JRTI's other function is to retrain judges in order to develop their capacity and enhance their knowledge. The training programs consist of training based on judicial experience and legal areas, and training in the form of judicial seminars. Training programs based on judicial experiences include the newly appointed judges' program, the municipal judges' program, etc.

51 Act on the Establishment and Management of Professional Law School, Art. 7(1). Currently, the annual quota of law school students is fixed at 2,000.

52 National Bar Examination Act, Art. 3.

state.[53] Although 25 newly established law schools are expected to produce around 1,500 lawyers, the problem of the homogeneity of judges' educational backgrounds may continue, because it is highly likely under the current state-controlled system that top law schools with better brand images would dominate over minor or regional law schools in the lawyer recruiting market, and, in particular, the judge selection process.[54]

This longstanding state-dominated system has its origin in the judicial personnel system of the Japanese colonial period, in which, like prosecutors, judges were selected by the Higher Civil Service Examination. Legal education reform together with reform of the judicial personnel system will change this bureaucratized legacy, but the continuing state control of law school admissions and the bar exam will extend the span of the old regime. At any rate, the fact that judges have been appointed from a state-controlled group with a highly homogenized and bureaucratic culture can at least partly explain why Korean courts are still criticized for their high level of bureaucratization and centralization.

4.2.3 The problem of early retirement

From the view of the term of office, Korea cannot be categorized as a country that protects the personal independence of its highest justices, because the Chief Justice can serve only for six years while the Supreme Court Justices serve six-year terms with one-time renewability. The combination of a relatively short term with renewability in Justices' final careers may cause two different but ultimately similar problems.

First, if a justice is interested in being reappointed, he or she cannot help but be aware of the political or social powers that may have an influence on the judicial appointment process. Under this system, regardless of the actual circumstances, the reappointed justice is likely to be suspected of political and/or social prejudice or bias. As the rate of reappointment is not high, this problem seems to have caused no serious harm to Korean society. However, the danger is still inherently embedded in the current system and may come to the surface if there is a change in the current trend of relatively early retirement of senior judges compared to that of judges serving in countries with tenure systems.

[53] In the first two bar exams (2011 and 2012), the pass rate was fixed at around 75 percent of the state-authorized total number of law school students each year, i.e. 2,000.

[54] It is also assumed that undergraduate university degrees of new judges would be likely to show the dominance of the traditional "Big 5" universities.

Second, more seriously, the early retirement of the highest or most senior judges in a hierarchical career system may increase the danger of judicial corruption. Due to a hierarchical and quasi-bureaucratic culture, most senior judges who fail to be appointed as Supreme Court Justices or Senior Judges (presiding judges) of high courts retire before their tenure expires[55] and become practicing lawyers. According to data from 2004, 92.9 percent of all judges were below fifty years of age.[56]

This means that the judiciary is not the final destination of most judges' careers but a "depot" for practicing lawyers. This cultural practice is the main reason why Korea has suffered from a peculiar syndrome, called "Jeon-gwan-ye-u" (前官禮遇), in which former judges who become practicing lawyers, especially those recently retired from senior judgeships, receive special treatment from their incumbent former colleagues or junior judges. This practice has been a major factor in the low levels of public confidence in the judicial system. Until 17 May 2011, when Article 31(3) and (4) of the Attorney-at-Law Act was adopted, prohibiting any former judge or prosecutor from opening a law office in the region in which his/her final year in office was spent, it was an open secret that newly retired Supreme Court Justices could easily amass great fortunes in their first or second year of retirement.[57]

4.2.4 The problem of the hierarchical career system

The underlying root of the abuse of judicial administrative power is the hierarchical career system. In principle, nobody, not even the Chief Justice as the ultimate holder of judicial administrative power, can intervene in a judge's decision-making process. A hierarchical career

55 Article 45(4) of the Court Organization Act stipulates that the age limit of the Chief Justice and Justices of the Supreme Court shall be seventy years of age, and of other judges, sixty-five years of age.

56 D. Kim, "Career patterns of the Korean judges," *Korean Journal of Law and Society*, 31 (2006), 180.

57 This has been indirectly verified in the hearing process for those retired senior judges who returned to the judiciary to be appointed as Supreme Court Justices. For example, the recently retired Chief Justice Lee Yong Hoon who served as a Supreme Court Justice until 2000 and then practiced before his appointment as Chief Justice in 2005 allegedly earned half a billion KRW (equivalent to roughly 4 million US dollars) for only five years as a practicing lawyer. From his report of his and his family's assets, it was assumed that he represented 397 cases, 70 percent of which were related to cases pending at the Supreme Court. See Views & News internet edition (22 September 2006) at www.viewsnnews.com/article/view.jsp?seq=6668 (in Korean).

system or decision-making process is incompatible with this principle. However, although there are no formal differences among judges in their legal status, actual hierarchical ranks between senior and junior judges and concomitant differences in terms of role and social recognition exist. Until now, a judge begins his/her career as a trainee of the JRTI and advances in the following hierarchical order: junior associate judge of a collegiate panel at the district court level → judge of a single-judge bench at the district court level → junior associate judge of a collegiate panel at the high court level → senior judge (presiding judge) of a collegiate panel at the district court level or judicial researcher at the appellate court level including the Supreme Court → senior judge (presiding judge) of a collegiate panel at the high court level → President of District/High Court or Supreme Court Justice. The standard of assignment of these ranks customarily has been exam records and performance evaluations conducted by senior judges of a panel or court presidents. The final say in regard to personnel matters lies with the Chief Justice, though he or she needs the consent of the Supreme Court Justices Council and the advice of the Judges Personnel Committee. It is likely that the hierarchical career system combined with the implicit influence of judicial administrative power tends to make judges (1) reluctant to take a liberal or progressive stance in interpreting laws and precedents, and (2) vulnerable to judicial administrative intervention.

4.2.5 Two contemporary issues relating to judges' personal independence

Recently, two issues regarding judges' personal independence were being debated in Korea. First, ideologically driven intimidation has begun to infringe upon judges' personal independence. Conservatives continually attack a research group of liberal judges, called *Uri-Bub-Yeonguhoe* ("UBY", the Research Group for *Uri* Law Study),[58] alleging that this

[58] This research group, known as an association of liberal judges, was founded in 1988 at the peak of the Korean democratization movement. In the wake of the fall of President Chun Doo Whan's iron-fisted rule, a number of liberal associations that had been oppressed under long-lasting authoritarian regimes blossomed in Korean civil society. Uri Law Group was one of this kind created along with other law academics' research groups (established with similar vision in this period like *Bub-Gwa-Sahoe-Yeonguhoe* (the Korean Law and Society Association) and *Minjujuui-Bubhak-Yeonguhoe* (the Democratic Law Studies Association) and liberal practicing lawyers society (*MinByun*, the Lawyers for a Democratic Society). With the advent of two liberal governments, i.e. the Kim Dae Jung and Roh Moo Hyun governments, the original members of Uri Law Group

group and its members intentionally damage the neutrality of the judiciary by deciding cases based on their personal ideology or political biases. During the Lee Myong Bak government, a number of civil and criminal cases of political significance were brought before the courts. In the so-called Representative Kang's violence case in 2010, a young judge of the Seoul Southern District Court delivered a not-guilty verdict to Representative Kang Ki Gap of the Democratic Labor Party, who was indicted for violent activities in the National Assembly. This judge consequently faced ideological and personal attacks by conservative media, politicians and activists. In several cases where a number of teachers belonging to the National Teachers' Union were indicted for their joint declarations on a couple of current issues, those judges who delivered not-guilty verdicts were also subject to serious criticism from conservatives. In the so-called "PD's Notebook" case, in which producers of an in-depth television report were indicted for defamation offenses, a judge of Seoul Central District Court delivered a not-guilty verdict and faced similar attacks from conservatives. In almost all these cases, conservatives have argued for the dissolution of UBY on the grounds that it has been the basis of a series of liberal decisions, regardless of whether or not those judges in those decisions actually belonged to it. The continual ideological attacks on a research group of judges and its members definitely raise serious concerns about judicial independence.

Second, judges' writing or other activities in the private sphere has become another hot potato in Korean society. Judge Seo Ki Ho of the Seoul Northern District Court became popular due to his derogatory comments about President Lee Myong Bak in his Facebook and Twitter messages. He was reported to ridicule President Lee by saying "Gakha" (literally "his highness" in Korean) should be "kicked on his ass" because of his oppressive policy toward online expression. He received a warning from his judicial administrator, and finally, in February 2012, he was dismissed from his post during his reappointment process on the grounds that his record in the career evaluation system was too poor for him to be reappointed. He challenged the dismissal and vowed to take legal action including filing a constitutional complaint. Since dismissal of

assumed important posts not only in the judiciary but also in the executive branch. For example, the first chairperson of Uri Law Group, Park Si Whan, was appointed as a Supreme Court Justice, while another outstanding founding member, Kang Geum Sil, was appointed as the first Minister of Justice in the Roh government.

judges is very rare in the reappointment process conducted every ten years, public suspicion grew that Judge Seo's dismissal was a political sanction for his online statements.[59]

4.3 Institutional independence: judicial budget and judicial administration

Institutional independence is another backbone of the functional independence of the judiciary. The independent functioning of the judiciary is unthinkable without effective budgetary and administrative support. However, judicial independence is not the only concern in deciding how much financial and administrative support is to be given to the judiciary. National budgets must be determined and controlled by the representatives of the sovereign nation according to the constitutional principle of democracy. The principle of checks and balances requires corroboration among branches in formulating and determining the size and portfolio of the national budget, depending on the financial situation of the nation. The principles of democracy and separation of powers also require functional specialization together with efficiency of administrative affairs so that court administration is not necessarily separated from other governmental administration. In sum, how to reconcile the need for judicial independence with other constitutional requirements depends upon the democratic will of the nation, unless the Constitution itself stipulates specific policies. The Korean Constitution leaves a wide margin of discretion to the National Assembly on these matters, and the current statutory arrangements very much cherish judicial independence, though the judiciary tends to demand more autonomy in this regard.

[59] Of course, the Supreme Court spokesperson speaking on behalf of the Chief Justice, who holds the power to reappoint Justices, denies this accusation, citing Article 45-2(2) of the Court Organization Act, which provides that "The Chief Justice of the Supreme Court shall not issue an official order of reappointment to the judges who are deemed to fall under any one of the following subparagraphs: 1. Where it is impossible for him to perform the normal duties as a judge due to the physical or mental handicaps; 2. Where it is impossible for him to perform the normal duties as a judge due to *a remarkable inferiority of service records*; and 3. Where it is remarkably difficult to keep the dignity of judge" (emphasis added). Although in the case of Judge Seo, only Article 45-2 Item 2 was applied, in Item 3 of the same clause (underlined in the above quotation), the standard of the dignity of the judge seems to be too vague to give a clear standard for dismissal, especially considering the constitutional safeguards of judges' personal independence.

4.3.1 Judicial budget

Article 82 of the Court Organization Act provides that "expenses of courts are appropriated independently in the national budget. The autonomy and independence of the courts should be respected in formulating the budget of the courts."

As the budget of the courts is a part of the national budget though independent from other government agencies, it is determined according to the general constitutional and statutory procedures regarding budget approval. With the deliberation and resolution of the Supreme Court Justices Council, the Chief Justice of the Supreme Court[60] prepares a request for the revenue and expenditure budgets and other statutory requirements and submits it to the Minister of Strategy and Finance no later than June 30 of each year.[61] However, as acknowledged in Article 82 of the Court Organization Act, the independence of the courts in formulating their own budget is crucial in keeping their functional independence at a sustainable level. This constitutional need requires special treatment of the courts' budget in the budget formulation and approval process. Therefore, the Executive, as the branch with the power of budget formulation, is required to respect the opinion of the Chief Justice to the fullest extent practicable and to consult with him in advance when it is necessary to make an adjustment according to the financial situation of the State.[62] If the Executive, notwithstanding its consultation with the Chief Justice, intends to reduce the amount demanded by the judiciary for its expenditure budget, it should seek the opinion of the Chief Justice during a meeting of the State Council, the highest deliberation body in the Executive. Aside from these consultation processes, if the Executive decides to reduce the expenditure budget demanded by the judiciary, the Chief Justice may submit his or her opinion on the size of and reasons for the reduction and on the reduction itself to the National Assembly.[63]

[60] As far as judicial administration, in particular external relations including budget affairs, is concerned, the role of the Chief Justice as the head of the judiciary is in practice performed by the Minister of the National Court Administration though under the direction and supervision of the Chief Justice. See Articles 69 and 70 of the Court Organization Act and the Supreme Court, *Introductory Book of the Supreme Court of Korea*, p. 32.

[61] Court Organization Act, Art. 17(4); National Finance Act, Art. 31(1).

[62] This special treatment is also given to the heads of other independent government bodies like the National Assembly, the Constitutional Court and the National Electoral Commission. See National Finance Act, Art. 40(1).

[63] National Finance Act, Art. 40(2).

4.3.2 The administration of the judiciary: the problem of instrumental judicial administration

4.3.2.1 Independent judicial administration As far as judicial administration is concerned, the judiciary is institutionally guaranteed to enjoy full-fledged autonomy unless it intends to contravene the limit set by the legislature. General judicial administrative affairs are to be handled by the National Court Administration ("NCA") affiliated with the Supreme Court. The ultimate power and responsibility of judicial administration lies in the hands of the Chief Justice, but, practically speaking, the Minister of the NCA appointed by the Chief Justice from among the Supreme Court Justices is in charge of the affairs of the NCA.[64] The Vice Minister of the NCA is appointed by the Chief Justice from among the senior judges to assist the Minister and to act on his or her behalf if he or she is absent or is unable to perform his or her duties.[65]

As the legislature delegates all relevant powers to the judiciary except the establishment of the offices, bureaus and sections themselves, the organization of the Court Administration Office is determined by the Rules of the Supreme Court.

4.3.2.2 The problem of instrumental judicial administration In his analysis of the Japanese judicial system, Professor Mark Levin defines "instrumental judicial administration" as "mechanisms or actions employed by judicial administrators to intentionally bias adjudicatory processes in favor of a particular party or result despite lacking authority as to the disposition of the subject case or class of cases. In other words, intentional actions, carried out through the exercise of judicial administration that aim to distort a structurally neutral court proceedings towards a result determined extrinsically from the litigation process between the parties."[66] According to Professor Levin, this negative feature[67] is in evidence in Japanese civil proceedings, though Japan's judiciary "enjoys a globally recognized reputation for its institutional

[64] Court Organization Act, Arts. 67(2) and 68(1).

[65] Court Organization Act, Arts. 67(3) and 68(2).

[66] M. Levin, "Civil justice and the constitution: limits on administrative judicial administration in Japan," *Pacific Rim Law and Policy Journal*, 20(2) (2011), 267–8.

[67] Since it inevitably has a detrimental effect on fairness, although, as Levin properly clarifies, this conception is not synonymous with corruption, its overall impact should be negative: M. Levin, "Civil justice and the constitution," 267–8.

integrity and the integrity of the judges within it."[68] As far as the peculiarities built into the Korean judiciary are concerned, the concept of instrumentality of judicial administration is applicable to it, in particular considering its highly bureaucratized and centralized but very independent judicial administration. Korea's judiciary has all the characteristics of instrumental judicial administration: an elite-oriented recruiting and selection system for judges, the lack of transparency in the judicial appointment process, a hierarchical career system, the proselytization of particular approaches to interpretations of the law, and rare but assumedly direct intervention in actual cases.

As we have seen above, the first tier of instrumental judicial administration, the elitist selection system, is now changing, though with very limited effect for the time being, through the introduction of a new legal education and judicial recruiting system. The problem with judicial appointments and career paths can be indirectly found in statistics showing (1) de facto patronage routes for promotion, and (2) lack of diversity in the judiciary. The constitutionally established omnipresent power of the Chief Justice together with the lack of democratic control of this power can also be a cause of the negative effects of independent judicial administration. The proselytizing aspect of judicial administration was also mentioned when we discussed judges' personal independence. Finally, a case of direct intervention can be found in the recent episode involving SCDC President Shin discussed earlier. Following are further descriptions and explanations regarding the relationship of judicial administration and promotion in the judiciary and the omnipresent power of the Chief Justice.

Article 71(4) of the Court Organization Act allows judges to be appointed as chiefs of the administrative organs, and practically all major administrative chiefs are appointed from among judges. In general, as those judges serving in the NCA have been regarded as promising judges with better chances of attaining senior judgeships, one's career in the NCA is an important element of a "royal route" to becoming a top judge in the notoriously hierarchical career system. As of September 2013, among 134 senior judges, 46 (34.3 percent) have worked at the NCA,[69]

[68] *Ibid.* 268–70.

[69] Yonhap News Agency, "Shadows of the judiciary (3): NCA, A royal route to senior judge," 25 September 2013 (http://news.naver.com/main/read.nhn?mode=LSD&mid=sec&sid1=102&oid=001&aid=0006498025) (in Korean). This circumstance has never been changed in the modern history of the Korean judiciary. For this, see Kim, "Career patterns of the Korean judges," Table 8, p. 177.

and 107 (79.9 percent) graduated from Seoul National University.[70] The dominant role of judges in judicial administration combined with the promotional effect of such service on judicial career paths may have contributed to the consolidation of the bureaucratization and centralization of the judiciary, as well as to the corrupted relationship between the Executive and the Judiciary.

The excessive empowerment of the Chief Justice may be another issue challenging judicial administration. The ultimate authority of the hierarchical judiciary in Korea is the Chief Justice. The constitutional status of the Chief Justice has become fortified. Under the current constitutional arrangement, the Chief Justice has immense independent power affecting not only the judicial system but also political or constitutional arrangements. First, within the judiciary, he or she has the ultimate administrative power: the power to recommend Supreme Court Justices, to appoint judges, and to assign judicial positions to judges, though there are some procedural controls like the consent of the Council of the Supreme Court Justices. Second, outside the judiciary, the Chief Justice also has powers of constitutional importance in being entitled to have a voice in the composition of other independent constitutional bodies: he or she can recommend three out of nine Constitutional Justices as well as three out of nine Commissioners of the National Electoral Commission. In particular, in the case of the latter, a well-entrenched practice is that one of the Commissioners is recommended by the Chief Justice from among the Supreme Court Justices and becomes the chairperson of the Commission.

Despite the excessive internal or external empowerment of the Chief Justice, however, his or her appointment is still dependent upon the political will of the time, as it requires the agreement of both the presidential and legislative powers. In tandem with all the other problems of the hierarchical career path, the early retirement of judges, the domination of judicial administrators, the almighty Chief Justice and his or her dependence upon the confidence of the other branches of government have reinforced the bureaucratization and centralization of Korea's judiciary.

What makes these pathological problems so entrenched in the judicial arrangements? Two hypotheses can be provided. First, the autocrats' conspiracy may explain not all but a part of the story. One may easily

70 Yonhap News Agency, "Shadows of the judiciary (3)."

assume that a centralized and bureaucratized judiciary, at the top of which is a Chief Justice with almost omnipresent administrative power, is easier for authoritarian rulers to control than a decentralized and less bureaucratic judiciary. Second, the special interests of judicial elites who have a strong sense of entitlement that is consolidated in the homogenized judicial culture would distort the constitutional principle of judicial independence by replacing it with judges' administrative independence. Instead of enhancing judicial control of authoritarian abuses of power and protecting the rule of law, this fortified bureaucratic administrative independence has a great impact on the exercise of judicial power in the direction of proselytizing particular approaches to interpretations of laws, especially in cases in which politically or socially sensitive matters are at stake.

5 Concluding remarks

Despite continuing micro-level advancements in judicial performance, the credibility of and public confidence in the courts still need to be improved. Judicial reforms at the macro-level, in particular those policies crucial to the eradication of fundamental problems of bureaucratization and centralization of the judiciary, are necessary to upgrade Korean constitutionalism. Having said that, whether or not we need judicial reform is no longer in question; rather, when, how, and, last but not least, by whom these reforms can be achieved, in the face of a built-in authoritarian legacy of centralization and bureaucratization, are the questions Koreans must tackle in the ongoing process of democratization.

References

Han, Kyun Woo. *Korean Administrative Law*, 3rd edn. (Seoul: Shin Young Sa, 2008) (in Korean)

Judicial Development Foundation. *The Judiciary in History* (Seoul: Judicial Development Foundation, 2009) (in Korean)

Kim, D. "Career patterns of the Korean judges," *Korean Journal of Law and Society*, 31 (2006), 165–86

Kim, J. "The structure and basic principles of constitutional adjudication in the Republic of Korea" in K. Cho (ed.), *Litigation in Korea* (London: Edward Elgar Publishing, 2010), ch. 6

Levin, M. "Civil justice and the constitution: limits on administrative judicial administration in Japan," *Pacific Rim Law and Policy Journal*, 20(2) (2011), 265–318

Moon, J.Y. *The Birth of Courts and Prosecutors – The Republic of Korea through the Spectrum of the Judicial History* (Seoul: Yuk Sa Bi Pyeong Sa, 2010) (in Korean)

The Constitutional Court of Korea. *A Brief Introduction to Practices of Constitutional Adjudication*, 2nd edn. (Seoul: The Constitutional Court of Korea, 2008) (in Korean)

The Constitutional Court of Korea. *Korean Constitutional Court Reports* (Seoul: The Constitutional Court of Korea)

The Supreme Court of Korea. *Annual Report of Courts 2012* (Seoul: The Supreme Court of Korea, 2013) (in Korean)

The Supreme Court of Korea. *Introductory Book of the Supreme Court of Korea* (Seoul: The Supreme Court of Korea, 2012)

4

Courts and judicial reform in Taiwan: gradual transformations towards the guardian of constitutionalism and rule of law

WEN-CHEN CHANG

Courts and legal institutions in Taiwan are modeled on a civil law system, a legacy of past imperial and colonial governance: first, by the Ch'ing Dynasty prior to 1895, then by Imperial Japan between 1895 and 1945, and finally, after 1945, by the Republic of China government.[1] In 1949, as a result of defeat by the Chinese Communist Party on the mainland, the government relocated all of the national institutions, including the Judicial Yuan (the highest judicial administrative organ), the Council of Grand Justices (the Constitutional Court)[2] and the Supreme Court, to Taiwan. Due to the ensuing warfare across the Taiwan Strait, however, martial law was declared, and the "Temporary Provisions"[3] that suspended a great many constitutional provisions and substantially expanded presidential powers were put into force. While the 1960s and 1970s saw miraculous economic growth, the implementation of constitutionalism and rule of law were compromised and the functions of courts significantly constrained. It was not until the mid-1980s, when civil society finally emerged with strong demands for social and political reforms, that the courts began to exercise effective functions.[4]

[1] For discussions of the legal system during the Japanese colonial period, see e.g. Tay-sheng Wang, *Legal Reform in Taiwan under Japanese Colonial Rule (1895–1945): The Reception of Western Law* (Seattle: University of Washington Press, 1992).

[2] The Council of Grand Justices was rechristened the Constitutional Court in 1993 due to the replacement of the 1958 Law on the Council of Grand Justices by the 1993 Constitutional Interpretation Procedure Act. The English text of the 1993 Act is available at www.judicial.gov.tw/constitutionalcourt/EN/p07_2.asp?lawno=73.

[3] The full name is the Temporary Provision Effective during the Period of National Mobilization for Suppression of the Communist Rebellion.

[4] For the development of social and political progress in Taiwan in the 1980s, see e.g. J.-r. Yeh, "Changing forces of constitutional and regulatory reform in Taiwan," *Columbia Journal of Chinese Law*, 4 (1990), 83–100.

A series of constitutional and political reforms were undertaken in the 1990s after the martial law was lifted in 1987. Additional articles were added to the ROC Constitution, which was amended a total of seven times until 2005. The first direct election of the legislature was held in 1992 and the first direct presidential election in 1996. Government power was transferred from the past ruling party, the Nationalist Party (Kuomintang, or KMT), to the opposition party, the Democratic Progressive Party (DPP), in 2000 and 2004, and shifted back to the KMT in 2008 and 2012.[5] Amidst these constitutional and political reforms, reforms regarding the court system and legal education were also placed high on the agenda. In September 1994, President Lee Teng-Hui appointed a new president of the Judicial Yuan along with the Grand Justices of the Constitutional Court who would serve until 2003. The Judicial Reform Committee, whose twenty-seven members included senior Grand Justices, judges from lower courts, prosecutors, private attorneys and law professors, was formed.[6] The Committee was tasked with the delivery of concrete and feasible proposals regarding four issues: the reform of the Judicial Yuan and Grand Justices, the reform of litigation systems, the facilitation of judicial independence, and the reform of legal education. While a few proposals regarding the reform of litigation systems and the measures to facilitate judicial independence were accepted and gradually carried out, others, such as the reforms of the Judicial Yuan and legal education, were not.[7]

In 1999, a national judicial reform consultative conference was called, again with the aim of reaching a consensus on comprehensive measures for judicial reform.[8] Notwithstanding the consensus reached, reform measures that would require further constitutional or legislative revisions for implementation became nearly impossible as the year 2000 saw a

[5] For further discussions on the constitutional and political reforms in Taiwan since the 1990s, see e.g. J.-r. Yeh, "Constitutional reform and democratization in Taiwan: 1945–2000" in P. Chow (ed.), *Taiwan's Modernization in Global Perspective* (Westport: Praeger Publishers, 2002), pp. 47–77; J.-r. Yeh and W.-C. Chang, "The emergence of East Asian constitutionalism: features in comparison," *American Journal of Comparative Law*, 59(3) (2011), 805–840.

[6] Judicial Yuan, *Meeting Records of the Judicial Reform Committee* (Taipei: Judicial Yuan, 1996) (in Chinese).

[7] W.-C. Chang, "Professor Weng Yueh-Seng and the reform of the Judicial Yuan" in J.-r. Yeh (ed.), *The Development and Transformation of Rule of Law: Public Laws of Professor Weng Yueh-Sheng* (Taipei: Angle Publishing, 2009), pp. 149–79 (in Chinese).

[8] Judicial Yuan, *Meeting Records of the National Judicial Reform Consultative Conference* (Taipei: Judicial Yuan, 1999) (in Chinese).

surprising DPP victory in the presidential election, which began a divided government of eight years characterized by serious confrontations between the DPP-led administration and the KMT-dominated legislature.[9] During this period, the progress of judicial reform was limited. However, as this chapter illustrates, certain progress was nevertheless achieved and facilitated by judicial decisions, particularly by the interpretations of the Constitutional Court. In 2008, the KMT once again controlled both executive and legislative powers. While comprehensive judicial reform was not undertaken as an important part of the government's agenda, piecemeal and incremental reforms have been carried out as the result of strong demands by the citizenry and legal community. The enactments of the Fair and Speedy Trial Act in 2010 to resolve the problem of prolonged trials in criminal litigation and the Judge Act in 2011 to diversify the recruitment of judges and further ensure judicial independence were two great examples. Also under consideration was a proposal for the creation of a "public trial observation system" which would function similarly to a jury system.[10]

It is against such dynamics of democratic transitions and political contexts that this chapter sets out to discuss the developments of courts and their functional transformations in Taiwan. The following begins with a general discussion of the judicial system and includes specific issues such as the appointment of judges, judicial training, judicial independence, access to justice, styles of judicial decisions and alternative dispute resolution mechanisms. Next is an elaboration of how certain reforms of courts and litigation systems – constitutional, criminal, civil and administrative – have been gradually undertaken and the influences these reforms have had on the functional transformations of courts. After a discussion of evaluations of judicial performance, this chapter concludes with some prospects for and challenges to Taiwan's judiciary.

1 General description of the judicial system

Article 77 of the ROC Constitution stipulates that the Judicial Yuan shall be the highest judicial organ of the state and shall be in charge of civil,

[9] For further elaboration of the eight-year political confrontation in the context of divided government, see J.-r. Yeh, "Presidential politics and judicial facilitation of political dialogue between political actors in new Asian democracies: comparing the South Korean and Taiwanese experiences," *International Journal of Constitutional Law*, 8(4) (2011), 911–49.

[10] For a brief policy statement regarding the "public trial observation system" made by the Judicial Yuan, see www.judicial.gov.tw/revolution/judReform03.asp.

criminal and administrative cases, as well as cases concerning disciplinary measures against public functionaries. Articles 78, 171 and 173 further provide the Judicial Yuan with the power to interpret the Constitution and review laws and regulations for their consistency with the Constitution. Article 79 stipulates that a number of Grand Justices are to be appointed to the Judicial Yuan.[11]

The design of the Judicial Yuan as the highest organ in the exercise of all judicial powers was inspired by the Federal Supreme Court of the United States.[12] However, the Judicial Yuan in this form has never been fully implemented. Prior to the promulgation of the ROC Constitution in 1946, the KMT government had already created both the Supreme Court, the court of last resort in civil and criminal cases, and the Administrative Court. Both courts, along with judicial bureaucrats, strongly opposed the implementation of Article 77, under which the Judicial Yuan would sit as a final court with jurisdiction over all types of cases. Eventually, the Judicial Yuan created in 1948 was housed with the offices in charge of judicial administration and the Council of Grand Justices that exercised the power to unify legal interpretations and to render constitutional interpretations. The Supreme Court and the Administrative Court have since continued to exercise their respective jurisdictions outside the Judicial Yuan, as illustrated by Figure 4.1.

This practice has left the Judicial Yuan as merely the highest judicial administrative organ and resulted in a separation between the highest judicial organ and the highest judicial administrative organ. In 2001, the Constitutional Court issued *J.Y. Interpretation No. 530*, which found such a separation to be inconsistent with the Constitution.[13] Despite the ruling, however, reform of the Judicial Yuan – as it inevitably involved a comprehensive restructure of the courts – continued to face strong opposition, and consensus on moving forward with reform was difficult to reach. As a result, Taiwan has maintained a judicial system with multiple final judicial organs alongside a separate judicial administrative organ (the Judicial Yuan) and the Constitutional Court. Notwithstanding the original design of a system based on the

[11] ROC Constitution, Art. 79.

[12] T. Ginsburg, *Judicial Review in New Democracies: Constitutional Courts in Asian Cases* (Cambridge University Press, 2003), p. 116.

[13] J.Y. Interpretation No. 530 (2001).

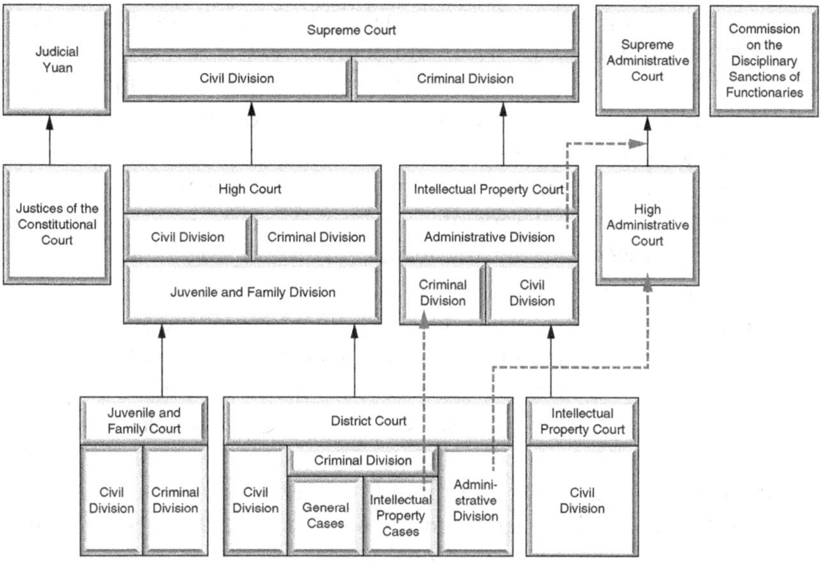

Figure 4.1: Structure of judicial system in Taiwan

American model, the present system largely reflects the framework of European judicial systems.[14]

1.1 *Structure of courts*

Figure 4.1 shows the structure of the judicial system with its multiple final judicial organs. With respect to civil and criminal cases, there are three levels of courts: the Supreme Court, the High Court with five other branches in major cities, and the District Court with 21 branches in all cities and counties. Regarding administrative cases, the Administrative Litigation Law of 2000 created two levels of administrative courts: (1) the Supreme Administrative Court, and (2) the High Administrative Court with three branches in Taipei, Taichung and Kaohsiung. In November 2011, the Administrative Litigation Law was revised to

[14] C.-f. Lo, *The Legal Culture and System of Taiwan* (Leiden: Kluwer Law International, 2006), p. 12. See also C.-f. Lo, "Taiwan: external influences mixed with traditional elements to form its unique legal system" in E. A. Black and G. Bell (eds.), *Law and Legal Institutions of Asia: Traditions, Adaptations and Innovations* (New York: Cambridge University Press, 2011), pp. 91–119.

create administrative litigation tribunals in the district courts that would deal with summary proceedings and adjudication of traffic offenses.

Aside from the Supreme Court and Supreme Administrative Court, the Commission on the Disciplinary Sanction of Public Functionaries is in charge of all disciplinary matters at national and local levels, and has authority over disciplinary measures against political appointees, ministerial officials and civil servants. Concerned by the judicial nature of disciplinary power, the Constitutional Court rendered *J.Y. Interpretation No. 396*, urging the Commission to be reconstituted as a disciplinary court, and the commissioners accorded the status of judges.[15] Up until now, however, the Commission has not been restructured or rechristened. Yet, nearly all appointed commissioners were qualified judges, most of whom had previously served in senior-level judicial positions.[16]

The Constitutional Court, known as the Council of Grand Justices prior to 1993, is empowered to interpret the Constitution and exercise constitutional review of laws and regulations. In 1992, a constitutional revision provided the Constitutional Court with adjudicative power to dissolve unconstitutional political parties.[17] In 1993, the Constitutional Interpretation Procedural Act was promulgated to replace the Law on the Council of Grand Justices.[18] Since then, the Council has been known as the Constitutional Court, and its procedures have been of an adjudicative nature. In addition, the constitutional revision of 1997 stipulated that the Constitutional Court be composed of fifteen Grand Justices with non-renewable terms of eight years appointed in a staggered manner.[19] Prior to this revision, the Council was often composed of sixteen or seventeen Grand Justices with renewable non-staggered terms of nine years.[20] The 1997 revision also stipulated that the President and Vice-President of the Judicial Yuan should serve concurrently as Grand Justices of the Constitutional Court, and the new system began in

[15] J.Y. Interpretation No. 396 (1996).

[16] The qualifications of current commissioners are available at http://tpp.judicial.gov.tw/indexen.asp?struID=17&contentID=661.

[17] The Constitutional Revision in 1992.

[18] 1993 Constitutional Interpretation Procedure Act.

[19] Additional Articles of the ROC Constitution, Art. 5.

[20] The first Council served from 1948 to 1960, the second from 1960 to 1969, the third from 1969 to 1976, the fourth from 1976 to 1985, the fifth from 1985 to 1994, and the sixth from 1994 to 2003. In 2003, eight justices were appointed for eight years while seven justices were appointed for only four years, allowing a new group of seven justices to be appointed in 2007.

2003. The 2005 constitutional revision further gave the Constitutional Court the power to adjudicate impeachment proceedings against the President and Vice-President.[21]

It should be noted that the Constitutional Court has the exclusive power to review the constitutionality of laws and regulations. If another court has doubts about the constitutionality of the laws or regulations it is about to apply, it must suspend the proceeding in question and request an interpretation from the Constitutional Court.[22] Moreover, the Constitutional Court can only exercise the power of "abstract review." In other words, it only reviews the constitutionality of laws and regulations and does not have the power to directly resolve cases brought by other courts or by individuals who have exhausted all available proceedings.[23]

Recent years have witnessed the proliferation of special courts. In 1997, the Law on Juvenile Criminal Matters created juvenile courts in metropolitan cities and juvenile tribunals in smaller cities and counties. In 2012, a new law – the Organic Act on Juvenile and Family Court – was promulgated, combining the juvenile and family courts and providing them with exclusive jurisdiction over family matters such as divorce, child custody and inheritance.[24] In addition, the Intellectual Property Court was created in 2008, with jurisdiction over first- and second-instance proceedings in disputes regarding intellectual property rights, and the Intellectual Property Case Adjudication Act also became effective in the same year.

There has been some effort to create a specialized court for members of Taiwan's indigenous communities, known as aboriginals. Aboriginals in Taiwan are primarily Austronesian and settled in Taiwan over 8,000 years ago. There are currently fourteen officially recognized tribes with several others still trying to obtain official recognition.[25] Due to the past policy of separation,[26] indigenous peoples have long suffered from

[21] Additional Articles of the ROC Constitution, Art. 5, s. 10.

[22] J.Y. Interpretation No. 371 (1995).

[23] For further discussion of various powers and jurisdictions of the Constitutional Court, see W.-C. Chang, "The role of judicial review in consolidating democracy: the case of Taiwan," *Asia Law Review*, 2(2) (2005), 73–88.

[24] Similar to administrative courts, the juvenile and family courts are established in metropolitan cities whereas the juvenile and family tribunals are established within the district courts.

[25] Council for Indigenous Peoples, Executive Yuan, www.apc.gov.tw/portal/index.html?lang=en_US&CID=B20D85423B8EED93.

[26] During the period of Japanese rule, the colonial government established separate legal and judicial systems for Han Chinese (including assimilated aboriginals) and aboriginals.

discrimination and the loss of traditional language and culture. In 2005, the Basic Law on Indigenous Peoples was enacted, reiterating the guarantee of fundamental rights of aboriginals and, more importantly, providing the legal basis for an indigenous court.[27] Regrettably, however, up until now, little progress has been made in establishing such a court.

Also worthy of mention is the military court. Article 9 of the ROC Constitution exempts all persons except those in active military service from being subject to trial by military tribunal. Before the 1990s, however, both civilians and military personnel under specified conditions could still be tried by military tribunals under the supervision of the Ministry of Defense without the full protection of due process or the opportunity to make appeals to ordinary courts. In *J.Y. Interpretation No. 436* of 1997, the Constitutional Court found such practices inconsistent with the Constitution and demanded the creation of a military court whose proceedings must be in full compliance with due process requirements.[28] In October 1999, the Military Trial Act was revised to reassert the constitutional command that no civilians be subject to military trials and to create a military court with military judges and prosecutors ensuring the application of criminal due process.

In 2012, the Constitutional Court also issued another ruling, *J.Y. Interpretation No. 704*, finding the power of military supervisors in suspending the service of military judges to be unconstitutional, as it is inconsistent with the maintenance of judicial independence.[29] The summer of 2013 saw a tragic case in which a soldier was tortured to death during his disciplinary confinement. The subsequent military investigation drew public attention to serious irregularities in the military judicial system. Thousands of people – particularly members of the younger generation who would still be required to serve in the military – took to the streets and demanded reform of the military justice system.[30] In response, the Military Trial Act was quickly revised to permit military trials only during wartime in armed conflicts.[31] As Taiwan has not been in a time of war involving any armed conflict, nearly all cases previously

See T.-S. Wang, *The Introduction to the Legal History of Taiwan*, 2nd edn. (Taipei: Angle Publishing, 2004), pp. 320–1 (in Chinese).

[27] Basic Law on Indigenous Peoples, Art. 30, s. 2.

[28] J.Y. Interpretation No. 436 (1997). [29] J.Y. Interpretation No. 704 (2012).

[30] R. Chang, "Thousands take to street for Hung," *Taipei Times*, 4 August 2013, www.taipeitimes.com/News/front/archives/2013/08/04/2003568877.

[31] Military Trial Act, Arts. 1, 34 and 137 as revised in August 2013.

under military jurisdiction are now subject to the jurisdiction of ordinary courts. Whether such suspension of the substantial functions performed by the military courts in peacetime would further result in their total abolition or reorganization is still under consideration on the legislative floor.

1.2 *Instances of trials*

In Taiwan, there are three instances of adjudication for all civil cases except for small or other similar claims stipulated in the Code of Civil Procedure. Typically the first trial is on both facts and law in the district court, the second trial – defined as a continuous trial from the first – is also on facts and law in the High Court, and the last trial is exclusively on law at the Supreme Court. In administrative cases, typically two instances are available at the High Administrative Court and the Supreme Administrative Court, with the former reviewing the cases on both facts and law and the latter only on law.

Criminal cases proceed with a similar route except that the second instance trial at the High Court is a trial de novo. In addition, the Code of Criminal Procedure sets no limits on the number of times that the parties, particularly prosecutors, may appeal or the Supreme Court may render remands. As a result, it has not been uncommon for criminal trials in Taiwan to proceed for more than a decade with countless retrials. To resolve this problem, the Fair and Speedy Trial Act was promulgated in September 2010. This law demands the issuance of acquittals to defendants whose trials proceed for more than eight years and sets limits on appeals if defendants are not found guilty under certain conditions.[32] The law also pays special attention to the length of trials if defendants are under detention and sets the maximum time of detention during trials to eight years.[33]

In the district courts, cases are presided over either by a single judge or a panel of three judges. At the High Court, cases are dealt with by a panel of three judges, and at the Supreme Court, a panel of five judges. Administrative cases are presided over by a panel of three judges at the High Administrative Court and a panel of five judges at the Supreme Administrative Court.

In 2010, the Judicial Yuan proposed "the Public Trial Observation System" in which a number of citizens would be selected to observe

[32] Fair and Speedy Trial Act, Arts. 7 and 8.

[33] Fair and Speedy Trial Act, Art. 5.

Table 4.1: *The Number of Courts and Judges in Different Jurisdictions in Taiwan*

	CC	PRDSC	SAC	HAC	SC	HC	DC	IPC	Total
Number of courts	1	1	1	3	1	6	21	1	35
Number of judges	15	12	23	58	81	421	1,443	17	2,070
Inhabitants	–	–	–	–	–	–	–	–	23,373,517
Judges per 100,000 inhabitants	–	–	–	–	–	–	–	–	8.86

[*]CC = Constitutional Court; PFDSC = Public Functionary Disciplinary Sanction Commission; SAC = Supreme Administrative Court; HAC = High Administrative Court; SC = Supreme Court; HC = High Court; DC = District Court; IPC = Intellectual Property Court

Source: Judicial Yuan, 2013, http://www.judicial.gov.tw/juds/index1.htm; Executive Yuan, 2013, http://www.dgbas.gov.tw/ct.asp?xItem=15408&CtNode=4594&mp=1.

criminal trials at first instance and provide their opinions to the presiding judges.[34] Unlike the jury system in the United States or elsewhere, the opinions of these lay observers are merely advisory. By proposing this system, the Judicial Yuan hoped to engage ordinary citizens in criminal proceedings and facilitate greater public trust in the judiciary.

1.3 Size and performance of the courts

Table 4.1 illustrates the numbers of courts and judges in various jurisdictions, and the ratio of judges to inhabitants in 2013. Taiwan has a fairly large Supreme Court for civil and criminal cases, with eighty-one judges. The district courts with all of their branches and special tribunals have a total of 1,443 judges and the High Court 421 judges. The administrative court is comparatively smaller, with fifty-eight

[34] For a brief policy statement regarding the "public trial observation system" made by the Judicial Yuan, see www.judicial.gov.tw/revolution/judReform03.asp.

judges at the High Administrative Court and twenty-three at the Supreme High Administrative Court. The recently created Intellectual Property Court has seventeen judges, and the Commission on Public Functionary Disciplinary Sanction has twelve commissioners. The Constitutional Court has fifteen Grand Justices, with one serving as the President of the Judicial Yuan and the other serving as the Vice-President. Altogether, in Taiwan there are about nine judges serving every 100,000 inhabitants.

Table 4.2 presents the case performance of courts in 2013. As can be seen, civil cases far outnumber criminal and administrative cases. Based on the clearance and congestion rates shown in Table 4.2, civil courts seem to perform more efficiently than criminal courts. Such a hasty conclusion, however, may not be warranted, as the number of civil cases in Table 4.2 includes non-litigation cases and cases of execution, which are less time-consuming. It is worth noting that the Constitutional Court, the Civil Division of the High Court and the High Administrative Court have the highest congestion rates. The worst appears to be the Constitutional Court as many cases have been pending for years, and the Constitutional Court has not yet made publicly available the average number of days that a case requires.

2 Judicial appointments, judicial independence and access to justice

Similar to most Asian jurisdictions, judges in Taiwan typically start as young law school graduates who pass competitive judicial exams and gradually climb to judicial seniority. Judges' lack of experience prior to entering the judiciary and their subsequent bureaucratization have often been the target of judicial reform efforts. The Judge Act, after nearly two decades of discussion, was finally promulgated in 2011 to address such problems. This law diversifies the recruitment of judges to include experienced lawyers and law professors.[35] The law also creates a judicial council under the Judicial Yuan that is in charge of judicial appointments and is composed of representatives selected by judges as well as representatives from the legal community.[36] To ensure the quality of judges, the law institutionalizes periodic evaluations of judges, and, more

[35] Judge Act, Art. 5. [36] Judge Act, Art. 4.

Table 4.2: *The Performance of Courts in Different Jurisdictions in Taiwan*

	CC	PFDSC	SAC	HAC	SC(Cr)	HC(Cr)	DC(Cr)	SC(Ci)	HC(Ci)	DC(Ci)	IPC
NCF/year	553	674	3,062	4,861	6,879	34,985	411,846	5,734	16,242	1,093,778	1,358
NCD/year	544	665	3,071	4,700	7,172	35,192	412,273	5,600	15,594	1,093,438	1,350
NCP/year	352	55	493	1,793	825	4,469	44,413	1,800	7,073	67,199	526
ClR	0.61	0.92	0.86	0.72	0.90	0.89	0.90	0.76	0.69	0.94	0.72
CoR	0.39	0.08	0.14	0.28	0.10	0.11	0.10	0.24	0.31	0.06	0.28
ADEC (day)		33.05	71.74	155.74	32.06	78.53	64.11	31.78	169.45	31.07	169.82

*NCF: Number of cases filed; NCD: Number of cases disposed (cases newly filed and lodged in previous years are both calculated); NCP: Number of cases pending (cases newly filed and lodged in previous years are both calculated); ClR: Clearance rate (cases newly filed and lodged in previous years are both calculated); CoR: Congestion rate (cases newly filed and lodged in previous years are both calculated); ADEC = Average duration of each case; (Cr): Criminal trial; (Ci): Civil trial.

**The administrative cases involve cases for judgment, ruling, and other procedural question; the criminal cases involve cases for judgment, ruling and others; the civil cases involve civil litigation, non-litigation and compulsory execution.

Source: Judicial Yuan, 2013, http://www.judicial.gov.tw/juds/index1.htm

importantly, it establishes a special disciplinary tribunal to oversee disciplinary measures and impeachment of judges.[37] The following discusses recent reforms concerning judicial appointment, judicial independence, and the related issues of judicial training, legal education and access to justice.

2.1 *Qualification and appointment*

With the exception of the Grand Justices of the Constitutional Court, who are appointed by the President with parliamentary confirmation, judges in Taiwan are typically recruited through judicial exams. After the exams, prospective judges must complete a two-year training program at the Judicial Training Institute.[38] The lack of practical experience on the part of judges and their potential bureaucratization have been strongly criticized. Prior to the promulgation of the Judge Act in 2011, certain reform measures were undertaken. For example, in 1999, when a new law expanded the administrative court into two layers, it also permitted the recruitment of judges from among practicing attorneys as well as law professors.[39] The Intellectual Property Court created in 2008 incorporates a similar recruiting measure. However, thus far, the number of judges recruited from those alternative sources has remained fairly small. We have yet to see if the Judge Act will really bring about greater diversification of judges and improvement in the quality of judicial decisions.

The qualifications for the Grand Justices of the Constitutional Court are different from those for ordinary judges. Article 4 of the Organic Act of the Judicial Yuan stipulates that a Grand Justice must meet one of the following five sets of qualifications: (1) served for ten years on the Supreme Court with a distinguished record; (2) served as a member of the Legislative Yuan for nine years; (3) taught for ten years at university level and published in the field of law; (4) served as a justice of the International Court of Justice or authored books on public or comparative law; or (5) obtained a legal education as well as experience and

[37] Judge Act, Arts. 30 and 47.

[38] It should be noted that in Taiwan, prosecutors are also chosen from those who pass the judicial exams. Those who pass the exams and the two-year training become judges or prosecutors depending on their exam results, their performance during the training period, the availability of positions in each category, and, of course, their own preferences.

[39] Organic Act of the Administrative Court, Art. 17.

renown in politics.[40] Also noteworthy is that the number of Grand Justices appointed from any one of the five categories should not exceed one third of the total of fifteen Grand Justices. Thus far, the practice has been that half of the Grand Justices appointed were previously career judges while the other half were law professors. In 2011, for the first time, a practicing attorney was appointed as the Grand Justice concurrently serving as the President of the Judicial Yuan.[41]

The life tenure of judges is guaranteed in Article 81 of the Constitution. This provision expresses that judges shall hold office for life and that no judge shall be removed from office unless he or she has been found guilty of a criminal offense, subjected to disciplinary measures, or declared to be under interdiction. No judge shall be suspended or transferred or have his salary reduced except in accordance with law. Under the principle of judicial independence, a judge cannot be retired, transferred to another office or discharged from office without his or her consent or by law.

2.2 *Judicial independence*

Judicial independence includes not only the independence of individual judges but also the institutional independence of the judiciary. One of the factors involved in institutional independence is the degree to which the judiciary may independently submit its own budget for parliamentary deliberation. The Constitution is silent on whether the Judicial Yuan may independently propose the judicial budget. In *J.Y. Interpretation No. 175* of 1982, the Constitutional Court decided that the Judicial Yuan, being the highest judicial administrative organ, should enjoy the power to make an independent submission of the judicial budget for parliamentary approval.[42] In practice, however, the Judicial Yuan has always submitted the judicial budget to the cabinet – also known as the Executive Yuan – which then submitted the overall national budget for parliamentary review. In the past, in order to balance the budget or address other policy concerns, the Executive Yuan has sometimes altered the judicial budget

[40] The text in English can be found at www.judicial.gov.tw/CONSTITUTIONALCOURT/EN/p03.asp.

[41] Hau-Min Rai is the present Chief Grand Justice and President of Judicial Yuan Hau-Min Rai. His curriculum vitae is available at www.judicial.gov.tw/constitutionalcourt/en/p01_03_01.asp?curno=24.

[42] J.Y. Interpretation No. 175 (1982).

without consulting the judiciary. In order to ensure judicial independence, the constitutional revision of 1997 added a provision – Section 6, Article 5 of the Additional Articles – stating that the Executive Yuan may not eliminate or reduce the judicial budget but may indicate its opinion when submitting the budget for parliamentary deliberation. For the last ten years, the annual judicial budget has typically occupied about 1 percent of the national government budget.[43]

The other issue regarding institutional independence of the judiciary is the distinctive separation between the supreme administrative judicial organ – the Judicial Yuan – and the multiple Supreme Courts. This has resulted in various conflicts between the Judicial Yuan in its capacity of judicial supervision over the entire judiciary and the Supreme Courts, which also have the power to supervise their respective lower courts. In *J.Y. Interpretation No. 530* of 2001, the Constitutional Court urged the government to undertake comprehensive judicial reforms to resolve this issue, but no progress has yet been made. The Constitutional Court subsequently rendered another two interpretations, *J.Y. Interpretation No. 539*[44] and *J.Y. Interpretation No. 665*,[45] attempting to resolve the issue by making clear that the Judicial Yuan may exercise its supervisory power over the entire judiciary, including the Supreme Courts, insofar as the exercise of such supervisory power would neither interfere with the judicial independence of the courts or their judges nor infringe on the fundamental rights of the individuals concerned.

2.3 *Judicial training and related legal education*

Judicial training and legal education are of particularly high importance in the quality of judges produced by a system like that of Taiwan, in which judges are primarily recruited through exams undertaken by young law school graduates. In Taiwan, various constitutional organs and government ministries are responsible for such matters. Judicial exams for judges and prosecutors, like other exams for civil servants, are under the jurisdiction of a special constitutional organ, the Examination Yuan. The training of prospective judges and prosecutors, however, is provided by the Ministry of Justice. Meanwhile, continuing legal

[43] For example, in 2011, the judicial budget was 19,341,773 in New Taiwan Dollars (NTD) while the national budget was NTD 1,769,844,184. See Directorate-General of Budget, Accounting and Statistics, Executive Yuan, www.dgbas.gov.tw/mp.asp?mp=1.

[44] J.Y. Interpretation No. 539 (2002). [45] J.Y. Interpretation No. 665 (2009).

education for judges is provided by the Judicial Yuan. Legal education, including the reform of law schools, is entirely under the charge of the Ministry of Education. The national bar association is only in charge of the training of prospective lawyers who pass the bar exams administered by the Examination Yuan. These various organs of competing capacities are indicative of the difficulties in pushing for reform. This may also explain why there have been many legal education reform initiatives in the last ten years, but none have so far succeeded in Taiwan, unlike in South Korea or Japan.

2.3.1 Training of judges

As discussed above, those who pass the judicial exams must complete a two-year training program at the Judicial Training Institute under the Ministry of Justice. Upon completion, some will become judges while others will become prosecutors, depending on their exam results, their performance during training, the availability of positions and their personal preferences.

The training program includes three phases. The first phase lasts for approximately six months. During this period, the candidates learn relevant legal subjects like those covered in law schools. This is followed by the second phase, lasting sixteen months, during which the candidates work either as law clerks to judges or prosecutors or as interns in administrative agencies. The third phase is only about one-and-a-half months, in which the candidates are each required to complete a short thesis on an important legal issue. Upon successful completion of the program, they will then become judges or prosecutors. Also noteworthy is the Judicial Yuan's establishment in March 2001 of a continuing legal education institute for judges.[46]

2.3.2 Legal education

Legal education in Taiwan has primarily been placed at the undergraduate level by university departments or colleges of law. Up until the early 1990s, there had been only eight such departments or colleges of law, mostly concentrated in Taipei and northern Taiwan. The democratization of the country brought demands for legal and judicial reforms, inevitably leading to calls for the reform of legal education.

[46] The website of the judge training institute is available at www.tpi.moj.gov.tw/mp092.html.

These calls for reforms were mainly twofold. One, a response to the long-held criticism that judges lacked experience, called for the adoption of an American-style system in which law schools recruit non-law college graduates to receive legal education and become lawyers. The first such program in Taiwan was created in 1991, by Soochow University College of Law, a private college of law renowned for its distinctive focus on Anglo-American law. After the success of this program, this model was followed in the 2000s by many other distinguished colleges of law in public universities.

The other reform demanded was to increase the number of departments or colleges of law, private or public, especially in the central and southern parts of Taiwan. For example, the first graduate institute of law in Tainan, a southern city renowned for its cultural heritage, was established in 1996 and later became a law department. In Kaohsiung, the largest city in southern Taiwan, a college of law was finally created at the National University of Kaohsiung in 2000.

The result of these reforms is evident. In 2006, the number of colleges of law was expanded to thirty-nine, spread throughout Taiwan. According to a survey done by the Ministry of Education that year, there were a total of 110 law departments, forty-two graduate institutes of law and nine doctoral programs in law. In the academic year of 2006, there were 5,365 law students enrolled. Among them, 1,275 students were enrolled in master of law programs while fifty were studying for doctorates.[47] In addition, the number of female law students gradually increased and is now almost equal to the number of male law students.

2.4 *Access to justice*

One of the points of consensus reached in the national judicial reform consultative conference of 1999 was the need to bolster efforts to ensure fair and equal access to justice. A task force was quickly formed to explore the creation of a legal aid system. As a result of forceful lobbying on the part of the bar association, in 2001, the draft of what became the Legal Aid Act was finally submitted by the Judicial Yuan for legislative consideration. Notwithstanding political confrontations between the DPP-led administration and the KMT-dominated legislature that obstructed many key legislative efforts, the Legal Aid Act, with its

[47] H.-S. Chen, "Reception from foreign legal system: the development of legal education in Taiwan," *Taiwan Law Review*, 188 (2010), 57–60 (in Chinese).

extensive support from the bar association and civic groups, was passed in December 2003 and promulgated in January 2004. In July 2004, the Legal Aid Foundation was established and now has twenty-one branches nationwide for the provision of legal aid to individuals.[48] In addition to discussing the institutionalization of legal aid, the following sections also discuss progress that has been made in related issues, including standing to sue, public interest litigation, litigation fees, the availability of legal interpreters and the availability of private legal counsel.

2.4.1 Standing to sue and the development of public interest litigation

In civil procedure, any persons, including incorporated or unincorporated associations, are recognized as having the capacity to sue.[49] The Code of Criminal Procedure – aside from public prosecution – also allows private initiations of prosecution with respect to a number of offenses.[50] The Administrative Litigation Act of 1998 expanded the types of administrative litigation permitted from, typically, the revocation of administrative acts to actions for declarative or prohibitive orders and injunctions.[51]

During the period of democratic transition in the late 1980s and 1990s, individual complaints made before the Constitutional Court were a very effective strategy for challenging laws or government regulations that were in violation of fundamental rights and liberties.[52] The interpretations of the Constitutional Court often had even greater impacts on legal and even social reforms. At the time, however, public interest

[48] A brief history and the mandate of the Legal Aid Foundation in English are available at www.laf.org.tw/en/a1_1.php.

[49] Article 40 of the Civil Procedure Act states that any person who has legal capacity has the capacity to be a party to a lawsuit. A fetus also has the capacity to be a party in a disputed case concerning the entitlement of its interests. An unincorporated association with a representative and a government agency at the central or local level has the capacity to be a party.

[50] Article 37 of Criminal Procedure Act stipulates that a private prosecutor shall authorize an agent to appear before the court by a power of attorney, provided that if the court considers it necessary, the private prosecutor may be ordered to appear in person. The agent referred to in the preceding section shall be a lawyer.

[51] These actions include appeals for mandatory administrative disposition; appeals for confirming invalidation, illegality and other legal relationships; appeals for mandatory agency actions other than administrative disposition; and citizen suits as prescribed in the Administrative Litigation Act, Arts. 4, 5, 6, 8 and 9.

[52] W.-C. Chang, "Public-interest litigation in Taiwan: strategy for law and policy reforms in course of democratization" in P. J. Yap and H. Law (eds.), *Public Interest Litigation in Asia* (New York: Routledge, 2011), pp. 136–60.

litigation in the ordinary courts had not emerged due to the lack of a legal basis for it.[53] The possibility was first given by the Administrative Litigation Act revised in 1998, which allowed individuals and public interest groups to bring lawsuits in the administrative courts against the illegal actions of government agencies, with the conditions further specified by the law. In 1999, the Air Pollution Control Act was amended to insert a clause permitting citizen suits, which was followed by the insertion of similar clauses in the Soil and Groundwater Pollution Remediation Act and the Marine Pollution Control Act in 2000, and the Water Pollution Control Act and the Environmental Impact Assessment Act in 2002. It was due to the provisions in these environmental statutes allowing citizen suits that public interest litigation began flourishing in Taiwan.[54] In keeping with the trend of citizen suits in administrative litigation, the Code of Civil Procedure was also revised in 2003 to allow for civil litigation initiated by public interest organizations.[55]

2.4.2 Litigation fees

In civil cases, litigation fees depend on whether the subject of the litigation involves a claim to property rights. If the litigation involves a claim to property rights, the court of first instance will assess the price or value of that claim and charge a litigation fee based on this assessment. If the litigation involves no such claim to property rights, the party need only pay a designated fee: currently 3,000 New Taiwan Dollars (NTD) for the court of first instance and NTD 4,500 for appeal to the second or third instance. If both property and non-property claims are involved, both kinds of fee must be paid. The cost of administrative litigation is NTD 4,000 for one proceeding. For criminal proceedings as well as constitutional litigation, no litigation fees are required.

2.4.3 Legal aid

In criminal cases, Article 31(1) of the Code of Criminal Procedure specifies the conditions under which criminal defendants may be assisted with legal counsel appointed by the court. The conditions include the following: (1) the minimum punishment in the case is no less than three years of imprisonment; (2) a high court has original jurisdiction over the case; or (3) the accused is unable to make a complete statement due to his or her mental incompetence. Should any of these conditions be met

[53] *Ibid.* p. 149. [54] *Ibid.* pp. 153–4. [55] *Ibid.* p. 150.

and the accused have no defense counsel, the presiding judge must appoint a legal counsel for the accused. However, this provision was poorly implemented due to an insufficient supply of legal counsel.[56] The shortage was eased with the full functioning of the Legal Aid Foundation in 2004 as described above. The Foundation receives funds from the government but is provided with institutional autonomy on its operation and management. Aside from legal aid to criminal defendants, the law also provides legal aid to any person with a reasonable case who meets certain financial eligibility criteria.

2.4.4 Legal interpreter

In order to guarantee the fairness of judicial proceedings, Article 98 of the Organic Act on Courts provides interpreter services to litigant parties, witnesses or other persons engaged in the proceeding who cannot speak Mandarin Chinese, such as aboriginals or foreigners. In reality, however, this service has been at best poorly supplied. First, the provision of interpretation services is not always mandatory: while the Civil Procedure Act requires the use of interpreters in civil proceedings, judges in criminal proceedings are given discretion over the use of interpreters. Second, interpretation services typically involve paperwork translation only. In the majority of cases, interpreters were not even present at the oral proceedings and could not speak or translate for those in need.

2.4.5 Availability of private legal counsel

A 2014 survey by the Ministry of Justice found that the number of registered lawyers in Taiwan at that time was 21,045.[57] At present, the total population in Taiwan is 23,373,517. This means that there is roughly one private legal counsel for every 1,111 inhabitants, or 90 per 100,000 inhabitants. This ratio is comparatively better than that of judges, in which there are nine judges for every 100,000 inhabitants, as illustrated in Table 4.1.

In the past, the bar exam was designed to be extremely competitive, and the pass rate was as low as 2 percent. The result was an insufficient

[56] Legal counsel may be private attorneys appointed by the court or public defenders. With the passage of the Legal Aid Act and the creation of the Legal Aid Foundation, the system of public defense has been gradually phased out. At present, there are only fifty public defenders, and courts in rather remote areas such as in the eastern part of Taiwan or the islets often find no such officers.

[57] Ministry of Justice, http://service.moj.gov.tw/lawer/notice.htm.

supply of lawyers, infringing fair and equal access to justice held by individuals. Lowering the threshold for passing the bar exam in order to increase of the supply of lawyers was the consensus reached in many discussions of judicial reform. The first increase of the bar pass rate took place in the early 1990s, and the rate has since been maintained at around 8 percent.[58] In a recent effort, the Examination Yuan decided to increase the pass rate further by changing the structure of the bar exam. The new structure involves a two-part exam, with the first part being a multiple-choice exam. Only 33 percent of the exam takers can pass the first part and continue to the second part, which involves more elaborate written questions. The new structure was implemented in 2011, and the pass rate rose to 10.64 percent.[59]

3 Sources of law and styles of judicial decisions

In a civil law system like Taiwan's, legal codes and statutes are the primary source of law. The styles of judicial decisions are also similar to those in a civil law system – relatively concise and short with primarily formalistic reasoning. With the exception of the Constitutional Court, judicial decisions are generally not rendered with the issuance of separate concurring or dissenting opinions. As early as 1977, the Constitutional Court began issuing interpretations together with dissenting opinions written by Grand Justices.[60] Since then, the number of individual opinions, including both dissenting and concurring opinions, has been escalating. Up until now, on average, every one interpretation by the Constitutional Court is accompanied by 1.40 individual opinions. Recently, in cases in which the interpretations involved key constitutional questions, the number of individual opinions even amounted to ten.[61] The styles of the opinions written by Grand Justices are also quite varied, with some employing policy or

[58] The numbers of bar examination applicants and pass rates are available at the Ministry of Examination, Examination Yuan. In 2002, the pass rate was 7.77%, and in 2003, 8.09%; from then until a new exam structure was implemented in 2011, the pass rate remained at about 8%.

[59] *Ibid.*

[60] The present legal basis is Article 17 of the Constitutional Interpretation Procedural Act.

[61] Note that the issuance of constitutional interpretations requires a two-thirds vote out of fifteen Grand Justices. Hence, ten opinions would mean many justices providing concurring opinions rather than dissenting opinions.

social sciences arguments or even literature. However, most courts still maintain a traditional style in issuing judgments.

3.1 Sources of law

Article 80 of the Constitution commands judges to render decisions independently in accordance with the law.[62] In addition, Article 1 of the Civil Code[63] and Article 1 of the Criminal Code[64] both accord primacy to the law. The hierarchy of norms is firmly guaranteed in the Constitution, with Articles 171 and 172 stating that any law in conflict with the Constitution shall be null and void, and that any regulation in conflict with the law or Constitution shall lose its legal effect.

As judges are strictly bound by the law, cases – even those rendered by the Supreme Courts – are not binding on judges, unlike the principle of *stare decisis* typically found in common law systems. Noticeably, however, in order to harmonize the application and interpretation of laws, a system of *Pan-Li* (precedent) was developed, in which a few decisions of the Supreme Court and the Supreme Administrative Court regarding how certain laws or regulations were interpreted or applied were selected and given binding status to the judges of the respective lower courts. In civil, criminal and administrative proceedings, the violation or misapplication of *Pan-Li* is deemed as one of the grounds for making appeals. Because of the binding status of *Pan-Li*, the Constitutional Court issued *J.Y. Interpretation No. 153* in 1978, asserting its power to review the constitutionality of *Pan-Li* and giving it a similar legal status to that of administrative regulations.[65]

Aside from laws, regulations, and *Pan-Li*, other sources of law may be considered in civil matters but not in criminal matters. Article 1 of the Criminal Code stipulates that no person shall be subject to criminal

[62] The Constitutional Court interpreted this provision and rendered J.Y. Interpretation No. 371 in 1995, stating that when ordinary courts have doubts about the constitutionality of the laws they are about to apply, they can only suspend the proceeding to request an interpretation from the Constitutional Court but cannot invalidate the laws themselves, as they should be bound by the laws according to Article 80 of the Constitution.

[63] Article 1 of the Civil Code states that if there is no applicable act for a civil case, the case shall be decided according to custom. If there is no such custom, the case shall be decided according to the jurisprudence.

[64] Article 1 of the Criminal Code also states that conduct is punishable only when expressly so provided by the law at the time of its commission. This also applies to a rehabilitative measure that puts restrictions on personal freedom.

[65] J.Y. Interpretation No. 153 (1978).

punishment without prior legislation. In contrast, Article 1 of the Civil Code allows customs and general principles of law, including principles inferred from foreign laws, as supplementary sources of law. Also worthy of mention is the general reluctance of judges to exercise lawmaking powers. Perhaps with only the exception of the Grand Justices, judges in Taiwan seldom interpret laws in ways that may amount to lawmaking, unlike their counterparts in common law systems.[66]

3.2 The style of judicial decisions and interpretive methods

The language of judicial decisions in Taiwan is Mandarin Chinese. Judgments are generally not lengthy, in a format that includes the holding, the claims of both parties, the facts of the case, and the reasoning behind the decision. As stated above, with the exception of the Constitutional Court, the courts – even the Supreme Court and the Supreme Administrative Court – are still not permitted to issue separate concurring or dissenting opinions. In a panel deliberation of three or five judges, the opinions of the judges are kept in a file that must be kept confidential before the issuance of the decision. Once the decision is released, only the litigant parties and their private counsel are given access to the file with the judges' opinions, but no copies or photographs may be made.[67]

Judicial decisions are typically rendered with formalistic reasoning and text-based interpretations of law. Other interpretive methods, such as structural, history-based or functional approaches or methods incorporating policy or economic arguments, are at times found in the decisions of ordinary courts but are mostly found in the interpretations of the Constitutional Court. Although foreign influences on the legal system are fairly strong, as evidenced in the educational backgrounds of most judges, practitioners and law professors,[68] direct citations of or

[66] See e.g. J.Y. Interpretation No. 706, Concurring Opinion by Justice Dennis T. C. Tang (2012).

[67] Organic Act of Courts, Art. 106.

[68] The majority of law professors in Taiwan obtained their doctorates abroad. Take the National Taiwan University College of Law, the top law school in Taiwan, as an example. Only one out of the forty-three faculty members is locally trained. The majority of faculty members have master's degrees or doctorates from Germany, the United States, Japan, England, and France, among others. Similar foreign educational influences are found in the Constitutional Court, in which eleven of the fifteen Grand Justices obtained master's degrees or doctorates abroad. See W.-C. Chang and J.-r. Yeh, "Judges as discursive agent: the use of foreign precedents by the Constitutional Court of Taiwan" in T. Groppi and M.-C. Ponthoreau (eds.), *The Use of Foreign Precedents by Constitutional Judges* (Oxford:

references to foreign or international authorities in judicial decisions are quite rare.[69] Take the Constitutional Court, for example. By the end of 2013, the Constitutional Court had issued a total of 716 interpretations. Among them, only four interpretations expressly refer to foreign judicial decisions in the majority opinion and only eight interpretations directly cite a foreign constitutional or statutory provision.[70] However, direct citations of foreign or international legal authorities appear in greater numbers in separate concurring and dissenting opinions.[71] This may point to the fact that direct citations of foreign or international authorities may not be a good indicator of foreign or international law influences. When interviewed, Grand Justices as well as judges of ordinary jurisdictions generally embrace a very open attitude towards the influence of foreign and international authorities.[72] Notwithstanding the scarcity of explicit citations, the interpretations of the Constitutional Court are rife with examples of foreign approaches like the principle of proportionality, the guarantee of due process, the political question doctrine, the distinction between content-based and content-neutral restrictions on expression, and the recognition of suspect classifications in equality cases.[73]

4 Courts and alternative dispute resolution

Courts are primarily engaged in formal judicial resolutions that are adversarial in nature. In such formal resolutions, courts are required to independently render decisions in accordance with pre-existing rules, and the results are often winner-take-all.[74] Albeit fair and just, such formal resolutions are also costly and time-consuming. More importantly, the

Hart Publishing, 2013), pp. 373–92, 379–80. It is also very common for private attorneys to obtain a foreign Master of Laws degree.

[69] Chang and Yeh, "Judges as discursive agent," pp. 381–84; D. S. Law and W.-C. Chang, "The limits of global judicial dialogue," *Washington Law Review*, 86(3) (2011), 557–58; W.-C. Chang, "An isolated nation with global-minded citizens: bottom-up transnational constitutionalism in Taiwan," *National Taiwan University Law Review*, 4(3) (2009), 203, 212–15.

[70] Chang and Yeh, "Judges as discursive agent," pp. 381–4; Law and Chang, "Global judicial dialogue," pp. 557–8.

[71] Chang and Yeh, "Judges as discursive agent," pp. 381–4; Law and Chang, "Global judicial dialogue," p. 557.

[72] Law and Chang, "Global judicial dialogue," pp. 558–62.

[73] Chang and Yeh, "Judges as discursive agent," p. 391; Law and Chang, "Global judicial dialogue," pp. 558–62.

[74] M. Shapiro, *Courts: A Comparative and Political Analysis* (University of Chicago Press, 1981), pp. 1–4.

adversarial nature of this type of resolution does not always fit into dispute resolution models across various cultures and legal systems.[75] Alternative dispute resolution, which emphasizes a less adversarial and more informal process with relaxed procedural rules, has thus become the focus of reform considerations. Not surprisingly, commercial or trade disputes in which time and cost are prime considerations have recently leaned towards such alternatives. Similar trends are also observable in Taiwan.

4.1 Arbitration

The predecessor to Taiwan's Arbitration Act was the Commercial Arbitration Act enacted in 1961, with two minor amendments in 1982 and 1986 respectively. In line with global trends, the Commercial Arbitration Act was renamed the Arbitration Act when comprehensive revisions were made in 1998. The revisions were mainly to extend the application of arbitration beyond commercial areas. According to the new law, any disputes that can be settled in accordance with law may be arbitrated.[76]

Notwithstanding the adoption of the new law, government entities are not particularly keen on using arbitration to settle disputes over government contracts. There seems to be a general distrust of arbitral awards due to concerns about the impartiality, objectivity, independence and qualifications of arbitrators. Hence, the impact of the new law remains to be seen. Interestingly, however, in sharp contrast with the rather conservative attitude of government entities toward arbitration, courts in Taiwan are much more open to this new form of alternative dispute resolution and are more willing to enforce arbitral awards.[77]

4.2 Mediation

Article 403 of the Code of Civil Procedure stipulates mandatory mediation for certain lawsuits involving property rights. Mediation may also take place when the parties have a mediation agreement but one party sues and the other party's defense is the breach of such mediation agreement. According to the law, such disputes must first proceed with mediation.[78]

[75] *Ibid.* pp. 8–17. [76] Arbitration Law, Art. 1(2).

[77] K.-L. Shen, "Government attitudes toward arbitration and judicial practice in Taiwan," *Contemporary Asia Arbitration Journal*, 1(2008), 149–70.

[78] Code of Civil Procedure, Art. 404.

Mediation proceedings are conducted primarily by summary court judges.[79] However, in order to facilitate its effectiveness, mediation may be conducted in advance by one to three mediators appointed by judges. To improve the credibility of mediators and ensure the right of litigant parties to select mediators, in cases where a party has objected to any appointed mediators or where the parties have agreed to appoint other persons, judges may reappoint or appoint such persons as agreed upon by the parties. The law also permits judges of trial courts to be mediators if both litigant parties have agreed to move the case from litigation to mediation, as these judges are already familiar with the case, and it is unnecessary for the mediation proceedings to be removed to summary court judges.

To increase the use of mediation, the Code of Civil Procedure was amended in 1998, adding two ways in which mediation may be undertaken other than by the agreement of both parties. The first is at the discretion of mediators or judges who decide the terms of settlement. In disputes over property rights, mediators may at their discretion propose the terms of settlement. If the mediators are unable to determine the proposed terms of settlement, judges may either determine the proposed terms with the consent of both parties or designate another mediation session. When judges propose the settlement terms, the mediation shall be deemed successful upon the entry of such terms in the mediation proceeding transcript by the court clerk. This is the so-called "med-arb" or "quasi-arbitration" model.[80] The second is by court-proposed mediation resolution. In disputes over property rights, if the parties are unable to reach an agreement but are nevertheless close to doing so, a judge may take all circumstances into consideration and propose a resolution on her or his own initiative. Such a proposed resolution should serve the interests of the parties, who have ten days to object to the proposed resolution.[81] The law also stipulates that in cases of unsuccessful mediation after both parties have appeared at the mediation session, the court may – on motions by one party – order an immediate oral argument to avoid procedural delay.[82] These new measures for mediation have given rise to a 93 percent increase in the use of mediation from 1999 to 2010, with the success rate of mediation also increasing from 10.97 percent to 37.04 percent in the same period.[83]

[79] *Ibid.* Art. 406-1, para. 1. [80] *Ibid.* Art. 415, s. 1. [81] *Ibid.* Art. 417, s. 1.

[82] *Ibid.* Art. 419.

[83] K.-L. Shen, "The alternative dispute resolution (ADR) systems in Taiwan" in J.-r. Yeh (ed.), *East Asian Courts in Transition: Models, Dispute Resolution and Governance* (Taipei: National Taiwan University Press, forthcoming 2014) (in Chinese).

5 Incremental reforms and functional transformations of courts

As stated at the beginning of this chapter, nearly all courts in Taiwan – including the Supreme Court and the Constitutional Court – were in place with the relocation of the KMT government in 1949. Prior to the lifting of the Martial Law Decree in 1987 and the beginning of the democratic transition and constitutional reforms in the 1990s, the functions of courts had been substantially constrained. Yet, today, the courts have become an effective institution with profound transformations in their functions. It is especially intriguing how the courts were able to sustain themselves through the authoritarian era and gradually transform into the institutions they are today.

5.1 Constitutional Court as the key player in the transformation

Already established in 1948, the Constitutional Court gradually became an effective court guarding constitutionalism and protection of fundamental rights as early as the mid-1980s.[84] During the democratic transition, the impact of the Constitutional Court reached an apex in 1990 with *J.Y. Interpretation No. 261*, in which it ordered the first-term national representatives elected in 1948 to leave office, as their continuous service without re-election was a violation of democratic principles.[85]

In the ensuing years of constitutional reforms, the Constitutional Court was often called upon to intervene in political conflicts resulting from the lack of clarity in the constitutional text caused by many rounds of constitutional revisions.[86] For example, the Constitution was silent on whether lower courts might exercise the power of judicial review, but the Constitutional Court issued *J.Y. Interpretation No. 371*, deciding that while lower courts could not directly review the constitutionality of laws, they nevertheless could request clarifications from the Constitutional Court should they have doubts on the constitutionality of laws.[87] In addition, it was not clear if the Constitutional Court could review the constitutionality of *Pan-Li* (precedent) selected by the Supreme Court. In *J.Y. Interpretation No. 185* rendered in 1984, the Constitutional Court asserted its power of review on the basis of the hierarchical order

[84] Chang, "Role of judicial review," 73–88.
[85] J.Y. Interpretation No. 261 (1990).
[86] Chang, "Role of judicial review," 73–88.
[87] J.Y. Interpretation No. 371 (1995).

embedded in the rule of law and constitutionalism.[88] As stated earlier, according to the Constitution, the Constitutional Court exercises "abstract review," as it may review only the laws and regulations themselves but not concrete cases and how those laws and regulations apply to concrete cases. Yet, if it finds it necessary in exceptional cases, the Constitutional Court may review the application of laws and regulations, as it did in *J.Y. Interpretation Nos. 242* and *582*,[89] or extend its power over concrete controversies, as in *J.Y. Interpretation No. 553*.[90] In particular, *J.Y. Interpretation No. 499*, in which the Constitutional Court granted itself the power to review constitutional amendments, demonstrates the extent to which the Constitutional Court may exert its interpretive power where the Constitution is silent.[91]

Ginsburg and Moustafa have identified several key functions of courts in both authoritarian and democratic contexts.[92] Among these functions, ensuring the smooth functioning of the market and shouldering decision-making for controversial policies are most evident in the decisions of the Constitutional Court. Regarding the provision of credible commitments in the market sphere, *J.Y. Interpretation No. 204* serves as a telling example.[93] In this interpretation, the Constitutional Court endorsed the constitutionality of a law that severely penalized the issuance of checks on accounts that are closed or that have insufficient funds. A more recent example is *J.Y. Interpretation No. 675*, regarding the constitutionality of the Act for the Establishment and Administration of the Financial Restructuring Fund.[94] The Asian financial crisis of 1997 came as a shock to many Asian countries including Taiwan. In order to improve the financial sector, the government pushed through a series of financial reform measures in 2002, one of which involved the establishment of the Financial Restructuring Fund, which would assume control of troubled financial institutions if deemed necessary. It came as no surprise when a deferential decision was made by the Constitutional Court and the government was provided with generous discretion.

Undertaking the review of controversial policies has always been a significant part of the functions exercised by the Constitutional Court,

[88] J.Y. Interpretation No. 185 (1984).
[89] J.Y. Interpretation No. 242 (1989); J.Y. Interpretation No. 582 (2004).
[90] J.Y. Interpretation No. 553 (2002).
[91] J.Y. Interpretation No. 499 (2000).
[92] T. Moustafa and T. Ginsburg, "Introduction: the function of courts in authoritarian politics" in T. Moustafa and T. Ginsburg (eds.), *Rule by Law: The Politics of Courts in Authoritarian Regimes* (New York: Cambridge University Press, 2008), pp. 4–5.
[93] J.Y. Interpretation No. 204 (1986).
[94] J.Y. Interpretation No. 675 (2010).

even prior to Taiwan's democratization.[95] This function became even more pronounced in the eight years of divided government between the DPP-led administration and the KMT-dominated legislature. The suspension of a nuclear power plant in 2000 and the resulting constitutional decision in *J.Y. Interpretation No. 520* was illustrative.[96] Soon after coming to power, the DPP government announced the termination of the installation of the country's fourth nuclear power plant, which angered the KMT members of the legislature. Both parties were in serious dispute over which branch – the executive or the legislature – had the final say on the policy. The Constitutional Court was called upon to resolve the dispute. Interestingly, however, the Constitutional Court conferred no such power to either branch but mandated that negotiations be held to resolve the dispute.[97]

As powerful as the Constitutional Court is, its interpretations have not always been implemented without challenge, nor has it never faced any setbacks. The most significant challenge to a decision of the Constitutional Court occurred in the implementation of *J.Y. Interpretation No. 530* regarding the restructuring of the Judicial Yuan, as previously discussed. In order to observe the original design of the Judicial Yuan in the ROC Constitution and to implement the consensus reached in various judicial reform conferences, the Constitutional Court strongly criticized "the separation of the highest adjudicative organ from the highest judicial administration" and mandated the completion of comprehensive legislative reform within two years.[98] However, as the restructuring of courts involves many stakeholders with vested interests in the status quo, this decision has not yet been implemented and is unlikely to be implemented in the near future.

The Constitutional Court has also faced political setbacks.[99] The first setback occurred after *J.Y. Interpretation No. 499*, in which the constitutional amendment of 1999 was rendered null and void. In 2000, while the National Assembly revised the constitutional amendment to comply with this decision, it also wrote into the amendment that the Grand

[95] Chang, "Role of judicial review," 73–88. [96] J.Y. Interpretation No. 520 (2001).

[97] J.-r. Yeh, "Democracy-driven transformation to regulatory state: the case of Taiwan," *National Taiwan University Law Review*, 3(2) (2008), 31–59.

[98] J.Y. Interpretation No. 530 (2001).

[99] W.-C. Chang, "Strategic judicial responses in politically charged cases: East Asian experiences," *International Journal of Constitutional Law*, 8(4) (2010), 885–910.

Justices not appointed from among career judges would not enjoy the privileges accorded to career judges after the end of their terms.[100] This revision was made due to the belief that those appointed outside the judicial circle were too liberal-minded. Another setback occurred after *J.Y. Interpretation No. 585*, in which the Constitutional Court decided that the parliamentary investigatory commission enjoyed only very limited power over the investigation of the shooting of the President of Taiwan in 2004, which occurred the day before the presidential election in which he was the DPP's candidate.[101] Dissatisfied with the ruling, the KMT-dominated legislature passed a bill cutting the salaries of the Grand Justices, which in turn was set aside by the Constitutional Court in another ruling, *J.Y. Interpretation No. 601*, as a grave violation of judicial independence.[102] Perhaps the most egregious instance of political revenge by the KMT occurred with the appointment of Grand Justices in 2007. The KMT-dominated legislature confirmed only four of the President's nominees and boycotted the other four on partisan grounds. Worse yet, the KMT further manipulated the process by leaving the four remaining positions open until the newly elected KMT president took office in 2008 and could nominate his own candidates.[103] Regrettably, these political manipulations have – to varying degrees – undermined the institutional integrity and credibility of the Constitutional Court and resulted to some extent in the "politicization of the judiciary."[104]

5.2 *Reforms of criminal, civil and administrative litigation*

The following illustrates how the interpretations of the Constitutional Court have triggered the reforms of criminal, civil and administrative litigation. Equally important were the political initiatives for judicial reforms as exemplified by the judicial reform committee of 1996 and the nationwide judicial reform consultative conference of 1999. These political efforts were reflective of strong citizen demands for comprehensive judicial reforms and were often intertwined with and mutually facilitated by the reforms initiated by the courts, especially the Constitutional Court.

[100] Additional Articles of ROC Constitution, Art. 5, s. 1, para. 2 as revised in April 2000.
[101] J.Y. Interpretation No. 585 (2004). [102] J.Y. Interpretation No. 601 (2005).
[103] Chang, "Strategic judicial responses." [104] *Ibid.*

5.2.1 Criminal justice reform

The criminal justice system was used for the purpose of political and social control under the authoritarian regime, resulting in grave human rights violations. No legislative amendments regarding the improvement of the criminal justice system were made prior to the early 1980s. In 1980, the Constitutional Court in *J.Y. Interpretation No.166* demanded the reform of the Act Governing the Punishment of Police Offences, which had granted the police the power of detention and imposition of forced labor, as it violated individual freedoms and due process.[105] Regrettably, this interpretation was ignored by the government. Ten years later, in 1990, the Constitutional Court rendered *J.Y. Interpretation No. 251*, declaring the same law unconstitutional and mandating that it be revised by the end of June 1991.[106] A few years later, the Constitutional Court made an even more important decision regarding the criminal justice system in separating the power of prosecution from the power of adjudication. In *J.Y. Interpretation No. 392*, the Constitutional Court found unconstitutional an entrenched practice from the authoritarian era in which prosecutors had the power to detain criminal defendants or suspects during criminal investigations.[107] Based upon Article 8 of the ROC Constitution, which incorporates habeas corpus, the Constitutional Court states that any infringement of physical freedoms must be reviewed by judges in accordance with due process.

In response to *J.Y. Interpretation No. 392*, the Code of Criminal Procedure underwent a substantial revision in 1997. In addition, one of the points of consensus reached in the national judicial reform consultative conference was the need to transform the inquisitorial nature of the criminal justice system to have more of an adversarial quality and to guarantee the due process rights of criminal defendants. Major revisions were undertaken in 2003, followed by a series of fine-tuning revisions. Meanwhile, the Constitutional Court continued to render decisions affirming the rights of individuals to be free from arbitrary detention or arrest,[108] as well as reaffirming the rights of criminal defendants to access legal counsel and other due process rights.[109] Up until now, the Code of Criminal Procedure has been amended about a dozen times and hundreds of provisions revised. Through these revisions, the criminal

105 J.Y. Interpretation No. 166 (1980).
106 J.Y. Interpretation No. 251 (1990).
107 J.Y. Interpretation No. 392 (1995).
108 J.Y. Interpretation No. 665 (2009).
109 J.Y. Interpretation No. 654 (2009).

justice system has been profoundly transformed, and the function of courts in criminal trials is very different from what it was in the past.

5.2.2 Civil litigation reforms

In the late 1980s and early 1990s, women's groups were among the first public interest groups to undertake constitutional litigation for advancing social reforms.[110] Their first goal was to challenge sex-based discrimination in the provisions of the Chapter on Family in the Civil Code. In *J.Y. Interpretation No. 365*, the Constitutional Court agreed with the women's groups and found unconstitutional a provision privileging the father in cases of parental disagreement on the exercise of parental rights.[111] This interpretation gave rise to a major overhaul of the Civil Code in 1995. Women's groups were encouraged to push the reform agenda even further to the Code of Civil Procedure regarding the adjudication of family and child matters. Their efforts succeeded in the passage of the amendments to the Code of Civil Procedure and the Act on Non-Litigation Matters in 1999, granting judges greater authority in the adjudication of family and child matters for the best interests of the child and the benefits of the family. In January 2012, an entire new law on the adjudication of family matters was promulgated and became effective in June of the same year. In 2013, the family court was created, providing a more friendly adjudicative setting in which sex and gender equality and the best interests of the child would be taken into full consideration.

Aside from the reforms pushed by women's groups, the consensus reached in the national judicial reform consultative conference of 1999 on the need to improve the efficiency and effectiveness of civil trials also resulted in a major revision of the Code of Civil Procedure in 2003. This and subsequent revisions have significantly altered the process of civil trials and emphasize a shift from party autonomy to greater responsibility for judges. By obligating judges to elucidate and to clarify main issues and evidence in civil trials, the new law is aimed at avoiding unnecessary delays or unexpected results and at delivering better and efficient justice. Also noteworthy in these amendments were the recognition of group standing and the institutionalization of public interest litigation.[112]

110 Chang, "Public-interest litigation in Taiwan," pp. 136–60.

111 J.Y. Interpretation No. 365 (1994).

112 K.-L. Shen, "Class action in Taiwan: a new system created using the theory of 'right of procedure options,'" *National Taiwan University Law Review*, 5(1) (2010), 39–71.

5.2.3 Administrative litigation reform

Prior to the substantial revision of the Administration Litigation Act in 1998, there was only one type of administrative litigation: revocation of an administrative disposition. Anyone whose rights were infringed upon by an unlawful disposition of an administrative agency at the central or local level would be entitled to bring a suit at the administrative court. This was the only way in which citizens could redress the wrongs committed by administrative agencies. During the authoritarian era, the definitions and concepts of administrative disposition, lawfulness, and standing to sue tended to be quite narrowly construed, substantially limiting the rights of individuals to sue administrative agencies.

Noticeably, however, since the 1980s, both the Constitutional Court and the administrative court have begun to develop much more generous readings into the above concepts, ensuring greater access to justice in administrative litigation. For example, as early as 1979, the Constitutional Court rendered *J.Y. Interpretation No. 156*, recognizing the alteration of an urban plan as an administrative disposition in order to permit the interested parties to sue at the administrative court.[113] Later, in *J.Y. Interpretation Nos. 423 and 459*, the Constitutional Court further elaborated on the concept of administrative disposition, stating that it includes notifications or classifications that may have profound impacts on the rights of individuals or the legal relationship between individuals and the state.[114] In *J.Y. Interpretation No. 469*, the Constitutional Court also expanded the concept of standing to sue by relying on a theory of "protective norms" in which "the overall structure of the law, the applicable party, and the intended regulatory effects and factors of social developments" must all be taken into consideration in deciding if individuals enjoy the standing to sue.[115] Similarly, the administrative court has also adopted a liberal construction of administrative disposition. In a recent decision, the Supreme Administrative Court again read an administrative plan regarding the network between local and mobile phones issued by the National Communication Commission as an administrative disposition.[116]

In addition to the above court-initiated reforms in administrative litigation, strong demands from citizens for a more accountable and transparent government have also resulted in a series of administrative

[113] J.Y. Interpretation No. 156 (1979).
[114] J.Y. Interpretation No. 423 (1997), J.Y. Interpretation No. 459 (1998).
[115] J.Y. Interpretation No. 469 (1998).
[116] Supreme Administrative Court, 98 Tsai-Tzu No. 1195 (Taiwan).

legislation.[117] These include the Environmental Impact Assessment Act of 1994, the Data Protection Act of 1995, major revisions to the Administrative Appeals Act of 1998, major revisions to the Administrative Litigation Act of 1998, major revisions to the Administrative Enforcement Act, the Government Procurement Act of 1998 and the Administrative Procedural Act of 2000, all of which place stronger judicial checks and balances on the exercise of government powers and hence strengthen administrative litigation.[118]

With the strengthening of administrative litigation, some judicialization of administrative governance has been inevitable.[119] As administrative courts step into more and more policy disputes, their professionalism, credibility and independence also face great challenges. The 1998 revisions to the Organic Act of the Administrative Court were right to diversify the sources of administrative court judges to talents outside the judicial circle.

6 Judicial compliance and evaluations

Judicial compliance is not easy to measure. As Taiwan has successfully transformed into a constitutional democracy with the rule of law, judicial compliance is generally not an issue. Interestingly, however, notwithstanding substantial progress made in judicial reform, public polls or evaluations of the performance of the courts have not been as positive, and the legal community still holds very critical views of the court system.

6.1 Compliance with judicial decisions

One possible index of compliance with the judiciary is the observance of judicial deadlines given by the Constitutional Court for the government to revise laws or regulations found to be unconstitutional but not yet rendered null and void. The first such deadline was mandated in *J.Y. Interpretation No. 218*, in which a tax regulation was found unconstitutional but provided with a grace period of six months

[117] Yeh, "Democracy-driven transformation to regulatory state." [118] *Ibid.*

[119] For further illustration of the judicialization of administrative governance, see T. Ginsburg, "The judicialization of administrative governance: causes, consequences and limits" in T. Ginsburg and A. H. Y. Chen (eds.), *Administrative Law and Governance in Asia: Comparative Perspectives* (New York: Routledge, 2009), pp. 1–19.

for revision.[120] While the six-month deadline was not met, the regulation was finally revised forty-five days after the deadline.[121] Since then, the Constitutional Court has imposed similar deadlines in a variety of cases, involving everything from penal laws to technical regulations, with deadlines ranging from six months to as long as three years. Overall, compliance with these judicial deadlines is high, at 66.7 percent.[122]

In general, the interpretations issued by the Constitutional Court – even those invalidating laws – have been observed. Since the late 1990s, the Constitutional Court has found nearly 30 to 40 percent of the impugned laws and regulations it has reviewed to be unconstitutional.[123] In *J.Y. Interpretation No. 499*, the Constitutional Court even found unconstitutional the constitutional revision of 1999 and invalidated it altogether.[124] This ruling was nonetheless followed by immediate action from the National Assembly to undertake another round of constitutional revisions.

Noticeably, however, compliance with decisions by the administrative courts, especially those regarding controversial policies, has not been as sound. A recent case concerning the environmental impact assessment (EIA) of the Central Taiwan Science Park serves as an example. Despite the annulment of the EIA by the Supreme Administrative Court, the government, under strong pressure from the business community, continued the construction of the science park, ignoring the decision as well as public criticism.

6.2 *Evaluations of judicial performance*

According to a telephone poll conducted in 2011 by the Judicial Yuan from 25 July to 10 August, 74.9 percent of the respondents considered themselves unfamiliar with the judicial system, and only 22.1 percent considered themselves familiar with it. Among those who had experience with litigation, 49.6 percent said that they were not satisfied. While over 65 percent of the respondents felt satisfied with the service of volunteers

[120] J.Y. Interpretation No. 218 (1987).

[121] J.-r. Yeh, "The politics of unconstitutionality: an empirical analysis of judicial deadlines and political compliance in Taiwan," paper presented in the Second International Conference on Empirical Studies of Judicial Systems, Institutum Iurisprudentiae, *Academia Sinica*, 24 June 2011.

[122] *Ibid.* [123] Chang, "Role of judicial review," 73–88.

[124] J.Y. Interpretation No. 499 (2000).

and staff at the court buildings, less than 40 percent felt satisfied with the integrity of judicial officers and the transparency of judicial information.[125] In another survey conducted in 2010, the credibility of judges, integrity of judicial officers and efficiency of the courts were considered most important by the majority of respondents. Yet, the rates of satisfaction with those issues were only 39.3 percent, 30.6 percent and 39.2 percent respectively.[126]

The Judicial Reform Foundation, a non-governmental organization that has advocated judicial reforms for decades, conducted a series of polls over the internet from 1999 to 2010. In 1999, only 13 percent of the respondents trusted judicial decisions.[127] In 2002, 65 percent of the examinees did not trust judicial decisions, while 13 percent of the respondents indicated their trust.[128] In the 2008 poll, 19 percent of the respondents held a skeptical attitude towards judicial reforms undertaken by the Judicial Yuan, and 56.1 percent of the respondents did not believe in the judicial reforms.[129] Polls conducted by the Academia Sinica, a renowned academic institution in Taiwan, indicated that in 2005, the number of individuals trusting courts was greater – by 2.75 percent – than those who did not.[130] However, in 2009, this margin increased to 14.14 percentage points.[131] Thus far, the respondents who consider the courts to be unjust have always outnumbered those who consider the courts to be just.

The legal and political communities generally hold critical views of judicial performance and integrity. A survey of legislative candidates in 1996 exhibited negative attitudes towards courts and judicial reforms: over 60 percent of the candidates felt unsatisfied with the outcome of

125 Judicial Yuan, Poll of judicial perception from the public (2011), www.judicial.gov.tw/juds/u100.pdf.

126 Judicial Yuan, Poll of judicial perception from the public (2010), www.judicial.gov.tw/juds/4_u99.pdf.

127 Judicial Reform Foundation, Perceptional evaluation of judicial system (1999), www.jrf.org.tw/newjrf/RTE/myform_search_result_detail.asp?txt=%E5%8F%B8%E6%B3%95%E4%BF%A1%E8%B3%B4%E5%BA%A6&Sumit=%E9%96%8B%E5%A7%8B%E6%90%9C%E5%B0%8B&id=856.

128 Judicial Reform Foundation, Perceptional evaluation of judicial system (2002), www.jrf.org.tw/newjrf/RTE/myform_detail.asp?id=1008.

129 Judicial Reform Foundation, Perceptional evaluation of judicial system (2008), http://tw.quiz.polls.yahoo.com/quiz/quizresults.php?stack_id=1607&wv=1.

130 Academia Sinica, Perceptional evaluation of courts (2005), www.ios.sinica.edu.tw/si/t6/si2008b/si2005a.fre.

131 Academia Sinica, Perceptional evaluation of courts (2009), www.ios.sinica.edu.tw/si/t6/si2008b/si2009a.fre.

judicial reform. Nearly 50 percent of the candidates considered there to be many serious problems in the judicial system, such as corruption among judicial officials, partisan judicial decisions, abusive detentions, and the extraction of evidence through torture or other illegal means. Not a single candidate responded that those problems did not exist.[132] A similar survey with private attorneys in 1997 indicated that the percentage of lawyers who considered the problem of bribery and corruption still to be serious was less than 20 percent. However, the survey also showed that these lawyers believe that serious problems remain, such as the attitude and performance of prosecutors and judges, the quality of judgments and the overall quality of the judicial system.[133] In a poll conducted by the Judicial Yuan in 2011, the lawyers surveyed considered it necessary to strengthen the quality of judicial decisions and improve the attitude of judges.[134]

7 Conclusion

The greatest strength of the courts in Taiwan is their capacity to gradually transform their functions in response to democratic transitions and social demands. It is not an easy task for any judicial system to sustain itself through political turbulence in both democratic transitions and divided governments while maintaining institutional integrity and judicial independence.[135] In the last two or three decades, the courts in Taiwan have succeeded in meeting such challenges. The quality of judges and of legal education has been maintained at a certain level, and the integrity of judges has been sustained, with corruption gradually decreasing over time. Admittedly, dissatisfaction with and criticisms of the judiciary still abound. Yet the judiciary has undoubtedly become an effective institution guarding constitutionalism, the rule of law and the rights of individuals. Perhaps even more importantly, facing ever-escalating

[132] Judicial Reform Foundation, Poll for legislators (1996), www.jrf.org.tw/newjrf/RTE/myform_search_result_detail.asp?txt=%E5%8F%B8%E6%B3%95%E4%BF%A1%E8%B3%B4%E5%BA%A6&Sumit=%E9%96%8B%E5%A7%8B%E6%90%9C%E5%B0%8B&id=1025.

[133] Judicial Reform Foundation, Poll for attorneys (1997), www.jrf.org.tw/newjrf/RTE/myform_search_result_detail.asp?txt=%E5%8F%B8%E6%B3%95%E4%BF%A1%E8%B3%B4%E5%BA%A6&Sumit=%E9%96%8B%E5%A7%8B%E6%90%9C%E5%B0%8B&id=1027.

[134] Judicial Yuan, Poll for attorneys (2011), www.judicial.gov.tw/juds/I100.pdf.

[135] Yeh, "Presidential politics," 885.

demands for economic development, courts in Taiwan have begun shouldering alternative functions to those of traditional arbiters.

At present, pressing challenges include the need to improve the quality of judges and to avoid judicial politicization. The lack of experience of judges is a result of the fact that legal education is typically provided at the undergraduate level. On average, law graduates are about twenty-one to twenty-three years old, and those who pass the judicial exams are about twenty-three to twenty-six years old.[136] After the two-year training, judges serving at the bottom level of the courts are mostly in their late twenties. As large-scale reform of legal education has not been in sight, one possible solution may be the diversification of the sources of judges. The other challenge is judicial politicization. As discussed above, the Constitutional Court and administrative courts in particular have begun to intervene in political or policy disputes. Such a trend has also been seen in other jurisdictions,[137] but it has placed judicial integrity and independence at high risk. Courts must exercise additional caution in stepping into such disputes, and judges with better and more professional training are needed in order to meet these demands.

References

Chang, R. "Thousands take to street for Hung," *Taipei Times*, 4 August 2013, www.taipeitimes.com/News/front/archives/2013/08/04/2003568877

Chang, W.-C. "An isolated nation with global-minded citizens: bottom-up transnational constitutionalism in Taiwan," *National Taiwan University Law Review*, 4(3) (2009), 203–35

Chang, W.-C. "Professor Weng Yueh-Seng and the reform of the Judicial Yuan" in J.-r. Yeh (ed.), *The Development and Transformation of Rule of Law: Public Laws of Professor Weng Yueh-Sheng* (Taipei: Angle Publishing, 2009), pp. 149–79 (in Chinese)

Chang, W.-C. "Public-interest litigation in Taiwan: strategy for law and policy reforms in course of democratization" in P. J. Yap and H. Law (eds.), *Public Interest Litigation in Asia* (New York: Routledge, 2011), pp. 136–60

Chang, W.-C. "Strategic judicial responses in politically charged cases: East Asian experiences," *International Journal of Constitutional Law*, 8(4) (2010), 885–910

[136] B.-c. Dong, "A new attempt for a new system of the bar and judicial exam in 2011," *Taiwan Jurist*, 100 (2011), 18–21 (in Chinese).

[137] Ginsburg, "Judicialization of administrative governance," pp. 1–19.

Chang, W.-C. "The role of judicial review in consolidating democracy: the case of Taiwan," *Asia Law Review*, 2(2) (2005), 73–88

Chang, W.-C. and Yeh, J.-r. "Judges as discursive agent: the use of foreign precedents by the Constitutional Court of Taiwan" in T. Groppi and M. C. Ponthoreau (eds.), *The Use of Foreign Precedents by Constitutional Judges* (Oxford: Hart Publishing, 2013), pp. 373–92

Chen, H. S. "Reception from foreign legal system: the development of legal education in Taiwan," *Taiwan Law Review*, 188 (2010), 54–69 (in Chinese)

Dong, B.-c. "A new attempt for a new system of the bar and judicial exam," *Taiwan Jurist*, 100 (2011), 18–29 (in Chinese)

Ginsburg, T. *Judicial Review in New Democracies: Constitutional Courts in Asian Cases* (New York: Cambridge University Press, 2003)

Ginsburg, T. "The judicialization of administrative governance: causes, consequences and limits" in T. Ginsburg and A. H. Y. Chen (eds.), *Administrative Law and Governance in Asia: Comparative Perspectives* (New York: Routledge, 2009), pp. 1–19

Judicial Yuan. *Meeting Records of the Judicial Reform Committee* (Taipei: Judicial Yuan, 1996)

Judicial Yuan. *Meeting Records of the National Judicial Reform Consultative Conference* (Taipei: Judicial Yuan, 1999)

Law, D. S. and Chang, W.-C. "The limits of global judicial dialogue," *Washington Law Review*, 86(3) (2011), 523–77

Lo, C.-f. *The Legal Culture and System of Taiwan* (Leiden: Kluwer Law International, 2006)

Lo, C.-f. "Taiwan: external influences mixed with traditional elements to form its unique legal system" in E. A. Black and G. Bell (eds.), *Law and Legal Institutions of Asia: Traditions, Adaptations and Innovations* (New York: Cambridge University Press, 2011), pp. 91–119

Moustafa, T. and Ginsburg, T. "Introduction: the function of courts in authoritarian politics" in T. Moustafa and T. Ginsburg (eds.), *Rule by Law: The Politics of Courts in Authoritarian Regimes* (New York: Cambridge University Press, 2008), pp. 1–22

Shapiro, M. *Courts: A Comparative and Political Analysis* (University of Chicago Press, 1981)

Shen, K.-L. "Class action in Taiwan: a new system created using the theory of 'right of procedure options,'" *National Taiwan University Law Review*, 5(1) (2010), 39–71

Shen, K.-L. "Government attitudes toward arbitration and judicial practice in Taiwan," *Contemporary Asia Arbitration Journal*, 1 (2008), 149–70

Shen, K.-L. "The alternative dispute resolution (ADR) systems in Taiwan" in J.-r. Yeh (ed.), *East Asian Courts in Transition: Models, Dispute Resolution and Governance* (Taipei: National Taiwan University Press, forthcoming 2014) (in Chinese)

Wang, T.-S. *Legal Reform in Taiwan under Japanese Colonial Rule (1895–1945): The Reception of Western Law* (Seattle: University of Washington Press 1992)

Wang, T.-S. *The Introduction to the Legal History of Taiwan*, 2nd edn. (Taipei: Angle Publishing, 2004) (in Chinese)

Yeh, J.-r. "Changing forces of constitutional and regulatory reform in Taiwan," *Columbia Journal of Chinese Law*, 4 (1990), 83–100

Yeh, J.-r. "Constitutional reform and democratization in Taiwan: 1945–2000" in P. Chow (ed.), *Taiwan's Modernization in Global Perspective* (Westport: Praeger Publishers, 2002), pp. 47–77

Yeh, J.-r. "Democracy-driven transformation to regulatory state: the case of Taiwan," *National Taiwan University Law Review*, 3(2) (2008), 31–59

Yeh, J.-r. "Presidential politics and judicial facilitation of political dialogue between political actors in new Asian democracies: comparing the South Korean and Taiwanese experiences," *International Journal of Constitutional Law*, 8(4) (2011), 911–49

Yeh, J.-r. "The politics of unconstitutionality: an empirical analysis of judicial deadlines and political compliance in Taiwan" in the Second International Conference on Empirical Studies of Judicial System, Institutum Iurisprudentiae, *Academia Sinica*, 24 June 2011

Yeh, J.-r. and Chang, W.-C. "The emergence of East Asian constitutionalism: features in comparison," *American Journal of Comparative Law*, 59(3) (2011), 805–40

5

Hong Kong: common law Courts in China

PUI YIN LO

Hong Kong came to the fore of modern history in 1841. That was the year Hong Kong Island was ceded by China's Qing Imperial Court to the British Crown at the end of the First Opium War. Subsequent expansions in 1860 and in 1898 into Kowloon and the New Territories, respectively, had led to European occupation of these parcels of Chinese territory and the establishment of an Administration along British colonial lines, maintaining law and order, providing basic sanitation and facilitating trade with the Mainland of China.[1] The Administration introduced policing and set up courts, and some lawyers migrated from other parts of the British Empire to ply their trade, in a system of adjudication of disputes styled after the common law based legal system. This was at first an exclusively European affair, with little participation from the growing Chinese population of the colony, who kept to themselves applying traditional or customary norms and the Qing Lü and Li codes. Indeed, for a short period after British occupation of Hong Kong and Kowloon, a yamen (magistrate's court) of Xinan County of Guangdong Province was maintained in Kowloon City. It took a bit of time, but eventually some members of the Chinese community distinguished themselves in the learning and practice of the laws and usages of the foreigners and practiced law in Hong Kong.[2]

The historical presence of Hong Kong as a British colony in the late nineteenth and early twentieth centuries may have precipitated or

The author gratefully acknowledges the provision of facilities by the Centre of Comparative and Public Law during his appointment as Visiting Fellow, which enabled him to complete his investigation of the courts in Hong Kong for this Study.

[1] See P. Wesley-Smith, *Unequal Treaty 1898–1997: China, Great Britain and Hong Kong's New Territories*, rev. edn. (Hong Kong: Oxford University Press, 1998).

[2] The first of them was Wu Choi, otherwise known as Wu Ting-fong, a barrister-at-law of Lincoln's Inn. Another who had had the benefit of Hong Kong education in the Anglican school that Wu once studied, founding, as it turned out, a subsequent career in the law, was Wang Chung-hui. Both later on served in governments of China as diplomats and legal reformers.

facilitated political change in neighboring countries. As for Hong Kong itself, its population grew with waves of immigration, particularly from Mainland China. In the earlier periods, many might have come to Hong Kong to work or trade but would eventually return to their native regions to retire. Later, with the conclusion of the Civil War by the establishment of the People's Republic of China (PRC) and the diminished ease of travel and interchange with Mainland China, Hong Kong acquired a more permanent population of ethnic Chinese who had to be fed, housed and made productive. The inflow of capital from Mainland China into Hong Kong from migrant entrepreneurs spurred the development of Hong Kong's industries, which, coupled with its geographical location as well as the market-driven economic policies and the welfarist social policies of the British Administration, led to gradual economic growth through trade, manufacturing and thereafter real estate development, culminating in prosperity.[3]

Then came 1979, when it was thought that the expiry of the term of the lease of the New Territories in less than twenty years' time might create uncertainty over the use of land granted by the British Administration as security for bank loans. The leaders of the PRC were approached by their British counterparts but they were uninterested in the legal niceties. Their fundamental position had been that Hong Kong as a whole was Chinese territory and one day it would be returned to the motherland.[4] The visit of Prime Minister Margaret Thatcher to Beijing in 1982 confirmed the intention on the part of the leadership of the PRC, represented by Deng Xiaoping, that Hong Kong would revert to China by 1 July 1997, if not earlier, and that there would be no compromise on their part to allow or tolerate British occupation and administration of Hong Kong beyond that date. Diplomatic negotiations between the United Kingdom and the PRC ensued under these parameters, resulting in the conclusion of the Sino-British Joint Declaration 1984, which paved the way for the relinquishment of British sovereignty over Hong Kong on 1 July 1997 and the resumption of exercise of Chinese sovereignty over Hong Kong on 1 July 1997.[5]

3 See L. Goodstadt, *Uneasy Partners: The Conflict between Public Interest and Private Profit in Hong Kong* (Hong Kong University Press, 2009).

4 P. Wesley-Smith, "Settlement of the question of Hong Kong," *California Western International Law Journal*, 17(1) (1987), 116–32.

5 Joint Declaration of the Government of the United Kingdom of Great Britain and Northern Ireland and the Government of the People's Republic of China on the Question of Hong Kong (hereinafter Joint Declaration), Beijing, 19 December 1984, in force 27 May 1985, 1399 UNTS 33; (1984) 23 ILM 1366, paras. 1 and 2.

The Joint Declaration of 1984 also set out the PRC's basic policies regarding Hong Kong upon the resumption of exercise of Chinese sovereignty. The Hong Kong Special Administrative Region (HKSAR) was to be established on 1 July 1997 and its economic, political, social and legal systems were to be prescribed by a law called the Basic Law of the Hong Kong Special Administrative Region of the People's Republic of China. The HKSAR was to be vested with executive, legislative and independent judicial power (including that of final adjudication), and the laws currently in force in Hong Kong were to remain basically unchanged. The Joint Declaration proclaimed that the social and economic systems in Hong Kong in 1984 "will remain unchanged, and so will the life style," and that these basic policies would "remain unchanged for 50 years."[6] The principle or concept behind these basic policies is known as "One Country, Two Systems," which was first conceived by the Central Authorities of the PRC as a principle for the reunification with Taiwan.

Following a five-year effort by a drafting committee organized by the Central Authorities of the PRC, of which less than half of the membership consisted of Hong Kong residents, the Basic Law of the HKSAR was adopted by the National People's Congress of the PRC on 4 April 1990. The President of the PRC promulgated the Basic Law on the same day, and it was to take effect on 1 July 1997.[7]

Hong Kong was "handed over" by the United Kingdom to the PRC at midnight, 1 July 1997, and the Basic Law of the HKSAR took effect. Judges and other members of the judiciary serving in Hong Kong before the establishment of the HKSAR were permitted to remain in employment and to retain their seniority with pay, allowances, benefits and conditions of service no less favorable than before.[8] Legislation passed shortly thereafter provided for the establishment of the courts of the

[6] Joint Declaration, para. 3(3), (5) and (12). For elaboration thereof, see Joint Declaration, Annex I, ss. I and II.

[7] I.e. The Basic Law of the Hong Kong Special Administrative Region of the People's Republic of China (adopted at the 3rd Session of the 7th National People's Congress on 4 April 1990; promulgated by Order No. 26 of the President of the People's Republic of China on 4 April 1990) (1990) 29 ILM 1511. The National People's Congress decided on the same date that the establishment of the Hong Kong Special Administrative Region would take place on 1 July 1997; see the Decision of the National People's Congress on the Establishment of the Hong Kong Special Administrative Region (adopted at the 3rd Session of the 7th National People's Congress on 4 April 1990) (1990) 29 ILM 1549.

[8] Basic Law of the HKSAR, Art. 93.

HKSAR, the continuity of service of judges and judicial officers, and the continuity of legal proceedings, the criminal justice system, and the administration of justice.[9] Continuity was achieved and maintained; this has thereafter been stressed judicially as a theme underlying the Basic Law.[10]

Despite the difference in the "two systems," the economy of Hong Kong is increasingly integrated with and dependent on that of the Mainland.[11]

1 General description of the judicial system

1.1 Independent judicial power of the HKSAR

Under the Basic Law of the HKSAR, the HKSAR is vested with independent judicial power, including that of final adjudication.[12] The HKSAR courts exercise the judicial power of the HKSAR and adjudicate cases in accordance with the laws applicable in the HKSAR, which are the Basic Law, the laws previously in force in Hong Kong, the laws enacted by the legislature of the HKSAR,[13] and a number of national laws of the PRC made applicable to the HKSAR as listed in an annex to the Basic Law.[14] The power of final adjudication is vested in the Court of Final Appeal, which may as required invite judges from other common law jurisdictions to sit on the Court.[15] When adjudicating cases, the HKSAR courts are authorized by the Standing Committee of the National People's Congress (NPCSC) to interpret on their own the provisions of the Basic Law that are within the limits of the autonomy of the HKSAR.[16] The HKSAR courts may refer to precedents of other common law jurisdictions.[17] Moreover, judicial power shall be exercised by the HKSAR courts independently without any interference.[18]

[9] Hong Kong Reunification Ordinance (110 of 1997), ss. 8, 9, 10(1) and 22(1).

[10] See *HKSAR* v. *Ma Wai-kwan David & Ors* [1997] HKLRD 761, CA; *Secretary for Justice* v. *Lau Kwok Fai Bernard* (2005) 8 HKCFAR 304, CFA; *The Catholic Diocese of Hong Kong* v. *Secretary for Justice* [2007] 4 HKLRD 483, CFI; *Luk Ka Cheung* v. *Market Misconduct Tribunal* [2009] 1 HKLRD 114, CFI; *Kong Yun Ming* v. *Director of Social Welfare* [2009] 4 HKLRD 382, CFI.

[11] See *Hong Kong in Figures*, 2013 edn., www.statistics.gov.hk/pub/B10100062013AN13E0100.pdf; A. Mason, "The rule of law in the shadow of the giant: the Hong Kong experience," *Sydney Law Review*, 33 (2011), 626–44.

[12] Basic Law of the HKSAR, Arts. 2, 19, 82 and 85.

[13] Basic Law of the HKSAR, Art. 8.

[14] Basic Law of the HKSAR, Art. 18.

[15] Basic Law of the HKSAR, Art. 82.

[16] Basic Law of the HKSAR, Art. 158.

[17] Basic Law of the HKSAR, Art. 84.

[18] Basic Law of the HKSAR, Art. 85.

According to Article 12 of the Basic Law of the HKSAR, the HKSAR, like any other province, national autonomous region or municipality directly under the Central Government, is a local administrative region of the PRC.[19] In this sense, the HKSAR is not a state, province or canton in a federation or confederation. Rather it is a unit of local administration in the unitary state of the PRC, directly under the Central People's Government and enjoying a high degree of autonomy.

On the other hand, in terms of the judicial system, the HKSAR courts do not form part of the system of people's courts of the PRC. The judicial system of the HKSAR is self-contained with its own power of final adjudication vested in a Court of Final Appeal sitting in Hong Kong.[20] There is no hierarchical relationship between the HKSAR courts and the Mainland Chinese courts.[21] A judgment of the Court of Final Appeal may not be further appealed or reviewed or otherwise examined by the Supreme People's Court in Beijing. Further, Articles 19 and 80 of the Basic Law provide that the HKSAR courts at all levels shall be the judiciary of the HKSAR, exercising the judicial power of the HKSAR and having jurisdiction over all cases in the HKSAR, except that the restrictions on their jurisdiction imposed by the legal system and principles previously in force in Hong Kong shall be maintained. As Cheng Jie of the School of Law of Tsinghua University has observed, judicial power has been "thoroughly devolved" to the HKSAR and its courts.[22]

[19] See the Constitution of the People's Republic of China 1982, Art. 30.

[20] See Basic Law of the HKSAR, Arts. 2, 19, 82 and 85.

[21] Article 95 of the Basic Law of the HKSAR makes provision for the maintenance of "juridical relations" between the HKSAR and the judicial organs of other parts of the People's Republic of China "through consultations and in accordance with law' and they "may render assistance to each other." Such consultations are conducted on an equal basis between the Hong Kong side (a combined effort of the Administration Wing, Chief Secretary of Administration's Office, the Department of Justice and the Registrar of the High Court) and the Mainland side (namely the Supreme People's Court). These consultations have yielded the conclusion of three arrangements on civil and commercial matters, including an arrangement on service of judicial documents, an arrangement on enforcement of arbitral awards, and an arrangement on recognition and enforcement of a limited category of civil and commercial judgments. There are also day-to-day matters of mutual assistance in criminal matters on an ad hoc or per case basis; see, for example, *HKSAR* v. *Hui Yat Sing & Anor* [2008] 4 HKC 577, CA (on the taking of evidence at the Jiangmen Intermediate People's Court).

[22] See J. Cheng, "The story of a new policy," *Hong Kong Journal*, 15 (July 2009), 1 (accessible at www.hkbasiclaw.com/hkjournal).

1.2 Structure and organization of the courts of the HKSAR

The system of courts of the HKSAR follows the tradition of the common law ordinary courts, and there is one single hierarchical system of courts, with the Court of Final Appeal serving as the apex "supreme court." The Chief Justice of the Court of Final Appeal is designated as the head of the Judiciary of the HKSAR and is charged with the administration of the Judiciary and such other functions as may from time to time be lawfully conferred on him.[23]

The system of HKSAR courts is divided along two broad jurisdictions: Civil and Criminal.[24] Figure 5.1 shows the structure of the HKSAR courts and their hierarchical relationship by way of appeals.

The civil jurisdiction of the Judiciary of the HKSAR may be exercised at first instance before a number of courts and tribunals, depending mainly on the monetary value of the claim and the nature of the claim. The Court of First Instance of the High Court is the superior court of record of unlimited jurisdiction in civil causes and matters.[25] The District Court is a court of record of limited jurisdiction in civil causes and matters,[26] the main limitation being the monetary value of the claim, which is set generally at HK$1 million in the case of a claim in contract,

[23] See the Hong Kong Court of Final Appeal Ordinance (Cap. 484), s. 6(1A).

[24] Sometimes it is difficult to determine whether a cause or matter is civil or criminal; see the High Court Ordinance (Cap. 4), s. 13(2) relating to the civil jurisdiction of the Court of Appeal and the cases litigating its meaning such as *Re George Tan Soon Gin* [1992] 2 HKLR 254, PC (application for judicial review from the proceedings before a district judge exercising criminal jurisdiction); *Hunsworth* v. *Attorney General* [1996] 3 HKC 519 (application for letter of request under the Evidence Ordinance (Cap. 8)); *Secretary for Justice* v. *Li Xin Nian* [2001] 2 HKLRD 851, CA (application for forfeiture of proceeds of drug trafficking); *So Wing Keung* v. *Sing Tao Ltd & Anor* [2005] 2 HKLRD 11 (application for a search warrant with respect to journalistic materials); and *Re Kennedy (No. 3)* [2009] 1 HKC 57, CFA (proceedings for the committal of a person for contempt of court).

[25] See the High Court Ordinance (Cap. 4), s. 3(2). The Court of First Instance maintains specialist lists, each with a designated judge in charge of the list with the power to regulate the business of cases assigned to the relevant list by practice directions; there are at present the Admiralty List, the Commercial List, the Construction and Arbitration List, the Constitutional and Administrative Law List, and the Personal Injuries List. Further, there is also designated a judge for the hearing of other categories of more specialized cases, such as bankruptcy and corporate matters (whose court is called the Companies Court), probate and administration of deceased's estates, and the administration of the estates of mentally incapacitated persons.

[26] The District Court incorporates the Family Court, which consists of a panel of judges designated to exercise the jurisdiction vested with the District Court under the Matrimonial Causes Ordinance (Cap. 172) and the Matrimonial Proceedings and Property Ordinance (Cap. 192), but with a separate registry.

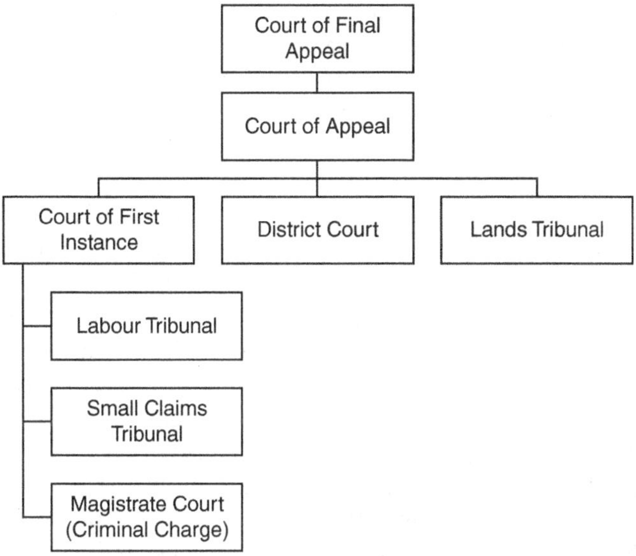

Figure 5.1: Structure of courts of the HKSAR

quasi-contract or tort, and at a rateable value of HK$240,000 where the action is for the recovery of land.[27] First instance hearings or trials in civil causes or matters are normally heard by a court consisting of one judge (be it in the District Court or in the Court of First Instance of the High Court).[28]

The Small Claims Tribunal and the Labour Tribunal are established for the purpose of providing avenues of expeditious access to justice in an informal setting with the presiding adjudicator or presiding officer having a duty to inquire, dispensing with formal procedures and legal representation. The Small Claims Tribunal has exclusive jurisdiction over monetary claims founded in contract, quasi-contract or tort where the amount claimed is not more than HK$50,000, whether on balance of account or otherwise.[29] Employment related claims, including claims for a sum of money arising out of a breach of a term of a contract of

[27] See the District Court Ordinance (Cap. 336), ss. 3, 32 and 35.

[28] See the High Court Ordinance (Cap. 4), s. 32(1) and the District Court Ordinance (Cap. 336), s. 6. Other provisions of the High Court Ordinance empower the Court of First Instance to hear first instance cases by a court consisting of a judge sitting with a jury or an assessor.

[29] See the Small Claims Tribunal Ordinance (Cap. 338), Sch.

employment, the failure of a person to comply with employment legislation, or a need for the determination of questions as to the rights of employees to payments and remedies under employment legislation, are exclusively handled by the Labour Tribunal.[30]

There are four other tribunals of specialized jurisdiction: The Lands Tribunal is a competent tribunal (with expert contribution from members qualified in surveying and valuation) whose jurisdictional remit covers matters under a number of Ordinances concerning land. It handles claims for compensation for resumption of land, action for recovery of vacant possession of premises rented out, rating and government rent appeals, and applications for compulsory sale of lots of land for redevelopment.[31] The Competition Tribunal hears and decides applications made by the Competition Commission to enforce statutory competition rules, applications for reviews made by persons subject to determinations made by the Competition Commission and private actions in respect of contraventions of the part of the statutory competition rules prohibiting anti-competitive agreements and abuse of market power.[32] The Coroner's Court is an inquisitorial mechanism for public investigation of questionable deaths, including accidental deaths, criminal or homicidal deaths, deaths following an operation, suicidal deaths, and deaths while in official custody or a mental hospital.[33] The Obscene Articles Tribunal is the most unusual judicial body in the Judiciary of the HKSAR, having under its statutory functions the administrative function of classification of articles submitted to it, and the exclusive judicial function of determining whether an article is obscene, indecent or neither obscene nor indecent when such a question arises in the course of civil or criminal proceedings.[34]

Criminal proceedings invariably begin in the magistrates' courts, which handle pre-trial proceedings, including whether the defendant should be freed on bail or detained. Criminal cases involving a defendant

[30] See the Labour Tribunal Ordinance (Cap. 25), s. 7, Sch.

[31] See the Lands Tribunal Ordinance (Cap. 17), s. 8, Sch.

[32] See the Competition Ordinance (Cap. 619), ss. 132 and 142.

[33] See the Coroners Ordinance (Cap. 504), s. 9. A coroner's inquiry operates by a coroner either sitting alone or sitting with a jury of three.

[34] See the Control of Obscene and Indecent Articles Ordinance (Cap. 390), ss. 8, 13 and 29. Even the judiciary itself has expressed a public view that this combination of functions is "unsatisfactory"; see Judiciary Administration, The Review of the Control of Obscene and Indecent Articles Ordinance ("COIAO") (Cap. 390): The Judiciary's Response (November 2008), www.judiciary.gov.hk/en/publications/coia_judiciary_response.pdf.

who is a juvenile below the age of 16 (excluding homicide) are to be heard and decided by the juvenile court, which is presided over by a magistrate.[35] Trial may take place before a magistrate, in the District Court or in the Court of First Instance of the High Court upon the application or choice of venue of the prosecution. Different levels of criminal courts have different sentencing powers, with the Court of First Instance having unlimited criminal jurisdiction, including the power to sentence a defendant to life imprisonment,[36] the heaviest penalty under the criminal jurisdiction of the HKSAR courts, as the death penalty was abolished in 1993.[37]

Criminal trials are heard and decided by a magistrate, a district judge, or a judge of the Court of First Instance sitting with a jury,[38] depending on the level of court to which the criminal case is applied for, transferred or committed for trial. The jury system was introduced in Hong Kong in 1845 when an Ordinance for the Regulation of Jurors and Juries was enacted. The system of trial by judge and jury is of constitutional importance. Article 86 of the Basic Law of the HKSAR maintains the principle of trial by jury previously practiced in Hong Kong but does not separately establish a right to jury trial.[39] Provisions for juries are now set out in the Jury Ordinance.[40]

Appeals of decisions of a magistrate are heard in the Court of First Instance.[41] Appeals of decisions of the District Court or the Court of First Instance of the High Court are heard in the Court of Appeal of the High Court, whether the decision in question is in the exercise of the civil or

[35] See the Juvenile Offenders Ordinance (Cap. 226). The juvenile court also hears and decides applications under the Protection of Children and Juveniles Ordinance (Cap. 213) for care or protection orders for infants and young persons.

[36] See the High Court Ordinance (Cap. 4), s. 3(2).

[37] For the history of abolition of the death penalty in Hong Kong, see *Lau Cheong & Anor* v. *HKSAR* (2002) 5 HKCFAR 415, CFA.

[38] A jury sitting in criminal trials on indictment before the High Court consists of seven jurors in ordinary cases. This can be expanded to nine jurors in long cases.

[39] See *Chiang Lily* v. *Secretary for Justice* [2009] 6 HKC 234, CA.

[40] I.e. Chapter 2 of the Laws of Hong Kong. Given that there has been maintained a requirement to understand the language in which the proceedings are to be conducted and that had for some time meant the English language, the list of jurors in Hong Kong may still have constituted a pool of the more educated class of the Hong Kong public: see P. Duff, M. Findlay, C. Howarth and T. F. Chan, *Juries: A Hong Kong Perspective* (Hong Kong: Hong Kong University Press, 1992). The criteria for service as jurors are at present the subject of law reform: see Report of the Law Reform Commission of Hong Kong (June, 2010), www.hkreform.gov.hk/en/publications/rjurors.htm.

[41] See the Magistrates Ordinance (Cap. 227), ss. 104 and 113.

criminal jurisdiction of the lower court, though the applicable procedural framework for appeals is different depending on whether a civil cause or matter or a criminal cause or matter is involved.[42] Appeals are generally heard in the Court of Appeal by a bench of three judges, but there are provisions for the handling of interlocutory appeals in a civil cause or matter, appeals against sentences in a criminal case and applications for leave to appeal by a bench of two judges or a single Justice of Appeal of the Court of Appeal.[43]

Appeals from the judgments of the Court of Appeal, and from the judgments of the Court of First Instance on magistracy appeals, are heard and decided by the Court of Final Appeal, the apex of the system of courts of the HKSAR. Its announced function is to decide questions of law of great, general and public importance and to put right substantial and grave injustice (particularly in criminal cases).[44] Hence the exercise of the Court of Final Appeal's jurisdiction is largely discretionary, administered by the Appeal Committee of the Court of Final Appeal consisting of a panel of three judges (be it the Chief Justice and two permanent judges or three permanent judges),[45] subject only to a provision for appeal as of right in a civil cause or matter where the matter in dispute on the appeal amounts to or is of the value of HK$1 million or more, or where the appeal involves, directly or indirectly, some claim or question to or respecting property or some civil right amounting to or of the value of HK$1 million or more.[46] Final appeals are heard substantively by a

[42] See the High Court Ordinance (Cap. 4), ss. 13, 14 and 14AA; the District Court Ordinance (Cap. 336), ss. 63, 83, 84; and the Criminal Procedure Ordinance (Cap. 221), ss. 81, 81A, 81D, 81E, 81F and 82.

[43] See the High Court Ordinance (Cap. 4), ss. 34, 34A, 34B and 35.

[44] See the Hong Kong Court of Final Appeal Ordinance (Cap. 484), ss. 22, 31. In addition, Part II, Division 3 of the Hong Kong Court of Final Appeal Ordinance provides for a special procedure by which an appeal in a civil cause or matter may lie to the Court of Final Appeal from a judgment of the Court of First Instance upon (1) certification by the Court of First Instance that a point of law of great general or public importance is involved in that court's decision, and that that point of law relates wholly or mainly to the construction of the Basic Law of the HKSAR or legislation and has been fully argued and fully considered before an appellate court, which produced a judgment binding on that court; and (2) the granting of leave to appeal by the Appeal Committee of the Court of Final Appeal.

[45] The Hong Kong Court of Final Appeal Ordinance (Cap. 484), s. 18.

[46] The Hong Kong Court of Final Appeal Ordinance (Cap. 484), s. 22(1)(a). The Court of Final Appeal has regarded the appeal as of right provision in its civil jurisdiction as an anachronistic diversion of judicial time and has called for its repeal by the legislature: see *Chinachem Charitable Foundation Ltd* v. *Chan Chun Chuen & Anor* [2011] 6 HKC 273,

bench of five judges, consisting of the Chief Justice, the permanent judges and one or more of the non-permanent judges drawn from lists of non-permanent Hong Kong judges and non-permanent judges from another common law jurisdiction.[47]

The HKSAR courts are authorized to interpret the Basic Law of the HKSAR, the constitutional instrument of the HKSAR, by the NPCSC, pursuant to Article 158 of the Basic Law. Accordingly, there is no separate constitutional court in the Kelsenian model. Rather, the Court of Final Appeal, being the final appellate court, controls the interpretation of the Basic Law by the courts through the doctrine of precedent and also decides whether the conditions for it to make a reference to the NPCSC for interpretation of certain categories of provisions of the Basic Law are met.

1.3 Size and performance of the courts

There is one Court of Final Appeal consisting of the Chief Justice, three permanent judges and six non-permanent Hong Kong judges, and twelve non-permanent judges from other common law jurisdictions.

There is one High Court consisting of the Court of Appeal and the Court of First Instance. The High Court is headed by the Chief Judge of the High Court. The Court of Appeal has ten Justices of Appeal, three of which hold the title of Vice-President of the Court of Appeal. A hearing of the Court of Appeal must be presided over by either the Chief Judge or a Justice of Appeal. There are twenty-six judges of the Court of First Instance. There are also nine recorders of the Court of First Instance, who are senior members of the Bar appointed for fixed terms on the

CFA App Ctte; *Champion Concord Ltd* v. *Lau Koon Foo (No. 2)* (2011) 14 HKCFAR 837, CFA; *Wealth Duke Ltd & Ors* v. *Bank of China (Hong Kong) Ltd* (2011) 14 HKCFAR 863, CFA. Draft legislation for the repeal of the appeal as of right provision in the civil jurisdiction of the Hong Kong Court of Final Appeal was introduced into the Legislative Council of the HKSAR in 2014.

47 See the Hong Kong Court of Final Appeal Ordinance (Cap. 484), s. 16. The appointment of a list of non-permanent judges from another common law jurisdiction and the sitting of one such non-permanent judge (NPJ) from another common law jurisdiction in final appeals on the invitation by the Court of Final Appeal gives effect to Art. 85 of the Basic Law of the HKSAR and is an important feature of the system of courts of the HKSAR. It has been suggested that the presence of a NPJ from another common law jurisdiction of stature (and the appointments to date have been retired or even serving judges of the courts of final appellate jurisdiction in Australia, England and New Zealand) has enhanced the reputation of the Court of Final Appeal in the common law world and facilitated transnational judicial dialogue and exchange: see P. Y. Lo, "The impact of CFA jurisprudence beyond Hong Kong," *Hong Kong Lawyer*, issue 8 (2010), 36–41.

condition that each year they will set aside a number of months of their time to sit in the Court of First Instance hearing cases.

There is one District Court consisting of the Chief District Judge, the Principal Family Court Judge and forty-one district judges.

There are seven magistrates' courts in Hong Kong, each covering a number of localities. Incorporated in each of five of the seven magistrates' courts is a juvenile court. Each magistrates' court is headed by a principal magistrate who handles the daily intake of criminal cases,[48] hears bail applications and sets down cases for trial; working under the principal magistrate are a number of magistrates who preside over up to three to four cases set down before each of them for trial on a daily basis. There are altogether one Chief Magistrate, ten principal magistrates, fifty-one permanent magistrates and nine special magistrates.[49] Judicial officers of the magistrate rank staff the Coroner's Court, the Small Claims Tribunal, the Labour Tribunal and the Obscene Articles Tribunal.

Apart from the above judges and judicial officers of the permanent establishment,[50] the Chief Justice has been empowered by statute to appoint from time to time and as the needs of judicial work requires, deputy judges of the Court of First Instance; deputy judges of the District Court and deputy magistrates; as well as temporary members of the High Court and District Court registries, the Lands Tribunal, the Small Claims Tribunal and the Labour Tribunal, for a specified duration of time. The deputy judges or magistrates can be from retired or former members of the judiciary, members of the lower ranks of the judiciary or members of the legal profession in private practice. At the time of writing (August 2014), there were at work nearly sixty deputy judges and judicial officers, including nine deputy judges of the Court of First Instance, nine deputy judges of the District Court, twenty deputy magistrates, nine deputy

[48] The daily intake of cases includes cases from the police force, the Independent Commission Against Corruption, the Customs and Excise Service and the Immigration Service. The remainder of the cases are hawker cases; departmental or private summonses (from government departments such as the Labour Department, the Department of Health, the Environmental Protection Department, the Inland Revenue Department, and the Agricultural, Fisheries and Conservation Department); and fixed penalty matters with respect to traffic, public cleanliness and smoking offenses.

[49] Special magistrates are appointed as a separate rank in the establishment with very limited power of imprisonment, and they are deployed to handle traffic, revenue and other regulatory penalty cases.

[50] The list of judges and judicial officers is accessible at: www.judiciary.gov.hk/en/organization/judges.htm.

special magistrates, five deputy adjudicators of the Small Claims Tribunal, and three deputy presiding officer of the Labour Tribunal.

There were at the time of writing 193 judicial posts in the establishment of the judiciary of the HKSAR, or 2.75 judicial posts per 100,000 inhabitants. However, the actual number of substantively filled posts was 164. Recruitment exercises had been under way since 2011 and announcements were made since the latter part of 2012 of appointments of fifty-odd judges and judicial officers at the ranks of Judge of the Court of First Instance, District Judge and permanent magistrate.[51]

The Annual Reports of the Judiciary of the HKSAR since 1997[52] have appendices on the caseload and case disposal of all levels of courts and tribunals of the judiciary, as well as the average waiting times for a case to be tried or heard, referenced against target waiting times set by the judiciary. These statistics show that while cases have generally been disposed of efficiently, there are bottlenecks at the levels of (1) civil appeals before the Court of Appeal, and (2) civil and criminal trials of more than moderate length before the Court of First Instance.

2 Sources and influences of the establishment of the judicial system

The establishment of British colonial administration in Hong Kong was followed by the establishment of a Supreme Court of Hong Kong and the creation of the offices of police magistrates by local legislation.

[51] See Judiciary Administration, *Judicial Manpower Situation at Various Levels of Court and Various Matters Relating to Judges and Judicial Officers* (May 2012) (LC Paper No. CB(2) 2107/11-12(01)), www.legco.gov.hk/yr11-12/english/panels/ajls/papers/aj0528cb2-2107-1-e.pdf; Judiciary Administrator, *Examination of Estimates of Expenditure 2013–14: Controlling Officer's Reply to Initial Written Questions* (JA018) (9 April 2013), www.legco.gov.hk/yr12-13/english/fc/fc/w_q/ja-e.pdf; Judiciary Administration, *Judicial Manpower Situation at Various Levels of Court and Court Waiting Times* (December 2013) (LC Paper No. CB(4)225/13-14(05)), www.legco.gov.hk/yr13-14/english/panels/ajls/papers/aj1216cb4-225-5-e.pdf; Legislative Council Secretariat, *updated background brief prepared on judicial manpower situation at various levels of court* (18 June 2014) (LC paper No. CB(4)822/13-14(04)), www.legco.gov.hk/yr13-14/english/panels/ajls/papers/aj0624cb4-822-4-e.pdf.

[52] The Judiciary Annual Reports are accessible here: www.judiciary.gov.hk/en/publications/publications.htm. See also *Controlling Officer's Report: Head 80 – Judiciary* (February 2012), www.budget.gov.hk/2012/eng/pdf/head080.pdf; Judiciary Administration, *Judicial Manpower Situation at Various Levels of Court and Court Waiting Times, ibid*; Legislative Council Secretariat, *updated background brief prepared on judicial manpower situations at various levels of court, ibid.*

The British manner of administration of justice and its basic principles, namely the independent administration of justice by the corps of judges, the judge being the sole interpreter of legislation, the adversarial system of administration of justice, habeas corpus, rules of evidence and legal representation, were introduced into Hong Kong. The coroner's jurisdiction was again a British import.

When the British Administration occupied the New Territories under a lease concluded with the Qing Imperial Court in 1898, farming communities organized under clans and lineages came under their colonial rule. The inhabitants of the New Territories did put up resistance to the British forces, notwithstanding assurances by the British that their customs and way of life would be respected. The first New Territories Ordinance, enacted in 1900, declared the land of the New Territories to be and to have been from 23 July 1900, the property of the Government, and that all persons in occupation of any such land were to be deemed to be trespassers against the Government, unless such occupation was authorized by grant from the Government, by other title allowed under the Ordinance, or by license from the Government,[53] irrespective of the title of the inhabitants of the New Territories derived under Qing law and customs.[54] However, section 13 of the Ordinance provided that subject to exceptions relating to the succession of landed property, in any proceedings in the Court of First Instance and the District Court in relation to land in the New Territories, the court would have the power to recognize and enforce any Chinese custom or customary right affecting such land. The assumption by the courts of the responsibility of recognizing and applying Qing law and Chinese customs in the personal affairs of the New Territories inhabitants helped reduce disruption of their daily lives and hence, to an extent, social disorder, thus making colonial rule more palatable.

The establishment of specialized tribunals is an indication of how the judiciary accommodates public demand for efficient and participatory justice. The establishment of the Small Claims Tribunal and the Labour Tribunal addressed a social necessity for expeditious and affordable

[53] See the New Territories Ordinance (Cap. 97), s. 8. Reference is made to the New Territories Regulation Ordinance 1899 and the New Territories Land Court Ordinance 1900.

[54] The existing occupation of land was allowed to continue under the grant of Block Crown Leases, subject to the power of the Crown landlord to re-enter and wield and of the Government's statutory power to resume the land for a public purpose.

justice proportionate to the amount of the monetary claim at stake and the claimants' ability to pay, so that in the circumstances, legal representation is dispensed with, to be compensated with a duty placed upon the tribunal to inquire into the claim. The establishment of the Obscene Articles Tribunal served a different purpose, which was to ensure some consistency in the determination of the nature of alleged obscene or indecent articles with community standards of morality, decency and propriety through the participation of a section of the public appointed for that purpose as members of a panel of adjudicators presided over by a magistrate.

Following the resumption of exercise of Chinese sovereignty on 1 July 1997, the HKSAR courts were established as the courts of a local administrative region of the People's Republic China enjoying a high degree of autonomy under the principle of "One Country, Two Systems."[55] The status of Hong Kong as a special administrative region of the PRC determines the position of its courts. This perspective is pronounced in Article 19(3) of the Basic Law of the HKSAR where the following is stated:

> The courts of the Hong Kong Special Administrative Region shall have no jurisdiction over acts of state such as defence and foreign affairs. The courts of the Region shall obtain a certificate from the Chief Executive on questions of fact concerning acts of state such as defence and foreign affairs whenever such questions arise in the adjudication of cases. This certificate shall be binding on the courts. Before issuing such a certificate, the Chief Executive shall obtain a certifying document from the Central People's Government.

In 2011, the Court of Final Appeal had to grapple with the meaning of this limitation to the jurisdiction of the HKSAR courts. Notwithstanding that the majority of the Court could reach a provisional conclusion on the issue for adjudication, namely the applicable doctrine of foreign sovereign state immunity, after considering the fact of the policy adopted by the Central People's Government of the PRC,[56] they determined that a reference must be made by the Court to the NPCSC under Article 158(3)

[55] See the Basic Law of the HKSAR, Art. 12.

[56] The relevant facts of the policy of the Central People's Government on foreign sovereign state immunity were conveyed to the Court of Final Appeal by virtue of three letters from the Office of the Commissioner of the Ministry of Foreign Affairs of the People's Republic of China in the HKSAR to the Constitutional and Mainland Affairs Bureau of the Government of the HKSAR and were made available to the Court by the Secretary for Justice, who intervened in the litigation between the parties.

of the Basic Law for interpretation of the Basic Law, and they referred to the NPCSC for interpretation of four questions, on the basis that the case cannot be resolved "without a determination of the questions of interpretation affecting the meaning of Articles 13 and 19 of the Basic Law, in particular in relation to the words 'acts of state such as defence and foreign affairs.'"[57] The NPCSC adopted on 26 August 2011 an interpretation of Article 13(1) and Article 19 of the Basic Law,[58] answering the four questions. The Court of Final Appeal then considered the NPCSC Interpretation of 26 August 2011 and declared the provisional judgment of the majority as final, making the orders proposed by the majority the final orders of the Court.[59]

While the spokesperson of the Ministry of Foreign Affairs of the PRC made a public statement that the Court of Final Appeal, in making the judicial reference, fulfilled "its obligations stipulated in the Basic Law [which] is of positive significance to the comprehensive implementation of 'one country, two systems' as well as the complete enforcement of the Basic Law," it has been submitted that the making of a judicial reference by the Court of Final Appeal in itself carried the implication of conjoining the judicial system of the HKSAR with the legal system of Mainland China; the HKSAR courts are no longer to be regarded as outside the PRC system but as PRC courts.[60]

3 Judicial appointments, judicial independence and access to justice

3.1 Judicial appointments and qualifications of judges

Judges and judicial officers in Hong Kong must be professionally qualified. Statutes establishing the courts of the HKSAR specify the professional qualifications for eligibility of appointment of judges of the Court

[57] *Democratic Republic of the Congo & Ors* v. *FG Hemisphere Associates LLC* [2011] 4 HKC 151, CFA at [406], [407].

[58] I.e. the Interpretation of Paragraph 1, Article 13 and Article 19 of the Basic Law of the Hong Kong Special Administrative Region of the People's Republic of China by the Standing Committee of the National People's Congress (Adopted by the Standing Committee of the Eleventh National People's Congress at its 22nd Session on 26 August 2011).

[59] *Democratic Republic of the Congo & Ors* v. *FG Hemisphere Associates LLC (No. 2)* [2011] 5 HKC 395, CFA.

[60] See P. Y. Lo, "The gateway opens wide," *Hong Kong Law Journal*, 41 (2011), 385–91; and further, P. Y. Lo, *The Judicial Construction of Hong Kong's Basic Law: Courts, Politics and Society after 1997* (Hong Kong University Press, 2014), pp. 371–441.

of Final Appeal, judges of the High Court, district judges, magistrates, coroners, and presiding officers and adjudicators of tribunals. Generally, in order to be eligible for appointment, a person must (1) be qualified to practice as a barrister, solicitor or advocate in a court in Hong Kong[61] or any other common law jurisdiction having unlimited jurisdiction either in civil or criminal matters; and (2) have, since becoming so qualified,[62] practiced as a barrister, solicitor or advocate in such a court, or been an officer of the Department of Justice, Legal Aid Department, Official Receiver's Office or the Intellectual Property Department of the HKSAR Government for at least a specified period of time, which is ten years in the case of a judge of the High Court[63] and five years in the case of district judge and other judicial officers.[64]

[61] The legal profession of the HKSAR is a divided profession consisting of barristers and solicitors in the English tradition. Barristers are advocates specializing in litigation and with general rights of audience before all courts of the HKSAR. Solicitors are lawyers qualified to conduct litigation and transactional business in law and with rights of audience limited to selected proceedings before the High Court (though legislative amendments have been enacted to enable them to undertake advocacy work in the High Court and the appellate courts after assessment), and generally in the District Court and before magistrates. Barristers are members of the Hong Kong Bar Association. Solicitors are members of the Law Society of Hong Kong. The Bar Association and the Law Society together constitute the mainstream voice of the legal profession.

[62] In order to be qualified as a lawyer in Hong Kong, a person usually goes through three stages: (a) studying for a relevant law degree, namely a law degree in the faculty of law of one of three universities in Hong Kong that offer undergraduate courses in law (namely the University of Hong Kong, the City University of Hong Kong and the Chinese University of Hong Kong); or a law degree from a Commonwealth institution, plus demonstrated competence, through examination, of additional subjects of Hong Kong Constitutional Law, Hong Kong Legal System and Hong Kong Land Law; (b) studying for the Postgraduate Certificate of Laws, a vocational course offered by the faculty of law of one of the three aforementioned universities in Hong Kong; and (c) undergoing a period of training, which is, to become a barrister, a total of one year of pupillage with one or more barrister(s) of at least seven years' standing, or, to become a solicitor, a total of two years of traineeship with a firm of solicitors. Practicing lawyers who are qualified outside Hong Kong can be qualified as lawyers in Hong Kong through passing, for barristers, an examination organized by the Hong Kong Bar Association (known as the Bar Qualification Examination) and, for solicitors, the Law Society of Hong Kong (known as the Overseas Lawyers Qualification Examination).

[63] See the High Court Ordinance (Cap. 4), s. 9(1). The period of at least ten years may include a period of time of service as a district judge or other judicial officer in the judiciary in Hong Kong, or a period of practice as a solicitor of a court in Hong Kong or any other common law jurisdiction.

[64] See the District Court Ordinance (Cap. 336), s. 5; the Magistrates Ordinance (Cap. 227), ss. 5AA and 5AB; the Coroners Ordinance (Cap. 504), s. 3AA; the Labour Tribunal Ordinance (Cap. 25), s. 4A; and the Small Claims Tribunal Ordinance (Cap. 338), s. 4AA.

The high offices of the Chief Justice and permanent judges of the Court of Final Appeal are limited, in terms of the pool of eligible appointees, to judges of the High Court, including the Chief Judge of the High Court, Justices of Appeal and judges of the Court of First Instance, and barristers who have practiced as a barrister or solicitor in Hong Kong for a period of at least ten years.[65] There are two classes of non-permanent judges of the Court of Final Appeal. Non-permanent judges from Hong Kong can be a retired Chief Justice or permanent judge of the Court of Final Appeal, a retired Chief Judge of the High Court, a Justice or retired Justice of Appeal, or a barrister who has practiced as a barrister or solicitor in Hong Kong for a period of at least 10 years, whether or not he or she is ordinarily resident in Hong Kong. Non-permanent judges from another common law jurisdiction can be a judge or retired judge of a court of unlimited jurisdiction in either civil or criminal matters in another common law jurisdiction, who is ordinarily resident outside Hong Kong and has never been a judge of the High Court, a district judge or a permanent magistrate in Hong Kong.[66]

Article 88 of the Basic Law of the HKSAR provides that judges of the HKSAR shall be appointed by the Chief Executive of the HKSAR on the recommendation of an independent commission composed of local judges, persons from the legal profession and eminent persons from other sectors. Article 92 of the Basic Law provides that judges and other members of the judiciary of the HKSAR shall be chosen on the basis of their judicial and professional qualities and may be recruited from other common law jurisdictions. Further, appointments of judges of the Court of Final Appeal and the Chief Judge of the High Court require the endorsement of the Legislative Council and reporting of the appointment to the NPCSC for the record, pursuant to Article 90 of the Basic Law.

These constitutional guarantees are implemented according to the terms of the Judicial Officers Recommendation Commission (JORC), the body corresponding to the independent commission referred to in Article 88 of the Basic Law and whose composition and mode of operation are established by statute.[67] The JORC consists of the Chief Justice (who shall be the Chairman); the Secretary for Justice (who is the chief

[65] See the Hong Kong Court of Final Appeal Ordinance (Cap. 484), s. 12(1) and (1A).

[66] See the Hong Kong Court of Final Appeal Ordinance (Cap. 484), s. 12(3) and (4).

[67] Namely, the Judicial Officers Recommendation Commission Ordinance (Cap. 92). For the annual report of the JORC, see www.judiciary.gov.hk/en/crt_services/pphlt/pdf/jorc_report2010e.pdf.

legal adviser to the Government); seven members appointed by the Chief Executive, of whom two shall be judges, one shall be a barrister and one shall be a solicitor, each holding a practicing certificate; and three shall be persons who are not, in the opinion of the Chief Executive, connected in any way with the practice of law. The Chief Executive is obliged to consult the Hong Kong Bar Association over the appointment of a barrister and the Law Society of Hong Kong over the appointment of a solicitor to the JORC, but he is not obliged to appoint the barrister or solicitor recommended to him for appointment by the Bar Association or the Law Society, as the case may be.[68]

Given the voting rules of the JORC requiring a dominant majority of the members present for a resolution to be effective,[69] government appointees consisting of the Secretary for Justice and the three eminent persons not having any connection with the practice of law may not dominate the decision-making of the JORC. While the Chief Executive can appoint members of the legal profession not recommended by the two legal professional bodies, such a move would be unwise, as it would indicate an overt intention of patronage, and there has so far been no attempt on the part of the Chief Executive to make an appointment different from those recommended by the two legal professional bodies.[70]

There is no training college for judges or judicial officers in Hong Kong. Rather the Hong Kong Judicial Institute (formerly the Judicial Studies Board) under the judiciary organizes lectures, conferences and workshops for judges and judicial officers to enhance the skills that are often requisite for effective judging, including judgment writing and mediation training.

3.2 *Judicial independence*

Article 85 of the Basic Law of the HKSAR provides that the HKSAR courts "shall exercise judicial power independently, free from any interference"[71] and makes provisions for immunity in the performance of judicial functions.

[68] The Judicial Officers Recommendation Commission Ordinance (Cap. 92), s. 3(1), (1A) and (1B).

[69] The Judicial Officers Recommendation Commission Ordinance (Cap. 92), s. 3(3A).

[70] This is not to say that the Chief Executive of the HKSAR may not do so: see J. Cheng, "Hong Kong's constitutional development and the executive-led system," *Faxue*, issue 1 (2009), 45–56.

[71] Cf. the Constitution of the People's Republic of China 1982, Art. 126.

Article 89 of the Basic Law of the HKSAR secures the tenure of judges of the HKSAR courts by providing that they "may only be removed" by the Chief Executive of the HKSAR on the grounds of (1) inability to discharge his or her duties or (2) misbehavior, and on the recommendation of a tribunal appointed by the Chief Justice of the Court of Final Appeal and consisting of no fewer than three local judges.[72]

Judges of the Court of Final Appeal and the Chief Judge of the High Court may only be removed by the Chief Executive of the HKSAR following the recommendation of a tribunal and the endorsement of the Legislative Council, and the removal must be reported to the NPCSC for the record.[73] In the case of the Chief Justice, the investigation into cause for removal would be carried out by a tribunal appointed by the Chief Executive and consisting of no fewer than five local judges.[74]

Article 91 of the Basic Law of the HKSAR maintains the previous system of removal of members of the judiciary other than judges, which is based upon the Judicial Officers (Tenure of Office) Ordinance.[75] The Ordinance provides for the establishment of a tribunal of investigation consisting of two judges of the High Court and one public officer, which would report its findings to the JORC so that the latter could make a recommendation to the Chief Executive of the HKSAR on disposal.

The administration of the HKSAR courts belongs to the judiciary itself. The Chief Justice of the Court of Final Appeal is assisted in the administration of the judiciary by the staff of the Judiciary Administration headed by the Judiciary Administrator. Apart from the maintenance of the running of the courts, the registries and the court buildings, the Judiciary Administration also provides the following support services: reporting and transcription, interpretation and translation, bailiff services (for execution of judgments and service of summonses), the resource center for unrepresented litigants, and library services. The number of people employed by the judiciary stands at 1,690 in 2013, with 184 posts for judges and judicial officers.

The budget of the judiciary in Hong Kong is not separately considered by the Legislative Council, which controls public finance in Hong Kong through its approval of the budget proposed by the Government of the

[72] This mechanism for removal to some extent follows the previous arrangement under the Letters Patent 1917–91, Art. XVIA.

[73] Basic Law of the HKSAR, Art. 90.

[74] Basic Law of the HKSAR, Art. 89.

[75] I.e. Chapter 433 of the Laws of Hong Kong.

HKSAR as well as public expenditure in accordance with Article 73(2) and (3) of the Basic Law of the HKSAR and the Public Finance Ordinance.[76] The estimated expenditure of the judiciary forms part of the General Revenue Account and is analyzed as a Head of Expenditure in the Estimates accompanying the budget proposed by the Government.[77] The estimated expenditure in a financial year is presented in terms of the programs on which it is proposed to spend resources, and the results are sought and compared with previous years. The effectiveness of the results is measured where possible in terms of unit cost or productivity indicators.[78] The preparation of the estimates of expenditure of the judiciary and its presentation by way of a controlling officer's report is done in-house by the Judiciary Administration, which categorizes expenses under the two programs of "courts, tribunals and various statutory functions" and "support services for courts' operation." The Judiciary submits its resource requirements to the Government prior to the Government's drawing up of the budget for the judiciary for incorporation as part of the Government's budget proposal to be submitted to the Legislative Council for approval.[79] The 2013/14 estimated expenditure of the judiciary of the HKSAR is HK$1,272.1 million, representing a 5.2 percent increase from the 2012/13 original estimates.

3.3 *Access to justice*

3.3.1 Substantive limits to access

Public interest litigation is recognized to some extent in Hong Kong. Certain developments in public law and the protection of fundamental rights guaranteed under the Basic Law of the HKSAR are owed to litigation filed by individuals or organizations aligned with a particular cause or interest group. Examples include an applicant that is a limited company established for the purpose of campaigning for the protection of the Victoria Harbour from reclamation, which launched an application for judicial review of the enforcement of legislation prohibiting reclamation

[76] I.e. Chapter 2 of the Laws of Hong Kong.

[77] See *Controlling Officer's Report: Head 80 – Judiciary* (February 2013), www.budget.gov.hk/2013/eng/pdf/head080.pdf.

[78] See *Estimates 2012/2013* (February 2013), Introduction, www.budget.gov.hk/2013/eng/pdf/introd_vola_e.pdf.

[79] See *Judiciary Administrator's Speaking Notes at the Special Finance Committee Meeting on 12 April 2013*, www.legco.gov.hk/yr12-13/english/fc/fc/sp_note/session2-ja-e.pdf.

unless overriding circumstances are shown;[80] and an applicant who claimed to be a male homosexual under the age of twenty-one and, in the absence of a criminal prosecution or arrest, commenced an application for judicial review to challenge the constitutional validity of the offense of buggery with a man under the age of twenty-one on the basis of discrimination on the grounds of sexual orientation.[81] These applicants were held to have sufficient interest to apply for judicial review of the decision or legislation under challenge.[82]

Applications for judicial review require the permission of the Court of First Instance. This acts as a filtering mechanism on the merits of the application at the beginning stage. The present applicable test requires the applicant to show that at least one of the grounds for review is "reasonably arguable with realistic prospects of success"; this is a threshold that was raised in 2007 from "potential arguability."[83] This approach requires a more than "quick perusal" of the papers by the responsible judge who might wish to call for an oral hearing with notice to the putative respondent in suitable cases. An applicant with limited access to the relevant case papers of the decision-maker would have difficulty in making an effective presentation of the merits of his grounds for review, especially where the issues in the matter may involve evaluation of all the facts against a policy directive as opposed to the interpretation of legislation or regulation.[84]

Studies have shown that social movements in Hong Kong have increasingly made use of the law as an instrument of mobilization to further their causes.[85] Further development in public interest litigation

80 See *Town Planning Board* v. *Society for Protection of the Harbour Ltd* (2004) 7 HKCFAR 1, CFA.

81 See *Leung* v. *Secretary for Justice* [2006] 4 HKLRD 211, CA.

82 For an analysis of the law on standing in judicial review of administrative decisions or legislation in Hong Kong, see P. J. Yap, "Understanding public interest litigation in Hong Kong," *Common Law World Review*, 37 (2008), 257–76.

83 See *Chan Po Fun* v. *Winnie Cheung* (2007) 10 HKCFAR 676, CFA.

84 Professor Johannes Chan criticized the 2007 *Chan Po Fun* decision of the Court of Final Appeal as "a retrograde step," noting that the lack of democracy in Hong Kong had left the courts as the only viable route to put pressure on government: see Johannes Chan, "A Retrograde Judgment," Ming Pao 13 February 2008, D5.

85 See A. Chen, "Social movements and the law in post-colonial Hong Kong" in K.-e. Kuah-Pearce and G. Guiheux (eds.), *Social Movements in China and Hong Kong: The Expansion of Protest Space* (Amsterdam University Press, 2009), pp. 65–90 (surveying cases of judicial review up to 2005); and A. Cheung and M. Wong, "Judicial review and policy making in Hong Kong: changing interface between the legal and the political," *Asia Pacific Journal of Public Administration*, 28 (2006), 117–41 (suggesting that applications

might require the HKSAR courts to take an active part in organizing and facilitating the exercise of evidence-gathering and fact-finding, and to be more ready to examine policy choices against the standards of constitutional and legal rights of HKSAR residents in order to hold governmental authorities responsible for carrying out their corresponding duties under the law.[86]

3.3.2 Institutional limits to access

The costs of litigation in Hong Kong are admittedly on the relatively expensive side. The gap between those in need of litigation and the professional services of litigators is met to a considerable extent in Hong Kong by the availability of legal aid, subject to the means and merits tests.[87] Organizers of social movements are well aware of the availability of legal aid and often pursue their causes through litigation in the courts commenced by a selected aggrieved applicant who is eligible for legal aid.[88] Legal aid thus provides for pursuit of the cause by legal means with (1) security against an adverse costs order in the case of failure, and (2) access to the professional services of public lawyers who are usually repeat players in the field of constitutional and administrative law and remunerated at near commercial rates. On the other hand, the courts have been inclined to caution against extravagant use of legal proceedings

for judicial review are being used as a political bargaining tool and a platform for agenda-setting by social movements).

86 See K. Kong, "Public interest litigation in Hong Kong: a new hope for social transformation?" *Civil Justice Quarterly*, 28 (2009), 327–43.

87 Civil legal aid is available in Hong Kong pursuant to the Legal Aid Ordinance (Cap. 91) under the Ordinary Legal Aid Scheme and the Supplementary Legal Aid Scheme. The former scheme is funded by general revenue funds and is relatively broad in scope, while the latter scheme is self-financing through contributions made by aid recipients who have been successful in their claims and is relatively narrow in scope, covering only personal injuries and professional negligence claims (which are most probably covered by insurance). Criminal legal aid is provided for representation at trials in the District Court and the Court of First Instance of the High Court, subject to a means test, and on appeals therefrom, subject to an additional merits test. Legal representation at trials before magistrates is provided by the Duty Lawyer Service. For an overview of legal aid in Hong Kong, see Legal Aid Services Council, *Legal Aid in Hong Kong* (Hong Kong: Legal Aid Services Council, 2006), www.lasc.hk/eng/publications/legal-aid.html.

88 A recent example is the case of *Yao Man Fai George* v. *Director of Social Welfare* [2012] 4 HKC 180, CA (where Mr Yao, a HKSAR permanent resident returning from Mainland China, was assisted by the Society for Community Organization in applying for judicial review to challenge the policy of the Director of Social Welfare in requiring applicants for social security payments to have resided in Hong Kong for not less than a specified number of days in the year immediately before the application).

merely to further a political cause or voice a socio-economic grievance. If an applicant fails in his application for judicial review, then the normal consequence of costs following the event should ensue; as Mr Justice Michael Hartmann indicated, "public interest litigation does not grant an immunity from costs or a 'free kick' in litigation,"[89] unless it can be satisfactorily shown that the proceedings were brought in the public interest.[90]

Access to simple legal advice does not usually present a problem, given the Free Legal Advice Scheme operated by the Duty Lawyer Service. However, access to quality legal advice is more difficult to obtain. While a HKSAR resident may apply for legal aid with the Legal Aid Department, whose staff are legally qualified and empowered to seek independent legal advice from private legal practitioners in suitable cases of difficulty, there remains a gap in meeting the needs of those who are refused legal aid and wish to obtain a second opinion or representation, apart from appealing the decision of the legal aid officer.[91] Pro bono or voluntary service provided by the members of the legal profession may serve to plug this gap. The Hong Kong Bar Association has been operating a Free Legal Service Scheme since 2000.[92] Nevertheless, the presence of unfulfilled need is demonstrated by the fact that at least one party in over 30 percent of civil trials before the Court of First Instance and about 50 percent of civil trials in the District Court is unrepresented.[93] A pilot

[89] See *Leung Kwok Hung* v. *President of the Legislative Council of the HKSAR & Anor* (unreported, 27 April 2007, HCAL 87/2006), CFI at [25].

[90] This means that it is incumbent upon the applicant to show: (1) that the legal proceedings have been properly brought to seek guidance from the court on a point of general public importance, such that, with regard to the proper role of the court in judicial review, the litigation is, viewed objectively, for the benefit of the community as a whole and has prospects for success that are real enough to warrant the costs of the litigation being borne by the public purse as costs incidental to good administration; (2) that the judicial decision has contributed significantly to the proper understanding of the law in question; and (3) that the applicant has *no* private gain in the outcome. Other relevant factors like the conduct of the litigants would also have to be considered: *Chu Hoi Dick & Anor* v. *Secretary for Home Affairs (No. 2)* [2007] 4 HKC 428, CFI at [29], [30].

[91] See the Legal Aid Ordinance (Cap. 91), ss. 26 and 26A.

[92] For more information, see the website of the Hong Kong Bar Association: www.hkba.org/the-bar/free-legal-service/index.html.

[93] See Judiciary Administration, *Statistics on Unrepresented Litigants* (December 2010) (LC Paper No. CB(2)571/10-11(01)), www.legco.gov.hk/yr10-11/english/panels/ajls/papers/aj1122cb2-571-1-e.pdf; Judiciary Administrator, *Examination of Estimates of Expenditure 2014–2015: Controlling Officer's Reply to Initial Written Questions* (JA026) (31 March 2014), www.legco.gov.hk/yr13-14/english/fc/fc/w-9/ja-e.pdf.

scheme was launched in 2013 to provide a service for those litigants in person who need advice on the rules and procedures relating to court proceedings in civil cases.[94] However, the real cure would be an expansion of legal aid, a matter with which the HKSAR Government has been proceeding at a rather slow pace.

4 Sources of law and styles of judicial decisions

4.1 Sources of law

Article 18 of the Basic Law of the HKSAR provides that the laws in force in the HKSAR shall be the Basic Law, the laws previously in force in Hong Kong as provided for in Article 8 of the Basic Law, and the laws enacted by the legislature of the HKSAR. Article 8 of the Basic Law maintains the previous legal system of Hong Kong basically unchanged, such that the laws previously in force in Hong Kong, that is, the common law, rules of equity, ordinances, subordinate legislation and customary law shall be maintained, except for any that contravenes the Basic Law, and subject to any amendment by the legislature of the HKSAR. Accordingly, the internal sources of law of the HKSAR consist of the common law, rules of equity, legislation (ordinances and subordinate legislation) and customary law, and all these internal sources may be amended by the legislature of the HKSAR.[95] Hong Kong's legal system thus maintains its nature as a common law based legal system. Hong Kong judges, in carrying out their task of declaring, elucidating and developing the common law, are to partake in the judicial function of establishing the common law of the HKSAR, which in reality amounted to a modified application of English common law, suited to local circumstances.[96] In this regard, the HKSAR courts may, in accordance with Article 84 of the Basic Law, refer to precedents of other common law jurisdictions in the adjudication of cases. In *Solicitor (24/07)* v. *Law Society of Hong Kong*,[97] Chief Justice Li indicated that the HKSAR courts should continue:

[94] See *Press Release: Pilot scheme on free legal advice for litigants in person to launch next Monday* (14 March 2013), www.info.gov.hk/gia/general/201303/14/P201303140430.htm.

[95] See, generally, P. Wesley-Smith, *Sources of Law of Hong Kong* (Hong Kong University Press, 1994).

[96] For example, the question of the applicability of the doctrine of lost modern grant for title to land by prescription in the context of Hong Kong was debated before the Court of Final Appeal in *China Field Ltd & Anor* v. *Appeal Tribunal (Buildings)* (2009) 12 HKCFAR 342.

[97] (2008) 11 HKCFAR 117, CFA.

> to derive assistance from overseas jurisprudence. This includes the decisions of final appellate courts in various common law jurisdictions as well as decisions of supra-national courts, such as the European Court of Human Rights. Compared to many common law jurisdictions, Hong Kong is a relatively small jurisdiction. It is of great benefit to the Hong Kong courts to examine comparative jurisprudence in seeking the appropriate solution for the problems which come before them. This is underlined in the Basic Law itself. Article 84 expressly provides that the courts in Hong Kong may refer to precedents of other common law jurisdictions.

The HKSAR courts have constantly drawn assistance from comparative law, including comparative human rights law; it has been commented that the HKSAR courts are thus "internationalist."[98]

Article 18 of the Basic Law then provides that national laws of the PRC shall not be applied in the HKSAR except for those listed in Annex III of the Basic Law.[99] Additions and deletions to this list of national laws are performed by the NPCSC on the basis of the criteria that the laws listed in Annex III "shall be confined to those relating to defence and foreign affairs as well as other matters outside the limits of the autonomy of the Region as specified by this Law."[100] However, in a declared state of war or a determination that the HKSAR is in a state of emergency, both decided by the NPCSC, the Central People's Government would be authorized by Article 18 to issue an order applying "the relevant national laws in the Region."[101] National laws are thus an external source of law of the HKSAR.

The Basic Law of the HKSAR is a source of law in itself. It is also more than that. Article 11 of the Basic Law indicates that in accordance with Article 31 of the Constitution of the People's Republic of China (which makes provision for the establishment of special administrative regions

[98] See P. Y. Lo, "An internationalist, consequentialist and non-progressive court: constitutional adjudication in Hong Kong (1997–2009)," *City University of Hong Kong Law Review*, 2 (2010), 215–35.

[99] National laws so listed are applied locally in Hong Kong by way of promulgation or legislation by the HKSAR. As for a legal challenge of legislation by the HKSAR legislature applying a listed national law, see *HKSAR* v. *Ng Kung Siu & Anor* (1999) 2 HKCFAR 442, CFA (over the National Flag and National Emblem Ordinance (116 of 1997) punishing flag desecration).

[100] As to how this provision may be policed, see B. Ling, "The proper law of conflict between Basic Law and other legislative acts of the National People's Congress" in J. Chan, H. Fu and Y. Ghai (eds.), *Hong Kong's Constitutional Debate: Conflicts over Interpretation* (Hong Kong University Press, 2000), pp. 151–70.

[101] See P. Y. Lo, *The Hong Kong Basic Law* (Hong Kong: LexisNexis, 2011), paras. 18.13–16.

and the specification of the systems practiced therein), the systems and policies practiced in the HKSAR[102] shall be based on the provisions of the Basic Law. Further, the article provides that no law enacted by the legislature of the HKSAR shall contravene the Basic Law. The combination of Articles 11, 18 and the authorized power of the HKSAR courts to interpret the Basic Law pursuant to Article 158, as well as the previous colonial judicial practice of reviewing colonial legislative acts against the constitutive legal instrument and imperial acts, ensures that the HKSAR courts acquire the power to exercise judicial review of legislation enacted by the HKSAR legislature, as well as the laws previously in force, and to declare on the question of constitutional validity of such legislation or law; it is the *Marbury* v. *Madison* type of judicial review carried out by virtue of the legal supremacy of the Basic Law and the power of the courts to interpret the same, thus performing the judicial functions of "saying what the law is,"[103] and acting as "a constitutional check."[104]

4.2 *The style of judicial decisions*

Judicial decisions in Hong Kong follow no fixed formatting of holdings and reasons. Rather, the judge writes discursively, identifying and addressing the issues and submissions, on both facts and law, raised in the hearing and requiring decision. On occasion, although it is not necessary for the decision or the substantiation of the decision, the judge may append his or her opinion on the merits of submissions from the parties on an incidental issue "in deference to counsel's submission" or "in case I am wrong" on the substance of the decision. This category of opinion is usually addressed as *obiter dicta*, to be distinguished from the *ratio decidendi*, the principal holding(s) of the judicial decision. There is also no fixed style of writing. Each judge may adopt a personal style. At times, the judicial decision is given *ex tempore*, recorded, and then transcribed into the judgment with a few modifications, and therefore adopts a more conversational style.

[102] These systems and policies include the social and economic systems; the system for safeguarding the fundamental rights and freedoms of its residents; the executive, legislative and judicial systems; and their relevant policies.

[103] See J. Chan, "Basic Law and constitutional review: the first decade," *Hong Kong Law Journal*, 37 (2007), 407–47.

[104] See *Ng Ka Ling & Ors* v. *Director of Immigration* (1999) 2 HKCFAR 4, CFA at 25I-J.

Another dimension is that the HKSAR operates in two official languages, namely Chinese and English. Important judgments are made available in both official languages, and here one experiences the challenge of translation, which is more pronounced when translating English (especially the idiomatic and subtle styles) into Chinese than translating Chinese into English.[105] A comparison between the Chinese and English judgments can indicate that writing judgments in Chinese may involve the use of more formal language. On the other hand, if a judgment is given in Chinese after a hearing in Chinese, the text of the judgment might be much terser than if the argument had been conducted in English, with the parties and the court tending to summarize the applicable common law precedents and case reports (which are usually available only in English).

4.3 *Judicial law-making and judicial policy-making*

There is no need in the present day to assume that judges working in a common law based legal system do not make law and only declare an existing corpus of common law. Sir Anthony Mason, in an extra-curial lecture, underlined the evolving common law:

> the reference in Article 8 to the common law and the rules of equity picks up the principles of the common law with its inherent capacity for further development by the courts of the HKSAR. To read Article 8, in conjunction with Article 18, as constitutionally freezing Hong Kong judge-made law in the condition in which it stood immediately before 1 July 1997 would be to insulate the principles and rules of judge-made law from the very process by which they come into existence and develop. Such a reading would deny to the Hong Kong courts of the HKSAR an important element of the exercise of the judicial power committed to them by Article 80 of the Basic Law, namely the elucidation and refinement of the principles

[105] For examples, see *Democratic Republic of the Congo & Ors* v. *FG Hemisphere Associates LLC* (FACV 5, 6, 7/2010, 8 June 2010), available in English at: http://legalref.judiciary.gov.hk/doc/judg/word/vetted/other/en/2010/FACV000005_2010.doc; and in Chinese at: http://legalref.judiciary.gov.hk/doc/judg/word/vetted/other/ch/2010/FACV000005Y_2010.doc (interpretation of the Basic Law of the HKSAR relating to the appropriate doctrine of foreign sovereign state immunity); and *LKW* v. *DD* (FACV 16/2008, 12 November 2010), available in English at: http://legalref.judiciary.gov.hk/doc/judg/word/vetted/other/en/2008/FACV000016_2008.doc; and in Chinese at: http://legalref.judiciary.gov.hk/doc/judg/word/vetted/other/ch/2008/FACV000016Y_2008.doc (the principles for division of matrimonial property in financial provision proceedings on divorce).

> and rules of the common law as an incident of the adjudication of cases. In the context of Article 8, "the common law" and "rules of equity" are the common law and rules of equity of Hong Kong.[106]

On the other hand, judges and lawyers in Hong Kong have long conducted debates in court on the terms of legality. For example, Chief Justice Geoffrey Ma in his 2011 Speech at the Opening of the Legal Year underlined that the beginning and the end of the administration of justice is "the law":

> The judicial oath requires judges to look no further than the law as applied to the facts . . . This is the true role of the courts. The courts do not serve the people by solving political, social or economic issues. They are neither qualified nor constitutionally able to do so. However, where legal issues are concerned, this is the business of the courts and whatever the context or the controversy, the courts and judges will deal with these legal issues.[107]

This assumption in judicial discourse does not negate the reality of judicial policies. Penal policies, especially the imposition of sentences for criminal offenses, have been regarded as within the competence and province of the courts, particularly the Court of Appeal, which is often called upon to expound principles and impose non-straitjacket guidelines to assist sentencing courts below. In doing so, the Court of Appeal often addresses the social and personal impact of the crimes involved, the prevalence of the commission of the offense, the need for deterrence, the need to mark community abhorrence, the need for punishment as an assurance to the victims and their families, and the need of the offender for rehabilitation. Civil procedure is another province of judicial policy, an area where party autonomy would compete with fairness between the parties and the fair allocation of judicial resources. The recent Civil Justice Reform has been an effort steered by the judiciary to enable a change in the culture of civil litigation in Hong Kong for the more expeditious and affordable (if not also practical) resolution of disputes. It is part and parcel of the implementation of the Reform for the HKSAR courts to exercise their powers and interpret any of the rules of court and practice directions to give effect to several systemic

[106] See A. Mason, "The role of the common law in Hong Kong" in J. Young and R. Lee (eds.), *The Common Law Lecture Series 2005* (Faculty of Law, the University of Hong Kong, 2006), p. 18.

[107] See G. Ma, *CJ's speech at Ceremonial Opening of the Legal Year 2011* (10 January 2011), www.info.gov.hk/gia/general/201101/10/P201101100201.htm.

objectives.[108] And the courts have made it a duty of the parties to the proceedings and their legal representatives to assist them to further those objectives.

4.4 *Interpretive method*

The interpretation of legal instruments is the daily work of judges working in a common law based legal system, with such legal instruments ranging from contracts, legislation (primary and subsidiary/delegated legislation) and constitutional instruments. The methodology of interpretation of legal instruments has been the thorough study of and commentary by legal scholars, lawyers and judges throughout the common law world,[109] and it is not proposed to produce an essay on this very substantial topic here.

The particular approach of constitutional interpretation adopted by the HKSAR courts at present can be described as a particular form of textualism. The Court of Final Appeal probably would have termed it as purposive interpretation when stating in the terms that the Court's role in interpreting the Basic Law of the HKSAR is to construe the language used in the text of the instrument, in light of its context and purpose, in order to ascertain "the legislative intent as expressed in the language." Interpreting the Basic Law is an objective exercise. Materials extrinsic to the Basic Law, whether pre- or post-enactment, cannot affect interpretation where the courts conclude that language construed in the manner above is clear. The Court by the above reasoning rejected categorically the suggestion that some extrinsic materials may have such force that it would, on the basis of such materials, depart from the clear meaning of the language of the Basic Law and give the language a meaning which the language could not bear. The Court in so doing placed particular emphasis on the character of a common law system that includes a separation of powers where "the interpretation of laws once enacted is a matter for the courts."[110]

[108] See the Rules of the High Court (Cap. 4 sub leg A), Order 1A rule 1.

[109] See, for example, F. Bennion, *Bennion on Statutory Interpretation*, 5th edn. (London: LexisNexis, 2008); A. Barak, *Purposive Interpretation in Law* (Princeton University Press, 2005); K. Greenawalt, *Legal Interpretation: Perspectives from Other Disciplines and Private Texts* (Oxford University Press, 2010); and A. Scalia and B. Garner, *Reading Law: The Interpretation of Legal Texts* (St Paul: Thomson/West, 2012).

[110] See *Director of Immigration* v. *Chong Fung Yuen* (2001) 4 HKCFAR 211, CFA.

By adopting this approach in a case where it was asked to consider and give significant weight to an indication of "legislative intent" of Article 24 (2) of the Basic Law by the NPCSC in its 1999 Interpretation of Article 24 (2)(3), the Court of Final Appeal had sought to ensure and enhance judicial autonomy of the HKSAR courts. The NPCSC may not, short of adopting an interpretation of a provision of the Basic Law, control the objective exercise of interpretation by the HKSAR courts of provisions of the Basic Law through exposition or signposting on the side of perhaps subjective "legislative intent."[111]

On the other hand, the Court of Final Appeal has accepted that, in construing the language of the Basic Law, the HKSAR courts "must avoid a literal, technical, narrow or rigid approach," bearing in mind that "[as] is usual for constitutional instruments, it uses general and ample language. It is a living instrument intended to meet the changing needs and circumstances." The adoption of a purposive approach, in the Court's view, was necessary in light of the Basic Law's nature as a constitutional instrument stating general principles and expressing purposes without condescending to particularity and definition of terms. "So, in ascertaining the true meaning of the instrument, the courts must consider the purpose of the instrument and its relevant provisions as well as the language of its text in the light of its context, context being of particular importance." As to context, the Court considered that the context of a particular provision of the Basic Law "is to be found in the Basic Law itself as well as relevant extrinsic materials including the Joint Declaration. Assistance can also be gained from any traditions and usages that may have given meaning to the language used."[112] It has been suggested that directing reference to the said materials and matters for context may, coupled with the theme of "continuity" said to be underlying the Basic Law, mean that Basic Law interpretation by the HKSAR courts would seldom involve the progressive adaptation of the constitutional text to new conditions, but instead would often look back to the state of the law, if not also of society, at the time of the drafting of the Basic Law to ascertain the meaning of the language.[113]

An exception to this "non-progressive" approach is probably the interpretation of provisions of the Basic Law protecting fundamental

[111] Lo, "Constitutional Adjudication in Hong Kong," 215; and Lo, *The Judicial Construction of Hong Kong Basic Law*, pp. 469–473.

[112] See *Ng Ka Ling & Ors* v. *Director of Immigration* (1999) 2 HKCFAR 4, CFA.

[113] Lo, "Constitutional Adjudication in Hong Kong," 215. Cf. *W* v. *Registrar of Marriages* [2013] 3 HKLRD 90, CFA.

rights and freedoms enshrined and entrenched in the Basic Law. Here, the HKSAR courts are to interpret these provisions generously in order to give to HKSAR residents "the full measure of fundamental rights and freedoms so constitutionally guaranteed."[114] In this connection, in *Shum Kwok Sher* v. *HKSAR*,[115] Sir Anthony Mason NPJ stated for the Court of Final Appeal that:

> In interpreting the provisions of chap. III of the Basic Law and the provisions of the Bill, the Court may consider it appropriate to take account of the established principles of international jurisprudence as well as decisions of international and national courts and tribunals on like or substantially similar provisions in the [International Covenant on Civil and Political Rights (ICCPR)], other international instruments and national constitutions.[116]

Apart from the General Comments[117] and views[118] of the United Nations Human Rights Committee, which is the treaty body of the ICCPR,[119] the HKSAR courts have also considered judgments of the European Court of Human Rights and the erstwhile House of Lords,[120] both of which interpret and apply the European Convention on Human Rights.[121] Further, the HKSAR courts have considered the judgments of final appellate courts of overseas jurisdictions enforcing a constitutional bill of rights, particularly the Privy Council,[122] the Supreme Court of

[114] See *Ng Ka Ling & Ors* v. *Director of Immigration* (1999) 2 HKCFAR 4, CFA.

[115] I.e. *Shum Kwok Sher* v. *HKSAR* (2002) 5 HKCFAR 381, CFA. [116] *Ibid.* at [59].

[117] I.e. the general comments the Human Rights Committee may adopt on thematic issues, more particularly the committee's interpretation of the provisions of the ICCPR. See ICCPR, Art. 40.

[118] I.e. the views adopted by the Human Rights Committee in considering individual communications of claims of violation by a state party of a right under the ICCPR pursuant to the Optional Protocol to the International Covenant on Civil and Political Rights, New York, 16 December 1966, in force 23 March 1976, 999 UNTS 302.

[119] Basic Law of the HKSAR, Art. 39 provides for the continuation of the provisions of the ICCPR as applied to Hong Kong and for restrictions to rights and freedoms of HKSAR residents to be prescribed by law and not to contravene those provisions of the ICCPR.

[120] In 2009, the judicial functions of the House of Lords were taken over by the Supreme Court of the United Kingdom. Courts of the United Kingdom take into account the jurisprudence of the European Court of Human Rights by virtue of s. 2(1) of the Human Rights Act 1998.

[121] European Convention for the Protection of Human Rights and Fundamental Freedoms, Rome, 4 November 1950, in force 3 September 1953, 213 UNTS 221.

[122] The Judicial Committee of the Privy Council, sitting in London, hears appeals by way of special petitions, from a slowly dwindling number of British Commonwealth countries and British overseas territories, including Mauritius, Jamaica, Belize, Dominica, Cayman

Canada, the Constitutional Court of South Africa, and the United States Supreme Court. On some occasions, even judgments of the German *Bundesverfassungsgericht*[123] and the Inter-American Court of Human Rights[124] were considered – the provision in Article 84 of the Basic Law that the courts may refer to precedents of other common law jurisdictions was viewed more as confirmation than as constraint. The invalidation record of the HKSAR courts suggests that there are occasions on which they considered that relying on international and comparative jurisprudence focusing on the relative importance of protecting particular fundamental rights[125] would lead to a more exacting intensity of review.[126]

Additionally, the courts have assumed an implied power, derived from the judicial power and jurisdiction invested in them by the Basic Law of the HKSAR, to adopt a "remedial interpretation" of a statute that goes beyond ordinary common law interpretation (i.e. a meaning which the language, understood in the light of its context and the statutory purpose, is incapable of bearing), in order to preserve the validity of a statutory provision that would otherwise have been impugned by inconsistency with the Basic Law, as opposed to declaring that provision to be unconstitutional and invalid.[127] A court engaging in an exercise of "remedial interpretation" may read words into and strike words out of the statutory provision in order to achieve an interpretation that complies with the

Islands, British Virgin Islands, Bermuda, Jersey, and Gibraltar. Many of these countries and territories either have a written constitution or a bill of rights.

123 See *HKSAR* v. *Ng Kung Siu & Anor* (1999) 2 HKCFAR 442, CFA, where the Court cited the Flag Desecration Case, BVerfGE 81, 278 (1990), as well as *Re Paris Renato* (1988), a judgment of the Corte Suprema di Cassazione, Italy to show how other ICCPR state parties reasoned against flag desecration. Similarly, in *Leung Kwok Hung & Ors* v. *HKSAR* (2005) 8 HKCFAR 229, CFA, the Court cited the Brokdorf Atomic Power Station Case, BVerfGE 69, 315 (1985) and the Mutlagen Military Depot Case, BVerfGE 73, 206 (1986) in considering the validity of the prior notification regime for public meetings and processions.

124 See *HKSAR* v. *Ng Kung Siu & Anor* (1999) 2 HKCFAR 442, CFA, where Advisory Opinion No. OC-6/86 (1986) was considered when elucidating the meaning of public order (*ordre public*) in human rights instruments.

125 Preference or great emphasis has been given to the enforcement of political rights and the protection of individuals from discrimination on the grounds of sex, race and sexual orientation, being grounds centrally associated with the dignity of the person.

126 See *Secretary for Justice* v. *Yau Yuk Lung* (2007) 10 HKCFAR 335, CFA; *Leung* v. *Secretary for Justice* [2006] 4 HKLRD 211, CA; *Chan Kin Sum & Ors* v. *Secretary for Justice & Anor* [2008] 6 HKC 486, [2009] 2 HKLRD 166, CFI.

127 See *HKSAR* v. *Lam Kwong Wai & Anor* (2006) 9 HKCFAR 574, CFA at [67] – [79].

Basic Law.[128] The courts do so in the belief that "the legislature intends its legislative provision to have a valid, even if reduced, operation than to have no operation at all, so long as the valid operation is not fundamentally or essentially different from what it enacted."[129]

5 Alternative dispute resolution (ADR) and the courts

In the ongoing bid to position Hong Kong as the leading center for dispute resolution in the Asia Pacific region, ADR by arbitration and mediation in civil and commercial disputes has thrived under Government and judicial support.[130]

The legal and judicial systems of the HKSAR are facilitative to the adoption of ADRs to resolve disputes. Legislation has been enacted to assist arbitration in Hong Kong or outside Hong Kong (including in relation to enforcement of the resultant arbitral award), as well as mediation in Hong Kong. Rules of court and practice directions made by the judiciary to regulate the conduct of civil proceedings in the HKSAR courts are geared towards encouraging early settlement, whether achieved through negotiations, mediation,[131] or other means through which a party can be made to view the merits of his or her case realistically and practically.[132] Pilot schemes incorporating an element of ADR have been introduced by the judiciary in suitable types of disputes.[133]

5.1 Mediation in court

There is recognition on the part of the HKSAR Government and many of the providers of mediation services in Hong Kong that greater use of mediation in litigation ought to be promoted and advanced proactively.

[128] See *ibid.* at [63], [65]–[66]. [129] See *ibid.* at [77].

[130] See R. Yuen, *Speech by the Secretary for Justice at Hong Kong Association forum in London* (27 September 2013), www.doj.gov.hk/eng/public/pr/20130927_pr1.html.

[131] A working definition of "mediation" is provided under the Mediation Ordinance (Cap. 620), s. 4(1): "a structured process comprising one or more sessions in which one or more impartial individuals, without adjudicating a dispute or any aspect of it, assist the parties to the dispute to do any or all of the following: (a) identify the issues in dispute; (b) explore and generate options; (c) communicate with one another; and (d) reach an agreement regarding the resolution of the whole, or part, of the dispute."

[132] See the Rules of the High Court (Cap. 4 sub leg), Order 13A and Order 22.

[133] The selected types of disputes have been financial dispute resolution and children's dispute resolution before the Family Court, and building management cases and compulsory sale cases before the Lands Tribunal.

Following Civil Justice Reform, the facilitation of settlement of disputes has been enshrined as one of the underlying objectives of the rules of court. The Court of First Instance and the District Court further this objective as part of their duty of active case management by encouraging the parties to use ADR if the court considers that appropriate.

Parties to a civil action in the Court of First Instance and the District Court are thus required by the rules of court to consider mediation,[134] and, pursuant to a practice direction, to indicate their views on the appropriateness of the resolution of the case through mediation by filing a notice with the court.[135] Where the parties are inclined to attempt settlement of the dispute by way of mediation, the court can order a stay of proceedings for a suitable period of time to give the parties time to arrange for and conduct the mediation. The confidentiality of things said or done, and of documents or information prepared for the purpose of or in the course of mediation, is protected by recently enacted legislation.[136]

Although the HKSAR courts have not assumed the power to conduct mediation as part of the court proceedings, and have left it mainly to the good sense of the parties in the face of procedural and other encouragements and facilitation to voluntarily enter mediation, the judiciary does recognize that litigants may not be familiar with mediation and ADR in general. In this regard, the judiciary has established a Mediation Information Office in the High Court Building to answer enquiries and provide information on mediation and legal proceedings.[137] Further, to facilitate the implementation of the pilot schemes, the judiciary has set up two Mediation Co-ordinator's Offices to hold free-of-charge information sessions on mediation and help litigants involved in building management disputes and family proceedings to consider and seek mediation as a means to resolve their disputes in a

[134] The parties' legal representatives are also obliged to inform their lay clients of the availability of mediation and to introduce them to mediation, including its advantages and facilities.

[135] See *Practice Direction 31 "Mediation."* See also *Practice Direction 15.10 "Family Mediation,"* concerning advice and referral to family mediation in matrimonial and family proceedings.

[136] See Mediation Ordinance (Cap. 620), ss. 8–10. These provisions do not apply to an agreement to mediate or a settlement agreement reached following mediation.

[137] For information on the Mediation Information Office, see mediation.judiciary.gov.hk/en/mio.html. The litigants can then approach the Joint Mediation Helpline Office, described below.

non-adversarial, cost-effective, timely and mutually satisfactory manner. A list of mediators is kept in the Offices.[138]

With the support of the Government and the judiciary, the Joint Mediation Helpline Office was founded by the professions[139] and mediation-related bodies in Hong Kong[140] as a non-profit-making organization to provide mediation services, including explaining the basic principles of mediation, answering general enquiries in relation to mediation, and putting users in contact with mediators of one of the participating service providers, who follow a standard practice, charge fees according to a prescribed schedule, and are subject to a common complaint procedure.[141]

5.2 *Arbitration and courts*

The HKSAR courts have adopted a pro-arbitration approach based on party autonomy. Civil actions before the courts may be stayed in favor of arbitration where the underlying transaction is governed by a contract containing an applicable arbitration clause. The HKSAR courts apply the Arbitration Ordinance, whose object is to facilitate the fair and speedy resolution of disputes by arbitration without unnecessary expense, and which is based on the principles that, subject to the observance of the safeguards that are necessary in the public interest, the parties to a dispute should be free to agree on how the dispute should be resolved, and that the court should interfere in the arbitration of a dispute only as expressly provided for in the Ordinance.[142] In this regard, the HKSAR courts partake in the promotion of the use of arbitration in Hong Kong for the resolution of domestic and international disputes, and contribute

[138] For information on the Mediation Co-ordinator's Offices, see http://mediation.judiciary.gov.hk/en/mcos.html.

[139] The professions are the lawyers, the arbitrators, the architects and the surveyors.

[140] The mediation-related bodies are the Hong Kong Mediation Council and the Hong Kong Mediation Centre.

[141] For information on the Joint Mediation Helpline Office Ltd, see www.jointmediation-helpline.org.hk/index.html.

[142] See the Arbitration Ordinance (Cap. 609), s. 3. The Ordinance provides for the provisions of the UNCITRAL Model Law expressly stated in the Ordinance as having the force of law in Hong Kong subject to the modifications and supplements as expressly provided for in the Ordinance (s. 4). The Ordinance applies to an arbitration under an arbitration agreement, whether or not the agreement is entered into in Hong Kong, if the place of arbitration is in Hong Kong (s. 5). Arbitral awards are given permission to be enforced in Hong Kong under Part 10 of the Ordinance under three routes: the UNCITRAL Model Law route (s. 86), the New York Convention route (s. 89), and the Mainland award route (ss. 93 and 95).

to the maintenance of Hong Kong's status as a leading international arbitration center.[143]

5.3 *Other ADRs*

The Financial Dispute Resolution Centre is another non-profit-making initiative established as a result of the encouragement, co-ordination and contribution of the HKSAR Government, the financial services regulators and financial service providers. Established on the heels of the experience of using mediation in resolving some of the many disputes arising out of the collapse of the merchant bank Lehman Brothers, the Centre administers the Financial Dispute Resolution Scheme, which requires financial institutions operating in Hong Kong, including banks and financial service providers, which are its members, to resolve monetary disputes with their customers through a process of "Mediation First, Arbitration Next."[144] The Centre aspires to deal with these disputes before they escalate and to support Hong Kong as an international financial center.[145]

6 Concluding remarks

Hong Kong's economic development into a free port; a separate custom area; aviation, logistics and communications hubs; and an international financial center has been accompanied by the need for efficient and reputable means of dispute resolution. Both the judiciary and the legal profession in Hong Kong must rise to the challenge. The market forces of global economic competition and foreign trade (including trade and investment with or in Mainland China) have shaped the requisite expertise of the judges and legal practitioners in diverse areas of law, including admiralty and shipping; carriage of goods by sea, land and air; securities, banking and finance; and telecommunications.

[143] Arbitration in Hong Kong is serviced by the Hong Kong International Arbitration Centre, an independent and non-governmental body, which has been designated under the Arbitration Ordinance (Cap. 609) as the appointing body to appoint arbitrators and to determine the number of arbitrators where the parties to a dispute are unable to agree. In 2012, 68 percent of all the Centre's arbitration cases (namely 199 cases) were of an international nature. Further, the International Court of Arbitration of the International Chamber of Commerce has established a branch in its Secretariat in Hong Kong since November 2008 to serve the ICC's arbitration in the Asia-Pacific Region.

[144] For the terms of reference of the Centre, see www.fdrc.org.hk/en/html/aboutus/aboutus_tor.html.

[145] For information about the Centre, see www.fdrc.org.hk/en/index.html.

Additionally, the moment for judicial action came when the Hong Kong Bill of Rights took effect in 1991, under which the courts were legislatively mandated to examine pre-existing legislation to reveal the extent of its inconsistency with the human rights enshrined in the Bill of Rights.[146] The practice prior to 1997 enabled the courts of the HKSAR to develop the constitutional jurisdiction underlining the courts' role as the check of the executive authorities and the legislature under the Basic Law of the HKSAR.[147] Basic Law and other public law litigation flourished thereafter, as disparate numerical and political minorities, including homosexuals, transsexuals, children with special education needs, new immigrants, individual political figures, and even political parties made applications for judicial review challenging legislation,[148] government policies[149] and infrastructure projects.[150] The proliferation of public law litigation, in numbers and, more importantly, in variety, complexity and urgency, has meant that to the judiciary, judges of a suitable caliber in terms of knowledge of the law, a clear understanding of the policy issues involved, and experience in managing competing demands of litigants have to be deployed to hear and decide constitutional and administrative law cases, often at short notice and within a constricted time frame.

Judges and the courts of the HKSAR, and their work in the administration of justice in Hong Kong, have consistently been rated highly by the public,[151]

[146] See the Hong Kong Bill of Rights Ordinance (Cap. 383), s. 3.

[147] See *Ng Ka Ling & Ors* v. *Director of Immigration* (1999) 2 HKCFAR 4, CFA.

[148] See, e.g., *Leung* v. *Secretary for Justice* [2006] 4 HKLRD 211, CA (concerning the constitutional validity of offenses of male homosexual activity); *Chan Kin Sum & Ors* v. *Secretary for Justice & Anor* [2008] 6 HKC 486, CFI (concerning the constitutional validity of the disqualification of prisoners from voting in elections).

[149] See, for example, *Fok Chun Wa & Anor* v. *Hospital Authority & Anor* [2012] 2 HKC 413, CFA (about the Hospital Authority's charging of a very substantial fee for the obstetric service package for mothers who were not HKSAR permanent residents, in implementation of the Government's population policy).

[150] See, for example, *Chu Yee Wah* v. *Director of Environmental Protection* [2011] 3 HKC 227, CFI (over the environmental impact assessment for the Hong Kong sections of the Hong Kong- Zhuhai-Macau Bridge project).

[151] The Public Opinion Programme of the University of Hong Kong has conducted opinion polls on core social indicators on a continuous basis since 1997, including the "compliance with the rule of law." These indicators have consistently been staying within the range of six to seven out of a rating scale of zero to ten. The combined charts on the rule of law indicators are accessible at: http://hkupop.hku.hk/english/popexpress/judiciary/overall/index.html. The same program has also asked the public to give a rating of the Chief Justice on a scale of zero to one hundred, and the ratings of both Chief Justice Andrew Li and Chief Justice Geoffrey Ma have stayed in the sixties in the majority of

the business community,[152] and the legal community in Hong Kong.[153] Judicial decisions are generally complied with. The HKSAR Government has, in spite of one notable exception,[154] thus far complied with judgments of the courts invalidating legislative provisions for being inconsistent with the Basic Law, not only at the micro-level of the individual case but also at

the polls. The rating tables are accessible at: http://hkupop.hku.hk/english/popexpress/judiciary/index.html.

152 In the Hong Kong General Chamber of Commerce's annual Business Prospect Survey in 2011, 91 percent of the membership returning the survey questionnaire regarded the legal and regulatory system of Hong Kong as "good," and this has been taken as one of Hong Kong's business strengths: see presentation of David O'Rear, Chief Economist, Hong Kong General Chamber of Commerce (December 2011), www.chamber.org.hk/FileUpload/201212171227441574/Business%20Survey%20Dec%202011%20(Final)_2.pdf.

153 The overall perception of the Hong Kong legal community of the courts of the HKSAR has consistently been positive; the courts have been considered as independent and impartial, and in a position to provide a fair hearing where all necessary issues for the proper adjudication of the case are heard and discussed. Indeed, members of the legal profession have stood ready to defend the independence of the courts of the HKSAR when crises arise. This was demonstrated in 1999 and 2005, when lawyers organized silent marches on each occasion to the Court of Final Appeal to express their distress and solidarity with the Court over the adoption of NPCSC interpretations at the proposal of the Central People's Government following consideration of a relevant report of the Chief Executive of the HKSAR; again, in 2011, when the Chief Executive of the HKSAR appeared to be making a public statement suggesting a successful legal challenge by way of judicial review on the basis of environmental impact legislation was somewhat illegitimate; and, yet again, in 2014, when a white paper released by the Information Office of the State Council of the Central Authorities of the PRC on the practice of the "One Country, Two Systems" policy in the HKSAR suggested that Judges in Hong Kong are among the administrators of Hong Kong who have the responsibility of correctly understanding and implementing the Basic Law of the HKSAR, of safeguarding the country's sovereignty, security and development interests, and of ensuring the long-term prosperity and stability of Hong Kong and that, in a word, Hong Kong's administrators (with Judges among them) are subject to the basic political requirement of loving the country.

154 The principal ruling in the *Ng Ka Ling* case [(1999) 2 HKCFAR 4, CFA] that invalidated the certificate of entitlement scheme that had sought to regulate entry into Hong Kong by Chinese citizen children of HKSAR permanent residents born in Mainland China for settlement was overturned by the HKSAR Government's approach to the NPCSC through the Central People's Government for an interpretation of the relevant provisions of the Basic Law of the HKSAR: see "The Interpretation by the Standing Committee of the National People's Congress of Articles 22(4) and 24(2)(3) of the Basic Law of the Hong Kong Special Administrative Region of the People's Republic of China" (adopted by the Standing Committee of the 9th National People's Congress at its 10th Session on 26 June 1999) in J. Chan, H. Fu and Y. Ghai (eds.), *Hong Kong's Constitutional Debate: Conflict over Interpretation* (Hong Kong University Press, 2000), pp. 478–9. The Interpretation included an interpretation of Art. 24(2)(3) of the Basic Law against the adjudication in a different but related case, namely, *Chan Kam Nga & Others* v. *Director of Immigration* (1999) 2 HKCFAR 82.

the macro-level of the treatment of like and prospective cases through legislative amendment. The judiciary has been entirely free of corruption. Although, as is usually the case in a community of diverse views, there have been a small number of commentators over the years who have held contrary views of the jurisprudence of the HKSAR courts and have been active in expressing those views in strong terms in their writing.[155] There have also been academic commentaries on the institution of judicial independence and the work of judges and judicial officers in Hong Kong.[156] While they make critical comments from time to time on the merits of individual cases, they have lauded the "reasonably impressive record [of the courts] in upholding civil and political rights" and the careful and sensible approach the courts adopted in "delineating the boundary of the division" of the powers between the Central Authorities and the HKSAR under the principle of "One Country, Two Systems." As Professor Johannes Chan indicated, "[on] the whole, the judiciary has maintained its independence and impartiality. It is true that it has been faced with an increasing volume of cases which have political implications, but this does not mean that its decisions are political."[157]

This "quite positive" verdict on the Judiciary of Hong Kong "in adhering to its proper role and in withstanding political pressure" will remain, as Professor Chan considered in 2007, as long as the political process in the special administrative region can effectively deal with matters of policy and resource allocation. Otherwise, calls for judicial intervention will intensify, putting the integrity and independence of the courts, and, with it, the Rule of Law in Hong Kong, to the test.[158]

Seventeen years have passed since 1997. The generation of judges that founded the jurisprudence of the HKSAR have retired or are to retire in the next few years. Chief Justice Andrew Li took early retirement in 2010 to enable his successor, Chief Justice Geoffrey Ma, to plan the generational transition in the judicial corps, including filling three

[155] See, for examples, S. C. Song, "'Constitutional review' system inconsistent with the Basic Law" (*Wen Wei Po*), 2 February 2005, http://paper.wenweipo.com/2005/02/02/WW0502020003.htm; B. Zhou, "Judicial independence and judicial self-restraint" (*Wen Wei Po*), 6 May 2011, A22.

[156] S. Tsang (ed.), *Judicial Independence and the Rule of Law in Hong Kong* (Hong Kong University Press, 2001); P. Wesley-Smith, "Judges and judicial power under the Hong Kong Basic Law," *Hong Kong Law Journal*, 34 (2004), 83–108; Chan, "Basic Law and constitutional review," 407–47; and P. J. Yap, "Constitutional review under the Basic Law: the rise, retreat and resurgence of judicial power in Hong Kong," *Hong Kong Law Journal*, 37 (2007), 449–74.

[157] See Chan, "Basic Law and constitutional review," 446.

[158] See *ibid*. at 447.

vacancies in the Court of Final Appeal that would arise in the next five years. More than fifty appointments have been made since 2012, the majority of which being judges or judicial officers from a lower court, as opposed to legal practitioners in private practice; this is perhaps an indication of a hierarchical ladder of promotion that judicial officers would expect from their careers.

The strong power of judicial review asserted by the HKSAR courts carries with it the responsibility to review and decide questions of constitutional validity properly presented to them in judicial review applications and to reach the right or satisfactory decision with all quarters, bearing in mind possible economic, social and political implications and consequences, some of which may not materialize until some time later in combination with other developments. By that time, it may be the next generation of judges who are presented with the task of explaining and elaborating on the original judgment and the principled rationale behind it, particularly the considerations for decontextualizing the Basic Law of the HKSAR's Mainland Chinese and socialist origins in favor of recontextualizing the same for Hong Kong's common law based legal system, tradition, and capitalist and democratic society.[159] This is an unenviable but undeniable responsibility.

The torch has been passed. The time may have come.

The Hong Kong population has since 2011 been in a state of some discontent over the unsatisfactory situation of a significant number of Mainland women giving birth in Hong Kong and putting strain on the limited obstetric services and socio-economic resources associated with the education and upbringing of these children, who qualify as permanent residents of the HKSAR (even though they are not linked to Hong Kong through a parent who is a permanent resident of the HKSAR).[160] Some commentators and even a political party have attributed this phenomenon to the 2001 judgment of the Court of Final Appeal a

[159] See P. Y. Lo, "Rethinking judicial reference: barricades at the gateway?" in H. Fu, L. Harris and S. N. Young (eds.), *Interpreting Hong Kong's Basic Law: The Struggle for Coherence* (Basingstoke: Palgrave Macmillan, 2007), pp. 157–81; and P. Y. Lo, *The Judicial Construction of Hong Kong's Basic Law*, pp. 469–493.

[160] The number of live births in Hong Kong to Mainland women whose spouses are not HKSAR permanent residents has increased from 1,250 in 2002 to 35,736 in 2011. By way of contrast, the number of live births born in Hong Kong to local women has grown much more slowly, from 39,703 in 2002 to 51,436 in 2011; see Food and Health Bureau, *Panel on Health Services: Use of obstetric services by non-local women* (February 2012), Annex A (LC Paper No. CB(2)1183/11-12(01)), www.legco.gov.hk/yr11-12/english/panels/hs/papers/hs0228cb2-1183-1-e.pdf.

decade ago[161] and have called for the Court to recant its "erroneous decision."[162] The incoming Administration under the leadership of Chief Executive Leung Chun-ying has vowed to the populace that these Mainland mothers should not expect their newborns to be entitled to HKSAR permanent resident status in 2013. Having tried unsuccessfully earlier in 2013 to persuade the Court of Final Appeal to seek an interpretation of the Basic Law from the NPCSC that would provide the NPCSC with an opportunity to pronounce the authority of the NPCSC's 1999 interpretation of the Basic Law over the Court's 2001 judgment,[163] the Administration has not yet announced its next move. A seismic crisis in the Rule of Law of Hong Kong has merely been temporarily averted, since several of the mooted approaches might involve the Court of Final Appeal under Chief Justice Geoffrey Ma being asked by the Administration to overrule his predecessor's judgment or to invite the NPCSC to supersede that judgment with an interpretation, thereby fracturing the seam of precedent that was conceived to be protective both of the right of abode of the individuals arriving within the clear terms of the language of the relevant provision of the Basic Law and of the judicial autonomy exercised in pronouncing and giving effect to such clear language.

If and when the HKSAR courts are confronted with constitutional cases of implications to the proper implementation of the "One Country, Two Systems" principle in Hong Kong, those at the helm would do well to recall the common law context of the Basic Law, which provides for a separation of powers, with the courts responsible for interpreting legislation once enacted, as well as for a methodology of judicial decision-making by reference to precedents (with the internal aspect of the decisions of the superior appellate courts binding on the lower courts and the external aspect of considering the non-binding but persuasive

[161] I.e. *Director of Immigration* v. *Chong Fung Yuen* (2001) 4 HKCFAR 221, CFA. The HKSAR Government implemented this judgment in 2002 with a legislative amendment.

[162] Among the commentators was the first Secretary for Justice of the HKSAR, Ms Elsie Leung, who has since become a Vice-Chairman of the Committee for the Basic Law of the NPCSC. She published a newspaper article expressing the view that the Court of Final Appeal was erroneous in 2001 on six fronts: see E. Leung, "The problem of 'doubly non-permanent' pregnant women coming to Hong Kong to give birth," *Hong Kong Economic Journal*, 10 March 2012, A17.

[163] See *Vallejos & Anor* v. *Commissioner of Registration* [2013] 4 HKC 239, CFA. The Court of Final Appeal refused the Administration's request on the basis that it was not necessary for the adjudication of the constitutional question before the Court to seek an interpretation from the NPCSC.

judicial reasoning from other common law jurisdictions), which has allowed the HKSAR courts to maintain trans-jurisdictional development of the common law in tandem with other common law jurisdictions, lest they allow themselves to be overwhelmed by Western "popular constitutionalism,"[164] if not Eastern "unification of the legal impact and the political impact."[165]

Features of the HKSAR judicial system that contribute to its strengths are likely to be the sources of its weaknesses. While Article 158 of the Basic Law establishes the link between the two legal systems and authorizes the HKSAR courts to interpret provisions of the Basic Law, the same provision has often been characterized as the weakest institutional feature in the judicial system of the HKSAR by virtue of its configuration of plenary interpretative power vested with the NPCSC. The separation of the power of final adjudication from the power of final interpretation of the constitutional instrument makes the judicial autonomy of the courts of the HKSAR vulnerable, as this plenary power of the NPCSC has been exercised to deprive a judgment of the Court of Final Appeal precedential value. As Sir Anthony Mason pithily noted, the Rule of Law of Hong Kong, like its courts, lies in the shadow of a Giant.[166]

References

Barak, A. *Purposive Interpretation in Law* (Princeton University Press, 2005)

Bennion, F. *Bennion on Statutory Interpretation*, 5th edn. (London: LexisNexis, 2005)

Chan, J. "Basic Law and constitutional review: the first decade," *Hong Kong Law Journal*, 37 (2007), 407–47.

Chan, J., Fu, H. and Ghai, Y. (eds.) *Hong Kong's Constitutional Debate: Conflict over Interpretation* (Hong Kong University Press, 2000)

Chen, A. "Social movements and the law in post-colonial Hong Kong" in K.-e. Kuah-Pearce and G. Guiheux (eds.), *Social Movements in China and Hong Kong: The Expansion of Protest Space* (Amsterdam University Press, 2009), pp. 65–90

Cheng, J. "The story of a new policy," *Hong Kong Journal*, 15 (2009), 1

Cheng, J. "Hong Kong's constitutional development and the executive-led system," *Faxue*, issue 1 (2009), 45–56

[164] See J. Rosen, "Judge mental," *The New Republic*, 15 March 2012.

[165] See B. Jiang, "The right understanding of the relationship between the judicial and the political," *Qiushi*, issue 24 (2009), 51–3. Grand Justice Jiang is a Vice-President of the Supreme People's Court of the PRC.

[166] Mason, "Rule of law in the shadow of the giant," 623.

Cheung, A. and Wong, M. "Judicial review and policy making in Hong Kong: changing interface between the legal and the political," *Asia Pacific Journal of Public Administration*, 28 (2006), 117–41

Duff, P., Findlay, M., Howarth, C. and Chan, T.-F. *Juries: A Hong Kong Perspective* (Hong Kong University Press, 1992)

Goodstadt, L. F. *Uneasy Partners: The Conflict between Public Interest and Private Profit in Hong Kong* (Hong Kong University Press, 2009)

Greenawalt, K. *Legal Interpretation: Perspectives from Other Disciplines and Private Texts* (Oxford University Press, 2010)

Jiang, B. "The right understanding of the relationship between the judicial and the political," *Qiushi*, issue 24 (2009), 51–3

Kong, K. "Public interest litigation in Hong Kong: a new hope for social transformation?" *Civil Justice Quarterly* 28 (2009), 327–43

Ling, B. "The proper law of conflict between Basic Law and other legislative acts of the National People's Congress" in Chan, Fu and Ghai (eds.), *Hong Kong's Constitutional Debate*, pp. 151–70

Lo, P. Y. "An internationalist, consequentialist and non-progressive court: constitutional adjudication in Hong Kong (1997–2009)," *City University of Hong Kong Law Review*, 2 (2010), 215–35

Lo, P. Y. "Rethinking judicial reference: Barricades at the gateway?" in H. Fu, L. Harris and S. N. Young (eds.), *Interpreting Hong Kong's Basic Law: The Struggle for Coherence* (Basingstoke: Palgrave Macmillan, 2007), pp. 157–81

Lo, P. Y. "The gateway opens wide," *Hong Kong Law Journal*, 41 (2011), 385–91

Lo, P. Y. *The Hong Kong Basic Law* (Hong Kong: LexisNexis, 2011)

Lo, P. Y. *The Judicial Construction of Hong Kong's Basic Law: Courts, Politics and Society after 1997* (Hong Kong University Press, 2014)

Lo, P. Y. "The impact of CFA jurisprudence beyond Hong Kong," *Hong Kong Lawyer*, issue 8 (2010), 36–41

Mason, A. "The role of the common law in Hong Kong" in J. Young and R. Lee (eds.), *The Common Law Lecture Series 2005* (Faculty of Law, University of Hong Kong, 2006), pp. 1–25

Mason, A. "The rule of law in the shadow of the giant: the Hong Kong experience," *Sydney Law Review*, 33 (2011), 626–44

Scalia, A. and Garner, B. *Reading Law: The Interpretation of Legal Texts* (St Paul: Thomson/West, 2012)

Tsang, S. (ed.) *Judicial Independence and the Rule of Law in Hong Kong* (Hong Kong University Press, 2001)

Wesley-Smith, P. "Judges and judicial power under the Hong Kong Basic Law," *Hong Kong Law Journal*, 34 (2004), 83–108

Wesley-Smith, P. "Settlement of the question of Hong Kong," *California Western International Law Journal*, 17(1) (1987), 116–32

Wesley-Smith, P. *Sources of Law of Hong Kong* (Hong Kong University Press, 1994)

Wesley-Smith, P. *Unequal Treaty 1898–1997: China, Great Britain and Hong Kong's New Territories*, rev. edn. (Hong Kong: Oxford University Press, 1998)

Yap, P. J. "Constitutional review under the Basic Law: the rise, retreat and resurgence of judicial power in Hong Kong," *Hong Kong Law Journal*, 37 (2007), 449–74

Yap, P. J. "Understanding public interest litigation in Hong Kong," *Common Law World Review*, 37 (2008), 257–76

6

As efficient as the best businesses: Singapore's judicial system

KEVIN Y. L. TAN

> To play their proper role in today's society, the Courts will have to be run as efficiently as the best businesses.
>
> Yong Pung How CJ (1991)[1]

From its earliest days, Singapore's existence as a port city and trading hub has been tied inextricably to trade and commerce. Its modern "founder," Sir Stamford Raffles, saw the island as "a great commercial emporium,"[2] a term that was adopted by a well-known local history textbook.[3] It thus comes as no surprise that the development of its judicial system owes much to the interests of businessmen and traders as well as its vibrant commercial sector. Prior to the British colonizing Singapore, the island was part of the Johor Sultanate, and justice was administered by the Temenggong (regional chief) under a mixture of customary law and Islamic law. The common law was formally introduced into Singapore in 1827 with the physical arrival of the Second Charter of Justice of 1826, which, among other things, extended the jurisdiction of the Court of Judicature at Penang (Prince of Wales' Island) to the territories of Malacca and Singapore. A Recorder presided over the court stationed at Penang and travelled on circuit to Singapore and Malacca several times a year to deal with cases in these two jurisdictions.[4]

[1] "In conversation: an interview with the Honourable Chief Justice Yong Pung How," *Singapore Law Review* 12 (1991), 1, 12.

[2] Raffles to Colonel Addenbrooke, 10 June 1819, reproduced in S. Raffles, *Memoir of the Life and Public Services of Sir Thomas Stamford Raffles* (London: John Murray, 1830), p. 379.

[3] C. G. Kwa, H. Derek and T. Y. Tan, *Singapore: A 700-Year History – From Early Emporium to World City* (National Archives of Singapore, 2009).

[4] For a history of the development of the Singapore legal system generally, see K. Y. L. Tan, "A short legal and constitutional history of Singapore" in K. Y. L. Tan (ed.), *The Singapore Legal System*, 2nd edn. (Singapore University Press, 1999), pp. 26–66; see also J. W. N. Kyshe, "A judicial history of the Straits Settlements 1786–1890," reprinted in *Malaya Law Review* 11 (1969). On the jurisdiction of the Singapore courts generally, see T. M. Yeo,

This situation lasted from 1827 to 1867 when the Court of Judicature was replaced by the Supreme Court of the Straits Settlements, which had a separate Court of Appeal. Final appeals lay to the Judicial Committee of the Privy Council in London. By the 1830s, Singapore had surpassed Penang in economic and political importance, and the court was situated in Singapore. One division of the court continued to sit in Penang, while judicial business of Malacca was conducted out of Singapore. It is useful to note that agitation for the grant of the Second Charter of Justice came from the locally based European merchants who felt that the uncertainty of the law was a major impediment to their doing business on the island. It was also the local Europeans who agitated for the Straits Settlements to be transferred from Indian control to the Colonial Office in 1867.[5]

Singapore's British-style legal system collapsed with the Japanese invasion of the island in February 1942 but was restored in 1945 after the Japanese surrendered. In the interregnum, British common law continued to be applied in most civil cases even though the local courts continued operating under a different guise. The Straits Settlements was disbanded in 1946, and Penang and Malacca joined the newly formed Malayan Union, which united these two territories with all other territories of the Federated Malay States and the Unfederated Malay States. This Union eventually led to the establishment of the Federation of Malaya in 1948. In the meantime, the Colony of Singapore came under the direct rule of the Colonial Office in London. The judicial system remained fundamentally the same as before the War.

Like most common legal systems, Singapore has a centralized judicial system with the Court of Appeal at its apex. The High Court has unlimited original jurisdiction as well as powers of supervision over the inferior tribunals and administrative bodies. Article 93 of the Constitution vests judicial power in the Supreme Court (comprising both the High Court and the Court of Appeal) and such subordinate courts as may be created by law. In addition, Article 4 of the Constitution declares the Constitution to be the supreme law of Singapore, thus giving the Supreme Court the power to declare laws that contradict the Constitution null and void. The two main statutes governing the administration

"Jurisdiction of the Singapore courts" in Tan (ed.), *The Singapore Legal System*, pp. 249–96.

[5] See generally, K. Y. L. Tan, "A short legal and constitutional history" in K. Y. L. Tan (ed.), *Essays in Legal History* (Singapore Academy of Law & Marshall-Cavendish Academic, 2005), pp. 27–72.

of the courts in Singapore are the Supreme Court of Judicature Act (Cap. 322, Singapore Statutes) and the State Courts Act (Cap. 321, Singapore Statutes).

1 Sources and influences in the establishment of the judicial system

With the grant of the 1826 Charter, a Court of Judicature was established for the territories of the Prince of Wales' Island (Penang), Malacca and Singapore (which collectively made up the Straits Settlements). The British authorities treated Singapore as *terra nullius* and administered English common law, having due regard for the "manners and customs" of the local population. This practice was judicially recognized in an 1858 decision of the Court of Judicature.[6] At the time of the introduction of the Charter, the population of Singapore was around 12,000 persons, most of whom were Chinese and Malays, with a few hundred European traders and businessmen.[7] Western law was, in that sense, imposed on a largely immigrant population.

1.1 Colonialism

As a British colony, Singapore's legal and judicial system was tied as if with an umbilical cord to that of the metropolis. Between 1827 and 1955, the entire judiciary was staffed by judges of the elite Colonial Legal Service, either from the United Kingdom or from different parts of the empire, such as Australia and Ceylon.[8] From the earliest years, the Recorder of the Court of Judicature was usually a knighted senior officer of the Colonial Legal Service. Most of them were well educated and connected and were expected to be the standard-bearers for English justice. Take the first two Recorders for example. The first Recorder for the Straits Settlements was Sir John Thomas Claridge (1792–1868). He was educated at the prestigious Harrow School where Lord Byron was his classmate. Later he studied law at Christ Church College, Oxford University. He was knighted in 1825, just before being sent out to the Straits.

[6] See *Regina* v. *Willans* (1858) 3 Kyshe 16.

[7] This figure is based on calculations on figures provided by S. H. Saw, *The Population of Singapore*, 3rd edn. (Singapore: Institute of Southeast Asian Studies, 2012), pp. 7–10.

[8] See generally, Sir S. Abrahams, "The colonial legal service and the administration of justice in colonial dependencies," *Journal of Comparative Legislation and International Law*, 30 (3) (1948), 1–11.

The second Recorder, Sir Benjamin Heath Malkin (1797–1837), was the son of the famous man of letters, Sir Benjamin Malkin. He studied mathematics and classics at Trinity College, Cambridge, before joining the Colonial Legal Service. Malkin was also a close friend of the noted Whig historian, Lord Thomas Macaulay, who drafted the Indian Penal Code.

Singapore remained under British rule until 1959 when it attained the status of a self-governing colony. It became independent only in 1963 when it became a constituent state of the newly formed Federation of Malaya. Throughout the colonial period, and right up until 1994, the Judicial Committee of the Privy Council was Singapore's highest court of appeal. These factors contributed to both the structure of the Singapore courts and the applicable law. English common law is applied as it would have been in England, but with modifications to suit local conditions.

Persons hoping to practice law in Singapore were all initially trained exclusively in the United Kingdom. It was only with the establishment of the Law Department at the University of Malaya in Singapore in 1956 that the first students were admitted for the study of law locally. The Department became a full-fledged Faculty of Law in 1959, and its successor institution – the Faculty of Law of the National University of Singapore – is now responsible for producing the bulk of lawyers in Singapore. Legal training was, for the most part, modeled on the English model of legal education, with law studied as an undergraduate honors degree. The use of English textbooks, precedents and authorities continued long after Singapore became independent in 1965. Today, the English common law forms the bedrock of Singapore's legal system even though legislative intervention has meant the enactment of many uniquely Singaporean laws.

1.2 Nationalism

Even after Singapore became an independent unitary state in 1965, its leaders consciously retained the Judicial Committee of the Privy Council as its final court of appeal. This was done to assure potential foreign investors that their property and contractual rights would not be jeopardized in any way, and that the judiciary remained independent throughout. Singapore's nationalism was thus tempered by an overriding practicality and an acknowledgment of the role of law in establishing a stable and viable business environment. Indeed, the old court system that Singapore operated under the Federation of Malaysia Constitution remained intact for some time after independence, with the Federal Court remaining Singapore's Court of Appeal. It was not until 1969 that the Singapore Parliament enacted the Supreme Court of Judicature Act to properly constitute its own judicial system.[9] That said, the system Singapore inherited from the British remained more or less intact. Significant departures from the colonial position included the abolition of the jury system and its replacement by a trial by two judges for capital cases, as well as radical changes to the legislative branch of government. None of this had any significant impact on the judicial system.

1.3 Tradition, religion and indigenous demands

Right up to the onset of the Japanese Occupation, the British treated all colonial subjects equally in law but discriminated between the various races in fact. Europeans were privileged above all others and were given the best positions in civil administration. However, at the end of World War II, the impending creation of the Malayan Union required the British state to treat the Malays differently and privilege them as the indigenous people of the land. And as most Malays were Muslim, the position of Islam within the Constitution would likewise be given a special place.[10] In Singapore, this manifested in the enactment of Article 152 of the Constitution, which provides that it "shall be the responsibility" of the Singapore Government to constantly "care for the interests of the racial and religious minorities in Singapore."[11] In addition, the Government is required to "exercise its functions in such manner as to recognize the special position of the Malays, who are the indigenous people of Singapore." It is thus "the responsibility of the Government to protect, safeguard, support, foster and promote their political, educational, religious, economic, social and cultural interests and the Malay language."[12] Article 153 goes further to empower Parliament to make law "regulating Muslim religious affairs and for constituting a Council to advise the President in matters relating to the Muslim religion." These constitutional obligations are met through the passage of the

[9] Supreme Court of Judicature Act, Act 24 of 1969, Singapore Statutes.

[10] On the historical foundations of this move, see K. Y. L. Tan, 'The legal and institutional framework and issues of multiculturalism in Singapore' in A. E. Lai (ed.), *Beyond Rituals and Riots: Ethnic Pluralism and Social Cohesion in Singapore* (Singapore: Eastern Universities Press, 2004), pp. 98–113.

[11] Constitution of Singapore, Art. 152(1).

[12] Constitution of Singapore, Art. 152(2).

Administration of Muslim Law Act; the establishment of the Majlis Ugama Islam Singapura (MUIS), or Islamic Council of Singapore; and the establishment of a Syariah Court (discussed above).

1.4 Global economic competition and foreign trade

Singapore's position as one of the world's most important trading centers has made the Government extremely responsive to shifts in demands for legal services. In view of these demands and the need to ensure a judiciary of the highest caliber, the Government significantly raised judicial salaries in the 1990s. Singapore's judges are the highest-paid judges in the world today. The Singapore Government has also made a conscious effort to position Singapore as a major international legal hub, providing legal services and arbitration facilities and expertise for the region. To this end, the Government has taken steps to liberalize the legal profession, giving selected foreign law firms special licenses to practice local law and thus compete with local law firms for business.[13]

2 Judicial appointments, judicial independence and access to justice

2.1 Judicial appointments and qualifications of judges

The Judges of the Supreme Court are appointed by the President of Singapore. In the case of the Chief Justice, the President makes the appointment "acting in his discretion" and concurring with the Prime Minister's advice.[14] In the case of other Judges of Appeal and the High Court, the Prime Minister is obliged to consult the Chief Justice before making his recommendations to the President. Qualification for appointment to the Supreme Court is fairly straightforward. The candidate only needs to be a "qualified person" under the Legal Profession Act (Cap. 161) or a member of the Singapore Legal Service (or both) for an

[13] See Jeffrey Chan Wah Teck, "Liberalisation of the Singapore legal sector," speech given at the 10th General Assembly of the ASEAN Law Association, Hanoi, 14–18 October 2009; and Steven Chong, "Liberalisation of legal services: freeing the legal landscape, is Southeast Asia ready?" speech at the International Bar Association's 3rd Asia-Pacific Regional Forum Conference, Kuala Lumpur, 27 November 2012. Chan and Chong were respectively Second Solicitor-General and Attorney-General of Singapore at the time they made their speeches.

[14] Constitution of Singapore, Art. 95(1).

aggregate period of not less than ten years. The threshold is not difficult to attain since almost anyone who has qualified with a law degree from Singapore or one of the recognized foreign law schools would be a "qualified person."

In the past twenty years, almost all judicial appointees have come from the Bar. Many of the judges were well-respected and highly experienced legal practitioners before being asked to serve on the Bench. Three appointees have been academics[15] while several have also been long-time Legal Service officers.[16] Due to the nature of the appointment process, there are no public hearings or campaigns by would-be judges. The Chief Justice consults regularly with senior members of the profession and other judges to determine the suitability of future appointees. The general public perception is that those who are eventually appointed to the Bench have been appointed primarily on the basis of merit.

2.2 *Tenure of judges and judicial independence*

In Singapore, all judges (including magistrates) are appointed by the President. In appointing the Chief Justice, the Judges of Appeal and the Judges of the High Court, the President acts in his discretion and must concur with the Prime Minister's advice. In the appointment of State Court judges (i.e. district judges and magistrates), the President acts on the Chief Justice's advice.

Article 98(1) of the Constitution in Singapore provides that "a judge of the Supreme Court shall hold office until he attains the age of 65 years or such later time, not being later than 6 months after he attains that age, as the President may approve." Article 98(6) provides that "Parliament shall by law provide for the remuneration of the judges of the Supreme Court, and the remuneration shall be charged on the Consolidated Fund." Furthermore, the Supreme Court judge's remuneration and terms of office, including pension rights "shall not be altered to his disadvantage after his appointment" (see Article 98(8)). This ensures that judges cannot be threatened with pay cuts or with the abolition of their offices.

[15] They were Professors Tan Lee Meng, Andrew B. L. Phang and George Wei who were appointed in 1997, 2005 and 2013 respectively. One judge, Philip N. Pillai, had been both an academic and leading corporate practitioner, prior to his appointment to the Bench in 2009.

[16] Among the Legal Service officers who have been elevated to the Bench since 1990 are: K. S. Rajah, Chan Seng Onn, Lee Seiu Kin, Tay Yong Kwang and Lionel Yee.

In 1971, the shortage of High Court judges led to an amendment to Article 94 of the Constitution to permit the appointment of "supernumerary" or "contract" judges. This allowed judges of the Supreme Court who were compelled by the Constitution to retire at the age of sixty-five to stay on as judges on a contractual basis, usually for terms of between one and three years. Difficulties in getting senior legal practitioners to accept appointments to the Bench led to an amendment to the Constitution in 1979 to create the post of Judicial Commissioner.

Judicial Commissioners can be appointed on a temporary basis, and this allows practitioners who take up such appointments to return to private practice when their terms are up. The term of appointment for a Judicial Commissioner, like that of a supernumerary judge, is between six months and three years, and is often viewed as a prelude to a full judgeship. In 1993, the Constitution was amended to enable the President to appoint Judicial Commissioners for very short terms and to hear long cases that would otherwise disrupt normal court hearing schedules. Indeed, under Article 94(5), a Judicial Commissioner may be appointed just to hear a single specific case. This last provision has never been utilized.

The provisions allowing for the appointment of supernumerary judges and Judicial Commissioners are problematic in that the appointees under these provisions lack security of tenure – one of the two key pillars to ensuring judicial independence. Even though there has never been any suggestion that any judge or judicial commissioner was appointed for political reasons, these provisions remain a challenge to full judicial independence.

2.3 *Judicial training and related legal education*

Like in many other common law countries, there is no formal training for judges prior to their appointment to the Bench in Singapore. Most appointees are highly experienced practitioners and typically undergo a brief orientation program before presiding over their first cases. Even for the specialist Syariah Court, there is no special training program for appointed judges.[17]

In April 2010, the Subordinate Courts established the Judicial Education Board (JEB). It was chaired by Judge of Appeal V. K. Rajah, and its

[17] See M. H. Hassan and S. T. S. A. Alhabshi, "The training, appointment, and supervision of Islamic judges in Singapore," *Pacific Rim Law & Policy Journal*, 21(1) (2012), 189–213.

members include Senior Counsel, leading law academics, the Chief District Judge and Senior District Judges. The JEB is responsible for the judicial education and training of district judges and magistrates in Singapore. Its training program comprises three main thrusts: (a) an induction program for new judges; (b) continuing training throughout judges' careers; and (c) the building of a learning community of judicial practice.[18]

3 Structure of courts and instances of trials

Trials in Singapore are held in both the State Courts and the Supreme Court. The State Courts, which are made up of the magistrates' courts and the district courts, have both civil[19] and criminal jurisdictions.[20] The High Court has both original and appellate jurisdictions[21] while all State Courts only have original jurisdiction. Criminal appeals from the State Courts go to the High Court.[22] Since 1994, when appeals to the Judicial Committee of the Privy Council were abolished,[23] the Court of Appeal has been the final arbiter on all legal matters in Singapore. There are no other final courts of special jurisdiction. As judicial power is vested in the Supreme Court, it has the power to pronounce on the constitutionality of statutes.

In September 1994, Article 100 of the Constitution was inserted to enable the President to refer "any question as to the effect of any provision" of the Constitution to "a tribunal consisting of not less than 3 Judges of the Supreme Court for its opinion . . ." When this provision is invoked, the tribunal has sixty days in which to render an opinion. Any dissenting opinions of any judge must accordingly be reflected in the opinion rendered to the President although the majority decision shall be considered the opinion of the tribunal and shall be pronounced in open court. The opinion is not subject to question in any court. This provision has only been invoked once, in 1995, when President Ong Teng Cheong referred a question concerning his powers in *Constitutional Reference No. 1 of 1995*.[24]

[18] V. K. Rajah, "Judicial education in Singapore: beyond the horizon," paper presented at the Asia Pacific Courts Conference, Singapore, 6 October 2010.

[19] See State Courts Act (Cap. 321, Singapore Statutes), ss. 19 and 52.

[20] State Courts Act, ss. 50 and 51.

[21] See Supreme Court of Judicature Act (Cap. 322, Singapore Statutes), ss. 15 and 19.

[22] Supreme Court of Judicature Act, s. 19. [23] Judicial Committee (Repeal) Act, 1994.

[24] *Constitutional Reference No. 1 of 1995* [1995] 2 SLR 201.

3.1 *Size and performance of the courts*

In Singapore, judges in both the superior courts and the subordinate courts sit alone. Section 10 of the Supreme Court of the Judicature Act provides that "Every proceeding in the High Court and all business arising thereout shall, except as otherwise provided by any written law for the time being in force, be heard and disposed of before a single Judge." Section 30(1) of the Supreme Court of Judicature Act further provides that "The civil and criminal jurisdiction of the Court of Appeal shall be exercised by 3 or any greater uneven number of Judges of Appeal."

As at the time of writing,[25] the courts are staffed by the following number of personnel:

(1) Court of Appeal: four judges (including the Chief Justice);
(2) High Court: fourteen judges (including the Chief Justice and two Judicial Commissioners);
(3) subordinate courts: ninety-eight judges;
(4) Syariah Court: panel of seven.

Singapore operates one of the most efficient court systems in the world. This was not always the case. In the early 1990s, there was a massive backlog of cases waiting to be disposed of. At the Supreme Court, there were more than 2,000 pending cases that had been set down for trial, but with trial dates available only three years or more in advance. There were some 10,000 inactive cases, some of which were more than a decade old, and some 44 percent of the cases took between five and ten years from commencement to disposal. Appeals took a further two to three years to be heard.

During the tenure of Chief Justice Yong Pung How (1990–2006), the court moved aggressively to deal with this problem.[26] Within some three years, the backlog was cleared by the introduction of the following measures: (1) appointing more judges; (2) changing the rules of procedure to empower the courts to be proactive in the management of cases; (3) denying adjournments; (4) giving hearing dates to moribund cases; and (5) expanding the jurisdiction of the subordinate courts.[27] The subordinate courts do not report their clearance rates, but since the

[25] The figures are accurate as of 31 August 2013.

[26] On the reforms introduced to clear the backlog, see W. H. Malik, *Judiciary-Led Reforms in Singapore: Framework, Strategies and Lessons* (Washington, DC: The World Bank, 2007).

[27] See Justice J. Prakash, "Making the civil litigation system more efficient," speech given at the Asian Pacific Judicial Reform Forum Roundtable Meeting in Singapore, 21 January 2009.

Table 6.1: *Disposal of cases by the Supreme Court 2012*

Civil cases	Filed	Disposed	Clearance rate
Civil originating process	7,068	6,387	90%
Civil interlocutory process	6,704	6,376	95%
Appeals before High Court	796	860	108%
Appeals before Court of Appeal	174	143	82%
Applications before Court of Appeal	90	89	99%
Criminal cases	**Filed**	**Disposed**	**Clearance rate**
Criminal cases	31	36	116%
Criminal motions	106	102	96%
Magistrates' appeal	221	229	104%
Criminal revisions	27	25	93%
Criminal appeals	17	23	135%

Source: Singapore Supreme Court, *Annual Report 2012*, pp. 53–9.

judicial reforms of the 1990s they have successfully cleared 99 percent of their cases.[28] Table 6.1 shows the number of cases handled by the Supreme Court in 2011 and 2012. The statistics are drawn from the latest available Supreme Court and Subordinate Courts Annual Reports 2012.[29]

Table 6.2 sets out the departmental targets and achievements by the Supreme Court in respect of the various courts:

Table 6.2: *Departmental targets and achievements by the Supreme Court*

Original civil jurisdiction			
Type of Proceedings	Departmental Target	Achievement	
		2011	2012
Trials in writ action	8 weeks from date of set down to trial	3.1 weeks	2.3 weeks
Originating summonses (OS)	5 weeks from date of filing of OS	4.3 weeks	4.1 weeks
	3 weeks from date of filing of OS	1.0 weeks	1.4 weeks

[28] See Supreme Court of Singapore, *Annual Report 2012*; and Subordinate Courts of Singapore, *Annual Report 2012*. In March 2014, the Subordinate Courts were renamed the State Courts.

[29] See Supreme Court of Singapore, *Annual Report 2012*; and Subordinate Courts of Singapore, *Annual Report 2012*.

Table 6.2: (*cont.*)

Original civil jurisdiction			
Type of Proceedings	Departmental Target	Achievement	
		2011	2012
Inter partes			
Ex parte			
Bankruptcy OS	6 weeks from date of filing of OS	3.4 weeks	3.5 weeks
Company winding up OS	4 weeks from date of filing of OS	3.4 weeks	3.5 weeks
Probate OS	5 weeks from date of filing of OS	4.1 weeks	4.2 weeks
Summonses	5 weeks from date of filing	4.6 weeks	4.7 weeks
Summary judgment	3 weeks from date of filing	1.9 weeks	1.9 weeks
Other summonses			
Probate summonses	4 weeks from date of filing	2.4 weeks	2.5 weeks
Bankruptcy summonses	4 weeks from date of filing	3.1 weeks	2.8 weeks

Original criminal jurisdiction			
Type of Proceedings	Departmental Target	Achievement	
		2011	2012
Trials of criminal cases	6 weeks from date of preliminary enquiry	5.0 weeks	4.5 weeks

Appellate civil jurisdiction			
Type of Proceedings	Departmental Target	Achievement	
		2011	2012
Appeal before 2 judges	12 weeks from notification to collect record of proceedings (ROP)	12.0 weeks	12.0 weeks
Appeal before 3 judges	16 weeks from notification to collect ROP	15.9 weeks	16.0 weeks
Registrar's Appeals to High Court Judge in Chambers	3 weeks from date of filing of appeal 4 weeks from date of filing of appeal against assessment of damages	2.2 weeks 2.8 weeks	2.2 weeks 2.9 weeks
Appeals to the High Court from the Subordinate Courts	4 weeks from receipt of ROP	3.3 weeks	3.6 weeks

Table 6.2: (*cont.*)

Appellate Criminal Jurisdiction			
		Achievement	
Type of Proceedings	Departmental Target	2011	2012
Appeal to the Court of Appeal	8 weeks from date of receipt of last confirmation of ROP	6.7 weeks	7.5 weeks
Appeals to the High Court from the Subordinate Courts	8 weeks from the date of receipt of the ROP	5.9 weeks	6.3 weeks
Trials of Criminal Cases	6 weeks from date of preliminary enquiry	5.0 weeks	4.5 weeks

Source: Compiled by author

3.2 *Courts of special jurisdiction*

3.2.1 The specialist commercial courts

In 2002, to handle the increasingly complex nature of commercial cases, the Supreme Court established the first specialist commercial court within the Supreme Court itself. The admiralty court is a court within the Supreme Court structure and does not have a separate existence. The need for greater specialization and expert knowledge led the Court to establish two other specialist commercial courts: the intellectual property court (also in 2002); and the arbitration court (2003). Puisne judges who are assigned to these specialist commercial courts fulfill their roles in addition to their general judicial duties.

3.2.2 The Syariah court

The Administration of Muslim Law Act (Cap. 3, Singapore Statutes) establishes the Syariah court.[30] The jurisdiction of the Syariah court is limited to disputes in which "the parties are Muslim or where the parties were married" under Muslim law. Specifically, the Syariah court has jurisdiction to hear disputes involving: (a) marriage; (b) divorce; (c) betrothal, nullity of marriage or judicial separation; (d) disposition or division of property upon divorce or nullification of marriage; and (e) payment of marriage gifts, marriage expenses, maintenance and

[30] See Part III, Administration of Muslim Law Act (Cap. 3, Singapore Statutes).

consolatory gifts.[31] Cases are heard by one of the Syariah court Presidents appointed by the President of Singapore.[32]

Appeals from the decision of the Syariah court lie to the Appeal Board of the Majlis Ugama Islam Singapura (MUIS, or Islamic Council of Singapore)[33] which comprises a panel of seven Muslims who are appointed by the President of Singapore (acting on the advice of the Council) every two years.[34] When an appeal is filed, the President of the Council will appoint a quorum of three persons from the seven-member panel to hear the appeal. The Appeal Board may "confirm, reverse or vary the decision of the Court, exercise any such powers as the Court could have exercised, make such order as the Court ought to have made or order a retrial, or award costs if it thinks fit."[35]

While the Syariah court is a separate and distinct court, it is part of the judicial system and is considered an inferior tribunal that is still subject to the High Court's general supervisory powers and judicial review.

3.2.3 The family court

The family court is a subordinate court established in 1995 as a specialized forum for disputes arising from family-related matters. The family court has jurisdiction over the following matters: (1) adoption proceedings under the Adoption of Children Act;[36] (2) divorce, nullity and judicial separation proceedings under Part X of the Women's Charter;[37] (3) guardianship, custody, care and control of and access to children under the Guardianship of Infants Act and Part X of the Women's Charter; (4) division of matrimonial assets under Part X and section 59 of the Women's Charter; (5) personal protection orders under Part VII of the Women's Charter; (6) spousal and child maintenance under Parts VIII and X of the Women's Charter; (7) enforcement of maintenance orders made by Singapore courts, the Maintenance of Parents Tribunal and the Syariah Court, under section 71 and Part IX of the Women's Charter and the Maintenance of Parents Tribunal Act,[38] respectively; and (8) reciprocal enforcement of maintenance orders made by foreign courts or tribunals under the Maintenance Orders (Facilities for Enforcement) Act[39] and Maintenance Orders (Reciprocal

[31] See Administration of Muslim Law Act, s. 35.
[32] Administration of Muslim Law Act, s. 34(2).
[33] See Administration of Muslim Law Act, s. 55.
[34] Administration of Muslim Law Act, s. 55(3).
[35] Administration of Muslim Law Act, s. 55(5).
[36] Adoption of Children Act (Cap. 4, Singapore Statutes).
[37] The Women's Charter (Cap. 353, Singapore Statutes).
[38] Maintenance of Parents Act (Cap. 167B, Singapore Statutes).
[39] Maintenance Orders (Facilities for Enforcement) Act (Cap. 168, Singapore Statutes).

Enforcement) Act.[40] While the family court has special functions, it operates as a court within the judicial system and is subject to the same kind of supervision and procedures as any other subordinate court.

3.3 *Citizen participation in the trials*

Jury trials were introduced into Singapore with the grant of the Second Charter of Justice in 1826. In 1960, it was restricted to only capital cases, with the jury sitting as a quorum of seven. An amendment to the Criminal Procedure Code in 1969 abolished trial by jury in 1970. The main reason for its demise was the government's view that Singapore juries were unsophisticated and were insufficiently educated to appreciate the proceedings in court and were thus more likely to be swayed by such non-legal or factual factors as the oratory and performance of the defence lawyer. Since then, citizens of Singapore have had no other opportunity to participate in the conduct of trials.[41]

3.4 *Access to justice*

3.4.1 Substantive limits to access: *locus standi*

While the courts are vested with extensive powers of judicial review, there are instances where judicial review is not permitted. Generally, courts will only pronounce on live disputes. The courts will not hear purely hypothetical cases or cases involving collusion of the litigants. Questions before the court must be real and not theoretical. The leading local authority on the requirement of standing in respect of declaratory relief is the Court of Appeal case of *Karaha Bodas Co. LLC* v. *Pertamina Energy Trading Ltd*[42] which laid down three requirements for *locus standi*: (a) the applicant must have a "real interest" in bringing the action; (b) there must be a "real controversy" between the parties to the action for the court to resolve; and (c) the declaration must relate to a right which is personal to the applicant and which is enforceable against an adverse party to the litigation. This decision was affirmed in two other Court of Appeal decisions: *Tan Eng Hong* v. *Attorney-General*[43] and *Vellama d/o Marie Muthu* v. *Attorney-General.*[44] In respect of alleged

[40] Maintenance Orders (Reciprocal Enforcement) Act (Cap. 169, Singapore Statutes).

[41] On the rise and demise of the jury system in Singapore, see A. B. L. Phang, "Jury trial in Singapore and Malaysia: the unmaking of a legal institution," *Malaya Law Review* 25 (1983), 50.

[42] [2006] 1 SLR(R) 112. [43] [2012] 4 SLR 476. [44] [2013] 1 SLR 439.

constitutional violations, the test laid down by the Court of Appeal in *Tan Eng Hong* v. *Attorney-General* was as follows:

> Constitutional rights are personal to each and every Singapore citizen by virtue of his or her citizenship, and are not contingent on membership of any society. Therefore, in the event that there is a violation of any constitutional right, a citizen's right to bring a constitutional challenge "arises not from membership of any society" . . . the mere fact of citizenship in itself does not satisfy the standing requirement for constitutional challenges . . . an applicant must demonstrate a violation of his constitutional rights before locus standi can be granted . . . Given the importance of constitutional rights, a citizen will prima facie have a "sufficient interest" to see that his constitutional rights are not violated . . . Sufficiency of interest still needs to be shown, but this is prima facie made out once there is a violation of a constitutional right.[45]

As such, before a court will adjudicate a case, three key conditions must be met: (a) the case must be "ripe" for decision; (b) it must not be a "collusive" case; and (c) the person bringing the case must have *locus standi* or standing to bring the case.

To show *locus standi*, a litigant must show that he or she has an interest to protect and is not merely an interested person. The law on *locus standi* has been exhaustively discussed by the Malaysian Supreme Court in the *Government of Malaysia* v. *Lim Kit Siang*.[46] By a majority, the Court held that to have standing, the applicant must have a "substantial" interest in the case or be acting by way of a relator action, in the name of the Attorney-General. The words of Buckley J in *Boyce* v. *Paddington Borough Council* were cited with approval:

> A plaintiff can sue without joining the Attorney-General in two cases: first, where the interference with the public right is such as that some private right of his is at the same time interfered with (e.g. where an obstruction is so placed in a highway that the owner of premises abutting upon the highway is specially affected by reason that the obstruction interferes with his private right of access from and to his premises and to and from the highway); and, secondly, where no private right is interfered with, but the plaintiff, in respect of his public right, suffers special damage peculiar to himself from the interference with the public right.[47]

This approach was, however, rejected by the two dissenting judges, who felt that a more liberal approach was in order. Subsequent cases in both Malaysia and Singapore have, however, adopted the majority decision in

[45] [2012] 4 SLR 476 at 514. [46] [1988] 2 MLJ 12. [47] [1903] 1 Ch 109 at 114.

Lim Kit Siang. This has meant that there have practically been no public interest litigation cases in Singapore.

Even after a court has established its jurisdiction to hear a case, it may still decline to hear it for a number of reasons. These may broadly be divided as follows: (a) political questions; (b) legislative prohibition; (c) laches; (d) *res judicata*; (e) executive prerogative powers; and (f) judgments of a superior court.

The political question doctrine has not been argued in the local courts, and there are no cases discussing it. Laches refers to an unreasonable delay or negligence in pursuing a right or claim, especially if it is an equitable one. Laches can occur when the aggrieved party is statutorily barred by being out of time, or where they have waited far too long to bring their case before the courts. Since laches proceeds on the equitable maxim *vigilantibus non dormientibus jura subveniunt*, meaning "the laws aid those who are vigilant, and not those who sleep upon their rights," in cases where the positions of the parties have changed substantially it would be inequitable for the court to have jurisdiction to entertain the suit.

3.4.2 Institutional limits to access

The main institutional limits to access to justice are factors related to the high cost of litigation and engaging legal counsel. Hearing fees – which were first introduced in 1993 for the Supreme Court, and in 1994 for the subordinate courts – are regarded as impediments to access to justice.[48] These fees were introduced to ensure that litigants "would use court time responsibly and expeditiously."[49] Fees were revised upwards in December 2002 as a necessary response to the increase in the total operating costs of the Supreme Court.[50]

Due to the high salaries of lawyers and the high overheads incurred in running a law firm in Singapore, the cost of legal expertise is high. At the same time, the entire process of preparing for an adversarial trial is prolix and expensive. This means that many erstwhile litigants may well be dissuaded from proceeding in court on account of cost. Naturally, this also means that less well-off litigants may well have to forego their rights since they are unable to afford legal representation in court. Some litigants have taken to defending themselves in court, but this is rare.

[48] See G. K. Y. Chan, "Access to justice for the poor: the Singapore judiciary at work," *Pacific Rim Law & Policy Journal*, 17(3) (2008), 595, 607–9.

[49] *Ibid*. 607. [50] *Ibid*. 608.

This is a matter of grave concern to the courts. As Chief Justice Sundaresh Menon noted recently at a conference on litigation:

> The first and probably the most critical hurdle is the high cost of litigation . . . the cost of legal services in Singapore must be acknowledged as being on the high side; and so we need to pay closer attention now than ever before to ensuring that it will be affordable to most. It is cold comfort to those who seek justice to say that we have a great legal system, if it is priced out of their reach.[51]

Since assuming office as Chief Justice, Menon has initiated a number of committees to study how the cost of litigation can be reduced. He has tasked Chief District Judge Tan Siong Thye to simplify the procedural rules for smaller civil cases so that costs can be reduced, and to find other ways to reduce the cost of litigation.[52] In line with the Chief Justice's call for finding ways to reduce legal costs, there have recently been various calls to review the rule against champerty in Singapore.[53] However, a recent decision of the High Court in a disciplinary proceeding against a lawyer for entering into a champertous agreement reiterated the public policy considerations that militated against such contingency fee arrangements:

> In our view, one of the key elements in effectively representing a client's interest is the ability of the lawyer to maintain a sufficient sense of detachment so as to be able to discharge his duty to the court. That duty is ultimately paramount and trumps all other duties. It follows that the considerations most engaged by the offence of champerty are those concerning the administration of justice and the related need to safeguard confidence in and the honour of the profession that is tasked with the vital role of assisting the judiciary in their mission . . .[54]

However, the Court went on to add that there was "an emerging trend in some jurisdictions towards recognizing that champertous fee

[51] See Chief Justice S. Menon, "Opening Address" at the Litigation Conference, Singapore, 31 January 2013, paras. 9–11.

[52] Speech of the Chief Justice at the Opening of the Legal Year 2013, 4 January 2013, para. 17. Tan Siong Thye was appointed Judicial Commissioner in October 2013, and Judge of the Supreme Court on 1 July 2014.

[53] See A. Ho, "Let David take on Goliath in court: champerty," *Straits Times*, 2 August 2013. Earlier calls include G. K. Y. Chan, "Re-examining public policy: a case for conditional fees in Singapore?" *Common Law World Review*, 33(2) (2004), 130–59; and A. Yeo, "Access to justice: a case for contingency fees in Singapore," *Singapore Academy of Law Journal*, 16 (2004), 76.

[54] See *Law Society of Singapore* v. *Kurubalan s/o Manickam Rengaraju* [2013] SGHC 135, para. 45.

arrangements properly regulated can help indigent litigants gain access to justice" but that it was "for Parliament rather than the courts, to decide whether and when such reform is to be undertaken."[55]

3.4.3 Legal aid

Legal aid for civil litigation is available through the Legal Aid Bureau[56] for persons of limited means. Applicants for such aid must meet the means and merits tests. The principle of legal aid for the poor was introduced by the Second Charter of Justice which brought into Singapore an old statute – An Act to Admit Such persons as Are Poor to Sue in *Forma Pauperis* dating back to 1494.[57] This was given legislative effect much later by the introduction of the Legal Aid and Advice Ordinance in 1956. This piece of legislation was modeled on the 1949 English Legal Aid Act and the 1943 New South Wales legal aid system. The Legal Aid Bureau was established on 1 July 1958 under this legislation. Initially, this scheme was to provide criminal legal aid but it was deemed to be contrary to public policy (in that the state could not be seen to be prosecuting an accused and helping him defend himself at the same time).

The Bureau is headed by a Director who is appointed by the Minister for Law and is currently staffed by about ten lawyers, all of whom are members of the Singapore Legal Service. More than 500 other lawyers in private practice have volunteered their services to the Bureau. Between them, they handle approximately 35 percent of the cases, while the permanent staff members of the Bureau handle the remaining 65 percent.

The Law Society of Singapore operates a Criminal Legal Aid Scheme (CLAS). Persons seeking criminal legal assistance must also pass a means test. Those persons who own private property (as opposed to state subsidized housing) or vehicles are ineligible. Persons having savings or equities exceeding S$3,000 (for singles) or S$5,000 (married); or disposable assets of more than S$5,000, are also not eligible under this scheme. In addition, the net monthly income of an applicant should not exceed S$1,300 (or S$1,700 in the case of a married applicant), plus S$160 for each dependant.

55 *Ibid.* para. 46.

56 On the Legal Aid Bureau, see C. Cheong and H. M. Lim, *Access to Justice: 50 Years of Legal Aid* (Singapore: Legal Aid Bureau, 2008); and H. M. Lim, "Helping the less privileged gain access to justice – the role of the Legal Aid Bureau in giving effect to the Women's Charter," *Singapore Journal of Legal Studies*, July (2011), 129–51.

57 11 Henry 7 c. 22.

4 Sources of law, styles of judicial decisions and the politics of judging

4.1 Sources of law

4.1.1 The common law

The grant of the Second Charter of Justice was significant not only in establishing the Court of Judicature, but also for its implicit importation of English law.[58] While there is no express statement in the Charter that English law was to be applied, the words of the Charter implied as much. Furthermore, the Court of Judicature had held in 1808 that English law had been introduced into Penang by the First Charter of Justice.[59] Key words in the Charter were interpreted to import English law into the Straits Settlements. This was affirmed in 1834, when Sir Benjamin Malkin R held that the introduction of the Charter into the Straits Settlements automatically introduced the existing law of England,[60] and yet again in the landmark decision of *Regina* v. *Willans*[61] in 1858, when Sir Peter Benson Maxwell R held that the Second Charter introduced the law of England as it stood in 1826 into the Settlements. In a later decision, Maxwell CJ (as he later became) held:

> ... in this Colony, so much of the law of England as was in existence when it was imported here, and as is of general and not merely local policy, and adapted to the condition and wants of the inhabitants, is the law of the land; and further, that law is subject, in its application to the

58 On the reception of English law in Singapore, see W. Woon, "The applicability of English law in Singapore" in Tan (ed.), *The Singapore Legal System*, pp. 230–48; A. B. L. Phang, "The reception of English law" in Tan (ed.), *Essays in Singapore Legal History*, pp. 7–26; M. F. Rutter, *The Applicable Law in Singapore and Malaysia: A Guide to Reception, Precedent and the Sources of Law in the Republic of Singapore and the Federation of Malaysia* (Singapore: Malayan Law Journal, 1989); M. Gopal, "English law in Singapore: the reception that never was," *Malayan Law Journal*, 2 (1983), xxv; A. B. L. Phang, "Of 'cut-off' dates and domination: some problematic aspects of the reception of English law in Singapore," *Malaya Law Review*, 28 (1986), 242; C. H. Soon and A. B. L. Phang, "Reception of English commercial law in Singapore: a century of uncertainty" in A. J. Harding (ed.), *The Common Law in Singapore and Malaysia* (Singapore: Butterworths, 1985), ch. 2; and G. W. Bartholomew, "The Singapore Statute Book," *Malaya Law Review*, 26 (1984), 1.

59 *Kamoo* v. *Thomas Turner Bassett* (1808) 1 Ky 1.

60 *Rodyk* v. *Williamson*, 24 May 1834, unreported. The transcript for the judgment is lost but the judgment was referred to by Malkin R in *In the goods of Abdullah* (1835) 2 Ky Ecc 8.

61 (1858) 3 Ky 16.

> various alien races established here, to such modifications as are necessary to prevent it from operating unjustly and oppressively on them.[62]

Once brought into Singapore, the common law in Singapore was on its own. English judges do not continue to make law for Singapore, and "subsequent developments in the common law in the English courts do not automatically apply to Singapore."[63] Developments of common law doctrine in England did not directly affect the development of Singapore, which continued to develop and flourish on its own, taking into consideration its unique social circumstances and the needs of its population. Post-1826 developments in the common law made by English courts do not apply to Singapore unless they are accepted as part of Singapore's law by a Singapore court.

In 1993, Parliament passed the Application of English Law Act (Cap. 7A)[64] to "declare the extent to which English law is applicable in Singapore." Section 3(1) makes it clear that "the common law of England (including the principles and rules of equity), so far as it was part of the law of Singapore immediately before 12 November 1993, shall continue to be part of the law of Singapore." Section 3(2) further provides that "[t]he common law shall continue to be in force in Singapore, as provided in subsection (1), so far as it is applicable to the circumstances of Singapore and its inhabitants and subject to such modifications as those circumstances may require."

4.1.2 Judicial precedent

Like most common law countries, judicial precedents[65] are a major source of law. The decisions of higher courts will bind lower courts if a similar issue of law should arise. This is known as the principle of *stare decisis* – literally "let the decision stand" – more commonly referred to as the doctrine of binding precedent. However, not everything in any particular decision is binding; only the *ratio decidendi* – that part of the judgment in which the law is applied to relevant and material facts – is binding. The usefulness of judicial precedent as a source of law is

[62] *Chua Choon Neoh* v. *Spottiswoode* (1868) 1 Ky 216.

[63] See Woon, "The applicability," p. 237.

[64] See generally A. Phang, "Cementing the foundations: the Singapore Application of English Law Act 1993," *University of British Columbia Law Review*, 28 (1994), 205.

[65] See W. Woon, "The doctrine of judicial precedent' in Tan (ed.), *The Singapore Legal System*, pp. 297–4.

predicated on the existence of a regular and reliable set of law reports and a judicial hierarchy that adheres to the doctrine of binding precedent.

Difficulties to be experienced in tapping this source of law arise from the complex legal history of the courts in Singapore. If decisions of higher courts are to bind those of lower courts, then it is important to determine which higher courts are relevant. In most jurisdictions, this is quite a simple matter, but in Singapore, this is rather more complicated because of its history. From a present-day standpoint, the rules of *stare decisis* are quite clear and simple. At the apex of the judicial system is the Court of Appeal. Decisions of the Court of Appeal naturally bind the High Court, and, likewise, those of the High Court bind the subordinate courts. This is what Woon calls "vertical *stare decisis*."[66] The main problems with vertical *stare decisis* can be found in two places. First, up until 1994, the Judicial Committee of the Privy Council was the last court of appeal for Singapore. Does this mean that all Privy Council decisions necessarily bind the Singapore courts? What if the appeal emanates from a jurisdiction other than Singapore? Going back further in time, does this mean that all decisions of the Privy Council emanating from the old Straits Settlements (1867–1946) will necessarily bind the current courts?

This difficulty was settled in July 1994 when the Court of Appeal issued a Practice Statement on Judicial Precedent that declared that with the abolition of the Privy Council, the Court of Appeal was no longer bound by its previous decisions or those of the Privy Council:

> We recognize the vital role that the doctrine of *stare decisis* plays in giving certainty to the law and predictability on its application to similar cases. However, we also recognize that the political, social and economic circumstances of Singapore have changed enormously since Singapore became an independent and sovereign republic. The development of our law should reflect these changes and the fundamental values of Singapore society.
>
> Accordingly, it is proper that the Court of Appeal should not hold itself bound by any previous decisions of its own or of the Privy Council, which by the rules of precedent prevailing prior to 8 April 1994 were binding on it, in any case where adherence to such prior decisions would cause injustice in a particular case or constrain the development of the law in conformity with the circumstances of Singapore.
>
> Therefore, whilst this court will continue to treat such prior decisions as normally binding, this court will, whenever it appears right to do so, depart from such prior decisions. Bearing in mind the danger of retrospectively

[66] *Ibid.* p. 301.

> disturbing contractual, proprietary and other legal rights, this power will be exercised sparingly.
>
> This statement is not intended to affect the use of precedent in the High Court or in any subordinate courts.[67]

The High Court continues to be bound by the decisions of the Court of Appeal as well as the old Privy Council decisions, and herein we encounter another problem. Up until 1994, Singapore did not have a permanent Court of Appeal even though the Supreme Court of the Straits Settlements sat as a Court of Appeal since the turn of the twentieth century. Would the High Court be bound by an old decision of the Straits Settlements Court of Appeal? Moving forward in time, how should the High Court treat the decisions of the courts of appeal of the Malaysian states, since Singapore was, for almost two years, a part of the Federation of Malaysia? Theoretically, this could possibly include pre-1946 courts of the former Malayan Union, such as the Court of Appeal of the Federated Malay States, as well as the Courts of Appeal of Johore, Kedah and Terengganu; the Sultan's Court of Kelantan and the Court of the Raja-in-Council of Perlis.[68] To make matters worse, one might include the Court of Appeal of Sarawak, North Borneo and Brunei after the formation of Malaysia in 1963. Woon suggests that a clean break may be necessary to avert a messy situation: the High Court should only be bound by the superior courts that have exercised jurisdiction in Singapore – the Privy Council, the Court of Appeal of the Straits Settlements, the Court of Appeal of Singapore and the Court of Criminal Appeal of Singapore, as well as the Federal Court of Malaysia (between 1963 and 1965), and the Federal Court of Malaysia sitting in Singapore (1965–9).

4.1.3 Custom

Customs are norms of established practice or behavior but are not laws as such. They only acquire the force of law if they are recognized as customs. Most of the customs that have been claimed in courts pertain to marriage[69] and to trade. The Second Charter of Justice provided for

[67] *Practice Statement (Judicial Precedent)* [1994] 2 SLR 689; [1994] SGCA 148.

[68] Woon, "The doctrine of judicial precedent," pp. 310–11.

[69] See generally, A. Ibrahim, "Developments in the marriage laws in Malaysia and Singapore," *Malaya Law Review*, 12 (1970), 257; K. W. K. Seng, "Customary marriages and the Women's Charter: lingering doubts," *Malaya Law Review*, 14 (1972), 93; K. W. K. Seng, "English law and Chinese family custom in Singapore: the problem of fairness in adjudication," *Malaya Law Review* 16 (1974), 52; and K. W. K. Seng, "The law of legitimacy in Singapore," *Malaya Law Review*, 18 (1976), 1.

application of English law with due regard to the "religions, usages and manners" of the local population. Prior to the enactment of the Women's Charter in 1961, the courts recognized the marriage rites and customs of the various ethnic communities, treating them with deference and taking judicial notice of their impact. In *Woon Ngee Yew & Ors* v. *Ng Yoon Thai & Ors*,[70] the Court of Appeal of the Federated Malay States pointed out, in relation to Chinese marriage customs:

> dealing with Chinese custom . . . is more in the nature of a trade custom, the recognition of the habits of a particular body of people in dealing with particular matters. Where it can be shown that the Chinese follow settled practices the Courts will give effect to those practices where no provision is made in local legislation, so far as these practices are of a character, not being contrary to reason or natural justice, to which effect can be given with propriety.[71]

Those asserting the existence of a particular custom must prove it in court. In the case of *Plaza Singapura (Pte) Ltd* v. *Cosdel (S) Pte Ltd*,[72] the respondent asserted the existence of a trade custom called "consignment trade." LP Thean J, in holding for the appellant, held, quoting Mellish LJ in the English Court of Appeal case of *Re Matthews, ex parte Powell*,[73] that:

> in order to establish a custom it must be proved to have existed so long, and to have been so extensively acted upon, that [those] . . . in his trade may be reasonably presumed to have known it.

Customary rites have been recognized for marriages contracted before 15 September 1961. Section 81(1) of the Women's Charter provides that:

> Nothing in this Act shall affect the validity of any marriage solemnized under any law, religion, custom or usage prior to 15 September 1961.

Furthermore, the Women's Charter also modifies the rules relating to marriage and divorce by exempting their application to Muslim marriages.[74] Likewise, section 2 of the Intestate Succession Act (Cap. 146) provides that the Act shall not "apply to the estate of any Muslim or shall affect any rules of the Muslim law in respect of the distribution of the estate of any such person."

[70] [1941] MLJ 37. [71] Per Murray-Aynsley J, *ibid.* 39.
[72] [1990] SLR 93; [1990] SGCA 9. [73] (1875) 1 Ch D 501.
[74] See sections 3(2) and 3(4) of the Women's Charter (Cap. 353).

4.1.4 Legislation

Pre-1826 English statutes of general application – as opposed to those of a local or parochial character – were brought into Singapore as part of its law by virtue of the Second Charter of Justice. Precisely which of these statutes applied to Singapore was never exhaustively determined, even though scholars have attempted to list Acts that have been declared to apply in the Settlements through local case law.[75] Even if an exhaustive list could be compiled, the list would be a short one. Few pre-1826 English statutes would continue to apply to Singapore, especially since local legislation has been passed in most of the areas covered by these pre-1826 statutes.

From 1833 until 1867, the Governor-General of India in Council was the sole source of legislative power in the Straits Settlements. This was known as the period of the Indian Acts. Though the Governor in Council in India passed numerous Acts, not all of them were applicable to the Straits Settlements. Indeed, in 1889, the Straits Settlements Legislative Council passed the Statute Law Revision Ordinance to establish a commission to enquire into which Indian Acts applied to the Straits Settlements. The Commission published a volume entitled *Indian Acts passed during the period extending from the twenty-second day of April 1834 to the thirty-one day of March 1867 both days inclusive and now in force in the Colony of the Straits Settlements as determined by the Commissioners appointed by His Excellency the governor of the Straits Settlements under the Provisions of the Statute Law Revision Ordinance 1889* listing Acts considered to be in force in the Straits Settlements as of 1890. It is not an exhaustive listing of all Acts that applied to the Settlements from the time of the 1833 Charter Act.[76]

In 1858, the EIC was abolished and the Straits Settlements came under the new Indian Government.[77] The Crown took over the direct administration of the territories formerly administered by the Company but this did not have an immediate effect upon the legal system of the Straits Settlements. On 10 August 1866, the Government of the Straits

[75] See, for example, Sir R. Braddell, *The Law of the Straits Settlements: A Commentary*, 2nd edn. (Singapore: Kelly & Walsh, 1931), Appendix V.

[76] See Bartholomew, "The Singapore Statute Book," 327–8. Perhaps the most comprehensive collection of all Acts passed by the Legislative Council in India is W. Theobald, *The Legislative Acts of the Governor-General of India in Council from 1834 to the end of 1867*, 5 vols. (Calcutta: Thacker, Spink and Co., 1870).

[77] 21 & 22 Vict. c. 106.

Settlements Act[78] was passed. It came into effect on 1 April 1867.[79] By Letters Patent dated 4 February 1867,[80] the Straits Settlements was granted a colonial constitution under which the Legislative Council had:

> full Power and Authority to establish such Laws, Institutions, and Ordinances, and to constitute such Courts and Officers[81] ... for the Administration of Justice and for the Raising and Expenditure of the Public Revenue, as might be deemed necessary for ... Peace, Order, and good Government ...[82]

From 1867 to 1942, the Legislative Council was responsible for passing law for the Straits Settlements. These laws were published in the *Straits Settlements Government Gazette*. From 1867, the Government Printer also published an annual volume of Ordinances passed in the preceding year.

The first revised edition of the legislation of the Straits Settlements was issued under the authority of the Statute Laws Ordinance 1917, which gave the Ordinance Law Revision Commissioners powers of revision. Five volumes of statutes were published as the first official revised edition in London in 1920.[83] This was followed by revised editions in 1925[84] and 1936.[85] These remain the main sources of written law for the period between 1867 and 1942.

During the Japanese Occupation (1942–5), the Legislative Council was abolished, to be replaced by Japanese military bodies, including the Supreme Command of the Southern Army Headquarters, the twenty-five Army Headquarters, the Military Administration Department, the Malai Malayan Military Administration Headquarters, and the City Government of Tokubetu-si. When the British returned in 1945, Singapore was placed under the British Military Administration and was governed under martial law. The BMA issued various Proclamations, Orders and Notices, which were published in the *British Military Administration, Malaya Gazette, Singapore Division*. This situation lasted until April 1946 when Singapore was returned to civilian rule.

[78] 29 & 30 Vict. c. 115. [79] See Braddell, *A Commentary*, p. 35.

[80] A copy of the Letters Patent is available in the Law Library of the National University of Singapore, and another at the Supreme Court Library.

[81] The Straits Settlements Act, Art. I. [82] The Straits Settlements Act, preamble.

[83] *The Laws of the Straits Settlements 1835–1919: Revised Up To and Including the 31st Day of December, 1919; But Exclusive of War and Emergency Legislation* (London: Waterlow & Sons Ltd, 1920).

[84] *The Laws of the Straits Settlements*, 5 vols. (London: Waterlow & Sons, 1926).

[85] *The Laws of the Straits Settlements*, 5 vols. (Singapore: Government Printing Office, 1936).

The Legislative Council functioned more or less like its pre-War predecessor until 1955, when it was transformed into a predominantly elected Legislative Assembly under the Rendel Constitution. That year, a new set of statutes was prepared as the Revised Edition 1955. It was the first revised edition to feature laws that applied solely to Singapore and was published in eight volumes.[86] Revised editions of the Singapore statutes were subsequently brought out by the Government in 1970 and 1985 under the Revised Edition of the Laws Act 1983 (Cap. 275).

Up until 1993, there was much confusion as to whether certain English statutes continued to apply to Singapore. This was because of the fact that various provisions in the statutes make reference to English law. For example, section 5 of the Criminal Procedure Code provides that:

> As regards matters of criminal procedure for which no special provision has been made by this Code or by any other law for the time being in force in Singapore *the law relating to criminal procedure for the time being in force in England shall be applied* so far as the procedure does not conflict or is not inconsistent with this Code and can be made auxiliary thereto [emphasis added].

Particularly problematic was section 5 of the Civil Law Act, which was repealed following the enactment of the Application of English Law Act in 1993. This landmark legislation makes it clear which English statutes continue to apply in Singapore. Section 5 removes all ambivalence by declaring that except where provided by the Act, "no English enactment shall be part of the law of Singapore." The list of English statutes and the extent of their application to Singapore is found in Schedule I to the Application of English Law Act.

4.2 The style of judicial decisions

The style and length of judgments is typical of that of most common law jurisdictions. In many instances, they will be longer than those of civil law jurisdictions, especially where the case involves complex common law issues. Since the law is invariably found in judicial authority, much of the judgment is dedicated to citing and elaborating on relevant

[86] *The Laws of the Colony of Singapore Containing the Ordinances and Selected Imperial Legislation in Force on the 1st day of May, 1955/ prepared under the authority of the Revised Edition of the Laws Ordinance, 1951 by E. J. Davies, C. H. Butterfield and A. H. Simpson*, 8 vols. (Singapore: Government Printer, 1955).

precedents and distinguishing those the court finds irrelevant or problematic. Court of Appeal decisions tend to be much longer than those of the High Court, especially when the Court of Appeal is trying to settle controversial points of law on which there are conflicting authorities. Judicial decisions of all jurisdictions can be cited before the Court of Appeal, which treats all common law decisions as being persuasive in value. The more authorities that are cited, the longer the judgments tend to be. In recent times, the longest judgment ran for over 130 pages.[87] Typical Court of Appeal judgments range between thirty and sixty pages on average. High Court decisions are typically half that length except where the facts are highly complex or where there are many witnesses.

All judgments of the Singapore courts are rendered in English, the administrative language of Singapore, and one of the four official languages under the Constitution. Since all Singaporeans study English as their first language in school, there is no need for the judiciary to give special consideration or accommodation for minorities. Foreigners appearing in court, either as the accused or as witnesses, are provided competent interpreters for the purposes of witness examination or cross-examination. The same facility is offered to Singapore citizens who are unable to follow the court proceedings in English.

4.3 *Can judges make law?*

Judges make law through their interpretation of the law and legislation. They are patently conscious of their unelected status and thus refrain from excessive judicial adventurism. Where a statute is applicable to the dispute at hand, the court will rely on the words of the statute and then interpret the law therefrom. Section 9A of the Interpretation Act further exhorts judges to adopt a purposive approach in the interpretation of statutes and makes legitimate the reference to legislative debates and *travaux préparatoires* to discern legislative intent. In subjects where no statute applies (e.g. a case involving only contract or tort, which are common law subjects), reference will be made to precedents of Singapore's highest courts, as well as to courts of other jurisdictions that decided on similar points of law.

[87] See *Review Publishing Co. Ltd & Anor* v. *Lee Hsien Loong & Anor Appeal* [2010] 1 SLR 52.

4.4 *Interpretive method*

It is not possible to generalize the courts' approach towards statutory interpretation. However, a few points may be made. First, the Court of Appeal, being the highest court in Singapore, is not bound by its own prior decisions[88] and allows the widest latitude in the reference to and citation of foreign case law, comparative material, and even academic writings. Second, section 9A of the Interpretation Act (Cap. 1) enjoins courts to interpret "a provision of a written law" in a manner "that would promote the purpose or object underlying the written law." To do this, the court may consider, among other things: (a) all matters not forming part of the written law that are set out in the document containing the text of the written law as printed by the Government Printer; (b) any explanatory statement relating to the Bill containing the provision; (c) the speech made in Parliament by a Minister on the occasion of the moving by that Minister of a motion that the Bill containing the provision be read a second time in Parliament; (d) any relevant material in any official record of debates in Parliament; (e) any treaty or other international agreement that is referred to in the written law; and (f) any document that is declared by the written law to be a relevant document for the purposes of this section.[89]

5 Function of courts

5.1 *Social control*

The Singapore courts see themselves as playing an important role in maintaining law and order and have acknowledged what Herbert Packer described as the "crime control model" of criminal justice,[90] which is:

> based on the proposition that the repression of criminal conduct is by far the most important function to be performed by the criminal process. The failure of law enforcement to bring criminal conduct under tight control is viewed as leading to the breakdown of public order, leading to law-abiding citizens being victimised by law-breakers. If the laws go unenforced, which is to say, if it is perceived that there is a high percentage of failure to apprehend and convict in the criminal process, a general

[88] See Practice Statement (Judicial Precedent) [1994] 2 SLR 689, [1994] SGCA 148.
[89] See Interpretation Act (Cap. 1), s. 9A(3).
[90] See H. Packer, "Two models of the criminal process," *University of Pennsylvania Law Review*, 113 (1964), 1.

> disregard for legal controls tends to develop. The law-abiding citizen then becomes the victim of all sorts of unjustifiable invasions of his interests. His security of person and property is sharply diminished and, therefore, so is his liberty to function as a member of society. The claim ultimately is that the criminal process is a positive guarantor of social freedom. In order to achieve this high purpose, the Crime Control Model requires that primary attention be paid to the efficiency with which the criminal process operates to screen suspects, determine guilt, and secure appropriate dispositions of persons convicted of crime.[91]

This point has been made consistently by Chan Sek Keong, first when he was Attorney-General,[92] and, more recently, as Chief Justice.[93] Chan CJ argued that although Singapore inherited a "due process model" from the British, a transition took place from 1959, when Singapore became a self-governing colony, and culminated in major revisions to its criminal procedure throughout the 1960s and 1970s. In summary, Chan CJ explained:

> The desired national goal of making Singapore a safe tranquil society would have been unattainable if the courts prescribe and apply a different set of values in the administration of criminal justice. In this regard, I would say the Singapore judiciary has played an effective role in crime control. It has delivered criminal justice quickly, efficiently and effectively. It has pursued a consistent policy of imposing punishments on retributive and deterrent principles consistent with legislative policies. These three elements are necessary to reinforce the philosophy that criminals have no place in Singapore.[94]

5.2 Legitimation of government policies

Philosophically, the Singapore Government is insistent that the state must have sufficient power to govern. A weak state results in weak governments that cannot govern effectively. As I have suggested elsewhere:

91 *Ibid.* 9–10.

92 See S. K. Chan, "The criminal process: the Singapore model," *Singapore Law Review*, 17 (1996), 433.

93 See S. K. Chan, "From justice model to crime control model," speech at the International Conference on Criminal Justice under Stress: Transnational Perspectives Conference, New Delhi, India, 24 November 2006.

94 *Ibid.* para. 20.

> The Constitution is thus not an instrument of limitation, but a charter of state power and authority which does not threaten the existence of the state nor fetter the Government's ability to govern.[95]

As a consequence, the courts do not see themselves as natural adversaries of the executive, waiting to pounce on the government at the slightest prompting. As Chan CJ recently stated:

> This idea of the courts being locked in an adversarial or combative relationship with the Executive and functioning as a check on administrative power is what Harlow and Rawlings, in their book, *Law and Administration*, label the "red-light" view of administrative law. I would like you to consider whether this is the right perspective for Singapore to adopt. There are, of course, pros and cons in such matters, depending on one's views on the social and legal values we should espouse and how society should be governed. One argument would be that what Harlow and Rawlings call the "green-light" approach is more appropriate for Singapore. This approach sees public administration not as a necessary evil but a positive attribute, and the objective of administrative law as not (primarily) to stop bad administrative practices but to encourage good ones. "Green-light" views of administrative law do not see the courts as the first line of defence against administrative abuses of power: instead, control can and should come internally from Parliament and the Executive itself in upholding high standards of public administration and policy.[96]

In this connection, the Court sees itself as an impartial referee, to ensure that the government stays on the correct side of the law:

> In other words, seek good government through the political process and public avenues rather than redress bad government through the courts. On a "green-light" approach, the courts play a supporting role by articulating clear rules and principles by which the Government may abide by and conform to the rule of law.[97]

5.3 Credible commitments in market functions of the economic sphere

As one of the world's most important trading and financial centers, the courts are particularly conscious of the need to provide the most

[95] See K. Y. L. Tan, "State and institution building through the Singapore Constitution 1965–2005" in L.-a. Thio and K. Y. L. Tan (eds.), *Evolution of a Revolution: Forty Years of the Singapore Constitution* (London: Routledge-Cavendish, 2009), pp. 50, 52.

[96] S. K. Chan, "Judicial review: from angst to empathy," *Singapore Academy of Law Journal*, 22 (2010), 469, 480.

[97] *Ibid.*

impartial and high-quality venue for dispute settlement. Most of the judges of the Supreme Court were top commercial lawyers before their elevation to the Bench, and the creation of three specialist commercial courts within the Supreme Court, for shipping, intellectual property, and arbitration, demonstrate the judiciary's commitment to the market.

5.4 Facilitation of compensatory or reparatory justice

As the rules of *locus standi* in Singapore require litigants first to establish sufficient interest in a case before the court will hear it, the use of litigation for compensatory or reparatory justice in environmental protection is practically non-existent. Pro-consumer legislation has hitherto not been robust, although the passage of the Consumer (Fair Trading) Protection Act in 2008 has ameliorated the situation somewhat. The passage of the "Lemon Law" in March 2012, an amendment to the 2008 legislation,[98] strengthens consumer protection by ensuring that defective products may be returned to their sellers within six months.

6 Courts and alternative dispute resolution (ADR)

6.1 ADR in Singapore

Singapore is now one of the leading Alternative Dispute Resolution (ADR) centers in Asia. Capitalizing on the quality of its arbitrators and legal expertise, and strongly supported by a government committed to ADR, Singapore is now one of the most popular arbitration venues in the world, sitting alongside established cities like London, Paris, Zurich, Geneva and New York. The Singapore International Arbitration Centre (SIAC) was established as an independent not-for-profit organization in July 1991 to promote international arbitration. Between 2000 and 2010, the SIAC handled 628 cases, making it the most popular arbitration center in Asia after the China International Economic and Trade Arbitration Commission (CIETAC).

In the International Chamber of Commerce's 2006 report, Singapore was ranked the top Asian city for arbitration, and in a 2010 survey by international law firm White & Case, Singapore ranked fifth among the "most preferred seats of arbitration," ranking below London, Geneva,

[98] Consumer (Fair Trading) Protection (Amendment) Act 2012.

Paris, and Tokyo.[99] In 2009, Maxwell Chambers, a dedicated arbitration venue with state-of-the-art facilities, was opened in Singapore. As a party to the Convention on the Recognition and Enforcement of Foreign Arbitral Awards 1958 (New York Convention), arbitral awards made in Singapore are potentially enforceable in more than 140 jurisdictions.

The Singapore Academy of Law established an ADR Directorate and charged it with promoting Singapore as the venue of choice for ADR. The Directorate is also responsible for developing and growing ADR in Singapore. The Academy has also established the Singapore Mediation Centre (SMC) in 1997 to provide ADR services, such as mediation and adjudication as well as ADR training (in subjects such as negotiation, mediation and conflict management). The SMC is also responsible for the accreditation of mediators, adjudicators and neutral evaluators.

6.2 Mediation in the courts

Mediation in the Singapore courts is institutionalized. There are two main categories of mediation practice: (a) court-based mediation, and (b) private mediation. Court-based mediation takes place in the courts after parties have commenced their suit. This type of mediation is mainly carried out by the State Courts and is coordinated by the e@dr Centre or the Primary Dispute Resolution Centre (PDRC). Private mediation in Singapore is spearheaded and mainly carried out by the Singapore Mediation Centre (SMC), a non-profit organization under the Singapore Academy of Law. A third facet of mediation practice is that which takes place in government agencies and industry-based bodies such as the Community Mediation Centres, the Tribunal for the Maintenance of Parents and the Consumers' Association of Singapore.

Since the early 1990s, the Singapore judiciary took active steps to encourage mediation. It initiated Pre-Trial Conferences (PTCs) for civil cases in 1992, in which registrars evaluated each case for optimal and efficient handling, and in which parties were encouraged to settle their disputes through negotiation on a "without prejudice" basis. This informal system was formalized in the High Court in 1996 through Order 34A

[99] White & Case LLP, *2012 International Arbitration Survey: Current and Preferred Practices* (School of International Arbitration, 2012); White & Case LLP, *2010 International Arbitration Survey: Choices in International Arbitration* (School of International Arbitration, 2010); see also Asian Legal Business, "Singapore vs Hong Kong: the arbitration battle intensified,"*Asian Legal Business* (2011).

of the Rules of Court. Under this procedure, courts can order parties to attend confidential PTCs or make other orders or directions to effect a just, expeditious and economic disposal of the dispute at any time before the commencement of proceedings.

In 1994, the judiciary launched the Court Dispute Resolution (CDR) scheme to encourage amicable pre-trial settlements of disputes. Court-led mediation is applied in criminal matters (such as for magistrates' complaints); small consumer claims (in the small claims tribunal); and in civil matters. Mediators for such cases are settlement judges who are specially appointed judges of the State Courts specializing in mediation. The PDRC schedules mediation sessions when all pleadings have been filed and all parties have consented to the mediation. In addition, the PDRC provides "neutral evaluation" for certain cases, such as motor accident cases. Such evaluations involve a settlement judge providing an indication of the likely liability of the parties at trial. The parties are then encouraged to negotiate on the basis of this indication.

Parties in divorce proceedings in the family court may be referred either to a resolution conference before a family resolution judge or a joint conference before a family resolution judge or a family resolution mediator. There is also the maintenance mediation chambers, which handles claims involving financial support for wife or child.

In 1996, the Singapore Government introduced a cross-profession Committee in ADR to study how mediation can be promoted in Singapore beyond the courts. This Committee recommended dividing the private mediation movement into commercial and community mediation by: (a) creating a commercial mediation center under the Singapore Academy of Law (the Singapore Mediation Centre), and (b) establishing a network of easily accessible community mediation centers to foster social cohesion. Community leaders and volunteers were trained to be mediators to enable communities to resolve their own disputes. This was implemented by the Ministry of Law, which created a Resource Panel on ADR to oversee the development of a national ADR infrastructure. The Community Mediation Centres Act (Cap. 49A) came into force in January 1998, and, shortly after, Singapore's first Community Mediation Centre was officially opened in November 1998. The Ministry of Law supervises the CMCs and remains an active promoter of mediation and ADR. Other initiatives to promote mediation as the primary tool of dispute resolution include the recommendation by the Attorney-General's Chambers that all government departments should use mediation as their first option for dispute resolution and that government contracts should include a mediation clause for referrals of disputes to SMC.

7 Concluding remarks

The Singapore judiciary is one of the country's most respected institutions. Based on public surveys conducted in 1999, 2001 and 2006, it can be said that public trust and confidence in the judiciary is very high. More than 90 percent of about a thousand interview respondents stated that "there is trust and confidence in the fair administration of justice in Singapore" and that "courts independently carry out justice according to law."[100]

In addition, the Singapore judiciary has also earned international acclaim. Based on the rankings given to Singapore's judiciary by the various international rating agencies, confidence in the judiciary is extremely high. The Hong Kong-based Political & Economic Risk Consultancy (PERC) has ranked Singapore's legal system among the top three in Asia, alongside Hong Kong and Japan, since 1999. The Institute of Management Development has ranked Singapore's legal framework among the top 5 percent of the sixty-one countries surveyed since 2002, and Singapore justice among the top 25 percent since 2006.

This is further buttressed by the high social regard the public has for judges and the high caliber of the judges themselves. The courts in Singapore are held in high esteem, and their orders are typically complied with without question. Singapore's judges are the highest paid in the world and have a stellar reputation for incorruptibility and impartiality. The fact that the Government ardently promotes Singapore as a major hub for legal services and adjudication and ADR adds further to the judiciary's strengths.

Throughout its history, Singapore's judiciary has responded to the demands of the markets and of business interests. At the same time, it has been made "as efficient as the best businesses" by a government that has long understood the importance of the need for its legal system to provide the Weberian stability required for capitalist expansion and development. And as long as the economy remains the *raison d'être* for Singapore's existence, much priority will be given to ensuring that the judiciary continues to be one of the best and most efficient in the world.

[100] "Survey on public attitudes & perceptions of the judiciary in Singapore," *Subordinate Courts Research Bulletin*, issue 12 (1998), 1 at 2.

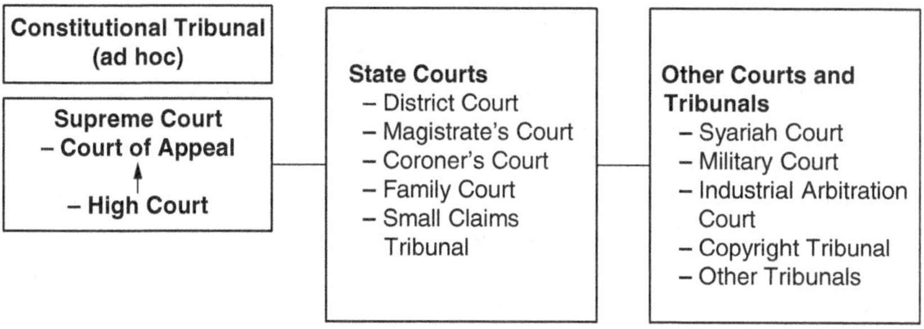

Figure 6.1: Structure of the courts in Singapore

References

Abrahams, Sir S. "The colonial legal service and the administration of justice in colonial dependencies," *Journal of Comparative Legislation and International Law*, 30(3) (1948), 1–11

Ahmad, I. "Developments in the marriage laws in Malaysia and Singapore," *Malaya Law Review*, 12(2) (1970), 257–76

Asian Legal Business. "Singapore vs Hong Kong: the arbitration battle intensified," *Asian Legal Business*, 1 December 2011

Bartholomew, G. W. "The Singapore Statute Book," *Malaya Law Review*, 26 (1984), 1–16

Braddell, Sir R. *The Law of the Straits Settlements: A Commentary*, 2nd edn. (Singapore: Kelly & Walsh, 1931)

Chan, G. K. Y. "Access to justice for the poor: The Singapore judiciary at work," *Pacific Rim Law & Policy Journal*, 17(3) (2008), 595–648

Chan, G. K. Y. "Re-examining public policy: a case for conditional fees in Singapore?" *Common Law World Review*, 33(2) (2004), 130–59

Chan, J. W. T. "Liberalisation of the Singapore legal sector," speech given at the 10th General Assembly of the ASEAN Law Association, Hanoi, 14–18 October 2009

Chan, S. K. "*From justice model to crime control model*," speech at the International Conference on Criminal Justice under Stress: Transnational Perspectives Conference, New Delhi, India, 24 November 2006

Chan, S. K. "Judicial review: from angst to empathy," *Singapore Academy of Law Journal*, 22 (2010), 469–89

Chan, S. K. "The criminal process: the Singapore model," *Singapore Law Review*, 17 (1996), 433–504

Cheong, C. and Lim, H. M. *Access to Justice: 50 Years of Legal Aid* (Singapore: Legal Aid Bureau, 2008)

Chong, S. "Liberalisation of legal services: freeing the legal landscape, is South-east Asia ready?" speech at the International Bar Association's 3rd Asia-Pacific Regional Forum Conference, Kuala Lumpur, 27 November 2012

Gopal, M. "English law in Singapore: the reception that never was," *Malayan Law Journal*, 2 (1983), xxv

Hassan, M. H. and Alhabshi, S. T. S. A. "The training, appointment, and supervision of Islamic judges in Singapore," *Pacific Rim Law & Policy Journal*, 21(1) (2012), 189–213

Ho, A. "Let David take on Goliath in court: champerty," *Straits Times*, 2 August 2013

Kwa, C. G, Heng, D. and Tan, T. Y. *Singapore: A 700-Year History – From Early Emporium to World City* (Singapore: National Archives of Singapore, 2009)

Kyshe, J. W. N. "A Judicial History of the Straits Settlements 1786–1890," *Malaya Law Review*, 11 (1969), 38–43

Lim, H. M. "Helping the less privileged gain access to justice – the role of the Legal Aid Bureau in giving effect to the Women's Charter," *Singapore Journal of Legal Studies* (2011), 129–51.

Malik, W. H. *Judiciary-Led Reforms in Singapore: Framework, Strategies and Lessons* (Washington, DC: The World Bank, 2007)

Menon, S. "Opening Address," speech at the Litigation Conference, Singapore, 31 January 2013

Packer, H. L. "Two models of the criminal process," *University of Pennsylvania Law Review*, 113 (1964), 1–68

Phang, A. "Cementing the foundations: the Singapore Application of English Law Act 1993," *University of British Columbia Law Review*, 28(1) (1994), 205–45

Phang, A. B. L. "Jury trial in Singapore and Malaysia: the unmaking of a legal institution," *Malaya Law Review*, 25 (1983), 50–86

Phang, A. B. L. "Of 'cut-off' dates and domination: some problematic aspects of the reception of English law in Singapore," *Malaya Law Review*, 28 (1986), 242–66

Phang, A. B. L. "The reception of English Law" in K. Y. L. Tan (ed.), *Essays in Singapore Legal History* (Singapore: Singapore Academy of Law & Marshall-Cavendish Academic, 2005), pp. 7–26

Prakash, J. "Making the civil litigation system more efficient," speech given at the Asian Pacific Judicial Reform Forum Roundtable Meeting, Singapore, 21 January 2009

Raffles, S. *Memoir of the Life and Public Services of Sir Thomas Stamford Raffles* (London: John Murray, 1830)

Rajah, V. K. "Judicial education in Singapore: beyond the horizon," paper presented at the Asia Pacific Courts Conference, Singapore, 6 October 2010

Rutter, M. F. *The Applicable Law in Singapore and Malaysia: A Guide to Reception, Precedent and the Sources of Law in the Republic of Singapore and the Federation of Malaysia* (Singapore: Malayan Law Journal, 1989)

Saw, S. H. *The Population of Singapore*, 3rd edn. (Singapore: Institute of Southeast Asian Studies, 2012)

Singapore Law Review. "In conversation: an interview with the Honourable Chief Justice Yong Pung How," *Singapore Law Review*, 12 (1991), 1–28

Singapore. *The laws of the colony of Singapore: containing the ordinances and selected imperial legislation in force on the 1st day of May, 1955 / prepared under the authority of the revised edition of the Laws Ordinance, 1951 by E.J. Davies, C.H. Butterfield, A.H. Simpson* (Singapore: Government Publications Bureau, 1955)

Soon, C. H. and Phang, A. B. L. "Reception of English commercial law in Singapore: A century of uncertainty" in A. J. Harding (ed.), *The Common Law in Singapore and Malaysia* (Singapore: Butterworths, 1985), pp. 34–70

Straits Settlements. *The Laws of the Straits Settlements* (London: Waterlow & Sons Ltd, 1920)

Subordinate Courts of Singapore. "Survey on public attitudes & perceptions of the judiciary in Singapore," *Subordinate Courts Research Bulletin*, 12 (1998), 1–12

Subordinate Courts of Singapore. *Annual Report 2012* (Singapore: Subordinate Courts, 2012)

Supreme Court of Singapore. *Annual Report 2012* (Singapore: Supreme Court, 2012)

Tan, K. Y. L. "A short legal and constitutional history of Singapore" in K. Y. L. Tan (ed.), *The Singapore Legal System*, 2nd edn. (Singapore University Press, 1999), pp. 26–66

Tan, K. Y. L. "A short legal and constitutional history of Singapore" in K. Y. L. Tan (ed.), *Essays in Singapore Legal History* (Singapore: Singapore Academy of Law & Marshall-Cavendish Academic, 2005), pp. 27–72

Tan, K. Y. L. "State and institution building through the Singapore Constitution 1965–2005" in L.-a. Thio and K. Y. L. Tan (eds.), *Evolution of a Revolution: Forty Years of the Singapore Constitution* (London: Routledge-Cavendish, 2009), pp. 50–78

Tan, K. Y. L. "The legal and institutional framework and issues of multiculturalism in Singapore" in A. E. Lai (ed.), *Beyond Rituals and Riots: Ethnic Pluralism and Social Cohesion in Singapore* (Singapore: Eastern Universities Press, 2004), pp. 98–113

Theobald, W. *The Legislative Acts of the Governor General of India in Council, from 1834 to the end of 1867*, 5 vols. (Calcutta: Thacker, Spink and Co., 1870)

Wee, K. S. K. "Customary marriages and the Women's Charter: lingering doubts," *Malaya Law Review*, 14 (1972), 93–102

Wee, K. S. K. "English law and Chinese family custom in Singapore: the problem of fairness in adjudication," *Malaya Law Review*, 16 (1974), 52–82

Wee, K. S. K. "The law of legitimacy in Singapore," *Malaya Law Review*, 18 (1976), 1–25

White & Case. *2010 International Arbitration Survey: Choices in International Arbitration* (School of International Arbitration, 2010)

White & Case. *2012 International Arbitration Survey: Current and Preferred Practices* (School of International Arbitration, 2012)

Woon, W. "The applicability of English law in Singapore" in K. Y. L. Tan (ed.), *The Singapore Legal System*, 2nd edn. (Singapore University Press, 1999), pp. 230–48

Woon, W. "The doctrine of judicial precedent' K. Y. L. Tan (ed.), *The Singapore Legal System*, 2nd edn. (Singapore University Press, 1999), pp. 297–324

Yeo, A. "Access to justice: a case for contingency fees in Singapore," *Singapore Academy of Law Journal*, 16 (2004), 76–167

Yeo, T. M. "Jurisdiction of the Singapore courts' in K. Y. L. Tan (ed.), *The Singapore Legal System*, 2nd edn. (Singapore University Press, 1999), pp. 249–96

PART II

Courts in fast developing economies

7

Legitimacy of courts and the dilemma of their proliferation: the significance of judicial power in India

JAYANTH K. KRISHNAN

Comparative law observers have long viewed India as a shining example of a democracy that has withstood enormous challenges since gaining independence from Britain in 1947. Such challenges have included the great wealth differentials between the "Haves" and "Have-Nots,"[1] grinding poverty for hundreds of millions of people, inadequate infrastructure, and the lack of basic needs such as reliably clean water, safe transportation, and quality primary education for children. In addition, corruption is taken almost as a given by everyday Indians since it inhabits so many aspects of daily life.

Yet in spite of these overwhelming problems, India has been able to uphold its democratic character for most of the past six-plus decades. India deserves praise for its representative system of government, structure of federalism, detailed rights-based constitution, and free press. It is a plural, multi-ethnic, multi-linguistic, and multi-religious society that has been able to retain cohesiveness, especially when compared to other post-colonial, Global South countries that have emerged since World War II. Furthermore, since the country liberalized its market in 1991, it has become an economic force on the world's stage, raising the standard of living of, and providing greater opportunities to, millions of Indians like never before. With all of its troubles, including its sad history of casteism that continues to this day, India is indeed an interesting, paradoxical, but also inspiring case study for scholars who follow comparative law and society issues.[2]

[1] See M. Galanter, "Why the 'haves' come out ahead: speculations on the limits of legal change," *Law & Society Review*, 9 (1974), 95.

[2] For citations that relate to points in this paragraph, see M. Galanter and J. K. Krishnan, "Bread for the poor: access to justice and the rights of the needy in India," *Hastings Law*

One important reason for India's sustained democracy is its strong, independent judiciary. This chapter will seek to explore this point in detail. To be sure, India's upper judiciary – its state High Courts but particularly its Supreme Court – has been at the forefront of rights-protection and rights-activism over the last thirty-five years. The courts here have been central in advancing the interests of the poor, minorities, and the socio-economically disadvantaged. Perhaps for this reason, there is a perception within the country that the judiciary – and again, especially the Supreme Court – is the most legitimate governmental institution in the country.[3]

The story is more complicated, however, within the "lower tier" of India's courts – the district courts, sub-district courts, specialized alternative bodies, and administrative, quasi-judicial tribunals – where tens of millions of cases are projected to be pending, many for more than a decade. Here, less is known about this universe of courts, but one study that has recently focused exclusively on this sector finds that in terms of civil cases, ordinary Indians have great difficulty accessing their rights.[4] Similarly, on the criminal side, other studies have uncovered that defendants wait extreme periods of time, often in custody, for their trials to commence, in what is a clear violation of India's due process doctrine.[5]

Still, what is interesting is that from these few studies of the lower tier, there is evidence that while litigants disdain the delay that is inherent within this process and blame lawyers, court staff, and other civil servants as the cause, there remains faith in one set of officials – the judges. Like with the higher judiciary, judges in the lower tier are seen as the protector of rights and defenders of justice, especially when compared to other public sector workers.[6]

Interestingly, governmental policy-makers have recognized this reality as well. For decades, the government has promoted the proliferation of additional courts at all levels of Indian society, as a means of helping

Journal, 55 (2004), 783; J. K. Krishnan, "Outsourcing and the globalizing legal profession," *William & Mary Law Review*, 48 (2007), 2221–6.

[3] See J. K. Krishnan, "Scholarly discourse, public perceptions, and the cementing of norms: the case of the Indian Supreme Court and a plea for research," *Journal of Appellate Practice & Process*, 29 (2007), 255–90.

[4] See J. K. Krishnan et al., "Grappling at the grassroots: access to justice in India's lower tier," *Harvard Human Rights Journal*, 27 (2014) (forthcoming).

Note, parts of this chapter will rely on and extract from this study in discussing the courts of India.

[5] See J. K. Krishnan and C. R. Kumar, "Delay in process, denial of justice: the jurisprudence & empirics of speedy trials in comparative perspective," *Georgetown Journal of International Law*, 42 (2011), 775.

[6] See Krishnan et al., "Grappling at the grassroots."

people redress their complaints in a timely fashion. The rationale is that because the regular system of courts is so clogged (and because elected officials resignedly acknowledge that they are perceived as ineffective), the best solution is to bypass the traditional routes for pursuing grievances by creating more adjudicatory forums where legitimately perceived judges can preside. While seemingly understandable at first blush, this chapter will contest the notion that simply constructing additional alternative judicial forums is the optimal answer to the problems of delay that plague India's judicial system. Indeed, such an unabated policy of creating more and more courts – without addressing the real structural deficiencies that exist in the regular judicial system – risks placing the one set of respected officials, the judges, in jeopardy of having their prestige and reputation lowered in the eyes of the public.

Before proceeding to this argument, however, the contents below will be discussed. Section 1 will outline how the courts in India are structured, with a focus on the powerful Supreme Court, along with providing a brief history on how the post-independent Indian judiciary has evolved into the system that we see today. Section 2 will address a subject that has recently been in the news, which relates to the appointment of judges in India and whether the current system needs to be revamped. Section 3 will discuss judicial training, legal education and the tactics of lawyering in India. Section 4 covers the sources of law to which judges refer and the norms and practices to which they adhere, including how personal/family law matters enter into this equation. Section 5 will then discuss how the judiciary was transformed, as well as how it transformed itself, following the Emergency Rule period that spanned from 1975 to 1977. Section 6, the conclusion, will analyze how there has been a massive proliferation of courts in India, particularly since the mid-1980s, with the point put forth that this policy has serious, negative, and unintended consequences for those trying to access justice.

1 The structure of the Indian judiciary – the Supreme Court and its progeny[7]

1.1 The structure of the courts

The Constitution of India became effective on 26 January 1950, and two days later an inaugural ceremony was held for the country's Supreme

[7] Parts of this section excerpt from Krishnan, "Scholarly discourse," 261–5. Note, because of space limitations here, the accompanying footnotes from that excerpt are not included.

Court. However, the British colonial influence on the post-independent Indian courts has been clearly visible. Like their UK counterparts, the Indian courts continued with the principles of *stare decisis* and common law. In addition, the judicial and lawyer decorum was patterned after the British. (For example, up until 1961, a divided bar was in place in India, and Indian judges were and still can be referred to as "lords." Attire by Indian judges and lawyers resembled that of the British as well.) Furthermore, India's lack of judicial federalism – where there are parallel federal and state tracks of courts – can be traced to the absence of this structural component in Britain.[8]

At the same time, influences of the American judicial model are present as well. Like in the United States, India's Constitution, particularly Articles 124 and 147, provides the constitutional basis for the Indian Supreme Court. Under these provisions, the Court is empowered with original, appellate, and advisory jurisdiction. The Court initially seated eight justices (including the Chief Justice), but over time that number has grown, where today there are thirty-one seats on the Court, with Justices usually hearing cases in small panels determined by the Chief Justice.

Article 124 also states that in order to be eligible as a justice, an individual must have served at least five years on a state supreme court, or what is called a High Court, or practiced as a lawyer in front of a state High Court or the Supreme Court for at least ten years, or be someone whom the President of India has deemed to be "a distinguished jurist."[9] In addition, Article 124 sets forth a mandatory retirement age of sixty-five. And justices are selected to the Court by the President of the country in consultation with sitting members of the Court itself. (For appointment to a state High Court, section 217 is the relevant constitutional section, where, along with the citizenship requirement, there is also the need to have either a certain amount of previous judicial experience or experience as a practicing lawyer. A fuller discussion of the appointments process will be provided below.)

(However, where there are direct quotes from that excerpt, those footnotes will be reproduced, and where there is material that was not part of that excerpt, there too footnotes will be added.) To see the accompanying footnotes from this Krishnan excerpt, please consult footnotes 23–43. The main authors cited in that excerpt were Granville Austin, Sunita Parikh and Alfred Darnell, S. P. Sathe, Stanley Wolpert, R. S. Gae, S. K. Verma and K. Kusum.

8 For a discussion of the evolution of the bar and bench in India from colonial times, see J. K. Krishnan, "Globetrotting law firms," *Georgetown Journal of Legal Ethics*, 23 (2010), 57.

9 Constitution of India, Art. 124 § 3(c).

In its formative years the Court seemed satisfied to give India's first Prime Minister, Jawaharlal Nehru, the leeway to follow through with his vision for creating a democratic-socialist republic. In several cases during the 1950s and early 1960s, the Court affirmed the government's initiatives nationalizing industries, creating monopolies over certain sectors, and regulating private businesses. But upon closer scrutiny of the case law during this time, there were certain occasions – namely in matters involving individual property rights and compensation thereof – when the Court refused to acquiesce completely to the government.[10]

The staunch position of the Court regarding landowners' rights during the first two decades of independent India could be seen as anti-democratic, especially given the dominance of Nehru's Congress Party at the local, state, and federal levels. But within the scholarly discourse an alternative narrative emerged: that while the Court "seemed to share the Nehruvian vision of socialist India, as evident in its decisions on the rights of industrial labor and regulation and control of the economy,"[11] it could not completely buckle to the government without losing its integrity. The property law cases that came its way gave the Court the opportunity to display its independence from the aggressive pressure being wielded by the national government.

Underneath the Supreme Court, but still considered part of the upper judiciary or upper tier, lie the High Courts. In many cases, different High Courts in India have also been aggressive in challenging government authority and in being at the forefront of protecting individual rights and civil liberties. While India has federalism – there is the central government, twenty-eight state governments, and seven union territories with their respective governing units – American-type judicial federalism, as stated above, does not exist in the same way in India. In India, there are twenty-four state High Courts.[12] (A few states share the same High Court.) Beneath these respective High Courts are district courts, which are divided into a civil side and criminal (or sessions) side. Below these district courts are sub-district courts, which hear more petty civil and criminal matters. (Depending on the location and language, these sub-district courts can be referred to as *Taluka* or *Tehsil* courts.) And one

[10] For the case law on these matters, Krishnan, "Scholarly discourse."

[11] See S. P. Sathe, *Judicial Activism in India: Transgressing Borders and Enforcing Limits* (Oxford University Press, 2002), p. 6.

[12] See J. Venkatesan, "3 New High Courts for NE," *The Hindu*, 26 January 2013, www.thehindu.com/news/national/3-new-high-courts-for-ne/article4345372.ece.

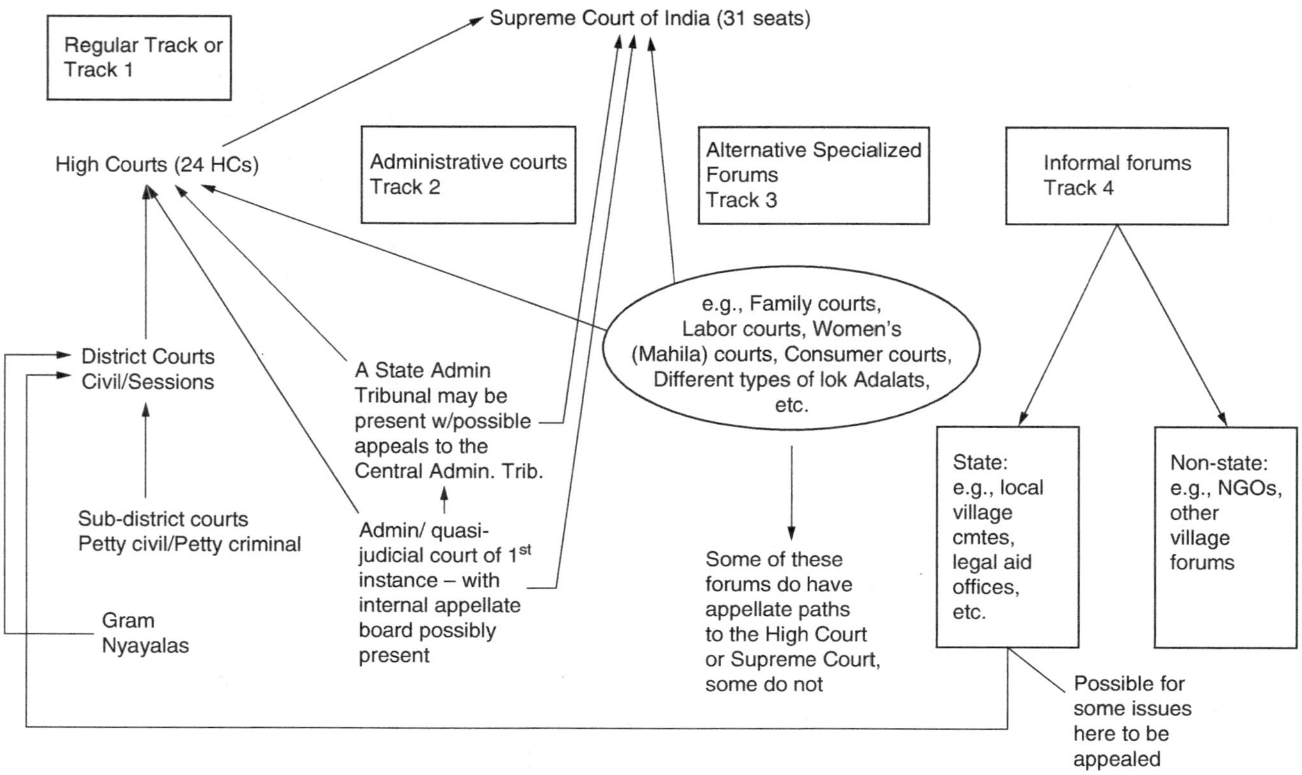

Figure 7.1: Court system in India

step below these forums are village (*gram*) courts, which deliberate on the most local of matters involving typically more rural claimants.

Judicial federalism is different in India than in the United States, because a case based on either a state or central governmental law may originate in the lower courts and work its way up this unified chain, ultimately to the Supreme Court. However, this is where the confusion lies, because in India, alongside these "regular" courts, there are other tracks of courts that exist as well. To begin, India has a vast array of administrative, "quasi-judicial" courts. (In India, such courts are referred to as "Tribunals.") These respective courts adjudicate matters regarding social security, government pensions, revenue matters, land disputes, and the like. Depending on the agency, there may be a higher administrative board within it to hear appeals, with a state or central apex agency being the final administrative court of resort. (If it is determined that a constitutional issue is involved, cases may be appealed to a state High Court or even directly to the Supreme Court after the initial administrative hearing.)

If administrative courts are considered a second track, then a third track would include a raft of alternative specialized forums, many of which have been created by special legislation at the central governmental level. These alternative forums come in many forms, with some of the more well-known being: family courts, labor courts, consumer courts, motor vehicle accident courts, women's courts (to hear crimes against women), and 'people's courts' or *Lok Adalats*, which can entertain a host of civil cases. A fourth track consists of more informal forums that may or may not necessarily be tied to the state. Courts within this sphere tend to be found throughout the many villages and rural communities in India. They can include: non-governmental organizations, women's protection homes, legal aid offices, non-legal village forums, and *Tanta Mukta Gaon Mohim* (dispute free village programs).[13]

1.2 *The size and performance of the courts*

Upon first impression, it may appear that the presence of so many different forums offers aggrieved parties a range of adjudicatory options. Furthermore, government leaders have sought to promote this proliferation because of the enormous backlog within all levels of the regular

[13] Excerpted from Krishnan et al., "Grappling at the grassroots."

court system. Consider that "[b]etween 2000 and 2010 the number of new admission matters that were filed with the Supreme Court [alone] nearly doubled from 24,747 to 48,677."[14] (As of the end of January 2013, there are thought to be some 66,000 cases pending in the Supreme Court.[15]) Overall, it is projected that all the courts in India have over 30 million cases that are awaiting decisions,[16] with over 4 million of those being in the states' High Courts.[17]

Problematically, however, with this type of court-proliferation there often is overlapping jurisdiction among courts within the different tracks. Otherwise put, two different sets of courts with two different sets of procedures can hear similar types of claims. And how a case ends up in one court versus another seems to have little to do with protocol or established procedure than with the idiosyncratic norms of where the matter is initially brought. Litigants (and sometimes even their lawyers) are thus left confused and uninformed on where they should proceed with their claims. Additionally, because courts in tracks 2, 3, and 4 are occasionally staffed with the same personnel as the regular lower judiciary, many of the practices that plague the district and sub-district courts migrate into these supposedly faster alternatives. The result is delays, inefficiencies, and overall frustrations – issues that are all meant to be avoided.[18]

On this issue of delay, there will be a full discussion of the causes later in this chapter. However, one point relevant here now is that a major contributing factor relates to the sheer lack of judges available on benches to hear cases. Above it was noted that there are thirty-one seats on the Supreme Court of India, but presently there are twenty-eight justices serving. If the shortage is only marginally noticeable in the Supreme Court, the story changes considerably at the High Court level and within the lower tier of courts. Consider some of these noteworthy figures that were released at the end of 2012. There are over 300 vacancies

[14] See N. Robinson, "A quantitative analysis of the Indian Supreme Court's workload," *Journal of Empirical Legal Studies*, 10 (2013), 570, 571.

[15] See "Over 3 crore cases pending in courts in India: Govt," *The Times of India*, 7 March 2013, http://articles.timesofindia.indiatimes.com/2013-03-07/india/37531045_1_apex-court-crore-cases-high-court.

[16] *Ibid.*

[17] See H. Dhawan, "Over 43 L cases pending before high courts," *The Times of India*, 5 October 2012, http://articles.timesofindia.indiatimes.com/2012-10-05/india/34278926_1_high-courts-crore-cases-supreme-court.

[18] Excerpted from Krishnan et al., "Grappling at the grassroots."

Table 7.1: *Vacancies of judges in High Courts*[a]

High Court	Approved strength [seats allocated by Government]	Vacancies
Allahabad	160	74
Delhi	48	13
Rajasthan	40	18
Bombay	75	20
Calcutta	58	17
Karnataka	50	13
Madras	60	10
Punjab & Haryana	68	26

Source: P. Thakur, "Over 300 posts of judges in High Courts vacant," *The Times of India*, 12 December 2012.

[a]See P. Thakur, "Over 300 posts of judges in High Courts vacant," *The Times of India*, 12 December 2012, http://articles.timesofindia.indiatimes.com/2012-12-24/india/35990853_1_high-courts-delivery-and-legal-reforms-mission-for-justice-delivery, citing the government Union Law Ministry as the source for the data.

throughout the country's state High Courts.[19] Table 7.1 provides some of the most severe shortages of judges in different states in India.

The effect of such vacancies is that those judges who are seated have overburdened dockets where they are not able to attend to the cases in front of them in a timely manner. For example, at the Delhi High Court "at least 30 per cent of cases are pending for five to ten years, including cases of sexual assault and murder. Of the [total] 61,000 cases pending … a record 5,000 are pending for more than 10 years."[20]

The problems within the lower tier are even more pronounced. One study has found that district court judges are supposed to have on average roughly 500 cases on their docket per calendar year; yet, instead the actual number is ten times this amount.[21] A report from the end of 2010 noted that of the 17,151 judgeships allocated by the central government within the lower tier, there were 3,170 vacancies, with the following states having the greatest number of empty seats: "Bihar (389 vacancies),

[19] See P. Thakur, "Over 300 posts of judges in High Courts vacant," *The Times of India*, 12 December 2012, http://articles.timesofindia.indiatimes.com/2012-12-24/india/35990853_1_high-courts-delivery-and-legal-reforms-mission-for-justice-delivery.

[20] *Ibid.* [21] See Krishnan et al., "Grappling at the grassroots."

Gujarat (361), Uttar Pradesh (294) and Maharashtra (234)."[22] Unfortunately, little has changed. A 2013 study found that whereas in advanced industrialized countries the ratio is of "50 judges per one million population … and 35–40 judges in some other developing countries,"[23] in India there are only "13 judges for every one million population."[24] It is true that the government is planning on increasing the number of judicial posts in the lower tier from its present number of around 18,000 to 37,000, but that 3,000-plus vacancies remain to be filled does not give attuned observers great hope.[25]

Why are there many judicial vacancies within the lower tier level? For one thing, India has around 1,000 law schools, but only a minute percentage adequately train students to pass the civil service tests to become a judge. (Even for those who do pass the exams, they are often not equipped with the full array of necessary skills to adjudicate the cases that come before them.) Then there is another problem: finding ways to incentivize a greater number of motivated, thoughtful, and talented people from the Bar to view the judiciary as a place where they would like to work. Consider, for example, the number of unappealing aspects to the job.[26]

First, as just stated, the dockets of such sitting judges are filled beyond capacity. In many districts and sub-districts, where populations are high, it is not unusual to find only a few judges present, and it is also not uncommon for one judge to be summoned to sit in multiple forums. Second, there are few enhanced training and continuing legal education opportunities for current judges who wish to keep abreast of developing trends in the law. It is true that India has established in many states highly reputable judicial academies. But there often can be a chasm that exists between what is being taught in the judicial academies and the everyday realities on the ground. Third, in many situations within the

[22] See M. Chhibber, "Justice delayed: SC down, Judge vacancies pile up," *The Indian Express*, 5 September 2011, www.indianexpress.com/news/justices-delayed-sc-down-judge-vacancies-pile-up/841693/.

[23] See Press Trust of India, "Only 13 judges for every 10 Lakh people in India," *Ibn-Live*, 9 May 2013, http://ibnlive.in.com/news/only-13-judges-for-every-ten-lakh-people-in-india/390705-3.html.

[24] *Ibid.*

[25] See P. Thakur, "All-India judicial service on track, Ashwani Kumar says," *The Times of India*, 8 April 2013, http://articles.timesofindia.indiatimes.com/2013-04-08/india/38372153_1_collegium-system-the-cji-law-minister.

[26] The following points below are excerpted from Krishnan et al., "Grappling at the grassroots."

lower tier, it is not the judges but rather the lawyers – because of their experience, reputation, social capital, and willpower – who control courtroom proceedings. The judges in these settings often take cues from the lawyers instead of vice versa. It is thus unlikely to expect the top lawyers practicing in the lower tier to leave their positions of prominence for the Bench. Fourth, the pay of lower-tier judges is comparatively much less than what top lawyers who practice in front of them earn. Some years back the government sought to implement a commissioned study that recommended providing higher judicial salaries, better living accommodation, and other increased perks. Still, such benefits pale in comparison to what the top lawyers in the lower tier earn. Of course, achieving parity may not be practical or politically possible, but, as it stands now, the financial adjustments made to date are not seen as attractive enough by those lawyers from whose service the judiciary could well benefit.

There are also other issues that give pause to those who might consider a judicial post. That judges are so frequently transferred (from district court to district court) is extremely unappealing, particularly for potential candidates who have families or working spouses. Then there is the lack of physical security that lower-tier judges feel they need, but frequently do not receive, both in and outside the courthouse.

The lack of camaraderie, which is a well-known complaint made by sitting lower-tier judges, is also a deterrent. There is little opportunity for social interaction, which is not only isolating for the judge but for accompanying family members as well. And lower-tier judges often work within dilapidated buildings with inadequate filing systems, inconsistent electrical power, sporadic air conditioning, and poor internet connectivity. Adding to these problems is the fact that judges do not have enough courtroom personnel assistance, and those staff members who are present not infrequently lack the skills, commitment, or incentives to carry out their duties in a professional fashion.

These obstacles clearly hinder judges from effectively doing their jobs, but they also serve as barriers to talented lawyers who might wish to pursue this career path. These vacancies that exist within the lower tier also have an upward effect. Typically, the norm is that roughly a third of High Court judges come to their positions after being promoted from the lower tier. But with there being so many gaps at the district court level itself, there are simply fewer judicial candidates from whom to select, which in turn contributes to the vacancy problems at the High Court level too.

2 Judicial appointments and judicial independence

The appointment process of judges to India's upper judiciary has been making news over the last several years. Above, section 124 was discussed, but in addition, sub-section 2 states that the President of India is to appoint the Chief Justice of the country. Furthermore, it goes on to note that the President is charged with naming the other justices of the Supreme Court, as well as the justices of the state High Courts. It is over this issue of appointing these other Justices (excluding the Chief Justice) that a row has occurred.

Beginning in 1982 and culminating in 1998, the Supreme Court, through decisions in three key cases,[27] concluded that in order to preserve the integrity and principle of judicial independence, the President had to receive the imprimatur of the Chief Justice and the four most senior justices of the Court before an appointment to the upper judiciary could be confirmed. This mandatory consultation with the Court's "Collegium," as it is called, has raised the ire of various observers. The objection stems from the sentiment that the Court has effectively solidified a "judges-pick-judge system"[28] where there is little transparency and a worry that the Collegium selects candidates based on factors not necessarily related to merit. As of this writing, the Collegium process continues, although there are those who believe that it should and will change in the near future.[29]

In terms of the lower tier, appointments can take one of two paths, with the latter paralleling more of what is found in civil law countries. On the one hand, a lawyer can be appointed to the lower bench after practicing in good standing for a certain period of time.[30] More frequently,

[27] *S. P. Gupta* v. *Union of India* [1982] 2 SCR 365; *Supreme Court Advocates-on-Record & Ors* v. *Union of India* [1993] 4 SCC 441; and *In Re Presidential Reference* [1998] 7 SCC 739.

[28] See P. Thakur, "Judges-pick-judge system may go," *The Times of India*, 11 April 2013, http://articles.timesofindia.indiatimes.com/2013-04-11/india/38462412_1_collegium-system-four-senior-most-judges-hc-judges.

[29] See *ibid.* Also see Press Trust of India, "Government must have say in appointment of judges to higher courts: Kapil Sibal," *The Times of India*, 2 June 2013, http://articles.timesofindia.indiatimes.com/2013-06-02/india/39690342_1_higher-judiciary-collegium-system-collegium-appointing-judges.

[30] See Law Commission of India, *One-Hundred Eighteenth Report on Method of Appointment of Subordinate Court/Subordinate Judiciary*, December 1986, http://lawcommissionofindia.nic.in/101–169/Report118.pdf. Also see A. Kumar, "Short essay on the subordinate courts in India," www.preservearticles.com/2011111216843/short-essay-on-the-subordinate-courts-of-india.html.

however, judges come to the lower court after having taken a series of civil service exams following their law school graduation.[31]

Aside from the appointment process within the regular courts, a final point is needed regarding judicial appointment in the other tracks. For judicial seats in the alternative specialized track, generally judges are drawn from the regular system and can either be presently sitting or retired. Administrative court judges are drawn from a similar civil service examination system that regular district and sub-district judges follow. And judges in the informal track can be selected through a variety of methods, which, not surprisingly, range from more informal processes (where the adjudicator may not have any formal legal training) to situations where an actual judge or lawyer serves as the respective body's decision-maker. For these informal courts, it simply depends on the forum and the parties involved.

This is the overall situation for how judges are selected in India. By and large, there is a common acceptance within the scholarly discourse that Indian judges are fiercely independent. The constitutional foundation of the judiciary and the Supreme Court's various decisions over the years have cemented this institutional norm. Even at the lower levels of the court system, there is evidence that judges are seen by litigants to be the one set of public officials who are most in a position to offer assistance.[32] More rigorous and larger-scale empirical work on this topic would be welcome, but it is safe to say that from both within the country and abroad, the Indian judiciary is perceived as a strong institution that helps keep the other arms of government in check.

3 Judicial training, legal education and the problem of lawyering

3.1 Legal education and the delivery of judicial and legal services[33]

Above it was mentioned that the vast majority of law schools in India do not adequately prepare students for a career as judges in the judiciary.

[31] *Ibid.* (at both cited). [32] See Krishnan et al., "Grappling at the grassroots."

[33] Please note that this section draws on the author's extensive work on legal education in India for over a decade. See, e.g., *ibid.*; J. K. Krishnan, "Professor Kingsfield goes to Delhi: American academics, the Ford Foundation, and the development of legal education in India," *American Journal of Legal History*, 46 (2004), 447; J. K. Krishnan, "From the ALI to the ILI: the efforts to export an American legal institution," *Vanderbilt Journal of Transnational Law*, 38 (2005), 1255.

That law schools overall in India are not solid institutions of education and pedagogy may come as a surprise to some. But such is the case; in fact it may be more accurate to say that there is a crisis in legal education within the country. It is true that since India liberalized its economy in 1991, the global marketplace has witnessed an influx of bright and talented lawyers entering the profession, notably those who are graduates from the country's dozen or so National Law Schools (NLS). The oldest of these schools was founded less than three decades ago, and the conventional wisdom is that these NLS graduates are helping to change the face of the Indian legal profession. And indeed many NLS alums have gone on to work at top Indian and foreign law firms; in multi-national corporations, legal academia, leadership positions in non-governmental organizations; and as successful Indian courtroom litigators.

However, what is regularly omitted from the discussion is the fact that these highly reputed NLS institutions only comprise a sliver of law schools in India. Although there is no reliably complete account of how many actual law schools exist in the country, figures range between 900 and 1,000, with there being great disparity in the quality of education dispensed. Law schools in India can be roughly categorized into the following groups:

(a) the National Law Schools (which are public),
(b) the historically reputed public law schools based in such cities as Delhi, Chennai, Mumbai, and Kolkata,
(c) another set of about twenty to thirty "decently-reputed" public institutions that are not in category (a) or (b),
(d) recently emerging private law schools (where there is variation here too), and
(e) several hundred local and regional law schools.

The legal training that occurs within the vast majority of law schools in category (e), which is where the bulk of lawyers and judges who work at the local levels study, is less than adequate. In these institutions, as well as some others in the different categories above, books are often outdated, English – the formal language of legal precedents from the upper courts – is not emphasized, infrastructure of the buildings frequently is abysmal, and often teachers are not present in a regular manner.

Additionally, the curriculum is based on learning statutes and regulations in a rote manner, and, especially in the more rural law colleges in the country, there is little opportunity to educate students through clinics or to have them engage in critical analysis of the daily problems they are likely to encounter in practice. Given this situation, it should not be surprising that in most law colleges from which these students graduate, the ability to deliver legal services in a routinized, efficient, and fair manner can be lacking.

And this last point is important because, after all, judges and lawyers are most frequently the first access points of claimants to the judicial system. Judges and lawyers are the ones who are supposed to serve as the protectors and representatives of the needy. They are to advise and guide them through the complicated maze of procedures that line the Indian courts. Ideally, they are to be the voice and champions of this constituency. For a country that was led out of colonial rule by eminent legal professionals who preached this same message, the Bench and Bar today should be vigorous in guarding the interests of the most disadvantaged.

But alas, such is not the case. As for the lawyers, many who work in India's courts suffer from apathy, self-interest, and a lack of critical skill sets; and in terms of the vast majority of judges (who work within the lower courts), the evidence suggests that while they have the respect of the claimants and seek to do the best that they can, they nevertheless despair because they are overworked and under-trained. From the start, then, with the training of law students, which leaves much to be desired, to the practice-setting, many judges and lawyers concede that their daily professional lives are a struggle to eke out an existence simply in order to do their jobs and support themselves and their families.

3.2 The number of lawyers in India and the disconnect between the Bar and clients

Given the immediate discussion above, it should not be surprising that many clients view lawyers in India with skepticism and frustration and often are unable to achieve satisfaction when seeking legal assistance. A few years back, the author requested the Bar Council of India – a statutorily created organization overseeing the licensing of lawyers in the country – to compile a state-by-state tabulation of the number of members that are currently enrolled within it throughout the country. The table below lists these figures and breaks them down by gender for most states as well.

The data reveal that there are over one million lawyers in India. But ascertaining the *real* number of practitioners has long been a challenge for those interested in empirical data collection, as the Bar Council

Table 7.2: *Statement of total number of advocates enrolled with the State Bar Councils*[a]

States	Men	Women	Total
1. Andhara Pradesh	58,147	9,605	67,752
2. Assam, Nagaland, etc	9,703	2,022	11,725
3. Bihar	N/A	N/A	104,464
4. Chhatisgarh	N/A	N/A	17,213
5. Delhi	N/A	N/A	38,549
6. Gujarat	38,586	9,208	47,794
7. Himachal Pradesh	4,680	741	5,421
8. Jammu & Kashmir	2,832	597	3,429
9. Jharkhand	5,407	485	5,892
10. Karnataka	N/A	N/A	60,539
11. Kerala	29,769	8,863	38,632
12. Madhya Pradesh	N/A	N/A	69,208
13. Maharastra & Goa	78,522	5,637	84,159
14. Orissa	N/A	N/A	37,993
15. Punjab & Haryana	42,411	4,265	46,676
16. Rajasthan	43,924	4,712	48,636
17. Tamil Nadu	46,575	5,902	52,477
18. Uttarakhand	N/A	N/A	7,505
19. Uttar Pradesh	N/A	N/A	244,691
20. West Bengal	N/A	N/A	59,535
Total			**1,052,290**

Source: Krishnan, "Globetrotting law firms," 57.
[a]This data was collected in 2008 for publication in 2010: see Krishnan, "Globetrotting law firms," 57.

does not provide information on how many actually practice law. (What is certain is that most are solo practitioners who work as courtroom litigators, and this author estimates that only about 50 percent of law degree holders are practitioners.[34])

Given that the population of India is over one billion, the percentage of available lawyers to assist needy clients is low. Moreover, there are

[34] See, e.g., Galanter and Krishnan, "Bread for the poor," 783; J. K. Krishnan, "Lawyering for a cause and experiences from abroad," *California Law Review*, 94 (2006), 575.

different hurdles that inhibit effective representation.[35] The first involves how lawyers structure their fees to clients. From the existing research, a repeated, bitterly made complaint from litigants is that lawyers routinely charge fees in an ad hoc manner. Fees are expected at an initial meeting, for phone conversations, for follow-up meetings, every time a court appearance occurs, and then for other random tasks. For many litigants, there is little explanation in how and when payments are required. Where they are unable to remit a demanded fee, work on their behalf stops, and, even where payments are properly made, cases continue for excessively long periods of time. Furthermore, given that lawyers on the whole are already viewed negatively, and even at times as corrupt, by clients, such a non-systematic, non-transparent fee collection structure only further enhances these perceptions. In contrast, an open and fair fee system would allow for the potential litigant to properly weigh the costs and benefits of pursuing court action, relying on the trusted guidance from the representing lawyer – just as how the system is supposed to work.

Another problem is the inordinate number of appeals that lawyers are allowed to make under the procedural codes. The presence of this interlocutory appeal system dates back to British times, whereby a party (namely the Crown) had the opportunity to petition any main or tangential judicial ruling up the chain of courts (all the way to the Privy Council in London) that it felt was wrongly decided. (Effectively, it served as a safeguard against an adverse decision made by local judicial officers who regularly staffed the lower courts in colonial India.) This system carried over to independent India, and because lawyers received payments per court appearance, a perverse incentive ensued whereby lawyers would abuse this appeals process to keep cases delayed, thereby allowing their fees to mount.

Today, politicians, judges, clients, and even the Bar are well aware of this "delay lawyering" employed by lower-tier advocates. But because of the Bar's political strength, legislators at the national, state, and local levels have been unable to amend the procedural codes enough to curtail and sanction those lawyers who abuse this system. Of course parties do need opportunities and avenues to appeal decisions that are adverse to them (or perceived to be adverse to them). All that is being

[35] The below discussion, for the next several paragraphs excerpts from Krishnan et al., "Grappling at the grassroots."

requested here, however, are reasonable measures to halt the clear patterns of abuse occurring at the expense of needy claimants.

And a third, readily observable, obstacle that exists relates to the physical difficulty in even having clients meet lawyers in the first place. Lawyers could increase their access, for example, by simply being willing to travel to where clients live. It can be painstakingly difficult for poorer claimants to trek from the remote areas where they reside to visit the chambers of lawyers; indeed, generally the arrow of movement works in this direction. Obviously, safer and more reliable transportation between villages and the courts would ease travel for both claimants and lawyers. But even without such improvements, lawyers certainly could increase their presence in rural townships.

4 The sources of law and norms of adjudication in India

India is a democratic republic that has a detailed constitution, common law, codified law, and administrative regulations all serving, formalistically, as sources that judges must consider when rendering decisions. The Constitution of India is considered the highest form and most important textual source of law within the country.[36] As provided for by the Constitution's Union List, the national Parliament is exclusively authorized to enact laws over nearly one hundred policy areas.[37] The Constitution also allows for states to have exclusive powers to pass laws that affect their own respective jurisdictions, and there is a Concurrent List, which enables both the Centre and States to legislate over similar policy domains, with the proviso that if there is a conflict, the former's law will trump the latter's.[38]

Additionally, the common law principle of *stare decisis* is to be adhered to by the Indian courts. The Supreme Court's judgments are considered binding on all lower courts and are supposed to have precedential value for future cases. (State High Court decisions similarly have precedential value over lower courts within their states.[39]) In a

[36] For a classic analysis of the Constitution, see G. Austin, *The Indian Constitution: Cornerstone of a Nation* (Oxford, Clarendon Press, 1966). For a more recent treatment, see S. Krishnaswamy, *Democracy and Constitutionalism in India: A Study of the Basic Structure Doctrine* (Oxford University Press, 2009).

[37] See Constitution of India, Part XI, List-I.

[38] See Constitution of India, Part XI, List-II–III.

[39] On precedent and its import, see N. Robinson, "The Supreme Court and its benches," *India-Seminar* (2013), http://india-seminar.com/2013/642/642_nick_robinson.htm; and

moment, we will discuss the powers and authority of the Supreme Court, but it is important to note that there is a civil law character to India as well. India has national codes relating to fields such as civil procedure, evidence law, criminal procedure, and criminal law, just to name a few.[40] With respect to criminal law, in particular, the main tome governing crimes that occur within the country is the Indian Penal Code (IPC), which was devised during colonial times (in 1862). It has been amended subsequently, but it did carry over to Independent India and continues to be in force to this day. In fact, there are two specific codes related to the IPC with which lawyers who practice in this area must be familiar. These include the Indian Code of Criminal Procedure that was passed in 1973 but has its roots in an earlier colonial incarnation that emerged in 1861, and the Indian Evidence Act, which although amended over the years remains basically in the form of when it was first passed – 1872.

In addition to having these types of codes in place, international law and administrative law also serve as sources of authority in India. In India, international treaties signed by the Prime Minister do not automatically come into force within the country's borders. Such treaties must receive the imprimatur by the national Parliament (through the passage of a statute) or the approval of the Supreme Court.[41] Once that is done, however, the treaty has the same weight as statutes and judicial decisions.

Administrative law is another key area that affects the everyday lives of so many Indians. India's reputation for having an incredibly large bureaucracy with mazes of rules and regulations is legendary. Infamously referred to as the "license raj," the administrative state in India has served as both a source of law and equally as a source of intense frustration for Indians dating back to the colonial era. From a professional services angle, administrative regulations from the central government down to the village-level units have been historically complicated and often contradictory – which has resulted in the country's very uneven path of development since independence. Beyond just commercial ventures, however, everyday living for most Indians can be extremely burdensome because of the inordinate number of administrative permissions and

N. Robinson, "Structure matters: the impact of court structure on Indian and US Supreme Courts," *American Journal of Comparative Law*, 61 (2013), 101.

40 Note states, under List-III, may also concurrently legislate on these cited areas of law too.

41 See S. K. Agarwal, "Implementation of international law in India: role of judiciary," Work-in-Progress Paper, http://oppenheimer.mcgill.ca/IMG/pdf/SK_Agarwal.pdf.

licenses required by the state. And while there are specialized agencies and courts designed to handle the range of matters across the administrative law spectrum, the combination of inefficiency, delay, and corruption continues to plague the India administrative state, even in this post-1991 liberalization context.[42]

Given this above description, not surprisingly it is difficult to overstate the omnipresence of the administrative bureaucracy in India. But there are two other sources of law that have even more institutional power than the rules and regulations set forth by the bureaucracy. One that has been already mentioned above comes via the decisions rendered by the Supreme Court of India. The other involves the power of customary law that is prevalent in India, particularly at the local and village levels. As Tariq Ahmad has succinctly put it: "The Courts of India have recognized custom as law only if the custom is (1) 'ancient or immemorial' in origin, (2) 'reasonable in nature and continuous in use,' and (3) 'certain.'"[43] Perhaps the most prominent display of customary law is in the form of how the personal or family law system in India functions. We discuss, in turn, each of these sources in greater detail.

4.1 *Interpretative authority of the Supreme Court*

The Supreme Court of India has established itself as the central institution in charge of finding whether the sources of law in India are valid or not. The Court has even concluded that it can determine whether Parliament may alter the country's Constitution – an obviously awesome power that scholars have studied, analyzed, and evaluated for decades.[44] The story of how the Court arrived at this conclusion requires a brief explanation.[45] In an effort to consolidate and bolster her authority in the late 1960s, the then Prime Minister, Indira Gandhi, sought, among

[42] The late Professor S. P. Sathe's classic administrative law work (which has been updated) should be consulted: see S. P. Sathe, *Administrative Law in India*, 7th edn. (Butterworths/LexisNexis, 2010).

[43] See T. Ahmad, "Research Guide: Customary Law in India," 2013, www.loc.gov/law/help/india-customary-law.php (citing B. J. Krishnan, "Customary law," *Seminar* (August 2000), www.india-seminar.com/2000/492/492%20b.%20j.%20krishnan.htm).

[44] On this point, see Krishnaswamy, *Democracy and Constitutionalism in India.*

[45] The following section is excerpted from Krishnan, "Scholarly discourse," 265–9. Please note that because of this volume's space limitations, the accompanying footnotes from this excerpt are not included. To see these references, please consult Krishnan, "Scholarly discourse," at footnotes 44–60.

other acts, to override the Supreme Court's power of judicial review, which was the main issue in the 1967 case of *Golaknath* v. *Punjab*. Here the question was whether Mrs Gandhi's majority-led Parliament could pass either a statute or constitutional amendment that contradicted or abridged the Fundamental Rights enumerated in the Constitution. In ruling against Mrs Gandhi, the Court reiterated that it alone was obligated to preserve these rights. The Parliament was too political a body, one which was too easily subject to the whims of politicians who were guided by majority will, a desire to remain in office, or sheer craven interests. The Fundamental Rights, on the other hand, were steadfast protections for the minority who needed an independent arbitrator to safeguard their interests; and in *Golaknath* the Court affirmatively opted to embrace this role.

Not one to be deterred, Mrs Gandhi, upon her party's victory in the 1971 parliamentary elections, pushed through a constitutional amendment that overturned the *Golaknath* decision. The amendment was challenged in the 1973 case of *Kesavananda Bharati* v. *Kerala*, in which the Court, sitting in a panel of thirteen, held by a seven-to-six margin that *Golaknath* had been incorrectly reasoned. According to the majority, Parliament could alter the Fundamental Rights in the Constitution through the passage of a constitutional amendment, but not through the passage of an ordinary legislative act. After all, even within the Fundamental Rights, exceptions existed indicating that these guarantees could be restricted. Nevertheless, while the Court was willing to reinstate Parliament's ability to amend the constitution, it set forth what has come to be known as the basic structure doctrine.

Under this principle, according to the Court, the Constitution had certain features to it that could never be compromised or abused by those entrusted with public authority – else India's democracy would cease to exist. For the Court, these features included constitutional, not parliamentary, supremacy; a republican form of government; secularism and federalism; separation of powers; a mutual respect for the Fundamental Rights and for establishing a welfare state; and preservation of the country's unity. For Mrs Gandhi and her supporters, the decision in *Kesavananda Bharati* was a direct repudiation. Although *Golaknath* had been overruled, the reversal was cold comfort to them, given the Court's firm pronouncement of the basic structure doctrine.

Nevertheless, this doctrine remains in effect and has contributed to the Court's increased institutional power. In Section 5, there will be a discussion of the other ways the Court has enhanced its prominence, especially following the period of Emergency Rule (1975–7) by Mrs Gandhi.

4.2 *Personal law in India*[46]

In India, it is important to highlight another key source of law, which has also been appropriated by the state judiciary: personal law. Systems or regimes of personal law refer to legal arrangements for the application within a single polity of several bodies of law to different persons according to their religious or ethnic identity. Personal law systems are designed to preserve to each segment its own law. Generally over the last several centuries, the most prominent instances have been personal law regimes in the areas of family law (marriage, divorce, adoption, maintenance), intergenerational transfer of property (succession, inheritance, wills), and religious establishments (offices, premises, and endowments).[47] Such personal law typically co-exists with general territorial law in criminal, administrative and commercial matters. On occasion, some commercial or criminal rules may be included in personal law.

The way personal law became institutionalized in India was during the colonial period when the British first established a general territorial law that operated in a common law style and was administered in a nationwide system of government courts. Over time the substantive law came to resemble its British counterpart, through infusion of common law and codification. At the same time, the British preserved enclaves of personal law. The Bengal Regulation of 1772 provided that in suits

[46] The discussion below on personal law excerpts from and draws on M. Galanter and J. K. Krishnan, "Personal law and human rights in India and Israel," *Israel Law Review*, 34 (2001), 101. Please note that because of this volume's space limitations, the accompanying footnotes from this excerpt are not included. To see these references, please consult Galanter and Krishnan, "Personal law and human rights," at footnotes 13–17 and 21–51. (One caveat, citations in this section will be provided where direct quotes from the excerpt are used or where post-2000 material has been incorporated.) The authors who are cited in the original *Israel Law Review* publication related to these excerpted sections include: Edouardo Vitta, M. B. Hooker, John H. Mansfield, Robert Baird, M. P. Jain, Martin Edelman, Marc Galanter, J. D. M. Derrett, Tahirm Mahmood, Rajeev Dhavan, Izhak Englard, Flavia Agnus, Carl Schneider, Luis Oropeza, Robert Dahl, Shyamla Pappu, B. K. Pal, Charles R. Epp, Anika Rahman, S. Raj, Ashgar Ali Engineer, Rajkumari Agrawala, Master Moos, and Namada Khodie.

[47] For a detailed discussion on personal law not included in the original Galanter and Krishnan, "Personal law and human rights" article because it was published subsequently, in 2003, see W. Menski, *Hindu Law: Beyond Tradition and Modernity* (Oxford University Press, 2003).

regarding inheritance, marriage, caste, and other usages and institutions, the courts should apply "the laws of the Koran with regard to Mohammedans, and those of the Shaster with respect to the Hindus."[48]

Under the British, the personal laws of Hindus and Muslims were administered in the regular courts by judges trained in, and familiar with, the style of the common law. Until about 1860, the courts had attached to them *pandits* and *kazis* (indigenous legal experts) to advise them on questions of Hindu and Muslim law respectively.[49] To make the law more uniform, certain, and accessible to British judges – as well as to check the discretion of the law officers – the courts relied increasingly on translations of texts, digests, and manuals, and on their own precedents. In 1860, when the whole court system was rationalized and unified, the law officers were abolished, and the judges took exclusive charge of finding and applying the personal law. These religious law systems were now reduced to texts severed from the living systems of administration and interpretation in which they were earlier embodied. Refracted through the common law lenses of judges and lawyers, and rigidified by the common law principle of precedent, there evolved distinctive bodies of Anglo-Hindu and Anglo-Muslim case law.

These bodies of personal law were administered by the courts of British India and, later, independent India. The Constitution of 1950 appears to envision the dissolution of the personal law system in favor of a Uniform Civil Code. Article 44, a non-justiciable Directive Principle, directs the state to "endeavor to secure for the citizens a uniform civil code throughout the territory of India."[50] After the Constitution came into force in 1950, the continued administration of separate bodies of personal law to the various religious communities was challenged as a violation of the guaranteed right to equality. The Indian courts upheld the continued validity of disparate personal laws and the power of the state to create

[48] Bengal Regulation of 1772. By 1793, the language was amended to "Mohamadan Laws" and "Hindu Laws": Regulation IV of 1793, s. 15.

[49] J. H. Mansfield, "The personal laws or a uniform civil code?" in R. Baird (ed.), *Religion and Law in Independent India* (New Delhi: Manohar Publishers & Distributors, 1993), p. 163.

[50] Constitution of India, Art. 44. But see *ibid.* Mansfield makes the argument that the 7th Schedule of the Constitution (Item 5 List III) and Article 44 might also lend support for the continuation of personal laws in the country. In addition, Mansfield argues that the language in Article 372, sections 1 and 3, along with Article 13(19) indicates that the framers intended for "laws in force" prior to 1947 (which included personal laws) to remain valid so long as they did not conflict with the Fundamental Rights section of the Constitution.

new rules applicable to particular religious communities. In the leading case during the 1950s (*State of Bombay* v. *Narasu Appa Mali*, 1952), the judges – a Hindu and a Muslim, both distinguished legal scholars as well as prominent secularists – were sanguine about the continued existence of personal law, presumably in anticipation of its early replacement.

However, there was an unwillingness of the Muslim minority to relinquish the *shari'a* (or the Anglo-Muslim amalgam administered in its name), which sidetracked plans for a uniform code during this time. Additionally, forces within the Hindu community fashioned a major codification and modification of Hindu law, enacting in 1955–6 a series of statutes known collectively as the Hindu Code. These Acts modified the Anglo-Hindu law in important ways. They abandoned the *varna* distinctions, the indissolubility of marriage, the preference for the extended joint family, and inheritance by males only and by those who can confer spiritual benefit. In their place, the new law emphasized the nuclear family, introduced divorce, and endorsed the equality of *varnas* and sexes. Very few rules remained with a specifically religious foundation.

The Hindu Code was in large measure tutelary: it mirrored "the values of [the] governing groups rather than those of … the congeries of communities that make up Hinduism."[51] While diluting if not effacing the traditional *dharmasastric* basis of Hindu law, the Hindu Code legislation rearranged the relationship between the state and religious authorities. It marked the acceptance of the Indian Parliament as a kind of central legislative body for Hindus in matters of family and social life. It discarded the notion, prevalent during the British period, that government had no mandate or competence to redesign Hindu society. In contrast to earlier times when the absence of centralized governmental or ecclesiastical institutions rendered impossible general or sweeping reforms, the modern Indian state now could accomplish across-the-board changes.

While retaining the personal law system, independent India introduced a note of voluntarism. The Special Marriage Act of 1872 had provided a code of general law by which couples could choose to marry and divorce, but in order to utilize this option they had to affirm that neither was a Christian, Jew, Hindu, or Muslim. In effect they had to renounce their religious and property relations with their families.

[51] Mansfield, "Personal laws," p. 168.

In 1954, Parliament passed a new Special Marriage Act that eliminated the onerous renunciatory costs of availing oneself of civil marriage.

There have been significant rulings on the issue of personal law by the Supreme Court of India over the past three decades, including in the famous cases of *Mohd Ahmed Khan* v. *Shah Bano* (1985), *Danial Latifi* v. *Union of India* (2001), and *Shabana Bano* v. *Imran Khan* (2009). Limited space here precludes a full discussion of these matters,[52] but, in short, India continues to retain a system in which certain family matters of Hindus, Muslims, Parsees, and Christians are governed by their respective religious laws. There is also a set of religiously differentiated public laws regulating religious endowments. While personal law in India covers issues of adoption, succession, and religious institutions, marriage and divorce are the main focus of public attention. Multiple pieces of national legislation deal with particular issues of marriage and divorce for the various religious groups in the country. The administration of these personal laws in India remains in the hands of state judges.

One final point worth noting here is that political conflict in India over personal law appears more prevalent between, rather than within, religious communities. This is not to say, however, that intra-religious dissension is entirely absent in India. Many Hindu women who champion equal rights for women support drastic reforms within (if not a complete abandonment of) Hindu personal law. Many Indian Christian women, similarly, struggle and protest against the obstacles Christian personal law poses for women who seek divorce. And there is a series of feminist critiques of Muslim law's treatment of women in divorce and maintenance.

Yet this intra-religious conflict is overshadowed by the tensions *between* religious communities in India. There is heated debate over whether or not India should adopt a uniform civil code and thereby abolish the various personal laws. Proponents of a uniform civil code (who typically are Hindus) point to Articles 14 and 15 of the Indian Constitution as well as to Article 44 as evidence that the "uniform civil code … [is] an ideal towards which the state should strive."[53] The Hindu-nationalist Bharatiya Janata Party (BJP) favors a uniform civil code, and enactment of the code was a tenet in the BJP platform in previous national election campaigns. On the other hand, opponents of

[52] For the most recent case here of *Shabana Bano* v. *Imran Khan*, see F. Agnus, "Shah Bano to Shabana Bano," *Indian Express*, 15 December 2009, www.indianexpress.com/news/shah-bano-to-shabana-bano/554314/.

[53] Mansfield, "Personal laws," p. 140.

a uniform civil code (typically members of the minority religious communities) argue that the framers respected the fact that various religious communities deeply identified with their own personal laws and never intended for the country to implement one set of rules and regulations for its diverse population. Many also contend that if a uniform civil code were adopted, the new laws would reflect the outlook of the majority Hindu population. The debate thus goes on.

5 Access to justice and the evolution of the Indian judiciary[54]

Following independence, a movement to restore an indigenous legal system flourished. Gandhians and socialists within the ruling Indian National Congress viewed the legal system inherited from the British as unsuitable to a reconstructed India, in which faction and conflict bred by colonial oppression would be replaced by harmony and conciliation. They proposed the displacement of modern courts by restoring traditional *panchayats* – a proposal that met with the nearly unanimous disdain of lawyers and upper judiciary judges and the vitriolic scorn of Dr B. R. Ambedkar, chair of the Constitution's Drafting Committee, who sidetracked the push for panchayats into a non-justiciable Directive Principle. As part of the Panchayati Raj (local self-government) policy of the late 1950s, judicial, or *nyaya*, panchayats were established with jurisdiction over specific categories of petty cases.

Although these *nyaya panchayats* derived sentimental and symbolic support from their appeal to the virtues of the indigenous system, they were quite different from traditional panchayats. They applied statutory law rather than indigenous norms; they made decisions by majority rule rather than unanimity; their membership was chosen by popular election from territorial constituencies rather than consisting of the leading

[54] This section draws upon and excerpts from Galanter and Krishnan, "Bread for the poor," 791–7. Please note that because of this volume's space limitations, the accompanying footnotes from this excerpt are not included. To see these references, please consult Galanter and Krishnan, "Bread for the poor," at footnotes 3–26 and 33–7. (One caveat: citations in this section from this excerpt will be provided where direct quotes, statistics, or ethnographic or empirical evidence are used.) The authors who are cited in the original *Hastings Law Journal* publication include: Marc Galanter, Lloyd Rudolph, Susanne Hoeber Rudolph, Upendra Baxi, Mauro Cappelletti, Bryant Garth, R. Kushawaha, Robert Hayden, Louis Dumont, Catherine Meschievitz, Richard Abel, S. N. Mathur, *Report on the Expert Committee on Legal Aid*, D. A. Desai, P. N. Bhagwati, Rajeev Dhavan, R. Sudarshan, Salman Khurshid, Smithu Kothari, Philip Oldenberg, Carl Baar, S. P. Sathe, Charles R. Epp, and S. K. Agarwal.

men of a caste. The focus on the "village" panchayat represented an attempt to recreate an idealized version of traditional society that emphasized democratic fellowship and ignored the caste basis of that society and its justice institutions.[55]

Like their traditional counterparts, these official *nyaya panchayats* encountered severe problems of establishing their independence from personal ties with the parties, enforcing their decrees, and acting expeditiously. They never attracted significant support from the villagers in whose name they were established. Their caseloads declined steadily while those of the courts continued to rise. In Uttar Pradesh, civil filings in the *nyaya panchayats* fell from 82,321 in 1960 to 22,912 in 1970 – just over four cases per *nyaya panchayat*.[56] During the same period, civil filings in the Subordinate Courts rose from 74,958 to 86,749.[57] One indicator of their demise is found in the experience of a researcher in Uttar Pradesh in the 1970s, frustrated by the rarity of *nyaya panchayat* sessions, whose villager hosts graciously offered to convene one to facilitate her research.[58]

In little more than a decade, *nyaya panchayats* were moribund. It is not clear whether they withered away because they lacked the qualities of the traditional indigenous tribunals or because they displayed them all too well. It was most likely because they represented an unappetizing combination of the formality of official law with the political malleability

55 Reviewing the literature on panchayats, Robert Hayden concludes that there was no such thing as a "village" panchayat, but only caste panchayats that, if sufficiently powerful locally, might decide matters involving members of other castes as well. See R. Hayden, *Disputes and Arguments Amongst Nomads* (Oxford University Press, 1999), pp. 83–109. See also L. Dumont, *Homo Hierarchicus: The Caste System and Its Implications* (University of Chicago Press, 1970), pp. 170–2 (noting *ibid.* (at p. 172) that "we conclude that on the eve of British conquest, and excepting exceptional cases, there was no village panchayat as a permanent institution distinct from caste panchayats. There was a panchayat of the dominant caste of the village, and there were meetings of ad hoc arbitrators or judges, of a temporary nature.").

56 M. Galanter and U. Baxi, "Panchayat justice: an Indian experiment in legal access" in M. Cappelletti and B. Garth (eds.), *Access To Justice, Vol. III: Emerging Issues and Perspectives* (Alphen aan den Rijn: Sijthoff and Noordhoff, 1978), pp. 341–85.

57 *Ibid.* at 78. See also R. Kushawaha, *Working of Nyaya Panchayats In India: A Case Study Varanas District* (Young Asia Publications, 1977), p. 99 (noting that in his study of Varansi district in Uttar Pradesh, "during the eleven years (1960–70) only 10,449 cases were instituted before 289 Nyaya Panchayats in the whole of the district. This works out at an average of 4 cases per Nyaya Panchayat per year.").

58 C. S. Meschievitz and M. Galanter, "In search of nyaya panchayats: the politics of a moribund institution" in Richard L. Abel (ed.), *The Politics of Informal Justice: Comparative Studies* (New York: Academic Press, 1982), vol. II, pp. 47–77, 55, 64–67.

of village tribunals. As Catherine Meschievitz concluded, "the N[yaya] P[anchayat] is thus a body of men … that handles disputes without regard to applicable rules and yet appears to villagers as formal and incomprehensible."[59]

Nevertheless, the panchayat idea continued to exert a powerful attraction on legal intellectuals. The 1973 report of the Expert Committee on Legal Aid, chaired by (and consisting of) Justice Krishna Iyer, a report that viewed itself as a radical critique of Indian legal arrangements, speaks glowingly of *nyaya panchayats* as part of a larger scheme of legal aid and access to the courts. Panchayats are endorsed as a method of incorporating lay participation into the administration of justice. But it is clear that the justice in mind is a more formal justice, the law of the land, and not that of the villagers or their spiritual advisers. Panchayats are commended as inexpensive, accessible, expeditious and suitable to preside over conciliatory proceedings. The *panches* envisioned by the report are not village notables but superannuated judges and retired advocates.[60]

A follow-up report by the Justice P. N. Bhagwati Committee, charged with proposing concrete measures to secure access to justice for the poor, endorses a system of "law and justice at the panchayat level with a conciliatory methodology."[61] The argument was that panchayats would remove many of the defects of the British system of administration of justice, since they would be staffed by people with knowledge of local customs and habits, attitudes and values, who were familiar with the ways of living and thought of the parties before them. Yet again the proposed panchayats do not depart from established notions of law. There was to be a presiding judge having knowledge of law, and the lay members were to receive rudimentary legal training. There would be no lawyers and the tribunal would proceed informally, its decisions subject to review by the district court. What was proposed was an informal, conciliatory, non-adversarial small claims court with some lay participation. These reports – written by distinguished, activist judges dedicated to enlarging access to justice – thus registered the appeal of the

[59] *Ibid.* p. 66.

[60] India Expert Committee on Legal Aid, V. R. Krishna Iyer, *Processual Justice to the People: Report of the Expert Committee on Legal Aid* (Department of Legal Affairs, India Ministry of Law, Justice & Company Affairs, 1973).

[61] See P. N. Bhagwati, *Report On National Juridicare: Equal Justice-Social Justice* (Ministry of Law, Justice & Company Affairs, 1976), pp. 33–4.

locally based "indigenous" forum under the guidance of an educated and beneficent outsider.[62]

The catalyst in the formation of a local justice template was an influential 1976 article by Upendra Baxi, one of India's most prominent legal academics, well connected to activist circles within the judiciary. Baxi described a "Lok Adalat" in a tribal area of Gujarat.[63] This forum was independent of the official law, both institutionally and normatively, although it bore no evident connection to traditional tribal institutions. As in the Krishna Iyer and Bhagwati reports, the imagery of indigenous justice was combined with celebration of conciliation and local responsiveness under the leadership of an educated outsider. These visions of paternalistic indigenous justice provided the basis for future developments.

The end of Emergency Rule and the return to democracy in 1977 brought great ferment in the Indian legal world and inspired hope that institutions and organizations could be fashioned to protect the rights of the powerless. Yet, the efforts on this front were advocated differently from before. Rather than promoting an enhancement of power for judges at the lower levels, legal elites in India sought to have the upper courts, and particularly the Supreme Court, take the lead. The Court's public reputation had been damaged during the Emergency era, as it was seen as not doing enough to protect the rule of law. As such, in order to repair its image and strengthen its legitimacy, the Court embarked on a series of unprecedented and electrifying initiatives. These included relaxation of requirements of standing, appointment of investigative commissions, appointment of lawyers as representatives of client groups, and a letter-based jurisdiction in which judges took the initiative to respond proactively to grievances brought to their attention by third parties, letters, or newspaper accounts. Public interest litigation, or social action litigation, as these initiatives have been called, sought to use judicial power to protect excluded and powerless groups (such as prisoners, migrant laborers, and the environmentally susceptible) and to secure entitlements that were going unredeemed.

These new initiatives envisioned purposive operations of a scale, scope, and continuity that would enable lawyers to acquire specialized expertise, coordinate efforts on several fronts, select targets and manage

[62] See *ibid.* for support for these statements.

[63] U. Baxi, "From Takrar to Karar: the Lok Adalat at Rangpur," *Journal of Constitutional and Parliamentary Studies*, 10 (1976), 52.

the sequence and pace of litigation, monitor developments, and deploy resources to maximize the long-term advantage of a client group. The notion was to relieve disadvantaged groups from dependence on extraordinary, spontaneous personal interventions and thus to enable legal work to be calculating and purposive rather than atomistic.

Public interest litigation has promoted important social changes, raised public awareness of many issues, energized citizen action, ratcheted up governmental accountability, and enhanced the legitimacy of the judiciary. But there have been limitations as well. For example, there has often been an inability to resolve disputed questions of fact, weakness in delivering concrete remedies and monitoring performance, reliance on generalist volunteers with no organizational staying power, and dissociation from the organizations and priorities of the disadvantaged. Furthermore, while affirming and dramatically broadcasting norms of human rights, the courts hearing public interest litigation claims frequently have been unable to secure systematic implementation of these norms.[64] And public interest litigation has at times aroused considerable resistance both from those who opposed its program and from those who were discomfited by the re-casting of the judicial role.[65]

For these reasons, and particularly since the mid-1980s, there have been efforts to find other ways to increase access to justice to those at the grassroots. A range of alternative dispute resolution bodies have emerged over the past three decades, which have sought to deliver remedies to claimants in a timely and just fashion. Yet the evidence to date on how well these forums work is both mixed and limited. For supporters, that these alternative bodies may provide actual judgments in a faster fashion than the regular courts is an enormous benefit that the parties (and regular lower court judges whose dockets are reduced) greatly appreciate. For others, however, the performance of these alternatives can be highly problematic, both in terms of effectiveness in resolving cases and in the quality of justice received by the parties. We turn to this issue in the final part of this chapter.

[64] For empirical support for these two sentences, see C. R. Epp, *The Rights Revolution: Lawyers, Activists, and Supreme Courts in Comparative Perspectives* (University of Chicago Press, 1998) at chapters 5 and 6. For an earlier critique of public interest litigation, see S. K. Agarwal, *Public Interest Litigation in India: A Critique* (Mumbai: N. M. Tripathi, 1985).

[65] See Galanter and Krishnan, "Bread for the poor," 791–7; Agarwal, *Public Interest Litigation in India*, p. 10–13 (identifying several Supreme Court judges who have expressed "a not-too-friendly posture to PIL [public interest litigation]").

6 Conclusion: more courts, more justice ... or not[66]

As has been intimated to this point but will be made explicitly now, a major issue concerning the Indian judiciary is the proliferation of courts – particularly as it has emerged within the lower tier, where legal life for most Indians is centered. Throughout the 1980s, 1990s, and into the 2000s, the government engaged in the expansion of specialized bodies to curb the tremendous backlog of cases in the regular district and sub-district courts. Specialized bodies are encouraged for all types of disputes that might otherwise enter into the regular courts. Again, the underlying premise is that if these matters could be disposed of rather quickly, then there would be no need to have the cases take up space in the regular courts.

Yet very little is known about how these bodies operate throughout the country. What do they look like? How do they function? Do they bring about settlements more regularly and equitably? Are people really able to obtain satisfaction on claims that they bring?

More needs to be investigated on these forums in greater detail, but what is known to date is that, given that there are so many different types of specialized bodies, it should not be surprising that there is great variation among these alternative settings. For example, some of these forums have very sophisticated lawyers; some do not. There is variation on the frequency of when hearings will be held. And whether the parties, lawyers, and judges appear varies from specialized forum to specialized forum.[67]

With this said, however, what is striking is how many similarities are present within these specialized bodies. For one thing, the process tends to be less weighted toward conciliation, mediation or negotiation, and much more adversarial in nature. Among the judges, there tends to be very little diversity of experience, with most being existing district court judges wearing the hats of specialized judges, or in some cases senior retired judges serving as specialized court judges. Relatedly, most specialized court judges are not skilled experts in the cases in which they are presiding. In addition, there is often informality and a lack of professionalism in these proceedings. At the same time, this informality

[66] This final section draws upon and excerpts work from Krishnan et al., "Grappling at the grassroots" and Galanter and Krishnan, "Bread for the poor."

[67] See *ibid.* at both cites, also see N. Robinson, "Failed by the lawyer," *The Hindu*, 6 July 2013, www.thehindu.com/opinion/op-ed/failed-by-the-lawyer/article4885640.ece.

can be simply a way of masking the lawyers' and judges' own unfamiliarity with the technicalities and nuances of the particular specialized court with which they are involved.

There is also often poor record-keeping across the specialized bodies – with no ability or method to reference precedent, properly manage files, or handle other administrative needs of the claimants. Consider as well the typically large power imbalances between the parties during the proceedings that have an obvious impact on the type of outcomes that are achieved. And many of the practices and norms that occur in the regular courts often are found in the specialized forums – particularly the negative feature of delay.

Overall, what is needed is for the system to be better streamlined, with the regular, specialized, and administrative courts organized in more efficient ways. Everyday claimants have great difficulty with the most basic aspects of trying to redress their grievances. There is, for instance, tremendous confusion on how to fill out paperwork required by the respective legal forums. Even before such forms are completed, there is the burden on the claimant to determine which court to enter to proceed with the complaint. Then, once in the forum that the claimant believes is correct, there is the likelihood that the claimant will be redirected to another institution that is thought to be the more appropriate one. In terms of legal procedures, there is no uniformity within the different legal forums for:

- what types of evidence are allowed;
- who is allowed to testify;
- how much lawyers are able to be involved in defending their clients; and
- whether appeals to higher bodies are permitted.

Essentially, therefore, what exist today are multiple tracks of courts with confusingly overlapping jurisdictions, where bureaucratic red tape is so overwhelming that its sheer presence frustrates many who participate within the process and likely deters others contemplating pursuing such a path. Moreover, how a case ends up in one track versus another seems to have little to do with protocol or established procedure than with the idiosyncratic norms of where the matter is initially brought.

This confusion and lack of synthesis has to come to an end. The amount of time and energy wasted trying to decipher the complicated procedures and pathways to the correct adjudicatory sites could all be saved if the government were simply to provide clear and proper guidelines to claimants. Concomitantly, the government needs to ensure that court staff are better equipped to deal with claimants' queries regarding the litigation process, because often these staff administrators themselves are unsure about what cases should go to which forums.

In conclusion, if India hopes to continue as an inspiring light as it has been for the last sixty years, its judicial system – particularly at the lower level – must address the many issues above and contemplate much-needed reforms. Since its upper judiciary has indeed served as a shining example of how law can be used as a source of empowerment, there is already a foundation upon which to build. This chapter has sought to highlight these positives as well as to note the challenges, all in the belief that India's future is nothing but hopeful and bright in the years ahead.

References

Agarwal, S. K. *Public Interest Litigation in India: A Critique* (Mumbai: N. M. Tripathi, 1985)

Austin, G. *The Indian Constitution: Cornerstone of a Nation* (Oxford: Clarendon Press, 1966)

Baxi, U. "From Takrar to Karar: the Lok Adalat at Rangpur," *Journal of Constitutional and Parliamentary Studies* (1976), 52–115

Bhagwati, P. N. *Report on National Juridicare: Equal Justice-Social Justice* (Ministry of Law, Justice & Company Affairs, 1976)

Dumont, L. *Homo Hierarchicus: The Caste System and Its Implications* (University of Chicago Press, 1970)

Epp, C. R. *The Rights Revolution: Lawyers, Activists, and Supreme Courts in Comparative Perspectives* (University of Chicago Press, 1998)

Galanter, M. "Why the 'haves' come out ahead: speculations on the limits of legal change," *Law & Society Review*, 9 (1974), 95–160

Galanter, M. and Baxi, U. "Panchayat justice: an Indian experiment in legal access" in M. Cappelletti and B. Garth (eds.), *Access to Justice, Vol. III: Emerging Issues and Perspectives* (Alphen aan den Rijn: Sijthoff and Noordhoff, 1978), pp. 341–85

Galanter, M. and Krishnan, J. K. "Bread for the poor: access to justice and the rights of the needy in India," *Hastings Law Journal*, 55 (2004), 789–834

Galanter, M. and Krishnan, J. K. "Personal law and human rights in India and Israel," *Israel Law Review*, 34 (2000), 101–33

Hayden, R. *Disputes and Arguments Amongst Nomads* (Oxford University Press, 1999)

Krishna Iyer, V. R. *Processual justice to the people: Report of the Expert Committee on Legal Aid, May 1973* (New Delhi: Department of Legal Affairs, Ministry of Law, Justice & Company Affairs, Government of India, 1974)

Krishnan, J. K. "From the ALI to the ILI: the efforts to export an American legal institution," *Vanderbilt Journal of Transnational Law*, 38 (2005), 1255–94

Krishnan, J. K. "Globetrotting law firms," *Georgetown Journal of Legal Ethics*, 23 (2010), 57–102

Krishnan, J. K. "Lawyering for a cause and experiences from abroad," *California Law Review*, 94 (2006), 575–616

Krishnan, J. K. "Outsourcing and the globalizing legal profession," *William and Mary Law Review*, 48 (2007), 2189–246

Krishnan, J. K. "Professor Kingsfield goes to Delhi: American academics, the Ford Foundation, and the development of legal education in India," *American Journal of Legal History*, 46 (2004), 447–99

Krishnan, J. K. "Scholarly discourse, public perceptions, and the cementing of norms: the case of the Indian Supreme Court and a plea for research," *Journal of Appellate Practice & Process*, 9 (2007), 255–90

Krishnan, J. K., Kavadi, S. N., Girach, A., Khupkar, D., Kokal, K., Mazumdar, S., Nupur, M., Panday, G., Sen, A., Sodhi, A. and Shukla, B. T. "Grappling at the grassroots: access to justice in India's lower tier," *Harvard Human Rights Journal*, 27 (2014) (forthcoming)

Krishnan, J. K. and Kumar, C. R. "Delay in process, denial of justice: the jurisprudence & empirics of speedy trials in comparative perspective," *Georgetown Journal of International Law*, 42 (2011), 747–84

Krishnaswamy, S. *Democracy and Constitutionalism in India: A Study of the Basic Structure Doctrine* (Oxford University Press, 2009)

Kushawaha, R. *Working of Nyaya Panchayats in India: A Case Study Varanas District* (Young Asia Publications, 1977)

Law Commission of India. *One-Hundred Eighteenth Report on Method of Appointment of Subordinate Court/Subordinate Judiciary* (Law Commission of India, 1986)

Mansfield, J. H. "The personal laws or a uniform civil code?" in R. Baird (ed.), *Religion and Law in Independent India* (New Delhi: Manohar Publishers & Distributors, 1993), pp. 139–78

Menski, W. *Hindu Law: Beyond Tradition and Modernity* (Oxford University Press, 2003)

Meschievitz, C. S. and Galanter, M. "In search of nyaya panchayats: the politics of a moribund institution" in Richard L. Abel (ed.), The Politics of Informal Justice: Comparative Studies (New York: Academic Press, 1982), vol. II, pp. 47–77

Robinson, N. "A quantitative analysis of the Indian Supreme Court's workload," *Journal of Empirical Legal Studies*, 10 (2013), 570–601

Robinson, N. "Structure matters: the impact of court structure on the Indian and US Supreme Courts," *American Journal of Comparative Law*, 61 (2013), 173–208

Sathe, S. P. *Administrative Law in India*, 7th edn. (Butterworths/LexisNexis, 2010)

Sathe, S. P. *Judicial Activism in India: Transgressing Borders and Enforcing Limits* (Oxford University Press, 2002)

8

Courts in Indonesia: a mix of Western and local character

HIKMAHANTO JUWANA

The judicial system in Indonesia resembles that of other countries that have adopted modern, Western legal systems. This resemblance is a result of European influence tracing back to the period when the Netherlands colonized Indonesia. At the time, the Dutch government did not apply Dutch law to indigenous Indonesians but instead created a separate judicial system. Dutch influence ended soon after Indonesia declared its independence in 1945. Interestingly, however, the newly independent government retained the laws and institutions of the colonial period, including the judiciary. This may explain to some extent the resemblance of the Indonesian legal system to those of European countries.

1 Structure and jurisdictions of courts

1.1 Structure of the courts

The judicial system is centralized in the Supreme Court. All courts except the Constitutional Court remain within and under the Supreme Court's structure. The first attempt to replace the law governing the court system was made in 1948. At the time, the government issued Regulation Number 19 concerning Judicial Bodies within the Republic of Indonesia (*Peraturan tentang Badan-badan Pengadilan dalam Daerah Republik Indonesia*), whereby the court system was structured into three tiers, namely, the District Courts (*Pengadilan Negeri*), the High Courts (*Pengadilan Tinggi*), and the Supreme Court (*Mahkamah Agung*).[1]

The author would like to thank M. Ajisatria Suleiman and Harjo Winoto for their assistance.

[1] See R. Tresna, *Peradilan di Indonesia dari Abad ke Abad* (*Indonesian Judiciaries from Century to Century*) (Jakarta: W. Versluys NV, 1957), p. 82.

Unfortunately, the regulation never took effect, as the Dutch clamped down on the "secessionist movements" of the colony.[2]

In 1964, the government introduced an Act governing the court system and replacing the Dutch colonial law. The Act is dubbed the Act on Basic Provisions of Judicial Power (the Act and its amendments will be referred to in this chapter as the "Judicial Power Act").[3]

The Judicial Power Act divides the court system horizontally into four jurisdictions, namely, General Tribunals (*Peradilan Umum*), Religious Tribunals (*Peradilan Agama*) or tribunals dealing with Islam religion matters, Military Tribunals (*Peradilan Militer*) and Administrative Tribunals (*Peradilan Tata Usaha Negara*).[4] The Act further divides the four tribunals vertically into three tiers, namely, courts of first instance, courts of appeal and the court of cassation.

In 1969, the government repealed the Judicial Power Act due to its inconsistency with the Constitution.[5] However, the Act states that its repeal would only take effect when an amending Act has been promulgated. Thus, theoretically the Judicial Power Act of 1964 was still effective at that time.

A little less than one year later, in 1970 an amending Act was promulgated. The new Judicial Power Act was dubbed Act 14 as it bears the number 14.[6] Act 14 completely amended the Judicial Power Act of 1964, although it still maintained some of its basic principles.

Act 14 of 1970 was amended by Act 35 of 1999 and repealed by Act 4 of 2004, which was in turn repealed and replaced in 2009 by Act 48 of 2009. Act 48 of 2009 is currently the law governing judicial power in Indonesia.

One of the purposes of the amendments was to foster judicial independence. Judicial independence was non-existent under the Judicial Power Act of 1970, as the organizational, administrative and financial aspects of the four types of tribunals of the lower and appellate courts were under the purview of the executive branch of the government.[7] The

[2] H. Juwana, *Dispute Resolution Process in Indonesia* (Japan: Institute of Developing Economics, 2003), pp. 7–10. Although Indonesia proclaimed its independence on 17 August 1945, the Dutch government did not recognize this and treated the proclamation by Soekarno and M. Hatta as a secessionist movement against which it had the authority to take forceful action under its internal law. It was not until 1949 that Indonesia gained recognition as a full-fledged sovereign state when the Dutch government finally recognized it as such.

[3] Act No. 19 of 1964, State Gazette No. 107 of 1964.

[4] Judicial Power Act, Art. 7(1).

[5] The Article that is inconsistent with the Constitution is Article 1, which states that "For the interest of revolution, dignity of State and Nations or the urgent interest of society, the President may intervene in judicial affairs."

[6] Act No. 14 of 1970, State Gazette No. 74 of 1970.

[7] Judicial Power Act of 1970, Art. 11(1). The article provides that "Institutions carrying out judicial power provided under Article 10(1) are under the purview of each Department."

general and administrative tribunals were under the purview of the Department of Justice and Human Rights, the religious tribunals were under the purview of the Department for Religious Affairs, and the military tribunals were under the purview of the Department of Defense.

The amendments of the Judicial Power Act effectively transferred to the judiciary the administrative affairs of the judges previously held by the executive branch. At the initial stage, the Department of Justice and Human Rights became the first executive branch with the obligation to transfer authority over the general and administrative tribunals to the Supreme Court. The transfer, as provided under the amending Act, was completed in 2004.[8] The other executive departments, the Department of Religious Affairs for the Religious Courts and the Department of Defense for the Military Courts, followed.

In addition, other Acts have stipulated certain provisions of the Judicial Power Act in greater detail. The detailed provisions on the Supreme Court, for example, are further elaborated under Act 14 of 1985 ("the Supreme Court Act"), which is amended by Act 5 of 2004 and Act 3 of 2009. The detailed provisions on the general tribunal are stipulated under Act 2 of 1986 ("the General Tribunal Act"), which is amended by Act 8 of 2004 and Act 49 of 2009.[9]

The court structure in Indonesia is complex.[10] First, it must be understood that the judiciary has two branches: (1) the Supreme Court and (2) the Constitutional Court.[11] The Supreme Court has four branches, which can be found in each regency and province in Indonesia. This is not the case with the Constitutional Court, which only sits in the capital city of Indonesia.

Under the Supreme Court, the jurisdiction of courts is divided into the four types of tribunals described earlier, namely, general tribunals, religious tribunals, military tribunals and administrative tribunals. These tribunals have their own jurisdictions, which are referred to in the Indonesian language as "*Peradilan.*"

[8] Amendment of Article 11 of the Judicial Power Act. This amendment also has consequences for the General Tribunal Act, Art. 5, para. 2, which states that the supervision of organization, administration and financial matters shall rest upon the Ministry of Justice.

[9] The provision on this matter is stipulated under Article 12 of the Judicial Power Act.

[10] For further reading on the history of the Indonesian courts, see K. Soetoprawiro, *Pemerintahan & Peradilan di Indonesia: Asal Usul dan Perkembangannya* (*The Government and Judiciary in Indonesia: The History and Its Development*) (Bandung: Citra Aditya Bakti, 1994).

[11] Article 18 of the Judicial Power Act of 2009. The article reads, "The power of the judiciary rests on a Supreme Court and courts below which work in four branches, namely the general court, the religious court, the military court and the administrative court, and a Constitutional Court."

Private disputes, except for cases regarding family law matters between Muslims, fall under the jurisdiction of the general tribunals (*Peradilan Umum*). Family law matters between Muslims fall under the religious tribunals (*Peradilan Agama*). This distinction is based on two criteria: the first is the nature of the case; the second is the religion of the disputing parties.

Public-initiated disputes, unless committed by a member of the armed forces, fall under the jurisdiction of the general tribunals (*Peradilan Umum*). Members of the armed forces are tried in the military tribunals (*Peradilan Militer*) even if the offense is not military in nature. Here, the distinction is not based on what offense is committed, but rather on whether or not the accused is a member of the military/armed forces.

Lastly, any public defendant dispute falls under the jurisdiction of the administrative tribunals (*Peradilan Tata Usaha Negara*).

In the event that there is conflicting jurisdiction between courts, the Supreme Court, under the Supreme Court Act, has the final say as to which court has jurisdiction over the case in question.[12] Of course, it will require a certain amount of time for the Supreme Court to decide on the issue.

Under the Judicial Power Act, the court hierarchy consists of three tiers. The lowest tier is the lower court, which is referred to in Indonesian as "*Pengadilan*."[13] The court of first instance is established by Presidential Decree.[14] The court in the next tier is the court of appeal, which is referred to as "*Pengadilan Tinggi*." The appellate court is established in each province by statute.[15]

The apex of Indonesian courts is the Supreme Court, which is referred to as "*Mahkamah Agung*."[16] Constitutionally, the Supreme Court is positioned at a level similar to that of the President and the House of Representatives (DPR). The Supreme Court as a court of last instance is vested under the Supreme Court Act with three broad powers.[17] First is

[12] Supreme Court Act, Art. 56.

[13] Jurisdiction and hierarchy are determined by the Judicial Power Act. Reference to jurisdiction in the Indonesian language is "*Pe**ra**dilan*" and hierarchy is "*Pen**g**adilan*."

[14] General Tribunal Act, Act No. 2 of 1986, *ibid.* Article 7 provides that the establishment of a district court is based on a Presidential Decree.

[15] *Ibid.* Art. 9 provides that the establishment of the High Court is by statute.

[16] Judicial Power Act, Art. 20(1); Supreme Court Act, Art. 2.

[17] The Supreme Court is also vested with other powers, such as judicial review, supervision of courts, and supervision of judges.

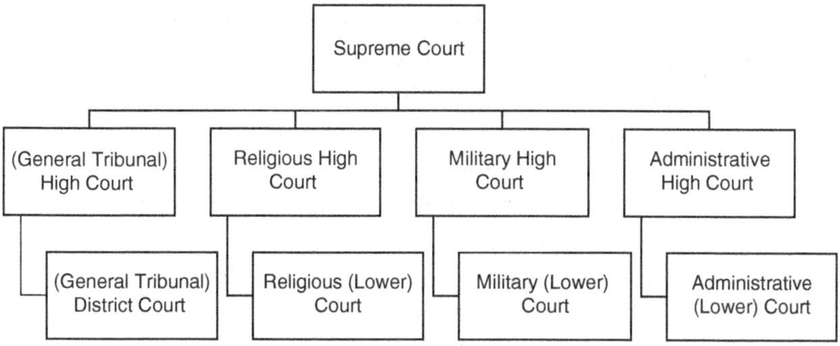

Figure 8.1: Judicial system in Indonesia
Source: H. Juwana, *Dispute Resolution Process in Indonesia* (Japan: Institute of Developing Economics, 2003), p. 15.

the power to examine and decide cassation applications.[18] Second is the power to examine and decide on conflicting jurisdiction between tribunals.[19] The third is the power to re-open or re-examine a case that has an enforceable verdict, referred to as *Peninjauan Kembali* (abbreviated as "*PK*").[20] Figure 8.1 above describes the jurisdiction and hierarchy of the Indonesian judicial system.

1.2 Special courts

Below are several specialized courts under the Supreme Court, specifically under the general tribunal category.

1.2.1 Syari'ah tribunals

The Nanggroe Aceh Darussalam Act establishes Syari'ah tribunals (*Mahkamah Syari'ah*), which are different from the religious courts. The religious courts have jurisdiction over family (civil) matters, while the Syari'ah tribunals have jurisdiction over cases involving Muslims who violate the syari'ah law.[21]

[18] Supreme Court Act, Art. 28(1) a. [19] *Ibid.* Art. 28(1) b.
[20] *Ibid.* Art. 28(1) c, Arts. 67–76; Judicial Power Act, Art. 24(1).
[21] The Nanggroe Aceh Darussalam Act was promulgated by virtue of Act No. 18 of 2001, State Gazette No. 114 of 2001, and was later repealed by Act No. 11 of 2006.

1.2.2 Commercial courts

The Amendment to the Bankruptcy Act, Act No. 4 of 1998, created special courts tasked specifically with resolving commercial cases, including bankruptcy, referred to as commercial courts.[22] Commercial courts are discussed in greater detail in Bankruptcy Act No. 37 of 2004, which replaced the previous Bankruptcy Act. The commercial courts are within the jurisdiction of the district courts and are first instance courts. The commercial courts were established through Presidential Decree No. 97 of 1999, and the first court was established in Jakarta at the Central Jakarta District Court. The Decree allows for the future establishment of additional commercial courts in Bandung, Semarang, Surabaya, and Medan. It is important to note that any appeal against a decision of a commercial court is submitted directly to the Supreme Court.

The commercial courts were established with at least two goals in mind. The first was to have a court with career judges knowledgeable about insolvency or other economic law matters. In the context of the Bankruptcy Act, the judges were selected from a list of career judges from all over Indonesia, who then had to undergo training in bankruptcy law. The second purpose of the commercial courts was to provide for the possibility of introducing new concepts to the court system without tampering with the generally accepted mechanisms and procedures governing the majority of cases. These new concepts include the introduction of non-career judges, dissenting opinions, and a scaled remuneration system.[23]

1.2.3 Tax court

Indonesia has had a Tax Review Tribunal (*Institusi Pertimbangan Pajak*) since 1915 (Staatsblaad No. 707/1915), based in Batavia (Jakarta). The Tax Review Tribunal was later renamed the Tax Review Council (*Majelis Pertimbangan Pajak*), and its primary function was to review and assess applications seeking a review of central and regional government taxes. The Council performed these functions until 1997, when these functions were taken over by the Tax Dispute Settlement Board (*Badan Penyelesaian Sengketa Pajak* or BPSP), which was established under the provisions of Law No. 17 of 1997.[24]

[22] The Amendment to the Bankruptcy Act was promulgated in 1998 by virtue of Act No. 4 of 1998, which was later replaced by Act No. 37 of 2004, State Gazette No. 208 of 2000.

[23] H. Juwana et al. (eds.), *Indonesian Legal System* (ASEAN Law Association, 2005), pp. 62–3.

[24] *Ibid.* pp. 65–8.

Despite the tax dispute settlement mechanisms in place, the government believed that the way to have an efficient, effective, and comprehensive way to resolve tax dispute matters was to have a court expressly created for that purpose. Therefore, Act No. 14 of 2002 on the Tax Court was enacted. The Tax Court is a special court with limited jurisdiction, as it is only able to hear and decide tax matters. Physically, the Court is a special Chamber of the Administrative Court system and as such is ultimately under the control of the Supreme Court (stated in the elucidation of Article 15, Act No. 9 of 2004 on Amendment of Act No. 5 of 1985 on Administrative Court).[25]

Prior to the submission of an application to the tax court, the taxpayer may file his or her petition to the relevant authority or the Directorate General of Taxation. In the event the petitioner is unsatisfied with the outcome of the petition, he or she may lodge an appeal at the tax court.

The decisions of the tax court are meant to be final and binding. However, a decision of the tax court can be appealed to the Supreme Court, seeking extraordinary legal remedy within three months of the decision, provided one of the following conditions is met: (1) the decision is considered to be based on an act of perjury or deception; (2) there is new and important written evidence that could have altered the decision if it had been discovered during the appeal or the original case; or (3) the decision clearly does not conform with prevailing tax regulations.

1.2.4 Labor court

Act No. 12 of 1964 requires that a "Pegawai Perantara" or a compulsory mediator process a labor dispute in the first instance. If the dispute is not settled amicably at this stage, the matter is assigned to the P4D (*Panitia Penyelesaian Perselisihan Peburuhan Daerah*) or Regional Committee for Labor Dispute Settlement. In the event that the decision issued by the P4D is rejected by one of the parties, that party could appeal to the P4P (*Panitia Penyelesaian Perselisihan Perburuhan Pusat*) or Central Committee for Labor Dispute Settlement. Essentially, the P4D and the P4P are arbiters tasked with resolving labor disputes.[26]

In December 2003 a new labor law was passed by the DPR and was enacted as Act No. 2 of 2004 on Settlement for Industrial Relations Dispute. The law is comprehensive and includes 8 chapters, 126 articles, and 204 sub-sections. A fundamental difference between the previous

[25] *Ibid.* [26] *Ibid.* pp. 68–9.

regulatory regime and the new regulatory regime encompassed in the new law is the establishment of the Industrial Relations Dispute Settlement Court. This court will ultimately be the highest judicial body in the resolution of all labor disputes.[27]

1.2.5 Children's court

The procedures in the children's court are basically the same as the procedures in a conventional criminal court. However, a few special provisions were enacted to ensure that the rights of the child are protected at all times.[28] Act No. 11 of 2012 on Juvenile Criminal Justice System ("Juvenile Criminal Law") further provides protection for both underage criminal perpetrators and witnesses, including the application of certain special procedures.

First, if the child who allegedly committed the crime was within the age range stated in the Law – that is, eight to eighteen years old – at the time of the crime but has reached the age of eighteen (but not yet reached the age of twenty-one) prior to the case reaching the criminal trial phase, the matter will still be heard in the children's court. Second, where a child alleged to have committed a crime has not yet reached the age of eight years, the child will still undergo investigation by a state investigator. The state investigator will then determine whether the child should remain with his or her parents or recognized guardian and be raised by them or instead become a ward of the state under the auspices of the Department of Social Affairs. Generally, the procedures to hear matters in the children's court are the same as those in the courts of criminal jurisdiction.

The children's court must ensure that the interests of the child are protected throughout the proceedings. Children who commit crimes in the company of adults will have their matters heard in the children's court, and the adults will be brought before the court with the relevant criminal jurisdiction. All children's court matters are to be heard in a closed court, thereby ensuring the confidentiality of the identity of the child. Nevertheless, the closed court principle is not absolute, and a judge may open the court to public access in the event that the subject matter of the trial warrants it. In any event the judge maintains the discretion to permit attendance of other individuals during the trial; however, this discretion still only allows the judge to permit attendance of individuals

[27] *Ibid.* [28] *Ibid.* pp. 71–2.

who have some relationship to the subject matter of the trial or who may contribute to bringing the matter to a conclusion.[29]

1.2.6 Human rights court

In 1999, the Indonesian government issued the Human Rights Act, Article 104 of which mandates that a court with specific jurisdiction over gross human rights violations be instituted. Following this mandate, in 2000, the government passed the Human Rights Court Act.

The Human Rights Court Act establishes the human rights tribunal and the ad hoc human rights tribunal, which are special chambers within the district court dealing with individuals accused of gross human rights violations. An ad hoc human rights tribunal hears cases involving gross human rights violations that occurred prior to the enactment of the Human Rights Court Act. The term "ad hoc" is used to refer to this type of tribunal because it is convened on an ad hoc basis by the President following approval from the DPR.

1.3 Constitutional Court and judicial review

The Constitutional Court was established during the third series of amendments to the Constitution that were enacted on 9 November 2001 after the fall of former President Soeharto.

Indonesia is the seventy-eighth country to establish a Constitutional Court, which in the Indonesian language is referred to as "Mahkamah Konstitusi."[30]

Prior to the establishment of the Constitutional Court, judicial review of legislation was one of the many functions of the Supreme Court. The Supreme Court still retains this function but on a much more restrictive mandate.

After the adoption of the relevant constitutional amendments, the People's Consultative Assembly (MPR) decreed that the Supreme Court would maintain the authority of the Constitutional Court until such time as the Constitutional Court was ready to assume its constitutional functions pursuant to Article III of the Transitional Provisions of the Constitution. However, this did not occur until the enactment of Act No. 24 of 2003 on the Constitutional Court.

[29] *Ibid.* [30] *Ibid.* pp. 58–9.

On 15 August 2003, the President swore in nine Constitutional Court Justices appointed from three branches of the government: the executive, the parliament and the judiciary each appointed three justices.

The Constitutional Court is a court of first and final instance in that justices have the authority to hold trials at both the first instance and appellate stages. The final decisions issued by the Court are deemed to be binding and may pertain to the following: (1) the constitutional validity of Acts; (2) disputes between state institutions; (3) the dissolution of political parties; (4) disputes related to the results of general elections; and (5) allegations of treason, corruption, bribery, and other serious criminal offences against the President and Vice-President.[31]

Judicial review of subordinate pieces of legislation (government regulations, presidential regulations, and ministerial regulations, among others), are still handled by the Supreme Court. Supreme Court Regulation No. 1 of 2011 serves as the guiding document for the Supreme Court's judicial review, according to which the process is basically one of document exchange, without any face-to-face trial or witness/expert hearing, in contrast to judicial review at the Constitutional Court.

1.4 Size and performance of the courts

The total number of judges in 2012 under the Supreme Court was 7,780.[32] The Supreme Court currently has sixty justice positions in total, of which, as of December 2012, only forty-four were filled, compared with an average of fifty-one justices in past years. These justices handled 13,412 cases in 2012; 13,480 cases in 2010; and 12,540 cases in 2009.[33] Those cases were filtered down from the following numbers of cases in the courts of first instance (also known as district courts): 3,037,036 cases in 2010; 3,531,613 cases in 2011; and 4,058,446 cases in 2012. In 2010, the total number of cases filed in all first instance courts was 3,037,036, with 104,444 cases remaining from 2009. Among the total of 3,141,460 cases, 3,028,916 cases were decided in 2010 and 112,564 cases remained. The details are distributed in the following Table 8.1.

[31] *Ibid.* p. 97. [32] *Annual Report of the Supreme Court of Indonesia 2012*, p. 36.

[33] *Annual Report of the Supreme Court of Indonesia 2010* and *2012*. Available at http://kepaniteraan.mahkamahagung.go.id/laporan-tahunan/120-laporan-tahunan-2010.html (accessed 28 July 2013), www.pembaruanperadilan.net/v2/content/2013/06/LAPTAH-MA-2012.pdf (accessed 4 September 2013).

Table 8.1: *Breakdown of cases by categories in first instance courts*

Type of tribunal	Remaining from 2009	Incoming in 2010	Amount	Decided	Remaining in 2010
General	36,938	2,705,231	2,742,169	2,703,265	38,904
Religion	56,478	320,904	377,382	314,407	62,975
Military	785	2,856	3,641	3,149	492
Administrative	420	1,348	1,768	1,107	661
Tax	9,823	6,697	16,520	6,988	9,532
Total amount	**104,444**	**3,307,036**	**3,141,480**	**3,028,916**	**112,564**

Source: Annual Report of the Supreme Court of Indonesia 2012, p. 57.

In 2010, the total number of cases filed in all courts of appeal was 14,681, with 2,643 cases remaining from 2009. Among the total of 17,324 cases, 14,172 cases were decided in 2010 and 3,152 cases remained. The details are distributed in Table 8.2.

Table 8.2: *Breakdown of cases by categories in courts of appeal*

Type of tribunal	Remaining from 2009	Incoming in 2010	Amount	Decided	Remaining in 2010
General	2,217	11,271	13,488	10,795	2,693
Religion	182	2,259	2,441	2,252	189
Military	128	332	460	374	86
Administrative	116	819	935	751	184
Total amount	**2,643**	**14,681**	**17,324**	**14,172**	**3,152**

Source: Annual Report of the Supreme Court of Indonesia 2012, p. 57.

The total number of cases filed in the Supreme Court in 2010 was 13,480, with 8,835 cases remaining from 2009. Among the total of 22,315 cases, 13,891 cases were decided in 2010 and 8,424 cases remained.[34]

2 Sources and influences of the establishment of the judicial system

2.1 Western influences under the pressure of modernization

Indonesia's legal system was not only influenced by the civil law system, but also by the common law system. Traditionally, the

[34] *Annual Report of the Supreme Court of Indonesia* 2010, p. 69.

Indonesian legal system was a civil law system due to the influence of the Dutch colonial government.

The influence of common law later became apparent due to the way in which the government drafted legislation. The government in many instances asked local scholars to advise them in drafting legislation. In the old days, many of the scholars were trained under the Dutch legal system and understood the Dutch language well. After 1980, this changed significantly.

The younger generation of scholars, due to their lack of fluency in the Dutch language, went to common law countries, such as the United States, the United Kingdom and Australia, to further their study. As a result, common law concepts have since been introduced in many pieces of legislation.

In addition, Indonesia has been assisted in its law reform efforts mostly by common law countries, especially post-1998. These countries in many instances dispatched their experts to Indonesia. These experts, in turn, have provided advice based on common law systems and have consequently influenced the law-making process and judicial behavior in Indonesia.

As a matter of fact, much of the commercial or business-related legislation, such as the Competition Act, Bankruptcy Act and Intellectual Property Act, were passed as a result of pressure from the International Monetary Fund and World Bank as a trade-off for receiving loans from these two international organizations. The Competition Act (Act No. 5 of 1999), for example, adopts numerous concepts from the US's Sherman Antitrust Act and Clayton Antitrust Act. One clear example is the introduction in Indonesia's Competition Act of the concept of trusts, which are prohibited under the Sherman Act but which were not previously recognized under Indonesia law.

Hence, there have been cases where a piece of legislation is based on the common law system, but the rules of procedure still use the civil law system. Also, there have been cases where legal institutions are established under the common law system where they are not known under the civil law system.

2.2 Colonialism

As mentioned in the first part of this chapter, the development of Indonesian law is intertwined with the history of Dutch colonialism. Indonesia was colonized by the Netherlands for almost 350 years and later occupied by Japan for three-and-a-half years during World War II. Some of the judicial system and substantive laws put in place by the Dutch are still enforced today.

In terms of the judicial system, the Dutch influence was arguably strongest during the Daendels Governorship. Under the Daendels Governorship many changes were made to the Indonesian system of justice that had been established by the Dutch. In 1798, Raad van Justitie became the Hooge Raad.

The period of English Colonialism saw the Raad van Justitie in Semarang, Batavia and Surabaya converted into the Courts of Justice. The Court of Justice of Batavia also became the Supreme Court of Justice and as such had the power to hear appeals of matters decided by the Courts of Justice in Semarang and Surabaya. With the return of the Dutch came the promulgation of St. 1819 No. 20 on Criminal and Civil Procedure which permitted a dual system of Indonesian justice to develop, particularly with respect to the hierarchy of courts.

Essentially, there were two separate judicial systems: one for indigenous Indonesians and one for Europeans. For Europeans, the functions and position of the Supreme Court were as follows: (1) to oversee the operation of the courts; (2) to act as "hov van casatie"; and (3) to serve as an appeal court for Raad van Justitie.

The Governor General Decree dated 3 December 1847 No. 2, which took effect on 1 May 1848 (RO), stated that the hierarchy of the courts in Madura and Java was as follows: Districtgerrecht, Regenschaptgerrecht, Landraad, Rechtbank van Omgang, and Hooggerechtshof (Supreme Court). Under this hierarchy, the courts were to be divided into two separate jurisdictions: one for the indigenous Indonesians and the other for Europeans. The Hooggerechtshof was a Supreme Court located in Jakarta. It had absolute authority over all jurisdictions in Indonesia to (1) oversee the operation of the courts; (2) supervise the conduct of the judges; and (3) settle disputes between the courts established on the authority of the King and any Adat Courts (courts with the power to hear matters related to indigenous law, or *adat*).[35]

After Independence, Government Decree No. 9/S.D. of 1946 stated that the Supreme Court was to sit in Jakarta. The Constitution of the Federal Republic of Indonesia stated that the Supreme Court was the highest federal court and was to sit in the capital city of the Federal State.

[35] H. Juwana et al. (eds.), *Indonesian Legal System*, pp. 51–2.

In terms of substantive laws adopted from the Dutch, some of the obvious examples are, *inter alia*, the Dutch Criminal and Civil Codes and the Code of Civil Procedure. There are three Dutch civil procedure laws that, with the exception of a few provisions, are still enforceable to date. First is the Revised Indonesian Rule of Procedures or *Reglemen Indonesia yang Diperbarui* (*Het Herziene Indonesisch Reglement* in Dutch).[36] Second is the Rule of Procedures Overseas (outside Java) or *Regelemen Daerah Seberang* (*Rechtsreglement voor De Buitengewesten* in Dutch).[37] The third is *Reglement op de Rechtsvor-dering*.[38] These three rules of procedure become the basis for civil litigation process in court.

2.3 *Democratization and social movements*

Democracy plays a central role in Indonesian history. In Soeharto's era, there were two particular flaws in the legal system and law making. First, the power of the executive branch pre-1998 was vast. It is not a coincidence that the first amendment to the Constitution during the post-1998 Reform Era shifted law-making power from the executive to the legislative branch.

This was done by amending Article 19 of the Constitution to explicitly stipulate that the House of Representatives has the power to make laws. The pre-1998 text stated that the President and the House of Representatives jointly make the laws. In addition, with regard to the structure of the judiciary, in the pre-1998 era, the judiciary was placed under the executive, i.e. under the Ministry of Justice. Thus, the Ministry of Justice had authority over the recruitment and supervision of judges. After 1998, during the Reform Era, the principle for which the judiciary advocated most was independence. As a result, the judiciary was completely separated from the executive branch and became viewed as a state organ equal to that of the executive and legislative branches.

2.4 *Tradition, religion and indigenous demands*

Tradition and religion affect law making to quite an extent. Indonesia still recognizes indigenous (*adat*) law, and *adat* law is closely connected to religion, belief and tradition.

[36] State Gazette No. 44 of 1941. [37] State Gazette No. 227 of 1927.
[38] State Gazette No. 52 of 1847 and State Gazette No. 63 of 1849.

Adat law applied to the indigenous community. The Islamic law applied to those who follow the Islamic teachings. The European legal system applied to the Dutch and other Europeans. *Adat* law has been upheld to a certain extent because it is considered a national treasure. Some principles under the various *adat* laws have been institutionalized in legislation at the national level. Islamic law is maintained due to the fact that the majority of the Indonesian population is Muslim.

In fact, in several important laws, *adat* law still plays a very important role. For example, the Agrarian Law explicitly recognizes the communal indigenous right to land (*hak ulayat*). The Marriage Law explicitly stipulates that a marriage institution is legal when it is carried out in accordance with the respective individual's religion.

2.5 Global economic competition and foreign trade influences

Global economic competition and foreign trade often exert influences upon the legal and judicial system in Indonesia. One of the indicators is the use of economic tests in the proceedings of KPPU (the Commission for the Supervision of Business Competition) to examine the implications of certain decisions on Indonesia's economic relationships with other states. Another example of the influence of global economic competition is in the field of arbitration, where consideration of national interests vis-à-vis foreign interests became the pivotal point of many judgments.

Also in the introduction of the competition law, nationalism is an issue prevalent in Indonesia today. However, its relationship to the judicial system and culture is not widely discussed. There seems to be a huge disconnect between the normative law and actual practice in Indonesia. To make this point clearer, one may turn to the competition law regime. Notably, the Competition Act (Act No. 5 of 1999) was among the series of laws enacted after the beginning of the Reform Era (1998). As a matter of fact, it was the fifth law enacted during the Reform Era.

Despite the controversy surrounding its enactment (being the result of political pressure from the IMF and World Bank), which is not the subject of the present discussion, the law adopts numerous concepts from US antitrust law, to the extent that some of the text is simply a translation of the text of the US law into the Indonesian language. However, in practice, due to the severe lack of coherence and clarity in the Competition Act, the authority in charge of implementing and elucidating it, the KPPU (the Commission for the Supervision of

Business Competition) issued numerous guidelines. These guidelines usually are consistent with the KPPU's decisions. Even when they are not consistent, the KPPU, in most of its decisions, relies on many of the European Union's competition law concepts. This is apparent from most of the references, standards, and economic tests that the KPPU has applied, which are based on the European Union's practices and decisions.

3 Judicial appointments, judicial independence and access to justice

3.1 Judicial appointments and qualifications of judges

Judges in Indonesia are appointed, not elected, and the Supreme Court and the Constitutional Court have different judicial appointment processes.

In the Supreme Court, candidates are first selected by the Judicial Commission. The selected candidates are then sent to the President, who will in turn ask the Parliament for approval of the candidates. The Parliament's approval is final, following which the President will then swear in the new Supreme Court justices. There are no strict criteria on which the Parliament must base its decisions in appointing judges to the Supreme Court. There have been several critics of the role of the Parliament when selecting Supreme Court justices.

Judges of courts under the Supreme Court are usually "career judges" who are appointed directly after law school. The main qualification to be a judge is to have an undergraduate law degree. The newly appointed judge will start work as a clerk before serving as a judge. Interested individuals can apply to the Supreme Court immediately after graduating from law school. The initial selection process is the same for candidates for the general courts and the administrative courts. The Supreme Court annually announces vacant positions and qualification criteria for all courts and conducts national examinations to fill those positions. The newly appointed judges will be appointed first as judicial candidates (*calon hakim*), and, once fully appointed, they will serve outside big cities and sometimes in remote places in Indonesia.

In the Supreme Court and its subordinate courts, judges may also be appointed from other legal professions. They are referred to as non-career judges. Candidates must, however, have been involved in a legal field for a certain number of years. Most are academics and practicing lawyers prior to becoming judges. All candidates must be at least 45 years of age and have an advanced degree in law and at least 20 years of experience.[39]

The appointment of Constitutional Court judges is completely different from that of Supreme Court judges. Each branch of the government – the executive, parliament and judiciary – has the power to appoint three candidates. The rationale for this is to minimize bias.

3.2 *Judicial independence*

Judicial independence can be assessed according the degree of interference of other branches of the government, i.e. the executive and the parliament, in the judicial process. The judiciary adopted a "one roof system" in 2004, pursuant to which all human resources management, budgeting, and planning were to be governed under the Supreme Court, as opposed to the previous system, in which the executive branch (through the Ministry of Justice) held administrative authority over the bureaucracy of the judiciary. At present, both administrative and judicial authority lie solely with the Supreme Court. However, the role of the parliament in the judicial selection process arguably reduces such judicial independence.

The eradication of judicial corruption is also a determinant in maintaining judicial independence. This is carried out by several programs, including case management reform, judicial transparency and dissemination of court decisions, and accessibility in judicial service provision.

However, in October 2013 the Chief Justice of the Constitutional Court was caught red-handed while accepting bribes. This has become a big issue that has severely weakened public trust in the Constitutional Court as an icon of integrity resulting from the Reform Era.

3.2.1 Tenure of judges

In general, judges in Indonesia can hold certain positions only for a certain period of time. The Chairman of the Constitutional Court, who is appointed by the Constitutional Court judges from amongst their midst, serves a term of two years and six months. The judges on the Supreme Court are appointed for five-year terms that are renewable once.

[39] Until Law No. 3 of 2009 changed it to 45 years of age, the minimum age requirement for Supreme Court candidates was 50 years of age.

3.2.2 Judicial budget

There is no explicit stipulation in the Constitution that allows the judiciary to independently propose its own budget, but one can infer from administrative practice that a state institution's budget requires certain levels of discussion with said institution. The House of Representatives is the authority that determines the budget and in doing so it will involve the judiciary.

3.2.3 The administration of the judiciary

As mentioned above, in the pre-1998 era, the judiciary was under the supervision of the Ministry of Justice, which thus had authority over the recruitment and supervision of judges. After 1998, during the Reform Era, the judiciary was completely separated from the executive branch and is viewed as a state organ equal to that of the executive and legislative branches.

However, the judicial system takes direct orders from the Supreme Court. In fact, it is said that judges dread the Supreme Court's circular letters more than the law itself. The Supreme Court has the authority to determine promotion, demotion and location of duty. This creates a high level of reward–punishment authority for the Supreme Court. This system can ensure more consistency and coherence between decisions, as judges will comply with the primary authority in determining procedural and substantive laws in certain issues.

3.3 Judicial training and related legal education

Legal education in Indonesia has a long history, having existed in Indonesia long before Indonesia became independent. The Dutch colonial government first established legal education at the secondary-school level, for the purpose of recruiting Indonesians to work as clerks in the courts. The colonial government gave this opportunity to Indonesians because importing Dutch clerks was very expensive.

At the time, however, Indonesians were not allowed to become judges. All judges were from the Netherlands. Later, the Dutch colonial government replaced the secondary-level legal education system with the university-level Rechthogeschool, or Higher School of Law. This school accepted Indonesians from middle-to-upper class Indonesian families whose parents were mostly public officials, such as mayors or civil servants.

After Indonesia's independence, the legal education system was transformed and supplied law graduates to fill all the various legal professions in the country. Currently there are a little over 200 Faculties of Law across Indonesia. This number does not include the Faculties of Sharia, which are faculties of Islamic law under Islamic universities.

There is a growing view that legal education and continuing legal education are very central to ensuring that judges have the abilities to carry out their duties well. The total amount of time required for candidate judges' training is 106 weeks.[40] There are six phases candidate judges must go through. Phase 1 is a two-week orientation, in which candidate judges receive training on administrative matters; in particular candidate judges are taught about the primary task and function of each court's secretariat. Phase 2 is an administrator internship. In this phase, candidate judges will be placed in their respective positions and secretariats in a court for roughly one month (in each department), and they are obliged to carry out their daily activities in order to eventually develop a proper understanding of the administration of the court.

Phase 3 is one in which candidate judges perform internship duties, for instance, as a substitute magistrate. In this phase, candidate judges will intensively study the hearing process and the primary tasks of a substitute magistrate for thirteen weeks. Phase 4 is a substitute magistrate internship, in which candidate judges will perform a local substitute magistrate's functions for twenty-six weeks. They will directly handle several pre-determined cases. These cases will be incrementally more difficult and complex to handle. Phase 5 prepares judges to perform the primary tasks and functions as a judge's assistant over a period of thirteen weeks. The primary aim is to teach candidate judges to deliberate and eventually formulate his or her own decisions. The last thirty-week phase requires candidate judges to serve as judge's assistants and to assist senior judges in analyzing cases and formulating decisions. Candidate judges must also handle several pre-determined cases of incrementally increasing difficulty.

3.4 Access to justice

3.4.1 Substantive limits to access

In Indonesia, there have been several progressive developments in terms of legal standing. The laws in several regimes, i.e. the Consumer Protection Law and Environmental Law, provide standing based on *actio*

[40] *Annual Report of the Supreme Court 2010*, p. 228.

popularis, better known as class action. In the Constitutional Court, however, legal standing is still quite rigid. In the current effort to amend the law regarding the Constitutional Court, many advocate the inclusion of the constitutional claim concept, in which the legal standing rule would be loosened.

In 2010, the Supreme Court issued a Circular Letter on Legal Assistance in Judicial Service Provision, covering the role of the Supreme Court in ensuring access to justice, including the provision of lawyers' assistance, fee exemptions, the court's legal aid center, and mobile courts. When Act No. 16 of 2011 on Legal Aid was enacted, the role of legal aid was to be transferred to the Minister of Law and Human Rights, although, to date, the process of transferring the authority has yet to be completed.

3.4.2 Institutional limits to access

The cost of judicial dispute settlement is a tricky issue in Indonesia. There are many components of judicial costs that are not readily available for examination or academic study. The primary reason is that a significant portion of judicial costs lies in private arrangements, for example, between lawyers and clients. This is assuming that there are no costs incurred in terms of bribery (which is still prevalent in Indonesia). In fact, at times, these two issues (lawyer's fees and bribery) are intertwined. Most lawyers charge very high fees because they include the bribery cost component in the lawyer's fee. They do so because they deal with foreign clients who adhere to strict budgetary transparency, and there is usually no line item in which to include a bribery component.

Although true judicial costs are difficult to determine, a recent World Bank report indicated that judicial costs are 122.7 percent of the amount of monetary compensation claimed.[41]

Public defense lawyers and pro-bono civil rights lawyers are scarce. The advocates' association, PERADI, recently issued an obligation for lawyers to set aside a certain number of hours for pro-bono work. This, however, is still an ongoing effort without immediate visible impact on the problem of access to justice. Lawyers are inclined to avoid this obligation and in any event circumvent it.

[41] "Doing Business, Measuring Business Regulations, Ease of Doing Business in Indonesia," see www.doingbusiness.org/data/exploreeconomies/indonesia/#enforcing-contracts (accessed 24 February 2012).

4 Sources of law, style of judicial decisions and politics of judging

4.1 Sources of law: codes or precedents, and the relationship between them?

Indonesia has adopted the civil law system; hence, the source of law is the codes. There is no formal recognition of precedent as a source of law. However, in the development of judicial practice and the body of laws, precedents in effect also serve as a source of law. Many practitioners, when arguing before the Supreme Court, refer to previous decisions of the Court regarding similar points of law. This is inevitable, as there are many cases in which the code is silent on certain issues and thus compels advocates or judges to resort to previous judgments. In terms of a judge's duty, judges are obliged to hear a case and decide on it even when there is no law governing the issue. The void is filled by the principle of *rechtsvinding*, which can be stated as "Judges may not reject a case or claim simply because there is no law governing it." In short, the relationship between the code and precedents is that precedents serve as gap fillers. However, it must be noted that in some instances practices that are developed through precedents are different from, if not contradictory to, the textual interpretation of the codes.

4.2 The style of judicial decisions: long? short? linguistic accommodation to minorities or foreigners?

There is no specific data as to whether judicial decisions in Indonesia are typically long or short. Ultimately, the length of a decision rests on the discretion of each judge and the nature of the case. However, judicial decisions tend to be long because judges commonly cite each party's entire argument.

One sharp criticism of Indonesian judicial decisions is that they fail to point out legal issues that are discussed and deliberated. In many judicial decisions, judges simply cite the arguments of the parties and decide whose arguments are accepted by the court without further elaboration on the reason one party's arguments are accepted and another party's arguments are rejected. Sometimes, one can find a long judgment (of 1,000 or more pages); however, the decision of the court is only five to twenty pages. The rest of the pages consist of a recital of the arguments of the parties to the dispute.

There is no linguistic accommodation for foreigners. Indonesian law does stipulate that illiterates and the underprivileged should be provided with legal assistance, i.e. the court magistrate shall write the claim for illiterates and the underprivileged in a format recognized by the law and judicial practice. However, even this obligation is not performed well in reality.

4.3 *Can judges make law?*

Since Indonesia has adopted a civil law system, in a formal sense, judges cannot make law. In practice, however, judges have certain influences on the law making, particularly in the sense of textual interpretation or providing context in understanding certain laws. These two tools are critical in understanding a law and hence affect the way a legal norm is actually formed.

In addition, the influence of precedents (*yurisprudensi*) that are prevalent in judicial practice also affirms the influence of common law in Indonesia's judicial practice. It is a common practice for a judge to observe and examine coherence between one judgment and the previous judgment, and hence, a certain dose of law-making authority is exercised by judges.

4.4 *Interpretive method*

There is no particular interpretive method adopted by Indonesia's judicial system. Further, it is difficult to tell whether certain judges and courts have adopted certain interpretive methods as Indonesia is vast, and different judges have received different kinds of legal education.

Indonesia's court does cite foreign laws. For example, the Indonesian Law on Human Rights, i.e. Act No. 26 of 2000 regarding the human rights court, contains numerous principles embodied in the Rome Statute (the statute of the International Criminal Court). Many provisions are direct translations from the English version of the Rome Statute. This is the reason why it is reasonable to assume that the decisions of the human rights court will observe international law, whether by nomenclature citation or by substantive citation.[42]

Citations of international law were made in several cases in the Constitutional Court. For example, in the case of the famous Bali Nine (nine Australians who were sentenced to death for drug offenses), concerning

[42] *Eurico Guterres* Case.

the constitutionality of the death penalty provision under Indonesian Law No. 22 of 1997, the Constitutional Court referred to Article 6, paragraphs 1 and 2 of the International Covenant on Civil and Political Rights (ICCPR). Taking Article 6(2) of ICCPR together with several expert testimonies, the Court concluded that a narcotics-related crime is categorized as a serious crime with far-reaching effects; hence, Article 6 (2) of ICCPR shall not apply.

In Decision No. 71/G.TUN/2001/PTUN-JKT, the administrative court employed the "precautionary principle" to address an environmental case. This principle is not contained in Act No. 23 of 1997 regarding Environment Management. Instead, the court referred to several international law authorities, i.e. the United Nations Convention on Biological Diversity, the Cartagena Protocol on Biosafety to the Convention of Biodiversity, and Article 15 of the Rio Declaration 1992.

5 Function of courts

5.1 Social control

At the end of the day, it is inevitable that the law will function as a form of social control. This is particularly true in Indonesia's context. In Indonesia, criminal law is primarily aimed at exercising social control. For example, the recent criminal provisions related to traffic control were meant to impose order and discipline on the streets. Motor vehicle users are now obliged to turn their vehicles' lights on for safety purposes. Failure to comply with this obligation may result in criminal sanction. Many provisions of the new traffic law are meant to exercise social control.

The majority of Indonesian laws use fines as one of the sanctions. The environmental protection, consumer protection and trade and competition laws are particular areas where fines, criminal fines, and monetary sanctions become the primary weapon of social or behavioral control. It is quite safe to conclude that the formal law and the practice in those areas use monetary sanction as their primary tool.

5.2 Controlling agents

There is no specific issue, at least not one that is widely known or formally raised, with regard to elite cohesion or controlling administrative agent. On the contrary, there is an ongoing phenomenon of friction among governmental organs: for example, the dispute between *Bank Indonesia* and Bapepam (Indonesia Investment Coordination Board) over which entity has authority in the event of overlapping of authorities. Similar problems can be found across governmental departments/ministries.

5.3 Credible commitments in market functions of the economic sphere

Indonesia's legal system and courts do not explicitly commit to ensuring the smooth functioning of the market. Among all the courts, the KPPU most frequently involves economic affairs. Many decisions of the KPPU gravitate toward relying on economic evidence rather than on strictly legal evidence. Despite the controversy of this precept and approach, the KPPU has been very judicially active in keeping abreast of the most up-to-date methodologies in economic testing, economic precepts and industrial organization concepts in the past five years. This is inevitable due to the nature of the cases the KPPU must handle. The KPPU must keep pace with the most recent business strategy and developments in the market.

However, the laws relevant to economic activities tend to be nationalistic. Competition law practice is one clear indicator, where the KPPU raised the issues of the national economy and consumers' welfare over and over. In fact, in several landmark cases (one involving Temasek and Carrefour), the KPPU has tended to go against foreign companies and to protect national interests. The rules in place in the capital markets also tend to gravitate toward government intervention rather than promoting free markets.

6 Courts and alternative dispute resolution (ADR)

Alternative dispute resolution (ADR) in Indonesia consists of both voluntary and mandatory means of settling disputes outside the court. According to some laws, certain disputes must be settled by government agencies that are outside the court. However, any challenges to these decisions will subsequently go to court.

The first part of this section will discuss matters concerning negotiation, mediation and conciliation. The second part will discuss matters concerning arbitration. The last part will discuss some of the mandatory ADR processes.[43]

[43] Juwana, *Dispute Resolution*, p. 40.

6.1 *Negotiation, mediation and conciliation*

Although Indonesian law does not recognize plea-bargaining, there have been instances where criminal offenses are settled outside the court. An example often cited is a driver in Indonesia. Most private disputes have been resolved by negotiation between the parties to a dispute to reach a common agreement on a solution. This process is referred to as *musyawarah mufakat*, which literally means "dialogue to reach consensus."[44]

There are many reasons for the parties in a dispute to opt for *musyawarah mufakat*. First, *musyawarah mufakat* is a settlement that likely maintains good relations among the disputing parties. For many Indonesians, maintaining good relations is very important. They see that the dispute has caused damage to a good relationship and that it will become much worse if the dispute is not settled amicably through *musyawarah mufakat*.

Second, settling a dispute by *musyawarah mufakat* is seen by many to have the prospect of resolving the dispute without any confrontation. Formal mechanisms, especially in court, are seen as more of a face-to-face confrontation. In addition, the contending parties will argue with each other based on their own perspectives without any consideration of the opposing party.

Another reason for opting for *musyawarah mufakat* is that the mechanism is consistent with traditional practices of settling disputes. Indonesians believe *musyawarah mufakat* is rooted in their culture.

In addition, *musyawarah mufakat* is cost efficient, since the process does not involve money. The parties, however, may agree to compensation in the form of money. Furthermore, in *musyawarah mufakat* the parties are in control of deciding the form of settlement, from a simple apology to a monetary compensation settlement. In this sense, justice is decided by the parties to a dispute themselves, and not by a third party. Many Indonesians have considered this to be the most appropriate dispute resolution mechanism.

If for some reason the dispute cannot be resolved through negotiation, the parties will refer the dispute to a third party. The third party will hear the case and try to find an acceptable settlement. This is referred to as mediation or conciliation.[45] In the mediation or conciliation process, the

[44] *Ibid.* pp. 40–3.

[45] The terms mediation or conciliation in this study will be used interchangeably as long as the process involves a third party who has no power to render a decision.

principle of *musyawarah mufakat* is also used. Mediation or conciliation is commonly used in village justice.[46] The third parties acting as mediators or conciliators include, among others, leaders of the community, religious leaders or respected elders within the community not holding leadership positions.

In 1999, the mechanisms for negotiation, mediation and conciliation processes were provided under the Arbitration and Alternative Dispute Resolution Act (hereinafter referred to as the "Arbitration Act").[47] Nevertheless, such ADR mechanisms are only limited to disputes of a commercial nature. A broader definition of ADR has not been provided by any law.

At one time, there was an effort by the Ministry of Justice and Human Rights to initiate an Act exclusively governing negotiation, mediation and conciliation dubbed as "*Rancangan Undang-undang tentang Alternatif Penyelesaian Sengketa*," or Draft Law on Alternative Dispute Resolution. There were two important objectives pursued in this initiative. The first was to recognize the existence of negotiation, mediation and conciliation as practiced by many Indonesians and to give a sound legal basis for such mechanisms. The second objective was to recognize enforceability of the amicable agreements resulting from negotiation, conciliation and mediation. This was because under the prevailing law only amicable agreements mediated and drawn before the court were enforceable. Amicable agreements concluded outside the court were not enforceable.

Unfortunately, the draft law has never been processed to the necessary higher authorities. One reason is that at the time the draft law was being discussed, the House of Representatives passed the Arbitration Act. There was a feeling among the drafters that the proposal to introduce a separate Act on ADR would be conceived as redundant by many, as the Arbitration Act also mentions "ADR."[48]

6.2 *Mediation in the courts*

There is a mandatory mediation requirement under Indonesian law. The Chief Justice of the Supreme Court has issued a circular letter to all heads of the district and religious courts to remind them of the importance of

[46] Hooker describes village justice as a "system of voluntary mediation under which villagers submit dispute to some indigenous form of settlement process." See M. B. Hooker, *Adat Law in Modern Indonesia* (Kuala Lumpur: Oxford University Press, 1978), p. 140.

[47] Act No. 30 of 1999; State Gazette No. 138 of 1999.

[48] Juwana, *Dispute Resolution*, pp. 40–3.

court-administered mediation.[49] The circular letter explicitly states that court-administered mediation is necessary in order to substantially overcome the backlog of cases at the Supreme Court.[50] The Chief Justice has asked judges to put real effort into mediating disputes, and not just treat mediation as a formality. Judges are given three months to mediate the dispute, and this time period can be extended with the approval of the head of the court. Judges who are successful in their mediation efforts will be given credit points in their performance evaluations for career advancement.

In Indonesia, the law requires that certain types of dispute be remedied by special government agencies. The first is the public defended dispute, in which an individual files a complaint against the government or its officials and seeks compensation. Tax issues fall under this category. The second type involves individuals or the public filing a complaint to the state against other individuals. The state becomes the referee, although the parties to a dispute do not face each other as they do in a civil case.

These refereeing agencies have attributes of judicial power based on two grounds. First, these agencies were intended by their framers to act as judicial bodies. Second, their decisions, if appealed, must be submitted to the courts.[51]

6.3 *Arbitration, ADR and the courts*

6.3.1 ADR under the Arbitration Act

The definition of ADR under the Act is "(a) resolution mechanism for disputes or differences of opinion through procedures agreed upon by the parties outside the court, namely, consultation, negotiation, mediation, conciliation, or expert assessment."[52]

[49] Circular Letter No. 1 of 2002 concerning the Empowerment of Court of First Instance to Apply Pacific Settlement (Article 130 HIR/154 RBg) dated 30 January 2002.

[50] Retnowulan Sutantio and Iskandar Oeripkartawinata have other opinions of court-administered mediation. They say, "Amicable decisions have good implications for the society at large and, in particular, those seeking justice. Disputes will once and for all be settled, quickly and inexpensively; apart from that, the animosity between the disputing parties will be lessened. This is by far better than if the dispute has to be decided by a regular decision, in which case the defendant loses the case and enforcement of the decision is carried out in forceful manner." See R. Sutantio and I. Oeripkartawinata, *Hukum Acara Perdata dalam Teori dan Praktek* (*The Law of Civil Procedure in Theory and Practice*) (Bandung: Alumni, 1986), p. 24.

[51] Juwana, *Dispute Resolution*, p. 53.

[52] Arbitration Act, Art. 1(1). Under the elucidation of the Arbitration Act it is stated that "ADR is a dispute settlement institution based on procedure agreed upon by the parties, namely resolution outside the courts by consultation, negotiation, mediation or expert opinion."

Under the Arbitration Act, Article 6 is the only article dealing with ADR. Article 6 consists of nine paragraphs. Paragraph 1 states that "Disputes or differences of opinion that are not of a criminal nature may be resolved by the parties through ADR based on their good faith by setting aside any resolution based on litigation at the District Court."[53]

The Act also provides that ADR shall be completed within fourteen days, and the outcome must be agreed to in writing.[54] If for some reason the process fails, the parties may make a written request for assistance from one or more advisers or a mediator to resolve the dispute.[55] The Act further provides that in the event that, after the lapse of fourteen days, the dispute is not resolved, parties may request that an arbitration center or an ADR institution appoint a mediator to mediate or conciliate the dispute.[56] In this situation, unlike the former, the mediator must be appointed by a certain institution.

The designated mediator must begin the mediation process within seven days (presumably, after his or her appointment, which the Act does not clearly mention).[57] Within thirty days, a written resolution must be signed by all parties concerned. The agreement must be registered at the district court within thirty days after its signing.[58] The Act further provides that within thirty days after registration the resolution must be executed.[59]

If amicable settlement through ADR fails, the Act provides that the parties may submit the dispute to be settled through institutional or ad hoc arbitration, based on a written agreement.[60] However, it is not clear under the Act whether the ADR process before submission for arbitration in this provision is compulsory or voluntary.[61]

6.3.2 Arbitration

The Arbitration Act, or *Lex Arbitri* of Indonesia, provides the legal basis for arbitration procedures in Indonesia, replacing the Dutch colonial provisions.[62] The Act defines arbitration as "(a) mechanism of settling private disputes outside the General Tribunal based on arbitration

[53] *Ibid.* Art. 6(1). [54] *Ibid.* Art. 6(2). [55] *Ibid.* Art. 6(3). [56] *Ibid.* Art. 6(4).
[57] *Ibid.* Art. 6(5). [58] *Ibid.* Art. 6(6). [59] *Ibid.* Art. 6(7). [60] *Ibid.* Art. 6(9).
[61] Juwana, *Dispute Resolution*, pp. 43–4.
[62] The Arbitration Act, apart from providing rules for ADR and arbitration, also provides for the issuance of binding opinions by arbitration institutions. Nonetheless, the provisions are very brief and general. One important point is that binding opinions, once issued, may not be appealed.

agreement entered in writing by parties to a dispute."[63] Under Article 5 of the Arbitration Act, the dispute that can be arbitrated is limited to "disputes of a commercial nature, or those concerning rights which under the law fall within the control of the disputed parties."[64] As the article further elaborates, "Disputes which may not be resolved by arbitration are disputes which according to prevailing regulations cannot be settled by amicable means."[65]

Disputes can be arbitrated if and only if the parties to a dispute have agreed in writing to reach a settlement through arbitration.[66] The agreement, however, can be executed before or after the dispute arises.[67]

The Arbitration Act provides exclusive jurisdiction once the parties have submitted their dispute to arbitration. A court should consider itself as lacking jurisdiction to settle a dispute that has been agreed by the parties to be settled in arbitration.[68] Further, the Act states that "The existence of an arbitration agreement in writing shall negate the right of parties to seek resolution of the dispute and difference of opinion provided under the agreement through the District Court."[69] If the district court were to receive such a dispute, it would have to refuse and refrain from intervening in the dispute, except as otherwise provided under the Act.[70] This provision is intended to eliminate a problem that has occurred time and again, whereby the courts will examine such cases, even though the parties to the dispute have concluded an arbitration agreement.[71]

The Arbitration Act recognizes two kinds of awards: the final award and the provisional award. A provisional award is issued if it is requested by one of the contending parties.[72]

Another important feature of the Arbitration Act consists of the provisions on enforcement and annulment of arbitration awards. The Arbitration Act provides a mechanism for the enforcement of foreign

[63] *Ibid.* Art. 1(1). [64] *Ibid.* Art. 5(1). [65] *Ibid.* Art. 5(2).

[66] *Ibid.* Art. 2. The article provides as follows: "This Act shall govern the resolution of disputes or differences of opinion between parties having a particular legal relationship who have entered into an arbitration agreement which explicitly states that all disputes or difference of opinion or which may arise from such legal relationship shall be resolved by arbitration or through alternative dispute resolution."

[67] *Ibid.* Article 9(1) provides that "In the event the parties select resolution for dispute by arbitration after a dispute has arisen, their agreement to arbitrate has to be drawn in a written agreement signed by the parties."

[68] *Ibid.* Art. 3. [69] *Ibid.* Art. 11(1). [70] *Ibid.* Art. 11(2).

[71] Juwana, *Dispute Resolution*, pp. 45–6. [72] Arbitration Act, Art. 32(1).

arbitral awards.[73] This is as a consequence of Indonesia becoming a party to the 1958 Convention on the Recognition and Enforcement of Foreign Arbitral Awards.[74] The Arbitration Act defines a foreign arbitral award as an award rendered by a permanent or ad hoc arbitration tribunal outside the jurisdiction of Indonesia, or an award considered foreign under Indonesian law.[75] There are five requirements for foreign awards to be recognized and enforced by the court.[76] First, the arbitration must be carried out in a country that is a party to a bilateral or multilateral treaty that reciprocates recognition and enforcement of Indonesian arbitration awards. Second, the award must concern a matter that is commercial in nature under Indonesian law. The third requirement is that the award does not contravene public order. Fourth, the award must have obtained an order of exequatur from the Central Jakarta District Court. And, lastly, if one of the parties to a dispute is the government of the Republic of Indonesia, the order of exequatur must be obtained from the Supreme Court.[77]

According to the Arbitration Act, a request for enforcement of a foreign arbitral award must be made by the arbitrator or the arbitrator's proxy, rather than a party to a dispute. This is uncommon to many arbitration laws around the world. In practice, however, if the request is made by one of the parties to a dispute, in particular the party desiring the enforcement, the court will allow it.

The Central Jakarta District Court is the only court that has jurisdiction over a request for recognition and enforcement of foreign arbitral awards.[78] The arbitrator or the arbitrator's proxy must register the award at the Central Jakarta District Court before submitting an application for enforcement.[79] However, the non-prevailing party may object to the application submitted by the party requesting enforcement. The non-prevailing party becomes the respondent in the process, and the application becomes adversarial between the party applying for enforcement and the party requesting that the court deny enforcement.

If the Central Jakarta District Court issues a decision in favor of enforcement, an appeal to the High or Supreme Court by the non-prevailing party will not be entertained.[80] However, if the enforcement

[73] *Ibid.* Chapter VI, Part II.
[74] Indonesia ratified the Convention in 1981 under Presidential Decree No. 34 of 1981.
[75] Arbitration Act, Art. 1(9). [76] *Ibid.* Art. 66.
[77] Juwana, *Dispute Resolution*, pp. 48–50. [78] Arbitration Act, Art. 65.
[79] *Ibid.* Art. 67(1). [80] *Ibid.* Art. 68(1).

is refused by the district court, the decision can be appealed. The appeal goes directly to the Supreme Court.[81]

An application for annulment of an arbitration award must be made in writing within thirty days after the award is registered at the district court.[82] The district court where the arbitration process was held has jurisdiction to annul. The application for annulment is addressed to the head of that district court.[83] The district court has thirty days to issue its decision.[84] Decisions by the district court can be appealed to the Supreme Court.[85] The Supreme Court will then have thirty days to issue its decision.[86]

6.3.3 Arbitration center

In Indonesia, there are several arbitration centers. These centers can be divided into two categories: those with general jurisdiction and those with limited jurisdiction. The latter is commonly referred to as a specialized arbitration center.[87]

6.3.3.1 Arbitration with general jurisdiction

6.3.3.1.1 *BANI* The oldest arbitration organization, which has very wide jurisdiction, is *Badan Arbitrase Nasional Indonesia* (BANI), or the Indonesian National Board of Arbitration. It was formed by the Indonesian Chamber of Commerce in 1977. BANI has a head office in Jakarta and maintains a branch office in Surabaya, East Java. It handles both domestic and international disputes. A reference of a dispute to BANI must be in writing, either in an arbitration clause, or in a contract or subsequent agreement between the parties to a dispute.[88]

6.3.3.1.2 *BAMUI* On 21 October 1993, at the initiative of the Indonesian Council of Religious Ulemas (*Majelis Ulemas Indonesia*) a new arbitration center was formed, called *Badan Arbitrase Muamalat Indonesia* (BAMUI), or the Indonesian Muamalah Board of Arbitration. BAMUI was established with the intention of providing a forum for the settlement of disputes arising from business transactions primarily

[81] *Ibid.* Art. 68(2). [82] *Ibid.* Art. 71. [83] *Ibid.* Art. 72(1). [84] *Ibid.* Art. 72(3).
[85] *Ibid.* Art. 72(4). [86] *Ibid.* Art. 72(5). [87] Juwana, *Dispute Resolution*, pp. 50–2.
[88] BANI suggests parties wishing to make reference to BANI for dispute settlement use the standard clause in their contracts as follows: "All disputes arising from this contract shall be binding and be finally settled under the administrative and procedural Rules of Arbitration of Badan Arbitrase Nasional Indonesia (BANI) by arbitrators appointed in accordance with said rules." See Brochure of BANI.

among Muslims, or disputes arising from Islamic transactions. BAMUI also provides binding opinions if requested.[89]

6.3.3.2 Specialized arbitration To date, there exists only one type of specialized arbitration center, which deals exclusively with capital market disputes. The center was formed in August 2002 and is called the *Badan Arbitrase Pasar Modal Indonesia*, or the Indonesian Capital Market Arbitration Center, and abbreviated as BAPMI. BAPMI was founded by capital market societies.[90]

There are three ADR mechanisms offered at BAPMI. The first is provision of a binding opinion when requested by parties to a dispute.[91] The second is settlement of a dispute through mediation and conciliation.[92] The third is settlement of a dispute through arbitration.[93]

7 Evaluations

Members of the upper middle class are much more likely to comply with judicial decisions than are members of the lower middle class. With respect to the upper middle class, foreign companies in particular are likely to comply because they usually must obey the law in their country of origin, which is usually strict regarding judicial decision compliance. Members of the lower middle class, due to illiteracy, lack of legal awareness and cultural factors, are more inclined not to comply with judicial decisions.

Although in the last three to five years the number of cases brought to court in big cities has steadily increased, it has not significantly changed the attitude of the general public in Indonesia toward the courts as a place to resolve disputes.[94]

It can be argued that Indonesian society is not a law-minded society, as opposed to most Western societies, which are law-minded societies. Asian societies tend to maintain harmony, with disputes being settled not by determining who is right or who is wrong. Therefore, dispute resolution employing the law and the court system is foreign to a non-law-minded society.

In recent times, Indonesian society has been in a period of transition from a non-law-minded society to a law-minded society. The society is

[89] Articles of Association of BAMUI, Art. 4.
[90] Juwana, *Dispute Resolution*, pp. 51–2.
[91] BAPMI Articles of Association, Art. 6(a).
[92] *Ibid.* Art. 6(b).
[93] *Ibid.* Art. 6(c).
[94] Juwana, *Dispute Resolution*, pp. 23–4.

torn between the past and the future, the non-law-minded and law-minded, the traditional system and the modern system, and even Asian values and Western values. Indonesian society is in flux. As such, it is difficult to make generalizations about perceptions toward law and the court system.

The perception of Indonesians depends on the social class to which they belong. Members of the upper middle class may have totally different perceptions toward the courts from members of the lower middle class.

Most of Indonesia's population is lower middle class, who live in villages and may have some basic education but often have none at all. The lower middle class does not have good exposure to or awareness of the formal legal system because of underdeveloped transportation and, sometimes, mass media. People who belong to this class conceive of law as more of a sanction than any other meaning of law. For this reason, they feel that they must keep away from the law. In their understanding, law is nothing but an act of government and is not helpful for dispute resolution. If they have a dispute, they will settle it amongst themselves or refer it to community and religious leaders.[95] A low level of awareness of the court system and legal procedures is another reason that members of the lower middle class tend to avoid formal legal remedies for resolving disputes. They do not know how to initiate legal procedures or who to approach. For them, access to justice is minimal or even unattainable. It is not surprising if in a remote area a district court only handles twenty to thirty cases per year, most of which are public initiated disputes (criminal cases).

Members of the lower middle class are deterred by many physical attributions of the courts. First, the judges wear robes and formal attire. Second, there are formal procedures to be followed. Third, the presence of police officers and prosecutors wearing uniform can easily be seen, as the district court handles civil and criminal cases. Lastly, even the court's building may look scary, as there exists a place for restraining those accused of criminal offenses who are waiting for their cases to be heard.

[95] According to Ohorella and Salle, "[I]f dispute arises among villagers, the disputes are rarely brought to court for settlement. The parties in dispute will be much happier and prefer most to settle their dispute in forums available within the village community and settle the dispute amicably." H. M. G. Ohorella and H. A. Salle, "Penyelesaian sengketa melalui arbitrase pada masyarakat di pedesaan di Sulawesi Selatan (Dispute settlement through arbitration in village community in South Sulawesi)" in A. M. Toar (ed.), *Arbitrase di Indonesia* (*Arbitration in Indonesia*) (Jakarta: Ghalia Indonesia, 1995), p. 106.

Furthermore, a member of the lower middle class will be reluctant to enter a courthouse wearing plain clothes and sandals. Indeed, the court is unfriendly to them, and they would not dare to resolve their disputes through this mechanism. Culture has partly played a role in the lower middle class's avoidance of courts. They usually believe that dispute resolution through a court may have the consequence of damaging their relationship with the contending party whom they may know from childhood and interact with on a day-to-day basis. They may even have concerns that the court process will cause greater problems, instead of solving the problem. Many lower-middle-class people assume that those who go to court are criminals, or they worry about losing face if they lose their case.

In view of the above, the lower middle class will avoid going to court at all costs. However, people will seek to resolve their problems through the courts when they have no other choice.[96]

On the contrary, the upper middle class mostly live in the cities and enjoy sufficient education. Perception of the upper middle class toward court dispute resolution is strikingly different. This is due to the fact that legal awareness among people living in the cities is much higher than that among those who live in remote areas. In addition, people's familiarity with the law has been improving in the last ten years or so, thanks to the media. Hence, people have become accustomed to the concept of law and the court system. They can easily distinguish between criminal and civil matters. They also have a good understanding of where to go if they want to resolve a dispute through the courts. In some instances, they will solicit lawyers, although there are occasions where lawyers approach them. The people who belong to the upper middle class do not have any problems with access to justice.

As members of the upper middle class become more and more individualistic, they have fewer qualms about resolving their disputes through the courts. They are not worried that such action may jeopardize their relationship with the contending party. People in the cities tend to not concern themselves with other people's business. Moreover, since people can distinguish between civil and criminal cases, those who resolve their disputes in court will not be considered criminals.

Nevertheless, the upper middle class, whenever possible, will avoid using the courts to resolve their disputes because they think that the

[96] Juwana, *Dispute Resolution*, pp. 25–6.

courts are not the best and most efficient mechanism. Even a retired judge would not turn to the courts for dispute resolution if he or she could avoid it. Judges know that court settlement involves a tangled regulatory and legal environment. It also involves a great deal of time, as well as large sums of money for legal fees and, most of the time, bribes and other irregular payments. Lastly, judges also have doubts as to whether a court can render a fair decision due to the lack of a credible justice system.

The upper middle class will listen to their lawyers' advice. Lawyers who are pragmatic and have full knowledge of the difficulty of resolving disputes through the court system tend to discourage their clients from going to court if it is unnecessary to do so. However, lawyers who are hungry for clients and litigation work may advise otherwise. This kind of lawyer has recently caused society to have a negative image of the profession.

In sum, members of the upper middle class, although their reasons are different from those of the lower middle class, also avoid using the courts to resolve their disputes.[97]

In discussing the perceptions of Indonesians toward the court system as a means of settling disputes, the perceptions of expatriates cannot be left out. The perceptions of expatriates toward Indonesian courts are similar to those of Indonesians, although the reasons for these perceptions are different. Expatriates will try to avoid resorting to Indonesian courts for settlement of their disputes; instead, they will resort to local or foreign arbitration or even foreign courts, which they feel are much more credible.[98]

There are many reasons why expatriates are not comfortable choosing Indonesian courts as a means to settle their disputes. First, businesses do not prefer court settlement. Second, local counsel have tended to advise their foreign clients not to settle their disputes in Indonesian courts. Third, investors have great doubts about the abilities of Indonesian judges when faced with complex transactions under an English contract. Fourth, investors often question whether the court can act impartially

[97] *Ibid.* pp. 26–8.

[98] It should be noted, however, that Indonesian courts under Article 436 Rv will not recognize the judgments of foreign courts. Dispute settlement through courts outside Indonesia can only be pursued if enforcement is not sought in Indonesia. This is not the case with respect to settlement through foreign arbitration. Indonesian courts in principle will recognize foreign arbitral awards, as Indonesia is a party to the Convention on the Recognition and Enforcement of Foreign Arbitral Awards.

when nationalism is at play. Fifth, investors have been made aware that the court system is not compliant with Western or international standards.[99] Lastly, the judiciary is not credible, as corruption is pervasive. Hence, foreign investors do not see the court system in Indonesia as an alternative for pursuing recourse, even as a last resort.[100]

From their experiences in Indonesian courts, most expatriates have complaints. Some say the process is time consuming and full of corruption, and that the procedure is difficult to follow. Others complain about the partiality of the judge when faced with local issues and interests. In addition, they feel that the courts' verdicts are not the result of thorough and comprehensive deliberations.[101]

References

Hooker, M. B. *Adat Law in Modern Indonesia* (Kuala Lumpur: Oxford University Press, 1978)

Juwana, H. "A survey on the influence of international economic policy on Indonesian laws: implementation and problems" in K. Hardjasoemantri and N. Sakumoto (eds.), *Current Development of Laws in Indonesia* (Tokyo: Institute of Developing Economies – Japan External Trade Organization, 1999), pp. 207–34

Juwana, H. *Dispute Resolution Process in Indonesia* (Japan: Institute of Developing Economics, 2003)

Juwana, H. et al. (eds.) *Indonesian Legal System* (ASEAN Law Association, 2005)

Ohorella, H. M. G. and Salle, H. A. "Penyelesaian sengketa melalui arbitrase pada masyarakat di pedesaan di Sulawesi Selatan (Dispute settlement through arbitration in village community in South Sulawesi)" in A. M. Toar (ed.), *Arbitrase di Indonesia (Arbitration in Indonesia)* (Jakarta: Ghalia Indonesia, 1995)

[99] One piece of advice that has been given to those foreigners investing in Indonesia for the first time is as follows: "The Indonesian court system has been said to be patrimonial in nature. Whether or not that is true, it seems to be the perceived condition by international investors. Patrimonial judicial authority is where the judicial office and its attendant powers are appropriated by the office-holder. In such a situation, judicial authority is exercised on the basis of specific and personal relationships between the individuals involved, not necessarily on the basis of law or fact." See: www.expat.or.id/business/twostepsforward.html.

[100] H. Juwana, "A survey on the influence of international economic policy on Indonesian laws: implementation and problems" in K. Hardjasoemantri and N. Sakumoto (eds.), *Current Development of Laws in Indonesia* (Tokyo: Institute of Developing Economies – Japan External Trade Organization, 1999), p. 217.

[101] Juwana, *Dispute Resolution*, pp. 28–9.

Sutantio, R. and Oeripkartawinata, I. *Hukum Acara Perdata dalam Teori dan Praktek* (*The Law of Civil Procedure in Theory and Practice*) (Bandung: Alumni, 1986)

Soetoprawiro, K. *Pemerintahan & Peradilan di Indonesia: Asal Usul dan Perkembangannya* (*The Government and Judiciary in Indonesia: The History and Its Development*) (Bandung: Citra Aditya Bakti, 1994)

Tresna, R. *Peradilan di Indonesia dari Abad ke Abad* (*Indonesian Judiciaries from Century to Century*) (Jakarta: W. Versluys NV, 1957)

9

The fledgling courts and adjudication system in Mongolia

BATBOLD AMARSANAA

To understand the development of the legal and judicial system in Mongolia, it is important to consider the country's geographical situation and population distribution. Mongolia is a landlocked country neighboring two world powers, the Russian Federation and the People's Republic of China. In terms of geographic area, it ranks as the nineteenth largest country, but it only has a population of slightly under three million, approximately one-third of which lives in the capital city of Ulaanbaatar. About half of the country's total population lives in urban areas while the other half lives a nomadic lifestyle.

Up until the 1990s, Mongolia was a socialist country with a legal and judicial system based on the Soviet system.[1] Around the time of the collapse of the socialist system, in 1992, Mongolia adopted a new Constitution inspired by democratic ideals and systems of governance.[2] During the socialist period, Mongolia had "telephone justice" similar to that in the Soviet Union, in which informal commands, requests or signals influenced formal judicial procedures.[3] With the adoption of the new Constitution, the concepts of rule of law and/or *rechtstaat*, separation of powers, protection of human rights and a free market economy were introduced, and such reforms are still in progress.

Due to the adoption of a Soviet-style legal system during the socialist regime, combined with the system's continued dedication to the civil law tradition,[4] most scholars and government authorities in Mongolia consider the legal system to be a member of the civil law family.

[1] See S. Narangerel, *Legal System of Mongolia* (Ulaanbaatar, 2004).
[2] See B. Chimid, *Concept of the Constitution* (Ulaanbaatar, 2002).
[3] The Communist party controlled the judiciary during this time. See Narangerel, *Legal System of Mongolia*, p. 49.
[4] Legal reform conference final paper (1997).

1 General description of the judicial system

The judicial system in Mongolia is fairly simple in terms of its structure. Mongolia has a single Supreme Court and a separate Constitutional Court (*Tsets*). The jurisdictions of the Supreme Court and Constitutional Court do not overlap. The Supreme Court adjudicates all civil, criminal and administrative disputes, while the Constitutional Court considers matters involving interpretation of the Constitution, such as the constitutionality of laws, decrees, and other decisions of the Parliament, the President and Cabinet, and the constitutionality of international treaties to which Mongolia is a party.[5] While justices of the Supreme Court and judges of lower courts are appointed by the President, members of the Constitutional Court are appointed by the Parliament. Article 47(1) of the Constitution stipulates that judicial power shall only be vested in courts and that courts shall be established only by the Constitution and other laws.

1.1 Structure of the courts

Mongolia is a unitary country. The Supreme Court, at the apex of the court system, oversees all legal disputes (except cases considered by the Constitutional Court) in Mongolia, including civil, criminal and administrative cases, through its specialized civil, criminal and administrative chambers. Administrative courts, which are the only specialized court in Mongolia, are within the hierarchy of the Supreme Court.[6]

There are two types of appellate courts in Mongolia: the administrative appellate court, which is a specialized court, and the courts of general jurisdiction. There is only one appellate administrative court, which sits in the capital city, Ulaanbaatar, while there are twenty-two appellate courts of general jurisdiction, one in each of the twenty-one aimags, the largest administrative and territorial unit, and one in the capital city. Courts of general jurisdiction adjudicate civil and criminal cases. Under the Mongolian legal system, civil cases also include labor matters, business and economic matters, and intellectual property matters.

[5] Constitution of Mongolia, Art. 66(2).

[6] Constitution of Mongolia, Art. 48(1).

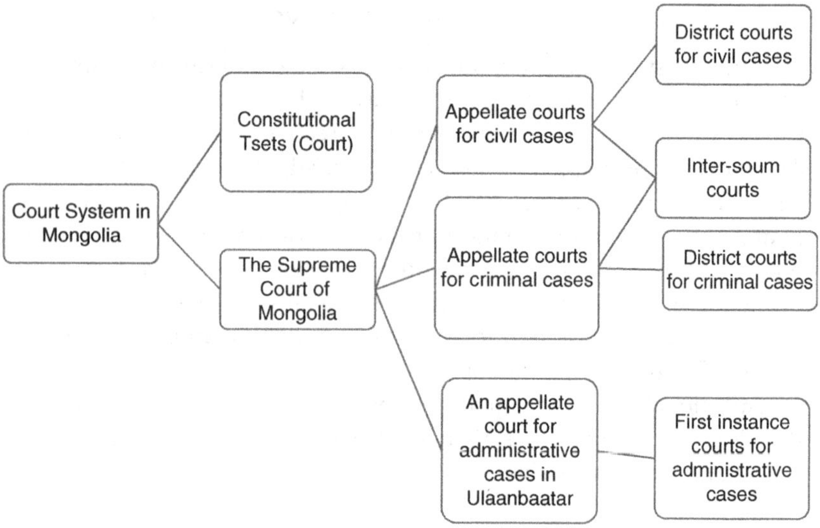

Figure 9.1: Structure of courts in Mongolia

1.2 Tiers of adjudication and functions of trials in general or special jurisdictions

As the following chart demonstrates, instances of trials in Mongolian courts are somewhat complicated. In civil proceedings, inter-soum and district courts act as courts of first instance. (A soum is the second-largest administrative unit, after aimags.) Some cases are deliberated with one judge presiding, while others are deliberated with three judges.[7] This level of courts considers both facts and law.

In the second instance of civil proceedings at appellate courts, a panel of three judges presides.[8] In the third instance of civil proceedings, only the Supreme Court can deliberate and the cases are heard by a panel of five justices.[9] At the Supreme Court, only matters regarding law can be considered.[10] At the discretion of the Chief Justice, an appeal of a civil judgment made in a third instance proceeding may be heard before a full bench of the Supreme Court.[11]

[7] Law on Civil Procedure, Arts. 81 and 82.
[8] Law on Civil Procedure, Art. 166(1). [9] *Ibid.* Art. 176(1).
[10] *Ibid.* Art. 172(2). [11] *Ibid.* Art. 176.

In criminal proceedings, inter-soum and district courts act as first instance courts. They decide matters of both fact and law[12] with one or three judges.[13] Appellate courts hear criminal cases as second instance courts with three judges.[14] In a second instance proceeding, matters of both fact and law are deliberated.[15] In a third instance proceeding, the Supreme Court deliberates matters of law with a five-judge panel.[16] In addition, the Supreme Court is required to hear any case in which a sentence of capital punishment is delivered.[17] After a third instance proceeding, the Chief Justice and/or Prosecutor General may submit the case to be re-examined by the full bench of the Supreme Court.[18]

Administrative courts adjudicate administrative disputes, as established by the Law on Establishment of Administrative Courts and the Law on Procedure for Administrative Cases, in accordance with Article 48(1) of the 2002 Constitution. Defendants in administrative cases falling under the administrative courts are always public authorities, including not only executive agencies but also public service authorities such as public schools or public hospitals. In some cases, even non-profit organizations, with which government powers may be entrusted, can also be defendants. In administrative cases, plaintiffs must be citizens or legal entities. Government agencies and public officials, in their capacity as such, are not eligible to submit claims to administrative courts asserting breaches of their rights.

In administrative proceedings, courts act with panels of one or three judges,[19] and matters of both fact and law are considered.[20] An appellate courts for administrative cases considers matters of fact and law with panels of three judges.[21] The Supreme Court deliberates administrative cases as a third instance court with a panel of five justices.[22] In this instance, it considers only matters of law.[23]

1.3 Constitutional Court

In response to the democratization of the late 1980s and early 1990s, the Constitutional Tsets (Court) was established in Mongolia. The Constitutional Tsets was established under Article 64 of the Constitution as "an

[12] Law on Criminal Procedure, Arts. 166 and 173(1).
[13] *Ibid.* Art. 32. [14] *Ibid.* Art. 32(3). [15] *Ibid.* Art. 308(1).
[16] *Ibid.* Art. 348(1). [17] *Ibid.* Art. 356(1). [18] *Ibid.* Art. 347(5).
[19] Law on Administrative Procedure, Art. 52(3). [20] *Ibid.* Art. 70(3).
[21] *Ibid.* Arts. 85(3) and 52(3). [22] *Ibid.* Art. 52(4). [23] *Ibid.* Art. 91(1).

organ exercising supreme supervision over the implementation of the Constitution, making judgment on the violation of its provisions and resolving constitutional disputes."[24] The Constitution of Mongolia does not specify whether the Constitutional Tsets is a part of the judiciary, and, as a result, there has been debate in the legal community and political circles on the nature of the Constitutional Tsets. This debate has been leaning toward the opinion that the Constitutional Tsets is a part of the judiciary although its jurisdiction is strictly limited to matters of constitutionality.

The Constitutional Tsets issues judgments on the following matters: (1) the constitutionality of laws, decrees and other decisions issued by the Parliament and the President, as well as of government decisions and international treaties signed by Mongolia; (2) the conformity with the Constitution of national referendums and decisions of the Central electoral authority on parliamentary and presidential elections; (3) breaches of law by the President, the Chairman and members of the State Ikh Hural (Parliament), the Prime Minister, Cabinet members, the Chief Justice of the Supreme Court and the Prosecutor General; and (4) the validity of the grounds for the removal of the President, Chairman of the Parliament and the Prime Minister, as well as for the recall of members of the Parliament.

The matters mentioned above can only be heard by the Constitutional Tsets under the following circumstances: (1) the Parliament, the President, the Prime Minister, the Supreme Court or the Prosecutor General submits a request; and/or (2) citizens of Mongolia submit a petition and relevant information. The Constitutional Tsets shall submit its judgment (called a "conclusion") to the Parliament for deliberation if the judgment finds any of the following to be unconstitutional: the laws and other decisions within the Parliament's jurisdiction, national referendums, and decisions of the Central electoral authority on parliamentary and presidential elections.[25] The Parliament then reviews the judgment and determines if it will accept it. If the Parliament decides to contest the judgment, the matter must be heard before a full bench of the Constitutional Tsets, which will make the final judgment (resolution). Resolutions by a full bench of the Constitutional Tsets in which the constitutionality or unconstitutionality of the matter under dispute is judged are final and binding.

The Constitutional Tsets has been fairly active since its inception and has rendered a number of decisions declaring the unconstitutionality of

[24] Constitution of Mongolia, Art. 64(1).

[25] Constitution of Mongolia, Art. 66(2).

laws and other government decisions within its jurisdiction. Each year, the Constitutional Tsets issues fewer than ten conclusions. Resolutions of disputed conclusions made by the Constitutional Tsets are rare, at two or three per year. Of note is the fact that the Constitutional Tsets has considered a dispute over a breach of law by the Chief Justice of the Supreme Court.

2 Judicial posts, appointments and independence

This section discusses judicial posts in Mongolia, the process of judicial appointment, and concerns relating to judicial independence.

2.1 Judicial posts and court caseloads

Courts are established in accordance with the Constitution and legislative acts. At present, there are seventy-nine courts excluding the Constitutional Court. As Table 9.1 shows, the Supreme Court of Mongolia is composed of twenty-four justices and one Chief Justice. Among the twenty-four justices, three justices are also the heads of the civil, criminal and administrative chambers. An appellate court for administrative cases deliberates on appeals of administrative cases nationwide and is composed of ten judges including a chief judge. In contrast, appellate courts of civil and criminal cases have territorial jurisdiction over the country divided into ten circuits. The first instance courts for administrative cases deliberate administrative cases in twenty circuits. As for the first instance courts, there are four district courts which sit in the capital city Ulaanbaatar and specialize in criminal or civil disputes. Besides, twenty-nine inter-soum courts which adjudicate both criminal and civil cases sit nationwide as the first instance courts. Altogether, there are about sixteen judges per 100,000 inhabitants.

Table 9.2 shows the performance of the courts in recent years. It is clear that civil cases outnumber both criminal and administrative cases, with criminal cases in second place and administrative cases in third. Each year, more than 40,000 civil cases are filed in inter-soum and district courts (the first instance courts), while only around 6,550 criminal cases and 1,500 administrative cases were filed in those courts in 2011. It is also apparent that the number of cases filed with the courts is steadily rising. Particularly, administrative court cases have increased at a faster pace than have civil and criminal cases.

Table 9.1: *Number of courts and judges in Mongolia*

	The Supreme Court	Appellate court for administrative cases	Appellate courts for civil cases	Appellate courts of criminal cases	First instance courts for administrative cases	District courts for civil cases	District courts for criminal cases	Inter-soum courts	Total
Court	1	1	10	10	20	4	4	29	79*
Judges	25**	10	48	55	67	62	52	144	463***
Maximum number of Judges****	25	12	78	78	78	88	88	198	645

Source:
*Law on Establishing Courts;
**According to Law on Courts of Mongolia, Art.16(1), the Supreme Court has at least 25 justices;
***Report of first half of 2014 of the General Council of the Courts, p. 59.
****Resolution #12 of Parliament of Mongolia (2013) has stipulated maximum number of judges to be hired except the Supreme Court.

Table 9.2: *The performance of courts in different jurisdictions in Mongolia*

		Supreme Court (civil cases)	Supreme Court (criminal cases)	Supreme Court (administrative cases)	Appellate court for administrative cases	Appellate courts for civil cases	Appellate courts for criminal cases	First instance courts for administrative cases	Inter soum courts and District courts for civil cases	Inter soum courts and District courts for criminal cases
Number of cases filed	2010	1334	726	427	573	2245	2129	1625	48170	6372
	2011	1135	822	331	551	1925	2159	1556	42538	6776
Cases disposed	2010	1282	692	407	544	2102	2016	1387	44090	5987
	2011	1089	809	322	504	1872	2065	1294	39018	6338
Cases pending	2010	52	34	20	29	98	69	238	4080	386
	2011	46	13	9	47	53	94	262	3520	438
Clearance rate %*	2010	96.1	95.3	95.3	94.9	93.6	94.7	85.4	91.5	93.9
	2011	95.9	98.4	97.3	91.5	97.2	95.6	83.2	91.7	93.5
Congestion rate %**	2010	91.6	94.1	86.8	89.1	90.4	91.9	74.3	84.4	88.2
	2011	91.7	94.5	91.7	86.9	92.5	92.7	72.1	83.7	88.7

Source: Court Report of 2011, the Supreme Court of Mongolia, (2012) pp.35–45; Court Report of 2010, the Supreme Court of Mongolia (2011) pp. 34–45; Court Report of 2009, the Supreme Court of Mongolia (2010) pp.25–35; Court Report of 2008, the Supreme Court of Mongolia (2009) pp. 38–49; Court Report of 2007, the Supreme Court of Mongolia (2008) pp.38–49;

*Done by the author based on the numbers mentioned in the same table.

**Done by the author based on the numbers mentioned in the same table.

***Court Report of 2003, the Supreme Court of Mongolia, (2004) p.14.

Interestingly, the rate of appeals is not high in Mongolia, which may suggest some degree of judicial efficiency. To take civil cases as an example, in 2011, there were 42,538 cases filed in the first instance courts; however, only 1,925 cases were appealed to the aimag and capital city courts, an appeal rate of less than 5 percent.

It is important to note that the clearance and congestion rates presented are not official published numbers but are calculated by the author. The clearance rate has remained high over the past several decades. With the exception of the first instance administrative court, the clearance rate in all courts has been over 90% in recent years. High congestion rates are common in the criminal and civil courts, while congestion rates are quite low for appellate and first instance administrative courts.

2.2 *Judicial appointments and qualifications of judges*

The Constitution of Mongolia stipulates the qualifications required for judges to be appointed.[26] Justices of the Supreme Court are required to be at least thirty-five years of age, to have completed a certain level of legal education and to have acquired at least ten years of professional experience. In practice, justices of the Supreme Court are usually over forty years old. Judges of all other courts are required to be at least twenty-five years of age, to have completed a certain level of legal education and to have acquired at least three years of professional experience. Additional qualifications are also stipulated by statute. For example, those who wish to become a judge should not have a criminal record and are required to have passed the bar exam.[27]

Mongolian law guarantees life tenure to judges once appointed. There are only a few grounds on which a judge can be removed from office: proven criminal liability, inability to perform his or her duties due to health or age, inability to perform his or her duties in a professional manner as proven by a professional committee, appointment or election to public office, or receipt of two or more disciplinary actions within one year.[28]

2.3 *Judicial budget and administration*

According to Article 28(2) of the Law on Courts, the judicial budget is a part of the state budget. It is composed of the budgets of the Supreme

[26] Constitution of Mongolia, Art. 51(3).
[27] Law on Legal Status of Judges, Arts. 5 and 6.
[28] *Ibid.* Art. 18(3) and (4).

Court, local courts, specialized courts and the General Council of Courts. The judiciary can propose its own budget through the General Council of Courts.[29] The judicial budget occupies only a tiny portion of the national budget, on average 0.5 percent. However, in recent years, the percentage has increased slightly.[30]

Higher salaries may be provided for judges with doctoral degrees or a certain number of years of public service. Compared to the average salary of public officials as a whole, the salaries of judges are higher and have been gradually increasing.

Administration of the judiciary is the responsibility of the General Council of Courts in Mongolia. It is composed of five members who are appointed by the President of Mongolia. Three of them are elected from the Supreme Court and the Judicial conferences of appellate courts and first instance courts. The remaining two members are proposed by the Minister of Justice and President of the Mongolian Bar Association.

There was originally some debate on whether judicial administration should belong to the Ministry of Justice. In the past, both the Minister of Justice and the Chief Justice of the Supreme Court chaired the Council. At present, the council is considered as independent from both judicial and executive branches.

3 Legal education and access to justice

The following section provides a brief introduction to legal education in Mongolia and the issues concerning access to justice in general.

3.1 Legal education

There are two primary paths of legal education in terms of educational duration: (1) a bachelor's degree to be completed in four or five years, and (2) a three- or four-year program for those who already have a bachelor's degree in another subject. There is a five-year bachelor's degree program at the National University of Mongolia School of Law. In all other law schools conferring a bachelor's degree, typically a four-year program dominates. Because of their popularity among the general public, over twenty law schools were created during the 1990s. However, recently the government

[29] Law on Administration of Courts, Art. 6(1)(1).

[30] The percentage provided here is calculated by the author based on numbers provided in the Court Report of 2003, the Supreme Court of Mongolia (2004), p. 19.

made plans to close down some law schools due to their low quality of teaching and their lack of resources including teaching staff.

Mongolia has a nationwide bar exam. On average, the pass rate of the bar exam is between 20 percent and 28 percent. Individuals passing bar exams can practice law as attorneys. Only those who pass the bar exam can apply to take further exams administered by the prosecutors' office and the courts. Those who pass the exams to become judges, prosecutors or advocates are then required to take training courses and fulfill a certain number of credits. These training programs are provided by the Mongolian Bar Association, a self-regulatory professional body established by statute.[31]

3.2 *Access to justice*

In Mongolia, any persons including natural and legal persons are allowed to sue.[32] In criminal proceedings, the law allows private parties to initiate prosecution. Moreover, the rules of administrative procedure permit legal and natural persons to sue the government.[33] However, there are no legal grounds for public interest litigation. Ecological problems associated with mining activities have spurred increasing demands from the general public and the legal community for public interest litigation.

The stamp fees paid by litigants may pose a barrier to access to justice for low-income individuals. Stamp fees are calculated based on the total amount of the claims made. Usually stamp fees are paid on submission of the claim. For example, if the amount of the claim is up to 130,000 tugrugs, the litigant pays 4,550 tugrugs. If the total amount of the claim is over 130,000 but less than 650,000 tugrugs, the litigant pays 4,550 tugrugs plus 3 percent of the amount over 650,000 tugrugs. If there is no property or estimable claim at stake, the stamp fee is 70,200 tugrugs. However, the stamp fee may be exempted in circumstances such as claims regarding pension payment, patent and copyright, and claims submitted by those legal persons financed by the national budget.[34]

Access to justice is also limited by the number of practicing attorneys available to serve ordinary citizens. There are approximately 1,000 advocates registered with the Supreme Court. In Mongolia, this means that there is one advocate for every 2,700 persons. However, many of those advocates work as in-house counselors and are mostly concentrated in

[31] Law on Legal status of Lawyers (2012), Art. 45(1)(3).

[32] Law on Civil Procedure, Art. 3. [33] Law on Administrative Procedure, Art. 12(1).

[34] Law on Stamp Fees, Art. 41(1).

the capital city. There are small soums that have no attorneys at all. Under Mongolian law, suspects and criminal defendants who are insolvent can have advocates hired by the government.[35]

4 Sources of law and influences on the judicial system

Modern courts and legal institutions in Mongolia are the products of modernization and nationalism. In the early twentieth century, Mongolia reclaimed its independence from foreign colonialism. Initially this process began as a result of nationalism and later became ideological. In the 1920s, Mongolia studied the constitutions of such countries as England, Japan and Korea[36] as models when it promulgated the Constitution of 1924. Later, however, Mongolia adopted a Soviet-style legal and judicial system until the early 1990s. During this time, ideology was very influential in determining the status of judges in society, and courts at every level of the judiciary were influenced to a great extent by the communist party.[37]

With the collapse of the Soviet Union, Mongolia became independent from the communist bloc. Since then, Mongolia has been able to control its destiny and has embraced such concepts as democratic government, separation of powers and an independent judiciary with the adoption of a new Constitution in 1992.[38] In line with this development and in response to political change, the Constitutional Tsets was created.

Mongolian lawyers and scholars usually classify its legal system as part of the civil law family. Indeed, there are no judge-made laws in Mongolia. The Constitution, statutes, regulations, customary laws and international treaties to which Mongolia is a party can all be sources of law under Mongolian law. At the top of these sources is the Constitution, and any rules not in compliance with the Constitution shall be considered invalid. In most cases, international treaties to which Mongolia is a party can prevail over domestic legislation if they are in conflict. Judges are bound by law according to the Constitution. In

[35] Law on Legal Aid for Insovent suspects and Criminal Defendants.
[36] M. Nakamura, "Conceptualizing the constitutional monarchy and the 1924 Constitutional of Mongolia: a review of the drafting process of the 1924 Constitution," paper presented to the 69th General Meeting at Ryukoku University on 3 and 4 June 2006, The Japan Society of Comparative Law.
[37] Narangerel, *Legal System of Mongolia*, p. 49.
[38] Preamble of the Constitution of Mongolia (1992).

addition to the Constitutional Tsets, the Supreme Court is permitted to deliver interpretations of statutes,[39] which has generated some criticism. As a result, the new Law on Courts has modified this interpretative power of the Supreme Court, which binds lower courts in deciding cases.

Judicial decisions are written in the Mongolian language only, and judicial decisions are relatively brief in comparison to those made by common law courts. Judgments typically do not incorporate detailed analyses of the cases, and they do not contain dissenting or concurring opinions. Judicial deliberation is not recorded and is kept confidential. Hence, there is no way to know the positions of the judges on any particular case.

The interpretive method used in judicial decisions is mostly one of text-based readings of the statute in question. However, if it is difficult for judges to determine the meaning of a particular law, a functional or historical approach may be employed, especially in private law. Scholarly publications, foreign laws or international legal authorities are not cited in judicial decisions. Although international treaties to which Mongolia is a party are considered to be part of the body of laws in Mongolia, and judges are empowered to apply treaties, there is no single case citing an international treaty. One of the main reasons for this lack of reference to international treaties may be quite technical: only international treaties published in the official gazette can be applied by the courts, but until recently, treaties were not published in the gazette.

5 Courts and alternative dispute resolution (ADR)

On 9 May 2003, a new Law on Arbitration based on the UNCITRAL (United Nations Commission on International Trade Law) Model Law on International Commercial Arbitration was adopted by the Parliament. In addition, the Civil Code, the Code of Civil Procedure and the Law on Court Enforcement of 2002 also apply to alternative dispute resolution in Mongolia. International conventions to which Mongolia is a party are also relevant sources of law regarding alternative dispute resolution. These include: (1) the 1958 New York Convention on Recognition and Enforcement of Foreign Arbitral Awards, (2) the 1965 Washington Convention on the Settlement of Investment Disputes Between States

[39] Law on Courts, Art. 17(3)(1).

and Nationals of Other States, (3) the 1972 Moscow Convention on the Settlement by Arbitration of Civil Law Disputes Resulting from Relations of Economic and Scientific-Technical Cooperation, and (4) the Mongolian and Chinese General Delivery Conditions between Foreign Trade Organizations. In principle, in the event of any conflicts with national legislation, international conventions to which Mongolia is a party prevail.

Under the Law on Arbitration, the following types of disputes are subject to arbitration: (1) any dispute that the parties agree to resolve through arbitration, and (2) any dispute required to be resolved through arbitration according to Mongolian law or any international treaty to which Mongolia is a party.[40] Types of disputes that are prohibited from being resolved by arbitration are those that are stipulated in Article 13(3) of the Civil Procedure Code and any other laws as being under the jurisdiction of courts or other authorized organizations and officials.[41]

There is only one arbitration center active in Mongolia, the Mongolian International and National Arbitration Center (MINAC), which was founded on 2 July 1960 at the Mongolian National Chamber of Commerce and Industry, a non-governmental organization. While the main function of the MINAC is to serve as an arbitration center, it also supports the development of other forms of alternative dispute resolution in Mongolia.[42]

Arbitration is not commonly used to resolve disputes in Mongolia. This is especially apparent when one compares the numbers of disputes resolved each year through arbitration with the numbers, provided earlier in this chapter, of civil cases resolved through the court system. In recent years, however, the number of cases resolved by arbitration has increased, ranging from ten to forty each year.[43] This is largely due to increased foreign investment in Mongolia, as foreign businesses are likely to prefer to resolve disputes through arbitration rather than through the Mongolian court system. If we look at the types of disputes resolved through arbitration, contractual disputes occupy the majority.

[40] Law on Arbitration, Art. 6(1); Code of Civil Procedure, Art. 13(2).

[41] Law on Arbitration, Art. 7(1); Code of Civil Procedure, Arts. 13(3), 13(4).

[42] Mongolia International Chamber of Commerce and Industry, http://en.mongolchamber.mn/index.php/departments-divisions/126-2011-12-21-114136.

[43] Mongolian National Chamber of Commerce and Industry, "Arbitration of Mongolia" (2012), http://en.mongolchamber.mn/documents/Arbitration_of_Mongolia.pdf.

According to the Law on Mediation, mediation can be used at courts in civil, labor and family disputes. Besides, the MINAC has taken steps towards encouraging mediation and has issued a set of mediation rules.[44] However, according to the MINAC's data, mediation is still underutilized.

6 Conclusion

In general, there is public recognition in Mongolia that judicial decisions need to be complied with. However, in reality, it is not uncommon to find that decisions are not actually followed. By some calculations, only 50 percent of judgments in civil cases are executed.

At present, the majority of the legal community and of the general public appear to hold negative perceptions of the court system. For example, a 2007 survey of the legal community as well as the general public showed that both populations had high levels of concern about the reliability and fairness of judges. Of the individuals surveyed, 24.3 percent of the respondents from the legal community and 31.4 percent of those from the general public considered the lack of reliability of judges to be a factor contributing to injustice in society.[45] Moreover, 50.3 percent of the respondents from the legal community opined that judges exercised their discretionary power inadequately.[46] On the question of whether the respondent was confident in his or her ability to obtain a fair judicial decision, 61.9 percent of the general public answered that they had some doubts or that it would depend on the prosecutor and judge on the case.[47]

It is clear from the above that public confidence in and respect for the judiciary still have a great deal of room for improvement. While the Mongolian judicial system has made great strides since the collapse of the Soviet bloc, it is important to bear in mind that its current

[44] Resolution No. 02 of the Council of the Mongolian National Chamber of Commerce and Industry, dated 16 June 2003.

[45] These were the second and third highest-ranking factors cited as contributing to injustice in society by the respondents from the legal community and those from the general public, respectively. The factor most frequently cited by the legal community as contributing to injustice in society was the inadequacy of statutes (34.8%). Among the respondents from the general public, the highest-ranking factors were the inadequacy of statutes (35.1%) and the inadequacy of the execise of police power (37.2%).

[46] Acceptance level of the legal reform in Mongolia, a sociological survey (2007) pp. 40, 45.

[47] See *New Straits Times*, 6 February 2007, p. 10.

Constitution was adopted just over two decades ago, and that many of the reforms that it engendered are still in progress. As these reforms continue to take root, and as external influences brought on by increasing globalization continue to shape the judicial system, it is hoped that the judiciary will become an institution in which a democratic society can place its trust. As the fledgling courts still lack Judicial independence, Mongolia needs to continue its efforts to reform and strengthen its Judiciary.[48]

References

Amarsanaa, J. and Chimid, B. *Judicial Reform in Mongolia* (Survey of Past Twenty Years) (Ulaanbaatar, 2010)

Chimid, B. *Concept of the Constitution* (Ulaanbaatar, 2002)

Mongolian National Chamber of Commerce and Industry. "Arbitration of Mongolia" (2012)

Nakamura, M. "Conceptualizing the constitutional monarchy and the 1924 Constitutional of Mongolia: a review of the drafting process of the 1924 Constitution," paper presented at the 69th General Meeting at Ryukoku University on 3 and 4 June 2006, The Japan Society of Comparative Law

Narangerel, S. *Legal System of Mongolia* (Ulaanbaatar, 2004)

Lundendorj, N., Unurbayar, Ch. and Batsuuri, M. *Strengthening Judicial Independence in Mogolia* (Policy review) (Ulaanbaatar, 2010)

[48] See N. Lundendorj, ch. Unurbayar and M. Batsuuri, *Strengthening Judisial Independence in Mongolia* (Policy review) (Ulaanbaatar, 2010).

10

The Philippines' post-Marcos judiciary: the institutional turn and the populist backlash

RAUL C. PANGALANGAN

The Philippine judicial system today is fundamentally shaped by the post-dictatorship constitution adopted in 1987 to protect a fragile democracy from the Marcos-era emasculation and manipulation of the judiciary. The result is a constitutional regime that protects judicial independence and secures the power of judicial review over the political and administrative arms of government.

The 1987 Constitution restored the separation of powers typical of liberal democratic constitutions: a bicameral Congress consisting of a Senate that is elected nationally, and a House of Representatives elected by district and by the party-list system; a president elected directly by the people in national elections; and a judiciary insulated from the elected branches by layers of institutional safeguards.

The Constitution itself defines the "judicial power" rather expansively. First, the power to decide becomes a "duty," that is, to settle disputes among litigants or enforce constitutional limits against the political branches of government. According to the Constitution, judicial power includes the "*duty* of the courts of justice to settle actual controversies involving rights which are legally demandable and enforceable, and to determine whether or not there has been a grave abuse of discretion amounting to lack or excess of jurisdiction on the part of *any branch or instrumentality of the Government*."[1] This was deliberately codified into the charter so that "the courts cannot hereafter evade the duty [to check the abuse of executive power] by claiming that [these] constitute a political question,"[2] a common excuse by overly deferential courts during the Marcos dictatorship.

[1] The 1987 Constitution of the Republic of the Philippines (hereinafter "Constitution"), Art. VIII, s. 1(2) (emphases supplied).

[2] *Francisco* v. *House of Representatives*, G.R. No. 160261 (10 November 2003), citing I Record of the Constitutional Commission 434-6 (1986).

Second, it recognizes the courts' traditional power to settle "actual controversies" between litigants and its power of judicial review over the other branches of government. But it pushes the envelope farther and expands the "grave abuse" standard way beyond its traditional scope, namely, the abuse of judicial discretion, to reach even political and administrative discretion exercised by "any branch or instrumentality of the Government." The "grave abuse" test had hitherto been used solely to review judicial decisions that were well circumscribed by law.[3] The 1987 Constitution now makes it applicable as well to the non-judicial, open-ended discretion exercised by political and administrative branches of government. It basically gives unelected judges a legal cover to substitute their discretion for that exercised by politically accountable officials.[4] In *Oposa* v. *Factoran*, it is stated that this "represents a *broadening of judicial power* to enable the courts of justice to review what was before forbidden territory, to wit, the discretion of the political departments of the government. As worded, the new provision vests in the judiciary, and particularly the Supreme Court, the power to rule upon even the wisdom of the decisions of the executive and the legislature."[5]

The judiciary clauses embody the institutional turn in the Philippines' post-Marcos democracy. On the one hand, the Constitution provides for an elected presidency[6] and Congress[7] and codifies the people's direct power of initiative for major decisions: to propose or repeal national and local laws;[8] recall local government officials, and propose or repeal local laws;[9] and propose amendments to the Constitution.[10] On the other hand, the Constitution installs institutional checks upon open-ended political discretion through the expanded jurisdiction of the courts, a power that the courts have seized upon with a populist flair. Twice the court has struck down even the people's "direct initiative" power to propose constitutional changes.[11] It is against this constitutional backdrop that this chapter discusses the functioning of the judiciary in the post-Marcos era.

[3] Rules of Court, Rule 69.

[4] *Oposa* v. *Factoran*, G.R. No. 101083, 224 SCRA 792 (30 July 1992).

[5] *Oposa* v. *Factoran*, G.R. No. 101083, 224 SCRA 792, 810 (30 July 1992) (citing Isagani A. Cruz, *Philippine Political Law* (Quezon City: Central Lawbook Pub. Co., 1991), pp. 226–7).

[6] Constitution, Art. VII. [7] *Ibid.* Art. VI. [8] *Ibid.* Art. VI, s. 32.

[9] *Ibid.* Art. X, s. 3. [10] *Ibid.* Art. XVII, s. 2.

[11] *People's Initiative for Reform, Modernization and Action* v. *Comelec*, G.R. No. 129754 (23 September 1997); *Lambino* v. *Commission on Elections*, G.R. 174153 (25 October 2006).

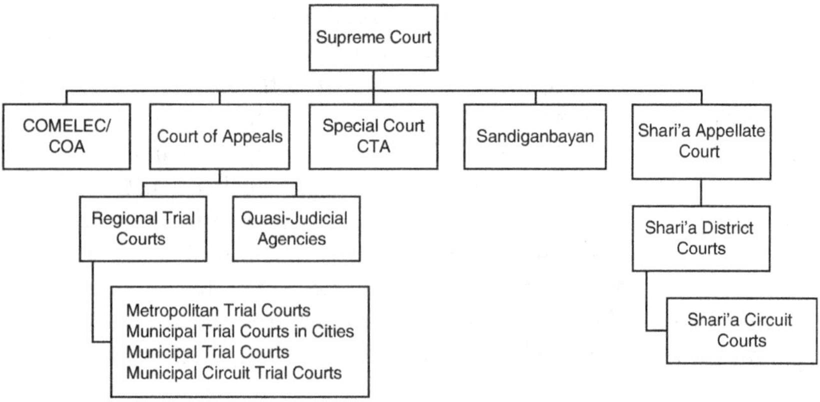

Figure 10.1: Expanded or total court system in the Philippines

1 Structure of the court system

1.1 Regular courts

The Constitution vests the judicial power in the "Supreme Court and such lower courts as may be established by law."[12] The Supreme Court thus stands at the apex of the court system. Below it are three tiers of lower-level courts, all of which trace their origin, in their current form, to the Marcos-era Judiciary Reorganization Act of 1980:[13] the Court of Appeals[14] and below it, the trial courts that initially decide controversies brought about by litigants in the first instance, namely, regional trial courts,[15] metropolitan trial courts, municipal trial courts in cities and municipal circuit trial courts.[16]

These courts are organized principally by geography, starting from the provincial level down, to cities and municipalities. Table 10.1 shows the number of courts in the Philippines.

1.2 Special courts

These refer to tribunals that have limited jurisdiction over specific types of cases or controversies. While special courts exercise judicial power

[12] Constitution, Art. VIII, s.1.

[13] The Judiciary Reorganization Act 1980, s. 3, as amended by Executive Order No. 33 (28 July 1986).

[14] Executive Order No. 33 (28 July 1986).

[15] The Judiciary Reorganization Act 1980, s. 13. [16] *Ibid.* s. 25.

Table 10.1: *The number of courts in the Philippines*

Courts	Total positions	Number of incumbents	Number of vacancies	Percentage (vacancies/ positions)
Supreme Court	15	15	0	0%
Court of Appeals	51	46	5	9.80%
Sandiganbayan	15	15	0	0%
Office of the court administrator	4	4	0	0%
Court of tax appeals	3	3	0	0%
Regional trial court	950	730	220	23.16%
Metropolitan trial court	82	64	18	21.95%
Metropolitan trial court in cities	141	102	39	27.66%
Municipal trial court	425	264	161	37.88%
Municipal circuit trial court	476	235	241	50.63%
Shari'a district court	5	2	3	60%
Shari'a circuit court	51	19	32	62.74%
Total	2,218	1,499	719	32.42%

just like the regular courts, they can hear only those cases specifically provided in statute.

The most prominent of the special courts is what in other countries would be called the anti-corruption court, the Sandiganbayan, created by statute[17] and codified into the Constitution.[18] The Sandiganbayan is unique in that it is a collegiate court tasked with trial functions to apply the Anti-Graft and Corrupt Practices Act.[19]

The second is the Court of Tax Appeals (CTA), created by statute as a collegiate court that reviews appeals from decisions in tax and/or tax-related cases.[20]

Finally, there is the family court, assimilated into the regional trial courts, which have exclusive original jurisdiction over child and family

[17] Republic Act No. 8249 (an Act Further Defining the Jurisdiction of the Sandiganbayan, Amending for the Purpose Presidential Decree No. 1606, as Amended, Providing Funds Therefore, and for Other Purposes) (5 February 1997).

[18] Constitution, Art. XI, s. 4; *see also* 1973 Constitution, Art. VIII, s. 5.

[19] Republic Act No. 1039 (12 June 1954). [20] Republic Act No. 1123 (16 June 1954).

cases[21] after the old juvenile and domestic relations courts were abolished in 1981.[22]

The Philippines, recognizing its Muslim minority population concentrated in the southernmost island of Mindanao, has created Shari'a courts to apply and adjudicate the Code of Muslim Personal Laws of the Philippines,[23] pertaining to civil relations between and among Muslim Filipinos. While the Shari'a court has the powers of the regular courts, it has jurisdiction only over Filipinos of the Muslim faith. The Supreme Court retains the power to review orders of lower courts through special writs, which includes decisions made by the Shari'a courts.

1.3 Quasi-judicial agencies

Although the judicial power is technically exercised exclusively by courts, administrative agencies have been allowed to exercise quasi-judicial functions to adjudicate disputes within their specialized expertise.

Standing alone in a separate category are the "constitutional commissions."[24] The Civil Service Commission is the central personnel agency for Philippine public officers and employees.[25] The Commission on Elections (COMELEC) enforces Philippine election laws.[26] The Commission on Audit (COA) examines all accounts pertaining to the use of public funds.[27] These bodies have been deliberately elevated to the level of constitutional agencies in order to insulate them from the political branches of government. Their decisions are appealable directly to the Supreme Court.[28]

On the other hand, the leading examples of quasi-judicial bodies that belong to the executive branch are the Securities and Exchange Commission and the National Labor Relations Commission.

1.4 Issues relating to judicial administration

Five main issues have been commonly identified in judicial administration. First is the problem of the delay in court trials and in deciding cases. Called by different names, e.g., court delay, "clogged dockets,"

[21] Republic Act No. 8369 (the Family Courts Act 1997) (28 October 1997).
[22] The Judiciary Reorganization Act 1980, s. 44.
[23] Presidential Decree No. 1083 (Code of Muslim Personal Laws of the Philippines), and the Judiciary Reorganization Act 1980, s. 45.
[24] Constitution, Art. IX, s. 1. [25] *Ibid.* Art. IX-B, s. 3. [26] *Ibid.* Art. IX-C, s. 2.2.
[27] *Ibid.* Art. IX-D, s. 2.1. [28] *Ibid.* Art. IX-A, s. 7.

"judicial backlog" and "docket congestion," it is foremost in the public mind as the main problem in the administration of justice in the country.

This problem was clearly recognized when the 1987 Constitution was being drafted. It provides for fixed deadlines for courts to decide cases, counted from the "filing of the last pleading, brief or memorandum required . . ."[29] According to the Constitution, all cases or matters filed after the effectivity of this Constitution must be decided or resolved within twenty-four months from date of submission for the Supreme Court, and, unless reduced by the Supreme Court, twelve months for all lower collegiate courts, and three months for all other lower courts.[30] The rule is so specific – and sufficiently realistic – that it provides for the consequence of missed deadlines, namely, the lapse of the period is officially notified to the parties with an explanation for the delay,[31] and the judge proceeds to resolve the case "without further delay."[32]

Not satisfied with that, the "Transitory Provisions" of the 1987 Constitution addressed the issue of pending cases. Within one year from ratification of the new charter, the Supreme Court was supposed to adopt "a systematic plan to expedite the decision" of all pending cases before all judicial and quasi-judicial bodies[33] and determine the "legal effect of the lapse [of the period] before the ratification of th[e new] Constitution."[34]

Today, more than a quarter-century since, the problem persists. It was rather pointedly recognized, to the chagrin of the Philippine judiciary, in a Canadian case denying the Philippine Government's request to extradite an accused in the murder of an anti-Marcos provincial governor right before the fall of Marcos. The Court of Appeal for Ontario concluded that "to surrender the appellant would be 'simply unacceptable' as the manner in which this prosecution has been conducted in the courts of the Philippines 'shocks the conscience', and that the cause of the unconscionable delay is the unexplained order of the Supreme Court of the Philippines [referring to successive Temporary Restraining Orders on interlocutory matter that effectively froze the trial]. The *shocking and unacceptable delay* in bringing the appellant's co-accused to trial and the *shocking and unacceptable period* of pre-trial detention and denial of bail fall far below Canadian standards."[35]

[29] Constitution, Art. VIII, s. 5(2). [30] *Ibid.* Art. VIII, s. 5(1).

[31] *Ibid.* Art. VIII, s. 5(3). [32] *Ibid.* Art. VIII, s. 5(4). [33] *Ibid.* Art. XVIII, s. 12.

[34] *Ibid.* Art. XVIII, ss. 13 and 14.

[35] The murder charge has since been dismissed, and the accused since acquitted. *Canada (Minister of Justice* v. *Pacificador*, Court of Appeal for Ontario, 60 O.R. (3d) 685 [2002] O.J. No. 3024, Docket No. C32995 (1 August 2002).

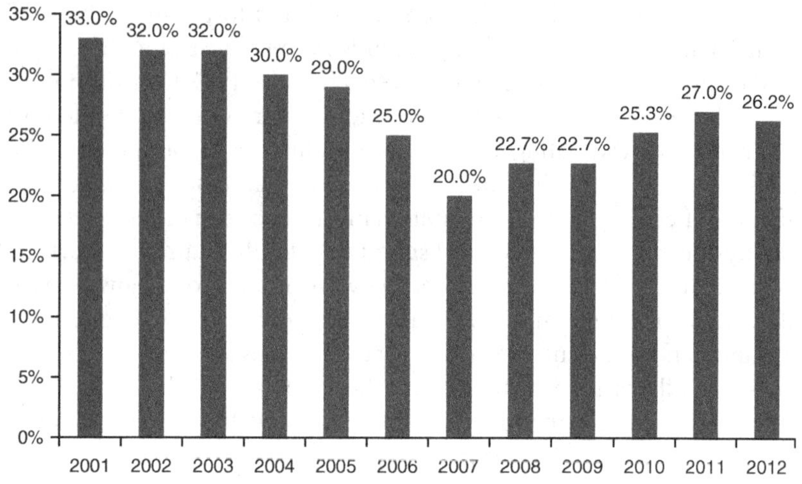

Figure 10.2: Vacancy rate for judicial positions
Source: Statistical Reports Division, Court Management Office – Office of the Court Administrator; Supreme Court of the Philippines, Annual Reports 2010, 2011, 2012.

Second, as the above Figure 10.2 indicates, the vacancy rate for judicial posts has remained around 20 percent to 30 percent and hence the need arises in filling up judicial vacancies and to improve judges' compensation and benefits to attract more and qualified applicants, and to make them competitive in the market. There have been ad hoc attempts to supplement judges' salaries with allowances from the local government units where they serve. However, a respected Supreme Court justice has warned that this "may give rise to a conflict of interest or weakened independence of judges."[36]

Third, the low "fill-up" rate has been identified as a potential source of abuse by enabling the court to "re-align" its budget by taking the unused salaries for the vacant seats and using them for staff bonuses. Conversely, the attempts by the executive branch to stop this practice have been seen as politically motivated attempts to curtail judicial independence.[37]

[36] Antonio T. Carpio, "Judicial reform in the Philippines" (speech delivered during the Central Luzon Regional Convention of the Integrated Bar of the Philippines, 29 June 2012), *The Bar Tribune*, August (2012), 13.

[37] Leila B. Salaverria, "Black color of protest in courts," *Inquirer News*, 25 September 2011, http://newsinfo.inquirer.net/64565/black-color-of-protest-in-courts; Cathy C. Yamsuan,

Fourth, the problem of judicial corruption persists. In 2008, then Vice-President Joseph Estrada, who was concurrently anti-crime chief, coined the term "hoodlums in robes" to refer to judges-for-sale.[38] A survey in 2005 estimated that corruption may exist in all courts. Overall, the survey suggested that only 14 percent of judges believed there is very little or no corruption in courts.[39] The estimated number of corrupt judges is more in lower courts and district courts. Seventeen percent of surveyed judges believed there are "very many" or "many" corrupt judges, and 44 percent believed there are "some" or "few" corrupt judges in district and lower courts. Surveyed judges estimated fewer corrupt judges in the Supreme Court and Shari'a courts.[40]

Fifth, the courts are under increasing pressure in populist politics. Given the political role that the courts have assumed, they have now been the subject of poll surveys regarding the public's trust and confidence. The rating shows that the trust of judicial appointees is relatively higher in comparison with that of cabinet appointees in the executive branch, but it is significant that non-political judges and politically appointed cabinet members are here measured by the same popular standards.[41]

2 Institutional safeguards for an independent judiciary

The courts are governed by the 1987 Constitution, which contains an entire section on the "Judicial Department."[42] The Constitution secures the independence of the courts from the political branches of government through institutional safeguards over its jurisdiction, personnel and budget. The courts' jurisdiction is protected from interference by the political branches in several ways.

2.1 *Jurisdictional safeguards*

To start with, the Constitution secures the Supreme Court's power of judicial review to strike down laws and international treaties;[43] its

"Judiciary money not going to hiring of new judges," *Inquirer News*, 24 August 2012, http://newsinfo.inquirer.net/256642/judiciary-money-not-going-to-hiring-of-new-judges; and Christine O. Avendaño, "Abad, Sereno end budget war," *Inquirer News*, 6 September 2012, http://newsinfo.inquirer.net/265030/abad-sereno-end-budget-war.

[38] GMA News, "Estrada and the 'hoodlums in robes,'" GMA News Online, 11 September 2008, http://www.gmanetwork.com/news/story/119704/news/estrada-and-the-hoodlums-in-robes.

[39] Social Weather Stations, 2005/06 Diagnostic Study of the Judiciary. [40] *Ibid.*

[41] *Ibid.* [42] Constitution, Art. VIII. [43] Constitution, Art. VIII, s. 4(2).

original[44] and appellate[45] jurisdiction over cases; and its rule-making powers[46] enabling the Supreme Court to create human rights remedies like the writs of *amparo*[47] (to stem the rise of extrajudicial killings) and *habeas data* (for the compulsory production of evidence);[48] the environmental remedy of the writ of *kalikasan*;[49] and the guidelines effectively de-criminalizing libel.[50]

Finally, the Constitution recognizes that the legislative power to allocate the courts' jurisdiction belongs to the Congress[51] but protects the Supreme Court's jurisdiction from being diminished by the Congress,[52] or increased without the Court's consent.[53]

2.2 *Appointment and tenure safeguards*

The most dramatic reform adopted by the 1987 Constitution pertained to the appointment of judges. Even under the independence constitution of 1935, which governed until Marcos installed one-man rule in 1972, major presidential appointees, including those of Supreme Court justices, were confirmed by an American-style Commission on Appointments comprised by senators and congressmen.[54]

Though that safeguard was restored in the 1987 Constitution,[55] judicial appointments were exempted from the confirmation process[56] to insulate them from political influence. Instead, the Constitution created a Judicial and Bar Council (hereinafter, "the JBC"), an independent body comprising a good balance between *ex officio* seat holders from the political branches of government and representatives from judicial stakeholders.[57] Its task is to "recommend [all] appointees to the Judiciary,"[58] and submit a short-list from which the president chooses.[59] Thus the old system of presidential appointment subject to congressional confirmation was replaced by a new system of JBC vetting and confined presidential choice.

44 *Ibid.* Art. VIII, s. 5(1). 45 *Ibid.* Art. VIII, s. 5(2). 46 *Ibid.* Art. VIII, s. 5(5).
47 A.M. No. 7-9-12-SC (25 September 2007).
48 A.M. No. 08-1-16-SC (2 February 2008).
49 A.M. No. 09-6-8-SC, Rule 7, s. 3 (13 April 2010).
50 A.M. No. 08-2008, *Guidelines in the Observance of a Rule of Preference in the Imposition of Penalties in Libel Cases* (25 January 2008).
51 Constitution, Art. VIII, s. 2(1). 52 *Ibid.* Art. VIII, s. 2(1). 53 *Ibid.* Art. VI, s. 30.
54 1935 Constitution, Art. VI, s. 12. 55 Constitution, Art. VI, s. 18.
56 *Ibid.* Art. VIII, s. 9 ("Such appointments need no confirmation").
57 *Ibid.* Art. VIII, s. 8. 58 *Ibid.* Art. VIII, s. 8(5). 59 *Ibid.* Art. VIII, s. 9.

Finally, to preclude the Marcos-era judiciary reform law[60] that gave the executive a proverbial "sword of Damocles" to hang over the judges' heads, the new Constitution expressly declares that "no law shall be passed reorganizing the Judiciary when it undermines the security of tenure of its Members."[61]

2.3 Budgetary and administrative safeguards

The Constitution affirmed congressional supremacy over the power of the purse[62] but gives the judiciary "fiscal autonomy,"[63] which means that appropriations for the judiciary may not be reduced below the previous year's and, once approved, shall be released automatically by the executive.[64]

Finally, the Constitution secures the administrative power of the Supreme Court to hire, compensate, promote and discipline its staff.[65] The Court is also given the gargantuan responsibility to administer the lower courts, for which a separate office, the Office of the Court Administrator, has been created.[66] It is tasked with the administration and finance of the lower courts and all of their personnel.

2.4 Remaining challenges to judicial independence

Notwithstanding the abovementioned safeguards, there remain serious challenges to judicial independence and legitimacy. The first problem is that the courts have overextended their reach into the political thicket, thus exceeding their expertise and jeopardizing their legitimacy. This is the classic counter-majoritarian dilemma in judicial review, played out in a Philippine context. Two excerpts from Supreme Court decisions exemplify this.

The 1987 Constitution has shifted to unelected judges the power to apply their own discretion in reviewing decisions by the politically

[60] Batas Pambansa 129 (14 August 1981) (the Judiciary Reorganization Act 1980).

[61] Constitution, Art. VIII, s. 2(2).

[62] Constitution, Art. VI, s. 29 ("No money shall be paid out of the Treasury except in pursuance of an appropriation made by law"), in relation to *ibid.* Art. VI, s. 24 ("All appropriation ... bill shall originate exclusively in the House of Representatives, but the Senate may propose or concur with amendments").

[63] *Ibid.* Art. VIII, s. 3. [64] *Ibid.* Art. VIII, s. 3. [65] *Ibid.* Art. VIII, ss. 5(6) and 6.

[66] Presidential Decree No. 828, as amended by Presidential Decree No. 842 (12 December 1975).

accountable branches of government and, worse, to dress up the review in the language of the law. The concurring opinion by Justice Feliciano in *Oposa* v. *Factoran* confronts that problem: "When substantive standards as general as 'the right to a balanced and healthy ecology' and 'the right to health' are combined with remedial standards as broad ranging as 'a grave abuse of discretion amounting to lack or excess of jurisdiction', the result will be, it is respectfully submitted, to propel courts into the uncharted ocean of social and economic policy making."[67] Such concern was also conveyed in the dissenting opinion by Justice Melencio-Herrera in *Garcia* v. *Board of Investments*, stating that "by no means, however, does [the Constitution] vest in the Courts the power to enter the realm of policy considerations under the guise of the commission of grave abuse of discretion. [The Supreme Court] has made a sweeping policy determination [on foreign investments] and has unwittingly transformed itself into what might be termed a 'government by the Judiciary', something never intended by the framers of the Constitution when they provided for separation of powers ... and excluded the Judiciary from policy-making."[68]

Second, and corollary to the first, this has led to the relaxation of legal doctrine and lessened the stability of legal outcomes. The Supreme Court itself has candidly recognized its capacity to "*brush aside technicalities of procedure*"[69] to carry out a "liberal policy ... on *locus standi*."[70] As regards the "grave abuse" standard, it has been said: "The catch, of course, is the meaning of 'grave abuse of discretion', which is a very elastic phrase that can expand or contract according to the disposition of the judiciary."[71]

Third, this has led to the charge that the courts have been politicized, and has provoked a similarly political backlash. Two chief justices have been the object of impeachment charges, though only the second impeachment attempt prospered. In 2003, the Supreme Court nullified

[67] Concurring opinion by Feliciano, J. in *Oposa* v. *Factoran*, G.R. No. 101083, 224 SCRA 792 (30 July 1992).

[68] Dissenting opinion by Melencio-Herrera, J. in *Garcia* v. *Board of Investments*, G.R. No. 92024, 191 SCRA 288 (9 November 1990).

[69] *Kapatiran ng mga Naglilingkod sa Pamahalaan ng Pilipinas, Inc.* v. *Tan*, G.R. No. 81311, 163 SCRA 371, 378 (30 June 1988).

[70] *Kilosbayan* v. *Guingona*, G.R. No. 113375, 232 SCRA 110, 137 (25 August 1994).

[71] *Oposa* v. *Factoran*, G.R. No. 101083, 224 SCRA 792, 810 (30 July 1992) (citing Isagani A. Cruz, *Philippine Political Law* (Quezon City: Central Lawbook Pub. Co., 1991), pp. 226–7).

the impeachment charge against Chief Justice Hilario Davide Jr, citing the one-year bar on a second impeachment against the same public officer. A first impeachment charge had been filed against Davide for having sworn in a new President while the incumbent had not yet left office. That charge was dismissed by the Congress, the sole authority to initiate impeachment proceedings. Soon thereafter, a second complaint was filed against Davide over irregularities in the use of a special, unaudited judiciary fund. It fell, however, within the one-year bar and was struck down by the Court.[72]

In 2012, the impeachment of Chief Justice Renato Corona for non-disclosure of certain assets led to his removal. The backdrop, however, was wholly political. A new president, Benigno Aquino III, had been elected in 2010 on an anti-corruption and anti-impunity campaign[73] but he was frustrated by the Supreme Court, and his first official act was to create a Truth Commission to inquire into corruption committed under his predecessor.[74] The Court struck it down on equal protection grounds, saying it had "singl[ed] out the previous [Arroyo's] administration" when it should have covered all past administrations.[75] Within one year, the Congress voted to impeach Chief Justice Corona,[76] followed by his removal in May 2012 after a full trial.[77]

Fourth, the Supreme Court's expansive use of its rule-making power has been labelled as the "extradecisional judicial activism,"[78] wherein the court advances substantive causes – for example, human rights, environmentalism, and press freedom – not by laying down precedent in the course of adjudication but by enacting rules purportedly in its administrative capacity over court procedure. Note that rule-making, when performed by any

[72] *Francisco* v. *House of Representatives*, G.R. No. 160261, 415 SCRA 44 (10 November 2003).

[73] Inaugural Address of President Benigno S. Aquino III (30 June 2010).

[74] Executive Order No. 1 (Establishing the Philippine Truth Commission of 2010) (30 July 2010).

[75] *Biraogo* v. *Philippine Truth Commission of 2010*, G.R. No. 192935, 637 SCRA 78 (7 December 2010).

[76] House of Representatives, *Verified Complaint for Impeachment (Articles of Impeachment)* (12 December 2011); see also *Chief Justice Renato C. Corona* v. *Senate of the Philippines sitting as an Impeachment Court*, G.R. No. 200242 (17 July 2012).

[77] Judgment, *In Re: Impeachment Trial of Honorable Chief Justice Renato C. Corona, Judgment*, Senate of the Philippines, Case No. 002-2011 (29 May 2012); *Lihaylihay* v. *House of Representatives*, G.R. No. 199509 (11 September 2012).

[78] B. D. G. Tiojanco and L. A. Y. Aguirre, "The scope, justifications and limitations of extradecisional judicial activism and governance in the Philippines," *Philippine Law Journal*, 84 (2009), 73.

other branch of government, is subject to judicial review, but rule-making by the Supreme Court is not reviewable by any court.

Fifth, the Court has also struggled with the role of politicians in the judicial appointments process and has recently reduced from two to one the seats allocated for the bicameral Congress in the Judicial and Bar Council.[79] There have been other attempts to shield judicial appointments from the elected branches but these have not prospered due to fears of in-breeding, privileging the judiciary's internal politics, and weakening the judiciary's ultimate accountability to the people.

3 The training of Filipino judges

The American influence in Philippine judicial tradition is best exemplified in the training and recruitment of judges. Unlike in the typical civil law jurisdiction where aspiring judges begin their judicial training in law school, the Filipino judge undergoes the same legal education received generically by any Filipino aspiring for a legal career. His civil law counterpart makes that choice earlier, typically in law school or as a fresh law graduate, whether he wishes to become a private law practitioner, or prosecutor or judge – and undergoes training specifically directed toward that career choice. In contrast, a Filipino judge – just like his American counterpart – is not expected to make that career choice until well into his life as a lawyer. Indeed, since a judicial applicant is required to have at least ten years' law practice, the Filipino judge has had extensive exposure to non-judicial work by the time he joins the bench.

3.1 Legal education

The American influence is reflected as well in the teaching of law. Given the country's long period as a Spanish colony, the study of law was originally designed along the lines of continental civil law. Modern legal education began at the oldest university in the country, the University of Santo Tomas, which formed its Faculties of Civil Law and Canon Law in 1734.[80] In 1899, the newly established government of the independence movement created a new state university, the Literary University of the Philippines, including a Faculty of Law with a six-year curriculum

[79] *Chavez* v. *Judicial and Bar Council*, G.R. No. 202242 (17 July 2012).
[80] Irene R. Cortes, *Essays on Legal Education* (Quezon City: University of the Philippines, Law Center, 1994), p. 5.

leading to a Bachelor of Laws degree and which included both broad courses in history and the social sciences, together with doctrinal courses in law.[81] In the same year, Felipe Calderon, one of authors of the 1899 Constitution, founded the Esuela de Derecho de Manila, which in 1924 would become the Manila Law College.[82]

It was only in 1911 that the American style of law teaching was introduced with the establishment of the University of the Philippines' College of Law, which offered initially a three-year professional course in law. Later, a two-year pre-law college course (eventually called the Associate in Arts degree) was required. In 1960, the pre-law requirement was upgraded to a four-year Bachelor of Arts degree.

The law program itself focuses on professional training, and is taught using the case method. A bar examination is conducted by the Supreme Court by virtue of its power over "admission to the practice of law,"[83] and covers the entire range of legal doctrine: civil law, commercial law, remedial law, criminal law, public and private international law, political law, labor and social legislation, medical jurisprudence, taxation and legal ethics.[84]

There are currently 105 law schools in the country. With but a few exceptions, instruction is carried out almost entirely by part-time lecturers consisting of private practitioners, judges, prosecutors and government officials, typically after office hours. Significantly, the state-funded University of the Philippines, declared by law as the "national university," is the only law school with a predominantly full-time faculty.[85] Today a Legal Education Board has been created by law to regulate the teaching of law.[86]

3.2 Continuing education for judges

To ensure and sustain the competence of Filipino judges, a Philippine Judicial Academy has been created by law.[87] The Academy conducts a

81 S. Guevara, *The Laws of The First Philippine Republic (The Laws of Malolos) 1898–1899* (Manila: National Historical Institute, 1972).

82 J. Bantigue, "History of the legal profession" in J. Coquia (ed.), *Legal Profession: Readings, Materials and Cases: An Introduction on How to Become a Lawyer* (Manila: Rex Book Store, 1993), pp. 5–20.

83 Constitution, Art. VIII, s. 5(5).

84 Rules of Court, Rule 138, s. 6.

85 Republic Act No. 9500 (University of the Philippines Charter of 2008) (29 April 2008).

86 Republic Act No. 7662 (the Legal Education Reform Act 1993) (23 December 1993).

87 Republic Act No. 8557 (An Act Establishing the Philippine Judicial Academy, Defining Its Powers and Functions . . .) (26 February 1998).

Pre-Judicature Program for applicants to judicial posts, a seminar for newly appointed judges, courses for other court personnel, and courses for judges with specialized jurisdictions (e.g. commercial courts). It is only at the Academy, in contrast to the regular law schools, that "all subjects are approached from a judicial perspective [that] departs from the provision-centered learning in law school."[88]

4 Foreign influences on the Philippine judicial system

The islands in the Philippine archipelago were governed by disparate tribal chiefs until the islands were colonized by the Spanish crown in 1565. In June 1898, Filipino revolutionaries proclaimed an independent republic. In the meantime, the Spanish-American War broke out and the United States defeated Spain in a token battle in Manila Bay in May 1898. By February 1899, open hostilities erupted between the Filipino revolutionaries and the United States and, by 1902, President Emilio Aguinaldo, leader of the revolution, was finally captured by the Americans after more than two years of guerilla resistance.

Though the Americans inherited a judicial system from the Spanish colonial government, the structure of the Philippine court system today is almost entirely American-influenced.

4.1 Transition from Spanish to American colonialism

The Philippine courts during the Spanish sovereignty consisted of superior courts, the Audencia Territorial de Manila, the Audencia de lo Criminal de Cebu and the Audencia de lo Criminal de Vigan.[89] The Audiencia was both a court, an advisory council, and acted as caretaker when the Governorship was vacant.

When the United States took over, the Philippine Commission, an American-appointed office, enacted Act No. 136 which abolished the Spanish Audencia and replaced it with a new American-style court system. Significantly, despite the American origins of the present judicial system, the colonial government deliberately did not adopt the jury system for the Philippines.

88 Philippine Judicial Academy website, http://philja.judiciary.gov.ph/programs.htm.

89 M. T. Chan, *The Audiencia and the Legal System in the Philippines, 1583–1900* (Manila: M.T. Chan, 1998). See also J. P. Bengzon, *The Philippine Judicial System* (Manila: G. Rangel and Sons, 1968), p. 6.

The current judicial system, however, traces its history to the passage by the Americans of the Judiciary Law of 1901,[90] which also created Courts of First Instance and Justice of the Peace courts. This was maintained in two subsequent constitutional documents enacted by the US Congress for the governance of the Philippines, namely, the Philippine Organic Act of 1902[91] and the Jones Law of 1916,[92] which both gave appellate powers to the United States Supreme Court over decisions by the Philippine Supreme Court.

Philippine criminal law derives from the Spanish Penal Code,[93] which was extended to the Philippine Islands, then a Spanish colony, in July 1887. A new government under the United States, the new colonial power, revised the Code and in 1932 issued the Revised Penal Code,[94] which remains in force today. Various criminal statutes or "special laws" have been since enacted.[95]

The Civil Code of the Philippines[96] derives mainly from the Spanish Civil Code of 1889,[97] and large parts have since been supplanted by veritable codes in themselves: e.g. Book One on Persons and Family Relations, by the Family Code of the Philippines which came into effect in August 1988[98] in order "to reflect contemporary trends and conditions."[99]

4.2 *Transition during the Commonwealth period*

In 1934, the US Congress eventually passed an independence bill that would enable the Philippines eventually to become independent.[100]

90 Act No. 136 (11 June 1901).
91 Public Act No. 235 (An Act Temporarily to Provide for the Administration of the Affairs of Civil Government in the Philippine Islands, and for Other Purposes) (1 July 1902).
92 Public Act No. 240 (An Act to Declare the Purpose of the People of the United States as to the Future Political Status of the People of the Philippine Islands, and to Provide a More Autonomous Government for Those Islands) (29 August 1916).
93 *US* v. *Tamparong*, G.R. No. 9527, 31 Phil. 321 (1915).
94 Act No. 3815, as amended (An act revising the Penal Code and other penal laws) (1931).
95 L. B. Reyes, *The Revised Penal Code: Criminal Law (Book One)*, 17th edn. (Manila: Rex Printing, 2012), p. 22.
96 Republic Act No. 386 (The Civil Code of the Philippines) (1950).
97 A. M. Tolentino, *Commentaries and Jurisprudence on the Civil Code of the Philippines* (Quezon City: Central Lawbook Publishing Co. Inc., 1990), vol. I, p. 12.
98 Executive Order No. 209 (1987), promulgated by President Corazon Aquino as law when she still possessed legislative powers during the transition after the ouster of Marcos in February 1986.
99 Tolentino, *Commentaries and Jurisprudence*, p. 218.
100 Tydings-McDuffie Law (1934).

A new Constitution would be adopted in 1935, and under which the country would be governed for the next decades: through independence in 1946, through six democratically elected presidents in an independent republic, and until Marcos proclaimed martial law in 1972.

The familiar structure today of a government of separated powers and an independent judiciary, though these existed in various degrees even before 1935, is usually traced to this 1935 Constitution. Significantly this Constitution transferred from the Congress to the courts the rule-making power over pleading, practice and procedure in all courts and the admission to the practice of law.

4.3 *The period of Japanese Occupation and its aftermath*

In 1942, the Imperial Japanese Forces occupied the City of Manila and placed the occupied territory under military administration. Courts remained in existence with no substantial change in their organization and jurisdiction "provided that their outlines be approved by the Commander in Chief of the Imperial Japanese Forces."[101] The Japanese interregnum left no recognizable influence in the Philippine judiciary.

When the war ended, a People's Court was created to try all the so-called "collaborators" during the Japanese Occupation.[102]

5 Concluding remarks

The Philippines, confronted with a dysfunctional democracy, has turned to the courts as the last institutional corrective mechanism short of military intervention or armed revolution. The 1987 Constitution codified a social reform agenda through its directive clauses, but democratic elections have not led to governments that would carry out that agenda. The courts are the default mechanism when electoral politics fails.

The drafters of the 1987 Constitution empowered the courts because they feared one-man dictatorship as much as the manipulability of the popular vote. Having shifted the onus to the courts, and now having seen the limits of adjudication and its manipulability as well, the nation turns to the political branches to "guard the guardians." If counter-majoritarianism required the perfection of the judiciary,

[101] T. A. Agoncillo, *History of the Filipino People* (Quezon City: Garotech Publishing, 1990), p. 395.

[102] Commonwealth Act No. 682 (1945).

popular constitutionalism assumes a functioning democracy where the sovereign chooses knowingly.

The recent judicial crisis, symbolized by the impeachment of the Chief Justice, signals an emerging consensus that the 1987 Constitution, after a quarter-century, is now reclaimed by "We, the sovereign Filipino people"[103] and restores the hope, expressed as far back as the 1935 Constitution, that "the people who are authors of this blessing must also be its guardians, their eyes must be ever ready to mark, their voice to pronounce aggression on the authority of their constitution" and that the true test of the constitution lies in the "crucible of Filipino minds and hearts than in consultation rooms and court chambers."[104]

The courts will remain secure in that role despite the crisis, but it cannot escape unscathed from the bruising showdown with the political branches. One possible positive legacy is that henceforth the judges will be more acutely aware of the limits of judicial power and recognize the place of the politically accountable branches of government in choosing and implementing public policy. One possible negative legacy is that the judges, instead of being attuned to the deep moral and social values of their time, will instead merely keep in step with fleeting political majorities, the very evil that counter-majoritarianism seeks to preclude.

References

Agoncillo, T. A. *History of the Filipino People* (Quezon City: Garotech Publishing, 1990)

Bantigue, J. "History of the legal profession" in J. R. Coquia (ed.), pp. 5–20

Bengzon, J. P. *The Philippine Judicial System* (Manila: G. Rangel and Sons, 1968)

Carpio, A. T. "Judicial reform in the Philippines," *The Bar Tribune* (August 2012)

Chan, M. T. *The Audiencia and the Legal System in the Philippines, 1583–1900* (Manila: M. T. Chan, 1998)

Coquia, J. R. (ed.) *Legal Profession: Readings, Materials and Cases: An Introduction on how to Become a Lawyer* (Manila: Rex Book Store, 1993)

Cortes, I. R. *Essays on Legal Education* (Quezon City: University of the Philippines, Law Center, 1994)

Cruz, I. A. *Philippine Political Law* (Quezon City: Central Lawbook Publishing Co., 1991)

Guevara, S. *The Laws of The First Philippine Republic (The Laws of Malolos) 1898–1899* (Manila: National Historical Institute, 1972)

[103] Constitution, Preamble.

[104] *Angara v. Electoral Commission*, G.R. No. 45081 (15 July 1936).

Reyes, L. B. *The Revised Penal Code: Criminal Law (Book One)*, 17th edn. (Manila: Rex Printing, 2012)

Tiojanco, B. D. G. and Aguirre, L. A. Y. "The scope, justifications and limitations of extradecisional judicial activism and governance in the Philippines," *Philippine Law Journal*, 84 (2009), 73

Tolentino, A. M. *Commentaries and Jurisprudence on the Civil Code of the Philippines* (Quezon City: Central Lawbook Publishing Co., 1990), vol. I

11

Courts in Malaysia and judiciary initiated reforms

YEOW CHOY CHOONG

Malaysia achieved her independence in 1957 and has adopted a system of parliamentary democracy with a constitutional monarch as the Head of the Federation of thirteen states and three federal territories.[1] The constitutional monarch or the *Yang di-Pertuan Agong* is elected by the rulers of the nine Malay states with rulers from among their own members. Elections are held every five years. Hence, the office of the *Yang di-Pertuan Agong* rotates among the nine rulers. The nine rulers and the governors or the *Yang di-Pertua Negeri* of the other four states form a Conference of Rulers or *Majlis Raja-Raja.*[2]

Its constitutional system of governance is based on a written Constitution (the Federal Constitution) as the supreme law of the Federation.[3] Malaysia is a secular state and the Federal Constitution clearly provides for separation of powers among the executive, legislative and judicial branches of the government.

Malaysia's legal history can be traced back to the Malacca Sultanate at the beginning of the fifteenth century. British colonial rule that began in the later part of the eighteenth century has had a major influence on the modern day legal setting of the country. Islamic or *Syariah* law and the customary laws of Malaysia's indigenous communities also form part of the corpus of laws in Malaysia.

Malaysia's legal system is based on the common law. The Civil Law Act 1956 authorizes the application of English law in the whole of Malaysia. A parallel *Syariah* law system exists alongside the civil justice system. The *Syariah* courts exercise jurisdiction over Islamic law and

[1] The thirteen states are Perlis, Kedah, Penang, Perak, Selangor, Negeri Sembilan, Melaka, Johor, Kelantan, Terengganu, Pahang, Sabah and Sarawak, and the three federal territories are Kuala Lumpur, Labuan and Putrajaya.

[2] The *Majlis Raja-Raja* is established by Article 38 of the Federal Constitution.

[3] See the Federal Constitution, Art. 4.

personal laws of persons professing the religion of Islam.[4] In addition, the various state Enactments (and Act, as in the case of the Federal Territories) provide for *Syariah* criminal offenses, and matters relating thereto. These include offenses in relation to the faith or *aqidah*, offenses relating to the sanctity of the religion of Islam and its institution, offenses relating to decency and other miscellaneous offenses.[5]

Malaysia has a robust judiciary that is committed to the rule of law. In *Pengarah Tanah dan Galian, WP* v. *Sri Lempah Enterprise*,[6] the Federal Court declared in clear terms that the executive branch of the government has limited powers. The Federal Court said that: "Unfettered discretion is a contradiction in terms . . . Every legal power must have legal limits, otherwise there is dictatorship . . . The courts are the only defense of the liberty of the subject against departmental aggression."[7] Such a pronouncement is clear testimony to the Malaysian judiciary's conviction and allegiance to the rule of law.

This chapter consists of five main parts. The first part provides a brief description of the legal and judicial system of Malaysia. This part of the report will elaborate on, among other topics, the organization and the jurisdiction of the courts. It will also examine statistics concerning the number of judicial positions within the judiciary and the data on the judge-to-population ratio.

This will then be followed by an elucidation of the sources of and influences on the establishment of the judicial system. The third part of this chapter will deal with issues relating to judicial appointments, judicial independence and access to justice. The relevance and importance of alternative dispute resolution processes within the context of the courts in Malaysia is discussed in the part entitled "Courts and alternative dispute resolution." The role and approaches of the courts relating to the promotion and facilitation of two specific alternative dispute resolution processes, namely, arbitration and mediation, are examined and discussed in this part of the report.

Two important aspects concerning recent reforms initiated and undertaken by the Malaysian judiciary and the performance of the courts in Malaysia are analyzed in the subsequent part of the report. This country

4 See the Ninth Schedule of the Federal Constitution, List II, Clause 1.

5 For a complete list of the offenses, see, for example, the Syariah Criminal Offenses (Federal Territories) Act 1997.

6 [1979] 1 MLJ 135.

7 Per Raja Azlan Shah Ag CJ (Malaya) (as HRH then was): [1979] 1 MLJ 135 at 148.

report will conclude with a number of observations pertaining to the areas and issues raised in the report.

1 General description of the judicial system

1.1 Organization of the courts and judicial posts

Although Malaysia is a federation, the courts in Malaysia are organized under a single unitary federal system. Currently, the Malaysian judiciary comprises the Federal Court, the Court of Appeal, two High Courts of co-ordinate jurisdiction – one for West Malaysia (the High Court of Malaya) and one for East Malaysia (the High Court of Sabah and Sarawak) and the subordinate courts (the sessions and the magistrates' courts). The Federal Court, the Court of Appeal and the High Courts are also commonly referred to as the superior courts and the sessions and magistrates' courts are commonly referred to as the subordinate courts.

Notably, there is no federal and state court dichotomy within the overall federal court system. However, there are state courts outside this federal system. As noted earlier, a parallel *Syariah* law system exists alongside the federal civil justice system. *Syariah* courts come within the purview of each of the states and the federal territories in the federation. *Syariah* courts are state courts established under various state laws, which also provide for their constitution, jurisdiction and procedure. Besides the *Syariah* courts, a hierarchy of state native courts exists in Sabah and Sarawak to hear disputes among natives.[8]

Although it is evident that there is now a three-tier system existing in the superior courts, it may be appropriate to provide a brief historical background of the structure of the superior courts, lest there be any confusion. The three-tier system has existed since Malaysia achieved independence in 1957. However, the superior courts were made up of the Judicial Committee of the Privy Council in London, the Federal Court and the High Courts.

In 1985, appeals to the Privy Council were abolished.[9] With the abolishment of appeals to the Privy Council, the Federal Court became the final court of appeal. At the same time, the Federal Court was

[8] For an exposition on the *Syariah* courts and native courts in Malaysia, see M. A. Wu, *Malaysian Legal System*, 3rd edn. (Kuala Lumpur: Longman, 2007), pp. 206–10 and pp. 244–58 respectively.

[9] It should be noted that appeals to the Privy Council in relation to constitutional and criminal matters had earlier been abolished in 1978.

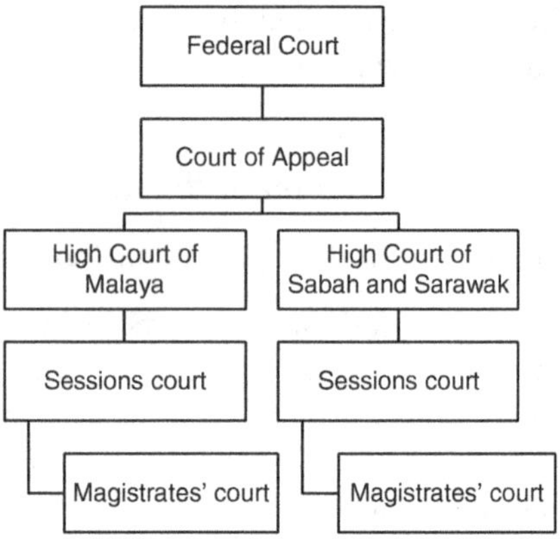

Figure 11.1: Structure of courts in Malaysia since 1994

renamed the Supreme Court. Hence, for the period between 1985 and 1994, there was only a two-tier system that existed in the superior courts.

In 1994, further changes were made to the structure and organization of the superior courts in Malaysia. The two-tier system was reverted back into a three-tier system. In the process, a new intermediary court between the High Courts and the Supreme Court was established, namely the Court of Appeal. At the same time the Supreme Court was once again renamed as the Federal Court.[10]

The abolishment of appeals to the Judicial Committee of the Privy Council, or severance of the umbilical link, in 1985 was understandable and not unexpected. It had become the "trend" in other commonwealth countries. As noted by Professor Wu Min Aun:

> With independence comes the desire to chart one's own destiny, including the field of jurisprudence, using one's own indigenously developed forum.[11]

However, the reason(s) for the change in the name of the apex court from Federal Court to Supreme Court and back to Federal Court is not as obvious or as easily explainable as the justification for, say, the severance of formal judicial links with the United Kingdom. The necessity for the change in the name of the apex court will remain a matter for speculation.

[10] The High Court of Borneo was also renamed the High Court of Sabah and Sarawak.
[11] Wu, *Malaysian Legal System*, p. 402.

The maximum number of judicial positions available at each of the superior courts is pre-determined by the Federal Constitution. Article 122(1) of the Federal Constitution provides that the Federal Court shall consist of: the Chief Justice of the Federal Court; the President of the Court of Appeal; the Chief Judge of Malaya; the Chief Judge of Sabah and Sarawak; and eleven other judges.[12] In the case of the Court of Appeal, Article 122A of the Federal Constitution provides that the Court of Appeal shall consist of the President of the Court of Appeal and thirty-two other judges.[13]

As of 2011, there are seventy-three authorized positions for the two High Courts. Article 122AA of the Federal Constitution provides for a maximum number of sixty judges for the High Court in Malaya and thirteen judges for the High Court in Sabah and Sarawak. Hence, the High Court in Malaya consists of the Chief Judge of Malaya and sixty other judges. The High Court in Sabah and Sarawak consists of the Chief Judge of Sabah and Sarawak and thirteen other judges.

The Federal Constitution also makes provision for the appointment of Judicial Commissioners. For all intents and purposes, judicial commissioners have all the powers of a High Court judge. Judicial commissioners sit as judges of the High Court. The only fundamental difference between a High Court judge and a judicial commissioner is that the latter is appointed for a fixed term, and such an appointment may or may not be renewed at the expiry of the term.[14] Unlike the other judicial positions in the superior courts as discussed above, there is no maximum limit on the number of judicial commissioners that may be appointed.

The number of judicial positions in the superior courts, authorized and filled, as of 2011 are as in Table 11.1:

[12] It should be noted the eleven positions may be varied by an order of the *Yang di-Pertuan Agong*. Article 122(1A) also empowers the *Yang di-Pertuan Agong*, acting on the advice of the Chief Justice of the Federal Court, to appoint, for such purposes or for such period of time as he may specify, any person who has held high judicial office in Malaysia to be an additional judge of the Federal Court.

[13] This number may be changed by order of the *Yang di-Pertuan Agong*.

[14] Judicial commissioners also draw marginally lower salaries when compared to those of High Court judges.

Table 11.1: *Number of judicial positions in superior courts (2011)*

Judges	Authorized positions	Filled positions
Federal Court (includes Chief Justice, President of the Court of Appeal and 2 Chief Judges)	15	11
Court of Appeal	32	25
High Courts	73	55
Judicial Commissioners	N/A	42
Total	120	133

Source: World Bank, *Malaysia: Court Backlog and Delay Reduction Program, A Progress Report*, August 2011.

As for the number of positions in the subordinate courts and other judicial and legal services,[15] as of 2011, the figures are as in Table 11.2:

Table 11.2: *Number of judicial positions in subordinate courts (2011)*

Judges	Authorized positions	Filled positions
Sessions court	157	117
Magistrates' courts	193	165
Other judicial and legal services	343	266
Total	693	548

Source: World Bank, *Malaysia: Court Backlog and Delay Reduction Program, A Progress Report*, August 2011.

The number of judicial positions *per se* does not tell us whether Malaysia is in need of more judges or has too many judges. Looking at the judge-to-population ratio and comparing this ratio to that in other jurisdictions may provide a better indication of the adequacy of the number of judges in Malaysia. With a population of roughly 28 million, the ratio of judges to population is said to be between 1.48 and 2.42 "judges" per 100,000 inhabitants (not counting roughly 30,000 lay justices of the peace), depending on whether the number of Judicial and Legal Service officers assigned to the courts but not on the bench

[15] These officers serve as deputy registrars or senior assistant registrars in the courts.

are included. As evident from the comparison, the ratio is very low. However, there is no correlation between the ratio and the efficiency of the courts. This aspect concerning efficiency and the performance of the courts in Malaysia is examined in a separate and later part of this report.

1.2 Jurisdiction and procedure of the courts

A civil action may be initiated in the magistrates' court, the sessions court or the High Court. The civil jurisdiction of the magistrates' and sessions courts is provided in the Subordinate Courts Act 1948.

The Subordinate Courts (Amendment) Act 2010, which came into force on 1 March 2013, has significantly increased the civil jurisdiction of the subordinate courts. The monetary jurisdiction of the magistrates' and sessions court has been increased from RM 25,000 and RM 100,000 to RM 100,000 and RM 1,000,000 respectively. In addition, the sessions court may now grant certain equitable remedies, such as injunctions and declarations.[16]

There is no limit on the jurisdiction of the High Court as far as the monetary amount and subject matter are concerned. The jurisdiction of the High Court is provided in section 23 of the Courts of Judicature Act 1964. It is pertinent to point out that unlike the jurisdiction of the subordinate courts, the jurisdiction of the High Court is extra-territorial in nature. A foreign defendant may be sued in Malaysia as long as it can be shown that she is one of several co-defendants in the suit and one of her co-defendants resides or has her place of business within the local jurisdiction of the court. The High Court is also conferred with appellate jurisdiction and hears appeals from the subordinate courts.

The Court of Appeal does not have original jurisdiction over civil matters. It has only appellate jurisdiction and appeals from the High Court lie to the Court of Appeal. Although the Federal Court is the court of final appeal, it is conferred with original jurisdiction in a number of matters. It has original jurisdiction over matters relating to the validity of laws made by Parliament or the legislature of a state and disputes on any other question between states or between the federation and any state.[17] The Federal Court is also conferred with advisory jurisdiction. The *Yang di-Pertuan Agong* may refer to the Federal Court for its opinion on any question that has arisen or appears to him likely to arise regarding the effect of any provision of the Constitution.[18]

[16] At the current exchange rate, US $1 is equivalent to about RM 3.2.

[17] See the Federal Constitution, Art. 128(1)(a) and (b).

[18] See *ibid.* Art. 130.

Civil proceedings in the subordinate courts and in the High Court are now governed by the Rules of Court 2012. The Rules of Court came into force on 1 August 2012. The Rules of Court 2012 replaced the Rules of the High Court 1980 and the Subordinate Courts Rules 1980. These rules of court have their roots in the former English Rules of the Supreme Court.

In relation to the criminal jurisdiction of the courts, reference must once again be made to the Subordinate Courts Act 1948 and the Courts of Judicature Act 1964. The jurisdiction of the courts is determined by the severity of the offense and sentence. Suffice it to say that cases punishable with the death penalty can only be tried by the High Court.

Criminal proceedings in the subordinate courts and in the High Court are governed by the Criminal Procedure Code. All cases in the subordinate courts are tried before a single judge of the sessions court or a magistrate. The sessions court judge or magistrate decides on questions of both law and facts. Likewise, cases before the High Court are tried before a single judge. Only the Court of Appeal and Federal Court operate in panels. The Court of Appeal will convene with a panel of three judges, while cases before the Federal Court may be heard by a panel of three or more judges in odd numbers.

Prior to 1995, criminal cases before the High Court of Malaya involving the death penalty were tried by judge and jury.[19] Trial by judge and jury has been abolished since 1995.

1.3 The civil and Syariah dichotomy

The existence of a dual legal system has no doubt enriched the legal jurisprudence of the country. Be that as it may, a number of challenging issues have arisen over the years. These range from jurisdictional issues to issues concerning the right of representation by counsel of choice in the *Syariah* courts.

In relation to the former, the amendment to the Federal Constitution in 1988 to demarcate the distinction between and remove whatever doubts that remain regarding the jurisdictions of the civil and *Syariah* courts has not produced the desired results.[20] Cases that expose the serious issue of conflict between the jurisdiction of the civil and *Syariah*

[19] However, cases triable under the Firearms (Increased Penalties) Act 1971, the Dangerous Drugs Act 1952 and security offenses under the Internal Security Act 1960 were still tried by a single judge.

[20] Article 121(1A) was introduced into the Federal Constitution in 1988 and it reads as follows: "The courts referred to in Clause (1) shall have no jurisdiction in respect of any matter within the jurisdiction of the Syariah courts."

courts, that is, whether a particular matter falls within the jurisdiction of one court or the other, continue to come before the courts.[21] As for the latter, a number of contentious and constitutional issues regarding the right of a non-Muslim counsel to appear before a *Syariah* court are currently pending appeal before the Federal Court.[22]

1.4 Other courts

It has been noted that the federal courts consist of three-tier superior courts and the subordinate courts. Other courts and tribunals also exist in the federal system. These include the courts for children, the industrial courts and the courts-martial. Specialized tribunals would include the tribunal for consumer claims, the tribunal for homebuyer claims and the public service tribunal. These are judicial bodies with specialized jurisdiction.

Unlike in some jurisdictions, there are no family, intellectual property, admiralty or constitutional courts in Malaysia. The High Courts in Malaysia were traditionally divided into criminal and civil divisions. However, further "sub-divisions" have been created administratively and as a result of the reorganization and specialization, family, intellectual property or admiralty cases, for example, are heard before designated courts within the civil division.

Of significance is the Special Court. This court was established in 1993.[23] The Special Court was set up to hear "any proceedings by or against the *Yang di-Pertuan Agong* or the Ruler of a State in his personal capacity." Article 182(3) of the Federal Constitution provides that the Special Court shall have "exclusive jurisdiction to try all offenses committed in the Federation by the *Yang di-Pertuan Agong* or the Ruler of a State and all civil cases by or against the *Yang di-Pertuan Agong* or the Ruler of a State notwithstanding where the cause of action arose."

The Special Court is composed of the Chief Justice of the Federal Court, who shall be the Chairman, the Chief Judges of the High Courts, and two other persons who hold or have held office as judge of the Federal Court or a High Court appointed by the Conference of Rulers.[24]

[21] Some of the more prominent and controversial cases include *Majlis Ugama Islam Pulau Pinag dan Seberang Perai* v. *Shaik Zolkaffily bin Shaik Nattar* [2003] 3 MLJ 705; *Lina Joy* v. *Majlis Agama Islam Wilayah Persekutuan* [2007] 4 MLJ 585; and *Subashini A/P Rajasingam* v. *Saravanan A/L Thangathoray* [2008] 2 MLJ 147.

[22] See *Victoria Jayaseele Martin* v. *Majlis Agama Islam Wilayah Persekutuan & Anor* [2011] 9 MLJ 194, HC; [2013] 6 MLJ 646, CA.

[23] See the Federal Constitution, Part XV.

[24] See *ibid.* Art. 182(1).

Two key characteristics regarding the Special Court that warrant mention are as follows. First, all proceedings in the Special Court are to be decided in accordance with the opinion of the majority of the members and its decision shall be final and conclusive and shall not be challenged or called into question in any court on any grounds.[25] Second, the consent of the Attorney General must be obtained before any action may be instituted against the *Yang di-Pertuan Agong* or the Ruler of a State in the Special Court.

To date, only two actions have been instituted against two rulers of two states in the Special Court. In the first case, the plaintiff failed in her bid to sue the ruler of one state for damages for libel. By a majority of four to one, the Special Court ruled that since the plaintiff was a non-citizen, she had no *locus standi* to commence proceedings against the ruler in his personal capacity.[26] In the second case, a financial institution successfully obtained judgment against the ruler of another state based on a standby letter of credit issued by the financial institution.[27]

2 Sources of law and influences of the establishment of the judicial system

2.1 Divergent sources of law

In his treatise *The Applicable Law in Singapore and Malaysia*, Michael F. Rutter very ably and admirably outlined, discussed and analyzed the sources of law in Malaysia and the extent to which the Malaysian courts are influenced by their own decisions and those of the courts in other

[25] See *ibid.* Art. 182(6).

[26] See *Faridah Begum bte Abdullah* v. *Sultan Haji Ahmad Shah* [1996] 1 MLJ 617.

[27] *Standard Chartered Bank Malaysia Bhd* v. *Duli Yang Maha Mulia Tuanku Ja' afar Ibni Almarhum Tuanku Abdul Rahman, Yang Di Pertuan Besar Negeri Sembilan Darul Khusus [2009] 4 MLJ 1.*

Also see *DYTM Tengku Idris Shah Ibni Sultan Salahuddin Abdul Aziz Shah* v. *Dikim Holdings Sdn Bhd & Anor* [2003] 2 MLJ 1. In this case, the plaintiff had filed an action in the High Court. Subsequently, the plaintiff was proclaimed the ruler of a state. One of the issues for determination by the Federal Court was whether the High Court had jurisdiction or power to transfer the suit to the Special Court established under Part XV of the Federal Constitution. For a more in-depth discussion of the composition, role and functions of the Special Court, see H. P. Lee, "Malaysian royalty and the special court" in A. Harding and P. Nicholson (eds.), *New Courts in Asia* (New York: Routledge, 2010), pp. 317–36.

commonwealth jurisdictions.[28] In dealing with the sources of Malaysian law, the learned author classified them into two distinct categories, namely (i) indigenous sources of law and (ii) foreign sources of law.

The indigenous sources of law are made up of customary law, Muslim law, Malaysian legislation (federal and state), and Malaysian case law. Customary law can further be sub-divided into Malay customary law, Chinese customary law, Hindu customary law and native customary law. Rutter sees foreign sources of law as those from: English statutes, English common law, Indian law, Singapore law, and case law from other jurisdictions.

It is indisputable that the doctrine of *stare decisis* or binding precedent has taken root in Malaysia's legal system. The courts in Malaysia have always applied both the concept of vertical *stare decisis* and horizontal *stare decisis* in their decision-making process. Vertical *stare decisis* means that decisions of higher courts are binding on the lower courts. The concept of horizontal *stare decisis* is slightly more complicated but, as a general rule, the apex court in Malaysia has affirmed on more than one occasion that the rules as laid down in *Young* v. *Bristol Aeroplane Company Ltd*[29] will apply in Malaysia. While decisions from the courts in the commonwealth jurisdictions are not binding on the courts in Malaysia, they are regarded as being of persuasive authority. Malaysia's jurisprudence has been greatly enriched by the practice of her courts in liberally referring to the judgments of and incorporating relevant principles that are propounded by the courts in England, India, Hong Kong, Australia, Singapore and other commonwealth countries.

On the topic of the applicable law in Malaysia, it is fitting to quote Michael F. Rutter, who opined that the applicable law in Malaysia "is a mosaic of differences, borrowed laws, continuing traditions and locally produced jurisprudence."[30]

2.2 *Colonial influences on the establishment of the judicial system*

Prior to British Colonial rule, the Portuguese and the Dutch had colonized Malacca for over 275 years. However, the most significant influence on the development of the Malaysian judicial system can be traced to British colonial rule from 1786 to 1957. The first territory in the Malay

[28] M. F. Rutter, *The Applicable Law in Singapore and Malaysia* (Singapore: Malayan Law Journal, 1989), pp. 413–548.

[29] [1946] AC 163.

[30] Rutter, *The Applicable Law in Singapore and Malaysia*, p. 551.

Peninsula to be held by the British was Penang in 1786.[31] This was followed by the cession of Singapore and the incorporation of the former Dutch colony of Malacca in 1824. All three colonies were incorporated as a single colonial entity called the Straits Settlements in 1824.

The period of the British Straits Settlements from 1824 to 1946 witnessed the establishment of the Courts of Judicature and the Supreme Court of the Straits Settlements. British intervention in the rest of Peninsula Malaya began with the introduction of its Residency system in Negri Sembilan in 1873, and its extension to Perak (1874), Selangor (1875), and Pahang (1888). They were constitutionally amalgamated into what came to be known as the Federated Malay States in 1895 and developed their own system of colonial courts with the Supreme Court of the Federated Malay States at its apex.

These courts, along with the Supreme Court of the Straits Settlements, were the precursors to the current courts in Malaysia. The influence of British Colonial rule does not stop at the structure and hierarchy of the courts but extends to court procedures, rules of evidence and the establishment of the Bar.

3 Judicial appointments, judicial independence and access to justice

This part of the report will explicate, discuss and comment on the process of judicial appointments, concerns relating to judicial independence, and the issue of access to justice.

3.1 The judicial appointment process

The judicial appointment process of judges to the subordinate courts differs significantly from that of judges to the superior courts.

3.1.1 Judicial appointments to the subordinate courts

Judges of the subordinate courts in Malaysia are drawn from a pool of legal officers from the Judicial and Legal Service. The Judicial and Legal Service is under the jurisdiction of the Judicial and Legal Service

[31] Justice J. Foong, *The Malaysian Judiciary: A Record from 1786 to 1993* (Singapore: Malayan Law Journal, 1994), said at p. 1 that "The history of the modern Malaysian judiciary may be said to have begun with the acquisition of the island of Pulo Penang (as Penang was then known) in 1786 by Captain Francis Light."

Commission and the Attorney General is a member of this Commission.[32] These legal officers are posted to and serve in all three branches of government. They are subject to periodic rotations within the three branches of government as a result of a promotion or with the aim of exposing these legal officers to the various types of legal work.[33]

In view of the fact that sessions court judges and magistrates are "officers" of the Judicial and Legal Service and that the Attorney General, who is the public prosecutor, is a member of the Judicial and Legal Service Commission, the impartiality of these judges may be questioned when they preside over civil cases where one of the parties is represented by the Attorney General's Chambers or criminal cases where the prosecution is carried out by the Attorney General's Chambers. This concern becomes more justifiable or real when the officer representing the Attorney General's Chambers is the Attorney General himself or a very senior member of the Chambers.

The issue concerning the likelihood of a magistrate being biased was raised before the Federal Court in *Cheah Yoke Thong* v. *Public Prosecutor*.[34] The Federal Court in that case held that the mere fear that the magistrate would be biased against the appellant was not a sufficient reason for the magistrate to disqualify himself. The Federal Court rightly held, it is argued, that an applicant must show evidence that the judge is in fact biased or is likely to be so.

It is further submitted that the fear of bias on the part of a sessions court judge or magistrate presiding over a case when one of the parties is represented by a "fellow" officer from the Judicial and Legal Service is understandable. However, if objections were to be allowed on this basis, the whole system of administration of justice would grind to a halt in the courts. As judges take the oath of judicial office, we have to place our trust in them to discharge their constitutional duties in a fair and impartial manner.

3.1.2 Judicial appointments to the superior courts

The appointments of judges to the superior courts are made by the *Yang di-Pertuan Agong*, acting on the advice of the Prime Minister, after

32 See the Federal Constitution, Art. 138(2)(b).

33 For a thorough discussion on the set-up of the Judicial and Legal Service, see World Bank, *Malaysia: Court Backlog and Delay Reduction Program: A Progress Report* (World Bank, 2011).

34 [1984] 2 MLJ 119.

consulting the Conference of Rulers.[35] Before the Prime Minister tenders his advice to the *Yang di-Pertuan Agong*, he is mandated by the Federal Constitution to consult the Chief Justice.[36] Despite the existence of a mechanism for consultation, it was thought that there was still a lack of transparency in the judicial appointment process. Such disquiet led to the overhaul of the judicial appointment process in 2009. A Judicial Appointments Commission was established in 2009 and the appointment process has changed substantially.[37]

The Commission is now made up of the top four members of the Judiciary, a Federal Court judge appointed by the Prime Minister and four other "eminent persons" who are not members of the executive or public service. These four eminent persons are also appointed by the Prime Minister, after consulting various stakeholders. The World Bank Progress Report entitled *Malaysia: Court Backlog and Delay Reduction Program* noted that "it is still too early to determine whether it has met the expectations."[38] The report went on to say that "all those interviewed for this study agreed that it represented a decisive improvement in the system for nominating judges."[39]

The qualifications for appointment as judges of the Federal Court, the Court of Appeal and the High Courts are provided for in Article 123 of the Federal Constitution. The two express requirements set out in the Constitution are that the appointee must: (i) be a citizen of Malaysia; and (ii) for ten years preceding the appointment, have been an advocate before any or all of those courts, a member of the Judicial and Legal Service of the Federation or of the legal service of one of the states, or some combination of the above. In view of the qualifications set out in Article 123, judicial appointments to the superior courts have always been drawn from the Judicial and Legal Service and the Bar. While there is nothing objectionable about this practice, the talent pool is limited to these two organizations.

During the leadership of Chief Justice Ahmad Fairuz, the judiciary took the sensible and, in the opinion of this author, correct move of tapping talent from the academic world. An academic member from one of the law schools was appointed as a Judicial Commissioner, and, within

[35] See the Federal Constitution, Art. 122B(1).

[36] See *ibid.* Art. 122B(2). Also see Art. 122B(3)–(6).

[37] See the Judicial Appointments Commission Act 2009. The long title provides *inter alia* that the Act is to uphold the continued independence of the judiciary and to provide for matters connected therewith or incidental thereto.

[38] World Bank, *Malaysia: Court Backlog and Delay Reduction Program*, para. 20.

[39] *Ibid.*

four months of her appointment, the Malaysian Bar Council commenced proceedings for a declaration that the appointment of Dr Badariah Sahamid was null and void and of no effect on the grounds that the appointment was in contravention of Article 122AB read with Article 123 of the Federal Constitution.[40] The argument raised by the Malaysian Bar Council was that since Dr Badariah had never applied for nor obtained a practicing certificate that would enable her to practice as an advocate and solicitor, she had failed to fulfill the second requirement in Article 123 of the Federal Constitution. It should be noted that Dr Badariah had been admitted as an advocate and solicitor of the High Court of Malaya for more than ten years preceding her appointment as a Judicial Commissioner.

The Federal Court was thus required to interpret the words "advocate of those courts" in Article 123 of the Federal Constitution. By a majority decision of three to two, the Federal Court held that the words "advocates of those courts" appearing in Article 123 of the Federal Constitution do not require an advocate to have been in practice for a period of ten years preceding his or her appointment as a judicial commissioner under Article 122AB of the Federal Constitution. The Malaysian Bar Council mounted another challenge to the appointment of Dr Badariah by urging the Federal Court to invoke its powers under rule 137 of the Rules of the Federal Court 1995 and/or its inherent jurisdiction to set aside its earlier majority judgments. This second application was unanimously dismissed by another panel of the Federal Court consisting of five judges.[41]

The above cases have amply demonstrated that parties are entitled to and will hold fast to their own interpretation of clauses and provisions in the Constitution and statutes. Opinions will inevitably differ. Although the issue regarding the appointment of an academic (or even a non-academic) who has been admitted as an advocate and solicitor but has never applied for and obtained a practicing certificate, should be regarded as settled in Malaysia, it would be ideal if Article 123 of the Federal Constitution were to be amended to provide for another category of persons to be appointed as a judge of the superior courts, as in the case of India.[42] This will indeed enlarge the talent pool for judicial appointments to the superior courts in Malaysia.

[40] See *Badan Peguam Malaysia* v. *Kerajaan Malaysia* [2008] 2 MLJ 285. Article 122(AB) of the Federal Constitution concerns the appointment of Judicial Commissioners.

[41] See *Badan Peguam Malaysia* v. *Kerajaan Malaysia* [2009] 2 MLJ 161.

[42] In the case of India, Article 124(3)(c) of the Constitution of India recognizes "a distinguished jurist" as a qualification for appointment as a judge of the Supreme Court.

3.2 *Judicial independence*

The topic or concept of judicial independence was discussed by the Federal Court of Malaysia in *Metramac Corporation Sdn Bhd* v. *Fawziah Holding Sdn Bhd.*[43] The Federal Court expressed the view that the concept of judicial independence refers to the neutrality of mind of the judge, to his impartiality and to his total freedom from irrelevant pressures. These virtues encapsulate freedom from both internal and external pressures. Hence, the courts in Malaysia must display these characteristics before they can claim to be truly independent. Whether there is judicial independence in Malaysia based on the above criteria is a highly debatable question. Any attempt to answer this difficult question can only be made upon considering some of the allegations and criticisms of improprieties hurled against the judiciary, which include: (i) that the post of the Chief Justice is a political appointment; (ii) that judges can be transferred at the discretion of the Chief Justice and/or the Chief Judges of Malaya, and Sabah and Sarawak; and (iii) that the Judicial Appointment Commission should have been established under the Federal Constitution rather than under a statute. These allegations and criticisms are not without merit. As long as these allegations and criticisms are not addressed, they will have a negative impact on the concept of judicial independence in Malaysia.

The Federal Court of Malaysia in *Metramac Corporation Sdn Bhd* v. *Fawziah Holding Sdn Bhd* also underscored the point that ensuring public confidence in the justice system is equally imperative. The Federal Court said in no uncertain terms that the goal of judicial independence is to ensure justice is done in individual cases and to ensure public confidence in the justice system.[44] Thus, whether or not there is judicial independence is a question of public perception.

It is inevitable that over a long period of time, and particularly so in the age of the internet, allegations of corruption or bias (in favor of the executive branch of the government or, for that matter, any party in the proceedings) against the judiciary have surfaced and will continue to do so from time to time. At the time of the writing, the mainstream media has in fact picked up on a posting in a blog alleging corruption against three judges of the superior courts.[45]

[43] [2007] 5 MLJ 501. [44] *Ibid.* at 528.

[45] See, for example, Shaila Koshy, "Bar comes to defense of judges," http://thestar.com.my/news/story.asp?file=/2012/3/15/nation/10912060&sec=nation.

The Malaysian Bar, through its Vice-President, has come to the defense of the three judges. The Vice-President has been quoted as saying that "the judges named, as far as I know, have impeccable integrity." The Vice-President went on to say that "it is very easy to make allegations, but one must have cogent evidence in hand before making allegations of corruption or fraud against judges" and that "it is also very unfair to judges who, by the very nature of their office, cannot retort or defend themselves in the media."[46] The last two statements are indeed very accurate. The fact that the Malaysian Bar, known for its fearless stance on all issues affecting the rule of law and society, has come up in defense of the judges, to a large extent, is a vindication of the integrity of these judges, in particular, and of the judiciary in general.

Be that as it may, continuing allegations of this nature will have a negative impact on the public perception of the judiciary. Until and unless the judiciary vindicates itself through contempt proceedings or other legal means available to them, these negative perceptions will continue to haunt the system.

3.3 *Access to justice*

This section will approach the subject of access to justice from the perspective of an individual litigant and a group of litigants (class action).

3.3.1 Access to justice by individual litigants

The right of access to justice is a fundamental right and is enshrined in Articles 5(1) and 8(1) of the Federal Constitution.[47] Unless one has been declared a "vexatious litigant,"[48] every person in Malaysia has a right to pursue her remedy or seek redress from the courts in Malaysia.

The provisions in the rules of court allow parties to appear in person.[49] However, considering the complexity of the law (both substantive and

[46] *Ibid.*

[47] Article 5(1) of the Federal Constitution states that: "No person shall be deprived of his life or personal liberty save in accordance with law." Article 8(1) of the Federal Constitution expressly provides that "All persons are equal before the law and entitled to the equal protection of the law."

[48] The power to declare a person a vexatious litigant is conferred on the courts under Article 17 of the Schedule to the Courts of Judicature Act 1964. One such rare occasion when the power was invoked was in *Sim Kooi Soon* v. *Malaysia Airline System (No. 2)* [2010] 9 CLJ 936.

[49] See Order 5 rule 6(1) of the Rules of Court 2012.

procedural), parties would be ill-advised to litigate without the aid of an advocate and solicitor. Representation by lawyers will inevitably increase the cost of litigation. This will be an impediment to parties seeking to pursue a claim in court. Although the general rule on costs, namely, that costs shall follow the event, to a certain extent will alleviate the hardship that a party may face in commencing (or defending) an action in court, an order as to costs is no guarantee that it will cover the expenses incurred by the winning party. In most cases, the winning party will still be out of pocket. Hence, the fundamental right of access to justice is illusory if the cost of legal advice and action is beyond the reach of the people. This is where legal aid becomes a necessity in the quest for justice in a judicial system.

In order to ensure that an indigent litigant has a right to counsel or that those who cannot afford to engage counsel would still have access to the courts, the Legal Aid Act 1971 was passed by the Malaysian Parliament. Legal aid available under the Act is limited in subject matter and eligibility is means-tested on the basis of capital and income. Legal aid under the Act is administered by the Legal Aid Bureau or *Biro Bantuan Guaman*.[50]

The Malaysian Bar also operates its own Legal Aid Centres throughout the country.[51] Despite these two organizations providing legal aid services, it has been reported that 80 percent of those accused of crimes have been unrepresented in court because they could not afford a lawyer.[52] Against the backdrop of this unsatisfactory state of affairs, the government of Malaysia established the National Legal Aid Foundation (hereinafter NLAF) or *Yayasan Bantuan Guaman Kebangsaan* in 2011.[53] The objective of this foundation is to ensure that all accused persons will not be deprived of legal counsel.

In his written reply to Parliament on 19 March 2012, the Prime Minister was reported to have said that NLAF would provide legal aid for all types of crimes except those which warrant the death penalty and that it was expected to begin operations by the end of March 2012.[54] The Prime Minister was also quoted to have said that legal aid and counseling on criminal matters will be given to Malaysians who need it during

[50] See Legal Aid Bureau, www.jbg.gov.my.
[51] See www.malaysianbar.org.my/legal_aid_centres.html.
[52] See www.themalaysianinsider.com/malaysia/article/najib-launches-legal-aid-foundation.
[53] See National Legal Aid Foundation, www.ybgk.org.my.
[54] *The Sun*, 20 March 2012 at 6.

arrest, remand/detainment and application for bail without income limit.[55] However, a capability test will be conducted to determine the recipient's eligibility for the hearing and appeal in court. Free legal aid will be provided to those with an annual income of not more than RM 25,000 (US $8,333) while those with an annual income of between RM 25,000 and RM 36,000 (US $12,000) will be imposed a RM 300 (US $100) fee.[56]

The establishment of the NLAF is indeed to be lauded. The NLAF officially began its operation on 2 April 2012, and we will be able to gauge its effectiveness in the coming years.

The right to counsel entails a number of aspects, one of which is the right to counsel without delay. This issue was put before the Federal Court in *Ooi Ah Phua* v. *Officer-In-Charge Criminal Investigation, Kedah/Perlis*.[57] In this case, the Federal Court held that the right to counsel could be delayed if this right interfered with police investigations. This case may be seen as a blight on the fundamental right of access to justice, with particular reference to the right to counsel. It is postulated that since the right to counsel under the second limb to Article 5(3) of the Federal Constitution is a non-derogable fundamental right, we await an occasion for the Federal Court to revisit this vital constitutional point.[58]

The issue pertaining to the right to counsel extends also to the counsel of choice. This issue was recently tested in *Victoria Jayaseele Martin* v. *Majlis Agama Islam Wilayah Persekutuan & Anor*.[59] This case involved an attempt by a non-Muslim counsel to appear on behalf of her client in the *Syariah* court. A number of constitutional issues were raised in this case, and the matter is pending appeal before the Federal Court. It is sincerely hoped that the apex court will give a liberal and broad interpretation of this fundamental right.

3.3.2 Class action and public interest litigation

The issue concerning access to justice is not limited to individual litigants or actions. A comprehensive legal system should make provision for group litigation or class actions. The issue concerning *locus standi* in public interest litigation is also a matter of utmost significance.

[55] *Ibid.* [56] *Ibid.* [57] [1975] 2 MLJ 198.

[58] Article 5(3) of the Federal Constitution provides that: "Where a person is arrested he shall be informed as soon as may be of the grounds of his arrest and shall be allowed to consult and be defended by a legal practitioner of his choice."

[59] [2011] 9 MLJ 194, HC; [2013] 6 MLJ 646, CA.

Class action is generally known as representative action in Malaysia. The formal rule that applies to a representative action in the courts in Malaysia is Order 15 rule 12 of the Rules of Court 2012. With this procedure, members in an identifiable group will be able to seek collective redress in the courts in Malaysia.

A preliminary issue of considerable importance in civil litigation is the concept of *locus standi*. How the courts interpret and apply the concept of *locus standi* in a given case may lead to the dismissal of an action without the matter being adjudicated on its merits. The issue concerning whether a plaintiff in a representative action has the standing to sue in that representative capacity is more profound when the representative action, by its nature, takes the form of public interest litigation.

Over the years, Malaysia has witnessed the concept of *locus standi* being interpreted and applied from the narrowest possible sense to a broad liberal approach.

It is generally accepted that the decision of the Federal Court in *Tan Sri Haji Othman Saat* v. *Mohamed bin Ismail*[60] represents the high-water mark in the law of *locus standi* in Malaysia. The Federal Court in that case endorsed the concept of liberalizing the scope of individual standing.

Unfortunately, the judicial attitude concerning the issue, scope and interpretation of individual standing in public interest litigation and class actions took a turn for the worst in *United Engineers (M) Bhd* v. *Lim Kit Siang*[61] (commonly referred to as the *UEM* case) and *Ketua Pengarah Jabatan Alam Sekitar & Anor* v. *Kajing Tubek & Ors and Other Appeals*[62] (commonly referred to as the *Bakun Dam* case). The judgments in these cases, also by the apex court, were delivered in 1988 and 1997 respectively. The majority decisions in the *UEM* case have left a blot on the field of public law litigation in Malaysia.

In both the *UEM* case and the *Bakun Dam* case, we see the pendulum of *locus standi* swing to one extreme, far away from a lenient stance or liberal approach. Whether these two cases signaled retrogression in the field of public law litigation is unclear. For the optimist, it may be argued that these two cases were based on their own peculiar facts, circumstances and policy considerations. Hence the insistence on a strict and pedantic, as opposed to a more enlightened and creative, approach on the issue of *locus standi* in public law litigation was a rarity and should not be taken to represent the preferred approach of the courts in Malaysia.

[60] [1982] 2 MLJ 177. [61] [1988] 2 MLJ 12. [62] [1997] 3 MLJ 23.

Gopal Sri Ram JCA in the *Bakun Dam* case did imply that we should not despair and that all is not lost in the field of public law litigation. His Lordship said that *locus standi* is a matter of pure practice that is entirely for the court to decide, and whether the strict or lenient approach is adopted really depends upon the economic, political and cultural needs and background of the individual society within which the particular court functions. His Lordship further said that "views upon standing in public law actions for declaratory or injunctive relief vary according to peculiar circumstances most suited to a particular national ethos" and that these views "fluctuate from time to time within the same country."[63]

Indeed, the view or approach has fluctuated once again, and the pendulum of *locus standi* has now swung away from the strict and pedantic approach as adopted in the *UEM* case and the *Bakun Dam* case. This is evident from the case of *QSR Brands Bhd* v. *Suruhanjaya Sekuriti & Anor.*[64] This decision signifies that the courts in Malaysia will regard *locus standi* as a flexible and vibrant concept. Therefore, the courts' attitude towards the notion of *locus standi* in the sphere of public interest litigation can now be regarded as falling in the middle of the spectrum.

4 Courts and alternative dispute resolution (ADR)

Alternative dispute resolution processes are widely practiced in Malaysia and exist alongside the traditional dispute resolution process of having a dispute adjudicated in the courts. In the context of the courts and alternative dispute resolution processes in Malaysia, this section will highlight and comment on the utilization of two such alternative dispute resolution processes in Malaysia's judicial system. These are arbitration and mediation.

4.1 Arbitration and the courts

It is not uncommon to find parties to a contract agreeing to refer any dispute that may arise between them for resolution by arbitration. Arbitration clauses or agreements in contracts are a vital aspect of the principle of party autonomy. In this respect, the first question is whether arbitration agreements are recognized by the laws in Malaysia. The

[63] *Ibid.* at 40. [64] [2006] 3 MLJ 164.

answer is without a doubt in the affirmative. As in the case of Hong Kong and Singapore, the government of Malaysia and the policy makers in the country have actively been, at least in the last decade, encouraging, promoting and supporting arbitration over litigation. The law on arbitration in Malaysia is governed by the Arbitration Act 2005. The most recent amendments made in 2011 to the Arbitration Act 2005 are testimony to the seriousness of the efforts of the government in supporting arbitration.[65] The Kuala Lumpur Regional Centre for Arbitration also plays an active role in promoting Malaysia as a preferred center for arbitration.[66]

This leads us to the more pertinent or important question: do the courts take a positive view of the efforts by the government and of the preferences of the parties in the individual contracts relating to their predilection for arbitration over litigation? The success or failure of the efforts of the government and policy makers in promoting arbitration will depend to a large extent on the attitude of the courts and the approach that the courts adopt. This is particularly true in situations when courts are called upon to give effect to an arbitration clause or to enforce an arbitral award. An attempt will have to be made to discern the trend or study the approaches adopted by the courts from the reported cases. These reported cases will provide an indication of the attitude or approach of the courts in taking either a pro-arbitration or an anti-arbitration stand.

4.1.1 Courts' attitude towards enforcement of arbitration agreements

As noted earlier, the law on arbitration in Malaysia is governed by the Arbitration Act 2005. Section 10 of the Arbitration Act 2005 expressly provides that "A court before which proceedings are brought in respect of a matter which is the subject of an arbitration agreement *shall* ... stay those proceedings and refer the parties to arbitration ..." The 2005 Act had replaced the Arbitration Act 1952. In the 1952 Act, section 6 provides that

65 See the Arbitration (Amendment) Act 2011. Prior to the coming into force of the Arbitration Act 2005, the applicable statute was the Arbitration Act 1952. The 2005 amendment was made as a result of lobbying by arbitration practitioners and parties who have an interest in the advancement of arbitration. One way of supporting and promoting arbitration is to ensure that the laws on arbitration are simplified and are modeled on the United Nations Commission on International Trade Law (UNCITRAL) Model Law.

66 See the website of Kuala Lumpur Regional Centre for Arbitration, www.klrca.org.my.

"If any party to an arbitration agreement . . . apply to the court to stay the proceedings, and the court . . . *may* make an order staying the proceedings."

The changes made to the law on stay of proceedings as evident from the above provisions have led many commentators,[67] particularly those who practice in the area of arbitration, and even the High Court in *Standard Chartered Bank Malaysia Bhd* v. *City Properties Sdn Bhd*,[68] to argue that when there is an arbitration clause, it is *mandatory* for courts in jurisdictions such as Malaysia to grant an order for a stay of proceedings. While a term "shall" in a statute concerning this aspect of the law would clearly denote or suggest some measure of directive to the courts or obligation on the part of the courts to grant an order for a stay of proceedings, the principle as contained in the Arbitration Act 2005 concerning the granting of an order for a stay is not absolute and is subject to many exceptions. The courts are still at liberty to strike down an arbitration agreement based on a wide variety of grounds. It is beyond the scope of this report to discuss each of these exceptions. Suffice it to say that the reported cases relating to this aspect of the law indicate that the courts in Malaysia will hold parties who have agreed to go for arbitration to their contractual obligation and will be slow to strike down an arbitration agreement.[69]

4.1.2 Courts' attitude towards enforcement of arbitral awards

Principles of international comity and finality of an award require national courts to uphold and enforce foreign arbitral awards. On the other hand, national courts are also required to defend the notions of morality and public policy of a state. Like in other jurisdictions, the courts in Malaysia have had to grapple with the policy tension that pits the principles of international comity and finality of an award against the notions of morality and public policy of a state.

[67] See, e.g., A. K. M. Ranai, "Malaysia" in S. Finizio and W. Miles (eds.), *The International Comparative Legal Guide to: International Arbitration 2010* (London: Global Legal Group, 2010), p. 68.

[68] [2008] 1 CLJ 496.

[69] For a general discussion on this area of the law, see, e.g., Y. C. Choong, "Public policy considerations in arbitral proceedings in Malaysia (and other selected common law jurisdictions)," paper presented at the 1st University of Malaya – Pusan National University Joint Seminar: Exploring Selected Issues, 31 May – 1 June, Pusan, Korea; and Y. C. Choong, "To arbitrate or to litigate?: Recent trend of judicial attitude towards the enforcement of arbitration clauses in Malaysia and in the UK," Conference proceedings, Wuhan University Press.

The courts in Malaysia have reiterated the point that the concept of public policy encompasses a narrow scope, and a very high threshold has to be met before the court will set aside an arbitral award.[70] In *Infineon Technologies (M) Sdn Bhd* v. *Orisoft Technology Sdn Bhd*,[71] after referring and quoting from two cases from Hong Kong and Singapore on this aspect of the law, Mohamad Ariff J said that "In both cases, the approach is not to refuse to register on the ground of conflict of public policy unless the most basic notions of morality and justice would be offended. Thus the approach is very restrictive, being grounded in the upholding of international comity. A less rigid approach should, in principle, apply where the award is a Domestic Arbitral Award, although the comparative jurisprudence on this matter cannot as yet be said as approximating a uniform approach."[72] Such a clear pronouncement concerning the approach that the courts in Malaysia will adopt sends an unmistakable signal that the principle of international comity will be upheld and enforced by the courts in Malaysia.

4.2 Mediation in the courts

A major development concerning the use of mediation as an alternative dispute resolution process first took place in August of 2010. A Practice Direction was issued by the Chief Justice of Malaysia directing all judges of the High Court and its deputy registrars, all judges of the sessions court and magistrates and their registrars to facilitate the settlement of disputes or matters before the courts by way of mediation.[73] This judiciary-led initiative is a major boost for mediation as an alternative mode for settlement of disputes.

The introduction of the Practice Direction has given, in the words of a Judicial Commissioner, "mediation in our courts a firmer procedural footing."[74] Every judge (and registrar) now plays an active role in facilitating and promoting mediation. Judges may suggest mediation to the parties and encourage them to settle their disputes at the pre-trial case management stage or at any stage in the proceedings, even after a trial has commenced.[75]

70 See, e.g., *Harris Adacom Corporation* v. *Perkom Sdn Bhd* [1994] 3 MLJ 504. Cf. *Sami-Mousawi Utama Sdn Bhd* v. *Kerajaan Negeri Sarawak* [2004] 2 MLJ 414.

71 [2011] 7 MLJ 539. 72 *Ibid.* at 572. 73 See Practice Direction No. 5 of 2010.

74 See S. S. Lee, "Mediation – 'A reflection, review and rediscovery,'" *The Law Review*, (2011), 663–4.

75 See Practice Note No. 5 of 2010, para. 3.1. See also paras. 5.2 and 5.3.

The Practice Direction further provides for the procedure to be followed if the mediation takes the form of a judge-led mediation.[76] In the event that the parties decide that the mediation should be referred to an independent mediator instead of being judge-led, they are at liberty to take their dispute to any of the certified mediators at the Malaysian Mediation Centre[77] or to any other mediator chosen by the parties.[78]

Regardless of whether the mediation is conducted by a judge (or registrar) or through "private" mediation, the legal effect of the settlement remains valid and binding on the parties. This is because in either of the modes, the settlement agreement will be recorded as a consent judgment.[79] The one advantage of a judge-led mediation is that it does not cost the parties any additional expenses or fees in terms of mediator's fees, administrative charges and room rental.[80]

In order to ensure that the practice of mediation be enhanced to its optimum, it may be worthwhile for the judiciary to seriously consider using the award of costs as leverage to secure the cooperation of the parties before the court to agree to mediation. This will send a clear signal to litigants that any party proven to have unreasonably refused to enter mediation may receive a lower cost award, no cost award, or even a penalty, even if that party succeeds at trial.[81]

It should be noted that as of 1 August 2012, the Mediation Act 2012 has been in effect. With this statutory law, mediation has established itself as a part of the formal civil litigation landscape in Malaysia.

4.3 *ADR as part of the court system*

Arbitration has had a strong foothold in Malaysia for a long time. Endeavors by the government and policy makers to promote arbitration and clear pronouncements by the courts that arbitration agreements and

[76] See Annexure A to the Practice Note No. 5 of 2010.

[77] The Malaysian Mediation Centre is set up under the auspices of the Malaysian Bar. See www.malaysianbar.org.my/malaysian_mediation_centre_mmc.html.

[78] See Annexure B to the Practice Note No. 5 of 2010.

[79] See para. 4 of Annexure A and para. 3.1 of Annexure B to the Practice Note No. 5 of 2010.

[80] For a comprehensive discussion of the practice of mediation in the Malaysian courts, see Justice M. W. Kwai, "Mediation practices: the Malaysian experience," paper presented at the 13th ASEAN Law Association General Assembly and Conference held in Bali, Indonesia.

[81] In this regard, the remarks by Brooke LJ in *Dunnett* v. *Railtrack plc* [2002] 2 All ER 858 (at para. 15) are germane. See also *Cable & Wireless plc* v. *IBM United Kingdom Ltd* [2002] 2 All ER (Comm) 1041 and the cases quoted therein concerning clauses in contracts or agreements to refer disputes to mediation.

awards, as a rule of thumb, are to be respected and enforced send an unambiguous message that arbitration as an alternative dispute resolution process has taken its rightful place alongside the traditional dispute resolution process of litigation.

The discussions in 4.1.1 and 4.1.2 demonstrate that the courts in Malaysia are not averse to arbitration as an alternative dispute resolution process. The reported cases show that the courts have given primacy to the principle of party autonomy.

On the other hand, the practice of mediation can still be regarded as being in its infancy. Be that as it may, we have seen that parties in the civil litigation process are encouraged in the course of the formal proceedings in the courts (through judges or registrars) to strive to reach a settlement by way of mediation. Through the issuance of Practice Direction No. 5 of 2010, the Malaysian judiciary has made known its desire that settlement of disputes without adjudication is a top priority. This initiative has had the effect of incorporating the alternative dispute resolution process of mediation into the traditional civil litigation landscape. Such a development augurs well for proponents of alternative dispute resolution processes, in particular, and for the overall good of the administration of the civil justice system in general. The judiciary must be applauded for taking this laudable step.

5 Performance and efficiency

As in many jurisdictions, Malaysia, at least prior to October 2008, had her fair share of the twin evils that beset the judiciary and the administration of justice system. The twin evils here of course refer to backlog of cases and delay in the litigation process. And as in most jurisdictions, efforts were made to overcome these problems.

In terms of reform, the period between 2008 and 2011 was very significant for the judiciary and the administration of the justice system in Malaysia. Under the leadership of Chief Justice Zaki Azmi, major reforms were introduced. These judiciary-led initiatives were introduced primarily to address the problems of backlog of cases and delay in the civil litigation process. What may not be apparent is that these reforms also have an impact on matters such as culture and mindset, corruption, efficiency, competency, transparency and technology.

In order to be able to better appreciate the resulting outcomes of the reforms of the Zaki court, a brief outline and discussion of the reforms introduced before October 2008 is in order. More importantly, one must also pay close attention to the current policies of the judiciary under the leadership of Chief Justice Ariffin Zakaria. This is with a view to finding out whether the reforms of the Zaki court are being pursued and continued and what further reforms, if any, have been introduced since September 2011.

5.1 Pre-Zaki court reforms

Prior to the reforms introduced by Chief Justice Zaki Azmi, reforms introduced were few and far between and not sweeping in nature. Some of the initiatives that were introduced are as follows.

5.1.1 Case management

Modern principles of case management are given due prominence under the new procedural landscape in many jurisdictions. Until September 2000, the only scheme that resembled modern-day case management practices that was in existence in Malaysia was the one that organized the High Court at Kuala Lumpur into a number of Divisions.[82] The objective was to achieve efficiency by having the same judge hear cases that raise similar issues. It was not until 21 September 2000 that the term "case management" appeared in the rules of court. The original Order 34 (Setting Down for Trial) of the Rules of the High Court 1980 was completely removed and substituted with a new Order 34 (Pre-Trial Case Management). The new Order 34 gave the judge the power to call for a first pre-trial conference and to "make any such directions as to the future conduct of the action to ensure its just, expeditious and economical disposal."[83]

Any attempt by the Rules Committee to introduce any reform into the civil litigation process is to be welcomed. However, the introduction of pre-trial case management was not carried out in a coordinated manner. For a start, the new procedure on pre-trial case management should have replaced Order 25 (Summons for Directions) instead of the former Order 34 (Setting Down for Trial). This fundamental error on the part of the Rules Committee gave rise to the problem of duplicity. Clearly, the matters to be dealt with at the first pre-trial case management conference

[82] Practice Note No. 1 of 1979 that came into force on 1 June 1979 organized the High Court at Kuala Lumpur into five Divisions, namely: Appellate and Special Powers; Commercial; Family and Property; Personal Claims; and Criminal.

[83] RHC 1980, Order 34 rr. 2 and 4.

are by and large the same as those to be considered at the stage of summons for direction. Both Order 25 (Summons for Directions) and Order 34 (Pre-Trial Case Management Conference) required the court to apply the same test when making any direction or order as to the future course of the action.[84]

Second, Order 34 did not promote the principal goal of case management because it did nothing to encourage settlement. What it did was basically to lay the groundwork and prepare the parties for trial. An ideal case management scheme should allow judges to take an active part to facilitate and encourage the parties to compromise and settle the dispute, or, alternatively, to determine the issues or make an order for summary judgment of their own motion. Where settlement is not possible or summary judgment is not appropriate, judges should then be given the power to ensure that cases proceed quickly to a final hearing. Order 34 was thus ineffective in that it left the conduct of proceedings entirely in the hands of the parties until just before trial.

5.1.2 Initiatives of Malanjum CJ (Sabah and Sarawak)

A number of initiatives that were introduced by the Chief Judge of Sabah and Sarawak, Richard Malanjum, deserve special mention in this report.

In early 2007, the country's first court video/teleconferencing facility between the Miri and Kuching courts was launched. It was reported that the objectives of the facility include helping to improve time management, quicken court proceedings and reduce the backlog of cases.[85]

In that same year, the courts in Sabah and Sarawak also launched the Short Messaging System (hereinafter SMS) and the File Tracking System (hereinafter FTS). While the former serves the purpose of notifying advocates of last-minute court hearings or rescheduling and to remind them of the status of their cases, the latter allows the court to keep track of the whereabouts of each individual file.[86]

Both of the above came close on the heels of the launching of mobile courts in Sarawak. Malanjum CJ (Sabah and Sarawak) was quoted to have said that rather than compelling rural residents to travel to the towns where the courts are located, the courts would go to the remote areas of Sarawak.[87] The role played by Malanjum CJ (Sabah and

[84] This "oversight" was finally noted and a Practice Direction was issued on 19 June 2001 suspending the application of Order 25 of the RHC 1980.

[85] See *New Straits Times*, 6 February 2007, p. 10. [86] *Ibid.*

[87] *Ibid.* The mobile courts service has since been extended to Sabah.

Sarawak) in enhancing access to justice by individual litigants, particularly those in remote areas, is extremely commendable.

5.2 *Reforms and legacy of the Zaki court*

The thriving transformation of the Malaysian Judiciary can be traced to the initiatives and efforts of Chief Justice Zaki Azmi. The success of the Zaki Reforms is documented in the World Bank Progress Report entitled *Malaysia: Court Backlog and Delay Reduction Program.*[88] The sweeping initiatives introduced and the statistics in the Report speak volumes about the accomplishment of the Zaki court.

Within a relatively short period of three years, Chief Justice Zaki Azmi overcame the problem of backlog of cases and has put in place a system where all new commercial and civil cases are now disposed of within nine months. Chief Justice Zaki Azmi achieved this by taking a step back to understand the underlying problems and then set out to work tirelessly with his fellow judges to overcome these obstacles. The strategies adopted by Chief Justice Zaki Azmi were not by any definition radical. They were in fact very simplistic and straightforward. However, these strategies were highly effective. The success of these reforms can be attributed to the unwavering commitment and desire on the part of the Chief Justice and his fellow judges to improve the overall system.

The reform process began with the preparation of a case inventory (file room audit). There was an overhaul of the court filing system, which was in a state of disarray. A tracking system (or case management) and an E-court program (such as e-filing) quickly followed suit. Specialized courts were established and managing judges were appointed to ensure that cases that were pending before the courts would progress smoothly. The Chief Justice and the senior judges worked tirelessly to conduct spot checks and make surprise visits to the courts. They also engaged the Bar, the Attorney General's Chambers and other government departments in finding solutions to ensure the success of these reforms.

Chief Justice Zaki Azmi did not merely address the problems that had beset the administration of justice in the country but went beyond that. He laid the groundwork to ensure that the judicial systems and procedures were up to date and on par with those in other developed nations. In the words of one commentator, he restored faith in the judicial system.[89]

[88] World Bank, *Malaysia: Court Backlog and Delay Reduction Program.*
[89] See N. S. Zeffreys, *New Straits Times*, 30 June 2012, p. 19.

In the opinion of this author, the singular brilliance of Chief Justice Zaki Azmi lies not just in the fact of the results achieved and the system put in place but in his ability to convince the judiciary, the bar and the public at large of the need for these reforms. This change in mindset will ensure that the reforms will not be undone in the future but instead will continue with more vigor.

5.3 *Post Zaki reforms – the Arifin court*

Chief Justice Arifin Zakaria succeeded Chief Justice Zaki Azmi in September 2011. Prior to his elevation to Chief Justice of Malaysia, Chief Justice Arifin Zakaria was the Chief Judge of Malaya. He had worked very closely with Chief Justice Zaki Azmi in ensuring that the reforms of the Zaki court were appropriately implemented. Thus, it is to be expected that the reforms introduced by the Zaki court will continue to be pursued and not abandoned. One such example is the Judicial Academy.

During the 2013 Judges' Conference, the Chief Justice outlined the policies to be pursued by the Arifin Court. One of these concerned the issue of transparency, integrity and the public's confidence in the judiciary. Chief Justice Arifin Zakaria has been reported as saying that he will have judges declare their assets.[90] He has also announced that all criminal and civil appeals at the Federal Court will be heard by a five-man quorum instead of a three-man panel. The Chief Justice explained that "it was a better figure as all the reasoning would be applied in the judgment and would improve the judicial system."[91] The Chief Justice has also announced the establishment of a special court to deal with matters concerning the environment.

The above developments bode well for the state of the judiciary and the administration of justice in the country.

6 Concluding observations

The reforms introduced by the Malaysian judiciary, particularly in more recent times, are both timely and praiseworthy. Despite these commendable initiatives, the Malaysian judiciary must continue to strive and embrace changes in the interest of the public at large.

[90] See *New Straits Times*, 16 January 2012, p. 13. [91] *Ibid.*

While it is necessary that the momentum of these initiatives be maintained, the one important factor that should not be overlooked concerns the appointment of judges. Judges play an essential role in determining the performance, efficiency and success of the judicial system. The stature and reputation of the judiciary will be determined by, to a large extent, the people who occupy judicial positions in the judiciary. There is thus an imperative to ensure that judicial positions are filled by the most qualified persons.

In this regard, the Judicial Appointments Commission established under the Judicial Appointments Commission Act 2009 has a very important role to play. Among the functions of the Commission are to select suitably qualified persons who merit appointment as judges and to formulate and implement mechanisms for the selection and appointment of judges.[92] In performing its function in selecting candidates, section 23(2) of the Judicial Appointments Commission Act 2009 expressly requires the Commission to take into account, amongst others, the following criteria: (a) integrity, competency and experience; (b) objectivity, impartiality, fairness and good moral character; (c) decisiveness, ability to make timely judgments and good legal writing skills; (d) industriousness and ability to manage cases well; and (e) physical and mental health.

The Commission has reaffirmed and refined the above criteria by categorically requiring that each candidate possess the following essential qualities as the minimum requirement for ensuring the successful performance of the judicial function in the superior courts: (i) integrity; (ii) legal knowledge and ability; (iii) professional experience; (iv) judicial temperament; (v) diligence; (vi) health; (vii) financial responsibility; (viii) public service; (ix) views on public issues; and (x) desirable special qualities.[93]

It is granted that some of the above qualities resist easy definition, and guidelines must be drawn to assist the Commission in determining the nature of these qualities. However, it is crucial that the Judicial Appointments Commission demand that these standards are met when it discharges its statutory duties in the judicial appointment process. This will ensure that the criteria and qualities outlined above will not remain as mere rhetoric but are translated into deeds.

[92] The Judicial Appointments Commission Act 2009, s. 21(1)(a) and (c).

[93] See Judicial Appointments Commission, www.jac.gov.my/index.php?option=com_k2&view=item&layout=item&id=28&Itemid=138.

References

Foong, J. *The Malaysian Judiciary: A Record from 1786 to 1993* (Singapore: Malayan Law Journal, 1994)

Lee, H. P. "Malaysian royalty and the special court" in A. Harding and P. Nicholson (eds.), *New Courts in Asia* (New York: Routledge, 2010), pp. 317–36

Lee, S. S. "Mediation – 'A reflection, review and rediscovery,'" *The Law Review*, (2011), 663–4

Ranai, A. K. M. "Malaysia" in S. Finizio and W. Miles (eds.), *The International Comparative Legal Guide to: International Arbitration 2010* (London: Global Legal Group, 2010), pp. 66–74

Rutter, M. F. *The Applicable Law in Singapore and Malaysia* (Singapore: Malayan Law Journal, 1989)

World Bank. *Malaysia: Court Backlog and Delay Reduction Program, A Progress Report* (2011)

Wu, M. A. *Malaysian Legal System, 3rd edn* (Kuala Lumpur: Longman, 2007)

12

Courts in Thailand: progressive development as the country's pillar of justice

PAWAT SATAYANURUG AND NATTAPORN NAKORNIN

The historical development of the court system in Thailand dates back to the thirteenth century with the establishment of the Kingdom of Sukhothai (1237–1348), the first of the series of kingdoms in the area that later became Thailand. Historical evidence shows that there existed an early judiciary or court system that allowed direct access by the public. Given the relatively small size of the first capital of Sukhothai, the societal structure was not complex; hence, the design of the court system did not need to be structurally complicated. At the time, the Kingdom was governed by the so-called (literally translated) "Father-protecting-his-children" system, where the King, the most revered figure of the Kingdom, had the highest authority and power to make law and issue judgments. With this power, the King became both the only source of law and the only guardian of justice. In the event of a dispute, the parties could directly ring a bell in front of the King's palace, without having to undergo any prior procedural requirements. Upon hearing the bell, the King would personally come out and adjudicate the case, and his decision would be final and binding.

Following the collapse of the Kingdom of Sukhothai was the establishment of the Kingdom of Ayutthaya (1440–1767). As the Kingdom expanded both in size and in population, a more complicated court system became necessary. The expansion was also a result of the change in the administrative regime, where the kingship rose to become that of a divine figure equipped with the highest power and authority, and the governance of the Kingdom became that of an absolute monarchy. During the Ayutthaya period, a group of experts and specialists were appointed to advise the King in deciding cases. These advisers later evolved to become judges who exercised judicial power in the name of the King.

The current Kingdom of Rattanakosin (1782–present) has seen a number of judicial developments in the country, which were due to a number of factors, particularly Western influences and societal changes. The foundation of the present courts and legal institutions in Thailand was established during the reign of King Rama V (King Chulalongkorn), whose vision led to many significant developments in the present system. Theoretically, the judicial system in Thailand is modeled after a civil law system, but some writers argue that certain common law elements are "mixed" into the Thai system, owing to the fact that many legal experts and judges in Thailand have been educated in common law countries. Most notably, HRH Prince Rapee Pattanasak, the son of King Rama V and praised as "the Father of Thai law," received his legal education in the United Kingdom. While such facts are true, it is premature to conclude that the judicial system of Thailand, officially a civil law country, receives influences from the common law system to the degree that it is a "mixed" system. At any rate, Thailand's judicial branch has progressed and developed from a "barbaric" system, as perceived by some Westerners during the mid-Rattanakosin period, to a judicial system that is on par with "Western" standards, and it now serves as the Kingdom's Pillar of Justice.

1 General description of Thailand's judicial system

The existence of the judicial system of Thailand is clearly stipulated in the Constitution of the Kingdom of Thailand B.E. 2550 (2007). According to the Constitution, the power to adjudicate cases belongs to the courts, "which must be proceeded in a manner serving justice in accordance with the Constitution and the law and in the name of the King."[1] These provisions reflect the incorporation of political theories that suggest that sovereign power belongs to the people and must be separated among different branches of government. Hence, the court shall have exclusive power to conduct trials and adjudicate claims. Nevertheless, the power to adjudicate must still be exercised in the name of the King owing to historical and customary influences. The King also has a role in establishing courts through the promulgation of Acts[2], as well as in the appointment and the removal of judges, except in the case of removal due to death.[3]

[1] Constitution of the Kingdom of Thailand B.E. 2550 (2007) (hereinafter "2007 Constitution"), s. 197.

[2] 2007 Constitution, s. 198. [3] *Ibid.* s. 200.

1.1 *Structure of courts*

Thailand has adopted a dual court system, in which civil and criminal matters are separated from administrative matters. Therefore, the structure of courts in Thailand is designed such that the trial and adjudication powers in civil and criminal cases are accorded to the Courts of Justice, while the trial and adjudication powers in administrative cases belong to the Administrative Courts. Judges in the courts of justice and in the administrative courts follow separate tracks and are recruited independently. However, in fact, there are four types of courts in Thailand. In addition to the courts of justice and the administrative courts, Chapter X of the Constitution establishes the Constitutional Court and the military courts.

1.1.1 Constitutional Court

According to section 204 of the Constitution, the Constitutional Court comprises one President and eight judges, appointed by the King upon the advice of the Senate.[4] The Constitutional Court has powers and duties in nine functions, which are prescribed in the Constitution.[5] First, the Constitutional Court is empowered to review the constitutionality of organic laws,[6] bills of law[7] and draft rules of procedure of the legislature[8] prior to promulgation so as to prevent any contrariness or inconsistencies with the Constitution.

Second, it has the power to review the constitutionality of laws already in force so as to prevent any contrariness or inconsistencies with the Constitution.[9] If a court or a party to a case casts doubt on the constitutionality of any provision of any law that is applied to the case, that court shall submit its opinion to the Constitutional Court for consultation. Furthermore, the Constitution provides for the right of a person whose rights and liberties are violated to submit a motion to the Constitutional Court for its decision concerning the contrariness or inconsistency of any provision of law with the Constitution.[10] Third, it also has the power to review the constitutionality of the conditions for enacting an Emergency Decree so as to avoid any contrariness or inconsistencies with the Constitution.[11] Moreover, it has the adjudicative power to rule on

[4] *Ibid.* s. 204.
[5] Constitutional Court, "Jurisdiction of the constitutional court," www.constitutionalcourt.or.th/index.php?option=com_content&view=article&id=153&Itemid=83&lang=thindex.php.
[6] 2007 Constitution, s. 141. [7] *Ibid.* s. 154. [8] *Ibid.* s. 155.
[9] *Ibid.* ss. 211 and 245. [10] *Ibid.* s. 212. [11] *Ibid.* s. 184.

whether or not a member of the House of Representatives, Senator or committee member has committed an act that results in a direct or indirect interest in the use of budgetary appropriations;[12] disputes or conflicts pertaining to the powers and duties of two or more organs with respect to the National Assembly, Council of Ministers or non-judicial constitutional organs;[13] resolutions or regulations of political parties, and cases concerning persons or political parties exercising political rights and liberties unconstitutionally;[14] the membership or qualifications of members of the National Assembly,[15] Ministers[16] and Election Commissioners;[17] and whether or not a treaty must be approved by the National Assembly.[18] In addition, it is empowered to consider appeals and exercise any powers or duties that are stipulated by the Organic Act on Political Parties B.E. 2550.[19]

1.1.2 Courts of justice

The courts of justice have the power to try and adjudicate all cases except those specified within the jurisdiction of other courts. The Statute of the Court of Justice[20] provides that there be three levels of courts: courts of first instance; courts of appeal; and the Supreme Court. Courts of first instance are divided into general courts and specialized courts. The former are situated in all provinces, while the latter are specially designated to adjudicate particular issues of dispute and consist of the following: the juvenile and family court; the labor court; the tax court; the intellectual property and international trade court; and the bankruptcy court. For courts of appeal, there are nine branches located in major provinces around the country. Very much similar to the circuit courts of the United States judicial system, each branch is responsible for its designated provinces.[21]

1.1.3 Administrative courts

The administrative courts are established by the Establishment of Administrative Courts and Administrative Court Procedure Act B.E. 2542 (1999). The Act stipulated that there be two levels of the administrative courts: the Supreme Administrative Court in Bangkok Metropolitan, and

[12] *Ibid.* s. 168. [13] *Ibid.* s. 214. [14] *Ibid.* ss. 198, 65 and 106(7). [15] *Ibid.* s. 91.
[16] *Ibid.* s. 182. [17] *Ibid.* s. 233. [18] *Ibid.* s. 190.
[19] Organic Act on Political Parties B.E. 2550 (2007), ss. 13, 14, 20(4), 31, 33, 41, 91, 93, 94 and 98.
[20] Statute of the Court of Justice B.E. 2543 (2000). [21] *Ibid.* ss. 3 and 4.

the Administrative Courts of First Instance.[22] Administrative courts of first instance are also divided into two types: (1) the central administrative court that has jurisdiction throughout the boundaries of Bangkok Metropolitan and the neighboring provinces of Nakhon Pathom, Nonthaburi, Pathumthani, Ratchaburi, Samutprakan, Samutsongkham, and Samutsakhon; and (2) nine branches of regional administrative courts to cover all other cities.[23] The administrative courts have the authority to try and adjudicate or give orders over cases involving disputes in relation to any unlawful act by administrative agencies or state officials, disputes in relation to any administrative agencies or state officials neglecting official duties, disputes in relation to wrongful acts or other liabilities of administrative agencies or state officials arising from the exercise of powers, and disputes in relation to an administrative contract.[24] In addition, the administrative courts are empowered to try and adjudicate cases stipulated by law to be submitted to or to be under the jurisdiction of the administrative courts.[25]

1.1.4 Military courts

Military courts are established by the Administration of Military Courts Act B.E. 2498 (1955) and have the authority to try, adjudicate and impose punishment on soldiers who violate military Acts.[26] Military courts are divided into three levels: military courts of first instance; central military courts, which are the appeal courts for military cases; and the Supreme Military Court.[27] Military courts of first instance are categorized into four types: provincial military courts; municipal military courts; Bangkok military courts; and the army unit courts.[28] However, in the event of war or a declaration of martial law, the Martial Court will be established and have jurisdiction over all relevant cases.[29]

1.2 Instance of trials

The instances of trials of courts in Thailand vary depending on the provisions of law that establish each court and stipulate its procedure.

[22] The administrative courts are established by the Establishment of Administrative Courts and Administrative Court Procedure Act B.E. 2542 (1999) (hereinafter "1999 Administrative Courts Procedure Act"), s. 7.

[23] 1999 Administrative Courts Procedure Act, s. 8. [24] *Ibid.* s. 9. [25] *Ibid.* s. 10.

[26] Administration of Military Courts Act B.E. 2498 (1955), s. 13 (hereinafter "1955 Military Courts Act").

[27] 1955 Military Courts Act, s. 6. [28] *Ibid.* s. 7. [29] *Ibid.* ss. 36 and 39.

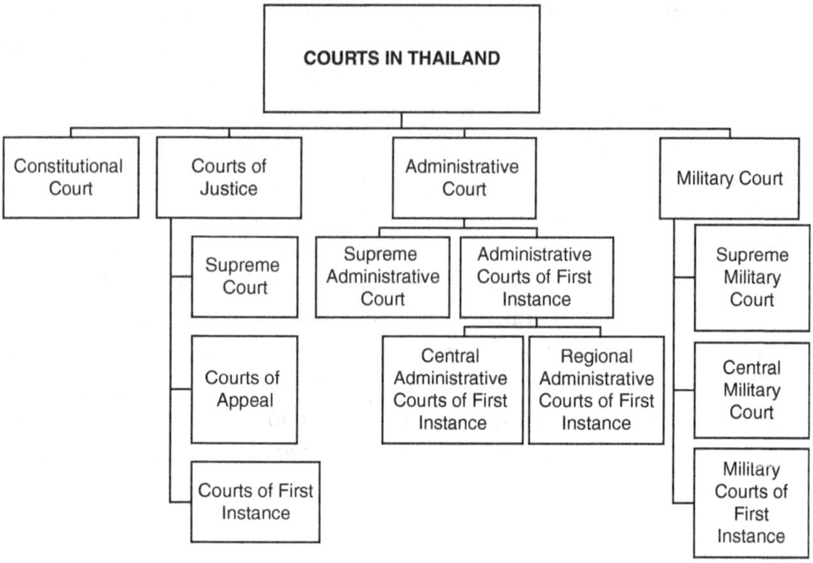

Figure 12.1: Structure of courts

For the courts of justice, which normally adjudicate civil and criminal cases on an adversarial basis, the Statute of the Court of Justice provides that there shall be the following three instances available for adjudication: the first instance, appeal, and last resort.[30] The first trial at the court of first instance must be based on both facts and law. The size of the claim and the location of the dispute determine the jurisdiction of each court of first instance (see Figure 12.1). Regarding size, any civil claim that concerns an amount of disputed money of less than 300,000 Baht or any criminal charge whose prescribed imprisonment does not exceed three years and prescribed fine does not exceed 60,000 Baht is under the jurisdiction of the municipal court.[31] Regarding location, since certain municipalities are large enough to have their own municipal courts, any claims occurring within those municipalities and falling within the aforementioned size requirement must first go to the municipal courts situated in those municipalities. For areas that do not have municipal courts, all claims must be instigated at the courts of first instance in those areas, such as the provincial courts.[32] The second trial on both facts and law

[30] Statute of the Court of Justice B.E. 2543 (2000), s. 1. [31] *Ibid.* ss. 17 and 25.

[32] Supreme Court, *The Supreme Court of Thailand*, www.supremecourt.or.th/file/dika_eng.pdf.

will be at the Court of Appeal, followed by the final adjudication, as the case may be, at the Supreme Court.

While there are typically three instances of trials at the courts of justice, certain cases require only two instances of trials. For instance, section 223*bis* of the Civil Procedure Code provides that an appellant may appeal a case directly to the Supreme Court if the issue being appealed involves only a question of law, and the appellee is not opposed to proceeding in such a manner.

The Administrative Court Procedure Act B.E. 2542 (1999) provides that there are two instances of trial for administrative cases. The administrative court of first instance adjudicates matters concerning fact-finding, statement hearing, and preliminary conclusion of the case file. Unlike the adversarial approach of the courts of justice, the administrative court adopts an inquisitorial approach in which the judges themselves are able to gather facts by directly questioning the parties on the facts of the case.[33]

The number of judges per panel varies depending on the level of the court. Cases at the municipal courts are adjudicated by a single judge,[34] while the panel is increased to two judges at the courts of first instance.[35] Both the Courts of Appeal and the Supreme Court require a panel of three judges to adjudicate a case.[36] For the administrative courts, a panel of three judges is required to adjudicate an administrative claim at the administrative court of first instance, whereas a panel of five judges is required at the Supreme Administrative Court.[37] For the Constitutional Court, a panel of nine judges is required to adjudicate a case within the jurisdiction of the Constitutional Court. The panel includes a combination of judges who are recruited *ex officio* and persons with demonstrated expertise in law, political sciences, or public administration.[38]

1.3 Courts with special jurisdiction

There are so-called "specialized courts" that were established in order to adjudicate cases requiring specialized knowledge. At the level of first instance, there are five specialized courts: the juvenile and family court; the labor court; the tax court; the intellectual property and international

[33] Administrative Court, "The administrative court proceedings," www.admincourt.go.th/amc_eng/01-court/procedure/courtproceed.htm.

[34] Statute of the Court of Justice B.E. 2543 (2000). [35] *Ibid.* s. 26. [36] *Ibid.* s. 27.

[37] The administrative courts are established by the Establishment of Administrative Courts and Administrative Court Procedure Act B.E. 2542 (1999), s. 54.

[38] Constitutional Court, "Jurisdiction of the constitutional court."

trade court; and the bankruptcy court. Each of them is established by provisions of law.

The Supreme Court also divides its operation into five specialized divisions. These five divisions are: the bankruptcy division; the criminal division for persons holding political positions; the environmental division; the consumer division; and the election cases division.[39]

1.4 Size and performance of courts

The size and performance of the courts of justice, with approximately 4,000 judges presently on duty,[40] can be assessed by means of considering the statistics published by the Court of Justice in its Annual Judicial Statistic Report.[41] Table 12.1 presents the number of civil cases, consumer cases, and criminal cases submitted in 2010 and 2011. Criminal cases ranked highest in terms of the number of cases submitted and pending, followed by consumer and civil cases respectively. Prior to 2008, consumer cases were classified as civil cases, and under this combined classification, civil cases always outnumbered criminal cases. However, with the promulgation of the Procedure for Cases Relating to Consumers Act B.E. 2551 (2008), consumer cases began to be separately recorded, resulting in a significant decline in reported civil cases.

Table 12.2 illustrates the performance of the Supreme Court by means of assessing the number of cases that remained pending or were disposed of in 2011. While the annual number of new cases is approximately half of the pending cases, this number is still well above the number of disposed cases, highlighting the likelihood that the number of pending cases will increase in the following years.

2 Sources and influences of the establishment of the judicial system

2.1 Western influence and nationalism

Prior to the current regime and its introduction of the principle of separation of powers, Thailand was under the rule of an absolute

[39] Supreme Court, "Jurisdiction of the supreme court," www.supremecourt.or.th/webportal/supremecourt/content.php?content=component/content/view.php&id=61.

[40] Due to the fact that the official number is not publicly disclosed, this number is an approximate number estimated by the authors.

[41] Court of Justice, "Annual judicial statistics of Thailand B.E. 2554 (2011)," www.oppb.coj.go.th/userfiles/file/AnnualStatistics55.pdf.

Table 12.1: *The number of civil cases, consumer cases and criminal cases in courts of first instance nationwide B.E. 2553–4 (2010–11)*

Year (B.E.)	Cases submitted to courts			Cases disposed of			Pending cases to following year		
	Civil cases	Consumer cases	Criminal cases	Civil cases	Consumer cases	Criminal cases	Civil cases	Consumer cases	Criminal cases
B.E. 2553 (2010)	253,019	382,958	544,258	202,256	339,400	487,711	50,763	43,558	56,547
B.E. 2554 (2011)	230,521	390,834	578,377	180,885	337,648	526,172	49,636	53,186	52,205

Source: The Court of Justice, *Annual Judicial Statistics of Thailand B.E. 2554 (2011)*

Table 12.2: *Statistics of civil and criminal cases pending and disposed of by the Supreme Court*

Court	Types of cases	Pending cases from previous years	New cases	Cases disposed of	Cases disposed of (%)	Pending cases to following year
The Supreme Court	Civil cases	14,682	7,466	4,313	19.47	17,835
	Criminal cases	19,074	8,206	7,879	28.88	19,401
	Total	**33,756**	**15,672**	**12,192**	**24.67**	**37,236**

Source: The Court of Justice, *Annual Judicial Statistics of Thailand B.E. 2554 (2011)*

monarchy, in which the King had the ultimate authority over legislation, administration, and judiciary. For instance, as previously described, during the Kingdom of Sukhothai the King would personally adjudicate a claim brought before him by a citizen having rung a bell.[42] Subsequently, during the Kingdom of Ayutthaya, adjudication power was accorded to the four ministries that formed the central administration – Interior Royal, Household, Finance, and Agriculture. Each of them had the authority to adjudicate both civil and criminal cases that were relevant to their operations, with the exception of the Ministry of Interior Royal, whose Metropolis Court could only adjudicate criminal cases. Civil cases that fell within the authority of the Ministry of Interior Royal were referred to the Central Civil Court and Kasem Civil Court.[43] In any event, the King had the ultimate authority over all adjudications.

The attempt by King Rama V to modernize the judicial system of Thailand in order to bring it in line with the standards of Western countries can be seen as the trigger for Western influences on the Thai judicial system. Thailand adopted a civil law system, as it would require less time to develop the entire system than it would a common law system. Nevertheless, while Thailand adopted a civil law system, certain traditions and cultural norms that are deeply rooted in the history of the Kingdoms of Sukhothai and Ayutthaya still find their place in the current modern system. For instance, the King still retains authority in some processes of the judicial system. According to section 191 of the Constitution, the King has the prerogative to grant a pardon. This power reflects the preservation of a deep-rooted tradition that has been present throughout the history of Thailand since the Kingdoms of Sukhothai and Ayutthaya.

2.2 Democratization and social movements

In the period immediately following World War II, Thailand encountered a number of political turning points, which, if handled incorrectly, could have jeopardized the country's political-legal status. Mom Rajawongse (M.R.) Seni Pramoj, the country's Ambassador to the United States at the time, refused to carry out his government's order to declare

[42] R. Lingat, *History of Thai Law* (Pathum Thani: Thammasat University Publishing, 2010), p. 463.

[43] W. Chitvaree, *Justice and Court System of Thailand* (Bangkok: Ramkhamhaeng University Publishing, 1973), p. 2.

war against the United States and the Allies, reasoning that such a declaration was made under duress from the Japanese government and did not reflect the genuine will of the Thai public at large.[44] As a result, Thailand was not considered part of the Axis, but after the war, Thailand's leaders were still targeted to be tried at the military tribunals of the Allies. In attempting to protect these former Thai leaders from being prosecuted at the Allies' military tribunal in Singapore, M.R. Pramoj proposed a promulgation of the War Criminal Act B.E. 2488 (1945), which defined "war criminals" as "those who committed any of the following acts (such as engaging in wars in violation of law or custom of wars), whether as an instigator or an accomplice, and whether such an act was committed before or after the promulgation of this Act."[45] This Act empowered Thai courts to try the alleged war criminals, including former Prime Minister General Plaek Pibulsonggram, domestically, preventing them from being retried in foreign military tribunals by virtue of the double jeopardy principle. However, General Pibulsonggram challenged the War Criminal Act on unconstitutionality grounds,[46] saying that it contravened section 14 of the Constitution of the Kingdom of Siam (relating to the liberty to life)[47] and must be voided pursuant to section 61 of the Constitution.[48]

The Supreme Court ruled that the War Criminal Act B.E. 2488 (1945)[49] was unconstitutional, as it was applied retroactively to cover an act committed prior to its promulgation, resulting in the deprivation of liberty to life of General Pibulsonggram and other convicts,[50] and ordered the release of all the convicts. Subsequently, since the Constitution did not expressly provide which entity – the Court or the House of Representatives – is authorized to decide questions of unconstitutionality, one member of the House of Representatives initiated a series of parliamentary debates on the topic.[51] Following the debates, the subsequent Constitution – the 1946 Constitution – created a Constitutional Tribunal mandated to decide questions of unconstitutionality but limited

[44] M.R. Seni Pramoj, *Biography* (distributed at his funeral service, published 1998).

[45] P. Udchachon, "War criminals Act: the origin of the constitutional court," *Journal of the Constitutional Court*, 42 (2011), 20.

[46] Defense testimony of General Plaek Pibulsonggram, dated 18 February B.E. 2489 (1946), p. 29.

[47] Constitution of the Kingdom of Siam B.E. 2475 (1932), s. 14. [48] *Ibid.* s. 61.

[49] War Criminal Act B.E. 2488 (1945).

[50] Supreme Court Decision No. 1/2489 and 2-4/2489, 23 March 1946.

[51] Report of the 20th Ordinary Meeting of the National Assembly B.E. 2489 (1946), p. 36.

it to only cases referred to it by the Court of Justice.[52] However, since the Tribunal was still structurally linked to political entities and was criticized on partiality grounds, subsequent amendments became necessary.[53] Ultimately, the Constitutional Tribunal was replaced by the Constitutional Court by virtue of the 1997 Constitution,[54] and its existence has been upheld by the most recent Constitution of 2007.[55]

Consequently, it is evident that Thailand upholds the principle of the Supremacy of the Constitution, which no law of inferior status can violate. The democratization and social movements, largely in response to the post-war situation, eventually led to the creation of an independent judicial body with an important mandate to uphold the Supremacy of the Constitution as the Supreme Law of the Land.

2.3 *Tradition, religion and indigenous demands*

Generally, a single legal system applies to the entire country, with certain exceptions due, mostly, to religion or ethnicity. In Thailand's southern provinces, the high percentage of Muslims, at approximately 80 percent, necessitates the application of religious laws in the area. Inevitably, Islamic law or "Sharia," considered as sacred,[56] governs many aspects of life for these Muslim populations.

As a result, Thailand allows the application of certain aspects of Islamic law in its four southernmost provinces. It promulgated the Application of Islamic Law in the Territorial Jurisdiction of Pattani, Narathiwat, Yala, and Satun Provinces Act B.E. 2489 (1946) to govern issues relating to family and succession, which are adjudicated by Islamic laws instead of the Civil and Commercial Code of Thailand when both parties are Muslim.[57] Moreover, as will be subsequently discussed, a specialist in Islamic law, called a *Qadi*, is appointed alongside ordinary career judges to adjudicate claims that fall within the scope of the Act.[58]

[52] *Ibid.* pp. 36–7. [53] *Ibid.* p. 46.

[54] Constitution of the Kingdom of Thailand B.E. 2540 (1997) (hereinafter "1997 Constitution"), s. 255.

[55] Constitutional Court, "Jurisdiction of the constitutional court."

[56] Constitutional Rights Foundation, "The origin of Islamic law," www.crf-usa.org/america-responds-to-terrorism/the-origins-of-islamic-law.html.

[57] Application of Islamic Law in the Territorial Jurisdiction of Pattani, Narathiwat, Yala, and Satun Provinces Act B.E. 2489 (1946), s. 3.

[58] See *ibid.* s. 3.1.4.

The promulgation of this Act provides an excellent example of how tradition and religion respond to the particular demands of the locals and can influence the judicial system in specific areas.

2.4 Global economic competition and foreign trade influence

Global economic competition and foreign trade prompt Thailand to adapt to the ongoing challenges they bring in order to remain competitive. In relation to trade, Thailand, similar to other World Trade Organization (WTO) Member States, is obliged to incorporate the WTO's rules, including the Trade-Related Aspects of Intellectual Property (TRIPS) Agreement, into its domestic legal system. Especially on issues relating to infringement of intellectual property, for which Thailand is heavily criticized, implementing the TRIPS rules tends to be a wise approach, in order to provide affirmation to the WTO community that Thailand complies with its international obligations and to increase foreign entities' confidence in Thailand. In enforcing intellectual property rights, Thailand has traditionally relied on police raids.[59] However, Article 50 of the TRIPS Agreement provides that judicial authorities have the power to order prompt and effective provisional measures to prevent any infringement of intellectual property rights from occurring.[60] As a result, the Central Intellectual Property and International Trade Court was established as a specialized court, with material jurisdiction over civil and criminal cases relating to intellectual property and over civil cases relating to international trade.[61]

3 Judicial appointments, judicial independence and access to justice

At the outset, the Regulation of the Judicial Service Act B.E. 2543 (2000) lists a number of judicial positions in hierarchical order, ranging from the Supreme Court Chief Justice down to a judge trainee (also known as a research judge).[62] Judges holding these positions are considered career

[59] V. Ariyanuntaka, "TRIPS and specialised intellectual property court in Thailand," *International Review of Industrial Property and Copyright Law*, 30 (1999), 360–76, at www.thailawforum.com/articles/trips-vichai2.html.

[60] Agreement on Trade-Related Aspects of Intellectual Property Rights, Art. 50.

[61] Central Intellectual Property and International Trade Court, "About the court," www.ipitc.coj.go.th/info.php?cid=1&pm=1.

[62] Regulation of the Judicial Service Act B.E. 2543 (2000), s. 11.

judges, who enter into the system as judge trainees and move upwards throughout their careers. In addition, the Act also permits three other types of judges – senior judges, associate judges, and *qadi* – to adjudicate cases.

3.1 Judicial appointments and qualifications of judges

3.1.1 Career judges

Judicial appointments of career judges in Thailand are regulated by the Regulation of the Judicial Service Act B.E. 2543 (2000). The Act requires that a qualifying judge must have already held a position as a judge trainee and successfully completed a judicial training program organized by the Judicial Training Institute.[63] To become a judge trainee, a candidate must pass a qualifying examination, which is administered in both written and oral forms. The written examination is divided into three levels: an open examination, a knowledge examination, and a special appointment examination.[64]

Of the three, the first level, the open examination, generally has the highest number of examinees. It requires that all examinees possess a Bachelor of Laws degree or its equivalent, as well as admission to the Thai Bar. In addition, examinees must have at least two years of experience in the legal profession, as prescribed by the Judicial Service Commission.[65]

The second level, the knowledge examination, generally has a smaller pool of examinees, as it requires more stringent qualifications. In addition to having been admitted to the Thai Bar, all examinees must have obtained certain qualifications, such as having obtained one of the following: one or more foreign law degrees higher than a Bachelor of Laws; a Master of Laws from a Thai university with a required minimum duration of study; or a certain level of professional experience.[66]

The final level, the special appointment examination, is the most restrictive, due to its specific prerequisites that are very difficult for potential examinees to achieve. In addition to having been admitted to the Thai Bar, being a person of integrity and good character, and exhibiting the kind of behavior and attitude appropriate to being a judge, qualified examinees of this category must currently be or previously have been one of the following: (1) a Professor or Associate Professor at a Thai public university; (2) a law lecturer at a law faculty of a Thai public

[63] *Ibid.* s. 15. [64] *Ibid.* s. 14. [65] *Ibid.* s. 27. [66] *Ibid.* s. 28.

university; (3) a civil servant with a title higher than a Directorship or its equivalent; or (4) a lawyer who has practiced for a minimum of ten years.[67]

Examinees who have passed the written examination will be short-listed to sit for an oral examination. At this stage, an examinee will be asked to orally answer a question in front of three to five examiners. Upon the completion of the judicial training program organized by the Judicial Training Institute, a judge trainee will then be elevated to the position of a judge.

3.1.2 Senior judges

Thai law permits the appointment of senior judges.[68] Appointments are governed by the Rules for Appointing and Holding Senior Judge Position Act B.E. 2542 (1999). Generally, a career judge retires at the age of sixty, after which he or she can be appointed to the position of senior judge if he or she has worked as a career judge for more than twenty fiscal years and has passed a duty performance fitness test.[69] A senior judge will then be appointed to adjudicate claims at the Court of Justice and is able to participate in the Grand Chamber of the Supreme Court as well as to adjudicate claims that can be decided by a single judge pursuant to the Statute of the Court of Justice.[70] A senior judge is required to retire at the age of seventy.[71]

3.1.3 Associate judges

An associate judge is a layperson who, due to his or her expertise in relevant fields, is recruited to assist career judges in adjudicating specific claims for a temporary term. Only certain specialized courts such as the juvenile and family court, the labor court, and the intellectual property and international trade court, have provisions allowing the recruitment of associate judges. Each court has its own recruitment rules and procedures. For instance, the Establishment of Juvenile and Family Court and Procedure Act B.E. 2553 (2010) requires that judges for each claim must consist of at least two career judges and two associate judges, at least one of whom must be female.[72] The qualifications of associate judges for the

[67] *Ibid.* s. 29. [68] *Ibid.* s. 12.
[69] Rules for Appointing and Holding Senior Judge Position Act B.E. 2542 (1999), s. 6.
[70] *Ibid.* s. 4. [71] *Ibid.* s. 9.
[72] Regulation of the Judicial Service Act B.E. 2543 (2000), s. 24.

juvenile and family court are prescribed by law.[73] An associate judge for the juvenile and family court must undergo special training and pass an assessment test relating to the judicial procedures of the juvenile and family court, as well as to psychiatry, social administration, and the protection of the welfare of children, juveniles, or families. Once appointed, an associate judge for the juvenile and family court serves for a three-year term, which can be renewed only once.[74]

As for the labor court, the Establishment and Procedure for Labor Court Act B.E. 2522 (1979) requires that each labor claim be adjudicated by both career judges and associate judges, the number of whom shall be fixed by the Committee for Administration of the Court of Justice according to the needs of each labor court. Generally, the King will appoint associate judges for the labor court from among a list of representatives of employers and employees who have been vetted by the Judicial Service Commission.[75] These representatives must have either participated in a trade union or been involved in labor-related organs.[76] The qualifications of associate judges for the labor court are also prescribed in detail by law.[77]

3.1.4 *Qadi* or *dato'* of justice

As mentioned above, a large number of Thai-Muslims reside in the southern part of Thailand, particularly in the four southernmost provinces – Pattani, Narathiwat, Yala, and Satun. Owing to their specific religious conditions, Thai law allows certain issues to be resolved according to Islamic law. Pursuant to the Application of Islamic Law in the Territorial Jurisdiction of Pattani, Narathiwat, Yala, and Satun Provinces Act B.E. 2489 (1946), when both parties are Muslim, issues relating to family and succession shall be adjudicated under Islamic law instead of the Civil and Commercial Code of Thailand.[78] In such cases, in addition to a bench of career judges, a *qadi* – referred to in the Act as "*Dato'* of Justice" – must also preside to adjudicate the case. A *qadi* shall apply Islamic law as necessary, and his decision with his signature in the judgment shall be final and binding.[79] Previously, a *qadi* was attached to each of the provincial courts in the four southernmost provinces, but with the introduction of juvenile and family courts in the region, two

[73] *Ibid.* s. 25. [74] *Ibid.*
[75] Establishment and Procedure for Labor Court Act B.E. 2522 (1979), s. 14.
[76] *Ibid.* [77] *Ibid.*
[78] Regulation of the Judicial Service Act B.E. 2543 (2000), s. 3. [79] *Ibid.* s. 4.

qadis are now appointed to each of the juvenile and family courts in each of the four provinces, with the exception of Yala, which has three *qadis*.[80] The qualifications of an applicant to become a *qadi* are prescribed by law.[81]

3.2 *Judicial independence*

In the past, the courts of justice were placed under the Ministry of Justice (referred to at the time as the Ministry of Court), which had responsibility for the administration and management of all courts.[82] Promulgation of the Statute of the Court of Justice Act B.E. 2477 (1934) affirmed the authority of the Ministry of Justice to administer and manage all courts in an orderly manner, even though the trial aspect of the judicial process, including the rendering of orders or verdicts, must remain within the specific discretion of judges.[83] From this initial structure, one may notice that the administrative matters of all courts, including personnel recruitment and budget administration, were not completely independent from administrative government agencies and possible political interference. Accordingly, this structure was heavily criticized by many, including legal professionals and the public at large.[84]

The Constitution deals with this criticism by affirming the independence of the country's judicial system. It stipulates that the courts of justice shall have an independent secretariat, with the Secretary-General of the Office of the Courts of Justice reporting directly to the President of the Supreme Court of Justice.[85] In addition, the Constitution ascertains that the Office of the Courts of Justice shall have complete autonomy in personnel administration, budget and other activities as provided by law.[86] To enforce the aforementioned constitutional requirement, the Regulation of the Administration of the Court of Justice Act B.E. 2543

80 N. Wongyuen, "Dato of justice: the origin worth recording," *Journal of the Ministry of Justice*, 4 (2012), 37, http://elib.coj.go.th/Article/courtP6_4_3.pdf.

81 Regulation of the Judicial Service Act B.E. 2543 (2000), s. 52.

82 Ministry of Justice, "Ministry of Justice: 118 years of serving the public," *Journal of the Ministry of Justice* (2011), 12.

83 Thammasat University Research and Consultancy Institute, *Complete Research Report entitled The Study of Social Attitude towards the Court of Justice after separating from the Ministry of Justice* (Thammasat University Research and Consultancy Institute, 2008), p. 72.

84 S. Cholpattana and P. Rui-on, "Current judicial reforms in Thailand: lessons and experience," presented in ASEAN Law Association 10th General Assembly, 2010.

85 1997 Constitution, s. 275.

86 *Ibid.* s. 275(3).

(2000) was enacted and came into force on 20 August 2000. This Act established the Office of the Judiciary, which is mandated to support the following aspects of judicial proceedings: administrative work, judicial affairs, and judicial technical affairs, including cooperation with other governmental agencies. Since then, administration of the courts of justice has been independent of the Ministry of Justice and protected from other political interference.

In addition to this affirmation of judicial independence with respect to administration of the courts of justice, the Regulation of the Judicial Service Act B.E. 2543 (2000) was enacted to guarantee the independence of the judicial process and took effect on 19 May 2000. This Act established the Judicial Commission, which consists of the President of the Supreme Court, twelve judges elected by all the judges of every court, and two commissioners from the Senate, to oversee the appointment, promotion and disciplinary procedures for judges.[87]

Both Acts include the following measures to further safeguard judicial independence:

3.2.1 Judicial appointment, promotion and discipline of judges

At the courts of justice, the ultimate authority to appoint a judge trainee to become a judge rests with the President of the Supreme Court.[88] A newly appointed judge must be approved by the Judicial Commission and take an oath of allegiance to the King, as this profession is considered to be working on behalf of the King. Of note is the fact that the entire process is conducted under the supervision of judges, without any external involvement or interference.

As with the appointment process, the reassignment of judges must be completely independent. Reassignment is only permitted with the consent of the judge to be reassigned, unless it results from one of the following: promotion of the judge; disciplinary action against the judge; the judge being an offender in a criminal case; a circumstance that compromises the judge's objectivity with respect to a particular case; *force majeure*; or some other non-violated necessity.[89] When a judge faces a disciplinary action, a three-step examination is required. First, an investigation commission must be established to gather all evidence, and

[87] *Ibid.* s. 274. [88] Regulation of the Judicial Service Act B.E. 2543 (2000), s. 14.
[89] *Ibid.* s. 18.

the judge accused of misconduct has the right to defend him or herself during the investigation. Second, the matter shall be re-examined first by the Judicial Subcommittee specified in each level of the court, and then by the Judicial Commission. Finally, the President of the Supreme Court, upon confirming that the evidence and facts presented are valid, shall approve the examination and issue an order of disciplinary action.[90] The entire process is designed to ensure the fairness and reasonableness of the process of investigating a judge facing disciplinary action, and to ensure the absence of external influences in reaching a conclusion.

In the administrative court, the appointment and removal of administrative judges must be approved by the Judicial Commission of the Administrative Court. The administrative courts also have an independent secretariat body, with the Secretary-General of the Office of the Administrative Courts reporting directly to the President of the Supreme Administrative Court.[91] The Office of the Administrative Courts is an independent government agency responsible for the administration of the administrative courts, and it has autonomy over personnel administration, budgeting and other activities.[92]

Appointment of judges to the Constitutional Court follows a specific mechanism. The Constitution provides that judges at the Constitutional Court shall be appointed in the following numbers from the following pools: five judges from among the judges of the Supreme Court and/or the Supreme Administrative Court, and four judges from among qualified persons.[93] A selection committee must be established to manage the appointments and must consist of the President of the Supreme Court of Justice, the President of the Supreme Administrative Court, the President of the House of Representatives, the Leader of the Opposition in the House of Representatives, and the President of one of the constitutional independent organs. Although the leaders of the House of Representatives have a role in the selection of Constitutional Court judges, the process is still under a system of checks and balances, in which the Senate must approve all those selected by the committee.[94]

[90] *Ibid.* s. 70. [91] 2007 Constitution, s. 227. [92] *Ibid.*

[93] Constitutional Court, "Jurisdiction of the constitutional court," www.constitutionalcourt.or.th/index.php?option=com_content&view=article&id=153&Itemid=83&lang=thindex.php.

[94] 2007 Constitution, s. 206.

3.2.2 Tenure of judges

To ensure the career security of judges, the tenure of judges at the courts of justice is legally protected. According to the Regulation of the Judicial Service Act B.E. 2543 (2000), judges can only be removed through death, resignation, disqualification, transfer to other civil servant position, retirement, and expulsion due to various reasons including health and malpractices.[95] The removal of a judge through impeachment is not an easy process, as it involves thorough investigation by several commissions and by the President of the Supreme Court. Therefore, judges are free to decide cases fairly and impartially without any fears about the security of their careers.

The Establishment of the Administrative Court and Administrative Court Procedure Act B.E. 2542 (1999) also specifies removal conditions for administrative court judges that are similar to those for judges at the Courts of Justice.[96] However, the mandatory retirement age for an administrative judge is sixty-five, as compared to sixty years of age for judges at the courts of justice.

The tenure of Constitutional Court judges is limited to one nine-year term.[97] They normally vacate their positions upon the expiration of their terms, but they may be removed prior to that time under the same conditions prescribed for judges at the courts of justice, although the mandatory retirement age for Constitutional Court judges is seventy years.[98] Additionally, a Constitutional Court judge can be removed from office upon the passing of a resolution by no less than three-fifths of the existing members of the Senate.[99]

3.2.3 Judicial administration

In contrast to the salaries of other civil servants, which are under the control of the Ministry of Justice or the Ministry of Finance, judges' salaries, including the salary scale and emoluments, are independently regulated, in accordance with the Annex to the Regulation of the Judicial Service Act B.E. 2543 (2000). As affirmed by the Constitution of the Kingdom of Thailand B.E. 2540 (1997), the Judicial Commission of the Courts of Justice regulates and approves the salary system, including salary increases. Consideration must be given to the position and the

[95] Regulation of the Judicial Service Act B.E. 2543 (2000), s. 32.
[96] The administrative courts are established by the Establishment of Administrative Courts and Administrative Court Procedure Act B.E. 2542 (1999), s. 21.
[97] 2007 Constitution, s. 208. [98] *Ibid.* s. 209. [99] *Ibid.* s. 274.

level of court to which a particular judge has been assigned.[100] Similar to those of judges at the courts of justice, the salaries, emoluments and other benefits of administrative judges must comply with the salary scale annexed to the Establishment of the Administrative Court and Administrative Court Procedure Act B.E. 2542 (1999).

The budget of the courts is also independently regulated. While the entire annual budget must be approved by the National Assembly each year, the Office of the Judiciary is the only entity that manages the budget.

Lastly, the Office of the Judiciary independently recruits its own personnel, with the exception of the Secretary-General, who is appointed by the President of the Supreme Court via the approval of the Judicial Commission.[101]

3.3 *Judicial training and related legal education*

The Judicial Training Institute operates a judicial training program, which is only available to those who have passed a qualifying test and become judge trainees.[102] The program is divided into four stages and normally takes more than a year to complete. The four stages are: (1) orientation; (2) initial on-site training; (3) substantive studies; and (4) final on-site training. The orientation stage is conducted right after a new batch of judge trainees is recruited, and the duration of this first stage ranges from four to six weeks.[103] All judge trainees are required to stay at the Institute of Judicial Training for the entire duration of this stage.[104]

The next stage is the initial on-site training. All judge trainees are trained at various courts of first instance in the Bangkok Metropolitan Area for eight months, which are allocated into two four-month periods at civil courts and criminal courts. The Institute barely has any training role at this stage, as career judges at the courts where judge trainees are sent supervise all the training, although the Institute occasionally conducts seminars in order to evaluate the progress of the on-site training.[105]

After the first eight-month on-site training, all judge trainees are called back to the Institute for the substantive studies stage. At this stage, the

[100] Regulation of the Judicial Service Act B.E. 2543 (2000), s. 13.

[101] Regulation of the Administration of the Court of Justice Act B.E. 2543, s. 22.

[102] S. Phonchai et al., *The Recruitment and Training of Judges at the Court of Justice* (Bangkok: Office of the Supreme Court, 2003).

[103] *Ibid.* at p. 38. [104] *Ibid.* [105] *Ibid.*

Institute offers substantive studies in various aspects of the judiciary, including information on rules and regulations for judges and the code of ethics for judges, as well as useful administrative matters. Field trips are also included. This stage normally takes twelve to sixteen weeks to complete. After this stage, all judge trainees will, again, undergo on-site training for sixteen weeks before completing the training program.[106]

At the end of the program, all judge trainees are tested for their mastery of the material covered in the training. Only those who pass the test will be elevated to become judges, and they will be assigned to one of the courts of first instance to complete three years of service on probation. Those who fail the test must continue the training, be dismissed from the judge trainee position, or be repositioned to become civil servants for the Office of the Judiciary. A judge who has completed three years at a designated court and displayed good performance will be appointed as a full-fledged judge at a court of first instance and will have complete authority to adjudicate claims.[107]

3.4 *Access to justice*

3.4.1 Instigation of cases

The Constitution affirms the right of a person to have access to justice.[108] Furthermore, such access must be uncomplicated, convenient and expeditious, and it must apply to the entire judicial process where trials are conducted in an accurate, swift and impartial manner.[109]

In civil cases, the Civil Procedure Code provides that any person whose rights or duties under the civil law are involved in a dispute or must be exercised through the medium of a court is entitled to submit his case to a civil court.[110] For criminal cases, the public prosecutor and the injured person are entitled to initiate a criminal prosecution.[111] However, the public prosecutor shall enter an action only if an inquisition has previously been made.[112]

For administrative cases, the Establishment of Administrative Courts and Administrative Court Procedure Act B.E. 2542 (1999) provides more protection by entitling a person who has not already been aggrieved or injured but "may" be aggrieved or injured to file a case at the

[106] *Ibid.* [107] *Ibid.* at p. 39. [108] 2007 Constitution, s. 40.
[109] *Ibid.* s. 40(1) and (3). [110] Civil Procedure Code, s. 55.
[111] Criminal Procedure Code, s. 28. [112] *Ibid.* s. 120.

administrative court. The Act stipulates that any person who is inevitably aggrieved or injured or who may inevitably be aggrieved or injured in consequence of an act or omission by an administrative agency or a state official or who has a dispute in connection with an administrative contract or other case falling within the jurisdiction of an administrative court, and the redress or alleviation of such grievance or injury or the termination of such dispute requires a decree, is entitled to file a case at the administrative court.[113]

For cases under the jurisdiction of the Constitutional Court, there are a number of channels to which various entities can refer cases. First, in any case in which one of the parties raises an issue of unconstitutionality of any legal provision, and the Constitutional Court has not yet decided on that issue, that party can raise the issue to the court in which the case is then being heard. That court shall deliberate the issue and shall have discretion over whether to submit its opinion to the Constitutional Court for its consideration and decision.[114] In other words, the party cannot submit the issue directly to the Constitutional Court but can instead raise the issue to the Constitutional Court via the support of the court in which the party's case is being heard. Second, a person can submit an issue of unconstitutionality of any legal provision to the Office of the Ombudsman for preliminary consideration. If the Ombudsman agrees with the petitioner, the issue shall be referred, together with the opinion of the Ombudsman, to the Constitutional Court.[115] Third, a person can submit an issue of unconstitutionality of any legal provision that he or she believes infringes on human rights to the National Human Rights Commission (NHRC). The NHRC shall then submit the issue to the Constitutional Court if it so agrees that the issue requires further deliberation by the Constitutional Court.[116] Lastly, a person who believes that his or her rights or liberties as recognized by the Constitution have been violated has the right to file a motion to the Court for a decision on whether a provision of law is contrary to or inconsistent with the Constitution. Nonetheless, this right shall be exercisable only in cases where all other means for the exercise thereof are exhausted.[117]

[113] The administrative courts are established by the Establishment of Administrative Courts and Administrative Court Procedure Act B.E. 2542 (1999), s. 42.

[114] 2007 Constitution, s. 211.

[115] *Ibid.* s. 245; see also the Organic Law on Ombudsman B.E. 2552 (2009), ss. 14 and 15.

[116] 2007 Constitution, s. 257.

[117] *Ibid.* s. 212.

3.4.2 Litigation fees

Litigation fees are by default compulsory. All civil and some administrative cases require payment of litigation fees before commencing legal proceedings. In civil cases where the relief applied for is not quantifiable in monetary terms, such as a request to appoint an administrator of an estate or a request to revoke the resolution of the meeting or the general meeting of the juristic person, the litigation fees are fixed at 200 Baht.[118] If the relief applied for is quantifiable in monetary terms, such as a plaint requesting compensation or a claim for damages according to a contract, the litigation fees vary depending on the amount of money requested or the value of the property in dispute.[119] For administrative cases, litigation fees must be paid only in: (1) cases involving a dispute in relation to a wrongful act or other liability of an administrative agency or state official arising from the exercise of power under the law or from a by-law, administrative order or other order, or from the neglect of official duties required by the law to be performed or the performance of such duties with unreasonable delay; and (2) cases involving a dispute in relation to an administrative contract in which a party requests money or the delivery of property. In similar fashion to civil cases, the litigation fees of the administrative court are computed based on the amount of money requested in the claim or the value of the property in dispute.[120]

Since litigation fees may impose considerable obstacles for some people, in the interest of equal justice, a party that is unable to afford the litigation fees required may file a request for fee exemption to the courts at all levels. Such a request must be accompanied by the plaint, the appeal, the interpreting request, or the answer to the court of first instance, the court of appeals, or the Supreme Court, as the case may be.[121] The court shall then grant an exemption from the litigation fee if it has reasonable grounds to conclude that without the ability to pay the litigation fee the applicant is likely to be in a disproportionately detrimental position in the case.[122] Of note, criminal cases and cases relating to the Constitution are heard without any litigation fee.

[118] Table 1 annexed to Civil Procedure Code. [119] *Ibid.*

[120] Administrative Court, "The court fee," www.admincourt.go.th/00_web/02_kadee/02_fee.htm.

[121] Table 1 annexed to Civil Procedure Code, s. 156. [122] *Ibid.* s. 156/1.

3.4.3 Legal aid

The Constitution affirms the right to receive legal aid in legal proceedings. It provides that a person shall have the right to proper legal assistance from the state in civil cases, and that in criminal cases, legal assistance from a lawyer must be guaranteed.[123]

The Criminal Procedure Code affirms that an arrested person or an alleged offender has the right to privately meet and consult with the person who will be his or her lawyer. The Criminal Procedure Code also provides legal aid for an alleged offender at every step of the process, in order to support the accused's right to a defense and to ensure fairness. Starting with the process of inquiry, in a case involving the death penalty or where the alleged offender was not over the age of eighteen as of the date when the alleged offender was notified of the charge against him or her, the inquiry official shall ask the alleged offender whether he or she has counsel prior to commencing the examination. If the alleged offender does not have counsel, defense counsel shall be provided by the state.[124] In addition, in a case having a penalty of imprisonment, the inquiry official shall ask whether the accused has counsel prior to commencing the examination. The alleged offender may request that counsel be provided by the state if he or she does not already have any counsel. If the inquiry official does not ask about the availability of the alleged offender's counsel or does not provide counsel, any statement that the alleged offender gives to the inquiry official is inadmissible as evidence to prove guilt.[125] Fees and expenses of the state-provided counsel are paid under the rules of the Ministry of Justice.[126] It is not the responsibility of the alleged offender to pay for his or her state-provided counsel.

The right to counsel is also affirmed in the trial process. The Criminal Procedure provides that in the case that the offence carries a death penalty or when the accused person is not over eighteen years of age as of the date when he is indicted, before the institution of the trial the court shall ask the accused person whether he or she has counsel. If the person does not have counsel, the court shall appoint a counsel for him or her. Similar to the process of inquiry, the court-appointed counsel shall be paid fees and expenses, and such payment is subject to the rule of the Administrative Committee of the Courts of Justice.[127]

[123] 2007 Constitution, s. 257.

[124] Table 1 annexed to Civil Procedure Code, s. 134/1, para. 1.

[125] *Ibid.* s.134/4.

[126] *Ibid.* s.134/1, para. 3.

[127] *Ibid.* s.173, para. 3.

In addition to the legal aid provided by the state during the process of inquiry and by the court during the trial, there are other organizations which play pivotal roles in providing legal aid. The two most notable organizations are the Lawyers Council of Thailand under Royal Patronage and the Legal Aid Office of the Thai Bar. The Lawyers Council of Thailand, established by the Lawyers Act B.E. 2528 (1985), is a professional organization that provides legal aid to people, provides defense lawyers to disadvantaged persons, and provides legal counseling to aggrieved persons in order to ensure fairness and protect the rights, liberty and equality of all people.[128] Legal aid provided by the Lawyers Council is not limited to criminal cases; it also covers most civil and administrative cases, cases relating to the environment, and cases of violations of human rights. From 1989 to 2003, the Lawyers Council counseled and provided legal aid for 235,605 cases, 189,740 of which were civil cases and 45,865 of which were criminal cases.[129] Furthermore, the Legal Aid Office of the Thai Bar, established under the Regulation of the Thai Bar Act B.E. 2507 (1964), provides recommendations and counseling on legal issues, and sometimes assists, free of charge, in civil and criminal litigation cases for disadvantaged people who are believed to have been treated unfairly.[130] From October 2012 to June 2013, the Legal Aid Office received 949 cases.[131]

4 Sources of law and styles of judicial decisions

4.1 Sources of law

As a civil law country, codes of law are the major source of Thai law. For instance, criminal cases are adjudged using the Penal Code, whereas civil cases use the Civil and Commercial Code. Criminal adjudications strictly follow the principle of *nulla crimen, nulla poena, sine lege*; hence, the Penal Code is the only source of criminal law. However, judges

[128] Lawyers Council of Thailand, "Lawyers council of Thailand," www.decha.com/main/showTopic.php?id=436&page=2.

[129] M. Thongpan, "The role of lawyer's council in giving public legal assistance," Part of the Training at College of Justice, the Office of Courts of Justice (2003), at http://elib.coj.go.th/managecourt/data/B7_28.pdf.

[130] Thai Bar under the Royal Patronage, "Legal aid office of the Thai bar," http://thethaibar.or.th/thaibarweb/index.php?id=166.

[131] Legal Aid Office of the Thai Bar, "Annual report for statistics on consultancy and litigation assistance of the fiscal year of B.E. 2556 (2013)," www.thethaibar.or.th/thaibarweb/fileadmin/DAM/2556/so.cho.no/chuailuea_55.pdf.

adjudicating civil cases can resort to other sources of law, provided that there are no other applicable laws. Section 4 of the Civil and Commercial Code of Thailand stipulates that in the case where there are no other applicable laws and no other applicable customs to fill the lacunae, recourse must be had by analogy to the provision most nearly applicable, and then to the general principle of law.[132] Regarding questions of constitutionality, the Constitutional Court interprets the relevant provisions in the Constitution.[133] For administrative matters, the administrative courts apply applicable administrative laws that are relevant to the matters in each case.[134]

4.2 *Styles of judicial decisions*

Judicial decisions are delivered and written only in Thai without any translation into foreign languages. As a result, Thai judicial decisions are inaccessible by foreigners who do not possess sufficient knowledge of the Thai language. Apart from the language barrier, the style and content of decisions are usually straightforward. Decisions are written in a way that is comprehensible, although they contain some legal terminology that may be difficult for non-lawyers to understand. Depending on the facts and issues of each case, civil and criminal decisions are usually not long. However, cases delivered by the Constitutional Court are usually long, as they must address many complicated factual and legal issues involving a number of parties, and the decisions may have political implications, which could potentially affect the public order of the country.

In terms of accessibility of the decisions of the courts of justice, only decisions issued by the Supreme Court are made available to the public,[135] whereas decisions by the courts of first instance and the courts of appeals can only be accessed by the parties to the case and any interested persons. Decisions can be obtained by authorized entities for a fee, but this can be waived.[136]

Regarding the styles of decisions, the judicial decisions of all courts generally conform to the following pattern: claims from both parties; a

[132] Civil and Commercial Code of Thailand, s. 4. [133] 2007 Constitution, s. 6.

[134] The administrative courts are established by the Establishment of Administrative Courts and Administrative Court Procedure Act B.E. 2542 (1999), s. 10; the Administration of Military Courts Act B.E. 2498 (1955), s. 13.

[135] Search engine is available at the website of the Supreme Court, www.supremecourt.or.th.

[136] Table 2 annexed to the Civil Procedure Code.

summary of facts obtained from hearings; reasoning on questions of fact and law; and then a verdict. In cases at the court of first instance where there is more than one judge on the panel or at the court of appeals, the duty to write the decision for the entire panel rests on the chief judge, although judges on the panel can write separate dissenting opinions. Having a dissenting opinion makes a difference in case the parties wish to appeal. As a rule, a civil claim that concerns a monetary dispute of less than 50,000 Baht is prohibited from appealing on the question of facts from the court of first instance to the court of appeals,[137] and monetary disputes of less than 200,000 Baht may not be appealed from the court of appeals to the Supreme Court.[138] Therefore, a civil claim that does not meet the monetary limitations but obtains a separate dissenting opinion is allowed to appeal to the court of appeals or to the Supreme Court, as the case may be.[139] It must also be noted that writing a separate opinion, whether concurring or dissenting, is totally at the discretion of judges. However, all judges at the Constitutional Court are required to prepare their own opinion of the decision if they are on the quorum and to orally deliver such opinion at the meeting before coming to a conclusion in each constitutional case.[140]

5 Courts and alternative dispute resolution (ADR)

The courts of justice have a heavy annual caseload, and the figure increases every year. A number of civil and criminal cases, large and small, are litigated, and this greatly affects the ability of the courts to deliver justice in a timely manner. The most frequently litigated civil cases are for the enforcement of loan agreements – a matter that can easily be settled outside the courts.[141] Recognizing this judicial restraint, the courts of justice have attempted to introduce alternative forms of dispute resolution in certain types of cases in order to alleviate the already-heavy caseloads of the courts of justice. Among these alternative forms are mediation in the courts of justice and arbitration.

[137] Table 1 annexed to Civil Procedure Code, s. 224. [138] *Ibid.* s. 248.
[139] *Ibid.* s. 224. [140] 2007 Constitution, s. 216.
[141] Department of Public Relations, Office of Permanent Secretary of Ministry of Finance, "Student loan fund cooperates with courts for possible mediation," *Royal Thai Government Press Release*, 9 November 2010, www.thaigov.go.th/th/news-ministry/2012-08-15-09-16-10/item/51101-.html.

5.1 *Mediation in the courts*

Mediation in the courts of justice dates back to 23 June 1994 when Justice Boonsin Tulagan, then the Chief Justice of the Civil Court, introduced mediation to the Civil Court by inviting Justice John Clifford Wallace of the US Court of Appeals for the Ninth Circuit to give an introductory lecture on the matter.[142] Since its introduction, mediation has proven more popular because it saves time and cost and maintains good relationships between the parties.

Given its advantages, mediation has been incorporated into the judicial system of the courts of justice. Mediation is given official support by being included in the "Strategy of the Court of Justice" as part of the "Strategy 1 concerning the Delivery of Justice."[143] The Strategy contains policies and plans to achieve greater efficiency in delivering justice by means of mediation. The ratio of cases during 2006–2009 that went through traditional litigation and conventional mediation was roughly 70:30, which met the target set in the Strategy.[144] Additionally, the proportion of successful mediation cases is 65 percent, which also met the target.[145] However, it must be noted that while all civil cases can be mediated, only criminal cases involving offenses that are compoundable can be resolved through mediation.[146] The limitation on criminal cases raises the question of whether an option to mediate can be extended to non-compoundable offenses.

One of the most important aspects of mediation is the mediator. Initially, judges were asked to serve as mediators, but due to the scarce number of available judges, mediators can now be recruited from among ordinary citizens.[147] Today, local courts recruit local mediators, for it is believed that the local courts have more information regarding the biographical details of potential local mediators. To register as a mediator, one must possess certain qualifications.[148]

In addition to local mediators, the Office of the Judiciary is in the process of developing a mechanism to recruit mediators to be specifically designated to one of the courts of justice. As a result, it seems that the future of mediation in Thailand is promising.

[142] A. Jitdhamma, "The development of mediation system in the court of justice," *Dulpaha*, 56 (2) (2009), 70, at http://elib.coj.go.th/Article/d56_2_9.pdf.

[143] S. Limparangsi, "Developing mediation work in the Court of Justice," *Journal of the Ministry of Justice*, May (2007), 113–14, at http://elib.coj.go.th/Article/50_5_9.pdf.

[144] *Ibid.* [145] *Ibid.* [146] Jitdhamma, "Development of mediation system," 74.

[147] Limparangsi, "Developing mediation work," 119–20. [148] *Ibid.*

5.2 *Arbitration, ADR and the courts*

Arbitration has proven to be a more effective method of dispute resolution in today's business transactions than traditional litigation. It is fast and efficient, and it maintains the secrecy of the details argued in the case. In fact, a number of jurisdictions tend to allow, or even promote, the use of arbitration as an alternative means of dispute resolution, for it promotes a more business-friendly environment where all parties are able to resolve their disputes more efficiently. The courts of justice also recognize this opportunity and have been supportive of such use.

Arbitration in Thailand can be performed both in and outside of the courts. For court-annexed arbitration, parties can determine which of the issues are to be resolved by arbitration.[149] Mostly, issues resolved by arbitration require deliberation on technical matters – something that is better done by specialized experts rather than judges. Also, the advantage of court-annexed arbitration is its timely enforcement; parties can directly ask the court overseeing the case to enforce the arbitral award without having to instigate a different claim.[150] Outside the courts, arbitration can be performed by means of *ad hoc* arbitration or institutional arbitration. For the latter, Thailand has established an Arbitration Office under the Ministry of Justice in 1990, and has developed a leading arbitration institution – the Thai Arbitration Institute (TAI) – under the Court of Justice.[151] For the past twenty-three years, TAI's caseload has increased annually, owing to the continuous promotion of the use of arbitration through various means, including public seminars and academic conferences. At present, the quality of TAI has proven to be on par with international arbitration institutions including the International Chamber of Commerce (ICC),[152] and TAI has greatly contributed to the development of arbitration in Thailand. In addition to TAI, the Arbitration Act B.E. 2545 (2002) is modeled after the Model Law on International Commercial Arbitration prepared by the United Nations

[149] Central Intellectual Property and International Trade Court and Institute of Developing Economies (IDE-JETRO) (IDE Asian Law Series No. 19, March 2002), *Alternative Dispute Resolution in Thailand*, http://elib.coj.go.th/Article/ADR.pdf.

[150] V. Ariyanuntaka, "Court-annexed ADR in Thailand: a new challenge," presented at LEADR's 7th International Alternative Dispute Resolution Conference (2000), www.thailawforum.com/articles/adr.html.

[151] IDE-JETRO, *Alternative Dispute Resolution in Thailand*, p. 2.

[152] Thailand Arbitration Institute, "Decoding arbitration," *Collections of Articles, Regulations, and International Agreements, Laws, and Supreme Court judgments relating to Arbitration commemorating 15 years of TAI* (Thailand Arbitration Institute, 2006), p. 15.

Commission on International Trade Law (UNCITRAL).[153] This ensures that Thai legal provisions on arbitration are also on par with international standards.

6 Functions, perceptions and challenges

Judicial decisions that are likely to have widespread impact on the entire justice system are generally rendered by the Constitutional Court, although the courts of justice and administrative courts also render decisions of this kind, albeit to a lesser extent. As previously mentioned, the Constitutional Court, along with its predecessors, has survived a number of changes in political and social paradigms, and it now stands firm as an entity that performs various functions that are expected of such courts. Following are examples of functions that are generally performed by courts in Thailand.

6.1 Functions of the courts

6.1.1 Social control

The function of courts in maintaining social order is generally understood as fundamental. The courts are, therefore, expected to perform this function not only as guardians of justice but also as enforcers of social order. There have been a number of landmark cases that illustrate the performance of this function by the courts.

For instance, the Supreme Court ruled in Decision 1176/2543 (2000)[154] that a defendant violated section 209 of the Penal Code[155] by being a member of the Barisan Revolusi Nasional Melayu Pattani (BRN), a terrorist organization based in Northern Malaysia that operates in Southern Thailand.[156] Such a classification is viewed as an attempt by the Court to maintain social order by suppressing terrorist activities. Subsequently, the Penal Code was amended to include Offences in Respect of Terrorization as a *sui generis* offense, giving the courts of justice another tool to maintain social order in this regard.

The Constitutional Court also plays an important role in this respect, particularly by monitoring adherence to the Principle of Equality.[157]

[153] *Ibid.* [154] Supreme Court Decision 1176/2543 (2000). [155] Penal Code, s. 209.

[156] National Consortium for the Study of Terrorism and Response to Terrorism, "Terrorist organization profile: Barisan Revolusi Nasional Melayu Pattani (BRN)," at www.start.umd.edu/start/data_collections/tops/terrorist_organization_profile.asp?id=4457.

[157] 2007 Constitution, s. 31.

A number of laws have been struck down due to their unconstitutionality with respect to this principle. For instance, section 12 of the Name of Persons Act B.E. 2505 (1962)[158] was rendered unconstitutional as it unjustifiably prohibited a woman from retaining the use of her last name after her marriage.[159] Additionally, section 26(1) of the Regulation of the Judicial Service Act B.E. 2543 (2000), which listed "a person having physical or mental condition unfit for being a judge"[160] as one of the grounds for disqualifying candidates from taking the written examination to become a judge, was struck down as unconstitutional, as the provision discriminatorily deprived persons with disabilities of the opportunity to become a judge.[161]

6.1.2 Legitimation of government policies

Another function of the courts is to legitimize government policies, or, alternatively, to strike them down due to their illegitimacy. One of the most notable cases illustrating the legitimation of a government policy by the Constitutional Court was Decision 11/2544 (2001).[162] This case involved the interpretation of section 15, paragraph 2 of the Narcotics Act B.E. 2522 (1979). Section 15, paragraph 1 of the Act prohibits the manufacture, sale, import, export and possession of narcotics unless authorized in writing by the Minister of Public Health.[163] Section 15, paragraph 2 provides that a person who possesses more than twenty grams of narcotics is presumed to have the intention to manufacture, import, export or possess to sell, which would automatically establish culpability pursuant to section 15, paragraph 1.[164] The defendant argued that this presumption violated the right to be presumed innocent in a criminal case.[165] However, the Constitutional Court dismissed this argument and legitimized the provision by ensuring that even with this presumption, the prosecution still must prove the culpability of the accused by successfully establishing that the accused indeed possessed the alleged amount of narcotics. The differences in the amount of narcotics in possession only result in different levels of severity of punishment. In other words, section 15, paragraph 2 is only applied after

[158] Name of Persons Act B.E. 2505 (1962), s. 12.
[159] Constitutional Court Decision 21/2546 (2003).
[160] Rules for Appointing and Holding Senior Judge Position Act B.E. 2542 (1999), s. 9.
[161] Constitutional Court Decision 15/2555 (2012).
[162] Constitutional Court Decision 11/2544 (2001).
[163] Narcotics Act B.E. 2522 (1979), s. 15, para. 1. [164] *Ibid.* s. 15, para. 2.
[165] 2007 Constitution, s. 33.

the successful establishment of culpability, without affecting the accused's right to be presumed innocent.[166]

Alternatively, the courts could also strike down a government policy due to illegitimacy. For instance, the Central Administrative Court recently ordered the National Water Resources and Flood Policy Committee, the Committee for Water Resources and Flood Management, and the Strategic Committee for Water Resources Management to redo their Framework Plan for Water Resources Management, as it violates section 165 of the Constitution as well as the Enhancement and Conservation of National Environmental Quality Act B.E. 2535 (1992) and the National Health Act B.E. 2550 (2007) by failing to conduct a referendum and public hearings.[167] Consequently, the relevant authorities must adhere to the procedures required by the Central Administrative Court, or their project will be rendered illegitimate.

6.1.3 Facilitation of compensatory or reparatory justice

Facilitation of compensation is another main function of all courts in Thailand. Regardless of the size and the nature of the case, or the number of injured persons, courts perform an essential function in facilitating the provision of compensation or remedy to those who have suffered. Two notable areas that illustrate this function of the courts are consumer protection and environmental protection.

Regarding consumer protection, the Consumer Protection Act B.E. 2522 (1979) affirms the consumer's rights to have access to accurate and sufficient information about goods or services, to have freedom of choice, to be assured the safety of usage, to have a fair contract, and to have an injury "considered and compensated."[168] Notwithstanding such an affirmation, consumers are still at a disadvantageous position due mainly to lack of knowledge on the quality of goods or services, as well as inferior negotiation power. While the default rule on evidence dictates that the accuser shall bear the burden of proof, consumers often lack access to useful information that is usually possessed by the provider of the goods or services in question. The Procedure for Cases Relating to Consumers Act B.E. 2551 (2008), enacted to offer separate procedural

[166] *Ibid.* s. 39.

[167] Manager Online, "Central Administrative Court orders government to conduct referendum for water resources management worth 3.5 billion baht," www.manager.co.th/politics/viewnews.aspx?NewsID=9560000078175.

[168] Consumer Protection Act B.E. 2522 (1979), s. 4.

requirements for cases relating to consumer protection, provides easier access for consumers to instigate a proceeding and assists consumers in a number of ways. For instance, consumers can make a verbal complaint instead of a complaint in writing,[169] and class action without court fees is permitted. Moreover, the Consumer Protection Commission and associations certified by it are able to represent consumers in a proceeding, and the burden of proof relating to information possessed by the provider of the goods or services in question is shifted to that person or entity. In addition to the compensation that ordinarily arises out of such cases, punitive damages may be awarded if the court finds that the operator of the business in question possessed intent to take unfair advantage of or to willfully, recklessly or negligently injure consumers, or that the operator of the business violated the public trust.[170]

6.2 *Challenges*

This chapter has illustrated a number of developments that contribute to the advancement of the system. While these developments provide the external framework of the system, it is the actual implementation of these changes that is also important in assessing whether the system is operating effectively and efficiently. While evaluation work generally requires the examination of carefully selected indicators, this research takes a rather humble approach by identifying three points of inquiry in order to assess the performance of the court system in Thailand. The points of inquiry are: (1) whether judicial rulings are complied with; (2) whether the system can effectively deliver justice; and (3) how the system is perceived by the general public.

6.2.1 Judicial compliance

As with other countries, decisions or rulings delivered by the courts in Thailand are duly complied with. For decisions by the courts of justice, the system provides that there be certain entities responsible for the implementation of the decisions. The implementation of civil decisions is carried out by the Department of Legal Execution, while the Department of Correction is responsible for criminal cases.

Decisions by the Constitutional Court are also duly complied with. For instance, of the cases referred to the Constitutional Court, those

[169] Procedure for Cases Relating to Consumers Act B.E. 2551 (2008), s. 20.
[170] *Ibid.* s. 42.

involving the affirmation of fundamental rights and liberty or relating to issues of unconstitutionality generally receive due compliance. To illustrate, section 12 of the Name of Persons Act B.E. 2505 (1962) became unenforceable after the Constitutional Court ruled that it was unconstitutional on the grounds of unjust gender discrimination.[171] Likewise, clause 3 of the Announcement of the National Executive Council No. 45,[172] which prohibited the selling of food and beverages during prohibited hours, became unenforceable after the Constitutional Court found that such a restriction was unconstitutional, as it was no longer justified by reason of national security.[173]

Cases relating to certain constitutional requirements also receive due compliance by relevant parties: for instance, issues relating to the interpretation of the treaty ratification process are a case in point. Previously, the Constitutional Court ruled that the Memorandum of Understanding (MoU) between Thailand and Cambodia[174] was a "treaty" subject to approval by the National Assembly pursuant to Section 190 of the Constitution.[175] As a result, the members of the executive branch could not enter into any international obligations arising from the MoU without receiving prior approval from the National Assembly.[176]

6.2.2 Institutional capacity

Annually, the courts of justice receive more than a million cases. In 2011 alone, the courts received 1,199,732 cases, categorized into civil, consumer, and criminal cases.[177] This extraordinary figure immediately prompts an inquiry into the ability of the courts to cope with such high demand while ensuring that justice is not unduly delayed. While the number of cases submitted to the courts increases every year, the number of newly recruited judges remains traditionally low. The recent open examination for judge recruitment saw only 15 out of more than 8,000 candidates successfully pass the examination, joining the already scarce number of judges on duty. The ability of the courts to dispose of cases

[171] Name of Persons Act B.E. 2505 (1962), s. 12.

[172] Clause 3 of the Announcement of the National Executive Council No. 45 dated 17 January B.E. 2515 (1972), as amended by Clause 1 of the Announcement of the National Executive Council No. 252 dated 16 May B.E. 2515 (1972).

[173] Constitutional Court Decision 12/2552 (2009).

[174] Memorandum of Understanding (MoU) between the Kingdom of Thailand and the Kingdom of Cambodia, signed on 18 June 2008.

[175] 2007 Constitution, s. 190. [176] Constitutional Court Decision 6-8/2551 (2008).

[177] Court of Justice, "Annual judicial statistics of Thailand B.E. 2554 (2011)."

can be assessed by comparing the number of cases submitted and pending. In 2011, the ratio between the numbers of civil cases submitted and pending is at approximately 4:1 (230,521:49,636), with consumer cases at 6:1 (390,834:53,816), and criminal cases at 10:1 (578,377:52,205).[178] Hence, at least one in every four civil cases, one in every six consumer cases, and one in every ten criminal cases will be pending. At the Supreme Court level, the annual percentage of pending cases is at 24.67 percent, meaning that one in every four cases will be pending.[179] These figures illustrate that the number of pending cases is still relatively high.

In responding to this high number of pending cases, the courts of justice initiated an off-office hours scheme, in which participating courts would operate during off-office hours, including Saturdays and Sundays.[180] From October 2012 to March 2013, the 120 participating courts, including the Appeal and Supreme Courts, disposed of a total of 53,401 cases during their off-office hours operation. However, parties that voluntarily opt for off-office hours operation must pay a nominal fee of an average of 1,400 Baht (approximately $45) per case. In addition to a more speedy delivery of justice, this operation conveniently accommodates parties that cannot come to the courts during normal hours of operation.

6.3 *Perceptional evaluation*

In addition to evaluations based on numbers, the perceptions of the general public can also be used as an indicator of the performance of the courts of justice. According to the poll by the National Institute of Development Administration (NIDA), one of the most advanced educational institutions for graduate studies in Thailand, the courts of justice are still perceived as the most trusted of all governmental bodies/systems.[181] The general public is of the view that corruption in Thai society is pervasive, with 85.85 percent of respondents indicating that the problem of corruption in law enforcement is the most prevalent. In light of this figure, the result of NIDA's poll in mid-2013 indicates that the judiciary ranks first out of the three branches of government with respect

[178] See Table 12.1 above. [179] See Table 12.1 above.

[180] Court of Justice, "Secretary-General commends the courts off-office hours operation as satisfactory," *The Courts Bulletin*, 17 January 2013, www.coj.go.th/iprd/system/Blue-news/56/june%202013/17%20June%202013.pdf.

[181] National Institute for Development Administration (NIDA), "Thai public opinion towards the constitutional court," www.nidapoll.nida.ac.th/main/index.php/en/2012-08-06-13-57-45/412-39-56.

to public confidence.[182] Similarly, the Suan Dusit Poll of Suan Dusit Rajabhat University, another trusted source of polls, reveals that 48.24 percent of 1,201 examinees believed that the courts of justice have significant roles in the judicial system, and that judges are highly respected.[183] Additionally, the public is satisfied with the operation of the Constitutional Court and the effectiveness of the implementation of its decisions.[184]

Consequently, it can be concluded that the courts of justice acknowledge the problem of delays. Instead of aggressively recruiting more judges, which might compromise quality, the courts of justice introduced this novel initiative in order to maximize their operational capability to meet demand.

7 Conclusion

This research reveals that Thailand's judicial branch has evolved from a system that was once criticized as "barbaric" to become one of the most efficient and recognized court systems in Asia and the world. The system is indeed charged with a lofty task – to serve as a "Pillar of Justice" in the name of the King. Therefore, one may notice a certain fusion between some traditional methods of dispute resolution and the so-called universal standard introduced during the colonial period in order to accommodate the specific needs of Thais while adhering to international standards. For instance, the Thai system is one of the very few that require at least one female judge to preside over a juvenile case, that replace family and succession laws with local religious laws, and that allow certain types of convicts to ask for Royal Pardons. At the same time, it is the very same system that promotes the use of alternative dispute resolution, that has a dedicated Constitutional Court to adjudicate cases of an important nature, and that has a number of judges with expertise in particular areas to adjudicate cases where such expertise is necessary. Consequently, a closer examination into Thailand's current court system clearly illustrates Thailand's competitive edge in light of the current global situation, as well as providing an affirmation that the system is fulfilling its role of serving the Kingdom as the Pillar of Justice.

[182] *Ibid.*
[183] Suan Dusit Rajabhat University, "Thai public opinion towards the judges at the appeals courts," http://dusitpoll.dusit.ac.th/polldata/2555/25551352194372.pdf (2002).
[184] *Ibid.*

References

Administrative Court. "The administrative court proceedings," www.admincourt.go.th/amc_eng/01-court/procedure/courtproceed.htm

Administrative Court. "The court fee," www.admincourt.go.th/00_web/02_kadee/02_fee.htm

Ariyanuntaka, V. "Court-annexed ADR in Thailand: a new challenge," presented at LEADR's 7th International Alternative Dispute Resolution Conference (2000), www.thailawforum.com/articles/adr.html

Ariyanuntaka, V. "TRIPS and specialised intellectual property court in Thailand," *International Review of Industrial Property and Copyright Law*, 30 (1999), 360–76, www.thailawforum.com/articles/trips-vichai2.html

Central Intellectual Property and International Trade Court. "About the court," www.ipitc.coj.go.th/info.php?cid=1&pm=1

Central Intellectual Property and International Trade Court and Institute of Developing Economies (IDE-JETRO). *Alternative Dispute Resolution in Thailand*, http://elib.coj.go.th/Article/ADR.pdf

Chitvaree, W. *Justice and Court System of Thailand* (Bangkok: Ramkhamhaeng University Publishing, 1973)

Cholpattana, S. and Rui-on, P. "Current judicial reforms in Thailand: lessons and experience," presented in ASEAN Law Association 10th General Assembly, 2010)

Constitutional Court. "Jurisdiction of the constitutional court," www.constitutionalcourt.or.th/index.php?option=com_content&view=article&id=153&Itemid=83&lang=thindex.php

Constitutional Rights Foundation. "The origin of Islamic law," www.crf-usa.org/america-responds-to-terrorism/the-origins-of-islamic-law.html

Court of Justice. "Annual judicial statistics of Thailand B.E. 2554 (2011)," www.oppb.coj.go.th/userfiles/file/AnnualStatistics55.pdf

Court of Justice. "Secretary-General commends the courts off-office hours operation as satisfactory," *The Courts Bulletin*, 17 January 2013, www.coj.go.th/iprd/system/Bluenews/56/june%202013/17%20June%202013.pdf

Department of Public Relations, Office of the Permanent Secretary of Ministry of Finance. "Student loan fund cooperates with courts for possible mediation," *Royal Thai Government Press Release*, 9 November 2010, www.thaigov.go.th/th/news-ministry/2012-08-15-09-16-10/item/51101-.html

Jitdhamma, A. "The development of mediation system in the court of justice," *Dulpaha*, 56 (2) (2009), 70, http://elib.coj.go.th/Article/d56_2_9.pdf

Lawyers Council of Thailand. "Lawyers Council of Thailand," www.decha.com/main/showTopic.php?id=436&page=2

Legal Aid Office of the Thai Bar. "Annual report for statistics on consultancy and litigation assistance of the fiscal year of B.E. 2556 (2013)," www.thethaibar.or.th/thaibarweb/fileadmin/DAM/2556/so.cho.no/chuailuea_55.pdf

Limparangsi, S. "Developing mediation work in the court of justice," *Journal of the Ministry of Justice*, May 2007, http://elib.coj.go.th/Article/50_5_9.pdf

Lingat, R. *History of Thai Law* (Pathum Thani: Thammasat University Publishing, 2010)

Manager Online. "Central administrative court orders government to conduct referendum for water resources management worth 3.5 billion baht," www.manager.co.th/politics/viewnews.aspx?NewsID=9560000078175

Memorandum of Understanding (MoU) between the Kingdom of Thailand and the Kingdom of Cambodia, signed on 18 June 2008

Ministry of Justice. "Ministry of Justice: 118 years of serving the public," *Journal of the Ministry of Justice* (2011)

National Consortium for the Study of Terrorism and Response to Terrorism. "Terrorist organization profile: Barisan Revolusi Nasional Melayu Pattani (BRN)," www.start.umd.edu/start/data_collections/tops/terrorist_organization_profile.asp?id=4457

National Institute for Development Administration (NIDA). "Thai public opinion towards the constitutional court," www.nidapoll.nida.ac.th/main/index.php/en/2012-08-06-13-57-45/412-39-56

Phonchai, S. et al. *The Recruitment and Training of Judges at the Court of Justice* (Bangkok: Office of the Supreme Court, 2003)

Plaek Pibulsonggram. "Defense testimony of General Plaek Pibulsonggram," dated 18 February B.E. 2489 (1946)

Pramoj, M.R. Seni. *Biography*, distributed at his funeral service, published in 1998

Report of the 20th Ordinary Meeting of the National Assembly B.E. 2489 (1946)

Suan Dusit Rajabhat University "Thai public opinion towards the judges at the appeals courts," http://dusitpoll.dusit.ac.th/polldata/2555/25551352194372.pdf (2002)

Supreme Court. "Jurisdiction of the Supreme Court," www.supremecourt.or.th/webportal/supremecourt/content.php?content=component/content/view.php&id=61

Supreme Court. *The Supreme Court of Thailand*, www.supremecourt.or.th/file/dika_eng.pdf

Thai Bar under the Royal Patronage. "Legal aid office of the Thai bar," http://thethaibar.or.th/thaibarweb/index.php?id=166

Thailand Arbitration Institute. "Decoding arbitration," *Collections of Articles, Regulations, and International Agreements, Laws, and Supreme Court judgments relating to Arbitration commemorating 15 years of TAI* (Thailand Arbitration Institute, 2006)

Thammasat University Research and Consultancy Institute. *Complete Research Report entitled The Study of Social Attitude towards the Court of Justice after separating from the Ministry of Justice* (Pathum Thani: Thammasat University Research and Consultancy Institute, 2008)

Thongpan, M. "The role of lawyer's council in giving public legal assistance," Part of the Training at College of Justice, the Office of Courts of Justice, http://elib.coj.go.th/managecourt/data/B7_28.pdf (2003)

Udchachon, P. "War Criminals Act: the origin of the Constitutional Court," *Journal of the Constitutional Court*, 42 (2011), 20

Wongyuen, N. "Dato of justice: the origin worth recording," *Journal of the Ministry of Justice*, 4 (2014) 37, http://elib.coj.go.th/Article/courtP6_4_3.pdf

13

Courts and the adjudication system in Bangladesh: in quest of viable reforms

RIDWANUL HOQUE

The present-day courts and adjudication system in Bangladesh as well as its legal culture have a history of several hundred years, including the 200 years of British rule in the Indo-Pak-Bangladesh subcontinent. The legal and judicial systems of Bangladesh have been greatly influenced by ancient Hindu, Buddhist and Muslim periods as well as by the English legal system. Prolonged British rule in the then British India, which ended in 1947, with law-making from Westminster and the local adjudication by British judges, culminated in the strongest and "most far reaching"[1] influence over the development of Bangladesh's laws.[2] The Bangladeshi legal system is fundamentally a common law system, but it has certain civil law attributes. It is a pluralist legal system built on a complex of pre-colonial indigenous legal cultures, received Anglo-Indian legal tradition, and post-independence developments. Its pluralistic nature is evident in the existence of customary laws, various personal laws, and semi-official or non-state justice systems alongside the secular state-law and justice systems. The legal system is more inclined toward societal or collective duties and public obligations rather than to Western-style individualistic rights.

Upon independence in 1971,[3] Bangladesh adopted the laws and legal institutions that existed in pre-1971 Bangladesh, i.e. the erstwhile East

I am indebted to a number of people for their assistance, information, and advice. I would especially like to thank Judge Md Zakir Hossain, Judge Abdur Rahim, and Judge Ruhul Imran, Rokeya Chowdhury, and my research assistant Khaled Saifullah.

[1] M. S. Alam, "Legal system of Bangladesh" in H. M. Kritzer (ed.), *Legal Systems of the World: A Political, Social and Cultural Encyclopedia* (Santa Barbara, California/Oxford: ABC-CLIO, 2002), vol. I, pp. 116–24, at 116.

[2] See, among others, P. K. Panday and M. A. H. Mollah, "The judicial system of Bangladesh: an overview from historical viewpoint," *International Journal of Law and Management*, 53 (1) (2011), 6–31.

[3] See the Proclamation of Independence Order of 10 April 1971 (with effect from 26 March 1971).

Pakistan.[4] Thereafter, the Constitution of the People's Republic of Bangladesh of 1972 (hereafter "the Constitution") in Article 149 provided that, subject to its other provisions, "all existing laws" shall continue to have effect. Needless to say, within the purview of these "existing laws" Bangladesh also adopted Muslim law, Hindu law and other religious personal laws alongside the British era laws that Pakistan inherited and internalized following its independence in 1947.

The following descriptions and analyses of functions of courts have to be considered in the light of the above features of the Bangladeshi legal system. Further, the reader needs to consider them in the context of two more important factors: the separation of the judiciary from the executive in November 2007, and the existence of exceptional adjudicative forums for some indigenous people as, for example, in the Chittagong Hill-tracts region.

1 General description of the judicial system

The judiciary of Bangladesh comprises the Supreme Court and other subordinate courts and tribunals. The Constitution establishes the Supreme Court, which lies at the top of the hierarchy of courts (the Constitution, Art. 94), and provides that other "subordinate courts" and "administrative tribunals" may be established by law (the Constitution, Art. 114).

Being a "unitary" country, Bangladesh has only one Supreme Court comprising two Divisions: (1) the Appellate Division (AD), the apex division, and (2) the High Court Division (HCD). The Supreme Court of Bangladesh is in effect the constitutional court of the country, having its seat in the capital. The Constitution (the Constitution, Art. 100), however, provides for holding circuit sessions of the HCD at any place beyond its permanent seat in Dhaka. Cases in the HCD are usually heard by two-judge division benches along with a few single-judge benches, which hear matters such as company or admiralty cases. In cases of particular import, the Chief Justice (CJ) may constitute a larger bench of three or more judges. Similarly, at present there are two benches in the Appellate Division. There is, however, a "chamber judge" in the AD to hear urgent and important matters during after-office hours and a vacation bench to hear matters when the court is in recess for vacation.

The traditional civil and criminal courts have their genesis respectively in the Civil Courts Act 1887 (hereafter "CCA") and the Code of Criminal

[4] The Laws Continuance Enforcement Order 1971.

Procedure 1898 (hereafter "CrPC"). Additionally, there are some special civil and criminal courts, established by special statutes. Apart from the Supreme Court, there are around 700 courts, and the approximate number of judges and magistrates (members of the Bangladesh Judicial Service) is 1,700.

There is no system of regional courts in Bangladesh. The seats of lower courts are allocated to administrative units, called districts. Some courts are placed in cities, and only a few courts are geographically placed in remote areas, i.e. in Upazillas (sub-districts), for the convenience of local people. The subordinate judiciary can thus be said to be only minimally decentralized.

The lower courts and tribunals are typically composed of single judges. A few special courts and tribunals such as the labor court, administrative appellate tribunal and international crimes tribunals are composed of more than one member. The system of jury trial, which was once part of the colonial-era judicial system, was discarded before Bangladesh's independence, in the early 1960s. Thus, in one sense, the scope of direct public participation in the justice-delivery system has become narrowed in modern times. There are no lay or non-stipendiary magistrates; nor is any court composed of expert non-lawyer members except for a few tribunals such as the administrative appellate tribunal and labor courts.

On the other hand, religious personal law issues governed by Muslim, Christian or Hindu laws, statutory and un-codified, are adjudicated in ordinary civil courts (CCA, s. 37(1)). As such, no shari'a courts exist to resolve disputes under the Muslim personal law. It is to be noted that disputes concerning, and offenses under, the laws applicable to the defense forces are adjudicated by military courts or courts martial.

1.1 The Supreme Court

The Supreme Court consists of the CJ, known as the "Chief Justice of Bangladesh," and of such number of other judges as the President may appoint in each of its two divisions, the HCD and the AD. In Supreme Court cases in which the government is implicated or is interested, the Attorney-General for Bangladesh represents the government.

1.1.1 The Appellate Division

The Appellate Division (AD) has only appellate power, with the exception of contempt and advisory jurisdictions. It hears appeals of any orders, decisions, judgments, and decrees or sentences of the HCD. An appeal to the AD lies "as of right" where the HCD certifies that the case involves a substantial question of law pertaining to the interpretation of the Constitution, where it has confirmed or imposed the death penalty or a sentence of life imprisonment, or where it has imposed punishment on any person for contempt. In other cases, an appeal to the AD shall lie only if the AD grants a *leave to appeal* (the Constitution, Art. 103). The AD also hears appeals of judgments and orders of some statutory tribunals such as the administrative appellate tribunal.

The AD has the extraordinary power of issuing any direction, writ or order "to do complete justice" in any case or proceeding pending before it (the Constitution, Art. 104). It is entrusted with advisory jurisdiction over any important question of law referred to it by the President. It is not bound, however, to issue any advisory opinion on such questions (the Constitution, Art. 106).[5] The AD is a court of record, has power to commit anyone for contempt of itself or of the HCD (the Constitution, Art. 108), and has rule-making power regarding its own procedures or that of the HCD, subject to prior approval of the President (the Constitution, Art. 107).[6] Its decisions are final, although it can review and depart from its own decisions under exceptional circumstances. In case of a final criminal appellate decision of conviction by the AD, a clemency petition may be made to the President.

1.1.2 The High Court Division and judicial review

The HCD of the Supreme Court hears appeals from judgments, orders and decrees of lower courts. It is a constitutional court having jurisdiction over constitutional matters, exercised through judicial review power. At the same time, it is also a civil and criminal appellate/revisional court.[7] It has original jurisdiction over contempt of court issues, company and admiralty matters,[8] certain Christian matrimonial issues,[9] trademarks and parliamentary electoral disputes.[10]

The HCD has the judicial review power under Article 102 of the Constitution to enforce constitutional rights and to remedy a legal or constitutional wrong as well as to enforce legal obligations. Judicial review on the grounds of breach of constitutional rights and the breach of legality can be sought against executive actions, judicial decisions, and laws.

[5] See *Constitutional Reference No. 1 of 1995*, III BLT (1995) (Spl.) 159.

[6] Its procedures are governed by the Supreme Court of Bangladesh (Appellate Division) Rules, 1988.

[7] See Chapter X (rr. 1 to 9) of the Rules of the High Court Division, and Order 48, CPC 1908.

[8] See the Admiralty Court Act 2000.

[9] See the Divorce Act 1869.

[10] See the Representation of the People Order 1972, Art. 49.

The constitutional supremacy clause of the Constitution (the Constitution, Art. 7) categorically declares that any other law inconsistent with the Constitution shall be void, while Article 26 enjoins the state not to legislate in derogation of fundamental rights. Article 26 further provides that any law, except a constitutional amendment (the Constitution, Art. 26(3)),[11] made inconsistently with these rights shall be void. Neither Article 7 nor Article 26 expressly vests in the HCD the judicial review of laws and the power to strike down any law. However, Articles 7, 26 and 102, taken together, make it adequately clear that it has the power to strike down any law as unconstitutional.[12] The Constitution indeed envisages a robust judicial constitutional review extending not only over administrative actions but also over legislative acts and constitutional amendments.

In recent days, the horizon of judicial review has expanded considerably. The court in appropriate cases has even dealt with policy issues or scrutinized sensitive economic and political decisions involving important questions of law.[13] Judicial review power is used against state contracts only sparingly. Importantly, judicial review in the form of "public interest litigation" (PIL) by persons who are not personally "aggrieved" has become an everyday phenomenon. The HCD (as well as the AD sitting on appeals) has used PIL largely appropriately in order to remove injustices in society or to improve constitutionalism.

The HCD, too, is a court of record and has power to punish anyone for contempt of itself or of other courts subordinate to it.[14] It has superintendence and control over all subordinate courts and tribunals. If in any case pending before any subordinate court any substantial question of law as to the interpretation of the Constitution or a point of general public importance is involved, the HCD may withdraw and dispose of the case itself or may send it to the subordinate court after determining the question.[15]

[11] Contradictory with this is the provision of Article 7B, inserted in 2011 via the Constitution (Fifteenth Amendment) Act 2011, which provides that fundamental rights provisions "shall not be amendable."

[12] See also Article 44 of the Constitution that guarantees the right to judicially enforce (through the High Court Division) constitutional rights.

[13] See, e.g., *Mohammad Badiuzzaman* v. *Bangladesh* (2010) 7 LG (HCD) 208, in which constitutionality of the Chittagong Hill-tracts "Regional Council" (a local government-type body) was successfully challenged.

[14] The Constitution, Art. 108.

[15] *Ibid.* Arts. 109–10.

1.2 Adjudication of civil disputes and civil courts

The procedures of adjudication of civil disputes in ordinary civil courts are governed by the Code of Civil Procedure 1908 (hereafter "CPC"), supplemented by certain British-era instruments[16] and situation-specific statutory instructions issued from time to time by the Ministry of Law. One of the basic principles of civil litigation is that every civil suit has to be instituted in the lowest court of competent jurisdiction (CPC, s. 15). Jurisdiction is determined principally with reference to territorial and pecuniary limits, but subject matter is also a key factor for jurisdiction. Pecuniary jurisdiction is determined by the monetary value of every claim in accordance with rules provided by the Suits Valuation Act 1887.

Before and during the hearing of any civil suit, the court may issue any order relating to discovery, production, compounding or return of documents or other material objects producible as evidence. In suits involving government interests, the government is represented by "government pleaders." As to the cost of suit, the governing rule is "cost follows the event," which requires the losing party to bear the cost. The court, for reasons to be stated, may, however, direct otherwise. The court may award both actual and compensatory costs (CPC, ss. 35–35A). Impoverished litigants may avail themselves of the benefit of legal aid in accordance with the Legal Aid Act 2000, or their court fees may be exempted by the court if they can prove themselves "paupers" or indigent persons (Order 33 of CPC).

1.2.1 Structure and jurisdiction of civil courts

Civil courts are classified into the following five tiers (CCA, s. 3): the court of the district judge; the court of the additional district judge; the court of the joint district judge; the court of the senior assistant judge; and the court of the assistant judge. In addition to the above, small cause courts have the power to adjudicate petty civil disputes of which the value does not exceed 25,000 taka. With the exception of certain orders, a decree or order by such courts is final.[17]

The courts of the district judge and of the additional district judge are usually the courts of second instance, with no original jurisdiction except

[16] See the Civil Rules and Order (CRO) of 1935, and the Manual of Practical Instructions for the Conduct of Civil Suits (1935).

[17] The Small Cause Courts Act 1887, ss. 5, 15 and 27.

for a few specified matters.[18] The pecuniary jurisdiction of the court of the joint district judge is unlimited, starting from suits whose value exceeds 400,000 taka. The court of the senior assistant judge may entertain suits valued at 200,000 taka and not exceeding 400,000 taka, while the court of the assistant judge may hear a suit of which the value does not exceed 200,000 taka.[19]

The court of the district judge has administrative supervision over all other subordinate civil courts based in a district, including the court of the additional district judge. The district judge and the additional district judge, however, enjoy similar power and jurisdiction. The latter court, of which there may be more than one in number in any district based on caseloads, hears such cases and appeals as are transferred to it by the court of the district judge.

An appeal from a decree or order of a joint district judge lies to the district judge if the value of the original proceeding does not exceed 500,000 taka, and to *the HCD* in other cases. An appeal from a decree or order of a senior assistant judge or an assistant judge lies to the district judge, who may transfer it for hearing to an additional district judge or a joint district judge (CCA, ss. 21–22). An appeal from a decree or order of a district judge or additional district judge (not being the appellate order/decree) lies to the HCD. Appellate orders or decrees, or revisional orders of these two courts, and any appellate order of the joint district judge may be challenged before the HCD by way of presenting a revision petition. Any civil court making a decree or order from which no appeal is allowed or has been preferred may review its own judgment (CPC, s. 115 and s. 113).

1.3 The criminal justice system and the ordinary criminal courts

The offenses that are tried by ordinary criminal courts (magistrates' courts or sessions courts) are all defined and criminalized in the Penal Code 1860. Rules relating to the trial procedure and penal powers of courts are provided by the Code of Criminal Procedure 1898. Supplementary rules of procedure are provided by the Criminal Rules and Orders (Practice Procedure of Subordinate Courts) 2009 issued by the Supreme Court.

[18] See, e.g., the Bengal Wills and Intestacy Regulation 1799; and the Succession Act 1925 under which proceedings are instituted with the district court.

[19] The Civil Courts Act 1887, S.19.

The accused has a statutory right of defense, and a constitutional right to a fair, prompt and independent trial. In non-bailable offenses, the granting of bail rests upon the court's discretion. When the accused cannot afford to engage a lawyer in a charge involving the death penalty, it is the duty of the court to appoint a state defense lawyer.[20] There is no separate prosecutorial department in Bangladesh. Criminal cases initiated through the police stations are prosecuted by public prosecutors appointed by the Law Ministry.[21] When any private prosecutor is appointed by the victim to prosecute the case, he or she has to work in partnership with the public prosecutor.

1.3.1 Structure of criminal courts

There are two classes of ordinary criminal courts: courts of sessions, and courts of judicial magistrates. Offenses carrying higher penalties are tried by sessions courts, while magistrates try offenses of lower gravity.[22] The Code of Criminal Procedure 1898 (Schedule II) determines by which court a particular offense defined in the Penal Code 1860 is to be tried. In terms of sentencing power, there are three classes of judicial magistrates, namely, magistrates of the first class (who in metropolitan areas are known as metropolitan magistrates), magistrates of the second class, and magistrates of the third class. In every district, there are courts of chief judicial magistrate, of additional chief judicial magistrate, and of judicial magistrates. In a metropolitan city, there are courts of chief metropolitan magistrate, of additional chief metropolitan magistrate, and of metropolitan magistrates. The Government may appoint special magistrates for the trial of certain specific offenses (CrPC, s. 12).

With respect to the jurisdiction of sessions courts, the whole country is jurisdictionally divided into certain sessions divisions, usually corresponding to districts. In metropolitan cities, criminal cases are tried by metropolitan courts of sessions. The following are the tiers of sessions courts: court of sessions/court of metropolitan sessions; court of additional sessions judge/metropolitan court of additional sessions judge; and court of joint sessions judges/metropolitan court of joint sessions

[20] The Legal Remembrancer's Manual 1960, Arts. 1 and 2, chapter 12.

[21] See the CrPC, ss. 492–495. Appointments of public prosecutors are mostly based on political considerations, which impinges upon the quality of criminal justice.

[22] For example, the maximum punishment that can be dispensed by a magistrate of the first class is imprisonment for a term not exceeding five years and a fine not exceeding 10,000 taka (CrPC, s. 32(1)(a)).

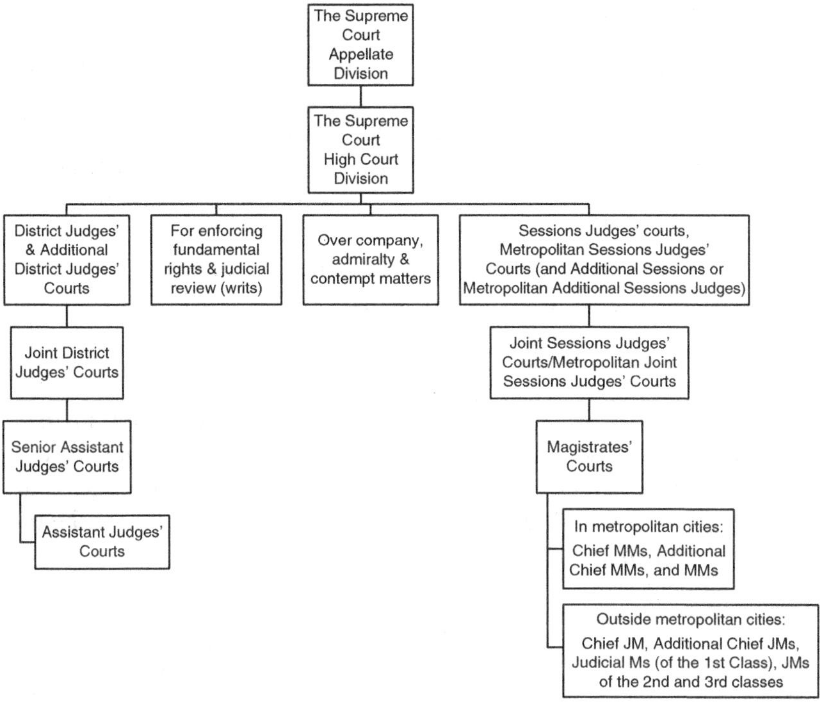

Figure 13.1: Structure of courts and tribunals

judge. The court of sessions judge and the court of additional sessions judge enjoy similar power and jurisdiction, but the latter hears such matters as are transferred to that court by the sessions judge.

Appeals of an order of sentence passed by a judicial magistrate of second/third class lie to the court of chief judicial magistrate. Appeals of a sentence of a joint sessions judge/metropolitan joint sessions judge or a metropolitan magistrate/judicial magistrate of first class lie to the sessions judge/metropolitan sessions judge as the case may be. Appeals against an order of sentence of more than five years' imprisonment passed by a joint sessions judge and appeals against a sentence passed by a sessions judge or additional sessions judge lie to the HCD.[23]

[23] In the case of an acquittal of the accused, an appeal may be filed only by the Government (CrPC, s. 417).

1.4 Special courts and tribunals of criminal jurisdiction

Not too long after the Independence of Bangladesh, the country began to face the challenge of combating newer offenses. At the same time, the volume of old crimes also increased significantly. The phenomenal growth in offenses led to the enactment of a series of special laws, establishing special tribunals. Of these specialist tribunals, which are discussed below, only the children's court is of a different genre, with jurisdiction to deal with breaches of criminal law generally by children. Other tribunals deal with specific offenses.[24]

1.4.1 Children's courts

The Children Act 2013[25] provides that any criminal allegation involving a child has to be tried by a children's court[26] to be constituted in every district and metropolitan area with an additional district judge. It also provides that no child (a person below the age of eighteen) can be tried together with an adult.[27] The Act of 2013 prohibits the death penalty and imprisonment (with certain strict exceptions) as a mode of punishing a child alleged to be in conflict with the law.

1.4.2 Special tribunal

The special tribunal is established under the Special Powers Act 1974 (hereafter "SPA"), with exclusive jurisdiction to try the offenses specified in the schedule to the Act, such as the offense of unlawfully possessing arms. Special tribunals, usually composed of session judges or additional session judges, follow summary procedures of trial (SPA, s. 27). An appeal against the order, judgment, decision or sentence of the special tribunal lies to the HCD and must be filed within thirty days of such order or judgment.

[24] In addition to the special criminal courts discussed below, the two International Crimes Tribunals (ICTs) established under the International Crimes (Tribunals) Act 1973 deserve mention. The ICTs have jurisdiction to try war crimes and crimes against humanity that were committed during the war of Bangladesh's liberation in 1971, and their orders are appealable to the Appellate Division of the Supreme Court.

[25] Act No. 24 of 2013. This new statute has repealed the Children Act 1974, which first established juvenile courts in post-independence Bangladesh.

[26] See the Children Act 2013, s. 16 (unofficial English translation of the term "Shishu Adalat").

[27] See the Children Act 2013, s. 15. It is to be noted that the age of criminal responsibility is nine (the Penal Code 1860, s. 82).

1.4.3 Nari O Shishu Nirjatan Daman Tribunal (NSNDT) and the suppression of acid crimes tribunal

These are two noteworthy special criminal courts to try, respectively, certain special offenses against women and children and the offense of throwing acid. The first tribunal, NSNDT, has been established under the Suppression of Repression against Women and Children Act 2000, while the suppression of acid crimes tribunal is established under Act No. 2 of 2002. Both tribunals are composed of an officer of the rank of a sessions judge or an additional sessions judge. When an offense under either of the two special statutes is conjoined with an offense under any other law, the concerned tribunal may simultaneously try both offenses together.[28]

1.4.4 The speedy trial tribunal and the law and order disruptive crimes (speedy trial) tribunal

The speedy trial tribunal, composed of an officer of the rank of a district judge, was established in 2002[29] with power only to try the most "sensational" cases involving grave offenses (such as murder, rape, offenses relating to arms, and so on) that may be transferred to it by the Government from among the cases pending elsewhere.[30]

On the other hand, the law and order disruptive crimes (speedy trial) tribunal, a time-bound tribunal, is established to hold speedy trial of offenses disrupting law and order.[31] Presided over by a magistrate of the first class, the tribunal has power to confiscate the tools, arms and vehicles used in committing the crimes in question, as well as to order the return of the proceeds of the crime to their rightful owners.

1.4.5 The court of the special judge (the anti-corruption court)

The court of the special judge is a special tribunal established under the Criminal Law Amendment Act 1958, section 3, for the speedy trial of "corruption offenses" (as described in the schedule to the Act). This anti-corruption court has the power to try corruption charges against any public servant as well as against private individuals. The Anti-Corruption Commission has the mandate to prosecute cases of corruption charges. As of December 2012, eight courts of special judges have been established

[28] See, respectively, the Suppression of Repression against Women and Children Act 2000, s. 27(3), and the Suppression of Acid Crimes Act 2002, s. 25.

[29] See the Speedy Trial Tribunals Act 2002, s. 4. [30] *Ibid.* ss. 5–6.

[31] See the Law and Order Disruptive Crimes (Speedy Trial) Tribunals Act 2002.

throughout the country. A limitation of this court that obstructs access to justice is that it may take cognizance of an offense only upon a written complaint or report by a police officer or the Anti-Corruption Commission.

1.4.6 Environment courts

First introduced in 2000, environment courts at the district level have been established under the Environment Courts Act 2010 (hereafter "ECA"). These are special tribunals of a predominantly criminal nature. They have, however, civil jurisdiction to entertain compensation claims. The ECA provides for the establishment of special magistrates' courts in all districts to try environment offenses as defined in the Environment Conservation Act 1995, which must be prosecuted by an inspector or the Director General of the Department of Environment or by any authorized officer. When it adjudicates a civil claim, an environment court may award any reasonable amount of compensation and may issue any protective, injunctive or restoration order.

1.5 Special courts and tribunals of civil jurisdiction

Unlike special criminal courts, special civil tribunals are small in number. Below, we discuss four such special civil tribunals. In addition to these four types of courts, there are a few other special civil tribunals in which career judges are appointed either exclusively or along with members of other professions.[32] The most notable of these special tribunals are the election tribunals (adjudicating disputes arising from local government elections) and the land survey tribunals (including appellate tribunals).[33]

1.5.1 Family courts

Established under the Family Courts Ordinance 1985 (hereafter "FCO"), family courts are specialist civil courts with an exclusive jurisdiction to "entertain, try, and dispose of any suit relating to, or arising out of" dissolution of marriage, restitution of conjugal rights, dower, maintenance, and guardianship and custody of children (FCO, s. 5). By virtue of a Supreme Court decision, any person following Muslim, Christian or Hindu personal law may invoke the family court.[34] As such, the family

[32] See, e.g., the Taxes Appellate Tribunal, composed of both judicial and other professional members. See the Income Tax Ordinance 1984, s. 11.

[33] The State Acquisition and Tenancy Act 1950, ss. 145A–145D.

[34] *Paschan Rishi Das* v. *Khuku Rani Das* (1997) 5 BLT (HCD) 174.

court may apply both codified and un-codified personal laws pertaining to one of its jurisdictional areas.

There are family courts in all districts except the three districts in the Chittagong Hill Tracts (CHT). There are roughly 350 family courts, and all assistant judges are *ex officio* judges of the family courts. An appeal from a family court lies to the court of the district judge. A special feature of this court is that it has a mandate to attempt, in camera, to reach an amicable resolution of the dispute between parties.

1.5.2 Money loan courts

These courts have been established to provide for the prompt recovery of loans that may become due to, mainly, private financial institutions and banks.[35] Public banks and other public financial institutions may, however, resort to this specialist court. Joint district judges preside over such courts, with exclusive and dedicated jurisdiction to adjudicate claims for the recovery of loans.[36] Although the court is bound to dispose of suits within 120 days, this timeline is often not maintained. As of March 2010, approximately 36,772 cases were pending before these special courts across the country, which proves their paucity against the caseload.[37]

1.5.3 Administrative tribunal

The administrative tribunal has exclusive jurisdiction to deal with disputes regarding the terms and conditions of service of public officials, including their appointment, tenure of office, dismissal, and recognition of service.[38] It comprises one member who is a sitting or former district judge, and appeals against its decisions lie to the administrative appellate tribunal. A further appeal lies to the Supreme Court's AD. The administrative appellate tribunal consists of three members, of whom one is a senior-level public servant, while the chairman is a person who is, or was, qualified to be a Supreme Court judge. Currently, there are seven administrative tribunals throughout the country and one appellate tribunal.

[35] See the Money Loan Courts Act 2003, s. 4. [36] *Ibid.* ss. 4 and 5.

[37] R. K. Byron, "Govt moves to settle loan cases out of court," *Daily Star*, 3 March 2010, www.thedailystar.net/newDesign/news-details.php?nid=128452.

[38] See the Administrative Tribunals Act 1980.

1.5.4 Labor courts and the labor appellate tribunal

There are seven labor courts across the country, established by the Bangladesh Labor Act 2006 (hereafter "BLA"), section 214. Based on a tripartite representation model, the labor court for the purpose of hearing an industrial or employment dispute consists of a chairman and two other members, one representing the workers and the other representing the employer. The Government appoints the chairman from amongst the district judges or additional district judges.

Appeal of the judgments, decisions or arbitral awards of any labor court lie to the labor appellate tribunal, which may be constituted with one or more members. The labor appellate tribunal's decisions are final (BLA, s. 217).

1.6 Administration of (local) justice in the Chittagong Hill-Tracts (CHT)

The indigenous people in the CHT and elsewhere in the country invoke their traditional adjudication system alongside the official or state courts.[39] In the CHT, the local aboriginal people follow the traditional justice system and go to courts of circle chiefs (*Raja's Court*) with petty cases involving tribal customs, usages and institutions such as marriage, divorce, adoption and inheritance.[40]

The CHT Regulation 1900 (s. 8) authorizes the Mauza headmen and circle chiefs[41] to resolve disputes in accordance with the family and customary laws, usages and traditions of the tribal people. Interestingly, the headman or the karbari (chief of a parha, a unit of the Mauza), the two revenue officers at the grass-root level, may also deal with petty criminal cases, with jurisdiction to levy fines or award compensation.

[39] For example, the Garos, an ethnic community of the northeast region of Bangladesh, follow their traditional adjudication system to resolve petty civil, property and family disputes based on the principle of collective responsibility for misdeeds by individuals. See M. R. Ullah, *The Garo Community: A Marginal Community of Bangladesh* (Dhaka: University Grants Commission, 2010), and J. Marak, *Garo Customary Laws and Practices* (New Delhi: Akansha Publishing, 2000).

[40] On customary laws and the adjudication system in the CHT, see R. D. Roy, *Traditional Customary Laws and Indigenous Peoples in Asia* (London: Minority Rights Group International, 2005), and *Aung Shwe Prue Chowdhury* v. *Kyaw Sain Prue Chowdhury & Ors* (1998) 18 BLD (AD) 33.

[41] The CHT is divided into three circles (Chakma, Mong and Bomang), each being controlled by a chief, called Raja. Each circle has several jurisdictional *mouzas*, each under a headman or dewan (revenue collector).

It is pertinent to mention that ordinary civil and criminal courts (with the exception of magistrates' courts) did not operate in the CHT until 2008. Earlier, senior government officials charged with the administration of the region used to discharge judicial functions. In 2008, following a court intervention seeking to enforce a 2003 amendment of the CHT Regulation 1900,[42] the government established district and joint district judges' courts and courts of sessions judges and joint sessions judges in each district of the CHT. However, courts of additional district judges, assistant judges and senior assistant judges and the special courts such as the family courts have not yet been established there.[43]

In the CHT, a source of law for the official courts when dealing with issues other than family law issues are the customs of the local indigenous people. Family issues of the tribal people of the CHT continue to be adjudicated in non-state forums. This aspect of legal pluralism has been statutorily recognized by the amended CHT Regulation 1900, which enjoins the civil courts to "try all civil cases in accordance with the existing laws, customs and usages of the districts concerned, except the cases arising out of the family laws and other customary laws of the tribes" (CHT Regulation 1900, s. 8(4)).

1.7 Remarks on the creation and function of special courts of criminal and civil jurisdictions

As seen above, the post-independence Bangladeshi judicial system has witnessed the proliferation of special courts. The rationales behind the creation of civil and criminal special courts are seemingly different. Most special civil courts were established to respond to the increasing market demands following the country's resort to financial liberalization in the 1980s, to respond to the demand for new adjudicative forums for certain technical issues, or to meet the challenges of ensuring access to justice, as was the case with, respectively, the money loan court, the environment court, and the family court. On the other hand, the creation of special courts of criminal jurisdiction was prompted by a motto to maintain "law

[42] *BLAST* v. *Secretary, Ministry of Law, Justice and Parliamentary Affairs* (2009) 61 DLR (HCD) 109.

[43] In the CHT, there are only a few special courts. For example, the joint district judge in each district has responsibility for the money loan court, while the sessions judges are responsible for the anti-repression of women and children tribunals and the special tribunals.

and order" by providing for new tribunals with stringent powers and a narrow timeframe for the trial of certain offenses.

In addition to the separate rationales behind the creation of the civil and criminal special courts, a common objective that was sought was the quick disposal of cases in the face of an excessively huge backlog, particularly in the lower courts. Despite some successes of these courts, however, the wider objectives of establishing them remain largely unfulfilled because, among other things, they often fail to complete the disposal of disputes or the trial of offenses within the stipulated timeline or because they lack adequate resources, such as staff and judicial officers, as well as well-trained judges for subject-specific special courts. The underperformance of these courts is, to some extent, attributable to hastily enacted statutes that established them without designing proper court structures and management.

2 Judicial appointments, judicial independence and access to justice

2.1 Judicial appointments and qualifications of judges

The administration of the judiciary can be said to belong to both the judiciary and the executive government. The Ministry of Law, Justice and Parliamentary Affairs (Law and Justice Division) significantly controls judicial governance, but the Ministry has to act in consultation with the Supreme Court in any dealings with lower court judges. With respect to internal matters, magistrates are under the administrative control of either the Chief Judicial Magistrate (hereafter CJM) or, in a metropolitan city, of the Chief Metropolitan Magistrate (hereafter CMM). The CMM or the CJM may regulate, manage, or distribute judicial businesses among magistrates under their administration (CrPC, s. 16). In the same way, the sessions judge or the district judge administratively controls the other judges subordinate to him.

As regards the Supreme Court, the President appoints its judges upon the advice of the Prime Minister. Currently, the approved number of judges in the AD is eleven, and there is no such approved number of judges to sit in the HCD. As of December 2013, there are nine judges (including the CJ) in the AD and ninety judges in the HCD.

Judges of the Supreme Court are appointed from amongst the advocates of the Supreme Court who have a professional standing of at least ten years before either of its divisions, or from amongst judges in the Bangladesh Judicial Service with a minimum experience of ten years.

Although there is no bar to direct appointment of qualified persons as judges to either of the divisions, the long-standing tradition has been to appoint "additional judges" in the HCD for a period of two years (the Constitution, Art. 98). Upon the expiry of her or his term as an additional judge, the judge may be appointed as a permanent judge in the HCD. Judges of the AD are drawn from amongst the judges of the HCD, but the Constitution keeps a leeway to appoint qualified persons from outside the HCD as judges of the AD.

Judges and magistrates of the lower judiciary are members of the Bangladesh Judicial Service and have been selected, since 2007, through a competitive entrance examination conducted by the Judicial Service Commission. The competition for judicial posts has become intense, and the pass rate is around 10 percent. In the latest intake of 2012, the pass rate was 6 percent (only 125 candidates were selected out of a total of 1,934). The test covers both legal and non-legal subjects and is divided into preliminary, written and viva-voce sub-tests. Qualifying candidates are appointed by the President (the Constitution, Art. 115). The President must consult the Supreme Court in respect of appointment, posting, transfer and discipline of judges and magistrates (the Constitution, Art. 116). In practical terms, for the control and direction of the lower court judges and for the approval of their appointments, the Supreme Court has a General Administration Committee (GA Committee), consisting of the CJ and three other judges.[44] Recommendations of the GA Committee are placed before the full court, comprising all the judges of the HCD, for approval.

In practice, both the appointments and disciplinary measures are carried out by the executive branch. The initiation of any scheme including disciplinary measures or the planning of posting of judges is made by the Ministry of Law. It is only after any proposal regarding the administration of services of the members of the Judicial Service is approved by the GA Committee that the Ministry can execute the proposal. An important aspect of the judicial administration is the Supreme Court's supervision over the subordinate courts. The HCD judges upon instruction of the Chief Justice randomly visit and inspect subordinate courts throughout the year, and, when assigned by the CJ, they hold inquiries about complaints, if any, against judges of lower courts.[45]

[44] See the Rules of the High Court Division, Part 1, Chapter 1, rr. 1–3.

[45] The discipline of judges belongs to the power of the President and is subject to a number of enactments. Apart from the Supreme Court, the Ministry of Law plays a vital role in

2.2 Judicial independence

Independence of the judiciary has been held by the court to be an unalterable "basic structure of the constitution."[46] Relevant constitutional provisions, taken together, reveal a scheme intended to guarantee judicial independence. For example, post-retirement appointment of Supreme Court judges to any "office of profit" other than a judicial/quasi-judicial post is prohibited (the Constitution, Art. 99).[47] In addition, Supreme Court judges are tenured and cannot be arbitrarily removed before they retire at the age of sixty-seven (the Constitution, Art. 96(1)). They are removable only through a peers-driven constitutional process (i.e. the Supreme Judicial Council comprising the Chief Justice and the two other senior most judges of the AD), which can be requested by the President on his own or upon receipt of an allegation of misconduct against a sitting judge (the Constitution, Art. 96(2)–(5)). The judges also enjoy financial and other benefits that are largely in accordance with the principles of judicial independence. For example, their salaries are disbursed from the "consolidated fund" and hence not subject to taxation (the Constitution, Art. 88(b)). The Constitution proclaims the functional independence of the judges of both the Supreme Court and the lower judiciary (the Constitution, Arts. 94(4) and 116A), and there are Codes of Conduct that govern their behavior. Nonetheless, problems of independence exist at both levels of the judiciary.

In appointing all judges of the Supreme Court except the CJ, the President is constitutionally required to act on the advice of the Prime Minister. In reality, all Supreme Court judges, including the CJ, are appointed by the executive government. By taking advantage of this unwritten prerogative, successive contemporary governments have indulged in various overt and covert actions to manipulate or exert political influence on the judiciary.[48] Political considerations in the

this process. On this, see S. A. Akkas, "Discipline of subordinate court judges in Bangladesh," *Chittagong University Journal of Law*, 5 (2000), 146–62.

[46] *Anwar Hossain Chowdhury* v. *Bangladesh* (1989) BLD (Special) 1. See also *Bangladesh* v. *Idrisur Rahman* (2010) 7 LG (AD) 137. On the much-debated issue of judicial independence, see, among others, R. Hoque, *Judicial Activism in Bangladesh: A Golden Mean Approach* (Newcastle upon Tyne: Cambridge Scholars Publishing, 2011), pp. 207–13.

[47] In *Ruhul Quddus* v. *Justice MA Aziz* (2008) 60 DLR (HCD) 511, appointment of a Supreme Court judge as the Chief Election Commissioner was held to be unconstitutional.

[48] Insiders' accounts confirm that some additional judges were in the past not appointed as permanent judges because their decisions displeased the Government. See R. Hoque, *Judicial Activism in Bangladesh*, p. 211.

appointment of judges of the Supreme Court are now an open secret. Another factor that has tarnished judicial independence is wide and non-transparent political discretion in elevating the HCD judges to the AD and in appointing the CJ. The convention (or good practice?) of appointing the most senior HCD judge to the AD in case of vacancy and of appointing the most senior AD judge as the CJ has more often than not been breached.[49]

In the past, the old convention of the President consulting with the CJ in appointing additional or permanent judges to the HCD was not often followed. In a 2010 decision, the AD has held that, while appointing new judges or confirming the service of additional judges, the CJ's recommendation shall have primacy over the wish of the President and that the convention of consulting the CJ was a binding constitutional norm.[50] Sometime after this verdict, the 15th amendment (of July 2011) of the Constitution reinstated the rule of consulting the CJ for the appointment of judges.[51]

The current scenario of institutional independence of the lower judiciary is the result of an AD decision in the famous case of *Secretary, Ministry of Finance* v. *Md Masdar Hossain* (1999),[52] which culminated in a tightly monitored verdict prescribing a number of measures for ensuring judicial independence. Seven years after the verdict, the government separated the magistracy from the executive and established the Judicial Service Commission for selection of judges, which took effect on 1 November 2007. Later, an independent Judicial Pay Commission for the determination of salaries of the members of the judicial service was established and the Supreme Court's financial autonomy was largely granted. However, the Judicial Pay Commission's recommendation as to the structure of salaries and benefits has not been fully implemented, allegedly due to bureaucratic obstruction.

Since 2008, the Supreme Court has been independently proposing its own budget. The draft budget proposal is sent to the government for its inclusion into the national budget proposal to be laid before

[49] In *S. N. Goswami* v. *Bangladesh* (2003) 55 DLR (HCD) 332, it was held to be a non-obligatory convention.

[50] *Bangladesh* v. *Idrisur Rahman* (2010), above, note 46.

[51] See the recently amended Article 95(1) of the Constitution: "[. . .] the other judges shall be appointed by the President after consultation with the Chief Justice." This consultation obligation was deleted from the Constitution in 1975 through the 4th Amendment.

[52] (2000) 52 DLR (AD) 82 (hereafter *Masdar Hossain*). For the HCD's judgment on this, see *Md Masdar Hossain & Ors* v. *Secretary, Ministry of Finance* (1998) 18 BLD (HCD) 558.

Parliament. The government, however, retains a check on the budget proposed by the judiciary. The government may approve the budget by perhaps slightly reducing the monetary threshold proposed; however, this is a rare possibility. Subject to constitutionally legitimate financial audits and checks, the judiciary has control over the budget allocated to it.[53]

The above shows that the law seeks to achieve and maintain the independence of the judiciary. Yet, as stated above, the judiciary is not immune from problems of independence, some of which are internal to the judiciary, including the quality of judges and representation in the Court.[54] Also, retired or sitting lower-court judges are being appointed to posts of an executive nature. On the other hand, the appointment procedures for the Supreme Court judges are somewhat arbitrary in that there are no legally determined selection criteria apart from the Constitution's broad-based qualification criteria. Nor is there any judicial commission for the appointment of Supreme Court judges. Advocacy and calls for reform of the appointment process for Supreme Court judges have been overlooked by successive governments in the post-democratic-transition years.[55] Moreover, the non-transparent appointment process and the lack of statutory criteria for the qualifications of potential judges have not only led to the politicization of the judiciary, but they have also significantly impacted the qualifications of judges and the quality of their decisions.[56]

[53] For example, parliamentary standing committees relating to the Ministry of Law and public accounts have indirect roles in this regard. The accounts of the Supreme Court and other courts are audited by the Office of the Comptroller and Auditor General.

[54] Note, for example, the CJ's personal administrative power to constitute benches of the HCD, which is not subject to any formal criteria or guidelines and hence susceptible to misuse.

[55] In 2008, a nine-member judicial appointment commission headed by the CJ was established by virtue of the Supreme Judicial Commission Ordinance 2008, promulgated during the emergency government in power at the time, which was later turned down by Parliament in 2009. There is a strong demand for the reinstallation of such a judicial commission. There is also a demand for a separate secretariat for the Supreme Court. See, for example, Institute of Governance Study, *The Judiciary: Policy Note* (Dhaka: IGS, BRAC University, 2010), http://www.igs-bracu.ac.bd/UserFiles/File/archive_file/Judiciary_Policy_Note.pdf. Recently, the Law Commission of Bangladesh issued a report (No. 118, 5 August 2012) suggesting certain selection criteria for Supreme Court judges and recommended the enactment of a statute in this regard.

[56] There is no detailed study on this. This claim is, however, borne out by certain recent controversial appointments as well as by unwillingness of some well-qualified lawyers to accept posts in the higher judiciary.

2.3 *Judicial and professional training, and legal education*

Since 1995, a specialized institute, namely, the Judicial Administration Training Institute, has been imparting foundational (basic) and continuing training to judges and judicial magistrates.[57] Also, for their professional advancement or promotion, judges must take certain departmental exams conducted by the Judicial Service Commission. They also must take certain other compulsory training courses imparted by other agencies of the government, such as the Bangladesh Public Administration Training Centre. Importantly, due to a policy implemented recently, candidates wishing to enter the judicial profession need first to qualify as advocates.

The Bangladesh Bar Council maintains the advocates' roll and holds examinations for admission to legal practice. To be enrolled as an advocate, a candidate must have a bachelor's degree in law from a university in Bangladesh or any recognized foreign university. The aspirant must appear for both written and viva-voce examinations to qualify as an advocate and then complete a pupilage of not less than six months under an enrolled advocate. Except for certain stipulated exceptions, an advocate must practice law in the lower courts for at least two years to be eligible to sit for the enrollment examination leading to practice in the HCD. An advocate having at least five years' practice in the HCD may be admitted by the CJ as an AD Advocate. Unlike the entrance examination for the judicial service, the entrance examination for the legal profession is not as competitive as it ought to be. However, the latest intake of 2012 was the most competitive in recent history, with a pass rate of 20 percent.[58]

Quality and independence of the judiciary depends largely on the quality of legal practitioners. The legal education at law schools/colleges and the continuing legal training at the Bar Council and the Judicial Training Institute have a significant role in the creation and maintenance of a strong and independent judiciary and legal profession. The great majority of members of the judicial service and the most successful members of the bar are graduates of leading law schools. The Bangladesh Bar Council has a statutory duty to oversee the standards of legal education. It has, however, largely failed to realize this role. The Bar Council

[57] The Judicial Administration Training Institute Act 1995.

[58] The Bar Council does not maintain and also refuses to disclose any data regarding such pass rates. The information used here is collected by the author personally.

has its own Legal Education Training Institute but it does not provide any continuing legal professional training as a standing program. On the other hand, Bangladeshi law schools do not seem to have any noticeable collaboration with the Bar Council or the Judicial Training Institute. Legal education providers should develop this connection, and their curriculum and teaching style will need to undergo a major overhaul if they are to contribute to raise the caliber of the country's judges and lawyers.

2.4 Access to justice and legal aid

The Constitution guarantees the rights of legal equality and of equal protection of law. It also guarantees the observance of due process of law (the Constitution, Arts. 27, 30 and 31). These provisions make it clear that the principle of access to justice is latently enshrined in the Constitution. However, justice for the marginalized or the poor sections of the public is not readily available. A 2010 UNDP report reveals that the rural poor have very limited access to justice, which often leads them to invoke the traditional *shalish* system, which in recent years has become synonymous with horrendous injustice against and torture on those who are vulnerable.[59] Absence of state courts other than quasi-judicial village courts at the rural level constitutes in itself a potentially retarding factor for the people's access to justice. Beyond this, other legal, procedural and systemic hurdles retard their access to justice. By contrast, the law on paper seems largely to be facilitative of universal access to justice.

Bangladeshi jurisprudence now recognizes the concept of PIL as a potent vehicle for bringing justice within the reach of the common people. Following a groundbreaking decision in *Dr Mohiuddin Farooque* v. *Bangladesh* (1996),[60] any "public interested" person may now petition the HCD to vindicate a cause of the rule of law or to enforce the constitutional rights of any marginalized or destitute group. In this case, an organization, which sought to challenge a big developmental project on the grounds that it breached the local people's rights and the principle of legality, was held to be a "person aggrieved" to be able to sue on behalf of the local people. Since then, the PIL-tool has changed the way people

[59] United Nations Development Program (UNDP), *Baseline Survey Report on Village Courts in Bangladesh* (Dhaka: UNDP and the Local Government Division, Government of Bangladesh, 2010).

[60] (1997) 17 BLD (AD) 1.

consider the role of the Supreme Court, and it has generated positive normative and social impacts. Filing of PIL in ordinary civil courts is also possible on a limited scale, under the principle of "representative suits," which allows numerous persons having a common interest to join in filing a suit.[61]

On the other hand, in the event of any public nuisance such as environmental damage, the Attorney-General or two or more persons with his written permission may file a suit for declaratory, prohibitory or any other "appropriate" relief, without having to prove any special damage.[62] Further, in a public nuisance case, criminal prosecution may be initiated by any member of the public.[63] Also, upon a police report or an application by any public-interested person, a criminal proceeding in the nature of a public interest action may be drawn by an executive magistrate requiring any person to stop or refrain from any act that causes public nuisance or infringes a "public right," such as a nuisance that is damaging to public health, the environment, and so on.[64]

Following the Legal Aid Act 2000, since 2006, the government has been administering a legal aid scheme through certain committees at different levels, predominantly in districts under the stewardship of the concerned district judge. Legal assistance, mainly financial, may be sought under this scheme by poor litigants/disputants for any civil or criminal court proceeding. The scheme is not free of defect (e.g. the costs of PIL are not, in effect, covered by the legal aid scheme), and is plagued by bureaucratic evils. As a result, most poor litigants either remain ignorant of the scheme or tend to shy away from taking advantage of it. Moreover, lawyers are largely disinterested to conduct cases on legal aid funds.

True, there are no formal substantive or institutional limits to the public's access to justice. The reality, however, is different. The breed of lawyers ready and willing to serve the poor has yet to emerge, and the fee regime of private lawyers is largely unregulated. On an institutional level, despite the existence of a flexible cost regime, the courts – both ordinary and superior – shy away from awarding costs in favor of the winning claimants. Thus, because of factors like corruption amongst court staff members, the high cost of litigation, virtually inaccessible private lawyers, and the lack of due care of government lawyers in conducting cases, access to justice continues to remain hurdled and problematic.

[61] See the CPC, Schedule 1, Order 1, rule 8. [62] CPC, s. 91.

[63] The Penal Code 1860, s. 268. [64] See, for details, the CrPC, ss. 133–143.

3 Sources of law, judicial law-making, and politics of judging

3.1 *Sources of law and judicial law-making*

As Bangladesh is a country of common law traditions, judicial precedents and common law principles are important sources of law. However, unlike many other common law countries, a large body of laws is found in codes, Acts or other statutes.

Also, most known equitable principles are statutorily codified. The existence of codes and statutes does not prevent the courts from "making" the law or relying upon judicial precedents. As mentioned, local customs and religious personal laws are also valid sources of law.

Judicial law-making is an accepted fact in Bangladesh. The judges, however, never recognize this explicitly in the sense of recognizing that they can and do make laws. Rather, senior judges often typically claim that their job is to "declare" what the law is, and not to make it. The rhetoric of the declaratory job of the judge has found its place in the Constitution itself. According to its Article 111, "the law declared" by the HCD is binding on all courts subordinate to it and the law declared by the AD is binding on the HCD and all other courts. This means, in effect, that decisions of either division of the Supreme Court have the same force of law as other statutes. The AD is not bound by its own judgments, but it is only on rare occasions that it will depart from its own decisions. Judgments of a larger bench of the HCD have binding effect on division and single-judge benches, while those of division benches have precedential authority over the judgments of any single-judge bench. Benches of equal stature can draw persuasive force from each other's decisions.

A landmark instance of law-making by the judiciary is a decision of the HCD in which the Court issued certain directives "in the nature of law" for the purpose of combating sexual harassment in workplaces and educational institutions and emphasized that these were to be strictly followed until any legislation was enacted. The parliament can, however, override the effect of any judgment by enacting legislation, which must not be in the nature of a parliamentary verdict.[65] The members of the lower judiciary are seen as having no chance, or power, to "make" law through their decisions, which are non-binding. Judges in the lower judiciary do interpret laws too, albeit not in the same scale

[65] On this, a useful source is *Dr Nurul Islam* v. *Bangladesh* (1981) 33 DLR (AD) 201.

and degree as the Supreme Court judges. The CCA (s. 37) provides that when a situation is not covered by any law or the applicable rules of Muslim law or of Hindu law, the civil courts can adjudicate by applying "justice, equity and good conscience." Needless to say, this functional discretion gives them a chance to "make" law, which is not adequately recognized.

3.2 *Style of judicial decisions*

Court judgments are usually of medium length, with the exception of politically important constitutional decisions[66] and some unnecessarily long decisions.[67] The lower courts rely more on statutes in their judgments. They also rely heavily on Bangladeshi precedents and rarely cite foreign judgments. By contrast, the Supreme Court tends to rely more on precedents, both domestic and foreign, than on statutes.[68]

Judgments in the Supreme Court are usually written by one judge as the leading judge, and the other fellow judges often issue their individual opinions either concurring with or adding new points to the leading judgment. Any judge disagreeing with the majority or the lead judgment may give his or her dissenting opinion. The sense of collegiality in the Supreme Court is remarkably strong, and the instances of dissenting opinions are rare.[69]

3.3 *Interpretive method*

It is hard to characterize the style of interpretation in Bangladesh. Sometimes, judicial interpretations have trodden the path of formalism,

[66] See, for example, the judgments in *Khondker Delwar Hossain* v. *Bangladesh Italian Marble Works* (2010) 62 DLR (AD) 298, and *Siddique Ahmed* v. *Bangladesh* (2011) 31 BLD (HCD) 84, which span 105 and 62 pages, respectively, in the law reports.

[67] For example, the reported version of the *13th Amendment Judgment* (*Abdul Mannan Khan* v. *Bangladesh* (2012) 65 DLR (AD) 169) is 349 pages including all opinions.

[68] This trend is more discernible in PIL. See, e.g., *BLAST* v. *Bangladesh* (2010) 30 BLD (HCD) 194, striking down a statute providing for the mandatory death penalty. In this case the Court cited decisions from the USA, the UK, India, South Africa, Jamaica, Malawi and Belize (Privy Council) jurisdictions, in addition to domestic precedents.

[69] For example, in constitutional decisions reported in the 2011 volumes of the *Dhaka Law Reports* and the *Bangladesh Legal Decisions*, one does not find any dissenting judgment. For a recent famous example of a dissenting judgment (4:3), see *Abdul Mannan Khan* v. *Bangladesh* (2012) 65 DLR (AD) 169 (*The 13th Amendment Case*).

while at other times the courts seem to have adopted purposive or functional interpretations. Given that teleological interpretation is practiced by a few activist judges, it would not be an overstatement to say that in most cases judicial interpretations are formalistic and swayed by legal positivism.[70]

Following Bangladesh's independence in 1971, the judges gradually began to abandon strict literalism in favor of a legal spirit-based method of interpretation. Importantly, they remarkably broke away from retrogressive judicial decisions of their former ruler, Pakistan. However, during extra-constitutional and emergency regimes they mostly followed mechanistic interpretations.[71]

In the area of public law, in particular, a discernible trend of interpretation is the reliance on transnational human rights instruments or foreign judicial decisions. In recent times, the Supreme Court has increasingly referred to comparative public law sources such as foreign judgments, international human rights instruments and foreign scholarly writing. It cites foreign case law in almost every decision, relying more on common law jurisdictions, especially the established jurisdictions,[72] and deriving both strong and mild persuasive force from them. The scenario of strong persuasive authority may occur not only in human rights adjudication but also in newer fields of jurisprudence or in cases concerning fundamental issues of constitutionalism.

Sometimes, the Court has used foreign comparative materials ornamentally, while at other times it has embraced the method of uncritical or selective comparison.[73] It should, however, be highlighted that the Court has largely remained conscious about the problems in blindly following foreign decisions, although there is so far no clear articulation of the legitimacy, desirability and method of transnational or comparative interpretation.[74]

[70] The principles of interpretation are largely subject to development by the judges themselves. But see the General Clauses Act 1897, which provides certain interpretational tools.

[71] See R. Hoque, *Judicial Activism in Bangladesh*, pp. 94–138.

[72] The most frequently cited jurisdiction is India. Other countries that have greatly influenced the Bangladeshi judges are the UK, the USA, Canada, Australia and Pakistan.

[73] See, e.g., *Md Faiz* v. *Ekramul Haque Bulbul & Ors* (2005) 57 DLR (HCD) 670, in which the Court seemingly relied only on those Indian decisions that took a largely restrictive view of the relation between freedom of expression and contempt of court.

[74] See, e.g., *Sajeda Parvin* v. *Bangladesh* (1988) 40 DLR (AD) 178, refusing to adopt the Indian Supreme Court's subjective satisfaction test in executive detention cases.

4 Courts and alternative dispute resolution (ADR)

4.1 General description of ADR in the judicial system

In Bangladesh, a number of alternative dispute resolution modes exist in the judicial system, such as negotiation, compromise, arbitration and conciliation. ADR is formally introduced to the adjudication system to achieve two main objectives: (i) to reduce undue litigation costs and inordinate delays; and (ii) to encourage public participation and honor the diversity in legal traditions.

Arbitration of disputes outside the courtroom has been an ancient practice. As far as court procedures are involved, certain statutes provide for court-sponsored or court-annexed ADR, which is either mandatory or voluntary. For example, the Bankruptcy Act 1997 (ss. 43–46) provides for voluntary settlement of claims after the court has made a declaration of insolvency. On the other hand, certain other statutes provide for both compulsory and voluntary settlement of certain specified disputes without the intervention of courts. For example, the Bangladesh Labour Act 2006 mandates a compulsory attempt to resolve industrial disputes through conciliation or arbitration before invoking the jurisdiction of labor courts.

Similarly, in order to lessen the exceedingly heavy load of customs disputes, voluntary ADR was introduced in 2012 under the Customs Act 1969, which allows the concerned parties to resolve their disputes through mediation or negotiation or to withdraw court challenges and resolve them extra-judicially.[75]

Alongside the formal system, there are state-led rural and urban semi-formal adjudicative forums that administer justice, such as the village courts under the union councils in rural areas and the reconciliation boards under municipalities in urban areas. These semi-formal bodies settle disputes in accordance with or under the coverage of the governing laws.[76]

[75] Other statutes that introduced compulsory ADRs are: the Bangladesh Energy Regulatory Commission Act 2003 (ss. 40–41); The Real Estate (Development and Management) Act 2010 (ss. 36–37); the Income Tax Ordinance 1984 (ss. 152F–152S); and the Value Added Tax Act 1991 (ss. 41A–41J).

[76] A traditional, informal dispute settlement system, called local *salish*, also exists alongside the state-led system. Salish (mediation) does not strictly follow any law but rather resolves disputes through a kind of negotiation under the leadership of any local elite/elder, taking into consideration local customs and age-honored societal traditions.

4.2 Arbitration and ADR within the formal justice system

Arbitration for settling civil disputes, especially commercial disputes, has a long historical and traditional base, the first arbitration law having been enacted in 1940. Now, arbitration is governed by the Arbitration Act 2001, under which a dispute may be arbitrated pursuant to any arbitration agreement, or the parties to any civil suit may agree to ask the court to refer it to arbitration. The fact remains, however, that an incremental rise in non-commercial disputes continues to add to the deadlock in the courts. Commercial disputes are not arbitrated in sufficiently high numbers, partly because of the voluntary nature of arbitration, a problem that has recently been addressed, and partly because of the unwillingness of the parties and lawyers involved.

To reduce the sheer volume of pending cases in civil courts, court-sponsored or compulsory ADR has been introduced within the formal justice system. It was first introduced in the family courts in 1985, in the form of court-sponsored mediation. The family court judge must attempt to foster a settlement between the parties before the hearing of the suit, failing which the suit proceeds to the hearing. In the second place, the family court judge has a duty once again to try to have the parties agree to a solution after the hearing is over but before pronouncing the verdict. When the parties agree and reach a solution at either of these two stages, the outcome is transformed into the court verdict.

This court-sponsored conciliation system worked marvellously in the past, although its success in recent years has slightly declined. As Alam reports,[77] pursuant to the launching of a pilot project in 2000 to make family-court-based mediation successful, the participating family courts in six metropolitan cities mediated 1,332 disputes within two years, realizing 48 million (48,500,309) taka in awards in favor of the women-plaintiffs. It seems that the degree of success of an ADR system, whether voluntary or compulsory, significantly depends on the enthusiasm, willingness, confidence, awareness and training of all actors concerned, including the parties to the dispute.

In 1990, the ADR system was introduced to another special court, the money loan courts. These courts, reconstituted under the Money Loan

[77] M. S. Alam, "Enforcing court-sponsored alternative dispute resolution (ADR) in Bangladesh: need for strengthening legislative, administrative and institutional measures," paper read in a seminar on *ADR in Bangladesh*, organized by Bangladesh Law Commission and SAILS, Chittagong, 7 August 2010, at p. 14.

Courts Act 2003, used to facilitate the settlement of claims of recovery of financial loans advanced by financial institutions through "settlement conferences" or arbitration. Now, by virtue of a 2010 amendment to the 2003 Act, it is mandatory for the court to send the dispute back to the parties or their pleaders for settlement. Conciliation of disputes relating to the recovery of financial loans is carried out by the mediator in an informal and non-adversarial manner. The court never exerts any influence but rather plays the role of a facilitator.[78]

The most notable ADR within the formal justice system is the one first introduced to ordinary civil courts by amending the CPC in 2003 and again in 2006. The amended law incorporated voluntary mediation of disputes or appeals by the court and allowed the parties to seek a referral for arbitration of their dispute. The defect of this system was that it was voluntary, and hence the parties were under no obligation to settle disputes out of court or through the court's mediation. In 2012, the CPC was once again amended to make court-sponsored mediation compulsory. The amended section 89A of the CPC now provides that, after all the parties to the suit are in attendance, the court, after adjourning the hearing of the suit, shall mediate the dispute or refer it to the engaged pleaders or to a panel of mediators in order to settle the dispute. If a compromise or solution is reached, the court may pass a decree accordingly, or, when the dispute is mediated by the pleaders or mediators, the court may transform the mediation report into a court verdict, against which no appeal is permitted. If the mediation led by the court or a mediator fails, the suit shall proceed towards hearing (CPC, s. 89A(7) and (9)). Mediation under section 89A of the CPC by ordinary civil courts is a non-formal, non-binding and consensual settlement process, and the court or the mediator only facilitates a compromise of the dispute between the parties without dictating the terms of such compromise (explanation (1), s. 89A). According to section 89C, the appellate courts are also required to attempt to mediate the appeal or to refer it to a mediator in order to settle the dispute.

On the other hand, by virtue of section 89B, the parties to a suit pending before a civil court may agree to settle the dispute through arbitration and may seek withdrawal of the suit. In such a case, the court must allow the withdrawal and permit the dispute to be arbitrated in accordance with the Arbitration Act 2001. Arbitration is an independent

[78] S. Khair, *Legal Empowerment for the Poor and the Disadvantaged: Strategies, Achievements and Challenges* (Dhaka: CIDA, 2008), p. 114.

process, and the court does not have any intervening power. An award of arbitration may be enforced as if it were a decree of the court. If the arbitration does not take place or an award is not issued, the parties to the suit so withdrawn may re-institute the suit (CPC, s. 89B(1)).

4.3 *Semi-formal justice system in rural and municipal areas*

At the rural (village) level, there are two streams of the state-led justice system. In every *union parishad,*[79] a local government jurisdiction, there is an "arbitration council," which operates on an ad hoc basis under the Muslim Family Laws Ordinance 1961 to oversee the Muslim divorce processes and adjudicate applications for permission of second marriage by Muslim husbands and for maintenance of Muslim wives. In the case of Muslim divorces, the arbitration council plays the role of mediator and attempts to reconcile the couple, failing which (after 90 days) the divorce becomes effective.[80] Appeals or revisions, as the case may be, against the orders or decisions of the arbitration council lie to the concerned assistant judge, whose decision is final.

In addition, there are village courts functioning within the jurisdiction of *union parishads*, which are permanent statutory forums, although their constitution varies from dispute to dispute. *Village courts*, earlier known as *panchayat*, are an age-old institution that has been administering rural-level justice since many, many years. The village court, first established in 1976,[81] is a quasi-judicial body and is now governed by the Village Courts Act 2006. Section 5 of the Act provides that a village court would consist of one chairman and four other members, of whom each party to the dispute nominates two. The chairman of the court is usually the chairman of the *union parishad*, unless he is alleged to be biased.

The 2006 Act confers on the village court jurisdiction to try specific petty civil disputes, where the monetary value of each does not exceed 25,000 taka. The village court can also try specific petty offenses that are listed in a schedule to the 2006 Act, provided that it can only award a fine up to a maximum amount of 25,000 taka and cannot commit anyone to prison. It has power to punish any recalcitrant person for contempt, and it can recover a fine or compensation that remains due as a public

[79] See the Local Government (Union Parishads) Act 2009.
[80] For these purposes, municipalities or city corporations also run arbitration councils.
[81] See the Village Courts Ordinance 1976 (repealed).

demand. The procedures before a village court are less formal and involve almost no cost, and lawyers are not allowed to represent the parties before it.

In municipal areas, *conciliation boards* functioning under *pourashavas* (municipal governments), amicably resolve petty civil disputes and certain specified criminal wrongs through "conciliation."[82] The five-member conciliation board is similar to the village court in terms of structure, procedures, powers and functions.

5 Function of courts and performance evaluations

Evaluating the functions and performance of courts is often an intricate task. There are factors, such as political and economic contexts, quality of legal education or the lack of judicial innovativeness particularly amongst lower court judges, that may affect the functions or performance of the judiciary as a whole. Practical issues such as the quantity of cases disposed, number of people served, and the average time spent in deciding cases are also important measures for weighing judicial performance.

5.1 Function of courts

Bangladeshi courts perform a number of important functions. They play a social control role by adjudicating crimes and thereby contributing to the maintenance of law and order. Importantly, the courts, especially the Supreme Court in exercising its criminal or constitutional jurisdiction, have in recent years made important strides towards ensuring justice for the victims, shying significantly away from the crime control model of criminal adjudication. The lower and intermediate criminal courts, however, largely adopt the crime control approach to the criminal justice system. These courts have sometimes shown excessive deference to the executive when dealing with arrests, bail and personal liberty issues.

With the Constitution having provided for a responsible government posited on the principle of the rule of law, the Supreme Court usually follows a strong form of judicial review and seeks to enforce constitutional limits on the executive. This does not necessarily mean that the Court does not legitimatize government policies. The Supreme Court of Bangladesh, except during times of extra-constitutional or overweening

[82] See the Conciliation of Disputes Boards (Municipal Areas) Act 2004.

governments, has often paid "due" deference to the government's policies, while at times intervening even in policy matters when constitutional ideals or norms are at stake.[83] Associated with its constitutionalism-enforcing role is the court's role in dispensing social or distributive justice through the unique tools of PIL. Although recent PIL decisions do not show a trend of judicial activism on behalf of the deprived and weaker sections of the public, the court's willingness to stand for, and its past activism on behalf of, those who would otherwise have been deprived of any access to justice is commendable.

On the other hand, the court has shown limited fulfillment of its commitments in the market sector, although the post-1980s laws have sought to generate a pro-business legal environment. This is, however, not to discredit the sensitivity and performance the HCD has shown in this field. The HCD, for example, upheld the laws that required only the losing defendant who is a borrower of any financial institution to deposit half of the decree money as a condition for an appeal to the higher court. In the Court's view, the alleged discrimination in those laws was constitutionally sustainable, as it aimed to ameliorate the country's ailing economy.[84] Yet, businesses and the revenue agencies of the government often claim that dilatoriness in the disposal of cases and the lack of efficient decisions in the corporate law sector continue to remain disincentives to business investment.

Another shortcoming that shadows the successes of Bangladeshi courts is their limited readiness to use litigation as a tool for reparatory and compensatory justice. Despite the creation of some new public law remedies, the trend of compensatory or reparatory justice in the court's jurisprudence is anything but remarkable.[85] There is a sustained disinclination to award civil compensation in constitutional adjudication, even in PIL cases in which damage to the public and the environment is alleged. As far as the role of lower civil courts is concerned, compensatory decisions in the area of tort law are few and far between. Indeed,

[83] See, e.g., *Shah Mohammad Hannan* v. *Bangladesh*, Writ Petition No. 2052/1998 (interim order 5 December 2001). Interestingly, the court does not explicitly recognize that it can deal with policy issues. See, e.g., *Dr Mohiuddin Farooque* v. *Bangladesh* (1998) 50 DLR (HCD) 84, 97 (there should be no judicial say regarding policy matters).

[84] *Chandpur Jute Mills* v. *Artha Wrin Adalat* (1997) 2 BLC (HCD) 49; *Abdul Gaffur* v. *Joint District Judge* (2005) 57 DLR (HCD) 138.

[85] R. Hoque, "Public law compensation in Bangladesh: looking within and beyond," *Journal of Law and Development*, 1 (2) (2009), 1–24.

the culture of invoking tort remedies or of seriously pressing for public law compensation is almost absent amongst the legal community.

5.2 *Judicial compliance*

The overall record of executive compliance with judicial orders is satisfactory. The Constitution (Art. 112) mandates all executive and judicial "authorities" to act in aid of the Supreme Court, which has power to commit for contempt anyone not complying with its order. Nevertheless, executive responses to judicial directives and recommendations are a mixed bag of compliance and defiance. In particular, when there is a lack of political willingness to implement the court's order, the executive branch resorts to the bureaucratic technique of dilly-dallying to comply, often on the grounds of lack of resources or institutional limitations.[86] To ensure executive compliance with its orders, the Supreme Court sometimes prescribes a timeframe for implementation and closely monitors the progress. The recommendations of courts are, however, often ignored by the government. On the other hand, compliance with decisions by ordinary courts, especially those involving public developmental works, has not been as consistent as that with Supreme Court decisions.

5.3 *Institutional capacity and delays in the administration of justice*

In Bangladesh, one judge (of the Judicial Service) serves one hundred thousand people, the ratio being one of the lowest in the world.[87] Notwithstanding such service capacity constraints, it is striking that the Bangladesh judiciary maintains a very strong commitment to defending its independence and is able to persevere through difficult political times. Although some judges almost abandoned their duty during extra-constitutional regimes, it has been a notable feature of the Supreme Court's strength that it can maintain institutional comity and a balanced

[86] Currently, for example, the Government is employing various techniques to delay the implementation of a court order, issued in the old case of *Masdar Hossain* (above, note 52), to implement the recommendations of the Judicial Pay Commission for increased salaries for judges.

[87] To date, there are about 1,700 judges and magistrates (including those placed in ministerial and non-adjudicative jobs) in the Judicial Service of Bangladesh. Of them, 185 are at the rank of district judge, 209 are at the rank of additional district judges, 246 are in the rank of joint district judges, and 360 are assistant and senior assistant judges. The number of judicial magistrates is about 525.

relationship with other branches of government even under such regimes. On constitutional issues of wider importance, the court has generally pursued a broader approach to the justiciability of politically charged issues, while it has remained at times strategically silent on complex political issues such as the legality of political strikes.[88]

On the other hand, one weakness is the absence of complete autonomy of the judiciary and the employment of lower court judges in non-adjudicative functions. The long-demanded separate secretariat for the Supreme Court has not yet been established. Another weakness is the inexperience of judges and the lack of diversity in professional orientation. Although the Constitution provides for only a minimum of ten years of experience as an eligibility criterion for appointment to the Supreme Court, the intent was to attract the most outstanding candidates even if they might not be too experienced. However, recent Supreme Court appointments have witnessed recruits who have merely completed ten years of experience and whose intellectual and professional caliber are open to question. As regards the lower judiciary, fresh law graduates, who are about twenty-three to twenty-five years of age, may join the Bangladesh Judicial Service, and there is no pre-appointment judicial training. The lower judiciary also faces the problem of integrity, and allegations of corruption are not rare, but an efficient system of dealing with corruption and misconduct charges is not in place.

Evaluation of judges' performance is intertwined with their efficiency and ability to deliver quality justice promptly. The most notorious and persistent problem that exists in the justice-delivery system is that of delays in both civil and criminal courts. Judicial reform in terms of easing the backlog has long been an item on the government's agenda.[89] In the post-independence period, Bangladesh adopted a series of reforms, with a view mainly to easing the backlog of cases. The reforms included the introduction of various forms of ADR into civil proceedings, creation of specialist courts and tribunals, introduction of first-track courts,[90]

[88] See *Khondaker Modarresh Elahi* v. *Bangladesh* (2001) 21 BLD (HCD) 352 (refusing to declare *hartal* (political strikes) illegal), and *Abdul Mannan Bhuiyan* v. *State* (2008) 60 DLR (AD) 49 (non-violent *hartal* is a democratic right of the citizens).

[89] On delays in civil courts see R. Rahman, *Civil Litigation in Bangladesh* (Dhaka: Nuruzzaman Chowdhury, 1986), M. Zahir, *Delay in Courts and Court Management* (Dhaka: BILIA, 1988), and Law Commission of Bangladesh, *Law Commission's Recommendations on Expediting Civil Proceedings*, Report No. 106 (Dhaka: Law Commission of Bangladesh, 2010).

[90] See the Special Courts (Additional Duty) Act 2003.

prescription of deadlines for the completion of trials, and so on. Yet, delays, particularly in civil courts, are still a major concern, and this situation impinges upon the people's right of access to justice. In most cases, the prescribed deadlines for trial completion have not been met, or the system of compensatory deposits by parties has failed. My investigation, based on a brief empirical survey of reported cases, shows that a civil suit on average takes more than five years to conclude, although the statutory timeline for concluding a trial is 340 days. One of the most significant factors that cause civil suits to linger for years is the system of applying to the court for execution of a decree/order when the defendant does not voluntarily comply. To achieve any viable improvement in the backlog problem, this system should be replaced by some type of court-supervised automated execution process backed by stricter consequences for defiance.

Delays in criminal trials are also a huge problem. This is undeniably a negation of the right to a fair trial for both the victims and the accused. To have a speedy trial of criminal charges is a constitutional right of the person accused (the Constitution, Art. 35(3)). The law seeks to achieve the conclusion of criminal trials within a reasonable timeline from the date of receipt of the case, which is 180 days for a magistrate's court and 360 days for a court of sessions (CrPC, s. 339C). Yet, inordinate delay in the criminal justice system has become a regular phenomenon. The ordeal of delays in criminal trials is further aggravated by delays in appeals, particularly in the HCD where criminal appeals often remain pending for five years on average.[91] Also, the average wait time in both divisions of the Supreme Court is quite long: three-and-a-half years on average.[92]

As Table 13.1 shows, the scenario of prolonged trials is improving gradually, but access to justice and a speedy trial is still a remote hope in Bangladesh. Despite improvements in the disposal rate, the backlog has not proportionately decreased. The rate of increase in the backlog of cases in the HCD in the last twelve years (1999–2011) is 262 percent, as against an increase of 300 percent in the rate of disposal in that period.

[91] My personal examination of decisions, reported in the 2009 volume of the *Dhaka Law Reports*, reveals that the average time spent by the HCD to conclude an appeal is nearly seven years. The timeframe for the appellate courts to dispose of a criminal appeal is ninety working days from the date of service of notice of appeal (CrPC, s. 442A).

[92] Based on my sample survey of forty cases reported in 2011 in the *Dhaka Law Reports* and the *Bangladesh Legal Decisions*.

Table 13.1: *Comparison of caseloads of different courts and a glimpse of backlog of cases in civil courts until early 2011*

Caseload of different courts in a comparative setting					
Years	Magistrates' courts	Sessions courts	Civil courts	High Court Division	Appellate Division
1999/ 2000	701,783 (87% disposed)	127,495 (100%)[a]	373,988 (76.85%)	106,711 (51.83%)	743 (43%)
2011				279,923 (153%)[*]	11,000+

A glimpse of backlog of cases in civil courts until early 2011		
At all lower courts	At the High Court Division	At the Appellate Division
161,9307	313,775	9,141[b]

Source: K. E. Hoque (2003); *The Bangladesh Supreme Court Report 2012*; Tahura (2012)

[a]This does not imply that all cases filed in 1998 were disposed of. The rate is calculated from the total number of cases disposed of against the new cases in that year.

In 2011 (Jan to Dec), a total of 44,686 cases/appeals were filed in the High Court Division, and a total of 68,425 cases were disposed of. Criminal cases (revisions/ appeals) filed that year (25,569) outnumbered other cases in the HCD.

[b]Supreme Court reports show that the number of pending cases in the Appellate Division in 2010 was 4,500, whereas by January 2012, the number rose to 12,000. According to a recent (April 2013) statement by the Law Minister, about 17,000 cases are now pending before the Appellate Division.

5.4 *Perceptional evaluation*

In Bangladesh, there is no organization that serves as a judicial watchdog. By contrast, judicial performance or judges' failures or successes are rarely discussed and debated in public discourse. Nor is there any polling or survey system to measure the public's trust in the judiciary and judges' efficiency. As mentioned, the public traditionally holds judges and the judiciary in high esteem. Despite this, there is also a widely held perception amongst the general public that those with enough money can obtain favorable court judgments, due to excessive litigation costs as well as corruption in the judiciary.[93] Yet, the public still regard the judiciary as the "last resort" for protection against any injustice or excesses.

As for the legal community's confidence in the judiciary, my personal survey shows that the majority of private legal practitioners largely seem to be dissatisfied with the judiciary; everyone feels that there should be appropriate reforms and that judges ought to apply and interpret the laws more generously and in a socially relevant way. By contrast, legislators as well as other politicians are often seen as more vocal about the deficient integrity and the inefficiency of the judiciary. In the same vein, the business community is quite critical of the efficiency and expertise of the judicial system. Businesses have long demanded more specialist benches in the HCD.

6 Conclusions

The present chapter sought to provide an overview of the system of courts in Bangladesh and their functioning. The courts in Bangladesh, having origins in colonial times, still appear to be swayed in many respects by the colonial legacy. In the post-independence era, however, Bangladeshi courts have attempted to build the public's confidence in them and to respond to the needs of society. The Supreme Court, in particular, except for its failings during the times of emergency rule and military intervention, has tended to defend constitutionalism and justice. Yet, it would be parochial to claim that its role vis-à-vis constitutionalism is beyond question.[94] There are certain problems that lie with the functioning of the judiciary as a whole. For example, despite the formal constitutional guarantee of its independence, the Supreme Court continues to suffer from some indigenous problems of non-independence, such as the absence of a pool of willing, active and efficient judges. On the other hand, it has not yet optimally used its judicial review power for the empowerment of the people, but rather has apparently tended to be more self-preserving on issues of its own autonomy and power. Nor are the lower courts adequately trained and sensitized to fully use their potential

[93] This does not necessarily mean "corruption by judges." See, however, a Transparency International Bangladesh (TIB) report in 2010 that found the judicial sector as the most corrupt sector, www.ti-bangladesh.org. See also TIB's *Policy Brief on the Judiciary* of 27 February 2011.

[94] See R. Hoque, "Constitutionalism and the judiciary in Bangladesh" in S. Khilnani, V. Raghavan and A. K. Thiruvengadam (eds.), *Comparative Constitutionalism in South Asia* (New Delhi: Oxford University Press, 2013), pp. 303–40.

in improving the justice delivery system. A number of factors are responsible for this scenario.[95] The major problems of judicial underperformance, passivity and "non-independence" are, as indicated above, connected to political maneuvering with respect to the appointments of Supreme Court judges, a lack of standards in the administrative/ministerial control of the lower court judges, a lack of society-specific and globally focused legal education and professional training, an absence of responsive and sustainable court management at all levels, and a paucity of judges.

The efficiency of the courts is significantly compromised by ever-increasing caseloads and delays in meting out justice, while the problem of people's unhindered access to justice continues. Unlike other courts in post-colonial societies, Bangladesh's courts have not undergone viable, thoughtful and society-specific reforms. For this, again, there are a number of factors that may be held responsible. Any sensible and pressing legal activism on the part of the legal profession regarding court reforms and a strong civil society are largely absent. Lack of political will has also contributed to the maintenance of the status quo. Moreover, the reform projects that have been initiated and implemented to date are donor-driven and not adequately based on necessities identified by those working within the system. As such, judicial reforms in Bangladesh have been in effect relegated to establishing certain new courts pursuant to special laws, without even properly designing these courts and adequately training their judges. Digitalization of judicial processes, reforms of case management and judicial administration, creation of a sufficient number of first-instance and intermediate courts, and institutional and personal capacity building of judges have been more talked about than implemented. If the Bangladeshi judiciary is to play an effective role as the protector of people's rights and the guardian of constitutionalism, there is no alternative to the installation of viable and progressive judicial reforms.

References

Ahmed, N. *Public Interest Litigation: Constitutional Issues and Remedies* (Dhaka: BLAST, 1999)

Ahmed, S. I. *Certiorari: An Administrative Law Remedy* (Dhaka: Mullick Brothers, 2011)

[95] Providing a detailed account of these problems and factors is beyond the scope of this chapter.

Akkas, S. A. "Discipline of subordinate court judges in Bangladesh," *Chittagong University Journal of Law*, 5 (2000), 146–62

Alam, M. S. "Enforcing court-sponsored alternative dispute resolution (ADR) in Bangladesh: need for strengthening legislative, administrative and institutional measures," paper read in a Seminar on Enforcing Court-Sponsored Alternative Dispute Resolution (ADR) in Bangladesh, Bangladesh Law Commission & SAILS, Chittagong, 7 August 2010

Alam, M. S. "Legal system of Bangladesh" in H. M. Kritzer (ed.), *Legal Systems of the World: A Political, Social and Cultural Encyclopedia* (Santa Barbara, California/Oxford: ABC-CLIO, 2002), vol. I, pp. 116–24

Hoque, K. E. *Administration of Justice in Bangladesh* (Dhaka: Asiatic Society of Bangladesh, 2003)

Hoque, R. "Constitutionalism and the judiciary in Bangladesh" in S. Khilnani, V. Raghavan and A. K. Thiruvengadam (eds.), *Comparative Constitutionalism in South Asia* (New Delhi: Oxford University Press, 2013), pp. 303–40

Hoque, R. *Judicial Activism in Bangladesh: A Golden Mean Approach* (Newcastle upon Tyne: Cambridge Scholars Publishing, 2011)

Hoque, R. "Public law compensation in Bangladesh: looking within and beyond," *Journal of Law and Development*, 1(2) (2009), 1–24

Hoque, R. "Taking justice seriously: judicial public interest and constitutional activism in Bangladesh," *Contemporary South Asia*, 15(4) (2006), 399–422

Hoque, R. "The recent emergency and the politics of the judiciary in Bangladesh," *National University of Juridical Science Law Review*, 2(2) (2009), 183–204

Islam, M. *Constitutional Law of Bangladesh*, 3rd edn. (Dhaka: Mullick Brothers, 2012)

Islam, M. and Neogi, P. *The Law of Civil Procedure*, 2 vols. (Dhaka: Mullick Brothers, 2006)

Jahan, F. and Shahan, A. M. "Access to justice for the poor in Bangladesh: conflict between Western model and Eastern culture," *Journal of Law and Development*, 1(1) (2009) 1–29

Khair, S. *Legal Empowerment for the Poor and the Disadvantaged: Strategies, Achievements and Challenges* (Dhaka: CIDA Legal Reform Project in Bangladesh, 2008)

Law Commission of Bangladesh. *Law Commission's Recommendations on Expediting Civil Proceedings*, Report No. 106 (Dhaka: Law Commission of Bangladesh, 2010)

Law Commission of Bangladesh. *Law Commission's Recommendations on Selection Criteria for Supreme Court Judges*, Report No. 118 (Dhaka: Law Commission of Bangladesh, 2012)

Marak, J. *Garo Customary Laws and Practices* (New Delhi: Akansha Publishing, 2000)

Mollah, M. A. H. "Independence of judiciary in Bangladesh: an overview," *International Journal of Law and Management*, 54(1) (2012), 61–77

Panday, P. K. and Mollah, M. A. H. "The judicial system of Bangladesh: an overview from historical viewpoint," *International Journal of Law and Management*, 53(1) (2011), 6–31

Pereira, F. "Dossier on *Fatwas* in Bangladesh," *Interventions: International Journal of Postcolonial Studies*, 4(2) (2002), 212–44

Rahman, R. *Civil Litigation in Bangladesh* (Dhaka: Nuruzzaman Chowdhury, 1986)

Roy, R. D. *Traditional Customary Laws and Indigenous Peoples in Asia* (London: Minority Rights Group International, 2005)

Serajuddin, A. M. "Family law, fatwa and society in Bangladesh" in K. Shahidullah (ed.), *Martyred Intellectuals Memorial Lectures* (Dhaka: Asiatic Society of Bangladesh, 2004), pp. 103–12

Supreme Court of Bangladesh. *Annual Report 2012* (Dhaka: Supreme Court, 2012)

Tahura, U. S. "Analytical assessment of civil litigation procedures, causes for delay and probable way outs: context Bangladesh," a paper presented in a seminar held at the Bangladesh Institute of Law & International Affairs, Dhaka, 10 March 2012

Ullah, M. R. *The Garo Community: A Marginal Community of Bangladesh* (Dhaka: University Grants Commission, 2010)

United Nations Development Program (UNDP). *Baseline Survey Report on Village Courts in Bangladesh* (Dhaka: UNDP and the Local Government Division, Ministry of Local Government, Rural Development and Cooperatives, Government of Bangladesh, 2010)

Zahir, M. *Delay in Courts and Court Management* (Dhaka: BILIA, 1988)

14

Courts in China: judiciary in the economic and societal transitions

WEIXIA GU

In 2009, the People's Republic of China ("China") celebrated its sixtieth birthday and thirtieth anniversary of economic reform and opening up. With respect to legal development, much has been accomplished: the courts, the bar, legal education, and the very idea of a rule-of-law system that was put into the Chinese Constitution.[1] Despite these considerable achievements, a judicial system rooted in an administrative governance society that is undergoing economic and political transformation such as China remains plagued by many pervasive shortcomings.[2] There have been concerns about Chinese courts such as the slow pace of case processing, lack of professional judges, varying quality of law enforcement across the nation, and the influence of local politics and social pressures on judicial decisions, despite the continuing efforts that China has made to improve the profile of its judiciary.[3]

It is in this context that this chapter discusses comprehensively the judiciary in China – the size and performance of the Chinese courts,

I am grateful to Professors Jiunn-rong Yeh, Wen-Chen Chang, and Kuan-Ling Shen at the National Taiwan University College of Law for inviting me to this wonderful book project. Thanks are also due to Professors Albert Chen, Hualing Fu, Xianchu Zhang, and Dr P. Y. Lo at the University of Hong Kong for helpful comments. Parts of this chapter excerpt from Weixia Gu, "The judiciary in economic and political transformation: *Quo vadis* Chinese courts?" *Chinese Journal of Comparative Law*, 1(2) (2013), 303–34, by the permission of Oxford University Press. Some parts of the research leading to this chapter have been financially supported by the Hong Kong Government Research Grants Council General Research Fund (Project Code HKU 742813H) and the University of Hong Kong Seed Funding Programme for Basic Research (Project Code 201211159094). Miss Crystal Lau at the University of Hong Kong provides excellent research assistance for the compilation of some of the judicial statistics and tables, which is acknowledged. All mistakes remain mine.

[1] The "rule of law" as a national policy was written into the Chinese Constitution in 1999.

[2] D. Clarke, "Empirical research into the Chinese judicial system" in E. Jensen and T. Heller (eds.), *Beyond Common Knowledge: Empirical Approaches to the Rule of Law* (Stanford University Press, 2003), pp. 164–92.

[3] *Ibid.*

judicial appointments and the training of judges, the actual operation of courts and judges in terms of independence and integrity, and finally, various judicial reforms over one-and-a-half decades. Moreover, the chapter analyzes the dialogues, tensions, compromises, and expectations of different currents in China's ongoing judicial reform, as it moves towards the goals of justice and independence against the macro backdrop of deepening marketization and social movements. In light of these challenges, this chapter argues that the Chinese government should reconsider the path and pace of China's judicial reform, as well as the importance and relevance of universal-value-based rule of law so as to render transitional justice into serious judicial justice.

1 General description of the judicial system

The traditional theory of the Chinese judiciary has been that the courts, together with other judicial organs (such as the procuratorate and public security), are "weapons" of the people's democratic dictatorship.[4] However, as the emphasis on the socialist market economy grew, it was increasingly stressed that the courts' task is to contribute to economic construction. Under the leadership of Xiao Yang, President of the Supreme People's Court (the "SPC") from 1998 to 2008, "justice" and "efficiency" were specified as the twin missions of the Chinese courts and the focus of judicial reform.[5] The importance of the leadership of the Chinese Communist Party (the "Party") and caution against the imitation of the Western practice of judicial supremacy were maintained,[6] although in general, Xiao affirmed the Chinese judiciary's commitment to justice (both substantive and procedural), fairness, conscientiousness, openness and professionalism.[7]

After Wang Shengjun assumed the Presidency of the SPC in late 2008, there was a shift of policy regarding the work and orientation of the courts. Older themes in the Party tradition emphasizing the political (rather than neutral or independent) and populist (rather than professional) nature of the Chinese judiciary have been revived, although in the meantime, Xiao's previous agenda of judicial modernization has not

[4] For example, the then President of the Supreme People's Court, Ren Jianxin, in his annual report to the National People's Congress in 1991, reiterated that it was necessary to strengthen the state machinery for the people's democratic dictatorship, and that the courts were a main instrument of such a dictatorship.

[5] SPC's work report to the National People's Congress (the "NPC"), addressed by X. Yang in March 2003 (the "2003 SPC Report").

[6] *Ibid.* [7] *Ibid.*

been completely abandoned.[8] Following the new Party line of the "Three Supremes"[9] and the concept of a "socialist rule of law,"[10] Wang stressed the duty of the courts to serve the goals and policies determined by the Party and to take into account the overall situation or circumstances of the society, thus implicitly downgrading the importance of strict adherence to legal rules. Wang encouraged the courts to pursue the "mass line,"[11] serve the needs of the people, and take public opinion into account, which would thereby increase the level of public satisfaction with and confidence in the work of the judiciary.[12]

1.1 Structure of the courts

Technically, the Chinese court system is structured into four levels. Corresponding to the governance system of China, there are thousands of basic-level people's courts at the district or county level (with many divisions in township and rural areas known as people's tribunals), hundreds of intermediate people's courts at the city or prefecture level within provinces, thirty-one high people's courts at the provincial level, and the SPC at the national level.[13] There are also specialist courts, such as military courts[14] and maritime courts.[15] These specialist courts have special jurisdiction over particular types of disputes. For example, maritime courts in various coastal cities handle exclusively maritime disputes, while military courts oversee all disputes relating to army servicemen.

In recent years, apart from national-level specialist courts, specialist tribunals have been established within the general courts at different levels. For example, over the past decade, in tandem with China's accession to the

[8] See generally SPC's work report on SPC to the NPC (addressed by Wang in March 2009) and the SPC's Third Five-Year Reform Plan for 2009–2013.

[9] The "Three Supremes" is the school of thought advocated by the Party during Hu Jintao's leadership, which involves three layers of meaning: the supremacy of the Party leadership, the supremacy of people's interests, and the supremacy of the Constitution and laws.

[10] SPC's work report on SPC to the NPC, addressed by Wang in March 2009.

[11] The "mass line" refers to "adjudication for the people" – it encourages the use of mediation and relies on Party leadership and consideration of socio-economic conditions in decision-making processes, with the law given secondary consideration.

[12] SPC's work report on SPC to the NPC, addressed by Wang in March 2009.

[13] For the structure of the Chinese court, see Article 2 of the Organic Law of the People's Courts. Regarding the numbers, see "About the People's Court" on the SPC website at www.court.gov.cn/jgsz/rmfyjj.

[14] Organic Law of the People's Courts, Art. 2.

[15] There are ten maritime courts in Chinese coastal cities such as Shanghai, Tianjin, Xiamen, Guangzhou, etc. The work of these maritime courts can be viewed on the China Foreign-related Commercial and Maritime Trial website at www.ccmt.org.cn.

World Trade Organization ("WTO") in 2001 and in an effort to foster judicial expertise in intellectual property protection, intellectual property tribunals have been established within each level of the Chinese courts. As of the end of 2012, there were 420 intellectual property tribunals across the country, with 2,759 judges engaged in intellectual property trials.[16] Other specialist tribunals include environmental tribunals, which have been established in accordance with China's rising concern for environment protection and sustainable economic development. A recent report shows that there are more than eleven environmental tribunals established at the municipal-level intermediate people's courts in Southwestern and Eastern China, dealing particularly with environmental tort disputes.[17]

As to the internal structure, each Chinese court consists of a number of divisions (*ting*) managing the pre-trial, trial and post-trial stages of cases. For example, the Filing Division (*li'an ting*) is in charge of the pre-trial filing of cases, and judges there are mainly tasked with resolving jurisdictional disputes.[18] The Enforcement Division (*zhixing ting*) handles enforcement petitions from parties (where the period of enforcement listed on the judgment has expired).[19] The trial divisions represent the core of the work of a court, and judges sitting on the panels of these divisions are those we narrowly define as real adjudicators, or judges (*shenpan yuan*).[20] They specialize in trials of different types of cases, such as criminal, civil and administrative. Amongst these trial divisions, the civil division is the most comprehensive one and may be sub-divided into several tribunals, known as Civil Divisions Number One to Four. The trend in recent years has been to have a more streamlined work division among different types of civil disputes, and to separately handle civil, commercial and intellectual property disputes by professional tribunals. Accordingly, Civil Division Number Three (*min san ting*) deals exclusively with intellectual property disputes (such as copyright, trademark and patent infringements). As previously discussed, this Division is more often referred to as the specialized intellectual property tribunal in China.[21] The difference between[22] Civil Division Number Two (*min*

[16] The 2012 SPC White Paper on Intellectual Property Protection (issued by the SPC on 22 April 2013), Part 4, available on the SPC website at www.chinacourt.org/article/detail/2013/04/id/949841.shtml.

[17] See A. Wang and J. Cao, "Environmental courts and the development of environmental public interest litigation in China," *Journal of Court Innovation* 3 (2010), pp. 38–9.

[18] The internal structure can be viewed through the SPC website, structure page, available at www.court.gov.cn/jgsz/zgrmfyjg.

[19] *Ibid.* [20] Organic Law of the People's Courts, Art. 3.

[21] SPC website, introduction page, available at www.court.gov.cn/jgsz/rmfyjj. [22] *Ibid.*

er ting) and Number Four (*min si ting*) is that the former focuses on domestic commercial cases (including contracts, companies and securities) while the latter specializes in those types of cases that also have a foreign-related element[23] as well as maritime disputes.[24] Traditional civil cases (such as personal and family relations, torts and labor) will then fall within the jurisdiction of Civil Division Number One (*min yi ting*).[25] For intermediate courts in some economically better developed cities, in response to the rising complexity of commercial disputes and associated challenges to manpower, there is an even more sophisticated division of civil tribunals. For example, there are land, labor and insolvency tribunals in the Shenzhen Intermediate People's Court (known as Civil Divisions Numbers Five, Six and Seven).[26]

1.2 Instances of trials

The instances of trials may be briefly summarized in the following way. Based on the four levels of the courts, the design of the litigation in China (both civil and criminal) follows the principle of "two trials to conclude a case" (one trial at first instance, and one trial on appeal, also known as *liangshen zhongshen zhi*).[27] The basic-level people's courts deal with the great majority of cases tried at first instance in the country.[28] The intermediate people's courts have appellate jurisdiction over cases appealed from the basic-level courts, as well as original jurisdiction over crimes against national security, criminal cases involving serious punishment (life imprisonment and death penalty) and foreigners, and important foreign-related civil and commercial disputes.[29] The high people's courts hear appeals from the intermediate courts and try first instance cases that are considered of provincial significance.[30] The SPC exercises original as well as appellate jurisdiction in important cases at the national level.[31]

[23] According to the judicial interpretations of General Principles of Civil Law and Civil Procedure Law, a case will be considered as "foreign-related" (or "with foreign-related elements") if any of the following three conditions can be satisfied: (1) one of the parties is not from Mainland China; (2) the subject matter of the dispute is outside the territory of Mainland China; and (3) the formation, change or revocation of the civil relationship is outside the territory of Mainland China. Hong Kong-, Macau- and Taiwan-related disputes are deemed as foreign-related under Chinese law.

[24] SPC website, introduction page. [25] *Ibid.*

[26] For the structure and scope of disputes handled by different civil divisions at the Shenzhen Intermediate People's Court, see www.szcourt.gov.cn/gaikuang.

[27] Organic Law of the People's Courts, Art. 12.

[28] For the jurisdiction of basic-level courts, see *ibid.* Art. 21. [29] *Ibid.* Art. 25.

[30] *Ibid.* Art. 28. [31] *Ibid.* Art. 32.

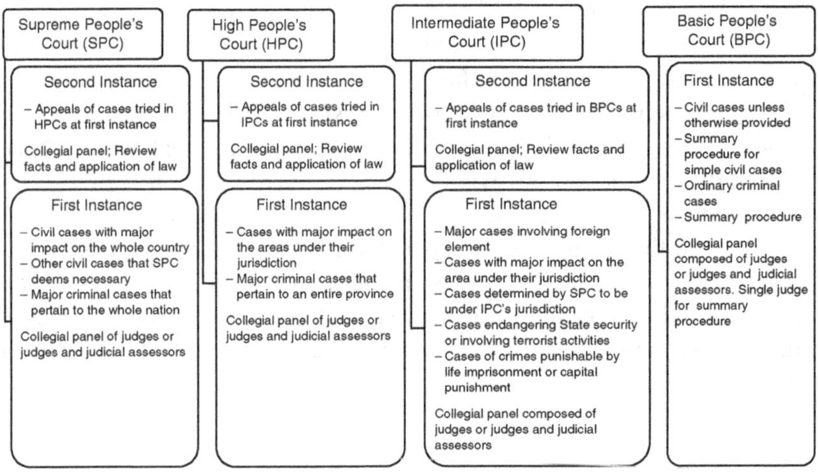

Figure 14.1: Structure of courts and instances of trial (civil and criminal procedure)

In addition to adjudication, the SPC has another important "legislative" power, whereby its judicial interpretations fill in the gaps of implementation of the laws and are considered binding rules in all Chinese courts.[32]

Cases in Chinese courts are usually heard before a collegiate bench of three judges, except those simple civil cases and minor criminal cases that may be heard before a single judge. According to the Organic Law of the People's Courts, in the district courts, a collegiate bench for first instance cases may consist either of judges and assessors or of judges entirely.[33] The people's assessors system is deemed to be a reflection of the ideal of popular participation in and democratic supervision of the administration of justice.[34] However, the use of people's assessors has declined over the years; it has been reported that those who participated in trials contributed little to the decision-making process.[35] For second instance trials, cases are heard before a panel of three judges at the intermediate court and high court, and at the SPC, by a panel of five judges. Figure 14.1

[32] *Ibid.* Art. 33. [33] *Ibid.* Art. 10.

[34] A. H. Y. Chen, *An Introduction to the Legal System of the People's Republic of China*, 4th edn (Hong Kong: LexisNexis, 2011), p. 184.

[35] *Ibid.*

summarizes the structure of the courts of China and their hierarchical relationship with respect to appeals.

1.3 *Size and performance of the courts*

Table 14.1 illustrates the number of courts and judges in various jurisdictions of China, and the ratio of judges to inhabitants in 2012. There is a fairly vast number of judges in the highest judiciary in China, with more than 500 judges serving the SPC. There are 31 provincial-level high people's courts in China that work directly under the SPC, and they have about 7,000 judges. Including all of their divisions and tribunals, the 409 intermediate people's courts, which are located in all major Chinese cities, have 36,000 judges. With respect to the district-level basic people's courts, which handle most of the first-instance civil and criminal trials in China, there are 3,117 such courts and 146,000 judges. These grassroots-level judges are considered to be the forerunners of Chinese judicial practices. At the end of the spectrum, the military and maritime courts are comparatively smaller due to their specialized jurisdictions, with the maritime courts being the smallest in size among all types of Chinese courts.

Table 14.1: *The number of courts and judges in different jurisdictions in China*

	SPC	HPC	MIC	IPC	MAC	BPC	Total
No. of courts	1	31	12	409	10	3,117	3,569
No. of judges	500	7,000	–*	36,000	–*	146,000	193,000
No. of inhabitants							1,343,239,923
No. of judges/ 100,000 inhabitants							14.37

SPC = Supreme People's Court; HPC = High People's Courts; MIC = Military Court; IPC = Intermediate People's Courts; MAC = Maritime Courts; BPC = Basic People's Courts

*Data unavailable

Source: Introduction to People's Courts, 2012, http://court.gov.cn/jgsz/rmfyjj/

Table 14.2: *Breakdown of cases by categories in 2011*

Category	Percentage (%)
Civil and commercial	62.46
Enforcement	20.85
Criminal	8.20
Parole	5.36
Administrative	1.49
Judicial supervision	0.90
State compensation	0.018
Others	0.059

Source: 2011 Judicial Statistics. These figures are available at the SPC website, www.court.gov.cn/qwfb/sfsj

The following figures appear in the SPC's report to the National People's Congress (the "NPC") in March 2012.[36] They are useful in providing an overview of the size and performance of the Chinese courts in a recent year (including numbers of cases, their categories and ratios). In 2011, the SPC handled a total of 11,876 cases (a decrease of 1.8 percent compared with 2010), and all the lower courts combined handled a total of 12.20 million cases (an increase of 4.4 percent compared with 2010). Since 2005, the number of cases has, on average, increased by 5.95 percent every year. The numbers of first instance civil, criminal and administrative (including administrative litigation and state compensation) cases decided by the courts in 2011 were 6.56 million, 839,973 and 136,361 respectively, which is an increase of 8.53 percent compared with 2010.[37] As shown in Table 14.2 above, among the cases concluded by the courts in 2011, the proportions of various types of cases were as follows: civil and commercial cases (62.46 percent); criminal cases (8.20 percent); administrative cases (1.49 percent); cases of enforcement of judgments and arbitral awards (20.85 percent); cases involving the reduction of criminal sentence and release under parole (5.36 percent); cases involving judicial supervision (examination of petitions and applications for

[36] SPC, *2011 Judicial Statistics.* These figures are also released at the SPC website, available at www.court.gov.cn/qwfb/sfsj.

[37] *Ibid.*

re-trial) (0.90 percent).[38] Not surprisingly, civil and commercial cases far outnumbered other types of cases. This is because in the course of deepening marketization, Chinese courts have more and more been expected to serve as impartial arbiters of civil and commercial disputes among citizens and market entities.

2 Judicial appointments, independence, training and legal education

2.1 *Judicial appointments and qualifications of judges*

With respect to judges, until the enactment of the Judges' Law in 1995, judges in China were not treated as legal professionals. Instead, they were treated as cadres of the State, and the personnel management system applicable to judges was identical to the one applicable to officials working in other government departments.[39] In the early 1980s, approximately two-thirds of the Chinese judges did not have a law degree, and one-third of them were demobilized members of the military.[40] Hence, the promulgation of the Judges' Law was seen as a major step towards the institutionalization and professionalization of Chinese judges and in the creation of a new personnel management system for judges that would be appropriate for the nature of the judicial profession. Related changes included the elaboration and rising of the qualifications for appointment as a judge to courts in China. The minimum eligibility criteria set out in the Judges' Law as amended in 2001 require new judges to pass the unified national judicial exam ("unified" for all prospective legal professionals such as judges, prosecutors and lawyers),[41] and moreover, to have one to three years of working experience in a Chinese court after obtaining a law degree or a non-law degree.[42] The number of years of work experience required depends on the degree the candidate holds and the level of the court.[43] For instance, with at least two years of work

[38] *Ibid.*

[39] D. Zhao (ed.), *Lectures on the Law on Judges* (Beijing: People's Court Press, 1995), pp. 5, 16.

[40] In the reconstruction of the court system that commenced immediately after the Cultural Revolution, demobilized soldiers became judges, since they were considered good candidates owing to their propensity to promote proletarian ideologies. Thus, many of their decisions were based not on law but on communist ideologies. See Y. Li, "Court reformation in China: problems, progress and prospects" in J. Chen, Y. Li and J. M. Otto (eds.), *Implementation of Law in the People's Republic of China* (The Hague: Kluwer Law International, 2002), pp. 253–4.

[41] Judges' Law, Arts. 12, 51. [42] *Ibid.* Art. 9. [43] *Ibid.* Art. 9(6).

experience, a holder of a Doctor's degree in a non-law specialty who is equipped with professional legal knowledge can also be appointed judge of a high people's court, in which case the candidate is assumed to demonstrate possession of professional legal knowledge. Existing judges without a law degree who were appointed before the Judges' Law was implemented are to be trained at the central or local judges' colleges.[44] This requirement ensures that even judges who were previously appointed based on their political background instead of their legal abilities would be qualified for their positions. The amended Judges' Law has further introduced a new system of judicial ranks, consisting of twelve grades grouped into the categories of chief justice (the President of the SPC, or *shouxidafaguan*), grand justices (vice-presidents of the SPC and presidents of provincial-level high courts, or *dafaguan*), senior judges (*gaojifaguan*), and judges (*faguan*).[45] Article 11 of the amended Judges' Law states that while the presidents of the people's courts at various levels are elected or removed by the people's congresses at the corresponding levels, the other judges, including the vice-presidents and members of the judicial committees, shall be appointed or removed by the standing committees of the people's congresses at the corresponding levels upon the suggestions of the presidents of those courts.[46] As of 2012, there were approximately 193,000 judges working in 3,569 courts in China.[47]

Although the recruitment standards for becoming a Chinese judge have been raised significantly, it is generally believed that the education of judges on commercial law practices is insufficient. For example, Chinese judges have limited knowledge of modern standards of commercial arbitration, let alone the global pro-enforcement approach in reviewing the effect of international arbitration awards.[48] Accordingly, local judges sometimes mistakenly apply legal principles and rules. In a series of arbitration reports published by the SPC Gazette, Chinese local judges usually ignore the applicable law rules when determining the validity of foreign-related contracts. This general shortage of judicial

[44] *Ibid.* Art. 9(6), para. 2. See also SPC President Y. Xiao's Report to the 4th Session of the 9th National People's Congress, Beijing, 10 March 2001.

[45] Judges' Law, Art. 18. [46] *Ibid.* Art. 11.

[47] Report by S. Wang (President of the SPC) to the 4th Session of the 11th National People's Congress, 11 March 2011. These figures are also released at the SPC website, available at www.court.gov.cn/qwfb/sfsj.

[48] W. Gu, "Judicial review over arbitration in China: assessing the extent of the latest pro-arbitration move by the Supreme People's Court in the People's Republic of China," *Wisconsin International Law Journal*, 27(2) (2009), 222–69.

expertise on commercial law has also caused some foreign arbitral awards to be unduly set aside or denied enforcement.[49]

The lack of a tenure system and decent salaries (as compared to lawyers) has also exacerbated the shortage of skilled judges. Some judges have committed corruption, while others have abandoned their posts for more lucrative practices in large law firms.[50] The caliber of local judges is also unbalanced across China and economically driven.[51] Economically well-developed areas attract more judicial talent, and judges in these areas are more likely to have the skills to deal with foreign cases and international arbitration norms. Therefore, judges in coastal areas are more competent, and they take a more liberal approach in interpreting contracts and agreements.[52] Rural areas, on the other hand, are ill-equipped to handle complicated commercial cases such as those involving arbitration. The unbalanced qualification of judges also creates uncertainty about and inconsistency of judicial enforcement in different areas of China. This uncertainty is also the reason why Hong Kong, in its 2000 agreement with the Mainland regarding mutual recognition and enforcement of cross-border arbitral awards, was reluctant to subject its arbitral awards to review by people's courts in all Chinese jurisdictions. Evidently, some of the intermediate courts have never taken up any Hong Kong or foreign-related cases, nor do they have qualified judicial personnel in dealing with such cases.[53]

[49] For example, the grounds for setting aside the award where an arbitral tribunal exceeds the scope of an arbitration agreement in its award was put to the test in *Shanghai Medical Equipment Factory for Tooth* v. *Hu Zhunren and Another*, which was decided by the Beijing 2nd Intermediate People's Court in 1996. In the comments by Mo, judges in that case did not understand what "scope of arbitration agreement" refers to. See S. Mo, *Arbitration Law in China* (Hong Kong: Sweet & Maxwell Asia, 2001), para. 10.40.

[50] One SPC judge commented that in 1998–9 alone, approximately 15 percent of all people's court judges left their positions for positions in law firms. See Interview Notes of S. Zhao, former SPC judge and now attorney at the Beijing Jingtian & Gongcheng Law Firm, reprinted in E. Reinstein, "Finding a happy ending for foreign investors: the enforcement of arbitration awards in the People's Republic of China," *Indiana International and Comparative Law Review*, 16 (2005), 37.

[51] Dean C. Wang, "Resolving business disputes in China," guest lecture at the NYU Law School, March 18, 2007.

[52] Gu, "Judicial review over arbitration in China," 263–4.

[53] X. Zhang, "Legal issues concerning the mutual enforcement of arbitral awards between the Hong Kong SAR and mainland China," *Arbitration and Law Journal (Zhongcai yu Falu)*, 2 (2002), 26–53.

2.2 *Judicial independence*

Contemporary scholarship on the Chinese legal system has explained the issue of judicial independence by creating two categories, *institutional independence* of the judiciary as a whole (the "thinner" layer of judicial independence) and *independent decision-making* by individual judges (the "thicker" layer of judicial independence).[54] Institutional independence requires the courts to be adequately funded so that they function free from governmental influences, while independent decision-making requires the judges' terms of office to be secured and their appointment depoliticized so that judges can perform impartially.[55]

In China, the Constitution and Organic Law of the People's Courts provide that Chinese courts have the right to be free from external interferences in their work.[56] However, the laws further require that individual courts at different levels must be administratively and institutionally accountable to the corresponding level of people's congresses.[57] In addition, courts in China are subject to dual leadership. They receive political supervision from the Party Committee (*dangwei*) within the court and the Party Political and Legal Affairs Committee (*zhengfawei*) outside the court (known as "horizontal supervision").[58] At the same time, their decisions and court judgments are scrutinized professionally by higher-level people's courts on the basis of judiciary hierarchy (known as "vertical scrutiny").[59] This stands in sharp contrast with the understanding of collective independence in Western ideologies where all individual courts enjoy functional independence. As such, the Chinese courts as a whole appear to enjoy institutional independence, although individual courts do not.[60]

The independence of local people's courts is further undermined by the way in which they are funded. Courts in China are financed by governments at their corresponding levels. Therefore, local courts are subsidized by the relevant local government. It is unfortunate that while the SPC supervises the adjudicative work of all lower level people's courts, it has no power over their budgets.[61] Local judiciaries are thus dependent on local governments for even basic necessities such as

[54] See, for example, R. Peerenboom (ed.), *China's Long March toward Rule of Law* (New York: Cambridge University Press, 2002), pp. 288–90.

[55] *Ibid.* [56] Constitution, Art. 126; Organic Law of the People's Court, Art. 4.

[57] Constitution, Art. 128.

[58] Peerenboom (ed.), *China's Long March toward Rule of Law*, p. 298. [59] *Ibid.*

[60] *Ibid.* [61] Constitution, Art. 127.

salaries and housing allowances. However, since local governments need to support themselves and local courts through local taxes, fees and charges collected from local businesses, an incentive for the court to lean on local businesses has formed.[62] By the same token, a locally subsidized court may be subject to local criticism if its rulings hamper local economic interests, and the court itself might be financially disadvantaged. Where state-owned enterprises ("SOE," *guoyouqiye*) or government-supported businesses ("GSB," *zhengfufuchichanye*) are at stake, the local court is more likely to seize its jurisdiction and refuse to refer parties to litigation outside the local jurisdiction.[63] Moreover, since Chinese local governments have a political responsibility to maintain social stability in their localities, they might interfere in a judicial ruling if its enforcement could hamper a major local business. From the perspective of government authorities, strict implementation of independent courts and judges may lead to the loss of *control* of the final outcomes of commercial dispute resolution and thus exert an adverse impact on the SOEs and GSBs as a political, economic and social safety net in China. Thus, the possible cash flow problems of the SOE or GSB would trigger the exercise of judicial intervention. Some commentators, however, argue that, in such cases, both the court ordering enforcement and the SOE receiving the order are governmental organs. Hence, local protectionism must be prevalent unless local courts can relieve themselves from the budget constraints.[64]

The courts' financial reliance on local governments has not only allowed local political and administrative powers to encourage local protectionism, but it has also led to the unbalanced development of local people's courts across the country. Former Dean Wang Chenguang of the Tsinghua University Law School notes that the court system in the coastal areas of China is better developed than its hinterland counterparts, as the economy in coastal areas has been better off and government administrations more liberalized in these regions.[65] By contrast, rural

[62] L. Lin, "Judicial independence in Japan: a re-investigation for China," *Columbia Journal of Asian Law*, 13 (1999), 199.

[63] In China, SOEs are thought to promote economic development and maintain social stability in that they produce jobs and provide various forms of social welfare to their workers, retirees and their family members.

[64] See A. Yuan, "Enforcing and collecting money judgments in China from a U.S. creditor's perspective," *George Washington International Law Review*, 36 (2004), 757.

[65] Interview notes of W. Chenguang, former Dean of the Tsinghua University Law School on 2 November 2004, reprinted in Reinstein, "Finding a happy ending for foreign investors," 37.

areas often suffer budget constraints due to their under-developed economies. As a result, the court system in these areas may be subject to more administrative interferences, which helps to explain the more frequent occurrence of biased judgments in hinterland and rural areas.

Regarding the administration of the judiciary, Article 123 of the Constitution states that, "[T]he people's courts of the People's Republic of China are the judicial organs of the state." This Article has been interpreted by scholars to indicate that the state's adjudicative power may be exercised only by the courts and not by any other organs, organizations or persons.[66] However, having been appointed by the people's congresses, the people's courts are also supervised by and accountable to the former.[67] For instance, Chapter 2 of the Law on Supervision by Standing Committees of People's Congresses at Various Levels, promulgated in 2006, provides for the examination by the NPCSC and the standing committees of local people's congresses of reports submitted by the courts.

The thicker layer regarding judicial independence, i.e. independent decision-making by Chinese judges, is another challenging issue. In the Chinese context, individual judges, by and large, do not have the right to decide cases on their own. Judges at all levels of people's courts, apart from their judicial ranks, are further divided into different administrative ranks: i.e. the President of the Court (*yuanzhang*), Vice-President (*fuyuanzhang*), and Division Heads of the Chambers (*tingzhang*).[68] The people's congresses at different levels decide on the appointment of the court presidents and the presidents then decide on the appointment of the vice-presidents and division heads.[69] Most cases are heard by a collegiate panel of three judges, and the presidents or division heads will determine which judge will act as the chair of the panel, and they may further review the panel's decisions if they deem it necessary.[70] In turn, collegiate panels are often required under the court's internal rules to obtain the approval of the division heads, vice-presidents, president and the court's Judicative Committee (*shenpan weiyuanhui*) before they render their judgments. The Judicative Committee is the highest adjudicative body inside the court, the establishment of which functions to guide the handling of difficult cases received by the court. The committee is composed of the Party Secretary, President, Vice-Presidents and

[66] Chen, *An Introduction to the Legal System of the People's Republic of China*, p. 174.
[67] *Ibid.* p. 172. [68] Organic Law of the People's Court, Arts. 19, 24, 27 and 31.
[69] *Ibid.* [70] *Ibid.* Art. 10.

Division Heads of the court concerned.[71] By submitting his or her tentative decisions to the Judicative Committee for approval, a judge in China is obliged to obey rank instead of reason and becomes little more than a bureaucratic clerk.[72] The administrative rank of the judges is important in determining the final outcome of the case, and the decision-making of individual judges is controlled indirectly through these administrative means.[73]

Outside the court, local governments and the Party Committee (*dang-wei*) may further influence judicial decisions on significant cases, and on the appointment, promotion, and removal of local judges. The Party Committee exerts tremendous influence at all levels of the court system. According to the Constitution, the local people's congress has the power to appoint the president of the relevant local court, and the president will then nominate the other lower-level judges.[74] However, in reality, the local Party Committee often selects judges, and the people's congress merely ratifies its choices. These judges serve on the Judicative Committee of each court, wielding considerable power in determining the outcome of controversial cases.[75] Once appointed, judges rely on salaries and housing benefits provided by the municipal government. Moreover, when appointing and promoting judges, the local political and administrative regime evaluates them in terms of obedience to its policies.[76] Hence, in cases in which local business interests are at stake, local judges are incentivized to render judgments favorable to those businesses: judges know that they will continue to be promoted if their judgments safeguard the court's financial position. As some leading scholars have commented on this issue, such personal dependence has resulted from the institutional dependence of the individual local people's courts, the combination of which have subjected the Chinese local judiciary to local politics and administration. Judicial interventions in adjudication and

71 See *ibid.* Art. 11.

72 S. Balme, "Local courts in Western China: the quest for independence and dignity" in Peerenboom (ed.), *Judicial Independence in China*, p. 169.

73 Dean Professor L. Wang of the People's University is one of the many scholars who have called for an end to the system of administrative ranking of judges.

74 Constitution, Art. 101.

75 Peerenboom (ed.), *China's Long March toward Rule of Law*, pp. 286–7.

76 Li, "Court reformation in China," p. 63; see also S. Lubman, *Bird in a Cage: Legal Reform in China after Mao* (California: Stanford University Press, 1999), pp. 55, 58–9. See also, Robb M. LaKritz, "Taming a 5,000 year-old dragon: toward a theory of legal development in post-Mao China," *Emory International Law Review*, 11 (1997), 262.

enforcement follow as a natural result.[77] In extreme cases, judges have even helped local companies with fraudulent transfer of assets as a way of evading enforcement.[78]

The SPC has become aware of the issues and has openly criticized the detrimental practices of local protectionism in the Chinese social legal system. Consequently, there have been some improvements in the general enforcement records. However, significant improvements have not been seen if we separate the judicial enforcement records by localities. The problem lies in the fact that, although China has a highly centralized judicial system in which the SPC supervises its lower level courts, local judicial powers may deviate from their central controllers in pursuing local economic interests. One author explains that local government needs to supply its own social welfare, to promote industries in its locality, and to finance itself in order to implement its plans.[79] Other leading experts in the field have commented that the Chinese courts could be more dependent upon the local governments due to a gradual administrative decentralization that is taking place alongside China's membership in the WTO.[80] This decentralization in the course of pursuing economic reforms may have fueled local judicial efforts to implement the national rules according to their own needs.[81] Thus, even though local judges might understand the SPC's reformist approach, they may not be able to implement it when a local interest must be protected.

2.3 *Judicial training and related legal education*

As mentioned earlier, existing judges in China who were appointed before the Judges' Law was implemented and did not have a law degree are to be trained at the central and local judges' colleges. The Chinese judiciary has recognized that continuing professional education of

[77] Lubman, *Bird in a Cage*, pp. 252, 279.

[78] See the *Revpower* case where the Chinese company appeared to be insolvent under the arrangement of the local people's court so that the enforcement was delayed, reported by F. Brown and C. A. Rogers, "The role of arbitration in resolving transnational disputes: a survey of trends in the People's Republic of China," *Berkeley Journal of International Law*, 15 (1997), 341–2.

[79] T. Inoue, "Introduction to international commercial arbitration in China," *Hong Kong Law Journal*, 36 (2006), 180.

[80] P. Potter, "Legal reform in China: institutions, culture and selective adaptation," *Law & Social Inquiry*, 29 (2004), 465, 473.

[81] *Ibid.*

existing judges is an important task. Chapter IX of the Judges' Law briefly outlines the type of training that judges are required to undertake, emphasizing the integration of theory with practice.[82] It is also stipulated that judges' colleges and universities of the state and other institutions are responsible for the provision of training.[83] Moreover, judges' performance during training shall be taken into account for appointment and promotion purposes.[84] Since 1985, various educational institutions specializing in judicial training have been established, the most famous being the National Judges' College affiliated with the Supreme People's Court. As of the year 2000, the great majority of Chinese judges had obtained their law degrees or diplomas through continuing professional education. The proportion of judges who held degrees increased from 7 percent in 1995 to 56 percent in 2006.[85] Despite the growing emphasis on judicial education and training, it was not until the introduction of the National Judicial Exam in China in 2002 that the standard of admission to becoming a Chinese judge was raised.

Legal education in China expanded even more rapidly in the 1990s and the first decade of the new century. In 2001, there were law schools or law departments in 241 institutions of higher education all over China (excluding Hong Kong and Macau).[86] By 2008, the number of law schools had risen to 634, among which 138 offered master's programs in law, and 29 offered law doctorates.[87] According to a report published by the Ministry of Education, the law student population in 2010 was 787,817, with an undergraduate intake of 197,878.[88] The bachelor of laws curriculum is a four-year program; the master of laws and doctor of laws are both basically three-year research programs. Interestingly, pursuant to the Judges' Law, the achievement of a law degree is not a prerequisite for sitting in the National Judicial Exam.[89] Hence, formal legal education is not the sole route to a professional law career in China.

However, although numbers of law students and schools have risen six-fold, job prospects have not kept pace. As some Western legal

[82] Judges' Law, Art. 26. [83] *Ibid.* Art. 27. [84] *Ibid.* Art. 28.

[85] J. Zhu, *China Legal Statistics Report* (2007), p. 34.

[86] Chen, *An Introduction to the Legal System of the People's Republic of China*, p. 255.

[87] CAAS (Chinese Academy of Social Sciences, Institute of Law) (ed.), *Three Decades of Rule of Law in China 1978–2008* (Beijing: Social Sciences Academic Press, 2008), p. 8.

[88] Source: Ministry of Education, "2010 Education Statistics," (教育统计数据) (released on 17 January 2012).

[89] As long as the candidate has a bachelor's degree, he or she can sit the National Judicial Exam.

scholars have most recently noticed, a flood of law graduates in China is facing dismal employment prospects, and Chinese law schools are advised to differentiate themselves from each other.[90] The proliferation of law schools and the devaluation of law degrees are pushing the Chinese authorities to re-evaluate the current system and the future direction of the Chinese legal education.

3 Legal aid and access to justice

3.1 Legal aid

The existing system of legal aid is governed by the Legal Aid Regulations enacted by the State Council in July 2003, which took effect in September 2003. The Regulations emphasize that the provision of legal aid is the government's responsibility.[91] However, the responsibility for generating financial support for legal aid is mainly assigned to local governments rather than to the Central Government. Donations from society are encouraged, and social organizations are also encouraged to provide legal aid services.[92] According to the Regulations, eligibility for legal aid is determined by a means test (the standards for which may vary in different parts of the country) and whether the case falls into one of the following categories. These cases include claims for social insurance or social security payments, claims for maintenance of spouses and children, claims for wages, and claims with respect to interests in civil actions generated by "voluntary acts of courage and justice."[93]

Moreover, the Regulations state that lawyers and lawyers' associations have obligations to participate in the legal aid service.[94] This participation corresponds with Article 42 of the Lawyers' Law, which prescribes a legal duty to lawyers to provide legal aid as required by the government. The Ministry of Justice and the justice bureaus at the local level are responsible for supervising the operation of the legal aid system.[95] For example, the justice bureaus of municipal- and county-level governments will designate a legal aid organ for the relevant city or county concerned, which will be responsible for processing legal aid applications and arranging for legal aid to be made available.[96]

[90] C. Minzner, "The rise and fall of Chinese legal education," *Fordham International Law Journal*, 36 (2) (2013), 335–337.

[91] Legal Aid Regulations, Art. 3. [92] *Ibid.* Arts. 7 and 8. [93] *Ibid.* Art. 10.

[94] *Ibid.* Arts. 4 and 6. [95] *Ibid.* Art. 4. [96] *Ibid.* Art. 5.

The number of full-time lawyers in China increased from 6,213 in 1981 to 192,546 in 2011.[97] The number of law firms increased from 3,716 in 1990 to 18,235 in 2011.[98] In 2010, almost 90 percent of licensed lawyers worked in large or medium-sized cities, whereas the remaining 20,000 lawyers served the large population in rural areas.[99] The profession of legal workers (also known as "barefoot lawyers" or "judicial assistants") was created by the government in the early 1980s to address the shortage of lawyers in rural areas.[100] Mediation was employed by these judicial assistants to resolve disputes in villages. The profession of township legal workers was later created and was regulated by the Ministry of Justice, which administered the licensing examination for entry into the profession.[101] In 2007, the Lawyers' Law was amended so as to allow only licensed lawyers (instead of "judicial assistants") to represent clients in courts,[102] although lawyer representation in the court is not required in China. An agent *ad litem* can be used in accordance with the Civil Procedure Law and Criminal Procedural Law, but the charging of fees is prohibited in such cases.

Access to justice is less visible and successful in rural county courts, which are weaker institutionally. It is extremely difficult to retain young and well-trained judges in the countryside or in district areas where work is both demanding and poorly compensated. In addition, most grassroots judges do not have the economic and social resources or long-established professional background to act fully independently.[103] County judges who have less professional experience and fewer legal qualifications continue to deal with cases through mediation. With the city courts relying more on adjudication, the county courts are the ones that have generated most of the petitions to extra-judicial organs.[104]

3.2 *Letters and visits system*

A particularly interesting feature of the Chinese courts system is that courts accept as part of their work the task of dealing with visits and

[97] Law Yearbook of China (2012), p. 1081. [98] *Ibid.*

[99] H. Fu, "Access to justice in China: potentials, limits, and alternatives" in J. Gillespie and A. H. Y. Chen (eds.), *Legal Reforms in China and Vietnam: A Comparison of Asian Communist Regimes* (New York: Routledge, 2010), pp. 163–87.

[100] Legal Aid Regulations, Art. 5. [101] *Ibid.* [102] See Lawyers' Law, Art. 13.

[103] Balme, "Local courts in Western China," p. 173.

[104] H. Fu and R. Cullen, "From mediatory to adjudicatory justice: the limits of civil justice reform in China" in M. Y. W. Woo and M. E. Gallagher, *Chinese Justice: Civil Dispute Resolution in Contemporary China* (Cambridge University Press, 2011), p. 62.

letters from people who have complaints and petitions to bring to court. This is known as the "letters and visits" system (*xingfang*), a concept that is applicable not only to courts but also to people's congresses and government departments.[105] By virtue of Article 41 of the Constitution, Chinese citizens have the right to make complaints and to petition state organs, and the relevant state organs must deal with such complaints.[106] In a court of first instance, a civil suit may be initiated orally by personally visiting the people's reception unit of the court, or it may be initiated by writing a letter to the court. Some courts now have designated halls for reception and initiation of such cases, with counters providing services for visitors. In 2011, more than 90 percent of the Chinese courts set up departments to receive complaint letters, petitions or visits concerning judicial grievances.[107] By way of letters and visits, petitions may also be made requesting the court to further review a case in which the right to appeal has already been exhausted (i.e. after two instances of a case).[108]

In recent years, the SPC has become increasingly concerned about the large volume of petitions and letters from and visits by aggrieved persons. In order to manage the letters and visits work by the courts, the SPC promulgated in 2009 Several Opinions on Minimizing Litigation-Related Xingfang from its Sources, and in 2010 the Measures on the Conclusion of Litigation-Related Xingfang Cases in the People's Courts.[109] These measures are seen, on the one hand, as a continuation of the channel in which ordinary citizens can file grievances against the judiciary, and, on the other hand, as a balance between judicial resources and efficacy. Most importantly, because petitions from letters and visits might have an adverse effect on the authority of judicial adjudication and, hence, exert a negative impact on social stability, the SPC has asked the lower courts to examine the merit of the complaints so that only those meritorious claims with real and substantial grievances can be entertained by the

[105] See the Regulations on *Xingfang* (2005) enacted by the State Council, which replace the Regulations on *Xingfang* (1995).

[106] Constitution, Art. 41.

[107] See Chief Justice and SPC President Wang Shengjun's report on the work of the SPC to the 5th session of the 11th National People's Congress on 11 March 2012.

[108] Civil Procedure Law, Art. 279.

[109] See SPC White Paper (2010). According to the SPC Report to the NPC in March 2010, in the five-year period from 2005–2009, the SPC handled a total of 719,000 litigation-related *xingfang* cases, and the lower courts handled a total of 18.76 million such cases.

court. Accordingly, in 2011, around 790,000 letters and visits were handled, and the figure was 25.9 percent less than that in 2010.[110]

4 Sources of law and styles of judicial decisions

4.1 Sources of law

Pursuant to the Legislation Law, legislation in China can be classified into six categories, amongst which the hierarchical order is as follows: (1) the Constitution; (2) national laws passed by the National People's Congress and its Standing Committee; (3) administrative regulations passed by the State Council; (4) administrative rules passed by various ministries and commissions directly under the State Council; (5) local regulations passed by provincial-level local people's congresses and their standing committees; and (6) local rules passed by local governments.[111]

The NPC is the supreme legislative organ in China, exercising the legislative power of the state. It has the power to enact and amend basic laws such as criminal laws, civil laws and laws relating to the organization of state organs. The NPC Standing Committee may enact and amend all laws apart from those that can only be enacted by the NPC. The Standing Committee may enact supplements and amendments to laws made by the NPC when the latter is not in session, but such supplements and amendments must not be contrary to the basic principles of the original laws. The State Council may enact administrative rules and regulations according to the Constitution and the laws.[112] People's congresses at the provincial level, as well as those of municipalities directly under the Central Government, and their standing committees may enact local regulations as long as they do not contravene statutes and administrative rules and regulations. In addition, people's congresses of national autonomous areas can enact regulations related to the exercise of autonomy and certain types of regulations, subject to the approval of the NPC Standing Committee.

Although the judiciary is not delegated with any legislative power under the Legislation Law, as mentioned previously, the SPC does exercise de

[110] See Wang's report on the work of the SPC to the National People's Congress.

[111] Y. Li, "The law-making law: a solution to the problems in the Chinese legislative system?" *Hong Kong Law Journal*, 30 (2000), 120–40.

[112] Constitution, Art. 89.

facto rule-making power in China under the Organic Law of People's Courts in that it interprets and clarifies national laws in judicial practice, and these interpretations have legal authority in the courtroom.[113] In the meantime, despite the fact that cases and judicial precedents are not formally recognized as sources of law in China, it is suggested that some judicial decisions of the courts, particularly those of the provincial and national levels, may be of persuasive value or even binding in practice.[114] Decisions published in the SPC Gazette are considered to be authoritative, and, in practice, precedents of the SPC are binding on lower courts.

4.2 Styles of judicial decisions and operation of courts

The typical judgment of a Chinese court is short and does not set out lines or steps of legal reasoning and logical analysis in as detailed a way as do judgments of common law courts, and even certain civil law courts. Relevant statutory provisions may be referred to, but the precise relationship between them and their application to the case will not usually be discussed at length. As there is no established doctrine of precedent, case law will seldom be referred to, with the exception of judgments delivered by the SPC, or certain leading judgments delivered by provincial-level high courts. Judgments do not usually include direct responses to lawyers' submissions, and dissenting judgments are not usually allowed under Chinese law.[115] However, in the last decade, the official policy has been to encourage judges to write more detailed judgments analyzing the evidence and elucidating the application of the law, and to publicize leading cases to a greater degree.[116] More cases are being published by the SPC Gazette, and collections of cases have appeared in some online databases. In 2011, the SPC introduced a "Guiding Case System" and announced the first batch of four model judgments on civil and criminal

[113] Organic Law of People's Courts, Art. 33, adopted by the NPC in 1979 and amended in 1983 and 2006; see also the *Resolution on Strengthening the Works for Interpretation of Law*, issued by the NPCSC in 1983. However, the scope of the SPC's interpretative power is not clearly defined between *interpreting law* and *making law* although there may be a literal distinction that legislation is the act of making a law, while interpretation is the art or process of ascertaining the meaning of existing laws.

[114] Chen, *An Introduction to the Legal System of the People's Republic of China*, p. 166.

[115] However, a member of the collegiate bench who dissents from the majority decision is entitled to have his or her opinion recorded, though this record does not apparently form part of the official judgment of the court. See Art. 148 of the Criminal Procedure Law and Art. 43 of the Civil Procedure Law.

[116] B. Liebman, "China's courts: restricted reform," *The China Quarterly*, 191 (2007), 625–6.

cases on its official website.[117] These judgments are expected to act as (1) guides for lower courts in ruling on issues of similar types, and (2) style guides for writing judicial decisions by Chinese judges. It is evident that in recent years, an increasing number of court judgments have been published on court websites in order to promote more analytical writing.

In terms of the operation of the courts, studies on contemporary Chinese law have identified a few distinctive features of the manner and style of Chinese courts that distinguish them from their Western counterparts. One is that, inherited from the Soviet legal system, the Chinese courts emphasize the educational function of law in their adjudicative work, with the intention of molding citizens' character and development. For example, the Organic Law of People's Courts requires the courts to use adjudicative activities to educate citizens to be loyal to the "socialist motherland."[118] The Party demanded that courts settle disputes using "democratic methods," that is, by persuading and educating disputants rather than adjudicating their disputes according to established legal principles.[119]

Before judicial reform, a very important feature of the operation of the Chinese courts was that judges themselves had a duty to conduct investigations and collect evidence, particularly in civil procedures.[120] The practice is partly an illustration of the inquisitorial rather than adversarial nature of China's adjudication system (following the continental European trial model), and partly an aspect of the principle of following the mass line of popular justice.[121] However, since the 1990s, under the global influence of placing more emphasis on due process, the general direction of judicial reform has been to introduce more adversarial elements into the trial process and, hence, to minimize the inquisitorial elements. This trend was reflected in the amendment to the Criminal Procedure Law in 1996, as well as in the promulgation by the SPC of

[117] Press conference on "SPC's Introducing the Guiding Case System" (20 December 2011), available at the SPC website, www.court.gov.cn/xwzx/jdjd/sdjd/201112/t20111220_168539.htm.

[118] Organic Law of the People's Courts, Art. 3.

[119] H. Fu, "Putting China's judiciary into perspective: Is it independent, competent and fair?" in E. G. Jensen and T. C. Heller (eds.), *Beyond Common Knowledge: Empirical Approaches to the Rule of Law* (Stanford University Press, 2003), ch. 6.

[120] X. Du and L. Zhang, *China's Legal System: A General Survey* (Beijing: New World Press, 1990), p. 100; see also C. Bian, "Thoughts on the reform of the courts," *Science of Law*, 1 (1990), 151.

[121] *Ibid.*

Provisions on Issues relating to the Reform of the Mode of Adjudication of Civil and Economic Cases in 1998 and Provisions on Evidence in Civil Litigation in 2001.[122]

Another peculiar feature of the operation of the Chinese courts is the existence of a referral system (*qingshi*) whereby lower courts may seek direction from the next higher court on a particular question or a particular case handled by the lower court.[123] Alternatively, the lower court may seek the approval of the higher court regarding a proposed way of deciding a case.[124] These practices have been seriously criticized for their lack of transparency and for rendering nugatory the right of parties to appeal,[125] as well as for violating judges' authority and independence.[126] Such practices would be considered extraordinary and even outrageous by contemporary Western standards.[127] The practice of referral should be gradually phased out. In this respect, the promulgation of the SPC in early 2011 of Several Opinions on Regulating the Relationship between Higher and Lower Courts' Adjudicative Work (the "Opinion") is a step in the right direction. The Opinion provides for the means by which a higher court may provide guidance to a lower court, whereby giving instructions on how the lower court should decide a particular case is not included as one of these means.[128]

5 Courts and alternative dispute resolution (ADR)

The legal and judicial systems of China, corresponding to its traditional legal culture, are facilitative to, and even favor, the adoption of ADR to resolve disputes. The emphasis on social harmony and the fulfillment of moral obligations have encouraged the use of mediation in dispute resolution in China, both inside (court-annexed mediation) and outside the court room (such as people's mediation committees and mediation combined with arbitration proceedings). Mediation in courts, known as "court-annexed mediation" (*susongnei tiaojie*), is emphasized at all levels of civil litigation in China, and this emphasis is one of the more unique characteristics of the Chinese system of civil procedure. With respect to

[122] X. Hu and P. Feng (eds.), *Research on Judicial Justice and Judicial Reform* (Beijing: Tsinghua University Press, 2001), pp. 265–68.

[123] *Ibid.* pp. 55, 139, 459; see also Peerenboom (ed.), *Judicial Independence in China*, p. 84.

[124] Chen, *An Introduction to the Legal System of the People's Republic of China*, pp. 188–9.

[125] Hu and Feng, *Research on Judicial Justice and Judicial Reform*, p. 60.

[126] For example, Gu, "Judicial review over arbitration in China," 262.

[127] *Ibid.*

[128] Opinion, Arts. 5, 8–10.

arbitration, China promulgated its Arbitration Law in 1994. The Law provides for the establishment in major cities of local arbitration commissions by relevant administrative departments acting jointly with local chambers of commerce. There are more than 200 such arbitration commissions, the most famous being the Beijing Arbitration Commission.[129] The general principle of arbitration in China, in line with modern international arbitration norms, is that where parties have entered into an arbitration agreement, the court will not exercise jurisdiction over a dispute covered by the agreement unless the agreement can be shown to be invalid.[130] Arbitral awards will be binding and enforceable unless the conditions for them to be set aside by the court are satisfied, which will be explained shortly.

5.1 Mediation in the courts

Chinese judges prefer to adopt mediation in their adjudicative work. Analysis of Chinese courts' preference for using mediation in their work has been offered in various aspects. There are strong cultural roots for this preference, such as Confucianism, which emphasizes amicable settlement. Irrespective of whether the dispute has been subject to mediation before the court action is brought, mediation efforts to bring about a settlement voluntarily accepted by both parties will be made at various points of the civil proceedings.[131] The first stage at which mediation is conducted by the court (as distinguished from mediation by people's mediation committees or by arbitrators in the course of arbitration) is before the trial. The court, acting either through one adjudicator or as a collegiate bench, may conduct mediation.[132] The second and more frequently occurring stage is mediation conducted during trial proceedings and can be requested by parties on a voluntary basis at any time before the court's judgment is rendered.[133] Furthermore, parties in a court-annexed mediation in China may invite other relevant parties to assist in the mediation process, such as working units that the litigation parties are attached to.[134] A mediation agreement prepared by the court, more frequently referred to as a "judicial settlement agreement," is binding and enforceable once it is delivered to the parties,[135] although the parties have

[129] W. Gu, *Arbitration in China: Regulation of Arbitration Agreements and Practical Issues* (Hong Kong: Sweet & Maxwell, 2012), p. 274.
[130] Arbitration Law, Art. 5. [131] Civil Procedure Law, Arts. 9, 85–91.
[132] *Ibid.* Art. 86. [133] *Ibid.* Arts. 88–91. [134] *Ibid.* Art. 87. [135] *Ibid.* Arts. 89, 211.

the residual right to apply for a retrial if it can be proved that the agreement was not entered into voluntarily or that it is contrary to law.[136]

From a political studies perspective, since 2006, in order to implement the state policy of building a "harmonious society," there has been an increasing emphasis placed on mediation in China – mediation is encouraged and even prioritized because it is viewed as being conducive to social stability and harmony.[137] Moreover, due to the economic boom over the past three decades, which has led to massive socio-economic changes, courts and formal adjudication are not equipped to resolve all the tensions and conflicts in Chinese society.[138] The current Party line reiterates Party control and an increase in the flexibility with which courts can decide cases, emphasizing "the feeling of the masses" and social conditions as well as the Constitution and laws. In response to public manifestations of discontent, as well as the more subtle societal changes that have occurred, the SPC has provided judges with training to deal with social unrest cases through mediation.[139] In 2007, the SPC published Several Opinions on the Further Development of the Positive Function of Mediation during Litigation in the Construction of a Socialist Harmonious Society, followed by Several Opinions on the Development of Coordination between Litigation and Non-litigious Means of Dispute Settlement in 2009. These judicial documents emphasizing mediation were followed by and consolidated into the SPC's Several Provisions on the Further Implementation of the Principle of "Priority of Mediation and Combination of Mediation and Adjudication" in 2010.[140] In this regard, the guiding principles of the justice system in China have evolved from the 1950s to the present, but the general theme of a preference for mediation over adjudication remains unchanged.

5.2 *Arbitration and the courts*

The involvement of the courts with respect to arbitration is necessary and unavoidable in China for the following reasons. To begin with, courts,

[136] *Ibid.* Art. 182.

[137] L. Stanley, "Chinese law after sixty years," *East Asia Forum*, 2 October 2009, available at www.eastasiaforum.org/2009/10/02/chinese-law-after-sixty-years.

[138] X. Qin, "Calling for judicial reform," *China Reform Magazine (Zhongguo Gaige)* (2010), 90: 316.

[139] These social unrest cases include, for example, mass torts claims such as the reported tainted milk case, the nail house demolition cases, derivative actions, etc., which involve a large number of litigants.

[140] SPC White Paper (2010).

particularly the SPC, issue important judicial interpretations that serve as important sources of regulations on arbitration. For instance, the SPC issued its Interpretation on Several Issues Relating to the Application of the Arbitration Law in late 2006, which elaborated on issues concerning the trial of arbitration-related cases by the people's court. This was published to consolidate the SPC's piecemeal judicial replies and notices on specific arbitration cases, indicating that the judiciary was trying to bring the development of arbitration in China closer to international norms and standards.[141] Moreover, in China, courts have the sole power to grant and enforce interim measures of protection to assist arbitration proceedings. These interim measures include property and evidence preservation orders that are granted upon the party and arbitral tribunal's request.[142] Courts also exercise the final check over arbitral jurisdiction, i.e. to rule on whether the arbitration agreement or clause is existent or valid. Pursuant to the Arbitration Law[143] and subsequent SPC judicial interpretations,[144] where parties dispute the validity of their arbitration agreement and one party requests the arbitral tribunal for a determination whilst the other party approaches a people's court for a similar determination, once the decision has been rendered by the tribunal, the court will seize its jurisdiction.[145] Some authors conclude that this kind of judicial involvement is indicative of the courts' supportive role towards arbitration.[146]

More powerfully, courts scrutinize arbitral awards, which they are asked to enforce or set aside. Arbitration commentators often refer to this as the courts' supervisory role over arbitration.[147] Under the dual-track system, arbitration in China is divided into domestic and foreign-related types. Correspondingly,[148] different standards of judicial scrutiny are applied to domestic and foreign-related awards, with domestic awards facing more severe scrutiny. Where cases with a foreign element

[141] Gu, *Arbitration in China*, p. 9.

[142] Arbitration Law, Art. 68. [143] *Ibid.* Art. 20.

[144] *The SPC Reply on Several Issues of Ascertaining the Validity of the Arbitration Agreement*, Fa Shi [1998] No. 27, issued by SPC on 26 October 1998.

[145] See more discussions below in Section 7.

[146] For example, J. Tao, *Arbitration Law and Practice in China*, 2nd edn. (The Hague: Kluwer Law International, 2008), paras. 99–100.

[147] *Ibid.*

[148] A foreign element is present in a foreign-related case if at least one contractual party is a foreign entity; the contractual subject matter is in a foreign country; or the act which affects the contractual rights and obligations at stake occurs in a foreign country.

are concerned, Chinese courts can only examine procedural aspects of the award, although exceptions are permitted on "public policy" or "social public interest" grounds, which are not explicitly defined.[149] For instance, according to Article 258 of the Civil Procedure Law, a people's court shall disallow the enforcement of an award if the party against whom the application for enforcement is made proves that he was not given notice of the appointment of an arbitrator or if the formation of the arbitral tribunal violates the arbitration rules.[150] However, where domestic awards are concerned, courts are permitted to review them on their merits as well as for procedural defects. According to Article 58 of the Arbitration Law, a party may apply to the court to set aside an arbitration award if he or she can produce evidence proving that the arbitration award was granted based on forged evidence[151] or that the other party has withheld evidence that is sufficient to affect the impartiality of the arbitration.[152] This shows that, apart from procedural irregularities, a party to a domestic award can refer to a mistake in the fact-finding process in order to have the award set aside. The reason why courts in China have been granted the power to review the merits of domestic awards is not addressed in the legislative annotation on the Arbitration Law, although many believe that it is mainly due to the concern that the quality of arbitral awards rendered by Chinese local arbitration commissions is unsatisfactory and thus requires substantial supervision.[153] In the past decade, the SPC has established a "pre-reporting" system for the lower courts that involves giving additional protection to the enforcement of foreign and foreign-related arbitral awards. Under this system, it is mandatory to report to and obtain the approval of the SPC regarding any decision that would revoke or deny enforcement of a foreign-related arbitration agreement or award. This development aims to counteract the

[149] There are reports that people's courts in some parts of China denied enforcement of foreign arbitral awards by citing "public policy" grounds simply because the enforcement could endanger the economic interests of a state-owned enterprise. To that extent, it may be argued that "public policy" is a shield behind which the Chinese government could exercise favoritism or local protectionism. See W. Gu, "Public policy under New York Convention: regional development and cooperation in Greater China," *Journal of Comparative Law*, 1 (2010), 90–9.

[150] Civil Procedure Law, Art. 258(2).

[151] Arbitration Law, Art. 58(4).

[152] *Ibid.* Art. 58(5).

[153] D. Brock and K. Sanger, "Legal framework of arbitration" in D. R. Fung and S. C. Wang (eds.), *Arbitration in China: A Practical Guide* (Hong Kong: Sweet & Maxwell, 2003), pp. 25–45.

influence of local protectionism on arbitration enforcement and, hence, to create a pro-enforcement environment for cross-border disputes.[154]

6 Judicial reforms and the changing functions of courts

6.1 *Judicial reforms since 1999*

Since 1999, the SPC has initiated reforms and measures to improve the infrastructure of the Chinese judiciary. One of the key reforms was the Five-Year Reform Plan of the People's Court (1999–2003) (the "First Five-Year Reform Plan"),[155] which focused on elevating the quality of judges through a more depoliticized judge selection system.[156] Subsequent to that, in October 2004, the SPC promulgated the Outline of the Second Five-Year Reform Plan of the People's Court (2004–2008) (the "Second Five-Year Reform Outline").[157]

The Second Five-Year Reform Outline appeared particularly bold in setting out no fewer than fifty objectives for upgrading the Chinese court system. As a whole, the provisions demonstrated a cautious awareness of the importance of increasing the professionalism, independence and integrity of the judiciary; reducing local protectionism; and stamping out corruption; while acknowledging the leadership of the Party and supervision of the courts by people's congresses at each level.[158] With respect to institutional independence, the SPC sought to enhance the autonomy of local people's courts and began to explore the establishment of a *guaranteed financing* system for local courts through the insertion of provisions in central and provincial government budgets.[159] Perhaps the

[154] Gu, *Arbitration in China*, p. 9.

[155] Five-Year People's Courts Reform Plan (Renmin Fayuan Wunian Gaige Gangyao 1999–2003), enclosed in the *Gazette of the SPC (Zhonghuarenmingongheguo Zuigaorenminfayuan Gonggao)* [1999] No. 6, 182–90, available at China Judge Website, http://china.judge.com/fnsx/fnsx386.htm.

[156] In the next five years, all the people's courts must adopt a selection system that requires that the higher court judges be selected from the most-qualified judges of lower courts, or high-performance lawyers, or other high-level legal professionals. Judges who are newly recruited from the recruitment examination should first work for the intermediate people's courts and basic people's courts.

[157] Outline of the Second Five-Year People's Court Reform Plan (Renmin Fayuan Di'erge Wunian Gaige Gangyao 2004–2008), available at www.law-lib.com/law/law_view.asp?id=120832.

[158] For the reassertion of the leadership of the Party and people's congresses, see *ibid.* Part Seven.

[159] *Ibid.* Art. 48.

program's boldest proposal concerned loosening the grip of local power holders over local courts. The SPC called for, "within a certain geographic area, the implementation of a system of *uniform recruitment* and *uniform assignment* of local judges in basic and intermediate courts by the upper level people's courts."[160]

Furthermore, judicial personnel were required to pass the national judicial exam to get qualified (which has been reflected in the amended Judges' Law of 2001 discussed previously). Under the Second Five-Year Reform Outline, judges thenceforth were required to participate in annual judicial training to keep their professional knowledge up to date.[161]

During this same period, opportunities for broader legal training for judges had also been increasing. In particular, in an attempt to respond to the country's accession to the WTO, legal education opportunities in the area of commercial law, particularly international commercial transactions, had begun to be offered in China. For example, since 1999, more than 500 provincial and intermediate-court-level judges have graduated from the Tsinghua-Temple International Business Law LLM program sponsored by the SPC.[162] Local judges from coastal area courts may have more opportunities to study abroad, due to the more developed economies and more liberal administrations of those areas.[163] This supports the findings of better enforcement rates regarding both judgments and arbitral awards in coastal city courts.[164] All of these measures have been seen as important steps in improving the institutionalization and professionalization of the Chinese courts.

However, in March 2009, following a rise in the types of social conflicts that come as a "by-product" of too-rapid economic growth, the SPC published its Third Five-Year Reform Plan of the People's Court (2009–2013) (the "Third Five-Year Reform Plan").[165] As compared with

160 *Ibid.* Art. 37.

161 *Ibid.* Art. 39. The SPC has trained the LHPC judges at the National Judge Institute, and those judges are responsible for training other judges.

162 Source: Ms Huang Ying, a judge from the Shanghai Higher People's Court who has participated in the Tsinghua-Temple LLM program in 2001.

163 For example, the Shenzhen Intermediate People's Court provides a Western legal training program to its judges. Each year since 1998, around fifteen judges have been sent to the University of Hong Kong Law Faculty to study in the Master of Common Law (MCL) program.

164 M. Gechlik, "Judicial reform in China: lessons from Shanghai," *Columbia Journal of Asian Law*, 19 (2005), pp. 122–32.

165 The Third Five-Year People's Court Reform Plan (Renmin Fayuan Di'sange Wunian Gaige Gangyao 2009–2013), available at www.pkulaw.cn.

the first two reform plans, the Third Five-Year Reform Plan places more emphasis on the "mass line."[166] The "mass line" refers to "adjudication for the people" – it encourages the use of mediation and relies on Party leadership and socio-economic conditions in decision-making processes, with the law given secondary consideration.[167] Some authors opined that this court reform agenda would help facilitate social harmony and reflect a distinction of transitional justice, while many others argued that the plan was characterized by "cautiousness" rather than touching on systematic issues under the Party leadership.[168] This seeming reversal in judicial reform policy and the stress placed on a more socialist direction can be analyzed from the perspective of the personal background of the leaders of the Chinese judiciary. When China acceded to the WTO in 2001, most of the presidents of the provincial-level high courts, if not all, had a formal, systematic legal education.[169] The then Chief Justice and President of the SPC, Xiao Yang, had received both a university-level legal education and practical qualifications in law.[170] His successor, Wang Shengjun, who took office in late 2008, had neither formal legal education nor any judicial experience. Wang, who previously worked as a Party Central-Political-Legal-Committee official, was appointed merely based on his political and administrative background.[171] In conjunction with Wang's appointment, the newly appointed presidents of the high courts of a few provinces also took office without any formal legal training.[172] These appointments were highly controversial and were strongly criticized as marking a reversal from the professionalism-building tone of judicial reform set by the Second Five-Year Reform Plan.[173]

The change in the tone of reform reflected by the Third Five-Year Reform Plan also needs to be analyzed and understood in the context of Party policy regarding the judiciary. On 28 November 2008, the Politburo of the Party Central Committee issued its Opinions on Deepening the Reform of the Judicial System and Its Working Mechanisms.[174] This

[166] *Ibid.* s. 1(3). [167] *Ibid.*

[168] See report by Q. Yudong, "Judicial reform: a new round," *Caijing Magazine*, 24 January 2009, available at http://english.caijing.com.cn/2009-01-24/110051303.html.

[169] J. A. Cohen, "Body blow for the judiciary," *South China Morning Post*, 18 October 2008, p. 13.

[170] *Ibid.* [171] *Ibid.* [172] *Ibid.*

[173] J. A. Cohen, "The PRC legal system at sixty," *East Asia Forum*, 1 October 2009.

[174] For a detailed report of the Opinions of the CCP, it is available at the China Legal Information Website, www.law-star.com/zt/zt0216/index.htm. The new trend of judicial reform and its failure to respond to systematic issues raised by the two previous rounds

document did not respond to increasing demands for major systematic reforms as raised by the previous two rounds of SPC reform plans, such as changing the ways in which the judiciary is funded, and judges are appointed, providing the court with more powers of judicial review and eliminating interferences with judicial independence. Instead, the document placed a great deal of emphasis on "Chinese characteristics" and "national conditions" in combination with "popularization of law."[175] Under these overarching themes, the tasks of judicial reform as set out by the Party agenda are to optimize the distribution of judicial functions and powers, balance the strict execution of criminal law with clemency in certain situations, ensure a healthy budget for the people's courts, stress the function of judicial service and achieve flexibility, while ensuring social stability and predictability.[176] In a sense, the development of the Chinese judiciary has closely followed and, moreover, concretized the so-called "Three Supremes" theory advanced by the Party leader Hu Jintao at the end of 2007. According to this theory, Chinese courts and judges should always regard as supreme the leadership of the Party and the interests of the people, as well as the Constitution and laws.[177]

To summarize the trajectory of these judicial reforms over one-and-a-half decades, it seems that the SPC early on introduced quite a few directives aimed at elevating the independence and integrity of the judiciary. It also attempted to provide education opportunities for lower-level judges. Greater independence and better education of judges was expected to generate increased judicial credibility and accountability. Although an optimistic view has been taken by scholars towards the implementation of the very ambitious Second Five-Year Reform Outline, so far, neither the practice of "guaranteed financing" of the courts nor that of "uniform recruitment" of lower level judges has been reported.[178] The Third Five-Year Reform Plan has also failed to touch upon implementation of these measures. As such, the real extent to which these reforms have actually been implemented has yet to be seen.

Insiders will know that these changes in judicial reform policy are actually reflections of the tensions and struggles present in political

of SPC Five-Year reform plans sparked wide-ranging discussions by legal academics and practitioners on that same website in 2009.

175 *Ibid.* 176 *Ibid.*

177 See the speech by Wang Shengjun, to the correlation between the new round of judicial reform and the "Three Supremes" theory advanced by Hu Jintao, available at the China Court Website, http://news.xinhuanet.com/legal/2008-06/23/content_8420938.htm.

178 Gechlik, "Judicial reform in China," p. 87.

reform. It also ties in well with an earlier observation by Professor Jerome A. Cohen, the "Godfather" of Chinese legal studies in the West. He insightfully points out that the political status quo in China does not allow the rapid expansion of judicial power, especially when such an expansion might threaten the primacy of administrative power.[179] This, seen from another perspective, explains the checkered path of Chinese judicial reform during economic and social transitions, as judicial reform has been largely dependent on the country's further political and administrative liberalization. Therefore, more groundbreaking changes need to take place to *empower* the courts and individual judges in the decision-making process. And the success of reform can only be tested according to its actual degree of implementation in practice.

6.2 Court functions

6.2.1 Role of the courts in society

In the course of China's economic and political development, the status of courts has risen significantly, and courts have played an increasingly important role in Chinese society. With deepening marketization, Chinese courts have been increasingly expected to serve as impartial arbiters of civil and commercial disputes among market entities, as well as of administrative law disputes between governmental organs and ordinary citizens. In contrast to the Maoist era, when disputes in economic and social life were resolved by mediation or executive organs, people have increasingly turned to the courts for remedies. The ever-increasing volume of litigation in the courts is testament to the rising consciousness among Chinese citizens of the law and of their rights under the law.

Over the years, the jurisdiction of the courts has expanded, and citizens and their lawyers have increasingly turned to the courts as "fora for the airing of rights-based grievances."[180] The judiciary is being asked to play a larger and more crucial role than in the past. Cases involving class actions, discrimination claims, women's rights and environmental protection have been brought before the courts. In the meantime, public interest litigation as a phenomenon has been born in China.[181] There are signs that lawyers are getting increasingly involved in sensitive policy areas. Lawyers are filing lawsuits against influential corporations for causing environmental

[179] J. A. Cohen, "China's legal reform at the crossroads," *Far Eastern Economic Review*, 2 (2006), 26.

[180] Liebman, "China's courts," 620.

[181] See discussions above in section 3.1, "Legal aid."

pollution, applying for judicial review against powerful government departments, and initiating litigation against the one-child policy and religious regulation. Scholars are of the view that despite its antagonistic stance towards cases involving critical and radical lawyering, the government is tolerant of moderate public interest litigation.[182] Although Chinese law does not formally allow representative litigation, the most recent change to the Civil Procedure Law has developed rules to extend standing to NGOs to litigate in mass torts such as environmental cases.[183] Such litigation has sometimes served to promote policy or legal change, primarily because of the media and public attention generated by the cases.

With Xiao Yang as the former Chief Justice, courts were more receptive to activist lawsuits. However, since Wang Shengjun took office in 2008, more constraints have been placed on legal activism and public interest litigation. Both the Party leadership and the courts themselves have set limits on the role of the courts in this regard, and a leading scholar even identifies a trend or logic of "dejudicialization" in cases that are too politically sensitive or socially controversial for the courts to cope with.[184] Courts have sometimes refused to accept such cases for adjudication. For example, in the "Sanlu tainted milk" case in 2009, which was about the mass product liability concerning melamine contamination in dairy products that affected 300,000 children nationwide, the Central Government decided to settle the case by compensating the children on a one-off basis, thus preventing the courts from exercising their adjudicative power. After claims were filed against Sanlu, the people's courts refused to accept the actions for more than six months, until after Sanlu was declared bankrupt and was subsequently taken over by a dairy producer with state controlling interest, as instructed by the government in order to continue operations. The SPC expressed that courts would not support all the claims filed as it would be more appropriate to use administrative measures to resolve the crisis.[185]

[182] H. Fu and R. Cullen, "The development of public interest litigation in China" in P. J. Yap and H. Lau (eds.), *Public Interest Litigation in Asia* (London: Routledge, 2011), p. 17.

[183] *Ibid.*

[184] This means that the courts may not have the capacity to deal with or may not be the appropriate forum for handling such cases. See R. Peerenboom, "More law, less courts: legalized governance, judicialization, and dejudicialization in China" in T. Ginsburg and A. H. Y. Chen (eds.), *Administrative Law and Governance in Asia* (New York: Routledge, 2009), ch. 9.

[185] X. Zhang, "Civil justice reform with political agendas" in G. Yu (ed.), *The Development of the Chinese Legal System: Change and Challenges* (New York: Routledge, 2011), p. 265.

In this regard, the role of Chinese courts in society, although much more important than before in achieving social justice, is still limited and is perhaps undermined by the political agenda of the Party. Further expansion of the role of the courts in addressing rights-based litigation (including class actions and public interest litigation) would require further empowerment of the courts by the Party.

6.2.2 Perception evaluations

There are studies suggesting that despite the positive general perception of and support for the Chinese courts, with non-users bearing "vague but benevolent notions of the judicial system and its effectiveness,"[186] the minute number of people who have experienced the system first-hand view it negatively.[187] Although economic development serves as a factor that improves popular perceptions of official justice, the practical effect of the judiciary and its recent reforms does not seem to be well appreciated by society. Judicial incompetence and corruption remain major concerns of the general public in China. Even more concerning are those cases in which dissatisfied losing parties in corrupted civil cases have attacked the people's courts with explosives or lethal weapons, reflecting discontentment with the imbalance of power in the system.[188]

The Working Report of the SPC, an important indicator of public satisfaction with judicial work, has in recent years reflected low satisfaction, and it was only in 2010 that the satisfaction rate was slightly improved.[189] In particular, personal experiences with the courts are assessed far more negatively in rural China than in big urban cities such as Beijing or Shanghai.[190] However, since the people with personal experience constituted a small percentage of the population, their evaluation may only have a trivial impact on public perception of the judiciary's performance. On the other hand, some studies point out that older, urban disputants employed in the state sector are more likely to feel disillusioned and powerless, whereas younger, rural disputants employed in the private sector are more likely to have positive evaluations of their judicial experience and to view the judicial

186 M. E. Gallagher and Y. Wang, "Users and non-users: legal experience and its effect on legal consciousness" in M. Woo and M. Gallagher (eds.), *Chinese Justice: Civil Dispute Resolution in Contemporary China* (Cambridge University Press, 2011), p. 204.

187 E. Michelson and B. L. Read, "Public attitudes toward official justice in Beijing and rural China" in Woo and Gallagher (eds.), *Chinese Justice*, p. 170.

188 X. Zhang, "Civil justice reform with political agendas," p. 256.

189 See Annual SPC Report to the NPC (2010).

190 Michelson and Read, "Public attitudes," p. 178.

system as capable of protecting rights.[191] While the older generation would petition before, during and after the civil proceedings and view the judicial system as a last resort, disputants in the younger age group tended to take their cases directly to the court.[192] One possible explanation is that the state sector is more intertwined with the government and political and administrative powers. Hence, corruption is more likely to take place when the court has to protect state interests and social stability.

A disconcerting issue suggested in various studies about perception evaluations of the Chinese judicial system is that people fail to distinguish between substantive (distributive) and procedural justice.[193] When people conflate procedural justice and distributive justice, they are more concerned about substantive outcomes than the fairness of the procedures that lead to those outcomes. This diversion of attention contributes to the disappointment of people and their negative assessment of justice.[194] Accordingly, people in the older generation tend to judge the experience based on distributive outcomes. Even when the law is applied correctly and fairly, procedural matters that obstruct a desired outcome will be considered illegitimate.[195] It has been suggested in some studies that only when people start defining the quality of their experiences in terms of procedural fairness that objective improvements in procedures will positively improve experience-based assessments of official justice in China.[196]

7 Concluding remarks and evaluations: transitional justice

To conclude, it is encouraging that some of the limitations of the Chinese court system have been seriously addressed in the past decade, in particular by the first two rounds of SPC reforms of the people's courts, which were promulgated in response to rising international pressures to establish an independent judiciary in China. Local protectionism and corruption may be mitigated by these SPC directives. The Second Five-Year Reform Outline (2004–2008) appears particularly bold in exploring a number of goals for upgrading the Chinese judicial system. However, the professionalism-building trend of reform of the Chinese courts and judges has been dampened recently, and the publication of the

[191] Gallagher and Wang, "Users and non-users," p. 206. [192] *Ibid.* pp. 225–30.
[193] Michelson and Read, "Public attitudes," p. 171.
[194] *Ibid.* [195] Gallagher and Wang, "Users and non-users," p. 232.
[196] Michelson and Read, "Public attitudes," p. 197.

Third Five-Year Reform Plan (2009–2013) has disappointed many legal scholars and judicial practitioners.

In assessing the development of the judiciary in China, particularly its discourse over the past fifteen years, the international literature on transitional justice, which is concerned with the development of rule of law in transitional political and economic regimes, might be of reference. As Professor Teitel observed, in a transitional period, the law is caught between the past and future, between retrospective and prospective, between the individual and the collective. Accordingly, transitional justice is the justice associated with this context and political circumstances.[197] In a context of political and economic flux, legal adjudication may have to struggle between settled and unsettled rules and ideologies; as a result, the features demonstrated by the judiciary can only be understood as responsive towards transitional economies and politics.[198]

Unlike other transitional economies where judicial justice has been developed to facilitate economic development and political reorientation, in China, the task of maintaining social stability has been assigned to the judiciary. With the rule of law as a developing concept,[199] the judiciary in China as part of the totalitarian regime cannot make decisions without considering their political and social consequences. Despite China's impressive economic growth over the past three decades, reform in China itself is entering a crucial stage in which conflicts caused by distribution inequality, wealth polarization, environmental pollution and labor violations that have accompanied deepening marketization is taking the country to many chaotic societal extremes. In this context, it is believed that any future judicial reform needs to take into account the social reality. Pragmatic compromise will be required to skillfully handle the complexity of political and economic transitions. In a huge developing country such as China, insufficient resources, developing legal institutions and enduring legal culture will all impact the manner of performance of the Chinese judiciary and the pace and ways of its future reform. During the process, the Chinese Party-state faces the pressures of maintaining both social order and regime legitimacy.

Many experts have argued that the Party should liberalize its ideology towards a universal-value-based rule of law (although this has been much

[197] R. G. Teitel, *Transitional Justice* (Oxford University Press, 2000), pp. 1–6.

[198] *Ibid.* p. 220.

[199] The rule-of-law principle was first written into the Constitution in 1999.

challenged as a "Western model" in some recent mainstream Chinese publications),[200] because a weak judiciary and its resulting limited institutionalization of dispute resolution will only undermine the ruling regime's legitimacy.[201] But as some scholars have observed, in China, once disputes are classified as politically sensitive, such as class actions, even those economic-based actions (product liability, derivative action), the attention of the Party will be expected.[202] Even after thirty years of economic and political reform, the Party's influence will still determine, either directly or indirectly, the results of these cases.[203] As such, judicial reform is bound to clash with the political agenda of the Party-state. With limited judicial independence, the judiciary may only carry out its judicial justice within the totalitarian environment, in which justice may not be measured by professional standards, but by social popularity, as the most recent SPC court reform indicates.

It is fair to say that China is still struggling to find the optimal judicial framework, with the Party leadership in a dilemma with respect to the role of the judiciary in Chinese society and governance during transitions. Although it has been strenuously argued that people's courts and individual judges should be significantly *empowered* to play a more active role in adjudication of cases, fundamentally reforming Chinese courts will be a very difficult and complex task that needs an entire rule-of-law system to be put into practice. The rule-of-law process, including the future reform of the Chinese judiciary, is increasingly pushed forward by the more progressive elements in Chinese society to transform towards real safeguarding of justice. In the long run, the trend of more serious judicial reform to support judicial professionalism, independence and efficiency is irreversible.

References

Balme, S. "Local courts in Western China: the quest for independence and dignity" in R. Peerenboom (ed.), *Judicial Independence in China: Lessons for Global Rule of Law Promotion* (Cambridge University Press, 2010), pp. 154–79

200 For example, F. Yizhang, "How to understand the so-called 'universal values,'" *People's Daily (Renmin Ribao)*, 10 September 2008; T. Zhou, "Universal values promoted are actually western values," *Guangming Daily (Guangming Ribao)*, 16 September 2008.

201 R. Peerenboom, "Between global norms and domestic realities: judicial reforms in China" in J. Gillespie and P. Nicolson (eds.), *Law and Development and Global Discourses of Legal Transfers* (Cambridge University Press, 2012), ch. 7.

202 Fu and Cullen, "From mediatory to adjudicatory justice," pp. 25–57.

203 X. Zhang, "Civil justice reform with political agendas," pp. 253–71.

Bian, C. "Thoughts on the reform of the courts," *Science of Law (Falu Kexue)*, 1 (1990), 146–7

Brock, D. and Sanger, K. "Legal framework of arbitration" in D. R. Fung and S. C. Wang (eds.), *Arbitration in China: A Practical Guide* (Hong Kong: Sweet & Maxwell, 2003), pp. 25–45

Brown, F. and Rogers, C. A. "The role of arbitration in resolving transnational disputes: a survey of trends in the People's Republic of China," *Berkeley Journal of International Law*, 15 (1997), 329–51

Chen, A. H. Y. *An Introduction to the Legal System of the People's Republic of China, 4th edn.* (Hong Kong: LexisNexis, 2011)

Chinese Academy of Social Sciences, Institute of Law (ed.), *Three Decades of Rule of Law in China 1978–2008* (Beijing: Social Sciences Academic Press, 2008)

Clarke, D. "Empirical research into the Chinese judicial system" in E. Jensen and T. Heller (eds.), *Beyond Common Knowledge: Empirical Approaches to the Rule of Law* (Stanford University Press, 2003), pp. 164–92

Cohen, J. A. "China's legal reform at the crossroads," *Far Eastern Economic Review*, 2 (2006), 26

Du, X. and Zhang, L. (eds.), *China's Legal System: A General Survey* (Beijing: New World Press, 1990)

Fu, H. "Access to justice in China: potentials, limits, and alternatives" in J. Gillespie and A. H. Y. Chen (eds.), *Legal Reforms in China and Vietnam: A Comparison of Asian Communist Regimes* (New York: Routledge, 2010), pp. 163–87

Fu, H. "Putting China's judiciary into perspective: is it independent, competent and fair?" in E. G. Jensen and T. C. Heller (eds.), *Beyond Common Knowledge: Empirical Approaches to the Rule of Law* (Stanford University Press: 2003), pp. 193–219

Fu, H. and Cullen, R. "From mediatory to adjudicatory justice: the limits of civil justice reform in China" in M. Y. W. Woo and M. E. Gallagher (eds.), *Chinese Justice: Civil Dispute Resolution in Contemporary China* (Cambridge University Press, 2011), pp. 25–57

Fu, H. and Cullen, R. "The development of public interest litigation in China" in P. J. Yap and H. Lau (eds.), *Public Interest Litigation in Asia* (London: Routledge, 2011), pp. 9–34

Gallagher, M. E. and Wang, Y. "Users and non-users: legal experience and its effect on legal consciousness" in M. Y. W. Woo and M. E. Gallagher (eds.), *Chinese Justice: Civil Dispute Resolution in Contemporary China* (Cambridge University Press, 2011), pp. 204–33

Gechlik, M. "Judicial reform in China: lessons from Shanghai," *Columbia Journal of Asian Law*, 19 (2005), 122–32

Gu, W. *Arbitration in China: Regulation of Arbitration Agreements and Practical Issues* (Hong Kong: Sweet & Maxwell, 2012)

Gu, W. "Judicial review over arbitration in China: assessing the extent of the latest pro-arbitration move by the Supreme People's Court in the People's Republic of China," *Wisconsin International Law Journal*, 27(2) (2009), 222–69

Gu, W. "Public policy under New York Convention: regional development and cooperation in Greater China," *Journal of Comparative Law (Bijiaofa Yanjiu)*, 1 (2010), 90–9

Gu, W. "The judiciary in economic and political transformation: *Quo vadis* Chinese courts?" *Chinese Journal of Comparative Law*, 1(2) (2013), 303–34

Hu, X. and Feng, P. (eds.), *Research on Judicial Justice and Judicial Reform* (Beijing: Tsinghua University Press, 2001)

Inoue, T. "Introduction to international commercial arbitration in China," *Hong Kong Law Journal*, 36 (2006), 171–96

LaKritz, R. M. "Taming a 5,000 year-old dragon: toward a theory of legal development in post-Mao China," *Emory International Law Review*, 11 (1997), 237–66

Li, Y. "Court reformation in China: problems, progress and prospects" in J. Chen, Y. Li and J. M. Otto (eds.), *Implementation of Law in the People's Republic of China* (The Hague: Kluwer Law International, 2002), pp. 55–84

Li, Y. "The law-making law: a solution to the problems in the Chinese legislative system?" *Hong Kong Law Journal*, 30 (2000), 120–40

Liebman, B. "China's courts: restricted reform," *The China Quarterly*, 191 (2007), 620–38

Lin, L. "Judicial independence in Japan: a re-investigation for China," *Columbia Journal of Asian Law*, 13 (1999), 199

Lubman, S. *Bird in a Cage: Legal Reform in China after Mao* (California: Stanford University Press, 1999)

Michelson, E. and Read, B. L. "Public attitudes toward official justice in Beijing and rural China" in M. Y. W. Woo and M. E. Gallagher (eds.), *Chinese Justice: Civil Dispute Resolution in Contemporary China* (Cambridge University Press, 2011), pp. 169–203

Minzner, C. "The rise and fall of Chinese legal education," *Fordham International Law Journal*, 36(2) (2013), 334–96

Mo, S. *Arbitration Law in China* (Hong Kong: Sweet & Maxwell Asia, 2001)

Peerenboom, R. "Between global norms and domestic realities: judicial reforms in China" in J. Gillespie and P. Nicholson (eds.), *Law and Development and Global Discourses of Legal Transfers* (Cambridge University Press, 2012), pp. 181–201

Peerenboom, R. (ed.), *China's Long March toward Rule of Law* (New York: Cambridge University Press, 2002)

Peerenboom, R. (ed.) *Judicial Independence in China: Lessons for Global Rule of Law Promotion* (Cambridge University Press, 2009)

Peerenboom, R. "More law, less courts: legalized governance, judicialization, and dejudicialization in China" in T. Ginsburg and A. H. Y. Chen (eds.), *Administrative Law and Governance in Asia* (New York: Routledge, 2009), pp. 175–201

Potter, P. "Legal reform in China: institutions, culture and selective adaptation," *Law & Social Inquiry*, 29 (2004), 465–95

Qin, X. "Calling for judicial reform," *China Reform Magazine (Zhongguo Gaige)*, (2010), 90: 316

Reinstein, E. "Finding a happy ending for foreign investors: the enforcement of arbitration awards in the People's Republic of China," *Indiana International and Comparative Law Review*, 16 (2005) 37

Tao, J. (ed.), *Arbitration Law and Practice in China*, 2nd edn. (The Hague: Kluwer Law International, 2008)

Teitel, R. G. *Transitional Justice* (Oxford University Press, 2000)

Wang, A. and Cao, J. "Environmental courts and the development of environmental public interest litigation in China," *Journal of Court Innovation*, 3 (2010), 38–9

Yuan, A. "Enforcing and collecting money judgments in China from a U.S. creditor's perspective," *George Washington International Law Review*, 36 (2004), 757–82

Zhang, X. "Legal issues concerning the mutual enforcement of arbitral awards between the Hong Kong SAR and mainland China," *Arbitration and Law Journal (Zhongcai yu Falu)*, 2 (2002), 26–53

Zhang, X. "Civil justice reform with political agendas" in G. Yu (ed.), *The Development of the Chinese Legal System: Change and Challenges* (New York: Routledge, 2011), pp. 253–71

Zhao, D. (ed.), *Lectures on the Law on Judges* (Beijing: People's Court Press, 1995)

Zhu, J. *China Legal Statistics Report* (Beijing: China Renmin University Press, 2007)

15

Renovating courts: the role of courts in contemporary Vietnam

PIP NICHOLSON

Constitutionally Vietnamese courts are both legal and political institutions. They are caught in a web of conflicting demands and expectations: reflecting, at least in part, the Party-state court-focused "renovation" strategies. This chapter offers a story of court/institution building in the Socialist Republic of Vietnam since 1945. Critical to this tale are the ways in which contemporary conflicts about judicial power (*quyền tư pháp*) in Vietnam are understood. I suggest that the Vietnamese courts are rapidly undergoing substantial reform, including escalating self-management, but remain Party controlled and directed, in an environment where the ultimate reform trajectory remains unclear and contested.

At the outset it is important to note that this is a partial reading offered by an outsider. My reading of court development in Vietnam may be quite different from that offered by Vietnamese scholars. However, one of the advantages of writing as an outsider on Vietnamese courts is the freedom to note how Party-state authority has enabled and constrained court development. Vietnamese scholars cannot necessarily be confident of publicly having the same license.

This analysis is structured in seven sections: each contributing to the mosaic of influences and expectations now impacting Vietnamese court operations. Section 1 outlines the history of the courts since 1945. Section 2 closely analyzes the courts' work over a ten-year period, followed in section 3 with a profile of courts, looking particularly at judicial appointments, independence and access to courts. Section 4 looks at sources of law, styles of judicial decisions and the politics of judging, while section 5 notes the

The author acknowledges the support of Australian Research Council Grant DPO880036 in the development of this paper. She also thanks Do Hai Ha and Samantha Hinderling for their excellent research assistance.

Please note that, throughout this article, names have been used following Vietnamese name-order: family name, middle names, first name.

escalating importance of alternative dispute resolution as a means of escaping the hybrid political-legal courts. Section 6 considers current influences on Vietnamese courts. In section 7, the courts are projected as both political and legal institutions by the Party-state with mixed signals about their reform trajectory and divergent stakeholders advocating different reform agendas.

1 Introducing the Vietnamese judicial system

There is not one Vietnamese court history. During 1945–1975 the people of Vietnam were involved in a devastating war that divided the country and produced two court systems. These divergent court systems were, in turn, built on different colonial legacies. In the northern Democratic Republic of Vietnam ("DRVN") a Soviet-inspired court system was constructed, although it did not mirror the Soviet system, which was built on very different roots.[1] Meanwhile, in the south of the country the French and then the Americans supported legal education and court-related reforms, working with the French colonial legacy, established during the period of French sovereignty in Cochinchina (1875–1954).[2]

More particularly, a system of people's courts, modeled on the Soviet system, was introduced in 1959 in the DRVN.[3] In the period 1945–1959, the northern courts were largely ad hoc, with a rudimentary attempt to systematize courts given the pressures of war. The courts of the 1960s, whether mobile or more formal, emphasized popular justice. The Party-state explicitly eschewed formal legal reasoning, exhorting the functionaries to deliver the ideals of the revolution in their decisions. If laws were not promulgated, judges were advised to adopt moral reasoning or give effect to current political ideology. Writing in 1974 then-judge Le Kim Que explains northern courts: "At present the people's courts only apply the new laws of the people's power. In the event of there being no legislative text they follow the principle of analogy or simply the general political line of the revolution."[4]

The most obvious example of the political role of courts was the short-lived introduction of the land courts/tribunals between 1953 and

1 P. Nicholson, *Borrowing Court Systems: The Experience of Socialist Vietnam*, London-Leiden Series on Law, Administration and Development (Leiden: Martinus Nijhoff, 2007).

2 *Ibid.* at pp. 211–22. See also, M. Osborn, *The French Presence in Cochinchina and Cambodia* (New York: Cornell University Press, 1969); Ministry of Justice and Legal Administration Branch USAID, *The Legal System of the Republic of Viet-Nam* (unofficial translation) (Saigon: Ministry of Justice, 1967).

3 Nicholson, *Borrowing Court Systems*, pp. 37–113.

4 Le Kim Que, "The people's courts" in *An Outline of the Institutions of the Democratic Republic of Vietnam* (Hanoi: Gioi Publishers, 1974), p. 99.

1956.[5] These were travelling courts introduced by the Communist Party of Vietnam ("CPV") to implement the redistribution of property and concurrently the eradication of political opponents (either through execution or long periods of political detention in now infamous jails) of the new regime.[6] Seen as arbitrary and brutal by their detractors, and not widely endorsed by the new regime's supporters, these courts were abandoned after just three years. Arguably, this tumultuous period produced distrust of the Ho Chi Minh-led government's arbitrary court decisions.

With the establishment of the Socialist Republic of Vietnam, after the defeat of the US-led allies in 1975, a divided Vietnam was unified. The post-war period saw the export of the northern socialist court system, established after the 1954 defeat of the French, south.

Vietnam today has a socialist legal system in which the CPV assumes the leadership of the state and society and functions as the vanguard of the Vietnamese working class and the whole nation under the teaching of Marxism-Leninism and Ho Chi Minh's thought (Article 4, 1992 Constitution). The CPV leads and manages the state, particularly its political, legal and economic reform. Political stability, economic growth and cautious incremental legal reforms are integral to Party-state reforms.[7]

There has been a series of legal reforms. In 1991, the CPV announced at the Communist Party's Seventh National Congress that it would introduce a socialist law-based state (*nhà nước pháp quyền xã hội chủ nghĩa*), based on Party leadership.[8] The doctrines of Party leadership and people's sovereignty, manifest through the supremacy of the National Assembly, which oversees the work of other state bodies, including courts, are set out in the 1992 Constitution.[9]

[5] Nicholson, *Borrowing Court Systems*, pp. 67–70; Pham Quang Ming, "Caught between tradition and modernization: local cadres in Hai Duong Province in the Renovation Period," Vietnam Update Conference, 28–29 November 2002, Canberra (paper on file with author).

[6] *Ibid.* at pp. 67–70; Bui Tin, *Following Ho Chi Minh*, translated by J. Stowe and V. Do (Bathurst: Crawford Publishing, 1995).

[7] Resolution No: 56/2006/QH11, SRVN Five-year Socio-Economic Plan, July 2006, Recommendation 11.

[8] J. Gillespie, "Concepts of law in Vietnam: transforming statist socialism" in R. Peerenboom (ed.), *Asian Discourses of the Rule of Law* (London: Routledge, 2004), pp. 146–82; Nicholson, *Borrowing Court Systems*, pp. 243–47; SRVN Constitution 1992, Art. 4.

[9] To Van Hoa, *Judicial Independence: A Legal Research on its Theoretical Aspects, Practices from Germany, the United States of America, France, Vietnam, and Recommendations for Vietnam* (Lund: Jüristforlaget i Lund, 2006), pp. 366–70. Commentators debate the unification of powers doctrine today: J. Gillespie, "The juridification of state regulation in Vietnam" in J. Gillespie and A. Chen (eds.), *Legal Reform in China and Vietnam: A Comparison of Asian Communist Regimes* (New York: Routledge, 2010), pp. 78–102.

Essentially, the one-party state has produced a unitary court system currently comprising a hierarchy of three court levels: district, provincial and central. To date, there are economic/commercial, civil, administrative, labor, family and criminal courts, appeals from all of which culminate in the Supreme People's Court (*Tòa án Nhân dân Tối Cao Việt Nam*), which sits at the apex of this system. The system of military courts, which today exists to try matters involving military personnel, is essentially independent of the civil court system comprising a hierarchy of central, regional and area military courts. At the central level, the Chief Judge of the Central Military Court is also a Deputy Chief Justice of the Supreme People's Court.[10] While a constitutional court system has been discussed, it is not likely that such a court will be introduced in Vietnam over the short term; nor is the introduction of Constitutional Council likely.[11]

Characterizing the court system in this way belies the diversity of courts and the divergent experience of dispute resolution they offer. Stark differences exist between urban, rural and mountainous courts, between district and provincial courts, and between courts in the north and the south.[12]

2 Courts in profile

2.1 Court reform

In April 2002, shortly after the publication of internal Communist Party Resolution 8, four fundamental court reforms were initiated. First, the new law revamped the qualifications required of staff. From 2002, judges were required to have a Bachelor of Laws degree, legal experience and completed adjudication training.[13] In 2006, it is suggested 80 percent of judges met this requirement.[14]

[10] Supreme People's Court, *Court System of the Socialist Republic of Vietnam* (Hanoi: Labour Publishing House, 2009), pp. 34–9.

[11] Gillespie, "Juridification of state regulation," pp. 83–9. Gillespie explains some people are now "smuggling" new ideas through invoking Ho Chi Minh and arguing that the revered leader was a champion of "rule of law spirit." That said, the proposed Constitutional Council was rejected in 2013 during the Constitutional Consultations.

[12] UNDP, *Report on the Survey of Needs of District People's Courts Nationwide* (Hanoi: Justice Publishing House, 2007). See also UNDP, *Report on the Survey of the Reality of Local Court Governance in Vietnam* (2013).

[13] Law on the Organization of People's Courts, 06/20002/L/CTN, 2002, Art. 37. Given that the courts did not receive enough applicants that met this requirement, it was also possible to be appointed if the appointee committed to legal training. See Resolution 131/2002/NQ-UBTVQH11 On Judges, People's Assessors and Prosecutors, 3 November 2002 and Joint Circular No. 01/2011/TTLT/TANDTC-BQP-BNV, dated 20 October 2011. See also P. Nicholson and Nguyen Hung Quang, "The Vietnamese judiciary: the politics of appointment and promotion," *Pacific Rim Law and Policy Journal*, 14(1) (2005), 1–34.

[14] UNDP, *District Courts Survey*, p. 49.

Second, the system by which judges and people's assessors were appointed and dismissed was changed. Rather than having all judges appointed by political institutions, a new hybrid system of appointment involving the courts and political institutions was introduced for most courts. More particularly, all judicial appointments to and dismissals from district and provincial courts were to be made by the Chief Justice of the SPC, on the advice of Judicial Selection Councils. SPC judges and the Chief Justice remained as appointments of the National Assembly.[15] People's assessors were to be elected by the Local People's Councils, but on the recommendation of the relevant branch of the Vietnam Fatherland Front.[16] Further, people's assessors can be dismissed by the relevant Chief Justice if he or she has the agreement of the relevant Vietnam Fatherland Front committee.[17]

Third, the connection between the courts and the Ministry of Justice, which had previously managed all budgets, was to be severed. From 2002, the SPC would apply to the National Assembly for the court budget.[18] Similarly, court staffing needs would be submitted by the Chief Justice to the Standing Committee of the National Assembly, which would determine staffing levels.[19] The department within the Ministry of Justice charged with court budgets was moved across to the SPC and continued its work on court budgets, albeit now reporting to the Chief Justice rather than the Ministry of Justice.[20]

Fourth, the court was to improve technology to assist the courts to do their work.[21] There have been many technology-based innovations. In Ho Chi Minh City there is an advanced electronic case management system, which, while apparently not replicated in Hanoi, has been taken up in other provinces.[22] Recently, limited publication of cassational review (*giám đốc thẩm*) judgments has also taken place, alongside the development of an SPC portal disseminating materials including the Bench Book, Court Clerks' Manual, legislation and cassational judgments.[23]

15 Law on the Organization of People's Courts, 2002, Arts. 25 and 40. 16 *Ibid.* Art. 41.
17 *Ibid.* 18 *Ibid.* Art. 44. 19 *Ibid.* Art. 42(1).
20 UNDP, *Local Court Governance Survey*, pp. 65–9 for a detailed discussion of budgets in local courts.
21 Law on the Organization of People's Courts, 2002, Art. 46.
22 UNDP, *Local Court Governance Survey*, p. 74 reports that the District Court of Vinh Long has adopted case management software and that the District Court of Da Nang also has plans to develop software.
23 UNDP, *Local Court Governance Survey*, p. 90. See P. Nicholson, "Access to justice in Vietnam: state supply – public distrust" in J. Gillespie and A. Chen (eds.), *Legal*

In many ways the 2002 reforms introduced great aspirations for court development. Yet, the implementation of the reforms has been uneven. Local people's committees have largely retained their influence over courts.[24] While the court budget is now approved by the National Assembly, this is not a fundamental shift from Party-state power, as the National Assembly remains controlled by the CPV. However, there has been an increase in court independence from the Ministry of Justice, although this is not to be confused with an increase in court independence from Party structures. There has been an uneven response to the challenges of introducing technology, perhaps reflecting competency and funds available to courts from provincial government budgets.[25] It is also suggested that the varying north/south practices reflect different north/south judicial attitudes to transparency and public access to court records, although this may be lessening.

Since 2002 the Party-state has made further statements about reform. Of most significance is the publication in 2005 of CPV Resolutions 48 (on legal reform) and 49 (on judicial reform). These Resolutions set out a more ambitious set of reform aspirations.

> To overhaul judicial procedures to make them more democratic, equal, open, transparent and consistent as well as more accessible; to ensure public participation and supervision of judicial activities . . .[26]

To cast these Resolutions as calling of the rule of law (however defined) is to misinterpret them. They set out a series of reform aspirations,

Development in East Asia: China and Vietnam Compared (London, Routledge, 2010), pp. 188–215. See also Toà Án Nhân Dân Tối Cao (2008) *Quyết Định Giám Đốc Thẩm Của Hội Đồng Thẩm Phán Tòa Án Nhân Dân Tối Cao 2006*, Hanoi (Supreme People's Court (2008) *Cassational Review Decisions of the Supreme People's Court Justice Council 2006*); Toà Án Nhân Dân Tối Cao (2008) *Quyết Định Giám Đốc Thẩm Của Hội Đồng Thẩm Phán Tòa Án Nhân Dân Tối Cao 2005*, Hanoi (Supreme People's Court (2008) *Cassational Review Decisions of the Supreme People's Court Justice Council 2005*); Toà Án Nhân Dân Tối Cao (2004) *Quyết Định Giám Đốc Thẩm Của Hội Đồng Thẩm Phán Tòa Án Nhân Dân Tối Cao 2003–2004, Quyển 1 va 2*, Hanoi (Supreme People's Court (2004) *Cassational Review Decisions of the Supreme People's Court Justice Council 2003–2004, vols. I and II*).

24 UNDP, *District Courts Survey*, pp. 208–9. See also UNDP, *Local Court Governance Survey*. It is alleged that the ongoing role of people's assessors elected by the local government undermines court independence.

25 Interview by the author in Ho Chi Minh City in 2007 suggesting that the Ho Chi Minh City Provincial People's Committee supported local court development of a case management system.

26 Resolution No. 48, p. 22. See also Resolution No. 49; Resolution No. 8; Resolution No. 900. See also Conclusion No. 92-KL/TW of the Politburo dated 12 March 2104.

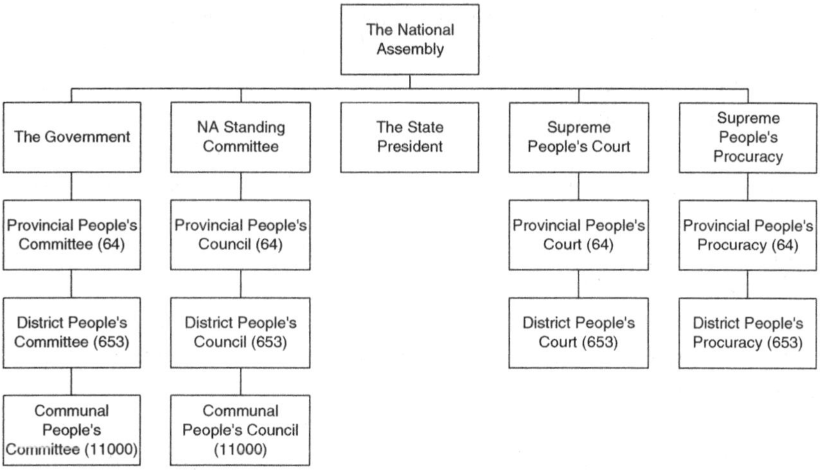

Figure 15.1: Vietnamese institutional map

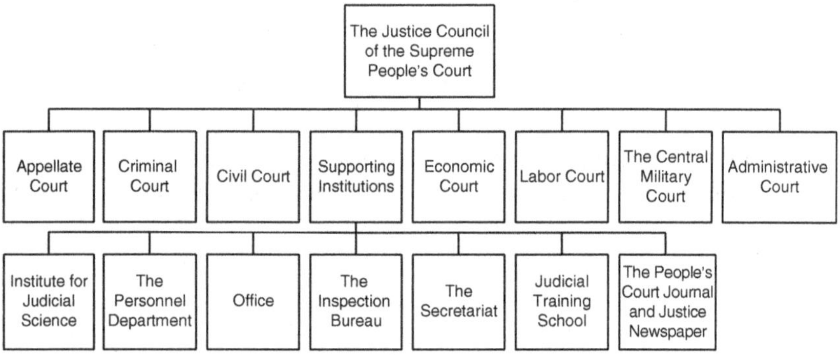

Figure 15.2: Vietnamese court institutions

including clearer demarcation of power between leading legal institutions such as courts, police and procuracy and as between courts and local government. Yet the call to reform remains largely rhetorical while large questions of policy, while debated, are not determined.

2.2 Courts across Vietnam

Across Vietnam there are 720 courts. Of these there are 3 Supreme People's Courts (Hanoi pre-eminent), 64 provincial courts and 653 district courts. Essentially the Vietnamese court system comprises a range of specialist courts at provincial and Supreme Court level, with trials originating in either the district (where the judges have to be able to work across diverse jurisdictions as there are no separate courts) or provincial courts. The system assumes two adjudicative levels: first instance trials and appeals with cases commenced in particular courts according to jurisdictional limits. The SPC offers cassational review (*giám đốc thẩm*). This involves either review of an error of law or a review on the basis of newly discovered facts.[27] The relationship with the National Assembly is set out below.

Put briefly, the Criminal Procedure Code 2003 provides that district courts should handle most criminal trials except where issues of national security, disruption of the peace, war crimes and crimes involving human lives are involved.[28] The pre-existing law gave district courts jurisdiction in matters where the maximum penalty was seven years and no foreigners were involved. The transitional provisions were to have seen all courts migrate to the new jurisdiction by 1 July 2009.[29]

In 2004, the jurisdiction of the district economic, civil and labor courts was also extended in some districts.[30] The Civil Procedure Code 2004 provided that in civil and family cases the jurisdiction of the district courts was unlimited where the changes were adopted, excluding those cases where a foreign judgment is involved.[31] District courts were given authority to determine all types of economic cases, with the exception of those related to transport, stocks, financial investment, banking, oil and gas, and operations of enterprises. This is a major change from the previous jurisdictional limit in economic cases of VND 50 million.[32]

Since 2005 there have been several plans to revamp court structure.[33] The reform was proposed to sever or reduce the connection between locality and court. The proponents of the change argued that by introducing new regional courts (comprising one or more administrative units) to hear district court appeals and some first instance trials) and three

[27] Law on the Organization of People's Courts, 2002, Art. 20.

[28] Criminal Procedure Code, 2003, Art. 170(1).

[29] Resolution of the Standing Committee of the National Assembly, No. 1036/2006/NQ-UBTVQH11, dated 27 July 2006.

[30] Resolution of the Standing Committee of the National Assembly 2006. This Resolution provides that, in 2006, 267 courts would continue to exercise "old" jurisdiction in civil, labor and economic matters as these courts did not have the staff to give effect to the changes. The transitional period was slated to end on 1 July 2009.

[31] UNDP, *District Courts Survey*, pp. 199–201. [32] *Ibid.*

[33] Resolution No. 49, 2005. See also UNDP, *Local Court Governance Survey*, pp. 99–100.

superior courts (again organized regionally and not reflecting existing administrative structures), the state would enable less influenced decision-making. The Supreme People's Court, it was suggested, would only hear cassational cases, devoting its expertise to guiding lower courts and developing jurisprudence. This reform aimed to break the budgetary hold on local courts by District and Provincial People's Committees and to cauterize People's Committees' hold on the appointment of judges and election of people's assessors, limiting influence on decisions. A limited pilot of this new arrangement has only been trialed to date.

While the mooted structural reform has not been realized, the numbers of court staff have increased. In 2006, of the 10,975 court staff 4,141 were judges.[34] The 2006 general report also indicates that the courts need 1,354 further staff, including a further 928 judges.[35] In 2008, the numbers of judges and court staff increased to 4,359 and 11,535 respectively.[36] Therefore, while the shortfall of judges has been marginally reduced (from 928 to 710), there are still, according to the Supreme People's Court, many courts understaffed. This has produced reports of the overwork of judges.[37]

Reflecting more broadly on the number of judges per head of the population, we see that there has been a marginal increase in a three-year period. As of 2006, there were, on average, approximately 0.0497 judges per 100,000 inhabitants.[38] In 2008, this ratio slightly increased to approximately 0.0512.[39]

The numbers of cases going to court in Vietnam have steadily increased in recent years. Over the four-year period 2005–9 there was an increase of

[34] SPC, *Báo cáo Tổng kết Công tác năm 2006 và Phương hướng Nhiệm vụ Công tác năm 2007 của Ngành Tòa án Nhân dân* (Report on the Performance of People's Courts in 2006 and their Task Orientations in 2007) (hereinafter "*2006 SPC Report*"), pp. 12–13.

[35] *2006 SPC Report*, p. 18. See also UNDP, *District Courts Survey*, which notes the shortfall of district court judges, pp. 210–11.

[36] SPC, *Báo cáo Tổng kết Công tác năm 2008 và Phương hướng Nhiệm vụ Công tác năm 2009 của Ngành Tòa án Nhân dân* (Report on the Performance of People's Courts in 2008 and their Task Orientations in 2009) (hereinafter "*2008 SPC Report*"), p. 12.

[37] In the years 2001–5 the SPC Annual Reports noted the number of unsettled cases. The 2005 report suggests 10 percent of all cases filed were not settled or 23,230 cases. It also notes this creates a heavy judicial workload. See UNDP, *District Courts Survey*, pp. 210–11.

[38] As mentioned, there were 4,141 judges in 2006. It is estimated by the GSO that Vietnam's 2006 population was 83,311,200 (www.gso.gov.vn/default.aspx?tabid=387&idmid=3&ItemID=11504).

[39] To recall, the number of judges was 4,359 judges in 2008. It is estimated by the GSO that Vietnam's 2008 population was 85,118,700 (www.gso.gov.vn/default.aspx?tabid=387&idmid=3&ItemID=11504).

just over 50,000 cases, an increase from 242,853 cases in 2005 to 295,986 in 2009. If we compare this with case numbers from the early 2000s we see a marked increase. In 2001, there were 191,835 cases accepted by the courts across all jurisdictions.[40] In effect, we see an increase of 104,151 cases over an eight-year period, as noted a steady increase and an increase of roughly 35 percent. At first blush this certainly suggests an increased interest in the courts as an institution relevant to the resolution of disputes.

However, there is uneven growth in case numbers across the different jurisdictions (see Table 15.1). There is almost no administrative or labor litigation in Vietnam, despite these courts having been introduced in 1996. The number of civil cases is quite stable between nearly 90,000 and 106,000 over a four-year period and no indication that the trend is rapidly increasing. It appears that there is a slow increase in criminal cases brought annually, arguably reflecting the population increases.[41] There is, however, a steady increase in the number of commercial cases filed at the economic court, established in 1994. While the increase is not voluminous, there is a suggestion of increased use, perhaps suggesting forum testing.[42] There is also steady growth in family cases. This may reflect a gradual decrease in the stigma associated with family breakdown and divorce and/or an increase in property claims.

However, the increase in case numbers needs to be assessed in terms of population growth. There is no net growth in criminal cases when viewed against Vietnamese population growth with 91.7 cases per 100,000 of the population in 1999 to 93.1 in 2009.[43] While there is an increase in the number of civil cases, it is small, from 114.4 cases per 100,000 in 1999 to 123.3 cases in 2009.[44] There is a marked increase in the number of economic cases over time per 100,000 of the population, from two cases in 1999 to ten in 2009.[45]

[40] Note the decrease in total numbers of cases accepted by the Vietnamese court between 1999 and 2001. This is discussed at Nicholson, *Borrowing Court Systems*, pp. 206–62.

[41] Analysis of criminal case numbers per 100,000 of the population over the period 1999–2009 reveals no increase.

[42] P. Nicholson and Minh Duong, "Legitimacy and the Vietnamese economic courts" in A. Harding and P. Nicholson (eds.), *New Courts in Asia* (London: Routledge, 2010), pp. 31–55.

[43] Source for population numbers: data from World Bank as displayed on www.google.com.au/publicdata/explore?ds=d5bncppjof8f9_&met_y=sp_pop_totl&idim=country:VNM&dl=en&hl=en&q=vietnam+population#!ctype=l&strail=false&bcs=d&nselm=h&met_y=sp_pop_totl&scale_y=lin&ind_y=false&rdim=region&idim=country:VNM&ifdim=region&tstart=793890000000&tend=1267275600000&hl=en&dl=en.

[44] *Ibid.* [45] *Ibid.*

Table 15.1: *Case numbers from all jurisdictions*

Year	1999	2000	2001	2002	2004	2005	2006	2007	2008	2009	2010
Economic	1,514	1,174	884	958	1,051	1,495	2,865	4,973	6,170	8,628	
Labor	665	762	967	976	844	1,129	1,043	1,275	1,907	1,990	
Admin	471	913	1,172	1,595	1,746	1,361	1,232	1,686	1,401	1,557	
Civil*	87,641	70,003	69,311	73,423	142,260	142,696	150,195	89,114	105,358	100,629	106,087
Family	55,366	53,968	59,573	63,140				71,865	77,561	83,856	97,620
Criminal	70,248	65,015	62,897	61,478	67,458	71,268	69,048	76,734	77,198	79,211	80,104

Source: Annual SPC reports for the years 1999–2010.

As Table 15.1 demonstrates, the economic court has demonstrated the greatest caseload increase in the current period. Over the ten-year period 1999–2009, total cases (including appeals and reviews) have increased by 569 percent, a five-fold increase in the number of economic cases heard overall. The number of trials has increased by 606 percent. The low ebb of economic cases in 2001 and 2002 is generally attributed to the lack of certainty about economic court jurisdiction that had become a well-recognized bar to effective use of the court in the six years after its introduction.[46]

Table 15.1 makes plain the divergent take-up of new courts in Vietnam. While the economic court has low overall case numbers in a country of over eighty million people, it has experienced substantial and sustained growth compared with the administrative and labor court use rates. There is commentary suggesting that formal labor law dispute resolution is low. The argument is that there has been little penetration of the new 2006 and 2012 Labor Code as a result of the lack of fit between the historical management of labor disputes and the new law and the use of ad hoc committees instead of courts.[47] In the case of administrative law, the explanation lies in lack of judicial independence, limited scope of juridical review of administrative action under Vietnamese law and lack of rules setting out judicial review processes.[48]

2.3 Clearance/congestion rates[49]

Courts have divergent clearance rates. The criminal court has the most consistently high clearance rate, hovering over 97 percent per year over the period 2006–9. This is followed by the family court with an average clearance rate of 94.15 percent over the same period. The civil and commercial courts have both improved their resolution rates from 2006 to 2009 from 85.98 percent to 87.43 percent and from 79.37 percent to 86.82 percent respectively. The percentage of cases where a plea of guilty is entered is said to be high, no doubt assisting the criminal court

46 Nicholson, *Borrowing Court Systems*, pp. 262–63.

47 Do Hai Ha, "Confirmation Report," Doctoral Studies Program, Melbourne Law School, 2011. See also Chang-Hee Lee, *Industrial Relations and Dispute Settlement in Vietnam* (ILO Office in Vietnam, 2006), cited by Do Hai Ha.

48 Nguyen Van Quang, "A comparative study of the systems of review of administrative action by courts and tribunals in Australia and Vietnam" (unpublished PhD thesis) (Latrobe University, 2007), p. 1.

49 The data discussed in this section is drawn from the SPC reports 2006–9. The data reflects estimates, on the bases of statistics within these reports.

clearance rate. Also, the law in criminal cases is relatively settled, when compared with the new law that applies in, for example, economic and labor cases. A relatively large number of family court cases are also resolved. When considering these together, it suggests that the stability of the law in these jurisdictions may support the high clearance rate. More particularly, it suggests the mix of law and ethics invoked to determine cases has not greatly altered, resulting in little review or appeal of earlier court decisions. Relatively newer jurisdictions (administrative and commercial) or jurisdictions where new laws have become operable (such as civil) have lower clearance rates. Labor law is an outlier here as it has high clearance rates despite substantial changes to the Labor Code. The low case numbers may explain this.

2.4 *Duration of cases*

There is limited statistical data explaining or reporting on the duration of cases. However, the courts' failure to comply with time limits prescribed by law is frequently noted in the SPC's annual reports.[50] It is estimated that more than 1,000 cases were not resolved within prescribed time limits in 2008 and 2009.[51] The SPC reports also suggest that it was civil cases where most of the lags occurred.[52] Problems also arose in connection with administrative,[53] business/commercial[54] and family[55] cases. Reportedly, criminal cases were largely settled within the prescribed time period.[56] The reports also suggest a correlation between the complexity of cases and incapacity to try and determine a case according to the legally stipulated time periods. More particularly, the majority of cases

[50] See *2006 SPC Report*, p. 2; SPC, *Báo cáo Tổng kết Công tác năm 2007 và Phương hướng Nhiệm vụ Công tác năm 2008 của Ngành Tòa án Nhân dân* (*Report on the Performance of People's Courts in 2007 and their Task Orientations in 2008*) (hereinafter "*2007 SPC Report*"), p. 6; SPC, *2008 SPC Report*, p. 15; SPC, *Báo cáo Tổng kết Công tác năm 2009 và Phương hướng Nhiệm vụ Công tác năm 2010 của Ngành Tòa án Nhân dân* (*Report on the Performance of People's Courts in 2009 and their Task Orientations in 2010*) (hereinafter "*2009 SPC Report*"), p. 15. This estimate is confirmed by the UNDP, Local Court Governance Survey, p. 38.

[51] *2008 SPC Report*, p. 15; *2009 SPC Report*, p. 15.

[52] *2009 SPC Report*, p. 15. See also *2006 SPC Report*, p. 15; *2007 SPC Report*, p. 6; *2008 SPC Report*, p. 15.

[53] *2006 SPC Report*, p. 15. [54] *2007 SPC Report*, p. 6; *2009 SPC Report*, p. 15.

[55] *2009 SPC Report*, p. 15.

[56] *2006 SPC Report*, p. 2; *2007 SPC Report*, p. 4; *2008 SPC Report*, p. 4.

not completed within time were in localities that had large and complicated caseloads, such as Hanoi, Ho Chi Minh City and Lam Dong.[57]

2.5 *Cancellation and revision of decisions*

The statistics on cases in which the judgment of a lower court is cancelled or revised by a higher court are hard to disaggregate as data on civil cases includes family, commercial and labor cases for the period 2007–9, and are variously reported before that. However, between 2007 and 2008, the overall rates of cancellation and revision of decisions averaged 1.15 percent and 3.82 percent respectively.[58] The data suggests that civil cases are not cancelled by the SPC. That suggests that the cases brought as civil cases commence in the right jurisdiction and are taken by appropriate parties. In that jurisdiction, however, cases are revised at very roughly the same level of cases as administrative cases, but again without knowing the breakdown between civil, labor, family and commercial cases revised, the data remains unhelpful. The criminal jurisdiction has the greatest number of revised cases and the least number of cancelled cases. In 2009, for example, 4.21 percent of criminal judgments were revised and 0.71 percent cancelled, compared to administrative judgments with 4.77 percent revised and 6.92 percent cancelled.[59]

2.6 *Compliance with decisions*

While there is a marked increase in court use, particularly in cases taken to the economic court, there are mixed messages about compliance with court orders. It is well understood in Vietnam that court orders are not necessarily enforceable. Fourteen years ago Ministry of Justice officials indicated that perhaps 15 percent of economic cases were enforced.[60] In 2005, survey work reveals that different actors have different perceptions of enforcement. More particularly, survey work out of six provinces indicated that businesses believed only 48.7 percent of judgments were enforced. Judges believed more judgments were enforced (67.8 percent), while lawyers maintained the enforcement rate was a low 24.2 percent.[61]

[57] *2009 SPC Report*, p. 15.

[58] *2007 SPC Report*, p. 3; *2008 SPC Report*, p. 3. [59] *2009 SPC Report*, p. 2.

[60] Interview by author with bureaucrats, Hanoi, 2002.

[61] LEADCO, *Report on Diagnostic Study on the Functioning of the Existing Commercial Dispute Resolution System in Vietnam: Formal and Informal* (Hanoi: DANIDA, 2007), p. 63.

In the course of an enforcement of a judgment there are many opportunities to delay or avoid a decision, and attempts to do that are allegedly very common. Comparative studies indicate that in 2011 it took 406 days to enforce a contract in China and 150 days in Singapore.[62] In Vietnam in 2011 it is suggested it took 295 days to enforce a contract, a decrease from over 350 days in 2003–4.[63] While the Ministry of Justice has worked to better manage the enforcement of civil and economic/commercial decisions, establishing registers of assets and a particular department with responsibility for enforcement, delays and uncertainty about enforcement remain problematic.

3 Judicial appointments, judicial independence and access to justice

3.1 Judicial appointments and qualifications of judges

In the early years after the Declaration of Independence in northern Vietnam, the emphasis was on access to justice and grassroots justice.[64] During this early period, judges largely had to demonstrate political, rather than legal, credentials and CPV policy guided judges.[65] As one Vietnamese scholar explains, revolutionaries in the north of Vietnam were expected to implement the "plan" rather than rely on legislation to guide decision-making.[66]

Over time the qualifications required of judges have become increasingly technical in focus, while retaining the need for judges to demonstrate political credibility. For the north of the country this has resulted in

62 World Bank, *World Bank Indicators*, www.google.com.au/publicdata/explore?ds=d5bncppjof8f9_&met_y=sp_pop_totl&idim=country:VNM&dl=en&hl=en&q=population+vietnam#!ctype=l&strail=false&bcs=d&nselm=h&met_y=ic_lgl_durs&scale_y=lin&ind_y=false&rdim=region&idim=country:VNM:CHN:SGP&ifdim=region&tstart=1046350800000&tend=1298811600000&hl=en&dl=en (accessed 28 February 2012).

63 *Ibid.*

64 Nicholson, *Borrowing Court Systems*, pp. 37–83. See also B. Fall, *The Viet Minh Regime Government Administration in the Democratic Republic of Vietnam* (Connecticut: Greenwood Press Publishers, 1956).

65 Nicholson, *Borrowing Court Systems*, pp. 37–55. See also Nguyen Nhu Phat, "The role of law during the formation of a market-driven mechanism in Vietnam" in J. Gillespie (ed.), *Commercial Legal Development in Vietnam: Vietnamese and Foreign Commentaries* (Sydney: Butterworths, 1997), pp. 397–412 and A. Forde, "The unimplementability of policy and the notion of law in Vietnamese communist thought," *Southeast Asia Journal of Social Science*, 1 (1986), 60–70.

66 Nguyen Nhu Phat, "The role of law," p. 398.

a seismic shift in terms of the skills sought in judicial personnel. As noted, where once political credentials and ethics were all important,[67] today an applicant for a judicial post should hold an LLB qualification and must also satisfy the general criterion of having "required political credentials."[68] In 2007, the Supreme People's Court noted that there were more than 200 judges who did not have an LLB.[69]

The 2002 Law on the Organization of People's Courts requires that candidates for judicial office have: "loyalty to the Fatherland and to the socialist Constitution, good ethical qualities, and capacity to protect socialist legislation."[70] As noted, judges had to be better qualified to be appointed. While initially the Party-state struggled to implement these changes,[71] more recent reports suggest that increasingly this requirement has been met.[72] Yet, many of the courts allegedly retain "old judges with the old mentality". As a result, it has been suggested, there has been little change in the work and efficiency of courts.[73] That said, the need for qualifications is a radical departure from previous practice.

The Party-state effectively retains a veto power over all judicial candidates at both the local and central levels. A recent survey suggests that 94.7 percent of provincial judges and 95.5 percent of district judges are Party members.[74] This is made possible by the requirement that those seeking judicial office include in their application dossier a letter of reference from the party cell of their current employer, referred to as an "opinion letter from the Communist Party cell"

[67] Nicholson, *Borrowing Court Systems*, pp. 74–82.

[68] Nicholson and Nguyen Hung Quang, "The Vietnamese judiciary," pp. 1–34.

[69] *2007 SPC Report*, p. 13.

[70] Law on Organization of People's Courts, 2002, Art. 37(1), Ordinance on Judges and Jurors of People's Courts 2002, Art. 5(1) and, in particular, Inter-Circular No.01/2003/TTLT/TANDTC-BQP-BNV-UBTWMTTQVN Guiding the Implementation of a Number of Provisions of the Ordinance on Judges and Jurors of the People's Courts, dated 1 April 2003, Art. 2.

[71] The Party-state issued Resolution 131/2002/NQ-UBTVQH11 On Judges, People's Assessors and Prosecutors, 3 November 2002 to by-pass the LLB requirement, by way of appointing staff prepared to study for an LLB after appointment.

[72] Interview by author with R. in October 2011, Hanoi. This claim has to be balanced against claims that only ten years ago 85 percent of judges and 70 percent of court officers had legal qualifications, but not Bachelor degrees. See Le Thi Thu Ba, "Công tác quản lý Toà án nhân dân địa phương và vấn đề nâng cao trình độ văn hoá xét xử của các Toà" (Local people's court management and judging cultural enhance of people's courts), *Judicial Science Information Review*, 7 (2001), 159.

[73] *Ibid.* [74] UNDP, *Local Court Governance Survey*, p. 50.

(*ý kiến của cấp ủy*).[75] The central endorsement is maintained by the requirement that an application dossier include a letter supporting the applicant's political credentials. Traditionally this has been supplied by completion of a program on political ethics at the National Political Academy. While the current law does not stipulate central endorsement by this academy, it does not set out other ways of evidencing endorsement, and so past practices continue.[76] Further, only Party members or those seeking membership can attend courses at the Political Academy.

Is the requirement for political endorsement instituting a system of patronage? On one view it is, with the ultimate patron being the Party-state, its officials holding the power to promote and appoint through their references. On another view, this requirement is no more than an employment check for suitability. Whichever is the case, these procedures concurrently allow relational practices in appointments (and dismissals) to continue through the discretion vested in various committees staffed by Party-state functionaries. While court staff members have not been analyzed for familial connections, limited research of the Ministry of Justice reveals that there is a long history of intergenerational appointments to the same institution.[77] Given the courts were once a part of the Ministry of Justice there is little reason to assume that it is different. It is also important to understand that judges are also public servants.[78] As a result, they are employees of the Party-state and expected to observe Party edicts as well as the law.[79]

The ideal composition of the bench is also much debated in Vietnam. In trials the elected people's assessors (*hội thẩm nhân dân*) have equal power to determine the issues before the court as the judge.[80] Some

[75] Nicholson and Nguyen Hung Quang, "The Vietnamese judiciary," 1–34; see also Inter-circular No. 05/TTLN of Ministry of Justice and Supreme People's Court, dated 15 October 1993 providing guidelines of Ordinance on People's Judges and Jurors 1993, Part III, Item 2.

[76] UNDP, *Local Court Governance Survey*, p. 50. This survey suggests that 87.3 percent of provincial judges and 61.5 percent of district judges had completed political training run by the Party.

[77] J. Gillespie, "The political-legal culture of anti-corruption reforms in Vietnam" in T. Lindsey (ed.), *Corruption in Asia: Rethinking the Governance Paradigm* (Sydney: The Federation Press, 2002), pp. 180–1.

[78] Nicholson and Nguyen Hung Quang, "The Vietnamese judiciary." [79] *Ibid.*

[80] Judges and people's assessors must be "independent and only act in accordance with the law": Law on the Organization of People's Courts, 2002, Art. 5. Further, "During trials, Assessors have equal authority with judges.": Ordinance on Judges and Jurors of People's Courts 16/2002/L/CTN, dated 11 October 2002, Art. 3. See also Art. 4, Law on the Organization of People's Courts, 2002.

Vietnamese commentators celebrate the continuity of lay involvement in trials. Others sharply criticize the continued use of people's assessors, arguing they know little of the law and are too easily subject to bias or coercion.[81] Further, whatever the merits of the continued involvement of people's assessors, it is suggested that judges have marginalized their capacity to participate through late production of case materials and consultation with senior courts.[82] People's assessors are elected by the relevant people's council (district, provincial) to represent the community and political ideals when determining disputes.[83] On appeal, a case is determined by a judge(s) sitting alone.

3.2 Judicial independence

It is best to understand courts as tribunals rather than as an entity vested with judicial authority to act as a check on government.[84] Sadly, this reality is all too often overlooked given the rhetoric of independence used in the Constitution and misunderstood by donors. However, this characterization better captures the ways in which courts are charged to determine facts and law on behalf of the National Assembly.

The courts are subservient to and members of the Party-state.[85] Courts also report to the National Assembly. They are concurrently bound to apply the law, including since 1992, to members of the Party. The issue becomes: how are cases resolved where the two duties, to Party-state and law, conflict? It appears that to date the ultimate duty to the Party-state will prevail.[86] That said, it is naïve to assume that the Party speaks with

[81] UNDP, *District Courts Survey*, pp. 208–9. Of forty-two interviewees only 36 percent maintained that people's assessors play an important role in determining cases.

[82] UNDP, *Local Court Governance Survey*, pp. 39–40.

[83] Ordinance on Judges and Jurors of People's Courts 16/2002/L/CTN, dated 11 October 2002, Art. 38.

[84] Nicholson, *Borrowing Court Systems*, pp. 33–4.

[85] *Ibid.* Resolution 48 and Resolution 49; P. Nicholson and S. Pitt, "Official discourses and court-oriented legal reform in Vietnam" in J. Gillespie and P. Nicholson (eds.), *Law and Development and the Global Discourses of Legal Transfers* (Cambridge University Press, 2012). See also 2011 Communist Party Statute of Vietnam, which sets out the duties of Party members. See also To Van Hoa, *Judicial Independence*, pp. 167–8 on the constitutional principle of Party leadership.

[86] Communist Party Statute, 2011, Art. 1 sets out the twin duties owed by Party members: "A member of the CPV is a revolutionary fighter in the vanguard of the Vietnamese working class, the working people, and of the entire nation as a whole who devotes his/her whole life to the Party's objectives and ideals, . . . who properly executes the Political Program, Statutes and resolutions of the Party and the law of the State . . ."

one voice. The CPV is not a homogenous entity.[87] Practically, the variety of attitudes severely complicates the work of judges.

There are debates within the Party, courts and legal sector in Vietnam about what constitutes an ideal court system and what notion of independence should be fostered. The current Vietnamese debate about independence asks, of what should the courts be independent and what powers should the court hold to make law? The more moderate pro-independence voice argues constitutionally to entrench "judicial power," and circumvents the issue of independence. Further, and as we have seen, many argue that the CPV has to remain all powerful and continue to lead courts. Others do not share this view. Some of those most critical of current arrangements are in jail, partly as a result of their outspokenness on issues of independence and the inappropriateness of Party leadership of courts.[88] While assuming ongoing Party leadership, some suggest that a vertical system of courts, where lower courts are led by higher courts, "enhances" court independence because it strengthens "judicial power, " particularly in its relationship with other state agencies.[89] There are others, however, that argue that a vertical system of courts produces a closed court system where influence and leadership by senior courts can undermine local court independence.[90] These issues remain unresolved, the Supreme People's Court usually referring to the need for transparent and accessible courts. Many agree that local courts need to be independent of local political leadership, but how to entrench this is less clear given the stalemate in the reform debates. Finally, most agree that courts should not be influenced by parties to a dispute.

Senior judges greatly influence the work of junior judges: 68.5 percent of district court judges indicated that they take the advice of senior courts into account when determining cases, although this was denied by provincial court judges.[91] Various mechanisms described how this advice

[87] Nicholson and Pitt, "Official discourses."

[88] Human Rights Watch, "The Party v. Legal Activist, Cu Huy Ha Vu," May 2011, pp. 4–5, www.hrw.org/reports/2011/05/26/vietnam-party-vs-legal-activist-cu-huy-ha-vu-0 (accessed 23 February 2012). See also the arrest and trial of lawyer Le Cong Dinh, details of which are set out in Human Rights Watch, "Rights Defenders Face Ongoing Harassment and Arrest," 16 June 2009, www.hrw.org/news/2009/06/23/vietnam-free-prominent-rights-lawyer-le-cong-dinh (accessed 23 February 2012).

[89] UNDP, *Local Court Governance Survey*, p. 18.

[90] *Ibid.*

[91] UNDP, *District Courts Survey*, pp. 250–1. The later 2013 UNDP, *Local Court Governance Survey*, pp. 40–2 confirms that consultation rates remain high.

was sought, including informal approach to those senior judges: 52.85 percent of district court judges indicated that they consulted decisions in like cases to assist them to determine disputes, and 25.56 percent of district court judges noted that they take the opinion of local government into account.[92]

Where formal documentation exists to assist lower courts, these sources are not always public and available, either because they are not published or on-line or because those seeking to rely on them do not have access to the resources (books, computers, internet) to access these materials.[93] Over the last five years, however, there has been a sharp increase in computer and internet access for judges. In 2006, district court judges reported having to finance the collection their own legal materials (58.5 percent), with only 15.37 percent of district court judges using the internet to access materials.[94] Current studies suggest that 83.3 percent of provincial court judges and 80.7 percent of district court judges have access to computers that are connected to the internet.[95]

At its most basic, the courts are CPV-led and this is maintained through appointments, short tenure, guidance of lower courts (see more below), and monitoring of staff by Party-cells within institutions. Within this context, there is also scope for relational lawyering (see below) and increasingly the intrusion of technical argument into court-based dispute resolution.

3.3 *Judicial tenure and remuneration*

Judges are appointed for five-year terms.[96] Appointments cannot be extended or a current judge promoted without a full fresh application.[97] The Party-state retains a hold on who it appoints with regular five-yearly opportunities to review their performance.

There are three pay scales for judges reflecting the place of their court in the hierarchy: supreme, provincial or district level. Typically a judge's salary includes a basic salary (*lương cơ bản*) and a responsibility allowance (*phụ cấp trách nhiệm*). The basic salary is calculated by multiplying the minimum salary (*lương tối thiểu*) under Vietnamese

92 *Ibid.* at p. 305. 93 *Ibid.* at p. 243. 94 *Ibid.*

95 UNDP, *Local Court Governance Survey*, p. 73.

96 Law on the Organization of People's Courts 2002, Art. 40(1) and (5).

97 Mai Bo, "Cần sửa đổi Pháp lệnh Thẩm phán và Hội thẩm nhân dân" (Ordinance on Judges and People's Assessors should be amended), *People's Court Journal*, 2 (2000), 3.

law, applicable to state officials and public servants,[98] with the applicable judge's salary level.[99] Broadly speaking, a first year Supreme Court judge will receive three times the salary increment of a first year district court judge, with a provincial judge between the two with double a district court judge's starting salary. Judges complain that salaries are not linked to skill or workload, only to length of service and locality.[100]

Typically, a Supreme People's Court judge with three years' experience would receive a salary of approximately US$ 312/month. A district court judge with seven years of experience would usually receive a salary of approximately US$ 138/month. Clearly judges are not well remunerated, although there has been an increase in the minimum salary (*lương tối thiểu*).

3.4 *Judicial budget*

As we have seen, the SPC must propose a budget to the Government, which is then submitted to the National Assembly.[101] The budget for military courts is, however, proposed by the Ministry of Defense.

The courts' budget for 2009 was VND 1,178,590 million (US $55,606,982.78 using VND 21,195 as the exchange rate).[102]

As noted, since 2002, the judiciary has increasingly been responsible for administering courts. Currently there appears to be some confusion about the bases of budget support locally. In a recent survey most, but not all, judges understood that they were funded by fixed or block grants that came to them from the SPC after its block grant from the National

[98] In early 2012, the monthly minimum salary for state officials and public servants is VND 830,000 (Decree 22/2011/ND-CP of the Government dated 4 April 2011 on the Nationwide Minimum Salary Level). This rate is expected to increase to VND 1,050,000 in May 2012 (Resolution 14/2011/QH13 of the National Assembly dated 10 November 2011 on the 2012 State Budget, Art. 2.3).

[99] Resolution 730/2004/NQ-UBTVQH11 of the Standing Committee of National Assembly dated 30 September 2004 Approving the Position Salary Schedule, Position Allowance Schedule for Senior Executives of the State and the Professional Salary Schedule for the Judiciary and the Procuracy. Although this resolution was amended by Resolution 823/2009/NQ-UBTVQH12 of the Standing Committee of National Assembly dated 3 October 2009, the professional salary schedule for the judiciary has remained unchanged.

[100] UNDP, *Local Court Governance Survey*, pp. 55–6.

[101] Law on the Organization of People's Courts 2002, Art. 46.

[102] *2009 SPC Report*, p. 10. Here and in various other places I refer to amounts in Vietnamese dong (VND). The approximate exchange rate (as of 11 June 2014) is US$ 1.00 = VND 21,195 (www.xe.com/).

Assembly.[103] Yet many courts, particularly those from more wealthy areas, also received payments from local government.[104] Technically this is not allowed. Payments supported activities such as sports and cultural events (very small payments) and computers and mobile hearings.[105] These payments are characterized as ad hoc. Some judges reject these payments (5 out of 18 courts surveyed) because they are illegal and link courts to local government.[106] There is also the real possibility that inter-agency support can increase the influence of local government over court decisions.

3.5 *Judicial training and related legal education*

As of 2012, judges are required to complete qualifications in adjudication.[107] At this time there is no court-run school offering judicial training, although the Korean International Aid Agency has completed a facility to house such a school.[108] Rather, judges are supposed to attend the Ministry of Justice's Judicial Training School,[109] which is also responsible for lawyer training. By way of background, the Judicial Training School was first established in 1998 as the Legal Profession Training School.[110] The Judicial Academy offers a year-long program for judges divided into three parts: six months for skills development; three months to develop academic skills; one month for special subjects (such as ethics, legal information literacy and deductive method); and two months for practice development. Various international agencies have assisted (with varying degrees of success) with the development of curriculum and materials,[111] which are seen as

[103] This complies with the Law on State Budget, Art. 20. See UNDP, *Local Court Governance Survey*, pp. 65–9.

[104] UNDP, *Local Court Governance Survey*, p. 67. [105] *Ibid.* [106] *Ibid.*

[107] Not all judges undertake the training. At one time candidates for the course had to sit an exam and if they met selection requirements they were admitted to the Judicial Academy (2003–4). Largely, however, judges are appointed to undertake the course by their courts. See Investconsult, *Report on the Survey on the Effectiveness of the Judge Training Program at the Judicial Academy* (hereinafter "*Investconsult Report 2009*"), 2009, p. 11.

[108] See Supreme People's Court Press Release, http://toaan.gov.vn/portal/page/portal/tandtc/299083?pers_id=1751931&item_id=11554238&p_details=1 (accessed 23 February 2011).

[109] The Judicial Academy was established under Decision No. 23/2004/ QD-TTg, dated 25 February 2004.

[110] The Legal Professional Training School was launched on 2 November 1998, under the auspices of the Ministry of Justice.

[111] Interview by the author with N., Australia, 29 August 2011 and O., Australia, 14 September 2011.

needing renewal.[112] Students report that the content in many textbooks is dated and "practical skills are hardly mentioned in the textbooks and documents."[113] Those who attend training also report the need to improve the availability of what currently exists.[114]

It is not suggested that Vietnamese judicial training is difficult only because of poor materials and resources. Commentators suggest that many of those currently appointed do not have the "mentality" to learn.[115] The quality of training offered is not celebrated by district court judges, 55 percent asserting the training is average and a further 2.76 percent stating it is low.[116]

In addition to the Judicial Academy, the courts run continuing legal education and provincial courts also offer professional training focusing on new regulations.[117] However, the suggestion from judges in provincial courts was that it was hard for the courts to hold this training regularly and much harder for those from rural or mountainous areas to attend training, whichever institution supplied it. Further, that basic training on new regulations was much needed.[118] Whereas only 4.4 percent of urban district court judges have not attended training, judges based in mountainous areas (21.5 percent) and rural areas (19.5 percent) find it much harder to access.[119] There is also a call for people's assessors to have qualifications beyond political credentials and ethics.[120] The involvement of donors in regional court training has been celebrated locally.[121]

3.6 *Access to justice*

In many countries non-governmental organizations and legal aid are key agencies that assist people to access justice. Generally, in Vietnam, these organizations are either coopted or managed by the Party-state and, as a result, have relatively little impact on the work of the court. More

[112] In 2009, 68.07 percent of graduates, 68.70 percent of trainees and 98.24 percent of staff interviewed cited a need for materials "renewal": *Investconsult Report 2009*, p. 33.
[113] *Investconsult Report 2009*, p. 45.
[114] *Ibid.* at p. 37.
[115] Interview by the author with P., Hanoi, October 2011.
[116] UNDP, *District Courts Survey*, pp. 270–1.
[117] *Ibid.* at p. 273.
[118] UNDP, *Local Court Governance Survey*, p. 60 where over 50 percent of local judges reported they were not updated on new regulations in a timely manner.
[119] *Ibid.* at p. 274.
[120] The training of people's assessors is set out at UNDP, *District Court Survey*, pp. 278–86.
[121] UNDP, *Local Court Governance Survey*, p. 59.

particularly, legal aid is delivered through the Ministry of Justice.[122] Vietnamese Legal Aid is misconceived if it is imagined as a challenge to state authority or catalyst for developing jurisprudence. For example, legal aid is not known for challenging the application of criminal procedure laws. This reticence to champion rights in criminal trials is not unique to legal aid, however. There are real challenges for those in custody seeking to access a lawyer.[123]

In large part legal aid exists to assist those needing legal advice, many of whom do not face trial, although assisting with court appearances is also part of the work of legal aid since 2007.[124] Since 2007 there has also been a concerted effort by the Ministry of Justice to ensure that a legal aid office exists in each of the 64 provinces (and in some communes and districts, a total of 117 branches) and according to the Vietnam Bar Association in 2009 there were 746 legal aid staff working nationally (206 of which had a legal aid assistant certificate) assisted by 8,043 collaborators (including over a 1,000 private lawyers).[125] The same report notes that 118,796 people were assisted by legal aid nationally in 2009, a radical increase on the 100,000 assisted over the ten-year period 1997–2007.[126]

However, employees of legal aid owe a twin duty to the client and to the Party-state. This essentially compromises their ability to defend client rights where they conflict with state order or Party edict. It also means that the legal aid lawyer is perceived as an arm of the state and not independent of it. That said, the National Bar Association notes that "people in rural areas have neither the habit nor any knowledge of how to rely on legal services to rescue them."[127] The same Bar Association also notes that lawyers and advisers, including those from legal aid, also confront the "evasive attitude of law enforcement officers."[128] These comments reinforce the struggle for legal aid to be accepted, both by those they serve – their clients – and other state institutions.

Similarly, analysis to date of the non-governmental sector suggests it has largely been coopted. Certainly, when the National Bar Association

[122] Nicholson, "Access to justice". See also Vietnam Bar Association report to Access to Justice Research, 2010, www.lawcouncil.asn.au/shadomx/apps/fms/fmsdownload.cfm?file_uuid=EFFCF7DE-EF7B-A30F-3704-FC8D566AD96F&siteName=lca (accessed 27 February 2012).

[123] UNDP, *Right to Counsel* (Hanoi: UNDP, 2012), pp. 56–8.

[124] Law on Legal Aid, Law No. 69/2006/QH11, 29 June 2006.

[125] Vietnam Bar Association report to Access to Justice Research.

[126] *Ibid.*

[127] *Ibid.*

[128] *Ibid.*

sought to set itself up independently and beyond the arm of the Party-state, the Law on Lawyers was changed, specifically setting out how the National Bar Association would be constituted and ensuring a Party-state veto of office holders.[129] Further, when the National Bar Association tried to establish its own fund to defend the indigent, "For Justice" (*Vì Công Lý*), this act was deemed illegal by the Hanoi Bar Association.[130]

Lawyers in contemporary Vietnam have grown in number, ability and tenacity.[131] There is also evidence of an increase in their use, particularly as advisers when establishing new businesses, for example. However, recently commissioned UNDP research on access to counsel indicates that there is still a large rhetoric practice gap when it comes to access to counsel in criminal matters. The Constitution enshrines a party's right to a lawyer as does the Criminal Procedure Code and the Law on Lawyers.[132] The recent UNDP report reveals that while courts will often ensure that a party has a lawyer, the investigating police and the procuracy are not greatly assisting those detained to obtain early or timely legal advice.[133] The report also notes the additional challenges an accused faces accessing a lawyer in rural and sol or mountainous regions.[134]

Lawyers generally maintain that court costs are not prohibitive and that most individuals and firms could afford to take a matter to court and possibly also a lawyer, if needed. For example, in civil and business cases if the value of the dispute is below VND 40,000,000 (US$ 1,887.24) the court fees (*án phí*) are VND 4,000,000 (US$ 188.72).[135] In cases involving

[129] See Nguyen Thi Minh, "Legal and professional challenges confronting practising lawyers in contemporary Vietnam" (unpublished PhD thesis) (University of New South Wales, 2008), pp. 110–13.

[130] M. Sidel, *Law and Society in Vietnam* (New York: Cambridge University Press, 2008), pp. 183–8.

[131] Nguyen Thi Minh, "Legal and professional challenges," p. 72. Minh notes that the number of national lawyers has increased as follows: 1991 - 369; 1996 - 727; 2001 - 2,100; 2007 - 4,357. The National Bar Association suggests that in 2010 there were 5,250 lawyers (Vietnam Bar Association report to Access to Justice Research).

[132] SRVN Constitution, Art. 132. See also Criminal Procedure Code, Arts. 11, 49 and 50.

[133] UNDP, *Right to Counsel*, pp. 35 and 41. Out of forty-five lawyer interviewees, forty-five noted that they had never been granted a Certificate of Defense in a criminal case during the investigation phase (before the decision to prosecute is made). A certificate of defense is required before a lawyer can access either his or her client or the dossier.

[134] *Ibid.* at p. 64. One interviewed judge said that in 2008 counsel only assisted in two to three out of forty criminal cases.

[135] Ordinance on Court Charges and Court Fees, 2009, Schedule of Court Charges and Court Fees. The exchange rate used here is US$1.00 = VND 21,195, calculated on the basis of the exchange rate quoted on 11 June 2014 at www.xe.com/ucc/.

larger amounts, court fees are largely set by reference to a set fee and then a component based on a percentage of the amount in dispute. For example, in civil and business cases where the amount in dispute is between VND 2,000,000,000 (US$ 94,362) and VND 4,000,000,000 (US$ 188,724), the court fee is VND 72,000,000 (US$ 3,397) plus 2 percent of the value of the dispute exceeding VND 2,000,000,000.[136] However, where a person is impecunious there are few avenues for assistance with court matters, although help with advice and negotiation is often forthcoming from bureaucrats and state functionaries, including more recently those employed by legal aid.[137] That said, lawyers suggest that 30 percent of defendants in criminal cases cannot afford a lawyer.[138]

The Ordinance on Court Charges and Court Fees also sets out court charges (*lệ phí Tòa án*). These charges usually apply to civil or business/commercial cases that do not involve a dispute, such as cases in which the petitioner requests the court to declare that an individual has lost his or her capacity for civil acts or is missing or is dead, or in which the petitioner requests the court to initiate bankruptcy proceedings. Court charges are low, not exceeding VND 4,000,000 (US$ 188.72).

4 Sources of law, styles of judicial decisions and politics of judging

4.1 Judging and sources of law: codes or precedents

Vietnam has a civil law system where judges are not able to make law, but are constitutionally empowered to "apply" the existing law. This is a particularly daunting task when the law is often vague, ambiguous, incomplete or regularly changing and, as already noted, training materials are dated and sparse. As now-jailed lawyer Le Cong Dinh explained when he was the Vice Chairman of the Ho Chi Minh Bar Association, constitutionally the Standing Committee of the National Assembly has the authority to interpret laws.[139] However, lawyer Dinh notes exercise of

136 *Ibid.*

137 Until 2007 legal aid workers were not able to assist with court proceedings. Since the introduction of the Law on Legal Aid, Law No. 69/2006/QH11, 29 June 2006 this position has changed and legal aid workers can now assist with court cases.

138 UNDP, *Right to Counsel*, p. 64. See also, OCCCF, Schedule of Court Charges and Court Fees.

139 Le Cong Dinh, "Role of precedent in judicial interpretation," paper presented at International Seminar on Legal Interpretation, Supported by Joint Programme Support Office, Hanoi, 21–22 February 2008.

this power is rare. Rather the practice is for implementing legislation introduced by government authorities to interpret/expand the operation of higher laws.[140] In addition, the court, more particularly the Justice Council of the Supreme People's Court, issues "summaries" in its internal journal, which are relied upon by courts to explain the law. Further, as we shall see below, increasingly the SPC issues, either alone or in combination with other state agencies, circulars and resolutions (normative documents) to explain the operation of provisions.[141]

What remains unresolved is whether, when an agency issues a statement of the law by way of circular or resolution, for example, it offers an interpretation of the higher law, or merely an expansion of the higher law, allegedly involving no interpretation. The latter view is plainly false according to Luu Tien Dzung, then head of the International Department of the Vietnam Lawyers Association.[142] It is impossible, writes Dzung, "to apply laws in a mechanistic way without any analysis and explanation of the reasons why a certain legal norm is understood like that and a related legal norm applicable in a certain situation in the case."[143] As Dzung argues, although the role of a judge in interpreting the law has not been realized in Vietnam, nevertheless a judge "implicitly interprets law before making a decision on applying a legal regulation/document," although this is not set out.[144]

There is no system of precedent in Vietnam, although some have argued for one. However, highly persuasive materials are available to inferior courts. More particularly, the court journal, the summary of cases in the SPC Annual Reports, and formal documents issued by the SPC, whether normative documents (such as circulars or resolutions) or guidance for particular cases (usually located in letters), influence the lower courts. This is because the SPC is charged with "protecting the socialist rule of law, the socialist regime and the people's mastery"[145] and the guiding of lower courts.[146] It realizes these responsibilities via its issue of normative documents and letters of advice.

140 *Ibid.*

141 See *Tạp chí Toà Án Nhân Dân* (*People's Court Journal*). First published under this name in 1972 and replacing the former *Justice Journal* (*Tạp chí Tư Pháp*). Nicholson, *Borrowing Court Systems*, p. 279.

142 Luu Tien Dzung, "Law application and interpretation in judgments in Vietnam," paper presented at *International Seminar on Legal Interpretation*, supported by Joint Programme Support Office, Hanoi, 21–22 February 2008.

143 *Ibid.* 144 *Ibid.*

145 Law on the Organization of People's Courts, 2002, Art. 1. 146 *Ibid.* Art. 19.

The SPC has been increasingly industrious in its production of normative documents, either alone or with other agencies,[147] issuing different types of documents to guide lower courts in different time periods. During the war years the SPC did little by way of officially guiding lower courts. The war and the reliance on popular justice and resolving cases by reason and sentiment in applying the law (*lý và tình trong việc chấp hành pháp luật*) explain this. Throughout the 1990s and into the twenty-first century the SPC has become increasingly active, particularly in issuing normative documents (resolutions, decisions and circulars). The increase in Official Letters (usually responses to queries from lower courts on application of law in particular cases) is most probably explained by courts' jurisdictional changes (see above) and the introduction of new courts, each resulting in lower courts seeking additional assistance from the SPC.

The power to issue guidance to lower courts might be characterized as a developing jurisprudence upon which to draw to assist with determining the applicable law. As noted above, there is a high degree of dependence on previous judgments and counsel from senior judges, although this is disputed by provincial court judges.

Constitutional interpretation is solely within the purview of the Standing Committee of the National Assembly.[148] And yet as academic Nguyen Dang Dung points out, this power had not been used up until 2008.[149] Dung also argues the power is wrongly vested in the National Assembly Standing Committee, arguing that those that legislate ought not also to interpret the Constitution. Moving from constitutional

[147] These statistics are sourced from LuatVietnam, www.luatvietnam.vn/VL/trang-chu/ (accessed 17 February 2012). A close inspection of this database suggests it is not entirely accurate. For example, known circulars are missing and some documents do not have legal content, but are about incidental matters, such as events. In the case of the latter they have been excluded from this analysis. That said, the numbers closely track numbers used on other Vietnamese Law Databases, such as LAWDATA, the National Assembly's law database for the period 1985–2012, and thus give a snapshot sufficiently accurate for these purposes. To the extent that there is disagreement between Vietnamese law databases, these can be explained by the fact that generally Vietnamese state agencies, and particularly the SPC, appear not to manage legal documents in a comprehensive or consistent manner. This is the case particularly for official letters, which did not have to be published in the Official Gazette (*Công Báo*).

[148] DRVN Constitution, Art. 91(3).

[149] Nguyen Dang Dung, "National Assembly Standing Committee and its interpretation of law," paper presented at International Seminar on Legal Interpretation, Supported by Joint Programme Support Office, Hanoi, 21–22 February 2008.

matters, the National Assembly Judiciary Committee determined that the Supreme Court had erroneously decided a decision in 2009.[150] This evoked substantial debate in elite circles about the finality of judgments and whether the National Assembly had the power to interfere with a court decision.[151] More recently, the SPC has been given power to annul a decision if asked to revisit a decision by the National Assembly in civil and administrative matters.[152]

Ultimately, decisions of the court remain under the purview of the Party either acting through the National Assembly or via tight communication channels between CPV internal committees and court leadership. Controversial cases are also closely monitored with regular (some say daily in the case of the notorious Nam Cam corruption trial of 2003), contact with Party leadership.[153]

4.2 *Style of judgments*

Vietnamese judgments are traditionally short. They comprise a preamble (setting out details of the parties and their legal advisers); a summary of the case (*nhận thấy*), which sets out the applicable law and submission of parties, if any; and the remarks of the court (*xét thấy*), which sets out the legal instruments used as the bases of the court's reasoning and, on occasion, the analysis of the court; and the decision (*quyết định*). Decisions also have to include a notice of the applicable appeal procedure and cost orders. Judgments do not record dissent, if any, between those determining the case. Nor do they set out in full the arguments made by defense counsel in criminal cases, although they include the full prosecutorial brief. Some of the judicial training undertaken at both the Judicial Academy and continuing legal education targets teaching judges how to write judgments.

[150] The case involved a contractual dispute between Tien Son Company and Chau Tuan Company. In this case the SPC and SPP accepted the decision of the National Assembly Judiciary Committee. See http://sggp.org.vn/chinhtri/2009/8/199691/.

[151] In late 2009 the UNDP together with the then Judicial Reform Steering Committee held a workshop at which these matters were discussed.

[152] The Law on Proceedings of Administrative Cases, Arts. 239 and 240, and the Law on Amendment of Law on Civil Proceedings, Articles 310a and 310b. See also *Report Judicial Committee of the National Assembly* No. 4745 of 2011 which sets out processes for and summarizes the incidents of review.

[153] Comments made on the basis of anonymity by Vietnamese official in 2003.

4.3 *Interpretive method*

Technically, judges rely on legislation and CPV documents and policies to assist with their application of law.

It is also suggested that, in addition to policy and law, judges turn to local situational reasoning and adopting legal fictions when exercising their judicial discretion to determine a case.[154] There is no doubt that Party policy and applicable law are key tools for the judge determining cases. It is also the case that judges will take into account facts and circumstances to assist with the determination of cases, using legal analogy where helpful. Yet the ways in which judgments are recorded leave this judicial approach, where used, implicit.

Direct guidance from the Party is also not unknown. As mentioned previously, one of the worst-kept secrets was that during the Nam Cam corruption trial, the Ho Chi Minh City provincial people's court were regularly on the phone (some say daily) to the Hanoi-based Internal Affairs Committee of the CPV.[155] There is also widespread acceptance within the profession of the need to liaise closely with judges and maintain "excellent relations" with them: the author is also aware of "under the table" payments being made to judges.[156]

5 Courts and alternative dispute resolution (ADR)

Negotiation and mediation are widely recognized in civil statutory laws as a major means to resolve civil disputes.[157] Civil disputes are broadly defined to include family and business disputes, among others.[158] Article 12 of the Civil Code 2005 emphasizes that "mediation between the parties in accordance with law is encouraged in civil relations."[159] Detailed provisions on mediation during court proceedings are set out

154 J. Gillespie, "Rethinking the role of judicial independence in socialist transforming East Asia," *International Comparative Law Quarterly*, 56(4) (2007), 837–70.

155 Nguyen Hung Quang and K. Steiner, "Ideology and professionalism: the resurgence of the Vietnamese Bar" in J. Gillespie and P. Nicholson (eds.), *Asian Socialism and Legal Change: The Dynamics of Vietnamese and Chinese Reform* (Canberra: Asia Pacific Press, 2005), pp. 202–4.

156 P. Nicholson, "Good governance and institutional accountability: the role of the Vietnamese courts" in T. Lindsey and H. Dick (eds.), *Corruption in Asia: Rethinking the Good Governance Paradigm* (Sydney: Federation Press, 2002), pp. 201–18.

157 See, for example, Civil Code 2005, Art. 12; Commercial Law 2005, Art. 317; Investment Law 2005, Art. 12; Labor Code 1994, Art. 158.

158 Civil Procedure Code 2004, Art. 1.

159 See also Civil Procedure Code 2004, Art. 10.

in the Civil Procedure Code 2004. Nevertheless, there are no specific rules governing mediation outside the courts, with the exception of labor disputes.

Vietnam began promoting the use of arbitration as a means of commercial dispute resolution in the 1990s. It ratified the New York Convention in 1995 and issued the Ordinance on Recognition and Enforcement of Foreign Arbitral Awards in the same year. Vietnam also promulgated the Commercial Arbitration Ordinance in 2003 to establish the legal framework for commercial arbitration. This ordinance and its successor – the Commercial Arbitration Law 2010 – replicate the UNCITRAL Model Law to a large extent. Arbitration is also provided for resolution of collective labor disputes. However, the practical impact of this mechanism is very limited.

5.1 Mediation in the courts

Mediation is a compulsory part of civil court proceedings. Under the Civil Procedure Code, a dispute must usually be mediated before a judge before the official hearing. The judge acts as mediator, and, if mediation succeeds, he or she will then issue a decision to acknowledge the mutual settlement between the parties. However, such a decision can be issued only if the parties have agreed to resolve the whole dispute.

The decision to acknowledge settlement between the parties is legally effective upon its issuance, and is enforced as a judgment. Neither disputing party may challenge the decision once it has come into force. Nonetheless, the decision can be reviewed through the judicial review procedures.

In reality, the rate of cases successfully mediated by Vietnamese courts is considerable. According to the SPC, more than 40 percent of cases were settled by the courts by mediation every year during the period between 2006 and 2009.[160]

5.2 Arbitration, ADR and the courts

Vietnam has two separate legal regimes for enforcement of commercial arbitral awards. Foreign arbitral awards are enforced under the Civil Procedure Code 2004, which largely replicates the New York

160 *2006 SPC Report*, p. 5; *2007 SPC Report*, p. 5; *2008 SPC Report*, p. 5; *2009 SPC Report*, p. 4.

Convention's regulations. The enforcement of domestic arbitral awards is set out in the 2010 Commercial Arbitration Law. The main difference between these two regimes relates to the procedure by which an award can be enforced.[161] Where a party holds a foreign arbitral award, the winning party is required to file its application with the Ministry of Justice, which will then forward the application to the court. Once the court issues a decision to recognize and enforce the award, the winning party has the right to request the relevant Department of Civil Judgment Execution to execute the award. Where a domestic award is involved, the winning party may go directly to the Department of Civil Judgment Execution to request enforcement, unless the losing party has challenged the award before a court within the timeframe prescribed by law. However, as we have seen, practical challenges to enforcement exist.

With the exception of labor disputes, there are no special rules on the legal effect of ADR outside the court. This does not mean that a settlement obtained outside the court is unenforceable. It only means that such a settlement will not be enforced as a court judgment as in the case of a settlement reached during court proceedings.

5.3 Commercial arbitration institutions

According to the Vietnam Lawyers Association there are eight arbitration institutions in Vietnam.[162] The Vietnam International Arbitration Centre (VIAC) is the biggest arbitration center, accounting for 118 of 207 arbitrators and the details of its caseload are set out below.[163]

There are various reasons why arbitration is attractive in Vietnam. First, as already noted, the procedures and applicable law closely resemble those used internationally. Second, while arbitration must proceed under Vietnamese law if all the parties are Vietnamese, where there is a

[161] See Civil Procedure Code, Chapter XXIX; Commercial Arbitration Law 2010, Chapters X–XI.

[162] Submission Paper No. 10/TTr-HLGVN, dated 4 August 2009 on the Draft Law on Arbitration. See also Vietnam Lawyers Association, *Report on the Implementation of the 2003 Commercial Arbitration Ordinance*, dated 30 April 2009 which names seven arbitration centres: the Vietnam International Arbitration Centre (VIAC); the Hanoi Commercial Arbitration Centre; the Asian International Commercial Arbitration Centre (AICA); the HCMC Commercial Arbitration Centre; the Pacific International Arbitration Centre (PIAC); the Can Tho Commercial Arbitration Centre; and the Vien Dong Arbitration Centre.

[163] VIAC was established on 28 April 1993. See Decision No. 240/TTg.

foreign party involved, the use of other laws can be agreed.[164] Third, the language of the arbitration can be other than Vietnamese where a foreign party is involved,[165] providing it is agreed by the parties. Fourth, the parties have the opportunity to seek particular expertise on the panel.[166] Fifth, six of the 120 arbitrators on the panel are foreign.[167]

There is an increase in the use of domestic arbitration at the largest arbitration center operating nationally. More specifically, a ten-fold increase occurred in cases arbitrated over a seventeen-year period, from just six cases in 1993 to sixty-three cases in 2010.[168] Just as significantly, caseload has approximately tripled in the ten years from twenty-three cases in 2000 to sixty-three in 2010.[169] This growth in case numbers was anticipated. Those closely watching developments in local arbitration alleged about ten years ago that many commercial disputants would steer clear of the formal court system and experiment with local arbitration because it was likely to be quicker, private and conducted by technically qualified people.

Over a twelve-year period, 1998–2010, roughly 66 percent of VIAC's work has involved a foreign party.[170] Yet while foreign-related disputes initially generated the bulk of VIAC's cases, disputing locals have increasingly turned to VIAC. In 2010, the number of local disputes arbitrated outnumbered (37:26) the number of foreign-related disputes.[171]

6 Sources and influences on the Vietnamese judicial system

The work of Vietnamese courts has, as we have seen, undergone some changes and new usage patterns have emerged, along with substantial institutional reforms. The Chinese, Russians, Japanese, French, Americans and, more recently, Western countries and organizations, have all at some stage sought to influence Vietnamese legal development,

164 VIAC, Rules of Arbitration (effective from 1 January 2012), Art. 22. See www.viac.org.vn/en-US/Home/default.aspx.

165 VIAC, Rules of Arbitration, Art. 21.

166 *Ibid.* Art. 11(4).

167 See list of arbitrators, www.viac.org.vn/en-US/Home/dieukhoanmau.aspx.

168 Vietnam International Arbitration Centre, www.viac.org.vn/en-US/Home/statistics/2011/01/353.aspx.

169 *Ibid.*

170 Over the same ten-year period VIAC heard 369 disputes involving foreign parties compared with 123 local disputes. See www.viac.org.vn/en-US/Home/statistics/2011/01/353.aspx.

171 See www.viac.org.vn/en-US/Home/statistics/2011/01/353.aspx.

sometimes only in particular parts of the country. As noted above, the Soviets had the most direct influence on the northern courts. This influence was then exported south after 1975.

Since 1986, with the adoption of "renovation" (*đổi mới*), and particularly after 1992, with the introduction of Vietnam's doctrine of *nhà nước pháp quyền* ("state rules or law-based state"), the legal sector was the target of potentially far-reaching reforms. These changes encouraged donors to become increasingly active in court reform.

The Vietnamese courts first engaged with donor activity in the early 1990s. The strategies of donors and their influence can perhaps be seen as involving three phases.[172] At this time the court was "hesitant" to collaborate with donors.[173] The Supreme People's Court, which was developing capacity to work with the international donor community, was learning why donors sought to work with courts and what the limits of their cooperation might be.[174] It has been suggested that constructive exchange and activity took place between 1995 and 2005, initially under a UNDP project, which also involved the Danish International Development Agency (DANIDA).[175] The Japanese International Cooperation Agency (JICA) was also very active over this period.[176] This decade witnessed a marked increase in court collaboration with donors, attributed to a "strong consensus" between those donors active in court reform and the Party-court leadership.[177] During this time the courts sought and obtained technical assistance to draft substantive laws and train judges. These activities were not politically sensitive.[178]

From 2005 to the present time, most donors (but not all, JICA is one notable exception) have agitated for rule of law reforms, however defined.[179] It is suggested that donors have either wrongly interpreted or deliberately misinterpreted Resolutions 48 and 49 as calling for rule of law reforms. As noted, the Party-state has not yet decided the pace and trajectory of legal reform as it impacts courts.[180]

As a result, the nadir of cooperation has passed and in the last eight years there is ideological conflict between some of the donors and the court's reform agenda, the former calling for rule of law based reforms

[172] Interview by the author with L., Hanoi, June 2011. [173] *Ibid.* [174] *Ibid.*

[175] UNDP Project, Strengthening Court Activity Project VIE 013. Interview by the author with L., Hanoi, June 2011 and O., Hanoi, September 2011.

[176] *Ibid.* interview by author with V. and X., Japan, October 2011.

[177] Interview by the author with L., Hanoi, June 2011. [178] *Ibid.* [179] *Ibid.*

[180] Interview by the author with L., Hanoi, June 2011 and O., Hanoi, September 2011.

like recognition of human rights and cessation of political influence on courts, while the latter still seeks technical cooperation.[181]

In the course of research that takes donor impacts on court reform as its focus, there are some examples of successful donor impacts that are frequently cited. More specifically, JICA's assistance with procedure laws and activities supporting training of judges are favorably reviewed by local commentators. USAID's STAR project, which took the publication of cassational review judgments as its focus, is also well reviewed.[182] Some comment favorably on the Australian government's funding of the development of a bench book, although this is debated by others. Most recently, the Canadian International Development Agency and JICA have both supported provincial courts to develop more transparent practices, including case management, to great internal acclaim.

Beyond donors, the engagement with international lawyers and businesses, and emerging domestic businesses, has produced debates about the place within Vietnam of international and domestic legal norms. In many ways there is a mass of new ideas circulating, some of which have penetrated the courts. How new ideas can be entrenched, however, is less clear.

7 Conclusion: role of Vietnamese courts?

The Vietnamese courts are in a vexed position. In 2013, more than ten years after the introduction of Resolution 8, and eight years after the 2005 passage of the detailed reform Resolutions 48 and 49, the Party-state has not endorsed an action plan. The public rhetoric and legal instruments characterize courts as independent and also beholden to the Party line. Yet the function of Vietnamese courts has changed over time. Where previously the northern courts aspired to deliver popular justice, we see that the contemporary Vietnamese court is concurrently a legal and political institution. Legal in that ideally it is bound by law, political in that ultimately it works for the Party-state and must resolve matters in accordance with a complex hierarchy of influences, only one of which is law. There is no doubt that technical legal skills of personnel are increasing, yet judges are poorly paid, frequently criticized by lawyers,

[181] P. Nicholson, "Prospects of legal technical assistance: from assistance to cooperation," Keynote Address to the annual JICA conference, Osaka, Japan, January 2012.

[182] Do Van Dai, "Về việc công bố bản án của Tòa án tối cao ở Pháp và ở Việt Nam" (About the publication of judgments of the Supreme Court in France and Vietnam), *Jurisprudence Science Journal*, 2 (2005).

sometimes lobbied through the press, not infrequently corrupt, and face an unclear reform trajectory. In such a climate it is hard consistently to attract people of a high caliber.[183] It is also difficult for judges independently to champion reform. Yet there are stories of great reformers working in their localities to improve access to justice and trust in decision-making.[184]

And yet the courts are used not only for criminal and civil matters brought by the state. And the courts have undergone a radical transformation in the last fifteen to twenty years, also attracting some reform champions. If the development of courts in Vietnam is compared with the development of courts in a range of other countries, the transformation is arresting. What cannot be assumed, however, is that the ultimate reform trajectory reflects court structures and practices common in the West.[185] If politics, the bedrock of the Vietnamese court system, should change, expectations of courts might radically alter. If not, an ongoing tension between various legally focused reform agendas and the status quo will be perpetuated, with the balance playing out differently in diverse jurisdictions and localities.

References

Bui, T. *Following Ho Chi Minh* (Bathurst: Crawford Publishing, 1995)

Do, H. H. *Confirmation Report* (Doctoral Studies Program) (Melbourne Law School, 2011)

Do, V. D. "Về việc công bố bản án của Tòa án tối cao ở Pháp và ở Việt Nam" (About the publication of judgments of the Supreme Court in France and Vietnam), *Jurisprudence Science Journal*, 2 (2005), 41–8

Fall, B. *The Viet Minh Regime Government Administration in the Democratic Republic of Vietnam* (Connecticut: Greenwood Press Publishers, 1956)

Forde, A. "The unimplementability of policy and the notion of law in Vietnamese communist thought," *Southeast Asia Journal of Social Science*, 1 (1986), 60–70

Gillespie, J. "Concepts of law in Vietnam: transforming statist socialism" in R. Peerenboom (ed.), *Asian Discourses of the Rule of Law* (London: Routledge, 2004), pp. 146–82

[183] Interview by the author with E., Hanoi, September 2010. While some successful lawyers admit they may work for the courts later in their careers, most are not rushing to join the court early in their professional lives.

[184] Interview by the author with A., Hanoi, 2011.

[185] B. Tamanaha, "The rule of law and legal pluralism in development," *Hague Journal on the Rule of Law*, 3(2) (2011), 1–17.

Gillespie, J. "Rethinking the role of judicial independence in socialist transforming East Asia," *International Comparative Law Quarterly*, 56 (4) (2007), 837–70

Gillespie, J. "The juridification of state regulation in Vietnam" in J. Gillespie and A. Chen (eds.), *Legal Reform in China and Vietnam: A Comparison of Asian Communist Regimes* (New York: Routledge, 2010), pp. 78–102

Gillespie, J. "The political-legal culture of anti-corruption reforms in Vietnam" in T. Lindsey (ed.), *Corruption in Asia: Rethinking the Governance Paradigm* (Sydney: The Federation Press, 2002), pp. 167–200

Harding, A. and Nicholson, P. "New courts in Asia: Law, development and judicialization" in A. Harding and P. Nicholson (eds.), *New Courts in Asia* (London: Routledge, 2010), pp. 1–27

Le, K. Q. "The people's courts" in *An Outline of the Institutions of the Democratic Republic of Vietnam* (Hanoi: Gioi Publishers, 1974)

Le, T. T. B. "Công tác quản lý Toà án nhân dân địa phương và vấn đề nâng cao trình độ văn hoá xét xử của các Toà" (Local people's court management and judging cultural enhance of people's courts), *Judicial Science Information Review*, 7 (2001), 159

LEADCO. *Report on Diagnostic Study on the Functioning of the Existing Commercial Dispute Resolution System in Vietnam: Formal and Informal* (Hanoi: DANIDA, 2007)

Lee, C. H. *Industrial Relations and Dispute Settlement in Vietnam* (Vietnam: ILO Office, 2006)

Mai, B. "Cần sửa đổi Pháp lệnh Thẩm phán và Hội thẩm nhân dân" (Ordinance on judges and people's assessors should be amended), *People's Court Journal*, 2 (2000), 3

Ministry of Justice and Legal Administration Branch USAID, *The Legal System of the Republic of Viet-Nam: An Unofficial Translation* (Saigon: Ministry of Justice, 1967)

Nguyen, H.Q. and Steiner, K. "Ideology and professionalism: the resurgence of the Vietnamese Bar" in J. Gillespie and P. Nicholson (eds.), *Asian Socialism and Legal Change: The Dynamics of Vietnamese and Chinese Reform* (Canberra: Asia Pacific Press, 2005), pp. 191–211

Nguyen, N. P. "The role of law during the formation of a market-driven mechanism in Vietnam" in J. Gillespie (ed.), *Commercial Legal Development in Vietnam: Vietnamese and Foreign Commentaries* (Sydney: Butterworths, 1997), pp. 397–412

Nguyen, T. M. "Legal and professional challenges confronting practising lawyers in contemporary Vietnam" (unpublished PhD thesis) (University of New South Wales, 2008)

Nguyen, V. Q. "A comparative study of the systems of review of administrative action by courts and tribunals in Australia and Vietnam" (unpublished PhD thesis) (Latrobe University, 2007)

Nicholson, P. "Access to justice in Vietnam: state supply – public distrust" in J. Gillespie and A. Chen (eds.), *Legal Development in East Asia: China and Vietnam Compared* (London: Routledge, 2010), pp. 188–215

Nicholson, P. *Borrowing Court Systems: The Experience of Socialist Vietnam* (Leiden: Martinus Nijhoff Publishers, 2007)

Nicholson, P. "Good governance and institutional accountability: the role of the Vietnamese courts" in T. Lindsey and H. Dick (eds.), *Corruption in Asia: Rethinking the Good Governance Paradigm* (Sydney: Federation Press, 2002), pp. 201–18

Nicholson, P. "Legal culture repacked: drug trials in Vietnam" in P. Nicholson and S. Biddulph (eds.), *Examining Practice, Investigating Theory: Comparative Legal Studies in Asia* (Leiden: Brill, 2008), pp. 71–108

Nicholson, P. and Duong, M. "Legitimacy and the Vietnamese economic courts" in A. Harding and P. Nicholson (eds.), *New Courts in Asia* (London: Routledge, 2010), pp. 31–55

Nicholson, P. and Pitt, S. "Official discourses and court-oriented legal reform in Vietnam" in J. Gillespie and P. Nicholson (eds.), *Law and Development and the Global Discourses of Legal Transfers* (Cambridge University Press, 2012), pp. 202–36

Nicholson, P. and Truong, K. "The modern propaganda trial: drugs prosecutions in Vietnam," *Monash Law Review*, 34 (2008), 430–56

Nicholson, P. and Nguyen, H. Q. "The Vietnamese judiciary: the politics of appointment and promotion," *Pacific Rim Law and Policy Journal*, 14(1) (2005), 1–34

Osborn, M. *The French Presence in Cochinchina and Cambodia* (New York: Cornell University Press, 1969)

Sidel, M. *Law and Society in Vietnam* (New York: Cambridge University Press, 2008)

Supreme People's Court. *Court System of the Socialist Republic of Vietnam* (Hanoi: Labour Publishing House, 2009)

Tamanaha, B. Z. "The rule of law and legal pluralism in development," *Hague Journal on the Rule of Law*, 3(2) (2011), 1–17

To V. H. *Judicial Independence: A Legal Research on its Theoretical Aspects, Practices from Germany, the United States of America, France, Vietnam, and Recommendations for Vietnam* (Lund: Jüristforlaget i Lund, 2006)

UNDP. *Report on the Right to Counsel* (Hanoi: UNDP, 2012)

UNDP. *Report on the Survey of Needs of District People's Courts Nationwide* (Hanoi: Justice Publishing House, 2007)

UNDP. *Report on the Survey of the Reality of Local Court Governance in Vietnam* (Hanoi: UNDP, 2013)

16

Conclusion

Challenges and prospects for Asian courts

JIUNN-RONG YEH AND WEN-CHEN CHANG

The recent rise of Asia, both economically and politically, has fundamentally shaped and re-shaped legal and political institutions in the region. The restructuring of courts and reconstruction of their functional dynamics are evident indications of this phenomenon. We cannot but become intrigued by what Martin Shapiro – given his leading institutional approach to courts – would say about these changing dynamics presented today by Asia's courts against their countries' respective distinctive political, economic, social and cultural contexts.

Using an institutional approach, we have in this book included the contributions of scholars of fourteen selected jurisdictions across Asia, who provided updated, systematic and contextual analyses of recent developments and related issues in these fourteen judicial systems and related issues. Relying on these insightful analyses, we have conducted a comparative study of these jurisdictions regarding the structures of courts, quality of judges, citizens' relationships with courts, and styles of judicial decisions. Attempting to understand these comparative dynamics in their corresponding contexts, we further elaborate on these dynamics against three conceptual dimensions: tradition and transplantation, transition and construction, and globalization and competition. We have discussed all of these findings in detail in the introduction of this book and will briefly highlight some of the key points before we address the challenges and prospects that lie ahead.

1 Asian courts in comparison

We find that courts in Asia have indeed become a pivotal institution and are likely to remain as such in the future. Nearly all of the jurisdictions covered in this book have recently undertaken judicial reforms to restructure the courts, improve the quality of judges, enhance citizens' access to courts, or ensure judicial accountability or judicial independence.[1] As a result of these reforms, in the majority of jurisdictions, judges have, to varying degrees, become better educated and more responsive or independent.

1.1 *Changing structures of courts*

Regarding the changing structure of courts, we find – first and foremost – that there has been an emergence of special courts or special tribunals across jurisdictions in Asia.[2] The creation of these special courts or tribunals has been primarily in response to economic and related challenges.[3] Nearly all jurisdictions have in recent years created commercial courts or intellectual property courts, and many jurisdictions have established labor courts, international trade courts, and tax courts, among others. The other main reason for creating special courts or tribunals is to provide accommodation for matters related to family, religion or indigenous communities.[4] The majority of jurisdictions have family or children's courts, and in a number of jurisdictions, especially those with Muslim populations, special religious courts or tribunals have been created, or, alternatively, special religious laws may be permitted in general courts.[5]

A second trend has been the establishment of constitutional courts with centralized powers of judicial review in a number of jurisdictions, from Taiwan, which was the first to establish such a court, to South Korea, Mongolia, Cambodia, Thailand, Indonesia, and Myanmar.[6] In a similar vein, constitutional litigation has also been strengthened in the courts of decentralized judicial review systems, for example in Bangladesh, Hong Kong, India, Japan and the Philippines.[7] Also noteworthy is that the adoption of a single or multiple supreme courts does not always correspond with the civil or common law division.[8] Last but not least is the rarity of judicial federalism in Asia. Even federal states such as India and Malaysia have adopted unitary, centralized judicial systems.[9]

[1] J.-r. Yeh and W.-C. Chang, "Asian courts in context: tradition, transition and globalization," this volume, section 5.2.1.
[2] *Ibid.* at 4.1.5. [3] *Ibid.* at 4.1.5.1. [4] *Ibid.* at 4.1.5.2. [5] *Ibid.* at 4.1.5.2.
[6] *Ibid.* at 4.1.3. [7] *Ibid.* at 4.1.3, fn 57. [8] *Ibid.* at 4.1.4. [9] *Ibid.* at 4.1.1.

1.2 *Quality of judges*

Regarding judges, we find that the number of judges per 100,000 inhabitants varies greatly across the Asian jurisdictions covered in this book: from 0.0512 in Vietnam, to 1.3 in India, 2.66 in Hong Kong, 4.9 in Korea, 8 in Taiwan, 14.37 in China, and 16 in Mongolia.[10] Overall, there seems to have been an increase in the number of judges in these jurisdictions in recent years, especially in those jurisdictions that have recently experienced economic or political transitions.

One salient feature regarding judges in Asia is the exam-based judicial recruitment process for entry-level judges.[11] In civil law jurisdictions, any law graduate or qualified individual who intends to become a judge must take an exam. Even among common law jurisdictions, where judges are usually recruited from among experienced lawyers, a number of jurisdictions in Asia still require exam passage for entry-level judges. These exams are usually very competitive.[12]

Also noteworthy is that in Asia, judicial appointments – except for those of constitutional court justices – are generally made by the chief executive, with very limited power-sharing mechanisms. Lower court judges are typically appointed by the chief executive based on exam performance or other qualifications.[13] For the appointment of Supreme Court justices, appointments are often made by the executive with consultation of the judiciary or judicial councils. In contrast, for constitutional court justices, a power-sharing appointment mechanism involving the executive, legislative and judiciary is typical.[14]

Life tenure is generally guaranteed for lower court judges across Asian jurisdictions. Interestingly, however, in Japan and South Korea, lower court judges enjoy only a ten-year term with the privilege of reappointment, as stipulated by both constitutions. Nevertheless, the practice has ensured that these judges hold office during good behavior until the age of retirement.[15] It is also important to note that the two socialist legal systems included in this book – China and Vietnam – do not provide tenure for judges. The powers of judicial appointment and reappointment remain in the strong control of the party-state.[16] In India and Singapore, "additional judges" or "contract judges" who are appointed due to a shortage of judges are also not granted tenure.[17]

[10] *Ibid.* at 4.2. [11] *Ibid.* at 4.2.1.1. [12] *Ibid.* at 4.2.1.1. [13] *Ibid.* at 4.2.2.1.
[14] *Ibid.* at 4.2.2.3. [15] *Ibid.* at 4.2.3. [16] *Ibid.* at 4.2.3. [17] *Ibid.* at 4.2.3.

1.3 Citizens and courts

Jury trials or other forms of citizen participation in trials are rare in Asia. The jury system was first introduced in Asia primarily in the common law jurisdictions of British colonies during the period of colonization. Interestingly, upon gaining independence, most former colonies abolished the jury system.[18] Hong Kong has retained the jury system in limited cases.[19] The Philippines, despite being a common law jurisdiction, never adopted the jury system.[20] In contrast, a few civil law jurisdictions such as Japan, South Korea and Taiwan have in recent years witnessed a trend of enhancing citizen participation in the judiciary by adopting systems incorporating citizen juries or lay judges.[21] Also noteworthy is the institution of people's assessors with the judiciary, which still remains in China and Vietnam, albeit with little usage.[22]

The availability of lawyers is crucial to ensuring citizens' access to justice. Generally, the number of lawyers has been rising across the Asian jurisdictions covered in this book. Particularly in China and Vietnam, the growth in the number of lawyers is astonishing.[23] Also noteworthy is the affordability of litigation. Only in Hong Kong and Singapore are litigation costs reported as being relatively high. In other jurisdictions, litigation costs appear to be more affordable.[24] In nearly all of the jurisdictions, legal aid is provided.[25]

Lastly, there is great disparity across Asian jurisdictions in the development of public interest litigation. A few Asian jurisdictions such as India and the Philippines have developed quite liberal doctrines to allow public interest litigation.[26] In recent years, the courts in Bangladesh, Hong Kong, Indonesia and Taiwan have also demonstrated – to varying extents – similarly liberal attitudes.[27] However, a few other jurisdictions have not recognized public interest litigation so liberally. As reported in the previous chapters, public interest litigation in China, Malaysia, Mongolia and Singapore has been non-existent or very limited in usage.[28]

1.4 The styles of judicial decisions

The styles of judicial decisions in Asian jurisdictions tend to be in line with the type of legal system of a given jurisdiction. Judgments in civil

[18] *Ibid.* at 4.3.1. [19] *Ibid.* at 4.3.1. [20] *Ibid.* at 4.3.1. [21] *Ibid.* at 4.3.1.
[22] *Ibid.* at 4.3.1. [23] *Ibid.* at 4.3.2.1. [24] *Ibid.* at 4.3.2.2. [25] *Ibid.* at 4.3.2.2.
[26] *Ibid.* at 4.3.2.3. [27] *Ibid.* at 4.3.2.3. [28] *Ibid.* at 4.3.2.3.

and socialist legal systems tend to be short.[29] In common law jurisdictions, judgments are likely to be lengthy.[30] Hong Kong serves as an interesting case, as the courts operate in two official languages, and the style and length of a judgment tends to be determined by the language in which the hearing is conducted.[31]

The text-based interpretive approach has gained the most popularity in Asia, while the purposive approach serves as a supplementary method of legal interpretation.[32] Judicial precedents are applied in common law jurisdictions. Interestingly, however, in some civil law jurisdictions, such as Indonesia, South Korea and Taiwan, the lower courts may also apply precedents, especially those rendered by the top courts or special courts in exceptional cases.[33]

Reference to foreign or international laws in court judgments has not been as evident in Asia as it is in other regions such as Europe or North America. We find two contrasting attitudes in courts across Asia towards references to foreign law: one embracing and the other resisting. On the side of embracing comparative and foreign law, the courts of Hong Kong stand out, followed by the courts of Japan, South Korea and Taiwan. On the side of resistance are Malaysia, Mongolia and Singapore.[34] It is particularly intriguing to note that the division of embracing or resisting does not correspond with whether a jurisdiction is one of civil or common law.

2 Contextual analyses: tradition, transition and globalization

What explains these comparative dynamics across Asian jurisdictions? As contexts do matter, we argue that the best approach to understanding the dynamics represented in Asian courts is to interpret them through their corresponding political, economic, social and cultural contexts.[35] We find three dimensions of contextual analysis crucial: (1) tradition and transplantation, (2) transition and construction, and (3) globalization and competition.

2.1 Tradition and transplantation

Colonial experiences have significantly shaped modern courts in Asia, with fairly complex paths and patterns. We find that jurisdictions with a

29 *Ibid.* at 4.4.1. 30 *Ibid.* at 4.4.1. 31 *Ibid.* at 4.4.1. 32 *Ibid.* at 4.4.2.
33 *Ibid.* at 4.4.2. 34 *Ibid.* at 4.4.3. 35 *Ibid.* at sections 2 and 5.

single colonial experience tend to maintain the judicial system established by the colonial regime.[36] However, multiple or even divided colonial experiences may complicate the patterns of legal and judicial transplantation. For example, in the Philippines, despite Spanish colonization, the courts and the operation of the judicial system have been more strongly influenced by the American model.[37] Similarly, in Vietnam, following French colonization, the country was divided, with the North influenced by the Soviets and the South by the French and Americans.[38] Also noteworthy is that not all colonization in Asia was simply from the West. Both South Korea and Taiwan were colonies of imperial Japan, and the establishment of their modern judicial systems was heavily influenced by Japan.[39]

Modernization also has had strong influences on the adoption of Western legal and judicial systems, both with and without the experience of colonial rule. For example, despite never having experienced colonial rule, Japan and Thailand began the modernization process by adopting Western laws and courts in the eighteenth and nineteenth centuries.[40] Yet, the emergence of nationalism in many Asian jurisdictions has complicated or undermined – to varying degrees – Western influence on their legal and judicial systems. For example, the chapters on Indonesia and Malaysia discuss the relatively greater influences of their respective post-independence constitutions on their present judicial structures.[41] The chapter on India notes that the ruling Indian National Congress after independence viewed the legal system inherited from the British as unsuitable to a reconstructed India.[42]

Tradition, religion, and indigenous cultures may further complicate the dynamics of Asian courts. For example, the emphasis on harmony in society may stand against the adversarial nature of modern litigation and favor informal mechanisms for dispute resolution.[43] The importance of family in Asian tradition may partly explain the trend across many jurisdictions in creating separate family courts in which family disputes are dealt with by applying different substantive and procedural

36 *Ibid.* at 5.1.1. 37 *Ibid.* at 5.1.1. 38 *Ibid.* at 5.1.1. 39 *Ibid.* at 5.1.1.
40 *Ibid.* at 5.1.1.
41 H. Juwana, "Courts in Indonesia: a mix of Western and local character," this volume, section 1, Y. C. Choong, "Courts in Malaysia and judiciary initiated reforms," this volume, section 1.3.
42 J. Krishnan, "Legitimacy of courts and the dilemma of their proliferation: the significance of judicial power in India," this volume, section 5.
43 Yeh and Chang, "Tradition, transition and globalization," this volume, section 5.1.3.

rules.[44] The heavy reliance on competitive exams for recruiting entry-level judges may be reflective of an imperial system in which exams are often regarded as a fair and merit-based institution facilitating social and political mobility.[45] Diverse religions in Asia may also be reflected in the creation of special religious courts or tribunals, especially in those jurisdictions with Muslim populations.[46] Last but not least, in a few jurisdictions such as Indonesia, Malaysia and Taiwan, indigenous peoples and their cultures have gradually gained recognition to allow the application of separate laws or the creation of separate indigenous courts or tribunals.[47]

The reliance on tradition, religion or culture in the construction of Asian courts has not been entirely without concerns. Such emphases may at times contradict modern legal concepts premised on neutrality of political community and equality between atomic individuals.[48] Considerable care must be undertaken to strike a balance between civil jurisprudence and cultural variations and to ameliorate jurisdictional conflicts between civil courts and alternative venues.

2.2 *Transition and construction*

Recent political and economic transitions have brought about significant changes in the structure of courts and the reconstruction of judicial functions in Asia. In response to these profound transitions, judicial reforms have been undertaken in nearly all of the jurisdictions covered in this book.[49] Advanced economies, particularly Hong Kong and Singapore, have demanded that their judicial systems be efficient and professional in order to attract more foreign investment.[50] Developing economies such as China and Malaysia have also undertaken judicial reforms in order to ease investor concerns and remove obstacles to the operation of more open and transparent markets.[51] Bangladesh and India have focused on the issues of incompetent judges and the delayed delivery of justice. Indonesia has put anti-corruption at the top of its judicial reform agendas.[52] Judicial reforms in advanced democracies such as

44 *Ibid.* at 5.1.3. 45 *Ibid.* at 5.1.3. 46 *Ibid.* at 5.1.3. 47 *Ibid.* at 5.1.3.

48 L.-a. Thio, "Constitutionalism in illiberal polities" in M. Rosenfeld and A. Sajó (eds.), *The Oxford Handbook of Comparative Constitutional Law* (Oxford University Press, 2012), pp. 133–4.

49 Yeh and Chang, "Tradition, transition and globalization," this volume, at section 5.2.1.

50 *Ibid.* at 5.2.1. 51 *Ibid.* at 5.2.1. 52 *Ibid.* at 5.2.1.

Japan, South Korea and Taiwan have unequivocally focused on enhancing citizens' participation in the judiciary, as reflected in their recent adoption of lay judge or citizen jury systems.[53]

These transitions have also altered the functional dynamics of the courts. In a few jurisdictions, for example Bangladesh, Singapore and Thailand, while the courts may continue to legitimize government policies, they have nevertheless not done so uninhibitedly and have even begun ensuring the government stay on the right side of laws and legal procedures.[54] In addition, a number of chapters note the enhanced capacity of courts to secure market functions or even to address market malfunctions, especially regarding consumers, workers, minorities or the environment. The courts in India stand out in addressing protections against market malfunctions.[55] Thai courts have also been praised as delivering this essential function, particularly in the areas of consumer protection and the environment.[56] Also noteworthy are the functions of courts in times of political transitions. In quite a number of jurisdictions, such as India, Japan, South Korea and Taiwan, among others, the courts may not only protect human rights and resolve political conflicts, but also, to varying extents, facilitate the process of democratization or uphold the results of democratic processes.[57]

Yet, effective judicial checks with the exercise of government powers remain sporadic in the jurisdictions with limited progress of political reforms or with relatively weak regime stability. As demonstrated by the experiences of Bangladesh, Indonesia, Malaysia, Thailand, among others, successful transformations of judicial functions continue to depend upon political contingencies and regime stability.[58] Absent the continuing progress in economic or political transitions, judicial reforms and the functions of courts may be constrained substantially.

[53] *Ibid.* at 5.2.1. [54] *Ibid.* at 5.2.2. [55] *Ibid.* at 5.2.2.

[56] P. Satayanurug and N. Nakornin, "Courts in Thailand: progressive development as the country's pillar of justice," this volume, section 6.1.3.

[57] Yeh and Chang, "Tradition, transition and globalization," this volume, section 5.2.2.

[58] R. Hoque, *Judicial Activism in Bangladesh: A Golden Mean Approach* (Newcastle upon Tyne: Cambridge Scholars Publishing, 2011), pp. 263–70; B. Dressel and M. Mietzner, "A tale of two courts: the judicialization of electoral politics in Asia," *Governance: An International Journal of Policy, Administration, and Institutions*, 25(3) (2012), 391–414, 404; C. C. Gan, "Administrative law and judicialized governance in Malaysia: the Indian connection" in T. Ginsburg and A. H. Y. Chen (eds.), *Administrative Law and Governance in Asia: Comparative Perspectives* (Oxen: Routledge, 2009), pp. 257–86; T. Ginsburg, "Constitutional afterlife: the continuing impact of Thailand's postpolitical constitution', *International Journal of Constitutional Law*, 7(1) (2009), 83–105.

2.3 *Globalization and competition*

The progress of globalization further brings Asian courts into a global context, connecting them to regional and international economic, political, and, eventually, legal and judicial systems. The first indication of globalization is an increased reference to foreign or international laws in the courts. We find that quite a number of jurisdictions in Asia have embraced comparative and foreign law in their judicial decisions, while a few have continued to resist such a trend.[59] A noteworthy finding is that in Asia, whether a jurisdiction has a common or civil law legal system is not necessarily associated with its attitude towards comparative and international law.[60]

A second indication of globalization is the recent mushrooming of special courts, which may be driven by market competition as well as global trade laws. For example, five intellectual property courts or tribunals have recently been created in China, Malaysia, Singapore, Taiwan and Thailand, reflecting the demand for protection of intellectual property under international trade frameworks.[61]

Last but not least is the emergence of alternative dispute resolution (ADR) as preferred by international trade agreements. Nearly all of the jurisdictions covered in this book have recently created or revised their systems of ADR or arbitration to resolve international trade disputes through much more efficient and flexible mechanisms. With the rise of global markets, judicial efficiency and capacity to deal with international trade disputes may become important benchmarks by which courts are evaluated and compared.

3 Challenges and prospects

The courts in Asia have responded in a variety of ways to the profound transitions that have occurred in the political, economic, social and cultural spheres throughout the region. Aside from resolving legal disputes, these courts have functioned to adapt foreign legal systems for local contexts, to facilitate economic development, to deliver social justice, to resolve political conflicts, or even to trigger democratic transitions. From the perspective of the institutional approach, it is clear that Asian courts have not only become pivotal legal institutions but also uninhibited political, economic, social and cultural institutions.

[59] Yeh and Chang, "Tradition, transition and globalization," this volume, at section 5.3.1.
[60] *Ibid.* at 5.3.1. [61] *Ibid.* at 5.3.2.

Meanwhile, problems and challenges remain. A few of these problems and challenges have been discussed in the individual country chapters or touched upon in the introduction of this book. We find that the four most pressing challenges are as follows: (1) the quality and capacity of judges; (2) judicial independence and corruption; (3) bureaucratization and politicization; and (4) competition with global courts and ADR mechanisms. We address them in the following.

3.1 *Quality and capacity of judges*

Notwithstanding judicial reforms undertaken to improve the quality and capacity of judges, concerns or even criticisms nevertheless remain. For example, in China, a law degree is still not a prerequisite for qualifying to be a judge. Even in the jurisdictions that require a law degree as a prerequisite, the quality of legal education may still be a concern. The chapters on India, Mongolia and China have all discussed the poor quality of legal education due to a lack of resources, especially in rural areas.[62] Perhaps due to concerns about the quality of legal education, many jurisdictions provide further training for judges. Yet, problems with the quality of this type of judicial training have also been reported in a few jurisdictions.[63] For example, in China, the lack of appropriate professional training, particularly for judges serving on special courts or tribunals, has already affected the quality of judicial decisions.[64]

In addition, the capacity of judges to respond to the challenges brought about by profound economic and political transitions may not be sufficient. For jurisdictions in economic transition, judicial capacity to secure contracts or transactions is crucial to a well-functioning market. Similarly, in the context of political transitions, courts may be requested to step into highly charged political conflicts or to guard the results of political compromises. As stated above, while some courts have shouldered these functions well, not all courts have delivered successful outcomes. For example, the Bangladesh and Indonesia chapters report poor judicial capacity and constrained functions of the courts in the economic

[62] Krishnan, "Legitimacy of courts," this volume, section 3.1; B. Amarsanaa, "The fledgling courts and adjudication system in Mongolia," this volume, section 3.1; and W. Gu, "Courts in China: judiciary in the economic and societal transitions," this volume, section 7.

[63] Yeh and Chang, "Tradition, transition and globalization," this volume, section 4.2.4.

[64] Gu, "Courts in China," this volume, section 7.

sphere.[65] As reported in Taiwan and South Korea, judicial politicization has occurred, and public distrust of the judiciary has emerged.[66] Poor performance or outright incompetence of the judiciary in dealing with political controversies during democratic transitions has also been a common complaint in Indonesia and Mongolia.[67]

As the quality and capacity of judges still need a great deal of improvement, the high level of public dissatisfaction with judicial performance observed in many jurisdictions, particularly in some jurisdictions such as China, India and Vietnam, is unsurprising.[68] Also noteworthy are the constraints placed by the political environment on judicial functions, as reflected in both the Bangladesh and China chapters.[69] Without some political reforms, the full realization of judicial functions will be quite difficult, if not impossible.

3.2 *Judicial independence and corruption concerns*

Judicial independence has been ensured to varying degrees throughout most of the Asian jurisdictions covered in this book. However, political interference with the judiciary still raises concerns. Noticeably, in the two socialist legal systems, China and Vietnam, judicial independence is yet to be ensured. In both places, life tenure has not been guaranteed for judges, and judicial independence has suffered from interference by both the communist party and the central and local governments.[70]

Very often the interference with judicial independence comes from the ways in which judicial administration is performed and decisions concerning judicial appointments or transfers are made. For example, the chapter on Japan has reports that the evaluations of judges that may affect promotions, salary increases or transfers have long been criticized

[65] R. Hoque, "Courts and the adjudication system in Bangladesh: in quest of viable reforms," this volume, section 5.1; Juwana, "Courts in Indonesia," this volume, section 7.

[66] J. Kim, "Courts in the Republic of Korea: featuring a built-in authoritarian legacy of centralization and bureaucratization," this volume, section 4.3.2.2; W.-C. Chang, "Courts and judicial reform in Taiwan: gradual transformations towards the guardian of constitutionalism and rule of law," this volume, section 5.1.

[67] Juwana, "Courts in Indonesia," this volume, section 5.2; Amarsanaa, "Courts in Mongolia," this volume, section 6.

[68] Yeh and Chang, "Tradition, transition and globalization," this volume, section 4.3.3.

[69] Hoque, "Courts in Bangladesh," this volume, section 5; Gu, "Courts in China," this volume, section 6.2.2.

[70] Yeh and Chang, "Tradition, transition and globalization," this volume, section 5.2.2.

as being carried out in a black box.[71] Similar issues concerning judicial appointments and transfers have also been reported in Malaysia.[72] In Thailand, it is reported that the operation of judicial administration has not been completely independent from the government or immune from political interference.[73]

At the same time, corruption continues to overshadow judicial independence and the progress of judicial reforms. A few country chapters have discussed or briefly touched upon this issue, namely, the chapters on Bangladesh, China, Indonesia, Malaysia, Taiwan and Thailand.[74] The extent of judicial corruption, however, remains to be further researched. Yet the enigma is that in some jurisdictions, for example Thailand, judicial corruption has not seemed to seriously affect judicial reputation. In other places, for example Taiwan, the legal and political communities are nevertheless quite critical of judicial integrity. Putting aside whether and how judicial corruptions may affect public confidence in the judiciary, it is at least clear that judicial corruption or even the charges of judicial corruption has negatively impacted judicial independence and the performance of the judiciary, and that there is a plenty of room for Asian courts to improve in this aspect.

3.3 *Bureaucratization and politicization*

In Asia, judicial recruitment of entry-level judges has primarily relied on competitive exams. In addition, the most popular method of judicial appointment is that in which the chief executive selects judges on the basis of these exams, with limited judicial or public consultation.[75] The result – unsurprisingly – has been an elite-centered judiciary in most jurisdictions. As reported in the chapter on South Korea, the judiciary consists primarily of graduates from the big five universities.[76] The

71 N. Kawagishi, "Towards a more responsive judiciary: courts and judicial power in Japan," this volume, section 4.

72 Choong, "Courts in Malaysia," this volume, section 3.2.

73 Satayanurug and Nakornin, "Courts in Thailand," this volume, section 3.2.

74 Hoque, "Courts in Bangladesh," this volume, section 5.3; Gu, "Courts in China," this volume, section 6.2.2; Juwana, "Courts in Indonesia," this volume, section 3.2; Choong, "Courts in Malaysia," this volume, section 3.2; Chang, "Courts and judicial reform in Taiwan," this volume, section 6.2; Satayanurug and Nakornin, "Courts in Thailand," this volume, section 6.3.

75 Yeh and Chang, "Tradition, transition and globalization," this volume, sections 4.2.1, 4.2.2.1.

76 Kim, "Courts in the Republic of Korea," this volume, section 4.2.2.

elite-centered and homogenous nature of Asian judges has two consequences that may seem contradictory but are in fact interrelated: bureaucratization and politicization.

As judges are recruited through competitive exams, and promoted by the chief executive based upon exam performance or other merit-based qualifications, they are easily rendered into a hierarchical system reflective of the nature of bureaucracies. This usually makes political interference from the government or the ruling political party relatively easy, and also results in judges being more likely to share political ideologies or social preferences with the ruling elite. This becomes a kind of "politicization" as a result of bureaucratization in the judiciary, a common epidemic, especially in authoritarian regimes in which the judiciary functions as a rubber stamp to legitimize the ruling government or political party.[77] Many jurisdictions in Asia, regardless of their extent of liberalization and democratization, continue to face this challenge, as reflected in the chapters on Bangladesh, South Korea and Taiwan.[78]

Another kind of "politicization" as a result of judicial bureaucratization occurs in the context of democratic transition. Since bureaucratic judges are more likely to be in collaboration with the ruling political elite, when they experience democratic transitions, these judges may still favor the departing ruling elite or their political ideology, a problem that has now been clearly identified in the study of comparative law and courts.[79] In such a context, politicization may occur in many ways: it may occur when the ruling elite manipulate these judges and judicial decisions in their favor, or alternatively, the democratic elite may decide to unpack the courts and install their own judges, and courts may eventually be involved in endless political confrontations, resulting in even further politicization. These vicious circles of politicization in the context of democratic transitions have already been witnessed in the constitutional courts or top courts of Mongolia, the Philippines, South Korea and

[77] See also T. Moustafa and T. Ginsburg, "Introduction: the function of courts in authoritarian politics" in T. Moustafa and T. Ginsburg (eds.), *Rule by Law: The Politics of Courts in Authoritarian Regimes* (Cambridge University Press, 2008), pp. 1–22.

[78] Hoque, "Courts in Bangladesh," this volume, section 5.1; Kim, "Courts in the Republic of Korea," this volume, section 4.3.2.2; Chang, "Courts and judicial reform in Taiwan," this volume, section 5.1.

[79] See e.g. T. Ginsburg, *Judicial Review in New Democracies: Constitutional Courts in Asian Cases* (New York: Cambridge University Press, 2003); R. Hirschl, *Towards Juristocracy: The Origins and Consequences of the New Constitutionalism* (Harvard University Press, 2007).

Taiwan.[80] Politicization may also occur with the constitutional courts that are given a wide array of ancillary powers such as adjudication of electoral disputes, impeachment, and dissolution of unconstitutional political parties.[81] As the recent experiences in Indonesia and Thailand have shown, judicial interventions in contentious electoral politics have rendered serious public distrust with the judiciary and at times may even trigger political setbacks for the courts.[82]

There is no easy cure for judicial bureaucratization and politicization. The recent reforms of legal education and bar exams in Japan and South Korea favoring the American model represent one way to tackle these intertwined issues.[83] High quality judges recruited from experienced lawyers have been adopted in some jurisdictions. Due considerations undertaken in the expansion of judicial ancillary powers may be another. More novel reform initiatives are needed. Asian courts and judges must effectively confront these challenges and find proper solutions.

3.4 Competition with global courts and ADR mechanisms

Last but not least of the challenges facing Asian courts are the competition between courts in different jurisdictions, and the competition between courts and alternative dispute resolution mechanisms.

The progress of globalization has brought courts into a global community of courts across different jurisdictions. The expansion of global markets has led to demands for efficient and cost-conscious dispute resolution, driving transnational corporations to forum-shop among the best and most efficient courts. Among the jurisdictions covered in this book, Hong Kong and Singapore have always been considered the most efficient.[84] In the chapter on Singapore, Tan comments that

80 Amarsanaa, "Courts in Mongolia," this volume, section 5; R. C. Pangalangan, "The Philippines' post-Marcos judiciary: the institutional turn and the populist backlash," this volume, section 1.4; Kim, "Courts in the Republic of Korea," this volume, section 4.1; Chang, "Courts and judicial reform in Taiwan," this volume, section 5.1.

81 See e.g. T. Ginsburg, "Beyond judicial review: ancillary powers of constitutional courts" in T. Ginsburg and R. A. Kagan (eds.), *Institutions and Public Law: Comparative Approaches* (New York: Peter Lang Publishing, 2004), p. 238.

82 See e.g. Dressel and Mietzner, "A tale of two courts," 404.

83 Yeh and Chang, "Tradition, transition and globalization," this volume, section 4.2.1.1.

84 *Ibid.* at section 5.3.

"Singapore operates one of the most efficient court systems in the world."[85] In contrast, some other courts may not fare better in the competition over judicial efficiency. For example, the courts in Indonesia have not been perceived as a credible forum for international investors.[86]

In a similar vein, forum competition may also take place between courts and ADR mechanisms. On the one hand, the emerging global market may call for more efficient ADR mechanisms with flexible rules. On the other hand, the recognition of certain special needs in cultural traditions or religions may also demand the use of ADR mechanisms. These dynamics may further alter the traditional functions of courts and compel courts and judges to adjust to the new frontiers.

In this book, we have provided an updated account of courts and their changing functional dynamics in fourteen selected jurisdictions across Asia. As these analyses have demonstrated, courts in Asia have indeed become a pivotal institution and will be likely to remain so in the future. These courts across different jurisdictions have – with varying degrees of success – responded to profound transitions in political, economic, social and cultural contexts. Challenges nevertheless remain. The challenges concerning the capacity of judges and judicial independence and integrity are not new and have been gradually addressed. The challenges concerning judicial bureaucratization and politicization, as well as the competition with different judicial and quasi-judicial venues, are relatively novel. There is no easy cure for these challenges. As a collective scholarly effort, we hope the discussions in this book will pave an intellectual foundation upon which more reform initiatives and solutions may be developed.

References

Dressel, B. and Mietzner, M. "A tale of two courts: the judicialization of electoral politics in Asia," *Governance: An International Journal of Policy, Administration, and Institutions*, 25(3) (2012), 391–414

Gan, C. C. "Administrative law and judicialized governance in Malaysia: the Indian connection" in T. Ginsburg and A. H. Y. Chen (eds.), *Administrative Law and Governance in Asia: Comparative Perspectives* (New York: Routledge, 2009), pp. 257–86

[85] K. Y. L. Tan, "As efficient as the best businesses: Singapore's judicial system," this volume, section 3.1.

[86] Juwana, "Courts in Indonesia," this volume, section 7.

Ginsburg, T. "Beyond judicial review: ancillary powers of constitutional courts" in T. Ginsburg and R. A. Kagan (eds.), *Institutions and Public Law: Comparative Approaches* (New York: Peter Lang Publishing, 2004), pp. 225–44

Ginsburg, T. "Constitutional afterlife: the continuing impact of Thailand's post-political constitution," *International Journal of Constitutional Law*, 7(1) (2009), 83–105

Ginsburg, T. *Judicial Review in New Democracies: Constitutional Courts in Asian Cases* (New York: Cambridge University Press, 2003)

Hirschl, R. *Towards Juristocracy: The Origins and Consequences of the New Constitutionalism* (Harvard University Press, 2007)

Hoque, R. *Judicial Activism in Bangladesh: A Golden Mean Approach* (Newcastle upon Tyne: Cambridge Scholars Publishing, 2011)

Moustafa, T. and Ginsburg, T. "Introduction: the function of courts in authoritarian politics" in T. Moustafa and T. Ginsburg (eds.), *Rule by Law: The Politics of Courts in Authoritarian Regimes* (New York: Cambridge University Press, 2008), pp. 1–22

Thio, L.-a. "Constitutionalism in illiberal polities" in M. Rosenfeld and A. Sajó (eds.), *The Oxford Handbook of Comparative Constitutional Law* (Oxford University Press, 2012), pp. 133–52

INDEX